W9-CDC-471

WORKS ISSUED BY
THE HAKLUYT SOCIETY

———

Series Editors
Gloria Clifton
Joyce Lorimer

———

THE ARCTIC JOURNAL OF
CAPTAIN HENRY WEMYSS FEILDEN, R.A.,
THE NATURALIST IN H.M.S. *ALERT*
1875–1876

THIRD SERIES
NO. 35

Photograph of Henry Wemyss Feilden (1838–1921) taken about 1890, by an unknown photographer. Courtesy of Norwich Castle Museum, Norfolk

THE ARCTIC JOURNAL OF
CAPTAIN HENRY WEMYSS FEILDEN, R.A.,
THE NATURALIST IN H.M.S. *ALERT*
1875–1876

Edited by

TREVOR H. LEVERE

Published by
Routledge
for
THE HAKLUYT SOCIETY
LONDON
2019

First published 2019 for the Hakluyt Society by
Routledge
2 Park Square, Milton Park, Abingdon, Oxon OX14 4RN

and by Routledge
711 Third Avenue, New York, NY 10017

Routledge is an imprint of the Taylor & Francis Group, an informa business

British Library Cataloguing-in-Publication Data
A catalogue record for this book is available from the British Library

Library of Congress Cataloging-in-Publication Data
CIP data applied for

ISBN: 978–0–367–35637–8 (hbk)
ISBN: 978–0–429–34082–6 (ebk)

Typeset in Garamond Premier Pro
by Waveney Typesetters, Wymondham, Norfolk

Routledge website: www.routledge.com
Hakuyt Society website: www.hakluyt.com

For Robert Anderson and Larry Stewart, and in memoriam David Knight, in grateful thanks for friendship over many years, invaluable criticism, and cheerful toleration of dissent.

CONTENTS

LIST OF MAPS AND ILLUSTRATIONS

Frontispiece

Photograph of Henry Wemyss Feilden (1838–1921) taken about 1890, by an unknown photographer, courtesy of Norwich Castle Museum.

Maps

For reference numbers of the original maps on which the sketch maps and charts are based, please see the Bibliography. However, the place-name spellings are those used by Feilden.

Colour Plates

See separate plate section between between pages 64 and 65.

Figures

Small Explanatory Sketches in the Text or Margin

All illustrations from Feilden's Journal are courtesy of the Royal Geographical Society, London.

PREFACE AND ACKNOWLEDGEMENTS

The disappearance of Sir John Franklin's Arctic expedition of 1846–7 and the failure of numerous attempts to find the ships and men made the British Admiralty reluctant to expend any more resources on Arctic exploration, despite appeals from the Royal Geographical Society and other scientific organizations.[1] However, in 1874 the leader of the Conservative Party, Benjamin Disraeli (1804–81), became Prime Minister and he decided, partly for political reasons, that a new expedition should be sent to explore towards the North Pole, carrying out scientific work en route. A British Arctic Expedition, commanded by George Strong Nares (1831–1915), was swiftly called into being, with detailed scientific as well as naval instructions. Henry Wemyss Feilden (1838–1921) was the naturalist in Nares's ship, HMS *Alert*, which wintered at the north-east corner of Ellesmere Island. This volume is an annotated version of the journal which Feilden kept during that expedition, including the preparations and the immediate aftermath, from 1 February 1875 until 7 January 1877. The original manuscript is in the archives of the Royal Geographical Society in London and it has never been published before, although Nares as leader produced a two-volume account of the expedition, to which Feilden contributed appendices on ethnology, mammalia, and ornithology. Feilden's journal has the immediacy of an account written day by day, illustrated by sketches, all of which have been reproduced.

My path to Feilden was not an obvious one. In the 1970s I was carrying out research on the role of science in Samuel Taylor Coleridge's intellectual labours. As a relief and release from some of the more opaque German philosophical works of the Romantic era, I read a selection of books on northern exploration and natural history, both subjects which I had long enjoyed. There were always two very different piles of books on my desk in the North Reading Room of the British Museum. By 1981, when I had finished my work on Coleridge, I knew that my next book would deal with natural history and other branches of science in relation to Arctic exploration.

My academic home was in Canada, and my previous research had been carried out in Canada and the United States, in Britain, and to a lesser extent in Europe. There were rich archival resources on both sides of the Atlantic and, given that most of my research had been in the nineteenth century, it seemed sensible to focus on the nineteenth-century exploration of what is now the Canadian Arctic archipelago. The islands in that archipelago constitute rather more than half the area of Nunavut ('our land' in Inuktitut). Nunavut is the largest Territory in Canada, which became formally separated from the Northwest Territories in 1999. The archipelago itself had been transferred to the Dominion of Canada in 1880, with startling imprecision; there was no rigorous definition of what was included in the transfer.

---

[1] Geography was then considered to be a science; several naval officers were elected to the Royal Society of London.

Most of the exploration throughout the nineteenth century had been in British ships, naval and private. The obvious starting place was the Scott Polar Research Institute (SPRI) in Cambridge University, where the library and archives were unparalleled. In the autumn of 1982, Terence Armstrong[1] very generously gave me an office in that Institute, and a set of keys so that I could work at all hours of the day (and night), and supported my application for a visiting fellowship at Clare Hall, of which he had been a founding fellow. Armstrong's co-authored *The Circumpolar North* had already given me an introduction to the field, and his seminar in polar studies, held at the SPRI, was stimulating and enriching. Clive Holland was the archivist at the SPRI. The book that he co-authored with Alan Cooke, *The Exploration of Northern Canada*, was invaluable as a preliminary guide to those expeditions which had carried out significant scientific work. Holland told me cheerfully enough that his work had doubled since my arrival. He could not have been more helpful. It was only halfway through my visit that I learned that 'my' office was in fact his. Harry King, the librarian there, was also unfailingly helpful. My research in the SPRI, guided by Armstrong, Holland, and King, enabled me to establish a foundation for my book published a decade later, *Science and the Canadian Arctic*.

While I was at the SPRI, it soon became apparent that one of the most important expeditions in the nineteenth century, prior to those of the first International Polar Year in 1882–3, was the British naval expedition of 1875–6, commanded by George Strong Nares in HMS *Alert* and *Discovery*. I first examined Feilden's journal of the expedition in 1982, when Christine Kelly's guidance was invaluable. Since then, in preparing this edition, I have returned to work in the library and archives of the RGS, where Eugene Ray has been most helpful. In 1982, Terence Armstrong was the acting director of the SPRI; we discussed Feilden's journal, and agreed that it should be published. Armstrong encouraged me to submit a proposal to the Hakluyt Society, of which he was the honorary secretary. The last time that we met, in 1988, at a conference in Toronto on the circumpolar Arctic,[2] he told me that he had one word as a reminder to me: 'Feilden'. Very belatedly, I have followed his advice.

Feilden was born in army barracks, to parents who were both themselves from military families. As the second son, Feilden could not inherit his father's baronetcy or the house and lands. Since commerce was not then a suitable career for a gentleman, his choices were restricted: the church, the law, or the armed forces. Given his family history, the army was the obvious choice; he went to the Royal Military Academy Sandhurst, and in 1856 his father bought him a commission as an ensign in the 42nd (Highland) Regiment of Foot. A year later he was in India with his regiment, engaged in the suppression of the Indian Mutiny. He never fully overcame the horror of that experience, but he remained a soldier throughout his life, taking part in most of the wars in his adult lifetime, in India, America (where he fought on the Confederate side, and married a southern belle), China, South Africa, and the First World War, when, coming out of retirement, he served as Paymaster and drilled with the recruits. The British Arctic Expedition of 1875–6 was his first Arctic voyage. He earned the respect and liking of Nares, who valued his

---

[1] Almost 40 years have passed since I began research on science in the Arctic. Sadly and inevitably, many of those who helped me have since died, Terence Armstrong among them. I shall simply refer to them by name, without adding 'deceased' or 'the late'.

[2] The proceedings were published: Franklyn Griffiths, ed., *Arctic Alternatives*.

contributions to the BAE as comparable to those of Sabine.[1] Feilden was subsequently on three other Arctic voyages, to Russian Lapland as it then was, and to islands in the Arctic Ocean at the western end of what was to become the Northeast Passage. On each of these voyages, as in the BAE, he proved himself an accomplished naturalist.

Feilden had the benefit of familiarity with the work of leading naturalists over the decades before the BAE. Charles Darwin's *Origin of Species*, Charles Lyell's *Principles of Geology,* and Joseph Dalton Hooker's 'Outlines of the Distribution of Arctic Plants' were the most important studies which informed Feilden's work; his journal shows how their work informed his own, and he thought deeply about the relevance of his observations to their seminal researches. He was also on friendly terms with leading ornithologists and zoologists, some of whom appear in his journal; they respected and welcomed his contributions. Some of his geological work in northern Ellesmere Island remained unsurpassed until the 1950s, and his observations laid down the geology along Smith's Sound for some 300 miles, supported by around 2,000 rock and fossil samples. His zoological and botanical specimens were numerous and important, finding their place in museums where they offered evidence for continuing research; Joseph Dalton Hooker (1817–1911), then Director of the Royal Botanic Gardens, Kew, and President of the Royal Society of London, was particularly impressed by Feilden's collection of Arctic plants. His Arctic collections went mainly to London museums, but some specimens went to the Castle Museum in Norwich. Feilden was not a born artist, but his sketches, sometimes technical, sometimes humorous, convey both scientific information and personal characteristics. Occasionally, during the Arctic summer, he appears dressed very much as an English gentleman in tweeds; in some of his geological sketches, where he is mainly concerned with stratigraphy, he is almost a stick figure. He seems to think with his pen in adding illustrative sketches to narrative or analysis. He had his bugbears, and was irritated by a couple of his shipmates, but overall he comes across as a very congenial companion, a gentle man for all his wartime service. He was active, and almost entirely uncomplaining, although he did find it hard to play the part of Widow Twankey in a theatrical performance of 'Aladdin', the Christmas pantomime on HMS *Alert*. Apart from Nares, Feilden was the oldest member of the ship's company, and he thought it a bit much to have to play the widow at his advanced age (37). There was a printing press onboard, and he kept copies of all the printed programmes for entertainments, along with menus, celebratory verses for important occasions (including birthdays), pencil sketches of encounters with unwilling sledge dogs, hauling overloaded sledges across pressure ridges, and of crowded tents; his journal is enriched throughout by enclosures and sketches. Geographical exploration was not his main task, although the expedition's principal goal was to get as close to the geographical pole as possible; nevertheless, he did contribute significantly to the geography of northern Ellesmere Island, almost a by-product of his geological, zoological and botanical work; and he was always ready to help with laying down depots or to succour sledge parties whose members were dropping from scurvy and exhaustion.

Nares, in his official report, gave Feilden a hearty commendation, and subsequently, with the support of Joseph Dalton Hooker, proposed him as a candidate for election to the Royal Society of London. Feilden's collection of rocks, minerals, and fossils were

---

[1] See below, Introduction, p. 4.

inevitably heavy, and sometimes obtained by sledge parties at considerable cost; his principal tools were a geological hammer, a magnifying glass, and pencil and paper. Feilden was a good field observer, in geology and the multiple strands of natural history: birds, animals, plants, and insects. He used a telescope, and as he became familiar with the species of birds in the high Arctic, he rightly trusted his identifications of distant birds more and more. But seeing a bird was not enough for the science of the day. For an identification to carry authority with zoologists, specimens were needed, and Feilden, a skilled shot, did what was necessary, sometimes with regret, usually with calm efficiency. The readers of this journal will be made uncomfortably aware that collecting zoological specimens in the 1870s generally meant shooting them, and the skins and skeletons of animals and birds found their way into major museums, neatly labelled with the date and place whence Feilden had taken them. There was an added reason for the hunt: fresh meat was always in short supply. Feilden's tools for botany were plant presses and paper, for zoology a rifle, knives, and saws. The crews of *Alert* and *Discovery* killed most if not all of the musk oxen in their neighbourhood, with the bulk of the bag a welcome treat on the dining table – even the musky-tasting meat of the old bulls was better than old salt beef. Hares and sea birds were similarly killed for the pot, sometimes on a large scale.

At one meeting of Armstrong's seminar at the SPRI, Vivian Fuchs was the main speaker; when asked what qualities he sought when choosing men for his Antarctic crossing, he said there were two main requirements: an equable temperament, and the ability to perform more than one essential role. Feilden fitted the bill.

In pursuit of Feilden, I have incurred debts to many individuals and institutions over several decades. In addition to those acknowledged above, I should also like to thank the following: the Arctic Institute of North America; Michael Barritt; the Natural History Museum (BMNH) and Dorothy Norman; Cambridge University Library; the Castle Museum, Norwich, and Tony Irwin and David Waterhouse; the Linnean Society, and Gina Douglas; the Public Archives of Canada, now Library and Archives of Canada (LAC); the Library of Congress; Rare Books and Special Collections, McGill University Library and Archives, and Jennifer Garland and Robert Michel; the Baldwin Room, Metropolitan Toronto Library; the National Maritime Museum (NMM); the National Museum of Natural Sciences (now the Canadian Museum of Nature), Ottawa, and David Gray and Stewart MacDonald; the library and archives of the Royal Artillery Institution; Royal Botanic Gardens, Kew, Herbarium archives (RBG) and Katherine Harrington and L. E. Thompson; the Royal Geographical Society (RGS), and Joy Wheeler and Jamie Owen; the Royal Society of London Library and Archives (RSL), Rupert Baker and Sally Grover; Urban Wråkberg, Center for History of Science, The Royal Swedish Academy of Science; the Scott Polar Research Institute (SPRI), and Robert Headland and Valerie Galpin; the South Carolina Historical Society and Molly Inabinett; the Public Record Office (PRO) and the Royal Commission on Historical Manuscripts, now subsumed into the National Archives (TNA) at Kew; the Map Library, University of Toronto, and Joan Winearls; the Fisher Rare Book Library, University of Toronto, and Richard Landon; and Mary P. Winsor, University of Toronto.

Although I retired from teaching more than a decade ago, Victoria College and the Institute for the History and Philosophy of Science and Technology in the University of Toronto have continued to provide an institutional home, and I have benefited from the university's excellent libraries, both paper and electronic. Keynyn Brysse unscrambled and edited drafts of parts of the original typescript. David Cox drew the maps and Kristen Schranz helped with the index. Finally, Gloria Clifton, series editor at the Hakluyt Society, has been unfailingly supportive and prompt with help and advice, which were very much needed; I am profoundly indebted to her keen eye, and rigorous and tactful editing.

In 1982–3 the Social Sciences and Humanities Research Council of Canada and the John Simon Guggenheim Memorial Foundation provided financial support, and the University of Toronto gave me sabbatical leave. Clare Hall provided a stimulating home in Cambridge while I was working in the SPRI.

To all of these, I extend grateful thanks.

Every effort has been made to trace and contact copyright holders prior to publication. If notified, all reasonable efforts will be made to rectify any errors or omissions.

ABBREVIATIONS AND SYMBOLS

ADM	Admiralty
BAAS	British Association for the Advancement of Science
BAE	British Arctic Expedition 1875–6
Bar	Barometer
BJHS	*British Journal for the History of Science*
BL	British Library
BM	British Museum, London
BMNH	British Museum of Natural History, South Kensington, London
C.	calm
CMB	Committee Minute Books
CRM	Clements Robert Markham
D. M. G.	Distance made good
EOL	*Encyclopaedia of Life*
FLS	Fellow of the Linnean Society
FRGS	Fellow of the Royal Geographical Society
FRS	Fellow of the Royal Society of London
GSL	Geological Society of London
h	hour[s]
HWF	Henry Wemyss Feilden
ITIS	Integrated Taxonomic Integration System
juv	juvenile
LAC	Library and Archives of Canada, Ottawa
Lat obs	Latitude by observation
m	midday
MS, MSS	Manuscript(s)
n.d.	No date
NF	Newfoundland (until 6 December 2001)
NL	Newfoundland and Labrador (since 6 December 2001)
N. L.	North latitude
NMM	National Maritime Museum, Greenwich
NRA	National Register of Archives
NS	New Series
o'c	o'clock
ODNB	*Oxford Dictionary of National Biography*
OED	*Oxford English Dictionary*
PC	Privy Councillor
Phil. Trans	*Philosophical Transactions of the Royal Society of London*

PP	Parliamentary Papers
PRO	Public Record Office, part of The National Archives, Kew, London
PRS	President of the Royal Society of London
PAC	Public Archives of Canada, now Library and Archives of Canada
RA	Royal Artillery
RBG	Royal Botanic Gardens, Kew, Herbarium archives
RGS	Royal Geographical Society
RN	Royal Navy
RSL	Royal Society of London
Sec.	Secretary
SPRI	Scott Polar Research Institute, Cambridge University
TNA	The National Archives, Kew, London
VCH	*Victoria County History*
W. L.	West Longitude
WoRMS	World Register of Marine Species

Symbols

♂	Male
♀	Female

WEIGHTS, MEASURES, AND CURRENCY

Weights and Measures

English mile	=	1.61 kilometres
Foot (12 inches)	=	30.48 centimetres
Gallon (8 pints)	=	4.55 litres
Inch	=	2.54 centimetres
Ounce	=	28.35 grams
Pint	=	0.55 litres
Pound (16 ounces)	=	453.59 grams
Ton	=	1,015.87 kilograms
Yard (3 feet)	=	91.44 centimetres

Currency

In the nineteenth century, the pound sterling was divided into 20 shillings and each shilling consisted of 12 pence, or 240 pence to the pound.

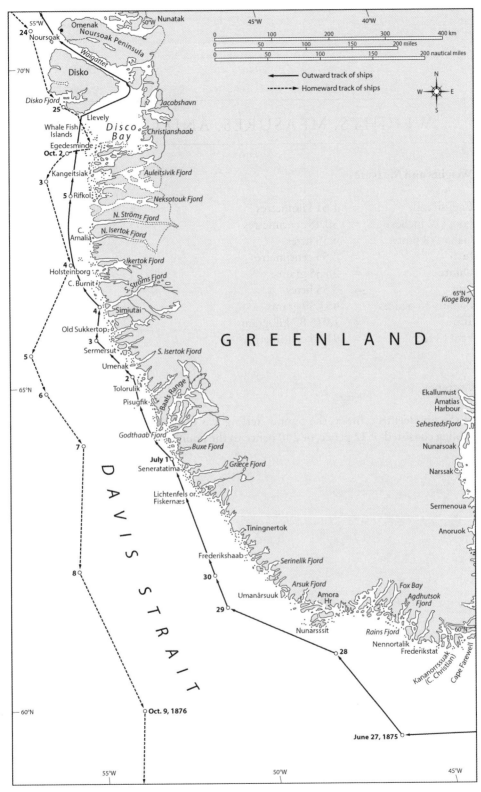

Map 1. Chart of Davis Strait and Greenland, showing the tracks of H.M. Ships *Alert* and *Discovery*, 1875–6, based on the National Map Collection, Library and Archives of Canada.

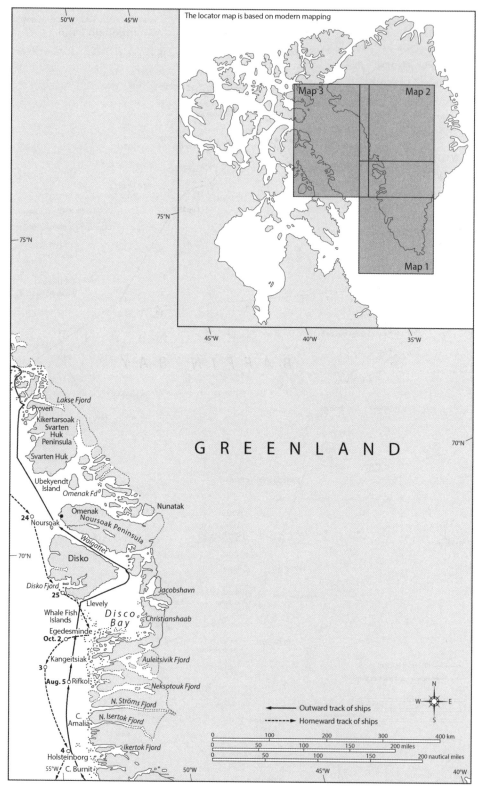

Map 2. Chart of Davis Strait and Disco Bay, showing the tracks of H.M. Ships *Alert* and *Discovery*, 1875–6, based on the National Map Collection, Library and Archives of Canada.

Map 3.   Chart of Baffin Bay, showing the tracks of H.M. Ships *Alert* and *Discovery*, 1875–6, based on the National Map Collection, Library and Archives of Canada.

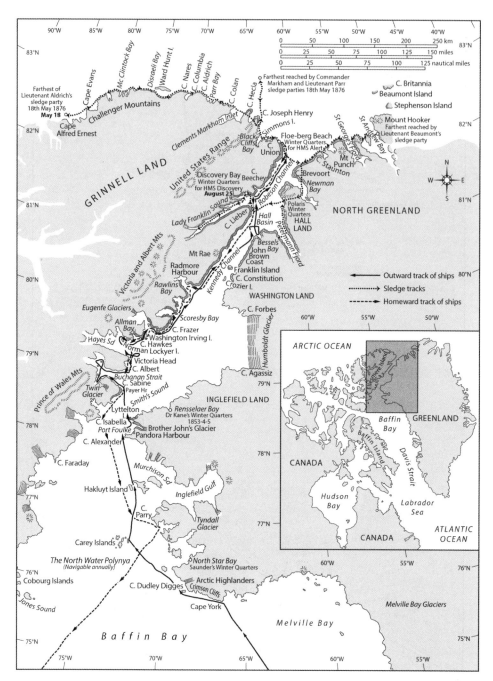

Map 4.   Sketch map of the tracks of the British Arctic Expedition from Baffin Bay to the Arctic Ocean, based on the map in Nares, *Narrative of a Voyage to the Polar Sea during 1875–6 of H.M. Ships 'Alert' and 'Discovery'*, 1878, vol. I, facing p. 1.

Map 5.   British Arctic Expedition 1875–6, Chart of Hall Basin and Robeson Channel, showing *Alert*'s winter quarters and the start of the route of the sledge parties led by Commander Markham and Lieutenant Parr, 3 April–13 June 1876. Based on the map *North America Polar Regions, Baffin Bay to Lincoln Sea*, Hydrographic Office of the US Department of the Navy, Bureau of Equipment, Washington, D.C., 1903.

INTRODUCTION:
HENRY WEMYSS FEILDEN, THE NATURALIST IN HMS *ALERT*, 1875–1876

1. Prelude and Preparation

The story of the British Arctic Expedition (BAE) of 1875–6[1] is a piece of natural history, the history of polar exploration, and imperial history, dealing with a Royal Naval scientific expedition to the north-eastern edge of the Canadian high Arctic five years before Britain transferred the Arctic islands to Canada. The expedition's destination was as remote from southern Canada as it was from southern England. It was the last major Victorian expedition to follow the nineteenth-century naval style of Arctic exploration, which had led to glory, disaster, and gains in scientific knowledge. It led in 1876 to suffering and death on the ice, but most of the men returned safely, and the scientific knowledge gained was extensive, especially in natural history: this was the most thoroughly planned scientific expedition that Britain had ever sent towards the Pole.

There had been a lull in British exploration of the Arctic after the disastrous expedition of Sir John Franklin (1786–1847) and the failure of subsequent attempts to find him or his ships and men. In May 1845 he set out with two ships, HMS *Erebus* and HMS *Terror*, intending to complete the mapping of the untravelled parts of the Northwest Passage. His ships were seen by whalers off the coast of Greenland in July of that year; some of Franklin's officers dined aboard one of the whaling ships, *Enterprise*. That was the last time that they were seen by Europeans. We now know that both ships were lost to the ice, that Franklin died in 1847, and that the survivors of the two crews set off overland towards Back River. They all perished. John Richardson (1787–1865) and John Rae (1813–93), who were both surgeons and explorers, and the Hudson Bay Company's trader and explorer John Bell (*c*.1799–1868), were sent by the Admiralty to search overland for Franklin and his men. From 1848 to 1869, many search expeditions, most of them naval, were in the Arctic. At first these were almost exclusively sent by the British Admiralty; then, encouraged by Lady Franklin's advocacy, there were private British searches, and, increasingly, American ones. The British Admiralty was growing reluctant to send more ships, cost being a major factor, but also the rapidly declining probability of success. The last British naval expedition to search for Franklin was commanded by Rochfort Maguire (1815–67) in HMS *Plover* from 1852 to 1854.[2] The Admiralty was by then heartily tired of so many failed searches, and for

---

[1] Its story has been told before. See, among others, Deacon and Savours, 'Sir George Strong Nares'; G. Hattersley-Smith, 'British Arctic Expedition'; Levere, *Science and the Canadian Arctic*, pp. 264–305.

[2] The final Franklin search was the American expedition of 1864–9, commanded by Charles Francis Hall (*c*.1821–71). There were several British search expeditions in these years, but they were not sent by the Admiralty. For Maguire, see Bockstoce, ed., *The Journal of Rochfort Maguire*.

1

the next twenty-one years refused to send expeditions to the high Arctic, whether in search of Franklin or of the Northwest Passage or of the geographic North Pole.[1] The search expeditions had filled in the map of sometimes navigable routes through Arctic waters, and if one put them together one could say that the Northwest Passage had been discovered piecemeal, but also that it was not a practical proposition.

The BAE, like others before it, had is origins in the enthusiasm of the President and Council of the Royal Geographical Society (RGS). That Society, under its president, Sir Roderick Impey Murchison, baronet (1792–1871),[2] decided to mount a thoroughgoing campaign, engaging the support of scientific societies at home and abroad, in a determined effort to awaken the Lords of the Admiralty from their post-Franklinian torpor, and persuade them to undertake renewed polar exploration. The scientific societies provided arguments to counter the Admiralty's reluctance. Murchison urged that any expedition should include someone 'capable of making the required geological investigations'. As for detailed proposals for geological work, these would be forthcoming as soon as the expedition was approved by government.[3] He first approached the senior society, the Royal Society of London, receiving in return a resolution that the proposed expedition, properly undertaken, would be 'highly advantageous in the advancement of several branches of Physical Science'. If the government sent out an expedition, then the Royal Society would propose a 'detailed statement of scientific objects which might be prosecuted with advantage without interfering with the main geographical purposes of the Expedition, and to specify in particular the instruments and methods of research available for such objects'. The primacy of geographical exploration reflects the origin of the proposal, as well as the Admiralty's relegation of natural science to a subordinate role, except where it bore on navigation. The stress on physical science also makes sense here; natural history and the human sciences had their separate advocates.

The Linnean Society, devoted to natural history and zoology, was next in order of seniority, and next to respond,[4] and, in spite of Joseph Dalton Hooker's conviction that there were probably no new species to be discovered in Arctic North America, they were very keen on the idea.[5] They argued not only that the expedition would be good for science, but that 'maritime adventure and voyages of discovery in the pursuit of science have an excellent effect upon the Naval Service' in training officers to cultivate their powers of observation.

Drawing on their experience around the world, they disposed briskly of 'the popular objection to North Polar Expeditions on account of the supposed danger'. Indeed, the Council of the society was:

---

[1] There was a British naval survey of the north-east coast of Labrador in 1867, commanded by William Chimmo (1828–91) in HMS *Gannet*, but that was scarcely an expedition to the high Arctic.

[2] Murchison was one of the leading geologists of his day, whose work on some of the oldest rocks in Britain established the Silurian system. In later life, he was a major figure in the Royal Geographical Society, of which he was one of the founders and, repeatedly, its President.

[3] London, The National Archives (TNA): Public Record Office (PRO), Admiralty, ADM 1/5934 [hereafter TNA: ADM], RGS proposals, 11 March 1865.

[4] TNA: ADM 1/5934, Linnean Society Sec. to Sec. RGS [n.d., 1865]. Founded in 1788, the Linnean Society received its charter in 1802.

[5] Joseph Dalton Hooker (1817–1911), the leading British botanist of his day and Fellow of the Linnean Society since 1842, was President of the Royal Society of London from 1873 to 1878, and in 1888 was one of the first two botanists to be awarded the Linnean Medal of the Linnean Society.

convinced that it rests on a fallacy. The Linnean Society has, during the last half century, enrolled among its Members almost all the scientific Officers of the surveying and exploring expeditions of our Naval and other public services. It has thus been deeply concerned in... judging of the comparative amount of loss and hardship incurred, the results showing a remarkable immunity from danger exemplified in the Polar voyages North and South, as compared with many others. With the exception of Sir John Franklin's party,[1] it is believed that not one Fellow of the Society has met with his death through Polar Discovery, whilst in those African Surveys and Explorations which are so warmly supported, there are very few of the numerous contributors to our publications who have not perished in the prosecution of their researches, and the numbers lost in, or in consequence of, scientific expeditions in India and other tropical countries, and in the interior of Australia, have been most deplorable.

Franklin's fate should be a guide to future expeditions rather than a warning against undertaking them. As for specific gains for science:

The most important results in natural history to be obtained from a voyage to the Arctic Ocean, are undoubtedly those that would extend our knowledge of the conditions of... life in those regions. It is now known that the Arctic Ocean teems with life, and that of the more minute organized beings, the multitude of kinds is prodigious. ...

The kinds of these animals, the relations they bear to one another, and to the larger Animals (such as whales, seals &c., towards whose food they so largely contribute), the conditions under which they live, the depths they inhabit, their changes of form, &c., at different seasons of the year, and at different stages of their lives, and lastly, their distribution according to geographical areas, warm and cold currents, &c., are all subjects in which very little is known.[2]

The Linnean Society also sought information about algae, diatoms, and other microscopic plant life of the polar seas. The skeletons of diatoms in particular could be correlated with fossil forms, and could thus contribute to dating rocks and to understanding ancient climatic changes. When it came to terrestrial plants, the most urgent questions were in phytogeography,[3] correlated with a study of currents and of the effects of climate. This would help to unravel anomalies; for example, 'the Spitzbergen Flora contains American plants found neither in Greenland nor in Scandinavia'.[4]

The enormous increase in the sophistication of the theoretical framework of natural history in the half century since the Napoleonic wars is abundantly clear from the Linnean Society's questions. Many developments had contributed to this increase, among them the evolutionary biology promulgated in Charles Darwin's *On the Origin of Species* in 1859. Darwin's work had contributed to a keen awareness of the interdependence of different forms of life, and of their adaptation to specific environments. Although the British Museum (Natural History) was not opened until 1881, the palaeontologist and comparative anatomist Sir Richard Owen (1804–92)[5] did admirable work to revive the

[1] Sir John Franklin (1786–1847), naval officer and Arctic explorer, led three Arctic expeditions, in the last of which both his ships were lost, and all hands died.

[2] TNA: ADM 1/5934, Sec. Linnean Soc., to Sec. RGS [1865].Winsor, *Starfish, Jellyfish* discusses taxonomic and other problems in invertebrate marine biology.

[3] Browne, *The Secular Ark*. Much of the book is devoted to phytogeography, but chapters 3, 4, and 5 are the most relevant here.

[4] Busk, 'Minute of the Linnean Society', p. 158.

[5] The British Museum (Natural History) opened its doors in 1881. It was a tool for research as well as education, and it was very much Owen's creation: Rupke, *Richard Owen*, makes these points beautifully.

British Museum's natural history collections following his appointment as their superintendent in 1856. The role of museums in preserving and organizing collections was a major stimulus to the growth of zoology, natural history, and palaeontology. Also related, and indeed seminal for Darwin's work and for natural history in general, was historical geology, combining stratigraphy and palaeontology, as well as studies of climate; these all owed much to the geologist Sir Charles Lyell, baronet (1797–1875), and his *Principles of Geology* (1830–33). Biogeography, stemming from the work of Alexander von Humboldt and others, had been advanced by Lyell, and was now passionately pursued by Hooker within a broadly Darwinian framework.[1] Also underlying the Linnean Society's questions were issues in marine biology and oceanography, sciences which had been developing since the Arctic expedition in 1818 of the naval officer and explorer Sir John Ross (1777–1856); oceanographic research had meanwhile gained greatly from significant improvements in sounding equipment.[2]

The Ethnological Society was founded in 1843 to study the physical and moral characteristics of the varieties of the human species. It was keen on using archaeological and modern evidence, and favoured polar exploration. Their Secretary, the eugenicist and biostatistician Sir Francis Galton (1822–1911), observed that 'it is a matter of notoriety that as compared with geographical Expeditions in other directions, those to the Polar regions have, on the whole, been attended with remarkably little loss of life ...'. To be properly useful, such observations, they urged, should be carried out by competent observers. The stress on properly skilled observers is a reflection of two complementary trends in natural history, one towards its growth as a branch of the sciences needing its own professional core, the other towards the increasing co-ordination of amateur contributions by those professionals.[3] It was no longer enough, if it had ever been, simply to assume that naval officers could satisfy the needs of qualitative natural science, while quantitative studies, like those pursued by the army officer and physicist Sir Edward Sabine (1788–1883), required formal preparation. Certainly, the naval officers Sir William Edward Parry (1790–1855), Sherard Osborn (1822–75),[4] and others had complained of their own unpreparedness for systematic natural history. As we shall see, recognition by serving officers of their scientific limitations, and criticism by scientists of those limitations, still failed to persuade the Admiralty to ensure the presence of an adequate scientific complement on naval expeditions.

One question to which the scientific societies responded with unanimity was about the best route to the Pole. If getting to the Pole was the main concern, then the Spitzbergen route might be acceptable; but for sciences other than geography, and even

---

[1] Hooker, 'Opinion of Dr Hooker, C.B.'.

[2] McConnell, *No Sea Too Deep*, chaps 4 and 5. Deacon, *Scientists and the Sea*, gives a wide-ranging history of oceanography; chap. 13–16, pp. 276–406, provide useful context.

[3] This is a principal theme throughout Allen, *The Naturalist in Britain* (chapter 14 discusses the combining of amateur and professional naturalists). Barton, 'An Influential Set of Chaps', explores the limitations of the amateur–professional dichotomy. Frank M. Turner, 'Victorian Conflict between Science and Religion' also explores emergent professionalism in a way that goes beyond that dichotomy.

[4] Rear Admiral Sherard Osborn (1822–75) had taken part in the search for the Franklin expedition, and in the Arctic expedition (1852–4) under Sir Edward Belcher (1799–1877). His interest in using steam in Arctic expeditions provided part of the impetus for the BAE in 1875–6. *ODNB*. Parry had explored the Arctic in 1819 and 1827. Sabine, an army officer, also took part in Arctic expeditions, to carry out research in the physical sciences.

for geography when it came to mapping the north shore of Greenland and the archipelago, the Smith Sound route was obviously superior, since many natural sciences cannot be studied in mid-ocean, and only the latter route had much land along it.

The Admiralty was not impressed by scientific arguments, and in any case, the First Lord insisted that he could not justify a second scientific expedition while paying for the oceanographic expedition then being undertaken by the *Challenger*.[1] Meanwhile, northern explorations were increasingly carried forward by other nations, including Sweden, Germany, Austria, and the United States. Arguments of national pride were joined to those of science.[2] Even this might not have changed the Admiralty's mind. But in 1874, the prime minister William Ewart Gladstone (1809–98), whose Liberal government had sent the *Challenger* expedition south, was defeated in his attempt to expand and secularize Dublin University,[3] and resigned. His arch-rival Benjamin Disraeli (1804–81) formed a Conservative government.

In October 1874, the Assyriologist and diplomatist Sir Henry Rawlinson (1810–95), as President of the RGS, wrote to Disraeli, urging him to approve an Arctic expedition. Mere days later, the new Hydrographer of the Admiralty, Captain Sir Frederick Evans (1815–85), prepared a confidential memorandum supporting the proposal.[4] He advanced arguments identical with those emanating from the RGS. Disraeli was keen on the idea, and wrote in November that 'Her Majesty's Government have determined to lose no time in organizing a suitable expedition'.[5] The BAE now had the support of government and the Admiralty.

Selecting the leader of the expedition was the Admiralty's responsibility, but their decision must have had a pleasurably ironic relish for Disraeli. Where Gladstone had sent an expedition south, Disraeli would send one north. Who could be better, in every sense, than the Aberdonian commander of HMS *Challenger*, Sir George Strong Nares, a man who was even now leading that great scientific expedition? He was at fifty-three the youngest surviving officer with sledging and sailing experience from the Franklin searches.[6] He was met at Hong Kong by a telegraphic message instructing him to return to England, there to make preparations for an expedition towards the North Pole.

The Admiralty informed the RGS and the Royal Society, whose Arctic committees were galvanized. The RGS undertook to prepare a selection of papers on Arctic geography and ethnology for the use of the expedition.[7] Sir Clements Robert Markham (1830–1916), Secretary of the Royal Geographical Society, explained to Hooker, since 1873 the thirty-second President of the Royal Society, that his aim was for the two

---

[1] Rawlinson, 'Address', pp. xxxiv–xxxv; [Royal Geographical Society], *The New Arctic Expedition*, pp. 8–9.

[2] Levere, *Science and the Canadian Arctic*, p. 260.

[3] *University Education (Ireland) Bill.*

[4] TNA: ADM 1/6313, Evans, 'Arctic Exploration 1874'.

[5] Disraeli to Rawlinson 17 Nov. 1874; Hattersley-Smith, 'British Arctic Expedition', pp. 17–26.

[6] Nares (1831–1915) had been on HMS *Resolute* under Henry Kellett and on McClintock's *Franklin* search expedition; Deacon and Savours, 'Sir George Strong Nares'.

[7] RGS, *A Selection of Papers on Arctic Geography*. The RGS was willing, through its most vocal advocate, Clements Markham, to take full credit for persuading other scientific bodies and the government to mount this new expedition: see C. R. Markham, 'The Arctic Expedition of 1875–76', pp. 536–55; C. R. Markham, *Threshold of the Unknown Region*. See also Caswell, 'The RGS and the British Arctic Expedition, 1875–76'. Clements Markham had formerly been in the Royal Navy and took part in one of the Arctic expeditions searching for Franklin in 1850–51.

societies to furnish the expedition with 'all that is known in the various branches'.[1] The Royal Society undertook the preparation of a 'Greenland Manual' covering natural history, geology, and physics, under the superintendence of the geologist and palaeontologist Thomas Rupert Jones (1819–1911), Professor of Geology at the Royal Military College, Sandhurst. The expedition was to leave at the end of May 1875, just four months after Hooker wrote to Jones.[2] Habits of organization at the Royal Military College may have helped; the *Manual* was ready in time.[3] It was really two books bound and presented as one, the relatively brief[4] *Instructions for the Use of the Scientific Expedition to the Arctic Regions, 1875*, and the much longer *Manual of the Natural History, Geology, and Physics of Greenland and the Neighbouring Regions*. The latter was a compilation of papers and extracts of works on the zoology, botany, geology and meteorology, compiled by T. Rupert Jones, and on the physical sciences, compiled by William Grylls Adams (1836–1915), Professor of Natural Philosophy and Astronomy in King's College, London.

The instructions covered sciences from the old *Admiralty Manual*,[5] with additions for branches of observation made possible by advances in instrumentation, notably in spectroscopy, and for categories of information required by theoretical advances.

The astronomical instructions concerned forthcoming eclipses of the sun and occultations; tidal observations; pendulum observations; and the detection of meteoric or cosmical dust in Arctic snow. There were no novelties in the magnetic instructions, the only advances since Franklin's day being modest ones in instrumentation. There was, for each of Nares's two screw steam ships, *Alert* and *Discovery*, a set of instruments containing a portable unifilar magnetometer, for determining the absolute horizontal force at a fixed station; a Barrow's or Kew pattern dip circle, for determining inclination, and fitted with special extra magnetic needles for determining the total force; a portable declination magnetometer, for differential observations at a fixed station; azimuth and sledge compasses for travelling; and a Fox dip circle, for observing the magnetic inclination and intensity in sledging or travelling parties.[6] Sabine's article in the *Admiralty Manual* remained authoritative for naval expeditions.

The meteorological instructions were also mostly standard.

The physical sciences were to be handled in a manner by now traditional in the navy, with naval officers receiving instructions, instruments, and where needed instruction from specialists. The officers would then carry out the programme of observations laid down for them; and the results, where reliable, and where money allowed, would be reduced following the expedition's return. There would be no dedicated astronomer or magnetician on this expedition.

---

[1] London, Kew, Royal Botanic Gardens, Herbarium Papers, Hooker Papers (hereafter RBG, Hooker Papers, Herbarium), ff. 174r–175r, C. R. Markham to J. D. Hooker, 11 Jan. 1875. *Alert* was a steam sloop that had been strengthened and fitted with new engines and boiler; *Discovery* had been a steam whaler, the *Bloodhound*, renamed for Arctic service. C. R. Markham, *Refutation of the Report of the Scurvy Committee*, p. 62.

[2] Cambridge, Scott Polar Research Institute (hereafter, SPRI), MS 336, Hooker to Jones 22 [Jan.] 1785.

[3] T. R. Jones, ed., *Manual*; London, Royal Society of London: Committee Minute Books, 2 (hereafter RSL: CMB 2) f. 89.

[4] 86 pages long.

[5] Herschel, ed., *Manual of Scientific Inquiry*, 3rd edn.

[6] For details, see Levere, 'Magnetic Instruments', pp. 68–9.

Although the scientific societies did not succeed in having geologists appointed to the BAE, their lobbying resulted in the appointment of a paid naturalist to each ship. This was something of a triumph. There had been unpaid naturalists: Joseph Banks (1773–1820) had sailed with Captain James Cook (1728–79); Banks was able to build a career in science on that foundation, transforming Kew Gardens into a major international establishment, and becoming President of the Royal Society in 1778. Charles Darwin (1809–82) had sailed with Captain Robert Fitzroy (1805–65) on HMS *Beagle*. Scientific work had been a feature of numerous prior nineteenth-century Arctic expeditions. Immediately following the French or Napoleonic wars, Edward Sabine, an artillery officer who eventually became a general, received a salary while on detached service carrying out important work on geophysics in the Arctic; he had gone on to become the leading British figure in geomagnetism, and from 1861 to 1871 was President of the Royal Society of London. But it soon became the norm for naval officers to do double duty, recording meteorological and magnetic data, and whatever other information of potential interest they could manage. Expeditions carried surgeons, and they were often the ones responsible for collecting specimens in natural history. The prime example of a surgeon-naturalist in the Arctic was John Richardson (1787–1865), who was on detached service in Franklin's first and second expeditions, but fortunately not on his final one. Surgeons were paid as surgeons, and simply added natural history to their portfolio when circumstances allowed.

The Admiralty's Arctic committee had originally taken the line that natural history on the BAE could be handled by naval personnel. This was perhaps not unreasonable, since many British gentlemen, naval and otherwise, were amateur naturalists, sometimes of no mean order. In spite of the barrier of Latin names, it generally seemed to require less training to be, say, an amateur botanist or ornithologist than to be an amateur magnetician or astronomer; experience in the field was more important for natural history. The Arctic committee recommended that the expedition should employ only naval officers, and no civilian scientists.[1] The general view of the scientific societies, however, was that there should be full-time naturalists on the BAE; this view prevailing with the Arctic committee, they reversed their earlier recommendation. With just two naturalists to be appointed, one for each vessel, it was desirable that they should each be acquainted with as many branches of natural history as possible.[2] The Royal Society was so informed, and was asked to suggest appropriate candidates. Their first recommendation was Chichester Hart (1847–1908), of Trinity College, Dublin, a young man whose principal distinctions were that he had 'worked up the flora of parts of the west of Ireland in the field', and that he had been awarded a 'pedestrian prize' in athletic sports at Dublin. Hart was to serve as naturalist on HMS *Discovery*, *Alert*'s sister ship in the British Arctic Expedition. The other naturalist, appointed to HMS *Alert*, was the army officer and naturalist Henry Wemyss Feilden (1838–1921), said to have been a distant connection of the magistrate and novelist Henry Fielding.

---

[1] TNA: ADM 1/6328, 4 Dec. 1874; RSL: CMB 2, pp. 55–6 re 4 Dec. 1874.
[2] TNA: ADM 1/6367, [Admiralty] Memorandum, 6 January 1875. *Arctic Blue Books*, 1875, [C. (2nd series) 1153], p. 27.

2. Henry Wemyss Feilden

Feilden was the second son of Sir William Henry Feilden (1812–79), the 2nd Baronet Feniscowles. A younger son, he was destined for a career in the army. He was born in barracks at Newbridge in County Kildare in Ireland, where his father, then in the 17th Lancers, was quartered. His mother Mary Elizabeth Feilden (1808–90) also came from a military family; she was the daughter of Colonel Balfour Wemyss (1759–1827). Feilden became an ensign in the 42nd Highlanders at the age of eighteen. While still in his teens, he went on to serve in the suppression of the Indian Mutiny at Cawnpore in 1857, and was scarred by the horrors he saw.[1] Then came Lucknow, where fighting ended in 1858, when he was a staff officer with the 1st Gwalior Infantry. He served in Bundelkhand in 1859. In his unfinished biography of Feilden, his friend, the traveller and naturalist Aubyn Bernard Rochfort Trevor-Battye (1855–1922) remarks that Feilden would never talk about the Indian Mutiny: 'He was only a boy at the time, and I think it had left a horror upon him.'[2] His next posting was to the 8th Punjab Infantry, with which he took part in the Second Opium War in China at the Taku forts.[3] In 1860 Feilden sold his commission in the British Army, and joined a ship that ran the blockade to South Carolina, then journeyed by train to Richmond, Virginia, where he offered his services to the Confederate cause. The details of his role in the fighting may be found elsewhere, but suffice it to say here that he was no spectator, had a horse killed under him, served on the staff of Confederate General William Joseph Hardee (1815–73) when opposing the Union General William Tecumseh Sherman (1820–91), and finally surrendered to Sherman in 1865. Altogether he spent three and a half years in South Carolina, during which he courted and married Julia McCord (1838–1920), the daughter of a prominent South Carolinian, returning to England with his bride in 1866. In 1867 he rejoined the British Army as Adjutant of the 8th Battalion of the Lancashire Volunteers, and later that year became paymaster of the 18th Hussars. In 1868 he and Julia sailed for India to join his unit, but he was invalided home at the end of the year.[4] After three years as paymaster of the 4th, followed by the same role in the brigade of the Royal Artillery in Malta, Feilden

---

[1] See his *Alert* journal entry for 6 Dec. 1875: London: Royal Geographical Society Library, MS 387B (hereafter Feilden, *Alert* Journal).

[2] Trevor-Battye, *A Noble Englishman*, p. 4.

[3] Ibid., pp. 1–12; *Debrett's Baronetage*, p. 205. C. R. Markham, *Threshold of the Unknown Region*, 4th edn, p. 401, summarizes Feilden's military career until 1875. See also 'Obituary', *Ibis*, 1921, pp. 726–32. Ensign in the 42nd Highlanders (Black Watch) 1856: suppression of the Indian mutinies at Lucknow (medal and clasp); staff officer, 1st Gwalior Infantry 1858, served against rebels in Bundelcund 1859; transferred to 8th Punjab Infantry, served with them at the Taku forts (medal and clasp); promoted to lieutenant in the 44th (East Essex) Regiment of Foot. American Civil War, captain and assistant adjutant-general on General Beauregard's staff, then senior officer on the staff at the siege of Charleston; on General Hardee's staff when opposing Sherman's march; returned to England 1866, adjutant of the Lancashire Rifle-Volunteers; paymaster of the 18th Hussars 1868, served briefly with them in India; 1869–73, Paymaster of the 4th and in 1873 of the brigade of Royal Artillery at Malta. Feilden went on to serve in the First Boer War, and again in Africa in 1890. During the Second Boer War, he was paymaster of Imperial Yeomanry, for which service he was made a Companion of the Order of the Bath. His rank when he retired was colonel. The Parliamentary Papers relating to the BAE refer to him as Captain Feilden, R.A. [i.e. Royal Artillery]. The Army List of 1875, however, shows that he was a member of the 4th (the King's Own Royal) Regiment. I am grateful to Mr C. L. Gardner for pointing out this discrepancy.

[4] Emerson and Stokes, *A Confederate Englishman*, pp. x–xxiii. The bulk of their edition concerns Feilden's participation in the Civil War, as does Trevor-Battye, *A Noble Englishman*, chap. 2, pp. 1–101.

enjoyed a brief spell in the Faroe Islands studying the avifauna, thereby gaining some reputation as a naturalist.[1] He was back in England when the Royal Society solicited applications for the post of naturalist on the coming British Arctic Expedition. There were only two applicants. Feilden's letter was suitably modest:

> Dear Sir, By the advice of Prof. Newton,[2] I write you a line to offer my services ... I am afraid my qualifications may be somewhat limited for such an undertaking ... I believe, however, that I am well acquainted with the birds that an Arctic expedition, even reaching the Pole is likely to meet with, I am fairly acquainted with the Mediterranean & Northern forms of mollusca and can make observations on the Geology of the countries I pass through.[3]

He was not an obvious candidate, but he was too modest about his abilities. He was to prove a highly skilled observer and highly effective collector of birds, a competent all-round naturalist, a tolerable palaeontologist, and a first-rate field geologist.[4] It also helped, though it was not mentioned in his application, that he was physically tough, eminently reliable, and a genial companion. He worked the dredges and towing nets, brought up samples from the tide hole[5] when the ship was at its winter quarters, and took part in making and recording physical and meteorological observations. He would turn his hand to whatever was needed, an important quality in a small community which became increasingly stressed by exhaustion, scurvy, and a harsh environment.

There was considerable pressure to appoint a geologist. Clements Markham, although no scientist, rated the work of a geologist as:

> the most important of all. Medical and other officers can carefully collect all plants and animals, and note localities and habits; but collecting is the very smallest part of geology; and it requires a thoroughly skilled man, well acquainted with all that is known, to bring back the information. Of course this branch of the work has the most interest for geographers, and I venture to think that a good geologist should certainly go.[6]

Markham combined the perspective of a geographer and naval officer with recognition of the need for study in the library and experience in the field. Nares was asked whether he could take a geologist, and replied that the ships were so small that each would have room for only one scientific officer, once the officers, crew, and stores were accounted for.[7] To take an additional scientist meant leaving a sailor behind, a poor idea since the crews were already minimal. 'I would point out', he continued:

[1] RSL: CMB 2/14/1, pp. 55–6, and CMB 2/14/2, pp. 61–4; C. R. Markham, *Threshold of the Unknown Region*, pp. 401–2. Levere, 'Henry Wemyss Feilden, Naturalist', 307–12.

[2] Alfred Newton (1829–1907), a zoologist and ornithologist of distinction, had taken a leading role in the creation of the British Ornithologists' Union in 1858, and was Professor of Comparative Anatomy at Cambridge from 1866 to 1907. See *ODNB*. He and Feilden became friends.

[3] RSL: MS M C.10.172, Feilden to Sclater, 25 Nov. 1874. Philip Lutley Sclater (1829–1913), zoologist, was Secretary of the Royal Society. See *ODNB*.

[4] Levere, 'Henry Wemyss Feilden (1838–1921)', pp. 213–18.

[5] The tide-hole, also called a fire-hole, was a hole kept open in the ice to provide a supply of water in case of fire, and it also contained a gauge for taking tidal observations.

[6] Royal Botanic Gardens, Kew, Hooker Papers, Voyage of HMSS *Alert* and *Discovery* (hereafter RBG, Hooker Papers, Voyage), JDH/1/15, ff. 174–174v, C. R. Markham to Hooker 11 Jan. 1875.

[7] For a list of Nares's officers and men, see Nares, *Narrative of a Voyage*, I, pp. ix–x. Brief biographical information about the officers is given in C. R. Markham, *The Arctic Navy List*, pp. 60–62. Nares took much larger crews than Franklin had done on his final disastrous expedition.

that two of the Medical Officers[1] have been appointed to the ships in consequence of their scientific accomplishments and knowledge of Natural History [in the old tradition of surgeon-naturalists], also that a gentleman specifically appointed for geological observations would have a very limited field for his Examination, as our number will render it impossible for him to travel any distance away from the ship by sledges.

... Regarding the subject of geological observations, great advantages would be gained if the Naval Officers who will be employed on sledging Expeditions, which if the [land] is [continued], must necessarily take them along two hundred, or three hundred miles of previously unexamined coast line, were to obtain such geological instruction as to make them at all events good collectors.[2]

In spite of his experience as commander of the *Challenger* expedition, Nares underestimated the preparation necessary for effective collecting. Although he would prove supportive of Feilden during the expedition and afterwards, he was unable to put scientific priorities to the fore when they conflicted with his primary mission, geographical exploration towards the pole, and the maintenance of naval discipline and efficiency.[3] In the event, he would be proved both right and wrong; naval officers contributed little to geology, but the geological work of Feilden, an amateur but official naturalist, was to stand unsurpassed until the middle of the twentieth century.[4]

The Admiralty accepted Nares's advice, and no geologist was appointed; Feilden would not have described himself as one. *The Scotsman* told the Admiralty what they should do: refuse the nomination of a botanist (i.e. Hart), put a geologist in his place, and turn over 'what little botanical work is required' to Edward Lawton Moss (1843–80), one of the surgeons, who was quite up to it.[5] Moss, in fact, believed that he had been appointed as surgeon in *Alert* partly because of his scientific achievements; that was true. But he appears to have considered himself an official naturalist to the expedition, and apparently was only disabused of this misunderstanding after *Alert* was in winter quarters. If that was the case, it is no wonder that he and Feilden came to be

---

[1] The two Medical Officers were Moss in *Alert*, and Coppinger in *Discovery*. Moss was born in Ireland in 1843, educated first at Dublin, and graduated in medicine from St Andrews in 1862. He entered the navy in 1864. By 1875 he had contributed several papers to the Linnean Society, the Zoological Society of London, and others. This information is from the biographical sketch in C. R. Markham, *Threshold of the Unknown Region*, p. 407. Richard William Coppinger (1847–1910) graduated MD from Queen's University, Dublin, in 1870. From 1889 he was Fleet Surgeon, Haslar Hospital. (*ODNB*).

[2] Library and Archives of Canada (LAC), Nares, 'Letterbook', Nares to C.-i.-C., 24 Feb. 1875.

[3] Instructions concerning equipment and fitting out are given in *Arctic Blue Books*, [C. (2nd series) 1153], 1875; the sailing orders for *Alert* and *Discovery* are in TNA: ADM 1/6367, 25 May 1875, 9 pp. printed. These were Nares's final instructions from the Admiralty, which he included in *Narrative of a Voyage*, I, pp. xi–xviii; see esp. p. xi. See also *Arctic Blue Books, continuation of* [C. (2nd series) 1153], 1876, pp. 3–6.

[4] De Rance and Feilden, 'Geology of the Coasts of the Arctic Lands'. Feilden and Jeffreys, 'Post-Tertiary beds of Grinnell Land and North Greenland'; Feilden, 'On the Geological Results of the Polar Expedition'; Feilden and Etheridge, 'On the Palaeontological Results of the Recent Polar Expedition'. Hattersley-Smith, 'British Arctic Expedition'; Blackadar, *Geological Reconnaissance*; Thorsteinsson and Tozer, *Geology of the Arctic Archipelago*.

[5] *The Scotsman*, 'From Private Correspondence', 1 March 1875, p. 5, cutting in RBG, Hooker Papers, Voyage, f. 38. See also *The Scotsman*, 13 Feb. 1875, p. 3, and 17 March 1875, pp. 6–7. Naval personnel were responsible for meteorological, magnetic, and other scientific work, although they were scarcely scientists; the ship's doctor frequently doubled as naturalist, and Moss had jumped the gun in assuming this would be the case on the BAE.

at loggerheads.[1] Feilden, although he was not a specialist, proved a careful and thorough botanist.

3. Instructions for the Expedition

The naturalists, like the officers responsible for physical observations, received instructions through the Royal Society. One of their main tasks was 'to ascertain all facts bearing upon the distribution or possibly gradual disappearance of Mammalian life in the direction towards the Pole'.[2] Geographical distribution and its change through time were important in zoology just as they were in botany, and for the same reason: the dominance of Darwinian theories of evolution. For the same reason, variations between southern and northern forms of the same species were to be carefully noted. There were a number of specific questions about endemic Arctic species, including polar bear, muskox, and Arctic fox; also of interest, should it occur, was the sickness among 'Eskimo dogs',[3] which had afflicted recent expeditions. Standard instructions were also given for observing cetaceans, and for collecting and studying birds and fishes, with due attention to distribution.

The instructions for observing and collecting molluscs made clear the importance of dredging, for palaeontology as well as zoology:

> The palaeontological basis of the glacial epoch consists mainly in the identification of certain species of Mollusca, which inhabit the Polar seas and are fossil in Great Britain and even as far south as Sicily. But such species may owe their present habitat and position to other than climatal causes, viz., to the action of marine currents. Certain small Spitzbergen species ... have lately been found everywhere in the depths of the North Atlantic as well as in the Mediterranean; and the question naturally arises what is the home of these species ...? That question cannot be answered for want of sufficient information ...
>
> It is hoped that each of the vessels to be fitted out for the Polar expedition will have a donkey engine,[4] by which the dredges can be lifted; and that a sufficient supply of necessary apparatus will be provided, regard being of course had to the limited space allowed for such a secondary object. The great experience of Capt. Nares renders any suggestions as to dredging quite superfluous.[5]

It is striking that even a scientific advisor to a scientific expedition could describe work in marine biology as secondary, presumably to geographical work.

Fossil shells were to be collected, and their position and height above sea level noted. 'The former conditions and climate of the Polar region may be thus ascertained, and a new chapter opened in the history of our globe.'[6]

---

[1] Appleton and Barr, *Resurrecting Dr. Moss*, pp. 95–6. Moss, *Shores of the Polar Sea*, pp. 95–6; Appleton claims that Moss did not know that he was not the official naturalist until the ships returned to England, but Feilden's *Alert* Journal, 7 Dec. 1876, makes it clear that he knew it by 7 Dec.

[2] Günther, 'Making Observations on, and Collecting Specimens of, the Mammalia', pp. 36–9.

[3] These were Greenland or Inuit working dogs, husky-type, brought from Siberia to North America by the Thule people at least one thousand years ago.

[4] A small portable engine, useful for raising objects and for pumping water.

[5] Jeffreys, 'Making Observations on, and Collecting the Mollusca of, the Arctic Regions', in T. R. Jones, ed., *Manual*, pp. 48–50. Jeffreys was a lawyer turned conchologist, active in in several scientific organizations, including the Royal Society (and the Royal Society club), the BAAS, and the Linnean Society.

[6] Ibid. p. 50.

Then came instructions for collecting and preserving hydroids and polyzoa, on the construction and use of the towing net, and notes on the animals that might thereby be obtained. These notes showed the considerable advance during the preceding decades in an understanding of the life cycles of some very curious creatures.[1]

Joseph Hooker gave instructions for botany. He thought it probable that there were no new species to be discovered in the Arctic, at least in North America. But there was still much to learn about their distribution, the conditions under which they grew, and their life cycles. There were questions of hybridization (how else to account for the number of intermediate forms of willow and saxifrage?); a need for the careful collection, hitherto lacking, of Arctic lichens and mosses; a study of the transportation of seeds by icebergs or other ice formations, and the resistance of those seeds to cold and to saline immersion, all central to any historical account of distribution, and therefore crucial for an evolutionary interpretation; and a study of marine algae and diatoms, including the depths at which they were found.[2]

There were instructions for geological work, given by Professor Andrew Crombie Ramsay (1814–91), Director of the Geological Survey, and Sir John Evans (1823–1908), since 1874 President of the Geological Society. The naturalists should tackle the identification of sedimentary rocks, recording their sequence, alignment, fossil content, and lithological character; the identification of igneous rocks, formed by upwelling through the earth's crust, their sequence, cleavage, and penetration by dykes; and they should make a similar study of metamorphic rocks, such as slate formed from clay. They should seek to identify major formations that could be compared lithologically or palaeontologically with such known American or European formations as the Silurian, Devonian, or Carboniferous. They should look for and record mineral lodes in fractures and faults. They should carefully record the fossil floras in north Greenland and Ellesmere Island. An article in *The Popular Science Review* informed a wider readership that the Miocene[3] flora was particularly rich and attractive, since at that time, as Scandinavian expeditions had shown, Greenland and other circumpolar lands had 'a luxuriant flora of ever-green trees and shrubs, oaks, magnolias, chestnuts, cypresses, redwoods (*Sequoia*), ebony, &c.'[4] In geology even more than in zoology, information brought back by numerous British expeditions was being integrated into a circumpolar picture. That picture was emerging from studies by several nations, notably in recent Swedish, Austrian, and, to a lesser extent, American polar work. The Austrians and the Swedes had worked largely to the east of Greenland, although Nordenskiöld[5] had led an expedition to west Greenland, the Americans had concentrated their energies along the Smith Sound route. Here were the beginnings of a true international enterprise. Clements Markham and the

---

[1] Ibid.; G. J. Allman, 'Collection and Preservation of Hydroids and Polyzoa'; Allman, 'Construction and Method of Using the Towing Net'. Winsor, *Starfish, Jellyfish* describes these advances.

[2] Hooker, 'Outlines of the Distribution of Arctic Plants', in T. R. Jones, ed., *Manual*, pp. 62–7.

[3] Miocene: the middle division of the Tertiary strata (as containing remains of fewer now-existing species than the Pliocene), and the geological epoch which it represents. Pliocene: the newest division of the Tertiary formation, distinguished from Eocene and Miocene as containing a larger proportion of fossil shells of still existing species. *OED*.

[4] R. Brown, 'The Arctic Expedition. Its Scientific Aims', p. 159.

[5] Baron Nils Adolf Erik Nordenskiöld (1832–1901), Finnish geologist, mineralogist, and Arctic explorer, who moved to Sweden, where he was prominent in science and politics. His first voyage to the west coast of Greenland was in 1870; in 1878–9 he made the first crossing of the Northeast Passage.

Royal Geographical Society might echo John Barrow (father and son)[1] in stressing the national glory accruing from polar exploration; but science, perhaps excluding geographical discovery, was increasingly dependent on international exchange and co-operation.

Distinct from the observations of rocks and fossils, but contributing to an understanding of erosion and other aspects of geological change, was the study of glaciers and icebergs; Ramsay and Evans proposed a more comprehensive set of questions and observations than had been given to previous British expeditions.

Mineralogy, once independent and then integrated with Wernerian geology with its Neptunist explanations of the formation of the earth's crust, now enjoyed a semi-autonomous existence, using chemical tools, such as the blow pipe, to identify specimens.[2] Much the most exciting prospect in mineralogy was the extension of Nordenskiöld's reported discovery of large masses of meteoric iron in Miocene rocks on the west coast of Greenland at Ovifak. Was the iron meteoric or not?[3] It would be good if the naturalists could visit the site again and settle the issue. Feilden, scrutinizing Nordenskiöld's account, clearly had some reservations. At Ovifak, the cliffs of basalt and red wacke (a sandstone-like rock derived from the breakdown of basalt) rise 2,000 feet above sea level. The ironstones lay together at the foot of the cliffs, which suggested that, if they were meteoric, they must have fallen before the cliffs were formed, and then been released by the action of the sea from the overlying cliffs. Perhaps Nordenskiöld's alternative explanation, of a terrestrial origin of the iron, was more probable. When Feilden got to Ovifak, a hand lens showed him that pieces of basalt were embedded in the iron, which argued against the latter's meteoric origin.[4]

Clearly, with responsibility for geology, mineralogy, and the full range of the life sciences, the naturalists would have their work cut out, since there would be only one of them on each ship. Equally clearly, neither of the naturalists selected possessed the kinds of qualifications, based on formal study and experience, to be able to achieve all that was required of them. The contrast with the scientific staffing of the *Challenger* expedition is striking, as is the lack of volunteers from the scientific community for Nares's expedition. The navy's attitude to non-naval personnel speaks volumes for the dominance of old models of control in the Arctic.

The spokesmen of the RGS, it will be recalled, had reserved for themselves the provision of advice about Arctic geography and ethnography. Among their offerings was a report from the Arctic committee of the Anthropological Institute, a group including Sherard Osborn and Clements Markham. They offered the opinion, on less than conclusive evidence, 'that there are or have been inhabitants in the unexplored region to

[1] Sir John Barrow, 1st baronet (1764–1848), promoter of exploration and author, had vigorously promoted the search for the Northwest Passage; his second son, John Barrow (1808–98), was, like his father, active in geographical and Royal Society circles, was a founder member of the Hakluyt Society (1846), and 'the only civilian member of the Arctic council established in 1851 to co-ordinate the search for Franklin'. *ODNB*.

[2] For the changing interrelations between mineralogy and the newer science of geology, see Laudan, *From Mineralogy to Geology*; Albury and Oldroyd, 'From Renaissance Mineral Studies to Historical Geology'; Porter, *The Making of Geology*, esp. pp. 175–6.

[3] For Nordenskiöld's report, including the discovery of the problematic iron, see his 'Account of a Voyage to Greenland' reprinted in T. R. Jones, ed., *Manual*, pp. 389–446. For a more detailed account of the iron, see Flight, 'On Meteoric Irons', in ibid. pp. 447–67; Maskelyne, 'Instructions for Making Observations', in ibid., pp. 80–81.

[4] Feilden, 'Notes from an Arctic Journal', 3rd series 2, 1878, p. 375.

the north of the known parts of Greenland. If this be the case, the study of a people who have lived for generations in a state of complete isolation, would be of the highest scientific interest.'[1] They listed general questions, including the diligent collection of skulls, and the collection of as complete a vocabulary as possible: enquiries about the 'Religion, Mythology, and Sociology of Eskimo Tribes'; questions about the remains of ancient races; about Eskimo warfare, art and ornamentation; and about their stature, intelligence, marriage and funeral customs, food, and kayaks and other forms of transportation.

Apart from this plethora of instructions, there were instructions from Dr Armstrong (1818–99), the Medical Director-General of the navy, for the maintenance of health and the avoidance of scurvy. Armstrong proposed a liberal diet of meat (two pounds daily) with a 'proportionate quantity of vegetables and antiscorbutics. ... [W]ith a scale of diet smaller than this I consider that debility of a scorbutic character must ensue, and that at an early period, if the men are much exposed to hard work and intense cold.' He recommended an alternation of fresh preserved meat with salt meat, and cabbage and preserved potato as the bulk of the vegetable food. Armstrong attached 'the greatest possible importance to the daily administration of Lemon juice', to begin the day after fresh vegetables ceased: 'but this must be carried out on the most rigid principles ... without one day's interruption'. To ensure that the men took their daily ration, it should be administered, mixed with sugar in water, in the presence of the officer of the watch. Away from the ship, when travelling by sledge, the same ration of lemon juice should be administered.[2] Nares copied Armstrong's recommendations into his 'Remark Book', which accompanied him on the voyage. When it came to sledging during the expedition, however, Armstrong's instructions were not followed, and there was a formal enquiry into the consequences of that omission.[3]

The ships were refitted and outfitted, and the crews assembled. Late in May the Admiralty sent formal instructions[4] to Nares on board HMS *Alert* at Portsmouth. His ships would be accompanied by the *Valorous* a little beyond Disko, Greenland, for the provision of extra coal and stores, and to bring back Nares's first reports; *Valorous* would also be available thus far for towing, if needed, and would perform dredging, sounding, and other scientific work before returning home.[5]

Alert and *Discovery* would continue north, picking up interpreters and dogs along the way, making vigorously for winter quarters. *Discovery* was not to winter beyond the 82nd parallel. This would enable her to serve for *Alert*'s crew to fall back on, if need be, so that the men could escape to the relief ship that would go to Smith Sound in the summer of 1877; *Alert*, no matter how far north she steamed, was not to winter more than 200 miles north of *Discovery*. '[I]t is not desirable, under any circumstances, that a single ship should be left to winter in the Arctic regions'. This, with instructions about marker cairns, supply

---

[1] Report of the 'Anthropological Institute' in [RGS], *A Selection of Papers on Arctic Geography*, p. 279.

[2] TNA: ADM 1/6361, pp. 33, 37. For details of the history of theories about the cause of scurvy, see K. J. Carpenter, *History of Scurvy*, esp. chap. 6, pp. 133ff.

[3] *Arctic Blue Books: Report to the Lords Commissioners of the Admiralty on ... Scurvy*. Nares was not disciplined, but was not wholly exculpated by the *Report*, which satisfied nobody. Clements Markham immediately published *Refutation of the Report of the Scurvy Committee*.

[4] [Admiralty], [Sailing Orders to Nares], see p. 10, n. 3 above.

[5] [Admiralty], Sailing orders for *Valorous*, TNA: ADM 1/6337. Wm. B. Carpenter, 'Report on the Physical Investigations'.

depots, and more, showed a proper post-Franklin concern with safety, allied to geographical ambition.

Nares was told that 'every reasonable facility should be given for the collection and preservation of such specimens of the animal, vegetable, and mineral kingdoms as can be conveniently stowed on board the ships. These specimens are to be considered the property of Her Majesty's Government and to be at their disposal.'[1] Feilden's precise observance of the latter part of the instructions was to earn him the displeasure of Hooker and the biologist and science educationist Thomas Henry Huxley (1825–95), respectively President and Secretary of the Royal Society of London.

4.   Outward Bound[2]

The expedition left England at the end of May, with Feilden observing sea birds and what he could of marine life. The 13 and 14 June saw a full gale, which did some damage, and there was still a heavy swell two days later, causing the ships to roll all night. The wind got up again on 18 June, and the following day there was another gale. They began to observe whales, continued north, and by 27 June were in drift ice, and saw an iceberg the following day. They saw the first walrus on 29 June, and by midnight were in another gale. They skirted the ice pack around Fiskernæs on the coast of Greenland, and on 2 July let down the dredge for the first time. Two days later, they crossed the Arctic Circle, and on 6 July reached Disko Bay, where they saw hundreds of icebergs, the discharge of Jacobshavn glacier. They did more dredging when at anchor, and 'the Greenlanders' brought specimens to the ships. Feilden went ashore, seeing the Arctic flora rapidly coming into bloom; he noted red snow, climbed the hills, and made geological observations. On 9 July, the Danish Inspector told Feilden about Ovifak, the place where Nordenskiold found meteoric iron, and Feilden went there in a whaleboat commanded by *Alert*'s Senior Lieutenant, Pelham Aldrich.[3] He collected ornithological specimens, some for science, some for the pot, recorded the geology, and noted signs of upheaval in the rocks. Wherever he could, he observed the dip of geological strata, and was able to give a good account of the geological structure of the land. Back at the Inspector's house, they were shown samples of the different nets used by the Greenlanders, some for hunting beluga whales, others for hunting seals. 'Eskimo dogs' were taken on board, in preparation for the sledging that the expedition planned for the following year. The expedition also needed help and advice from a Greenlander, and fortunately for them, 'Frederick the Greenlander' agreed to join them at Lievely. Nares wrote of him that 'his character is most excellent, and above all he is unmarried'.[4]

[1] *Arctic Blue Books: Papers and Correspondence* [C. (2nd series) –1153], pp. 42–51, 1875; Nares, 'Sailing Orders', in *Narrative of a Voyage*, I, pp. xi–xviii.

[2] The overall route taken by the expedition after passing to the south-west of Greenland is shown in Map 1, p. xxvii. More detailed information from Melville Bay and Baffin Bay northwards is shown in Maps 2–5, pp. xxviii–xxxi.

[3] Pelham Aldrich (1844–1930) had previously served under Nares on the *Challenger* expedition. He later became Admiral Superintendent of Portsmouth Docks and ultimately retired as Admiral in 1908. The Hakluyt Society had commissioned Dr Ian Jackson to edit Aldrich's journals from that expedition, as well as the British Arctic Expedition, commanded by Nares; however, the Society's ambition had to be deferred when Jackson died in 2017.

[4] Nares, *Narrative of a Voyage*, I, p. 24.

On 16 July the ships anchored near the settlement of Ritenbenk, where Feilden collected ornithological specimens, and Clements Markham left to return to England on *Valorous*. On 20 July, they landed at Proven, and visited the Governor. Again they let down the dredge. Two days later, they went onshore, and bagged 122 guillemots. 'Nothing could excuse the wanton shooting and wounding of these beautiful birds, but the fact that they are excellent eating.'[1] Feilden also noted the manner in which the Greenlanders prepared seal skins. That day, they saw their first polar bear. They made their way through ice that was generally broken and disintegrating, and had navigable leads, but every so often they had to break through the thinner ice. They saw another bear, and landed on the ice to pursue it, but 'Mr Bruin went much faster than we could'.[2] Whenever the ship stopped for sounding, Feilden used the dredge net.

They were at the Cary Islands on 27 July. Feilden went ashore, collected birds and flowers, and made geological observations. Geological and palaeontological specimens, i.e. rocks, were heavy, and getting them back to the ship over scree, boulders, ice and snow was exhausting. As they went farther north, the ice became thicker, and there were great piles of floe to scramble over before reaching shore. Wherever the ship paused, Feilden collected specimens and made observations, but if there was a lot to record, his field pocket notes[3] were too long to transfer to his journal. The pages of the journal were folios, but each page had to do service for each day, which, since the expedition went from May 1875 until October 1876, and since Feilden kept using the journal after the ships returned, generally meant that two dates (for a given date in 1875 and for the same date in 1876) had to be fitted onto a single page.

It was fortunate, indeed crucial, that the ships had reinforced hulls, and also crucial that they had steam engines as well as sails; fortunate also that there were a couple of open seams of coal to replenish fuel in the high Arctic. The ships went up the west coast of Greenland, and up Kennedy Channel, sailing, steaming, cutting and battering their way north through the ice. Sometimes they sought shelter from icebergs, sometimes progress was painfully slow, and on occasion they had to blast a way through the ice with powder. At other times they had open water, and briefly made rapid progress. They found muskox skulls and reindeer bones on shore, as well as the remains of Inuit camps, and saw narwhals. *Discovery* had killed one at Cape York. But as they went farther north, they found little life around them. Feilden, on 22 August, noted that the 'open water we have passed through during the last 24 hours is almost devoid of beast or bird life'. When he was able to use the dredge, he found little in the way of life; in shallow water, icebergs had scraped along the bottom, which helped to explain this paucity.

The 25th of August marked their first sighting of muskoxen, a group of nine. All of them were killed by the naval officers; they provided fresh meat, some for immediate consumption, some for later, and some for salting. The temperature at this point was above freezing, but low enough to keep the meat fresh for a while.

Discovery wintered in Discovery Harbour, on the north shore of Lady Franklin Bay on Ellesmere Island, and almost on the site of the future Fort Conger; *Alert* went on up Robeson Channel to the north-east of Ellesmere Island, and on the shores of the Arctic

[1] Feilden, *Alert* Journal, 22 July 1875.
[2] Ibid., 24 July 1875.
[3] Most of these have not been preserved.

Ocean, a few kilometres east of the modern military and meteorological station at Alert, named after the ship. Ice conditions made for hazardous moments, but *Alert* was able to shelter behind floebergs, great slabs of ice up to 30 feet thick that had run aground and built a formidable barrier, which protected *Alert* through the winter and into the spring and summer of the following year. The expedition named their icy harbour and refuge Floeberg Beach.

5. Winter Quarters

The first dog sledging trip set out 9 September. Snowdrifts required the men and dogs to pull together; the average weight of each sledge was 400 lb. They set up camp. On 10 September Aldrich took two sledges to put out a depot to the northward, while Feilden, Moss, and engineer George White headed back to camp; Feilden remarked on White's great strength, a godsend in hauling sledges. Feilden noted the geological strata, and the shells giving proof of the recent elevation of the land. He returned to the ship on 11 September, Aldrich's sledge returned the next day, and Commander Albert Hastings Markham's[1] on 14 September, having weathered a storm, and with the men too exhausted to cover the final leg to the ship; they were all rescued by a party from *Alert*.

Feilden was by now aware of the difficulties facing naturalists collecting specimens in the high Arctic, both from his own brief experience, and from the narratives of previous expeditions. There were only four to six weeks in the year when the ground was free from snow, but those weeks were precisely the best for navigation. Even then, the use of the towing net was hampered by sea ice. Feilden came to be very appreciative of Nares's support:

> Few persons have had the advantage of sailing with so thoughtful a person as Captain Nares, on no occasion has he ever omitted to send me on shore when feasible, or to give me every assistance. In spite of this I feel that the results in my department are somewhat meagre. From the 29th of July to the 1st of September, the date on which we attained our highest northern latitude, we were battling with the ice in Smiths Sound. The frequent delays were of great service to me as I was enabled to go frequently on shore, and I have traced the geology of the coast with tolerable accuracy.[2]

But with the best support in the world, there were uncertainties because of variable ice and variable weather. When the snow began to melt in June, the ground was a morass, unsuitable for sledge travel. Feilden was concerned to devise a means of transport that would be able to carry '100 lbs of impedimenta'.[3] At this stage he thought that loading the dogs with pack saddles would be the best solution. Unfortunately, some of the dogs had already sickened, becoming useless because of fits, and one was not 'pulling his value in food'; Nares ordered that two of them be killed.[4] Minor fits, with symptoms suggesting epilepsy, were common among the sledge dogs, but they recovered from them and made their own way back to the ship.

---

[1] A. H. Markham (1841–1918), born in France, a cousin of Clements Robert Markham, retired as Admiral Sir Albert Hastings Markham, KCB [Knight Commander of the Bath].
[2] Feilden, *Alert* Journal, 31 Dec. 1875.
[3] Ibid., 19 Sept. 1875.
[4] Ibid., 8 Oct. 1875.

By the end of the month, Feilden had the use of his own new workshop on the main-deck. He began to make 'small, almost microscopic collections of most of the specimens',[1] animal, vegetable and mineral, in case it became necessary to leave the main collections behind; given the vicissitudes of Arctic travel, that was a prudent precaution. He was extremely grateful to Nares for the smooth running of the ship; his experience saved them from failures.[2]

Feilden dated the beginning of real winter from 1 November in the 24-hour Arctic night, when it was no longer possible to read the *Times* leader at noon on the floe. But it was always necessary to have water within reach, in case of fire, so throughout their time at Floeberg Beach, a hole was kept open in the ice next to the ship. Feilden used it to sample the marine organisms there, sometimes by baiting it with a dead but inedible animal.

Keeping everyone fit meant exercise as well as lime juice;[3] keeping them cheerful meant providing occupation, entertainment and instruction. The ship's routines kept officers and men busy; Feilden had no time for himself. The ship carried a printing press, and produced news bulletins. There were lectures, often on scientific subjects, by the officers, who also gave instruction to the men, including basic reading and writing for those who lacked these skills. There were musical evenings, with a ship's orchestra, and songs where all joined in the chorus; magic lantern shows and recitations. Officers and men put on plays from 25 November to 17 February, in 'The Royal Arctic Theatre', with printed playbills, and with scenery painted by Moss. Feilden, making his first appearance on the stage, found it 'a great effort to join the troupe, … it is rather hard lines at the age of seven and thirty, to make ones first appearance on the boards'.[4] There were birthday celebrations, with verses for the occasion, and elaborate dinners with printed menus. And the officers hotly debated the ventilation of the ward room mess, differing about the appropriate temperature and the risks of poisoning by excessive carbon dioxide. The rest of the ship, of course, was heated and ventilated according to Nares's orders.

On 20 November, aided by N. C. Petersen, the 'Eskimo interpreter', Feilden began building a snow house for storing some of his effects; Petersen finished the job. Petersen also taught Feilden about Eskimo hunting weapons, their drills used to start fires, and a good deal more about their way of living.

By mid-December, explorations and observations by Feilden and the other officers and crew led them to conclude that there was no 'Open Polar Sea'. The existence of such an open sea had been hypothesized since at least the sixteenth century and was revived in the nineteenth century by the German cartographer and geographer August Heinrich Petermann (1822–78). The American Arctic explorer and physician Isaac Israel Hayes (1832–81) believed that it existed.[5] But Feilden clearly understood that the only 'real

---

[1] Ibid., 7 Oct. 1875.

[2] Ibid., 3 Nov. 1875.

[3] Lemon juice had been prescribed by Alexander Armstrong, Director General of the medical department of the Admiralty (MS ADM. 6361), but the expedition was supplied instead with lime juice, which has less effectiveness as an anti-scorbutic. Armstrong, as Surgeon on *Investigator* during its search for Franklin in 1850–54, had long-held and clear views about the importance of lemon juice: Armstrong, *Observations*, 1858.

[4] Feilden, *Alert* Journal, 24 Dec. 1875. Feilden played the Widow Twankay (the spelling used in *Alert*, now usually 'Twankey') in their Christmas pantomime 'Aladdin'.

[5] See e.g. Hayes, *The Open Polar Sea*.

"Open Polar Sea", with which we are acquainted, is the "Old Greenland", cleared, entirely by the action of the Gulf Stream'.[1] North of the Arctic archipelago, there was ice, and variable seasonal areas of open water. Feilden in his journal wrote that he had coined a new term for it: 'Paleocrystic', meaning ancient ice.[2] That became the expedition's name for it. The programme for the 'Thursday Pops' on 10 February 1876 featured 'the original and only true PALE-O CHRISTY MINSTRELS', and the last 'Thursday Pops' of the winter, on 2 March 1876, included the Rev. Pullen's 'Grand Pæleocrystic Sledging Chorus', which became 'henceforth, as it were, the "Arctic National Anthem"'.[3]

Keeping the fire hole open was a painful chore; Nares made it less so by ordering that a snow house be built over it, with a covered way to it, which made dredging easier; it was thenceforth, with Nares's encouragement, a frequent operation.[4] Feilden went out regularly with a water bottle and an axe, took samples through the ice, and, examining them through the microscope, found beautiful diatoms.

On New Year's Eve, he reflected on his findings to date:

> I have traced the geology of the coast with tolerable accuracy. ... As far as possible I have taken notice of the effects of all the old glacial action that we have met with, and my journal is replete with references to this important subject. I believe I can claim as original <remarking> the difference between ancient sea-beaches and the terraces made by the snow-foot, a new fact for the geologist. A collection of several hundred specimens of rocks and fossils illustrating every point visited has been made and carefully labelled.
>
> In plants my collection is considerable, at every point visited since entering Smith's Sound, I obtained as many specimens of the Flora, as lay in my power. I can see no variation in the flora of the American side from the Greenlandic. The dredgings obtained, often full of diatomacea have been carefully preserved.
>
> Invertebrates – our chances of dredging were limited, but we had the good fortune to obtain a new and beautiful species of crinoid, and amongst other good things two ~~or more~~ species of Terebratula hitherto unrecorded, from ~~arctic seas~~ <Smith's Sound>. All the results of our dredgings have been most carefully preserved. Insects required due share of attention and a tolerably rich collection has been made.[5]

New species of birds had been added to the list. The main finding about mammals was that whales did not venture that far north, except for narwhals at Cape Sabine. On land, muskoxen were found almost as far as the expedition had ventured northwards.[6]

Even in the far north, and in the depths of an Arctic winter, hares and ptarmigan were active, feeding mostly on Arctic willows, preserved in the microclimate beneath the snow. Feilden was eager to discover 'whether the willow does not put forth its buds, and seeds germinate under the snow, many weeks before the sun exposes the plant, and this will be elucidated by a careful examination of the crops of Ptarmigans and stomachs of Lemings [sic]'.[7] A month later, on 11 February, he came across the tracks of a hare that had been

[1] Feilden, *Alert* Journal, 16 Dec. 1876.

[2] Ibid., 15 Dec. 1795. Nares used 'Pæleocrystic' in his *Narrative of a Voyage*.

[3] A. H. Markham, *The Great Frozen Sea*, pp. 246–7 and 422. The chaplain in *Alert*, Anglican clergyman and writer William Henry Pullen (1836–1903), served as their principal writer of verse, plays and songs, and directed the ship's choir. See *ODNB*.

[4] Feilden, *Alert* Journal, 28 Dec. 1875.

[5] Ibid., 31 Dec. 1875.

[6] Ibid.

[7] Ibid., 8 Jan. 1876.

feeding on exposed shoots of a saxifrage (*sax. oppositifolia*); the temperature that day went down to −55°F, showing that at least some Arctic plants 'retain vitality at extremely low temperatures'. Joseph Hooker had commented on the importance of combinations of local circumstances for determining the abundance or scarcity of vegetation. Feilden was keen to elaborate this insight.

He did not merely collect data, he pondered them with insight and care. Animal and plant distribution was a subject that most naturalists were content to study by the compilation of lists and the collection of specimens; Feilden wanted to go further, and the long winter night gave him plenty of time to digest his observations. He gave careful consideration to the effects of climate, of climate change, of ocean currents, of changing levels of land and other impacts of the geological history of the north. He commented on variability and stability in plant and animal populations, with frequent recourse to the writings of Charles Darwin. The ship had a good library of Arctic science and exploration,[1] and he mined it vigorously, seeking to understand how his own work fitted in with that of his predecessors.

With the end of the winter came the possibility of sledge travel, and opportunities for collecting and observing well away from *Alert*.

6.   Sledging in Earnest[2]

The sledging expeditions began on 3 April, some establishing depots to be used along the way by the heavily laden sledges exploring the northern parts of Ellesmere Island and Greenland. Although Feilden was not on the longest of these explorations, he spent some fifty days travelling by sledge and collecting, apart from his work in and around the ship. Some of his sledging journeys were gruelling, and camping conditions were frequently awful. Magnetic, meteorological, tidal, and other observations were kept by the naval personnel, with Feilden assisting, mainly in record-keeping, when asked.[3]

---

[1] Some of the books he consulted may have been from his own library: 'Feilden had a remarkable library, for the buying of books had been through many years his one extravagance. He kept his booksellers' catalogues and bound them into volumes, and had a reliable knowledge of the market value of obscure and secondhand works, esp. of those upon Natural History. I believe his collection of local Natural Histories to have been complete, and his library of Arctic literature (presented to the Royal Geographical Society) has never been approached in comprehensiveness.' Trevor-Battye, 'A Noble Englishman', 'Introduction', pp. 7–8. The books that Feilden donated to the RGS may be consulted there.

[2] For the routes of the main sledging expeditions, see Maps 5–10, pp. xxxi, 224–8.

[3] Feilden wrote the appendix on ornithology in Nares, *Narrative of a Voyage*, II, pp. 206–17; co-authored the appendix on geology in ibid., pp. 327–45; contributed specimens that were described by specialists in the other appendices on natural history, with whom he discussed his findings; and was named (with Nares) as co-author of the physical observations from the expedition: *Arctic Blue Books: Results Derived from the Arctic Expedition 1875–76. I. – Physical Observations by Captain Sir George Nares, R.N., and Captain Feilden, &c.. II. – Medical Report on the Eskimo Dog Disease, by Fleet Surgeon B. Ninnis, M.D.*, in *Accounts and Papers: 1878*, VII, *Arctic Expedition* [C. (2nd series) 2176], pp. 3–146. Within the report on physical observations, Moss wrote the 'Observations on the Specific Gravity of the Sea Water, by Buchanan's (Challenger) Method and Chlorine Estimations', in ibid. pp. 85–7; Lieut. A. C. Parr wrote the section on 'Auroras observed, 1875–1876, at Floeberg Beach and Discovery Bay', in ibid., pp. 113–19; Staff-Commander E. W. Creak, attached to the Admiralty Compass Department, wrote the 'Report to the Hydrographer of the Admiralty, on the Results of the Magnetical

Geology was his forte. He explored the west coast of Robeson Channel and the north coast of Ellesmere Island; his findings remained the major ones for this area until 1953. The rocks, part of the Franklinian geosyncline, were produced by heavy sedimentation between the late Precambrian and late Devonian periods, and saw heavy and complex folding in the Palaeozoic. Feilden's geological notes and sketches were careful and informed, and incorporated detailed sketches, for example one made on 27 March 1876 showing folding of beds of argillaceous sandstone and clay slates. He was repeatedly struck by evidence for the elevation of land. For example, on 19 January he pondered in his journal about the shape of the coastal bays, generally circular with narrow inlets from the sea. 'One thing is certain', he remarked:

> that the numerous lakes spread over the country, have been scooped out by the same forces as made the bays now connected with the sea, the mud deposits around them now teeming with shells of recent testaceous mollusca, shows that it is not so very long ago, since they were elevated above the sea level, and in all probability before very long many of our bays will be converted into chains of circular fresh water lakes by the advancing elevation of the coast.

Since the lakes and bays were surely gouged out by ice, 'we have evidence of alternations of depression and re-elevation of this district during the glacial period'.

With the return of light, Feilden was able to go out regularly shooting specimens for science. His ornithological notes and collections were comprehensive – ornithology was, after all, his avocation, alongside soldiering. Preparing skins was an art, and he was good at it. He studied mammals, alive and dead, performing elaborate autopsies on sledge dogs when they died of mysterious fits, or, though rarely, on muskoxen; when the latter were butchered to provide fresh meat, their remains were useless as specimens. He used the microscope to identify small marine organisms. He organized his collection of plants. Botany was a field in which he was a fast learner, and his observations would prove very welcome to Hooker; he made important observations about sea ice; indeed, he tackled every field of natural history, on shore and, although in a limited fashion, in the ocean; he performed yeoman service.

The expedition had planned to spend two years in the far north, but when the sledge teams returned, suffering from exhaustion and ravaged by scurvy, and after deaths from those causes, Nares determined not to spend another winter in the ice. Feilden, who with others from the ship had gone out to bring the sufferers among the northern party back, was shaken by their condition:

> I cannot pretend to write an account of the hardships and sufferings that these poor fellows went through. In latitude 83°.19′ they dug through the ice and sounded in 71 fathoms mud, the little they were enabled to obtain is full of foraminifera.[1] I guard this with a watchful eye as one of the most precious relics of the expedition.[2]

Observations made by the Officers of the Arctic Expedition, 1875–1876', in ibid. pp. 119–45; and there was an 'Extract from Pages 13 and 15 of the "Report on Atmospheric Electricity"' by Prof. J. D. Everett of Queen's College, Belfast, in ibid., p. 146. Thus Nares and Feilden wrote the bulk of the report on results, and I cannot determine what parts they each played here.

[1] An order of Rhizopoda (protozoan amoebas) with a shell, usually perforated by pores.

[2] Feilden, *Alert* Journal, 14 June 1876.

7. Out of the Ice, and Homeward Bound

It was time to head south. Feilden was particularly frustrated by his hitherto 'long and weary search for the nest of the Knot.[1] I must have walked some hundreds of miles on the errand',[2] and in the end it was a party of crewmembers who found what he had so long sought.[3]

Before HMS *Alert* could move, it was necessary to get the propeller back into the shaft; all efforts at doing this at first failed, because the water constantly froze in the boss.[4] Indeed, although Floeberg Beach had provided a safe shelter through the winter, getting out of it was brutally hard work. On 31 July, blasting the ice-cradle around *Alert* succeeded, the propeller was in place, and the ship floated free, although pack ice made progress slow and uncertain. Nares's concern for the ship led him to advise Feilden 'to pack two or three small tin cases, with samples of my collection and put them on deck ready to throw out on the ice, in case of the ship going'.[5] Since some of the floebergs which they used for mooring were more than 40 feet high, Nares had reason for his warning to Feilden. Feilden was worried too: 'The sombre colouring of the rocks, the contrast with the snow and ice, the sun hidden behind a leaden mist and a strong gale howling down the ravines and whistling through the rigging combined with the knowledge of our perilous position is anything but enlivening.'[6] In spite of the conditions, they tried using the dredge, but found nothing but sand; they did dip 'a couple of beautiful hydroids, very delicate they fell to pieces almost immediatly [sic]'.[7] Sometimes they raised a full head of steam, but progress southward was intermittent, in fits and starts, and repeatedly required raising the ship's screw and rudder.

On 7 August, Feilden went ashore while the ship was once again iced in; he found Eskimo relics, part of a sledge, a stone lamp, and a scraper, and on the following day found the remains of three or four Eskimo encampments. He made careful records, and sketched the implements found at 81°50′N, farther north than any previous discoveries of the remains of man, and far north of then-existing limits of human habitation; his observations led him to theorize about the antiquity of such remains, and the long history of settlement in the north.

By 12 August, *Alert* was able to join *Discovery* in the latter's winter quarters. Hart had discovered a coal seam, and he and Feilden went to examine it. Feilden was clear that it did not belong to the Carboniferous Period, but, on the evidence of fossil plants, it was Miocene, a much younger geological epoch.[8] He returned to the 'coal-mine' with Nares and a party on 17 August, and collected more fossils. Repeated nips from the ice had Feilden concerned for his collections: 'As for ourselves suppose the ship is crushed we

[1] Knot, red knot, *Tringa Canutus*.
[2] Feilden, *Alert* Journal, 26 July 1876.
[3] Ibid., 30 July 1876.
[4] Ibid., 27, 30 July 1876.
[5] Ibid., 31 July 1876.
[6] Ibid., 1 Aug. 1876.
[7] Ibid.
[8] Oswald Heer, 'On the Miocene Flora of North Greenland', in T. R. Jones, ed., *Manual*, pp. 378–89, was Feilden's evidence for this conclusion. Today we reckon that the Miocene Epoch was from 23 million to 5 million years ago, whereas the Carboniferous Period was from 359 million to 299 million years ago. Feilden, *Alert* Journal, 8–17 Aug. 1876.

have simply to step on shore, but I have my collections to look after, and unless I got the boxes out myself not a scrap will be saved'.[1]

The ships made their way fitfully through the ice, with Feilden taking every pause as an opportunity for geologizing and collecting fossils, and, where there was open water, dredging. By 25 September they were back at Disko, and were delighted to see their Danish friends again. The Royal Inspector of South Greenland, Sophus Theodor Krärup Smith (1834–82), allowed Feilden to make a selection from his collection of Eskimo antiquities. On 1 October Fred the Greenland dog driver was in tears when he said farewell to Feilden: 'They are real good fellows these Greenlanders, for 15 months we have been shipmates, and many a night we have slept under the same blanket, and Fred has always been a good messmate'.[2] The ships steamed off the next day, under a salute from the three guns of the settlement. What with ice and rough weather, *Alert* damaged her rudder, which made for slow sailing and slower manoeuvring. They roughly retraced their outward journey, sailing and steaming southward, although farther out in the straits and away from the coast of Greenland. They crossed the Arctic Circle on 4 October, fifteen months to the day since their outbound northward crossing. Bottlenose whales played around the ship on 6 October; the next day saw great numbers of Little Auks flying south in flocks. The 12th of October saw the onset of a full gale, with tremendous seas; Feilden's cabin was flooded. A break in the weather gave them the opportunity to make some repairs to the rudder, but it was still a weak point. On 18 October Nares signalled to *Discovery*: 'Will not risk *Alert* with damaged rudder up channel. If we separate rendezvous at Queenstown sighting Cape Clear',[3] the latter being the southernmost inhabited part of Ireland. Foul weather succeeded good, with head winds; then they were briefly becalmed, before favourable winds returned; *Alert* reached Valentia, the most westerly point of Ireland and, since 1866, the eastern end of the first commercially viable transatlantic telegraph cable. Nares, Feilden, Moss, and Pullen landed there on 27 October. Nares, Feilden and Moss went on to Dublin. They were in London on 29 October.

8.   Home again: Science, Politics, and the Military

Before the expedition had returned, Clements Markham announced that he anticipated splendid results. Answers would be forthcoming to important theoretical questions linking botany, palaeobotany, and geology; significant information would be gained in economic geology, marine ecology and zoology, both vertebrate and invertebrate; plant geography and the study of glaciation would illuminate one another; mysteries of bird migration would be elucidated; the list went on, for it was a long one, and it ended in the confident expectation of valuable unforeseen results besides. When the expedition returned, Markham judged that his confidence had been well placed. For Markham, the geographical and hydrographical results had been the most important, and next in importance came the geological ones. Then there was Feilden's collection of the biology

---

[1] Ibid., 8 Aug. 1876.
[2] Ibid., 1 Oct. 1876.
[3] Ibid., 18 Oct. 1876.

of the land north of the 82nd parallel, hitherto almost unknown to science; a complete flora of the region; exhaustive examinations of the zoology; and remarkably complete zoological collections. Most of this was Feilden's achievement.[1] Nares praised Feilden, generously and accurately, in his official report to the Admiralty: 'no[t] one moment has been lost by this indefatigable collector and observer. ... I am only doing him justice when I state that he has been to this Expedition, what Sabine was to that under the command of Sir Edward Parry.'[2] This was high praise indeed. Sabine had been the most distinguished natural philosopher on any Royal Naval vessel in the Arctic since the beginning of serious British exploration there, had gone on to become a key figure in the establishment of an international network of magnetic observatories, had been knighted for his work in astronomy, geophysics, and ornithology, and had served as the thirtieth President of the Royal Society.

Feilden's initial reception by British scientists was cordial, especially among geologists and ornithologists. He was appropriately modest, telling Hooker that he was working on 'a small typical collection' that he had brought from his cabin, with the bulk of the specimens remaining on board. As soon as he had something ready, he would send it to Hooker, but this would have to be through Nares, 'as I am on the full pay of the Admiralty'.[3] He gave Hooker a quick preview. There were invertebrates from Smith Sound, echinoderms whose distribution confirmed that Greenland was an island, a flora that seemed Greenlandic in character, with between twenty and thirty species of flowering plants between 82° and 83° north. There were no whales in Smith Sound, a circumstance that Feilden attributed to overhunting by whalers. There were terrestrial mammals, with lemmings unsurprisingly being the most numerous, and serving as the bottom of the food chain for other creatures. There were evidences of old Eskimo settlement, indicative of an earlier milder climate; pieces of driftwood arguing for an oceanic drift from Siberia and Bering Strait; and, best of all, geological observations and specimens. He told Hooker, 'I think the Geology is our strongest point'.

9. Geology and Specimens

Feilden was right. His work in geology was indeed his most valuable and enduring contribution to the scientific results of the expedition. He summarized his findings in a letter to Hooker, when he wrote that the geologist Robert Etheridge (1819–1903), who was palaeontologist to the Geological Survey and curator of the Museum of Practical Geology on Jermyn Street, was

> kindly helping me with the few fossils,[4] I have by me, and I am happy to say that the result of his examination, so far, endorses my determination of the formations we met with ... From C.

[1] C. R. Markham, 'The Arctic Expedition of 1875–76', and RGS, MS CRM 65, 'Arctic Expedition 1875–76'; pp. 182–95 of the latter are about Feilden's work in the expedition.

[2] Nares, *Official Report*, p. 47.

[3] RBG, Hooker Papers, Voyage, ff. 222–227, Feilden to Hooker, 12 Nov. 1876.

[4] Feilden, 'Arctic Expedition. Feilden. Post-pliocene & Recent Specimens from Arctic Localities', 1875–6, London, BMNH, Palaeontology MSS, Feilden Collection, MSS FEI; Feilden, 'Rock Specimens and Collecting Sites Including Some Collected by H. C. Hart, and Some Deposited in the Museum of Practical Geology [1875–6]', included in Henry Wemyss Feilden, 'Diary of an Expedition to the Arctic', BMNH, Palaeontology

Isabella in 78° to Hayes Sound in 79°, Gneiss, Syenite and Hornblendic rocks prevail.[1] These are overlaid in lat 79° by massive beds of Silurian[2] conglomerates, dipping generally E to W. The[se] conglomerates are overlaid by beds of grey limestone upper Silurians replete with fossils, these continued to Cape Collinson. From that point we stood over to the E. Greenland coast and anchored in Bessels Bay. There we found the same Silurian Rocks, and our explorers up Petermann Fiord ditto.

Crossing over to Discovery Bay, the geological characteristics alter entirely. The fossiliferous limestones (if ever they existed there) have been denuded, altogether, and are replaced by an enormous series of unfossiliferous Slates and hard limestones, which I presume are the equivalents of the Azoic rocks underlying the Silurians of the American geologists. These strata exhibit the wildest tokens of contortion and disturbance, for miles you sail along them, the strata almost vertical, they appear to have been crumpled up like a puckered ribbon, and then some tremendous denuding agent has shaved them off, and after that the glacier and ice action has grooved them with peaks and hollowed them out into valleys. This formation I followed to 82° and at that point a great anticlinal ridge passes from E. to W. the northern strata on this line dipping to N.N.E. following these up I found them in Lat 82°44 covered with carboniferous limestones dipping N.N.E. the thickness of those beds increased until in Lat 82°46′. Mount Julius 2000 feet high was entirely composed of this formation. Considering the difficulties of transport I brought a good collection of fossils from this point. In Lat 81°44′ near to the Discovery's winter quarters, is a fine development of Miocene strata, it occurs in a valley which has been eroded out of the azoic slates I have before mentioned, and the Miocenes rest unconformably[3] on them, dipping at a moderate angle to the E, and disappearing under Robeson Channel. There we found a fine seam of coal over 20 foot thick, and the shales and sandstones lying above the coal beds produced a rich hard wood flora.

The post-pliocene beds are very interesting they consist of fine muds, sometimes 400 feet thick filling up valleys and climbing the hill sides to a height of 1000 feet, they contain many shells, and I have taken out of them bones of Musk-ox, seals and driftwood &c. that they were deposited under almost similar circumstances as at present exist, and under glacial influences is clear from the number of ice worn and highly polished erratics found in these beds.[4]

Feilden, meanwhile, was working hard on all the collections from the expedition. He was also in a whirl of visits to geologists, ornithologists, zoologists, and ichthyologists, among them museum curators, academics, and educators.[5] He was energetic in his visits to scientific societies; on 4 November 1876 alone, he visited the Royal, Geological, and

---

Manuscripts, Small Library MSS FEI. pp. 44–77. There is a partial list of specimens collected while dredging: Feilden, Fishing and dredging specimens, 1875–76, BMNH, MSS FEI. The bulk of Feilden's collections went to the BMNH, and a smaller number went to the Castle Museum in Norwich, now part of Norfolk Museums.

[1] Gneiss: a metamorphic rock, composed, like granite, of quartz, feldspar or orthoclase, and mica, but distinguished from it by its foliated or laminated structure. Syenite: a crystalline rock allied to granite, mainly composed of hornblende and feldspar, with or without quartz. Hornblende: a mineral closely allied to augite, and having as its chief constituents, silica, magnesia, and lime. It is a constituent of many rocks, as granite, syenite, and diorite, and has numerous varieties. *OED.*

[2] Silurian: the name given to the system or series of Palaeozoic rocks lying immediately below the Devonian or Old Red Sandstone. *OED.* (Silurian today has a more restricted meaning.)

[3] Feilden is here referring to angular unconformity: 'A discordant surface of contact between the deposits of two episodes of sedimentation in which the older, underlying strata have undergone folding, uplift, and erosion before the deposition of the younger sediments, so that the younger strata truncate the older.' *Dictionary of Geology,* 2013.

[4] RBG, Hooker Papers, Voyage, f. 548, Feilden to J. D. Hooker, 12 Nov 1876.

[5] See e.g. Feilden, *Alert* Journal, 31 Oct. 1876.

Geographical Societies. The same day saw him calling on Captain Evans, Hydrographer of the Admiralty, and he unpacked some of his specimens in a room allocated to him at the Zoological Society of London. At the end of November, he was busy getting boxes out of the hold in *Alert*, and packing them up. On 7 December, he dined at the Royal Society Club as a guest of the palaeontologist, lawyer and conchologist John Gwyn Jeffreys (1809–85), went on to a meeting of the Linnean Society, and wrote to Nares about his Arctic specimens collected during the expedition.[1]

He separated marine specimens brought up by the dredge from the crowded stew in which they had travelled to London; he had sent a muskox carcass to the British Museum, since it was deteriorating rapidly; and generally, he sought to put the collections in order. He hoped that it would be possible for him, under Nares's supervision, to work up the natural history of the expedition, and that appropriate arrangements could be made for his salary and out-of-pocket expenses. As he had told Hooker, he considered himself still under Nares's command. Nares supported his request.[2] Although Feilden had begun to send Hooker plants, and to ask his advice about other specimens, that wasn't enough for Hooker, who felt that the specimens should at once have been at his disposal, not Feilden's. Nares sought to smooth things over, explaining that Feilden was still under Admiralty orders, reporting to his superior officer. '[A]ll his information is at the disposal of the Royal Society and no one else – but it must be sent through the Admiralty until he is released.'[3] Hooker was not satisfied with that, and said so. Feilden told him:

> I have been brought up from boyhood as a soldier. I was employed by the Admiralty, and consequently waited for orders from them. Who ever heard of a soldier leaving his post until duly relieved. Now that you tell me that the council of the R.S. is the body to which I am *wholly* and *entirely* responsible you will find me as willing a servant as ever you met with.[4]

Early in the new year, on 4 January, Feilden packed up his collection of Arctic plants and gave them to Hooker at the Royal Society in Burlington House, and conversed for some time with him and Huxley, who were civil enough, but cool towards him, under the unfortunate impression that the 'Arctic Expedition has treated them with want of courtesy and ingratitude, which is a most mistaken idea'.[5] Hooker was indeed impatient, and Feilden had read him correctly at their meeting. The very next day, Feilden 'packed up boxes containing sea beasts &c.', and sent them to the Royal Society.[6] One day later, Feilden 'packed up birds and Miocene fossils in readiness to transport them to Burlington House'.[7] This still wasn't enough for Hooker, who was described even by his close friend Darwin as 'impulsive and somewhat peppery in temper'.[8] Nares told him that he had jumped the gun, but agreed that the sooner Feilden and Hart were under Royal Society orders, the better. Then the Hydrographer, Evans, had to poison the waters by expressing

---

[1] Ibid., 7 Dec. 1876. In 1875, Jeffreys had done some dredging on board HMS *Valorous* in Baffin Bay during Nares's expedition.

[2] RBG, Hooker Papers, Voyage, ff. 222–227, Feilden to Nares 7 Dec. 1876; Nares, 'Letter Book', 15 Dec. 1876, LAC MG 29 B 12, III.

[3] Nares, 'Remark Book', 27 Dec. 1876. LAC, MG 29 B 12, III.

[4] RBG, Hooker Papers, Voyage, f. 65: Feilden to Hooker 27 Dec. 1876,

[5] Feilden, '*Alert* Journal', 4 Jan. 1877.

[6] Ibid., 5 Jan. 1787.

[7] Ibid., 6 Jan. 1877.

[8] Darwin, *Autobiography of Charles Darwin*, p. 105.

astonishment that the naturalists were so wanting in the proprieties as to turn their backs on the Royal Society.[1] Hooker, thoroughly irritated, wrote icily to Feilden:

> Let me remind you, in the spirit of true friendship that the expedition is widely regarded as a failure & waste of money. Viz it appears that the *two* paid naturalists (the first ever paid on an arctic Expedition) cannot bring out their *one year's* collections from the 'limits of life' without paid aid, there will be the most disagreeable comments made on the Royal Society's choice of Naturalists and on the Naturalists themselves. The world still looks to the scientific results of the Expedition for the salvation of its credit.[2]

Feilden responded by writing to the Treasury, with a copy to Hooker, announcing that he would no longer undertake any work under the direction of the Council of the Royal Society, but that he would within three months submit a report to the Treasury, on his own responsibility and without remuneration, on leave from his regimental duties.[3] Hooker realized that he had gone too far, and wrote to amend the affair. Feilden, while willing to accept a friendly gesture, justified himself, explained that arrangements with the Treasury would no longer allow him to work under the original terms, and offered to meet Hooker and return his letter if a friend of Hooker's and a member of the Royal Society's council would read both parties' letters. The meeting took place.[4]

A new arrangement was struck. Hart was not producing much. Feilden undertook to write up the ethnology, mammals, and birds collected during the expedition, while specialists would write up other subjects. Some of the specialists, predictably, published the results of their work independently, to Nares's and Feilden's chagrin. Relations between Hooker and Feilden nevertheless regained cordiality.[5] Hooker examined the plants; he was deeply interested in phytogeography. In 1856 Charles Darwin had asked Hooker to comment on the section of his 'big species book' that dealt with the similarities between Arctic and alpine floras. Hooker was in broad agreement with Darwin about the southward migration of Arctic plants during ice ages, and their return to the north as the glaciers melted and the climate warmed, and also where he claimed that, as climate warmed, Arctic plants would also retreat up mountains, whose peaks were effectively Arctic refuges. Hooker, however, believed that land bridges provided the only sure route for the migration of plants, whereas Darwin had also indicated an important role for icebergs in this migration. In 1861, Hooker had written a major paper on the distribution of Arctic plants; part of that paper had been reprinted in the *Manual* provided to the expedition by the Royal Society in 1875.[6] Hooker did prepare the appendix on botany in Nares' *Narrative* of the expedition.[7] He was delighted at the thoroughness of the collection, which included 69 identifiable flowering plants from north of 82°, as well as

[1] RBG, Hooker papers, Voyage, ff. 66–68, Feilden to Hooker 2 and 8 Jan. 1877; ff. 192–193, Nares to Hooker 20 Jan. 1877; f. 53, F. J. Evans to Hooker 5 Jan. 1877.
[2] Ibid., ff. 139–141, Hooker to Feilden 10 March 1877.
[3] Ibid., f. 81, Feilden to Lingen, Permanent Under-sec. Treasury, cc. Hooker, 14 March 1877.
[4] Ibid., f. 82, Feilden to Hooker 14 March 1877.
[5] Ibid., ff. 96–97, Nares to Hooker 6 May 1877; ff. 101–103, Feilden to Hooker 15 May 1877; ff. 196–197, 211–213, 'Instructions to Naturalists'. Hooker's original 'Instructions to Botanists' are in T. R. Jones, ed., *Manual*, pp. 62–7.
[6] Hooker, 'Outlines of the Distribution of Arctic Plants', pp. 251–348; in T. R. Jones, ed., *Manual*, pp. 197–238; Levere, *Science and the Canadian Arctic*, pp. 234–8.
[7] Hooker et al. 'Appendix No. XIV', in Nares, *Narrative of a Voyage*, II, pp. 301–26.

nearly as many again from the Greenland coast to the south – ten more than had been obtained by all previous explorers of Melville Island 5° to the south. That autumn he told Feilden:

> I am busy with your phænogams[1] & more interested than ever. There are sixty-nine flowering plants and ferns from 80°[–83°] … No fewer than 15[2] are neither in Spitzbergen or Melville Island, & of these 2 are not even in Greenland! On the other hand there are only 12 common to Melville & Spitzbergen (both so much farther South) that are not in your collection … and of these 5 are not Greenland plants at all. Of Spitzbergen plants not found in 80–83°, there are only 5, & none of these are Greenlandic. Of Melville Island plants not in 80–83 there are 10, and only two of them are Greenlandic and these two are confined to E. Greenland! Thus your Flora of 80–83 is a northward extension of the Greenlandic, & with two plants added that are not Greenlandic or Melville Isd. or Spitzbergen! – and which are not found anywhere in the Arctic circle for many degrees further south. … [3]

This meant that the flora included Greenland plants lacking in other islands of the Canadian archipelago to the west, and in Spitzbergen to the east, while it lacked plants that either or both of those regions possessed, but which were also lacking in Greenland.[4] Distribution and its causes in climate, winds, and currents were vitally important to Hooker: 'To my mind all this indicates occasional warm winds or warmth of ocean currents which other polar lands do not enjoy – also … that the interior of Greenland enjoys a climate & vegetation that its coasts do not [betray]. Will you dine with me at the R.S. …?'[5] Cordiality had been fully restored.

10.   Palaeobotany

As the botanist and explorer Robert Brown of Campster[6] had pointed out, parts of the Arctic had once enjoyed a much warmer climate, and a correspondingly luxuriant flora. The distinguished Swiss palaeobotanist Oswald Heer (1809–83) had worked on Arctic fossil collections made from the Canadian archipelago to Spitzbergen, and was working on a magisterial *Flora Fossilis Arctica*. The *Manual* prepared for Nares's expedition made sure that the naturalists were properly alerted to the existence of Miocene and other fossil plants.[7]

The exposed coal seam, 25–30 feet deep, that lay four miles north of *Discovery*'s winter quarters did indeed contain the fossils the naturalists had hoped for. Fossilized impressions of plants were collected by the naturalists from both ships, and by Moss, who sketched and painted careful records of the expedition. Moss was a better artist than Feilden, as was

---

[1] Phænogams, or phanerogams, are flowering plants.

[2] This number was subsequently revised downward to 12. See Hooker et al., 'Appendix No. XIV. Botany' in Nares, *Narrative of a Voyage*, II, p. 301.

[3] RGS, Correspondence Block 1871–80, Hooker to Feilden, 2 Nov. 1877.

[4] Hooker et al., 'Appendix No. XIV. Botany', in Nares, *Narrative of a Voyage*, II, p. 302.

[5] RGS, Correspondence Block 1871–80, Hooker to Feilden 20 Nov. 1877.

[6] This Robert Brown (1842–95) was often referred to as being 'of Campster', to distinguish him from the great botanist of the same name, Robert Brown (1773–1858); for the latter, see Mabberley, *Jupiter Botanicus*. Phytogeography was for geographers as well as botanists. See Thistleton-Dyer, 'Lecture on Plant-Distribution as a Field for Geographical Research', pp. 412–45.

[7] See Heer, 'Miocene Flora and Fauna of the Arctic Regions', in T. R. Jones, ed., *Manual*, pp. 368–89.

Thomas Mitchell (*c*.1833–1924), Assistant Paymaster on *Discovery*.[1] Moss was jealous of Feilden's status as official naturalist, judging him too ignorant for his duties,[2] but they managed to co-operate on this occasion. Hart seems to have done nothing with his collection, but Feilden left carboniferous Arctic fossils with Etheridge.[3] Moss and Feilden independently sent their specimens to Heer. Feilden sent twenty-six species to Moss's fourteen; three of them were new to Heer.[4] The result was another volume in Heer's series on Arctic flora, comparing these collections with others made in Greenland and in Spitzbergen.[5] Heer also compared the fossils with the modern range of species around the 'coal mine'. Not only were the species different, but in all but two cases (willows and sedges), even the genera were different. There was a general coincidence between the Miocene fossil flora of Grinnell Land[6] and that of Greenland, just as there was between their living floras. The fossil flora was as luxuriant as Robert Brown had hoped, with horsetails, yews, cypresses, beech trees, elms, viburnums, and many more. There were the usual problems of taxonomy. Heer renamed a genus of yew after Feilden, and four species within it became *Feildenia rigida H[ee]r.*, *F. major Hr.*, *F. bifida Hr.*, and *F. Mossiana Hr.*;[7] the last embodied a form of subordination that Moss could scarcely have welcomed. Heer published these findings in his *Flora Fossilis Arctica*. In 1877, but even before this volume was published, Heer received the Royal Society's Royal Medal for his palaeobotanical researches. He was working in a difficult field, and was one of the few whose results were trustworthy. As Hooker wrote to Sir John William Dawson[8] (1820–99) of McGill University in January 1879:

> I agree with you that the Veg. Palaeontology of the Arctic regions has to be redone: but I do not limit this redoing to those regions, I would make it include all [known] regions, for that we have as yet no approximate conception of the extent, or composition, or affinities, or chronology, or geographical distribution, of the vegetation of any one past epoch. I believe that we are in the dark as to the affinities of perhaps 90 per cent of the [enumerated] fossil plants; & that [our methods] of determining the ages of beds, by these means are very feebly tentative. In saying this I do not [undervalue] the definite results obtained by Heer ... and others.[9]

---

[1] See Moss's sketches in the Scott Polar Research Institute, Cambridge (SPRI) and his *Shores of the Polar Sea*. Moss also painted the scenery for the Royal Arctic Theatre; see e.g. 'Thursday Pops', 'Boots at the Swan' and 'Aladdin', 23 Dec., and 'Area Belle' on 27 Jan. The finest paintings from the expedition were made by Thomas Mitchell, Assistant Paymaster on *Discovery*: Bell, 'Thomas Mitchell, Photographer and Artist'. At Nares's request, *Alert* and *Discovery* carried photographic equipment; Mitchell and George White, Assistant Engineer in *Alert*, were trained at the Army School of Photography in Chatham. Nares's published *Narrative of a Voyage* contains some of the photographs from the expedition, and four of them are reproduced in this edition.

[2] The friction between Moss and Feilden is clear from numerous passages in the latter's *Alert* Journal 1875–76.

[3] Feilden, *Alert* Journal, 6 Dec. 1876.

[4] RGS, Correspondence Block 1871–80, Heer to Feilden 10 Nov. 1877.

[5] Heer, *Flora Fossilis Arctica*, V, Pt. I; for a summary, see Heer, 'Notes on Fossil Plants'.

[6] The central portion of Ellesmere Island, named for Henry Grinnell during the first Grinnell Expedition (1850) by Edwin de Haven, expedition leader.

[7] In modern usage, mossiana would be in lower case; there is a good deal of variation in Victorian usage when it comes to naming plants, birds, and so on, and here I follow Heer.

[8] Dawson was a man of energy and many talents. His entry in the *Dictionary of Canadian Biography* describes him as 'geologist, palaeontologist, author, educator, office holder, publisher, and editor'.

[9] Hooker to J. W. Dawson 4 Jan. 1879. The square brackets here indicate uncertain readings.

Classifying fossil plants was and is a difficult discipline. Feilden and the others rightly did not try to sort them out; sending them to Heer showed good judgement.

11. Zoology

Feilden was competent in zoology. We have already noted that he wrote up the ornithology himself. In the appendix on ornithology in Nares's *Narrative*, it is clear that the finding of eggs of the red knot gave him particular satisfaction, but the only colour plate in Nares's two volumes was of the eggs of the sanderling.[1] Feilden also published accounts of his collecting and observing in *Ibis*, the leading British ornithological journal, and in the *Proceedings* of the Zoological Society of London.[2] He did the same for the mammals.[3] There were no surprises, but many fine observations, and confirmation of the suggestions of others. He noted the profusion of flowers immediately around the den of an Arctic fox, whose presence had fertilized the soil. He found several dead lemmings, their skulls penetrated by the canine teeth of foxes, as well as two ermines killed in the same way:

> Then to our surprise we discovered numerous deposits of dead lemmings: in one hidden nook under a rock we pulled out a heap of over fifty. We disturbed numerous 'caches' of twenty and thirty, and the ground was honeycombed with holes each of which contained several bodies of these little animals, a small quantity of earth being placed over them.

Here was confirmation of the suggestion that foxes laid up supplies of food for the winter. Feilden also found remains of a hare, and wings of young brant geese from the previous season – evidence that the foxes used the same den in successive years.[4]

They had seen no living polar bears around Floeberg Beach, there being little there to tempt them away from the richer hunting grounds of Baffin Bay's open North Water,[5] although ringed seals penetrated as far as the icy polar sea. Feilden was quite clear that whales could not inhabit the frozen polar ocean to the north of Grinnell Land; there was little hope that Arctic discoveries in that region could further extend the range for whaling.

His extensive observations on the muskox were accurate; so too was his perception that 'the number of muskoxen in Grinnell Land is extremely limited, whilst the means of subsistence can only supply the wants of a fixed number; consequently, after an invasion such as ours, when every animal obtainable was slaughtered for food, it must take some years to restock the ground'.[6] He was right; the game list for *Alert* included eighteen muskoxen.[7]

[1] Nares, *Narrative of a Voyage*, II, pp. 206–17; Sanderling eggs, facing p. 210.
[2] Feilden, 'List of Birds'; Feilden, 'On the Birds of the North Polar Basin'.
[3] Feilden, 'Appendix II. Mammalia', in Nares, *Narrative of a Voyage*, II, pp. 192–205.
[4] Feilden, 'Appendix II. Mammalia', in Nares, *Narrative of a Voyage*, II, p. 194.
[5] The north water is a 'recurring polynya'; see Dunbar and Dunbar, 'The History of the North Water'.
[6] Feilden, 'Appendix II. Mammalia', in Nares, *Narrative of a Voyage*, II, p. 201.
[7] Anon., 'Appendix XVII. Game List', in Nares, *Narrative of a Voyage*, II, pp. 352–3.

Ten species of fish were collected between latitudes 78° and 83°N, some previously known from the western Arctic, others from Spitzbergen, and one new species, which the ichythiologist Albert Charles Lewis Gotthilf Günther (1830–1914) of the British Museum named after Nares, *Salmo naresii*. There was comprehensive coverage of the other zoological collections, to which Feilden had contributed most of the specimens: molluscs, insects, crustacea, echinoderms (including holothurians, starfish, and sea urchins), sponges, and more besides.[1]

Feilden had been surprised to find butterflies on the shores of the polar ocean, but overall had not been impressed at his collection of insects. The entomologist Robert McLachlan (1837–1904), however, who wrote up the insects and spiders,[2] had no hesitation in stating that the entomological collections were the most valuable of all the zoological ones, because they proved the existence 'of a comparatively rich insect fauna, and even of several showy butterflies, in very high latitudes'. Their presence posed a puzzle, since '[o]ne month in the year is the longest period in which they can appear in the perfect state, and six weeks is the period in each year in which phytophagous [i.e. plant-eating] larvae can feed; so it appears probable that more than one season is necessary, in most cases, for their full development ...' Also remarkable was the paucity of beetles, elsewhere so numerous as to make it clear that the Creator loved them. The incidence and distribution of species was, here as elsewhere, a major pre-occupation of naturalists.

In like manner, the historical dimension of distribution patterns was repeatedly addressed throughout the zoological essays, so that, for example, similarities were noted between the Arctic crustacea and the fauna of 'the Post-tertiary glacial beds of Scotland, and also, of course, to that of the North British seas.[3] Geology's imperialism could find an ally in historical zoology.

12. Coda

After the British Arctic Expedition of 1875–6, Feilden served with the 6th (Inniskilling) Dragoons in the First Boer War in 1881. In 1888 he was posted to the North America and West Indies Station in Bermuda. Two years later he was again serving in Africa. In the early 1890s, he retired from the army, only to re-enlist as Paymaster of Imperial Yeomanry

[1] The following are Appendices from Nares, *Narrative of a Voyage*, II: Feilden, I, 'Ethnology', II, 'Mammalia', III, 'Ornithology', and, with de Rance, XV, 'Geological Structure of the Coasts'; Günther, IV, 'Ichthyology'; Smith, V, 'Mollusca'; McLachlan, VI, 'Insecta'; Miers, VII, 'Crustacea'; McIntosh, VIII, 'Annelida'; Duncan and Sladen, IX, 'Echinodermata'; Busk, X, 'Polyzoa'; Allman, XI, 'Hydrozoa'; Carter, XII, 'Spongida'; Brady, XIII, 'Rhizopoda Reticularia': Hooker, XIV, 'Botany'; Coppinger, XVI, 'Petermann Glacier', XVII; Anon., 'Game List', XVIII, 'Meteorological Abstract'; Haughton, XIX, 'Tidal Observations'. Other reports on the expedition's collections include: Cambridge, 'New and Little-Known Spiders'; Miers, 'Report on the Crustacea'; Duncan and Sladen, 'Report on the Echinodermata Collected'; Carter, 'Arctic and Antarctic Sponges'; Brady, 'On the Reticularian and Radiolarian Rhizopoda; Busk, 'List of Polyzoa Collected by ... Feilden'; McIntosh, 'Annelids of the British North-Polar Expedition'; Duncan and Sladen, *Memoir on the Echinodermata*; Feilden, 'Arctic Molluscan Fauna'; Smith, 'On the Mollusca Collected during the Arctic Expedition of 1875–76'.
[2] McLachlan, 'Insecta and Arachnida'.
[3] Miers, 'Appendix VII. Crustacea', in Nares, *Narrative of a Voyage*, II, p. 255.

in the Second Boer War. Whenever time allowed, he studied the birds and plants around him. And, when the First World War broke out, Feilden, then 76 years of age, drilled with the recruits and worked in the Army Pay Department.[1]

He had also made further visits to Arctic Europe and Asia. When Henry John Pearson (1850–1913), industrialist, ornithologist, naturalist, and explorer, planned summer voyages to Novaya Zemlya, the islands of the Barents Sea, and the coast of what was then Russian Lapland, he invited Feilden to join the expedition. Feilden's experience in Arctic work proved invaluable:

> In these days, when new books on travel in the Artic regions appear almost every season, it requires some courage to add yet another to the list. I have done so in order to bring into one volume the papers written by Colonel Feilden and myself in *The Ibis* with those by the former on the Botany and Geology of Novaya Zemlya, Waïgatch, and other countries visited by us in 1895 and 1897, together with some fuller details of the voyage.[2]

When Albert Hastings Markham sailed to Novaya Zemlya in 1879, he asked his old shipmate Feilden to write an appendix about the birds collected on that expedition.[3] Feilden obliged. He was also active in local and national zoological, geological, botanical and other scientific societies.

In 1899, Nares, 'acting on the advice of friends', took the first steps towards getting Feilden elected a Fellow of the Royal Society of London (FRS).[4] By now, Feilden's relations with Hooker were cordial; Hooker, no longer President of the Royal Society, but still a man of force and weight, wrote to him on behalf of the signatories for his candidature: 'I need hardly say we think your claims are full to overflowing'.[5] The citation is as follows:

> COLONEL HENRY WEMYSS FEILDEN, Wells, Norfolk. Chief Pay master, Army Pay Department (Retired). Was Naturalist to Sir George Nares's Polar Expedition of 1875–6, when, besides making large and valuable zoological observations and collections, he laid down the geology of 300 miles of the coast of Smith's Sound, and brought home 2,000 specimens, carefully localised, illustrating and confirming his surveys. On the same voyage he discovered the Miocene Flora of Grinnell's Land, his collection and observations on which form an important contribution to Heer's 'Flora Fossila Arctica'. He has made three subsequent voyages to Arctic Europe and Asia, visiting Novaya Zemlya, Barentz Land, Kolguev Island, Spitzbergen, and Russian Lapland, for the purposes of collating the geology, zoology, and botany of Arctic Europe with those of America. During his military services in Malta, Natal, and the West Indies he assiduously devoted himself to studying their natural history, and has published valuable papers relating to their zoology. He was an active member of the

---

[1] Trevor-Battye, 'A Noble Englishman', 'Introduction', pp. 11–12.

[2] Pearson, *Beyond Petsora Eastward*, pp. xi, xii–xiii. The title of Pearson's book is taken from Milton's, *Paradise Lost*, Book X, ll. 289–93: 'As when two Polar Winds blowing adverse / Upon the Cronian Sea, together drive / Mountains of Ice, that stop th' imagin'd way / Beyond Petsora Eastward, to the rich / Cathaian Coast'.

[3] Feilden, 'Note on the Birds Collected by Captain A. H. Markham, R.N.; A. H. Markham, *The Great Frozen Sea*.

[4] McGill University, Blacker-Wood Library, Woodward correspondence, Nares to Henry Bolingbroke Woodward, 8 March 1899. Henry Bolingbroke Woodward (1832–1921) was a geologist and palaeontologist. Confusingly, Henry Woodward (ca. 1838–98) was a member of the Geological Department of the British Museum.

[5] Trevor-Battye, 'A Noble Englishman', 'Introduction', p. 8.

Committee of the British Association for Scientific Research in the West Indies. The results of Colonel Feilden's labours are published in the Journals of the Geological, Linnean and other scientific societies, whereby he has extended our knowledge, especially of the geology, zoology and botany of the North Polar area.

[*Signed by:*] George S. Nares.   Archibald Geikie.   J. W. Judd.   T. McK. Hughes. A. Newton.   A. Günther.   F. Leopold McClintock.   William T. Thiselton-Dyer. W. B. Hemsley.   Joseph Dalton Hooker.   W. T. Blanford.   John Murray. H. Woodward.   William J. L. Wharton.   T. H. Tizard. Clements R. Markham.   R. Etheridge.   R. McLachlan.   J. Y. Buchanan. Henry H. Howorth.   T. R. Jones.   H. B. Woodward.   E. Hull.[1]

Feilden was balloted for thrice, from 1899 to 1901, but in spite of his own merits and Hooker's optimism, he was not elected. His claims were at least as great as those of several candidates who were elected in those years. When a friend showed natural resentment at what he perceived as an insult, Feilden

> merely said with his kindly smile, 'I have done my work, it could make no difference to me, where it is everything to these boys, it means their bread and butter'. Then, pointing to the unique array of distinguished names upon his Form of Recommendation, 'There is the *real* honour!' And perhaps he was prouder of that piece of paper than of anything else, unless it were his Polar medal.[2]

13.   Editorial Practice

Feilden used Letts's Perpetual Diary, No. 51, folio, cloth boards, price 14 shillings, with one page for every date in the year. Since the expedition set out from England on Saturday 29 May 1875, and Feilden left the ship with Nares, Moss, and Pullen at Valentia on Friday 27 October 1876, most pages bear entries for the same date in different years, e.g. Saturday 29 May 1875 shares the page with Monday 29 May 1876. Since the diary was a perpetual one, printed dates but not days or years are given at the top of each page, e.g. May 29. Feilden has added the year and, after 15 April 1875, the day, sometimes in the margin, and sometimes beginning in the margin and extending into the part of the page devoted to the

---

[1] Sir Archibald Geikie (1835–1924), geologist and historian; Professor John Wesley Judd (1840–1916), geologist; Professor Thomas McKenny Hughes (1832–1917), geologist; Alfred Newton (1829–1907), zoologist; zoologist; Admiral Sir Francis Leopold McClintock (1819–1907), Irish explorer in the Royal Navy; Sir William Turner Thiselton-Dyer (1843–1928), botanist and 3rd director of the Royal Botanic Gardens, Kew; William Botting Hemsley (1843–1924), botanist; William Thomas Blanford (1832–1905), geologist and naturalist; Sir John Murray (1841–1914), oceanographer, marine biologist, and limnologist; Henry Bolinbroke Woodward (1832–1921), geologist; William James Lloyd Wharton (1843–1905), naval officer and hydrographer; Thomas Henry Tizard (1839–1924), naval officer and hydrographer; Robert McLachlan (1837–1904), entomologist; John Young Buchanan (1844–1925), chemist, oceanographer, and Arctic explorer; Sir Henry Hoyle Howorth (1842–1923), politician, barrister, and geologist; Horace Bolingbroke Woodward (1848–1914), geologist; Edward Hull (1829–1917), geologist, director of the Geological Survey of Ireland.

[2] Trevor-Battye, 'A Noble Englishman', 'Introduction', p. 5. It is not known what politics, if any, was involved. Admiral Sir Erasmus Ommanney, FRS, had opposed Feilden's appointment to the expedition. The folder in the archives of the Royal Society of London dealing with elections for the years of Feilden's repeated nomination and rejection is missing. The biographical folder on Feilden in the Norwich Castle Museum is also missing. Trevor-Battye's account suggests that Feilden had the document proposing him in his possession. If he did have it, it would probably have gone to the archives of the Norwich Castle Museum.

main body of his text. Sometimes he abbreviates the month, e.g. Sept., at other times he writes it in full. I have used the unabbreviated spelling for the month, then combined the two parts of each date and italicized them, although Feilden was erratic in his use of italics: *Saturday 29 May 1875*. The entry in the journal for each day usually bears a heading presented variously in upper case letters, lower case letters, single underlining, and double underlining. I have used single underlining throughout. Feilden's journal is continuous, with entries day by day but with no chapter breaks. I have divided the journal into parts, adding titles to guide the reader.

Feilden's punctuation, like his capitalization, is erratic. Where the lack of punctuation makes smooth reading difficult, I have silently added or altered punctuation marks. Feilden's spelling is generally consistent and accurate, but there are some words (e.g. unmistakably, govenor) which are consistently misspelled, and after indicating this on the first appearance of a word, I have thereafter let his spelling stand without comment. Rare errors are indicated in the text by [*sic*]. Feilden presents the names of ships in a variety of ways, e.g. 'Alert', "Alert", *Alert*, <u>Alert</u>. I have used italics throughout for ships' names, thus *Alert*, *Discovery*, *Pandora*. Feilden uses different versions of abbreviations concerning time, e.g. O'c, am, and so on. I have standardized these to read o'c, a.m. and p.m.

Legible deletions in the journal are shown with single crossings out, thus, e.g., ~~Moss~~. Feilden also blacks out some passages using dense ink scribbles; most of these passages are impossible to make out, and I have indicated such passages in the text as [... *lines crossed out*]. In one instance, he has taken a razor or sharp knife to physically excise much of an entry, and I have indicated this by [... *lines excised*]. Feilden's insertions of words in the text are indicated by angle brackets, < ... >. Square brackets [ ] are used to indicate uncertain readings or editorial interventions. Notes or comments in the margin, apart from dates, are given in the form [*Margin*: words].

Feilden has added numerous insertions to the bound journal, where they remain today; where these appear to have been inserted during the expedition, or at least to have been sketched or written during the expedition, I have included them in this edition. Sometimes sketches were taped in, and this is apparent from the marks of tapes on those sketches. Feilden kept field notes in small notebooks that he used when geologizing or collecting botanical and other specimens. For the most part, these notebooks have been lost, but some pages from them are inserted in his journal, and I have included these geological and other sketches. But Feilden also used his journal as a kind of scrap book after the expedition, and has added newspaper cuttings and even extensive journal articles bearing dates after the return of the expedition to England. These are not part of his expedition narrative, and I have not included them here.

THE ARCTIC JOURNAL OF
CAPTAIN HENRY WEMYSS FEILDEN, R.A.,
THE NATURALIST IN H.M.S. *ALERT*
1875–1876

PRELUDE: 1 FEBRUARY – 15 APRIL 1875

Feilden's journal, written during the British Arctic Expedition of 1875–6 is in the archives of the Royal Geographical Society, Library Manuscript MS 387B. He presented it to the library of the RGS on 13 May, 1919. Feilden began his journal on 1 February 1875, when he was appointed by the Admiralty to the post of naturalist on HMS *Alert*. On his return to England, he had to prepare scientific reports on some of his collections, and arrange for specialists in different areas of natural history; this work extended into 1877, and his journal ends on Sunday 7 January 1877.

[*The journal bears Feilden's bookplate on the verso of the front cover, with the motto*:] VIRTUTIS PRÆMIUM HONOR [*This is normally translated as 'Honour is the reward of virtue', but may also be rendered as 'Honour is the reward of courage', appropriate for a family with a military tradition.*]

[*Also on the verso of the front cover, overlapping the bookplate, is a plate bearing the RGS's coat of arms and the inscription*:] 'This work was presented to the Library of the Royal Geographical Society by Col. H. W. Feilden, 13th May, 1919'.

[*On the printed title page*, Lett's Perpetual Diary ..., *Feilden wrote this inscription*:]
H. W. Feilden Captain.
& Paymaster Royal Artillery.
Naturalist Arctic Expedition.
H.M.S. *Alert*.

[*Single printed sheet pasted on recto facing front cover*:]

DIRECTIONS FOR COLLECTING AND PRESERVING THE SKELETONS
OF ANIMALS.[1]
ALTERED FROM THOSE BY W. H. FLOWER, F.R.S.,
Conservator of the Museum of the Royal College of Surgeons.
IF THE ANIMAL is of small size – say not larger than a fox – take off the skin, except from the feet below the wrist and ankle joints, as otherwise there is danger of losing the small bones of those parts, and the toes. If it is intended to preserve the skin for purposes of stuffing, as well as the skeleton, the bones of the feet should all be left in the skin; they can be easily extracted afterwards, and will be preserved much more safely in their natural

---

[1] This is a transcript of a single printed sheet pasted on to the inside cover of Feilden's journal. William Henry Flower (1831–99) also wrote 'On Collecting Specimens of Cetacea of the Arctic Seas, and Making Observations Thereon', in T. R. Jones, ed., *Manual*, pp. 39–45.

covering. Remove all the entrails, together with the heart and lungs: also the wind-pipe, gullet, and tongue. In doing this be careful to leave attached to the base of the skull the chain of bones which support the root of the tongue. These may either be left in connection with the skull, or cleaned separately and tied to the skeleton. Then with a knife clear away the meat from the head, body, and limbs, without cutting or scraping the bones, or separating them from each other. At any intervals that may be necessary during this process it will be desirable, if practicable, to leave the body in water, so as to wash away as much of the blood as possible from the bones, and a few days' soaking in water frequently changed will be an advantage: but, if not easily managed, this is by no means absolutely necessary,

The body, with all the bones held in connection by their ligaments, should then be hung up to dry in a place where there is a free current of air, and out of the way of attacks from animals of prey. Before they get hard the limbs may be folded by the side of the body in the most convenient position, or there is no harm in detaching them and placing them inside the trunk. A few hours' exposure will be sufficient to dry any skeleton of moderate size: and all the operations described above may be easily performed in a room in an hotel without any unpleasant consequence.

When thoroughly dry the skeletons may be packed in boxes with any convenient light packing material between them. Sawdust, especially Pine sawdust, will be found very convenient as it absorbs moisture, and prevents any unpleasant smell. Each should be securely wrapped in a separate piece of paper or canvas, as sometimes insects will attack the ligaments and allow the bones to come apart.

If the animal is of larger size, it will be most convenient to take it partially to pieces before or during the cleaning. The head may be separated from the neck, the backbone divided into two or more pieces, the ribs detached from the backbone and the breastbone, and the limbs from the trunk; but in no case should the small bones of the feet be separated from one another. The parts should then be treated as above described, and all packed together in a canvas bag.

In the Cetacea (porpoises, &c.), look for two small bones suspended in the flesh, just below the backbone, at the junction of the lumbar and caudal regions (marked externally by the anal aperture or 'vent'). They are the only rudiments of a pelvis, and should always be preserved with the skeleton.

If there is no opportunity of preserving and transporting entire skeletons, the skulls alone should be kept. They should be treated as above described, picked nearly clean, the brain being scooped out through the large hole at the back of the skull, soaked, if possible, for a few days in water, and then dried.

Every specimen should be carefully labelled with the scientific or popular name and sex of the animal, the exact locality at which it was procured, and the date.

For the purpose of making entire skeletons, select, if possible, adult animals, but the skulls of animals of all ages may be advantageously selected.

[*Next, pasted in, is a MS leaflet of 6 pages describing and portraying Arctic flowers. Feilden used these notes during the expedition, although the handwriting is not his. These pages are reproduced in Figures 1–6, pp. 39–44.*]

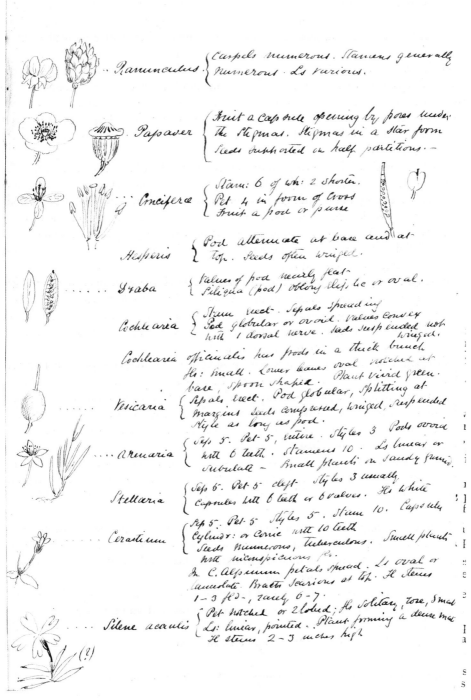

Ramunculus { Carpels numerous. Stamens generally numerous. Ls various.

Papaver { Fruit a Capsule opening by pores under the Stigmas. Stigmas in a star form Seeds supported on half partitions. —

Cruciferæ { Stam: 6 of wh: 2 shorter. Pet: 4 in form of cross Fruit a pod or purse

Hesperis { Pod attenuate at base and at top. Seeds often wriged.

Draba { Values of pod nearly flat. Siliqua (pod) oblong ellip, tic or oval.

Cochlearia { Stem erect. Sepals spreading Pod globular or ovoid. Values convex with 1 dorsal nerve. Seeds suspended not wriged.

Cochlearia officinalis has pods in a thick bunch Fls: small. Lower leaves oval notched at base, spoon shaped. Plant virid green.

Vesicaria { Sepals erect. Pod globular, splitting at margins Seeds compressed, wriged, suspended Style as long as pod.

Arenaria { Seps 5. Pet: 5, entire. Styles 3 Pods ovoid with 6 teeth. Stamens 10. Ls linear or subulate — Small plants on sandy places.

Stellaria { Seps 6. Pet: 5 cleft. Styles 3 usually Capsules with 6 teeth or 6 valves. Fls white

Cerastium { Sep 5. Pet: 5 Styles 5. Stem 10. Capsule Cylindr: or Conic with 10 teeth Seeds numerous, tuberculous. Small plants with inconspicuous fls. In C. alpinum petals spread. Ls oval or lanceolate. Bracts scarious at top. Fl stems 1–3 fld, rarely 6–7.

Silene acaulis { Pet notched or 2 lobed; fls solitary, rose, small Ls: linear, pointed. Plant forming a dense mat Fl stems 2–3 inches high.

Figure 1.   First of six manuscript sheets listing and illustrating Arctic plants, tipped into Feilden's journal after the first fly leaf. It is not known who drew these, but they are not in Feilden's hand.

39

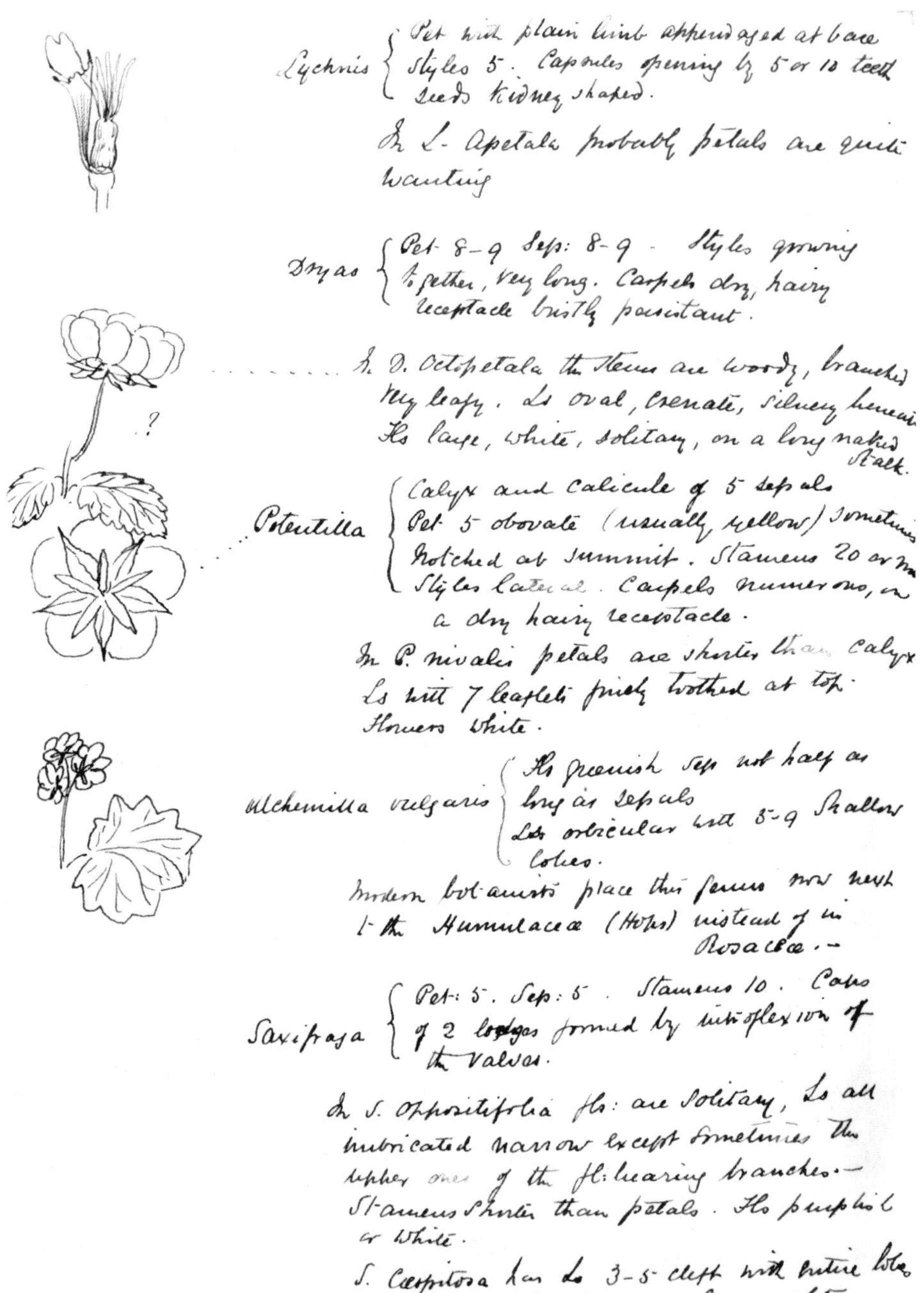

Lychnis { Pet with plain limb appendaged at base
Styles 5. Capsules opening by 5 or 10 teeth
Seed kidney shaped.

In L. Apetala probably petals are quite
wanting

Dryas { Pet. 8-9 Sep: 8-9 . Styles growing
together, very long. Carpels dry, hairy
receptacle bristly persistant.

In D. Octopetala the stems are woody, branched
very leafy. Ls oval, crenate, silvery beneath
Fls large, white, solitary, on a long naked
stalk.

Potentilla { Calyx and calicule of 5 sepals
Pet. 5 obovate (usually yellow) sometimes
notched at summit. Stamens 20 or m
Styles lateral. Carpels numerous, on
a dry hairy receptacle.

In P. nivalis petals are shorter than Calyx
Ls with 7 leaflets finely toothed at top.
Flowers white.

alchemilla vulgaris { Fls greenish seps not half as
long as sepals
Ls orbicular with 8-9 shallow
lobes.

Modern botanists place this genus now next
to the Humulaceæ (Hops) instead of in
Rosaceæ.—

Saxifraga { Pet: 5. Sep: 5. Stamens 10. Caps
of 2 lodges formed by introflexion of
the valves.

In S. Oppositifolia fls: are Solitary, Ls all
imbricated narrow except sometimes the
upper ones of the fl: bearing branches.—
Stamens shorter than petals. Fls purplish
or white.

S. Cœspitosa has Ls 3-5- cleft with entire lobes
Pet oval, sessile, twice as long as obtuse
divisions of Calyx.

Figure 2.   Sheet 2 of manuscript list of Arctic plants.

40

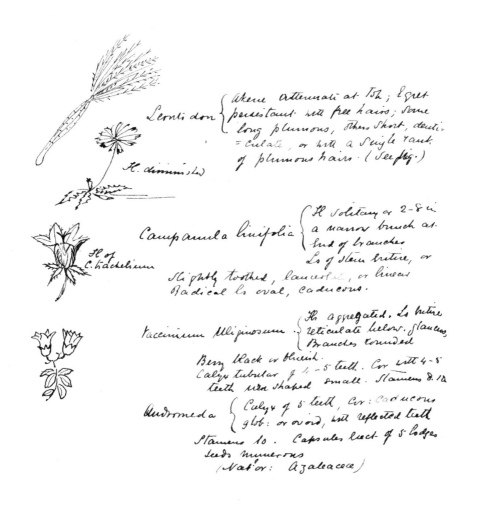

Figure 3.   Sheet 3 of manuscript list of Arctic plants.

Pyrola chlorantha { Style bent, 5 stigmas erect
sometimes soldered together.
Ls nearly round. Capsule
with woolly borders.

Fls. greenish in a few fls? spike

Bartsia Alpina { Cal campanulate with
4 div: Lower lip of Cor
with 3 lobes. Anthers velvet

Caps: oblong compressed with 2 lodges.
Spike of flg leafy. Bracts coloured
much larger than Calyx, wh is
shorter than Capsule. —

Pedicularis { Calyx ventricose. Upper lip of
Cor: helmet shaped, compressed

Ls generally pinnatifid.

Armeria { Calyx with 5 ribs & 5 teeth soldered
in a ring at base — Styles 5,
plumous soldered at base. –

Fls in a head on a radical stalk, surrounded
by an involucre of imbricated leaves, wh are
prolonged into a sheath surrounding the peduncle
Leaves all radical, matted.

Polygonum { Pet 5 usually. Stamens 4–9 generally
5–8. Anthers moveable. Styles 3–4

P. Viviparum. Lower ls attenuate at base
fls: white or rose. Spike oblong
fruit ovoid with obtuse angles.

Oxyria { Fls with 4 divisions, the interior larger
fls in branching bunches in O. digyna
Stamens 6. Stigmas 2. Fruit winged

Empetrum
Nigrum { Fls of 3 pet (withering) & 3 sepals.
Stamens 3 - Stigmas with 5-6-9
lobes on a short style. Berry round
Seeds bony, whitish.

Betula { Catkins cylindrical. In male flr
perigone has 1 leaf 4 stamens
Female with scales 3 lobed, 3 fl?
membranous & caducous.

B. Nana has smooth orbicular crenate leaves,
fruit elliptic, winged

Figure 4. Sheet 4 of manuscript list of Arctic plants.

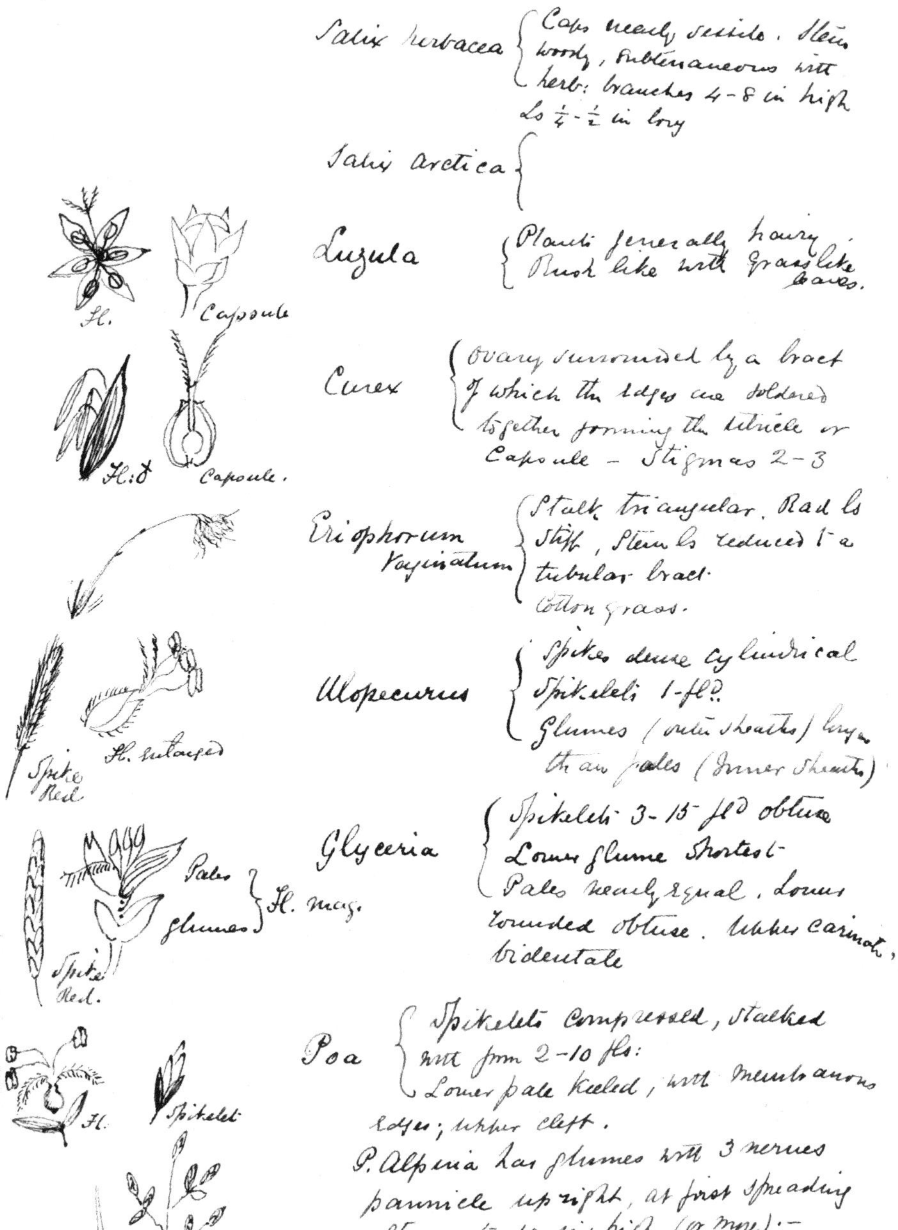
Salix herbacea { Caps nearly sessile. Stem woody, subterraneous with herb: branches 4-8 in high Ls ¼-½ in long
Salix arctica {
Luzula { Plants generally hairy. Rush like with grasslike leaves.
Fl.
Capsule
Carex { Ovary surrounded by a bract of which the edges are soldered together forming the utricle or Capsule - Stigmas 2-3
Capsule.
Eriophorum vaginatum { Stalk triangular. Rad ls stiff, Stem ls reduced to a tubular bract. Cotton grass.
Alopecurus { Spikes dense cylindrical Spikelets 1-fld. Glumes (outer sheaths) longer than pales (Inner sheaths)
Fl. enlarged
Spike Red.
Glyceria { Spikelets 3-15 fld obtuse Lower glume shortest Pales nearly equal. Lower rounded obtuse. Upper carinate, bidentate
Pales
glumes
Fl. mag.
Spike Red.
Poa { Spikelets compressed, stalked with from 2-10 fls: Lower pale keeled, with membranous edges; upper cleft.
P. Alpina has glumes with 3 nerves pannicle upright, at first spreading Stems 5-10 in: high (or more).-
Fl.
Spikelet
Panicle.

Figure 5. Sheet 5 of manuscript list of Arctic plants.

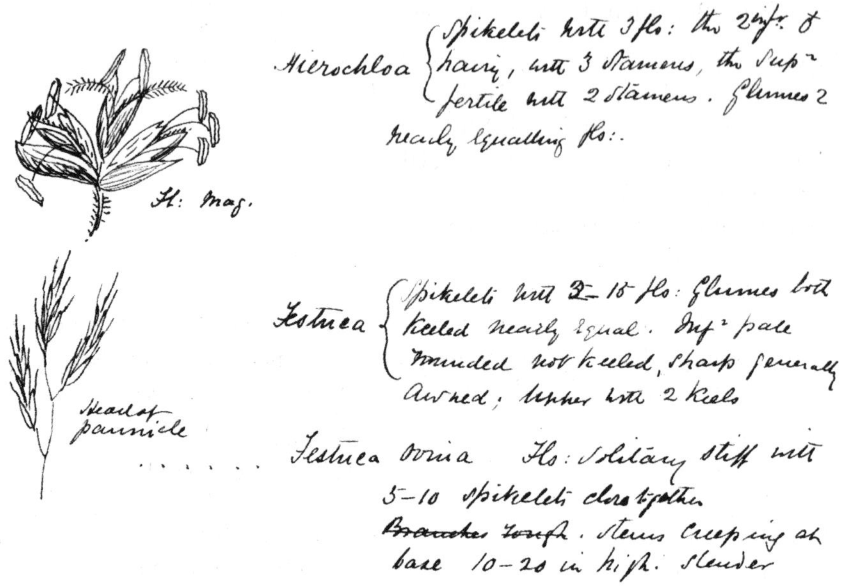

Microchloa { Spikelets with 3 flo: the 2 inf. ♂
hairy, with 3 Stamens, the Sup.
fertile with 2 Stamens. Glumes 2
nearly equalling flo:.

Fl: mag.

Festuca { Spikelets with 3–15 flo: Glumes both
keeled nearly equal. Inf.ᵃ pale
rounded not keeled, sharp generally
Awned; upper with 2 Keels

Head of
panicle

Festuca ovina   Flo: Solitary stiff with
5–10 Spikelets close together
Branches rough. Stems creeping at
base 10–20 in high. slender

Figure 6.   Sheet 6 of manuscript list of Arctic plants.

[*On blank pages before the journal begins, HWF has transcribed, in indelible pencil:*]
Extract from "Bulletin de la Société de Geog.", Paris, Mars 1875.

L'Expedition Polaire Américaine, lettre du Docteur Bessels. Washington 19.7.74.[1]
"nous observâmes les marées avec la plus grande attention."
L'etablissement du port est de 12h.13m.
Le flux le plus haut observé = 8 pieds anglais.
Le reflux le plus bas = 2, 5
Moyenne de haute et basse marée = 3, 8
Moyenne de grande marée = 5,47
Moyenne de basse morte-marée = 1,83
La faune et la flore de la terre de Hall sont assez riches, mais, hélas! Presque toutes nos collections sont perdues. Nous avons rencontré huit espèces de mammifères, vingt-trois sortes d'oiseaux, quinze espèces d'insectes, dix-sept especes de plantes.

Les mammifères[2]
1. Ursus maritimus. (L)[3]
2. Canis Lagopus. (L)
3. Phoca barbata. (Fabr)[4]
4. Phoca groenlandica (Müll)[5]
5. Phoca hispida (Erxel)[6]
6. Lepus glacialis. (Leach)[7]
7. Myodes. Sp[r]. Pallas[8]
8. Ovibos moscatus. (Zimm.)[9]

Les phanérogames.
1. Ranunculus nivalis (L).
2. Papaver médicale (L).
3. Draba alpina (L).
4. „ corymbosa. (Durand)[10]

Les oiseaux
1. Falco arcticus (Holb).[11]
2. Strix nyctea (L).
3. Corvus corax (L).
4. Emberiza nivalis (Naum).[12]
5. Strepsilas interpres (L).
6. Tringa maritima (Brünn).[13]
7. Calidris arenaria (Lin).
8. Lagopus (Briss.) sp.
9. Xema sabini (Sab).[14]
10. Larus Glaucus (Brünn).
11 „ eburneus (Phipps).[15]
12. Sterna macrura (Naum).
13. Larus tridactylus (Linn).

---

[1] In the same envelope as Feilden's Journal at the RGS is a folder containing sheets that were associated with the journal. Included there is an offprint of Bessels, 'L'éxpédition polaire américaine, sous les orders du Capitaine Hall'.

[2] See Appendix D for the names of animals and plants observed by Feilden during the BAE.

[3] L and Linn refer to the Swedish taxonomist, botanist, and zoologist Carl Linnaeus (1707–78), whose binomial nomenclature was the basis of modern taxonomy.

[4] Otto Fabricius (1744–1822), author of *Fauna Groenlandica*.

[5] Otto Friedrich Müller (1730–84), Danish naturalist.

[6] Not identified.

[7] William Elford Leach (1791–1836), naturalist.

[8] Peter Simon Pallas (1741–1811), Prussian zoologist and botanist.

[9] Eberhard August Wilhelm von Zimmermann (1743–1815), German zoologist and geographer.

[10] Probably Elias Durand, né Élie Magloire Durand (1794–1873), French-born American botanist and pharmacist.

[11] Not identified.

[12] Johann Friedrich Naumann (1780–1857), German ornithologist.

[13] Morten Thrane Brünnich (1737–1827), Danish ornithologist.

[14] Joseph Sabine (1770–1837), natural historian.

[15] Constantine John Phipps, 2nd Baron Mulgrave (1744–92), naval officer and politician.

5. Cochlearia fenestrate ((R. Brown).
6. Cerastium vulgatum (L).
7. Lychnis apetala (L).
8. Dryas octopetala (L.)
9. Taraxacum palustre (L.)
10. Polygonum viviparum (L).
11. Oxyria digyna (L. Campd).[1]
12. Salix arctica (Pallas).
13. Juncus biglumis (L).
15. Carex dioica (L).[2]
16. Poa arctica (R. Brown).[3]

14. Stercorarius cephus (Baird)[4]
15.   „   parasiticus (d[itt]o)
16. Procellaria glacialis (L.)
17. Bernicla branta (Pall).
18. Harelda glacialis (L.)
19. Somateria mollissima (L.)
20.   „   spectabilis (L.)
21. Uria grylle (L).
22. Uria troile (L) ? *Brunnichii H.W.F.*
23. Mergulus (alle L).

List of tradesmen's bills incurred on account of the natural history outfit of the *Alert*, by Captain H. W. Feilden.

Ladd,[5] optician 11 & 12 Beak Street Regent Street	£43.14. 0
Keene & Ashwell[6] (glass tubes) 74 New Bond Street	4. 4. 0
Troughton & Simms,[7] 138 Fleet Street	9.12. 0
Hatchard[8] (Booksellers) Picadilly [*sic*]	28. 7. 6
William Laughlin[9] Polperro, nets (£13.1.0) ?60 to the ship	6.10.11
Hatchett[10] (Stationer) 426 Strand	22.14. 3
Boucard[11] (Naturalist) opposite Brit. Mus.	10.15. 1
Bourne & Taylor[12] (35 Castle Street, Holborn) Wholesale Chemist	18.10. 2
Reynolds & Co.[13] (57 New Compton Street W.C.) Copper sieves	7. 4. 6

Feilden Cash paid;

White[14] [Woolwich] 6 tin cases	£6.12.0	
Quaritch.[15] Thompsons [B?] of Ireland[16]	2. 2.0	

[1] Francisco (François) Campdera (1793–1862), botanist.

[2] Bessels, 1875, p. 297 has: '14. Eriphorum vaginatum (L).', here omitted by Feilden.

[3] Robert Brown (1773–1858), Scottish botanist.

[4] Spencer Fullerton Baird (1823–87), American ornithologist.

[5] William Ladd.

[6] Manufacturing homoeopathic chemists. See Ashwell, *Companion*, advertisement p. 1.

[7] Scientific (including navigational) instrument makers. See McConnell, *Instrument Makers*.

[8] Hatchard's is still on Piccadilly. For the early history, see Humphreys, *Piccadilly Bookmen*.

[9] Page, *VCH: Cornwall*, I, p. 114, refers to a William Laughlin of Polperro, coastguardsman and contributor to marine fauna of Cornwall, but gives no date.

[10] Frances Hatchett, manufacturing stationer.

[11] Adolphe Boucard (1839–1905), French ornithologist and trader in specimens, Foreign Member of the Zoological Society of London 1865, moved permanently from Paris to London.

[12] *Year-Book of Pharmacy*, 1874, advertisement p. 668 describes Bourne & Taylor as smelling bottle manufacturers and general druggists' sundrymen, and shows respirators, electro-magnetic apparatus, insect powder apparatus, and a new spray producer for the throat, all identified as their own.

[13] Reynolds & Co., wirework manufacturers. See advertisement in Berly, *Universal Directory*, 1884, p. 213.

[14] William W. White's Royal Artillery Agency, 8 Frances St, Woolwich, military outfitter and army contractor: see Hazard, *Army and Navy Calendar for the Financial Year 1893–94*, advertisement on verso of title page.

[15] Bernard Quaritch, bookseller and publisher, 1819–99, see *ODNB*. He moved his business to 15 Piccadilly in 1860. Feilden had a superb library of works on natural history: see Trevor-Battye, 'A Noble Englishman', pp. 7–8.

[16] Thompson, *Natural History of Ireland*.

Ray Society Proc[1]	1. 0.0	
Holtzappel & Co.[2]	2. 2.0	
Th[ʔen]ier[3]	4.0	
Tennant[4]	1. 4.0	13. 2. 0

Supplement to Parry's voyage in 1819–20. London 1824[5]

Lists Mammalia, Fish, Insects, Birds

January temperatures of Arctic expeditions 1822–1876

List of animals observed by M'Clintock, Melville, Patrick & Emerald I. 4th April–19 July 1853[6]

List of animals observed by Pullen. *North Star*, Beechey Island 52.53.54.[7]

Temperature for February 1876. N. Lat. 82°.27'

Monday 1 February 1875

Appointed by Admiralty to the post of Naturalist with Arctic Expedition.[8] Rate of pay 1[6]/–[9] per diem until date of sailing, £1. afterwards. Food & clothing as a lieutenant of R.N.

27 February 1875

Arrived at Gibraltar in steamer *Thibet*.[10] Lunched with 1st. Batt. 4th. K.O. Royals.[11]

6 March 1875

I arrived at Southampton in P&O steamer *Thibet* from Malta, 13 days out. Paid Army pay to this date by W.O.[12] that depar^mt. considers that Admiralty should bear all my expenses from this date. Subsequently altered to 1[5]/- per diem to date of sailing 6/- after departure.

12 March 1875

Met Captain G. S. Nares at Grosvenor Hotel. Medically surveyed at the Admiralty and passed as fit for Arctic service.

18 March 1875

Elected Corresponding Member of the Zoological Society of London.

[1] The Ray Society, founded in 1844, still publishes works on natural history.

[2] Holtzappfel & Co., 64 Charing Cross, London, known for woodworking tools, lathes and scales. See Turner, *Scientific Instruments*, p. 278.

[3] Not identified

[4] Possibly Charles Tennant, Sons & Co., chemical manufacturers, London and Glasgow.

[5] [Parry], 1824.

[6] Francis Leopold McClintock (1819–1907) was Commander of *Intrepid* in 1852–4. *ODNB*. I have not found the list, nor the source from which Feilden may have extracted it.

[7] William John Samuel Pullen (1813–87) was Commander of *North Star* in 1852–4. *ODNB*. I have not found Pullen's list of animals.

[8] Feilden was chosen by the Royal Society from the two candidates who had applied for the job. Royal Society of London, GB MS CMB 2/14/1.

[9] 1[6]/– is 16 shillings, but the reading is uncertain as the figures are hard to decipher.

[10] Peninsula & Oriental Steam Navigation Company; *Thibet* was built in 1874.

[11] King's Own Royal Regiment (Lancaster). The 4th Battalion was a Territorial battalion.

[12] War Office.

25 March 1875
From London to Portsmouth, called on Sir Leopold M'Clintock[1] went onboard H.M. Ships *Alert* and *Discovery*.

15 April 1875
Arctic Expedition; *Alert* and *Discovery*, commissioned at Portsmouth.

[1] (Francis) Leopold McClintock (1819–1907), *ODNB*. See above, p. 47, n. 6.

PART I: OUTWARD BOUND
20 MAY–1 SEPTEMBER 1875

20 May 1875
Banquet given by the Mayor of Portsmouth to Captain G. S. Nares & officers of the Arctic Expedition.

21 May 1875
H.R.H. the Prince of Wales and Duke of Cambridge visited the *Alert* and *Discovery*.

22 May 1875
H.M. the Ex-Empress of the French,[1] paid a visit to the arctic vessels in Portsmouth dockyard.

Saturday 29 May 1875 <u>Departure from England</u>
Bar. Max. 29°.96'. Min. 29°.95".57'.[2] At 4 p.m., precisely H.M. ships *Alert* and *Discovery* cast off from the dockyard wharf Portsmouth, and proceeded to sea. H.M.S. *Valorous*, having gone to Spithead previously, there joined the squadron.[3] Before our departure Captain Nares received the following telegram, dated Balmoral from her gracious Majesty.[4]

"I earnestly wish you and your gallant companions every success, and trust that you may safely accomplish the important duty you have so bravely undertaken".
Captain Nares replied.

"I feel the great honour Her Majesty has done myself and the other members of the Arctic Expedition in wishing us success, Her Majesty may depend upon all doing their duty".

The intense interest taken by the country at large in this expedition culminated today in the demonstration attending its departure. No person in our two ships will ever forget the farewell that the people of England gave to their 'discovery vessels' on this occasion.

---

[1] Empress Eugénie (1826–1920), widow of Napoleon III, former Emperor of France, who had died in 1873. The couple had gone into exile in England after the defeat of France in the Franco-Prussian war of 1870–71.

[2] Bar[ometer]. Naval officers normally used the height of a column of mercury in inches, so 29.96". Feilden is erratic in his use of the signs for inches (should be "), as he also is in his use of the signs for latitude and longitude. Sometimes he simply gives numbers, with no signs. The context shows whether he means inches (barometer), degrees, minutes, and even seconds (latitude and longitude). Nares, *Narrative*, 1878, II, Appendix XVIII, Meteorological Abstract, pp. 354–5, shows correct naval usage for this date.

[3] HMS *Valorous* was an old steam-powered paddle-wheel sloop, serving here as a supply ship for *Alert* and *Discovery*. *Valorous* carried extra coal, supplies, and food (including sheep) for the expedition. *Valorous* accompanied the expedition as far as Ritenbenk, returning to England with mail and reports. See below, entry for 16 July 1875.

[4] Queen Victoria (1819–1901), who reigned from 1837.

Closely packed multitudes occupied each pier and jetty on both sides of the harbour, whilst Southsea beach as far as the castle[1] was covered to the waters edge with one dense crowd, the regiments of the garrison being drawn up amongst it. All the ships in port manned their rigging, and as we passed greeted us with deafening cheers, whilst the air rang with the shouts of the people on shore, as well as from the steamers yachts and small craft of every description which crowded the waters. When abreast of the south shores of the Isle of Wight the squadron made sail down channel. It was a lovely night and we sat up late watching the shores of old England gliding past us.

Sunday 30 May 1875 <u>Off Plymouth</u>
Wind westerly. Bar. Max. 30°.02′. Min. 29°.92″. Thermo*meter* 59°.

At 10.30 a.m., made the number of *The Princess Royal* bearing the flag of Vice Admiral Sir H. Keppel,[2] coming out of Plymouth, the gallant Admiral came on board, but only stayed a few minutes, taking our letters, and then went to our consort. Towards evening Captain Nares made signal for the *Valorous* to close and at 7 p.m., our budget of letters was despatched by her to Queenstown.[3]

Monday 31 May 1875. <u>Scilly Isles</u>
Wind N.W. Bar. Max. 30°.19′.56″. Min. 29°.98. Temp. 56°. Lat. 50.14 N. Long. 6°.32′.30. W.

At 8 o'c. a.m., abreast of the Scilly Isles, and passing between them and the Lands End, observed a Cormorant, *Phalacrocorax carbo*, a single Gannet *Sula bassana*, and several parties of Puffins, *Fratercula arctica*, a few Common, and Lesser Black-Backed Gulls, *L. canus* and L. *fuscus*,[4] following in our wake.

Tuesday 1 June 1875 <u>Bantry Bay</u>
Wind ~~N.N.W.~~[5] <N.E. by E – C. 3–4.[6] Bar. Max. 30°.25. Min. 30.18. Temp. 54°–63°. Bantry Bay.

Another splendid day, at 8 o'c. a.m., we were off the Fastnet light, and Cape Clear.[7] Entering Bantry Bay, noticed several Guillemots *Alca troile*,[8] Gannets, *Sula bassana*, Herring Gulls *L. argentatus*, Cormorants *Phal. carbo*, and one Great Northern Diver, *Colymbus glaci*alis, this latter was in adult plumage. Came to anchor at Beerhaven at 3 p.m. Went ashore and walked through the village of Castletown, sent off, and received some telegrams. The inhabitants of Castletown are evidently Roman Catholics, as in most

---

[1] Southsea Castle, near Portsmouth, begun by Henry VIII, was turned into a modern fortress in 1814.

[2] Sir Henry Keppel (1809–1904), *ODNB*.

[3] Known as Queenstown 1849–1920, now known as Cobh, on the south coast of Ireland.

[4] Feilden generally uses *L.* for *Larus*. He did not always italicize Latin names.

[5] Ship's log has 'N.N.W.' as standard compass course. Bearings struck through by Feilden are standard compass courses, not wind directions.

[6] C is calm. The numbers for the strength of wind are from the Beaufort Scale, which is a 'series of numbers from 0 to 12 assigned by Captain (later Admiral Sir Francis) Beaufort to indicate the strength of the wind from a calm, force 0, to a hurricane, force 12'. *OED*.

[7] A promontory at the south-western point of Clear Island, the most southerly inhabited land in Ireland, 51°25′41″N 09°31′41″W. Fastnet Rock and Lighthouse are the most southerly part of Ireland.

[8] Guillemot, known as the murre in North America. Dresser, *History of the Birds of Europe*, VIII, p. 567, called it *Alca troile*; now *Uria aalge*.

of the shops rosaries and cheap pictures of saints are exposed in the windows. The Union workhouse is a very large stone building surrounded by extensive walled in grounds, inside of which many men were working. It ~~was~~ <caused> an unpleasant reflection to see so many able-bodied men thus employed. The people we met, were healthy, comely looking folk. The geological formation is micaceous slate, which in the coast sections exhibits *great distortion in its stratification.*

Wednesday 2 June 1875 <u>Irish Coast</u>
Wind E & S.E. 3–4. Bar. Max. 30.20 Min. 30.67. Temp 65°–56. Of sea 62 ½ to 55°.

At 11 a.m., left Beerhaven[1] [*sic*] under steam, joining the *Valorous* outside Bantry Bay, by her we received letters from Queenstown, and papers of the 31ˢᵗ ult., the latest news of the busy world that we shall receive for many a long day and night. Inside of the bay noticed one example of the Black Guillemot, *uria grylle*, outside many Kittiwakes, *rissa tridactyla*,[2] Common Gull, *larus canus*, many Gannets *sula bassana* were sailing about, and a small cetacean[3] with a high back fin[4] passed us going to the westward. Between three and four in the afternoon we passed the islands known as the Bull, Cow, and Calf, the latter surmounted with a light house.

Thursday 3 June 1875 <u>Sun-fish</u>
Wind <W.>N.W. Light. Bar. Max. 30.095–30.10. Temp. 59°–51. Of sea 56½–55. Lat. D.R.[5] 51.40 N. Long. 11.6 W.

Making little progress under sail, light westerly wind. During the afternoon two Sunfish were observed near the surface, close to the ship. I did not see them, neither was it determined whether they were examples of *Orthagoriscus mola*, or *Ortha. truncatus*.[6] The smooth sea was alive with *Salpæ*.[7] A boat was lowered for a floating bottle, which proved to be a hock flask well corked, the cork showed no sign of decay, but the bottle had about a fourth or fifth of its capacity filled with sea water, the exposed surface was bare, but the submerged half, had a heavy growth of *Lepas anatifera*[8] attached to it, many young barnacles were fastened to the old ones, and numerous sea-creatures were crawling amongst the attachments of the Barnacles. I threw this bottle back into the sea, lest hereafter they might get mixed with our Arctic collections, and cause confusion. Captain Markham[9] informed me that whilst cruising in the *Arctic*, July 1873, in Lancaster Sound,

---

[1] Castletown Berehaven.

[2] Black-legged kittiwake (the only species of kittiwake in Europe).

[3] Order of mammals including whales and their congeners.

[4] Orcas or killer whales have a strikingly high dorsal fin.

[5] Dead reckoning. 'The estimation of a ship's position from the distance run by the log and the courses steered by the compass, with corrections for current, leeway, etc., but without astronomical observations.' *OED*. Originally the log was a thin piece of wood, loaded so that it floated upright in the water, and attached to a line with knots. The log was thrown behind the ship, and the rate at which the knots were fed out gave the ship's speed through the water. By the date of the Nares expedition, however, naval ships often used mechanical rotating logs, often called patent logs, with dials to record the distance run.

[6] Ocean sunfish, slender sunfish.

[7] In the 19th century, regarded as a genus of soft-shelled or tunicated acephalous molluscs which float in the sea, now classified as a degenerate branch of *Chordata*. *OED*.

[8] The pelagic or smooth gooseneck barnacle in the family *Lepadidae*.

[9] Albert Hastings Markham (1841–1918), second-in-command on HMS *Alert*.

two Narwhals, *monodon monoceros*, were seen from the crows-nest, a boat was lowered in pursuit, which Captain Markham steered. These animals turned out to be at the time *in copula* their position in the water upright, the heads visible at the surface. The harpoon struck the ♀ which was captured, the harpoon also struck the ♂[1] which escaped wounded.

Thors[2] one of our ice-quartermasters tells me that during his whaling and sealing cruises, extending over eighteen seasons, he has frequently seen the acts of copulation performed between the Right Whales *B. mysticetus*.[3] According to his observations it is always performed whilst the animals are in an upright position, he described to me one ocurrence [*sic*] when the monsters had their tails exposed on the surface, and lashed the water into foam with violent blows of their extremities. Thors also told me that when approaching a sleeping, or apparently sleeping *B. mysticetus* he has observed its whalebone expanded outwards like an opened umbrella, and that at a considerable distance the rattling of the *baleen* may be heard as the animal brings it into its normal ~~con~~<pos>ition.

Friday 4 June 1875 Shearwaters & Kittiwakes
Wind N.W.<b.[4]N.> 3–4. Bar. Max. 30°.12–30°.018. Temp. 56°–54½. Of sea. 55–52½. Lat. 52°.26 N. Long. 11.57 W. Distance 56 miles.

Bright morning, fresh breeze. Hove to, waiting for the *Valorous*. Before breakfast a school of porpoises passed the bows of the ship followed by a flight of *Puffinus anglorum*.[5] Several Kittiwake gulls around the ship, in the afternoon at least a dozen of these birds were following us, two or three were adult, but the majority not in adult plumage having the ends of the tail feathers black. This bird often scratches its head when on the wing with its foot. Usually the legs and feet are carried close to the body, and entirely hid from view by the snowy plumage of the under-parts. Considering that this is the breeding season, and that most of their fellows are now busy with the cares of incubation, I am somewhat surprised at meeting with adult birds, so far out in the Atlantic. A single *Puffinus anglorum* passed the ship, flying at great speed to the westward.

Saturday 5 June 1875 Duties of Naturalists
Wind ~~N.W.ᵇN.~~[6] <W.S.W.> (1–4). Bar. 29.95–29.67. Temp. 55–53½. Of sea. 54–54½. Lat. D.R. 53°.12 N. Long. 14°.9 W. Distance made good 87 miles.

Read over and initialed the Admiralty instructions which Captain Nares has sent round for our information.

Par 27, which relates to me, reads as follows.
"You will also receive assistance from the two gentlemen who have been appointed as naturalists to the Expedition; and every reasonable facility should be given for the collection and preservation of such specimens of the animal, vegetable, and mineral

---

[1] Feilden uses the same symbol for male and female, with a cross rather than an arrow for both sexes. If the cross is downwards '♀', that signifies female; if upwards '♂', that signifies male, where we would write '♂'.

[2] John Thors or Thores. 'Ice quartermaster': a whaling captain or mate, experienced in navigation in ice-covered seas, who advised the officers and piloted the vessel through the ice. See Belcher, *Last of the Arctic Voyages*, I, p. xvii.

[3] *Balaena mysticetus*, the bowhead whale, a species of the right whale family Balaenidae.

[4] 'b.' is 'by', so passage reads Wind N.W. by N.>.

[5] Manx shearwater.

[6] Ship's log has 'N.WᵇN' as standard compass course. Bearings struck through by Feilden are standard compass courses, not wind directions.

kingdoms as can be conveniently stored on board the ships. These specimens are to be considered the property of Her Majesty's Government, and to be at their disposal."
x x x

"As in previous expeditions all journals, diaries, notebooks, charts &c, kept by officers of the ship, are on the expiration of the voyage to be handed over to the Commanding officer."[1]

Sunday 6 June 1875 <u>Fulmars</u>
Wind *Calm.* ~~N.W.N.~~ <W.S.W.> (1–4) Bar. 29.88–29.75. Temp. 58–54. Of sea 55–53½. Lat. D.R. 53°.12 N. Long. 14°.9 W. Distance made good 48 miles.

A fine clear day, making 8 knots for a shor*t* time during the day. Two examples of *Procellaria glacialis*[2] made their appearance round the ship. I can find no record of these birds having been before met with in such low latitudes at this season of the year. I have previously fallen in with them as the Shetlands were passed. Thompson (Nat. Hist. Ireland. vol. iii p. 406)[3] gives this bird as extremely rare on the Irish coasts. Our position today at noon was about 170 miles due west from the coast of Galway in Ireland, and S.W. 360 miles from St Kilda, its nearest known breeding station to us. It is just possible that some of this species may breed on one of the loan [*sic*] islands that stud the W. coast of Ireland.
(Note subsequent. "two days after we left Stromness, I noticed numbers of the Mollemoke, or fulmar petrel (*Procellaria glacialis*) following us, besides one or two passing Rotges (*Allea* [*sic*] *alle*).[4] When to the southward of lat 53°, they disappeared entirely, but whenever we were to the northward of that parallel, the whaler's constant companion the 'Molly' again made its appearance, and we were never without numbers of them to enliven us, throughout the remainder of the voyage." Arc. Voyage. R. A. Goodsir. 1850)[5]

Monday 7 June 1875
Wind ~~N.E.~~ <calm. – N.W.> (1–5) Bar. 30.16–29.74. Temp. 60 ½ –54°, of sea. 55°–52½°. Lat. 54°.35′ N. Long. 16°.52′ W. Distance made good 81 miles.

Bright and clear, wind light. Issue of lime juice commenced today. allowance ½ oz. per head it contains 90% of pure expressed juice of the fruit and 10% of spirit.

Made out a list of all the instruments books, supplies &c brought on board by me and provided out of Government grant, which handed over to Captain Nares.

Tuesday 8 June 8 1976
Wind N.W. <to W.> (1–3) Bar. 30.17–29.95. Temp. 61°–56°, of sea. 53°½–52½. Lat.56°.5.N. Long.17°.21 W. Distance made good 92 miles.

A bright and lovely day, did some towing with a small net.

---

[1] Given the extent of Feilden's vigorous deletions in this journal, he must have for a while forgotten or ignored this directive.

[2] Fulmar, now known as *Fulmarus glacialis*.

[3] Thompson, *Natural History of Ireland*, VIII, p. 406.

[4] *Alle alle*, the little auk or dovekie.

[5] Goodsir, *Arctic Voyage*, pp. 5–6, quotation slightly abridged.

[June 8th. <53> S. Osborn P.P.[1] p. 225. Shot 9 ptarmigan today: Brent geese and phalaropes plentiful but very shy] Osborn has certainly confused the phalarope with some other species. H.W F.

[June 8th. 1853. P.P. p. 160. shoots 2 geese on Pr Royal I[sland]. Allard.]

Wednesday 9 June 1875 Great Shearwater

Wind ~~N,W. — W.S.W.~~<W.S.W. to N.W.> [2–6] Bar. 29.84–29.52. Temp.57 ½– 51½. Of sea 53–52. Lat. 56°35′ [Long.] 19.21. D.M.G. 74 miles.

Cloudy with rain. Egerton[2] called me on deck immediatly[3] after breakfast, to see two birds which from his description were probably *Puffinus major*.[4] By the time I reached the deck, they were too far distant for me to recognize more than that they were Shearwaters. The *Valorous* was visible this morning on our front quarter, the *Discovery* on our port bow.

Thursday 10 June 1875 Oceanic Birds

~~S.W.ᵇW — W.ᵇS.~~ <N.N.W.> [4–6]. Bar. 29.60–29.56. Temp. 52–51. Of sea 53°–51°. Lat. 54.53 N. Long. 20.54 W. D.M.G.[5] 114 *miles.*

Moderate S.W. gale. Several Fulmars following the ship. Markham tells me he saw a *Puffinus major* today. There is considerable variety in the plumage of the *Procellaria glacialis*, the Greenland quartermasters have an idea that the darker are the younger birds.[6] Most of the information supplied by these men is traditional, not founded on their own observation.

Friday 11 June 1875 Porpoises

~~W.ᵇS. — W.ᵇS.~~ <N.N.W.> 5–7 Bar. 29.60–29.74. Temp. 50½ –52. Of sea. 48 –54. Lat. 53.27 N. Long. 21.49 W. D.M.G. 92 *miles.*

Moderate gale and high sea running, ship with its heavy deck load knocking about a good deal. A large school of Porpoises during the morning played round the ship. Dr Colan[7] returned me £5. which I had advanced for the mess at Bantry Bay, and I handed it over to Mr Clements Markham,[8] to pay for my entrance and subs for 1876 as F.R.G.S.

Saturday 12 June 1875 Marine Forms

~~W.ᵇS — W.~~ <N.W.–N.> 7–[6]. Bar. 29.74–29.65. Temp 51–57 of sea 54 –52 Lat D.R. 52.33 N. Long. 22.36 W. D.M.G. 61′.[9]

---

[1] Sherard Osborn (1822–75) who achieved the rank of admiral, had taken part in the search for Sir John Franklin from 1850 to 1851; from 1852–4 he was commander of HMS *Pioneer*. He wrote a popular account of the first 18 months of his search in Osborn, *Stray Leaves* (1852). *ODNB*. John Hilary Allard was second master of *Pioneer* in 1850–51, and master in 1852–4. P.P. are *Parliamentary Papers*, in *Arctic Blue Books*, 1855, p. 225.

[2] Sub-Lieutenant George Le C. Egerton, HMS *Alert*.

[3] Feilden consistently uses 'immediatly' for 'immediately'.

[4] Great shearwater, renamed *Puffinus gravis*.

[5] The first letters and numbers in this entry refer to wind direction, and to force on the Beaufort scale. Distance made good. In this journal, D.M.G. is always in miles, as given here, although Feilden often uses ′.

[6] There are two colour morphs of the northern fulmar in the Atlantic, light and dark.

[7] Thomas Colan, MD, RN (1831–85), Fleet-Surgeon; subsequently Inspector General of Hospitals and Fleets.

[8] Clements Robert Markham (1830–1916), geographer, cousin of Albert Hastings Markham, had taken unauthorized leave from the India Office to sail to Greenland with the Nares expedition. *ODNB*.

[9] i.e. miles.

At noon the wind abated, and we were tossed about in a calm, the towing net put over brought up *Salpæ*[1] and *Lucerinaridæ* [*sic*].[2] Towards midnight the wind blew from the W.

Sunday 13 June 1875 Tern. Heavy Gale

W.N.W. ~~WᵇN.~~ 3–10. Bar. 29.608. 29.22. 28.820. 28.862. Temp 54–50½ of sea 54–48.[3] Lat. 53.41 N. Long. 23. D.M.G. 70 *miles*.

2 p.m. Reefed F. topsail 3.50 Furled foresail. 4 o'c. Reefed M. topsail,[4] in F. topsail. Furled fore topsail. 8 p.m. Strong westerly gale. 8.30 lost sight of *Discovery*. 9. Block of main trysail[5] sheet carried away. 9.30 obs*erved* a steamer standing to westward. 10 o'c. wore[6] ship. Mid night Bar. rose from 28.820″ to 28.862″.

The wind increased by 2 a.m. and continued to do so, with a rapidly falling barometer. Many *Thalars* [*sic*] *pelagica*,[7] and *Proc. glacialis*, following the ship. The probable reason that these birds follow ships more in rough weather than in calm is that their usual food, small *cephalapoda*[8] and minute sea water organisms sink as soon as the surface of the sea becomes agitated by wind. Captain Nares informs me that this sinking of sea animals when the surface water is disturbed was satisfactorily proved on the *Challenger*. A single *Sterna hirundo* (*Arctic tern*)[9] [*sic*] flew round the ship, seemingly rather tired, it alighted on the head of a biscuit cask thrown overboard, and floated on this raft, rising to the top of the great green seas. By nine at night it was blowing a full gale the Bar. sank to 28°.80 and at 10 p.m. Captain Nares wore ship, as we were evidently approaching the centre of a cyclone or circular storm, almost immediatly after this, the barometer which before we could see falling, began to rise slowly but steadily. Still a strong gale of wind blew, and the ship laboured a great deal, and took in green seas forward which swept aft, one of these came down the ward room skylight, and flooded my cabin. The starboard whaler was stove in and destroyed.

Monday 14 June 1875 Fulmars

~~WᵇN. N.W.~~ – N. 8–3. Bar. 29.09–29.82. Temp. 57–52½ of sea. 52½–5. Lat. 53.57 N. Long. 23.34. D.M.G. 26 *miles*.

1 a.m. Heavy sea struck the ship, carried away after slings in starboard whaler. Secured wreck. Mid-day under reefed F. Topsails, F. staysail, Trysails & spanker.[10]

The gale has not yet blown itself out, although the barometer today has risen a full inch above the lowest point recorded last night. The *Fulmars* are increasing in numbers around us.[11]

---

[1] See above, p. 51, n. 7.

[2] Lucernariidae, a family of Hydrozoa, which includes jellyfish.

[3] These are temperatures, in degrees Fahrenheit.

[4] F. Topsail is fore topsail, i.e. the sail above the topsail set on the fore-top mast. M. topsail is the corresponding sail on the main mast.

[5] 'A small fore-and-aft sail, set with a gaff, and sometimes with a boom, on the fore- or mainmast, or on a small supplementary mast abaft either of these.' *OED*.

[6] 'To come round on the other tack by turning the head away from the wind'. *OED*.

[7] Presumably the storm petrel, *Thalassidroma pelagica*, renamed *Hydrobates pelagicus*.

[8] *Cephalopoda* are members of the phylum Mollusca, with a head and tentacles attached to it; e.g. octopus, squid.

[9] *Sterna hirundo* is the common tern. *Sterna paradisaea*, formerly *S. macrura*, is the Arctic tern.

[10] 'A fore-and-aft sail, set with a gaff and boom at the aftermost part of the ship.' *OED*.

[11] Fulmars were then found mainly in sub-Arctic regions of the North Atlantic; they have recently extended their distribution significantly to southern England.

Tuesday 15 June 1875 Great Skua

N.N.W.–N. 62. Bar. 29.85–30.186. Temp. 52–50. Of sea 51–49. Lat. 52.36. Long. 25.32. D.M.G. 107 *miles*.

Westerly wind, caught a *Proc. glacialis* with a bare hook attached to a line hung over the taffrail, on being hauled on deck, it vomited amber coloured oil, some of which I examined under the microscope but it showed no trace of animal structure mixed with it. One or two of this species that I have captured in the island of Väagoe,[1] Fäeroe, vomited a red fluid, about the tint of salmon roe. Professor Newton remarks "On picking up one (Fulmar.) which fell on the dry land, I was rather surprised to find its plumage tinged in several places with a bright reddish orange hue. I at first thought it was stained by oil which these birds, when killed, sometimes discharge; but I found subsequently that the effect so produced was entirely different." Ibis April 1865.[2]

When placed on the deck the *Proc. glacialis* cannot take wing, without being ~~raised~~ <assisted> from the deck.

Following the ship, I noticed what I took to be a *Ster. Catarractes* [*sic*],[3] it was very white on the scapulars, also a Long-tailed Skua, *Ster. longicaudatus*.

Noting any birds out of the common, seen at sea is unsatisfactory, and I feel averse to state that I have observed such and such a species unless they have been in my hand.[4]

Wednesday 16 June 1875

L' air to N.N.W. 3. Bar. 30.17–30.12. Temp. 53. Of sea. 49–51. Lat. 52.42 N. Long. 27.36. D.M.G. 69 *miles*.

Heavy swell and we rolled much all <last> night hardly got a wink of sleep.

Thursday 17 June 1875

Wind W.N.W. 3–7. Bar. 30.068–29.77. Thermo*meter* 56–52 of Sea 50–46. Lat. D.R. 54.14 N. Long D.R. 30.32. D.M.G. 140 *miles*.

The usual sea-birds following the ship, between 9 and 10 p.m., they all disappear.

Friday 18 June 1875 Storm Petrel

W.N.W.–N.W. 5-7. Bar. 29.78–29.46. Temp. 57–49½ of sea 48–47. Lat. 57.26. Long. 31.4. D.M.G. 193 *miles*.

I kept the middle watch with Aldrich,[5] as I wished to see about what time the sea birds re-appeared in the morning. By ten last night all had disappeared. At 2 a.m., this morning we noticed a single *Thalas. pelagica*, hawking round the ship, it was very rough, and I could just detect in the gloom this small black bird flying round the ship sometimes at an elevation above the water, as <high as> our mainyard. This conduct was so unlike that of the Storm Petrel generally, that I felt certain it must have been some species of

---

[1] There is now no Faeroese island of that name; Feilden may have meant the island of Vágar.

[2] Newton, 'Notes on the Birds of Spitsbergen', p. 203.

[3] *Stercorarius Cataractes*: the great skua,

[4] This often involved shooting and recovering, or otherwise catching and killing the bird, a standard procedure in the years before good binoculars, cameras, and field guides.

[5] Pelham Aldrich, lieutenant on HMS *Alert*; see p. 15, n. 3 above.

Hirundine,[1] which would soon alight on the rigging. Increasing light however showed its real species, shortly after this a Fulmar or two came hurrying towards the ship, and gradually they collected in our wake. They certainly do not follow the ship during the hours of darkness. The wind increased much during the day.

nSubsequent noten. This is the last date on which I saw *Thal. pelagica*.

Saturday 19 June 1875 <u>Gale. Lying too</u> [*sic*]
Wind N.W. 6.9. Bar. 29.60″–29.77″. Temp. 53°–45°. Of sea 47°–45°. Lat. 57°.2′ N. Long. 31°.48′ W. D.M.G. 31 *miles*.

Lying too [*sic*] under close reefed topsails and fore and main trysails, gale from N.W. true, battened down fore and aft.

Sunday 20 June 1875
N.Wᵇ.W.–W. 9–1. Bar. 29.85–30. Temp. +53°–50° of sea +47. Lat. 57°.34′ N. Long. 31°18 N. D.M.G. 36 *miles*.

Weather moderated after breakfast set plain sail, 4 p.m., wore ship – 9 p.m., up steam.

Monday 21 June 1875
Wind *Ligh*ᵗ air to WᵇN. 3–5. Bar. 29.714″–29.21″. Temp. 54–52. Of sea 47–45. Lat. D.R. 58°.3 N. Long. 33.45. D.M.G. 100 *miles*.

Banked up fires and stopped engines at 3 a.m. Bar. falling rapidly, the wind, however, did not increase to any great extent.

Tuesday 22 June 1875
WᵇN–W.S.W. 5.2.6. Bar. 29.27. 29.50. 29.27. Temp. +48–54 of sea. 45–41. Lat. 59.23 N. Long. 35.46. D.M.G. 102′.

Almost becalmed, caught a Fulmar with a baited hook, as soon as it was pulled on deck, Nellie the retriever belonging to Markham, killed it. There is a very marked difference in the plumage of Fulmars, some, but they are the minority, perhaps one in ten, are of a uniform smoke-gray colour. These ones seem more wary than the white ones, and I could not succeed in hooking one. Too much swell on, or would have asked the Captain to lower a boat, in hopes of procuring a specimen of the fine Shearwaters, that are now about the ship. I take them for *Puffinus major*, some are of a uniform sooty hue, others are white on the underparts, with a neck band of white, top of head dark brown, back dark brown, with a band of white across the tail feathers. The flight of these fine birds is very striking, my eye cannot <always> detect the movement of the beat of the wings, they appear to sway their bodies keeping the pinions always expanded and in a horizontal plane with the body, and to guide their course without beats of the pinions.

In Scotland the act of cutting grain with scythe or sickle is called Shearing. v. Miss Mulock. "Shearing the corn-fields of Ardbeg aboon sweet Rothsay Bay".[2] it is possible that the sweeping scything flight of the *Procellaridæ* may have originated their trivial name. The towing net brings up multitudes of needle shaped *Diatomacæ*[3] which give a greenish

---

[1] Member of the swallow family.

[2] Craik, *Poems*, p. 49. Fielden slightly misquotes Craik, who wrote: 'Shearing the corn-rigs of Ardbeg, / Aboon sweet Rothesay Bay'.

[3] *Diatomacae*, or diatoms, are an order of microscopic unicellular algae. *OED*.

tinge to the water, hundreds of *Entromostraca* [*sic*],[1] *Thalassicola*,[2] &c, are also included in the *mess* brought up in the net.

Wednesday 23 June 1875 <u>Fulmars. Diatoms</u>
Wind W.[C]. N.N.W. 5.0.6. Bar. 29.20. 30.32. 29.50. Temp. 45. 54. 43. Of sea. 40–43. Lat. 59°.36 N. Long. 39.5. W. D.M.G. 107 *miles*.

The morning broke fine and clear, at 8 a.m. temperature of air +42½, wind south, steering our course. At mid day captured a *Fulmar* ♂. Iris dark hazel brown. Eyelid brown. culmen to nares, light sea green Orbit of nares black. Bill (split-pea) yellow, under mandible greenish yellow. Tongue large and fleshy, delicate pink. Legs and feet delicate French gray, soles of feet ditto. numerous parasites on it.

Length entire 19 inches, wing 13 inches, upper mandible 1¼ in. Tarsus 2 in. Testes small and dark blue. Contents of stomach offal from ship. When placed on deck ran with ease but could not rise on the wing.

Many of the large *Shearwaters*, with white bands across the tail, flying round the ship.[3] Several *Kittiwakes* put in an appearance this afternoon the first we have seen on this side of the Atlantic.

Many fragments of seaweed floating past, secured some pieces, the slime scraped off when placed under the microscope, appeared to be diatomacæ, some of them belonging to the genus *Licmophora*[4] (v. Carpenter Micro. p. 322.[5])

Thursday 24 June 1875
Wind W.N.W. 6–4.3. Bar. 29.54. 29.72–29.80. Temp. 42. 45 of sea 42–40½ Lat. D.R. 58.00 N. Long. 40.22. W. D.M.G. 104 *miles*.

Hardly enough wind to move the ship ahead. This has been so far a very long passage. Today the temperature feels much colder. A flock of *Kittiwakes* remained sometime round the ship.

Friday 25 June 1875 <u>Floating Corpse</u>
Wind N.W. S.E. N.E. 1.4.5. Bar. 29.73. 29.57. 29.41. Temp. 44. 49. 47. of sea 42. 41. Lat. D.R. 58.5 N. Long. 41.43 W. D.M.G. 41 *miles*.

Early this morning up steam, the breeze increasing, fires let down about 9 o'c. a.m. Sighted a barque steering to the E. Probably from the Arksut fiord,[6] where the *cryolite*[7] mines are situated. Quartermaster Bury[8] reported to me seeing three Bottle-nosed Whales,

---

[1] Entromostraca was 'a subclass of Crustacea comprising the Branchiopoda, Ostracoda, Copepoda, and Cirripedia, groups regarded by most modern systematists as too diverse for inclusion in a single subclass, the name then being used as a term of convenience without taxonomic implications'. *Merriam–Webster Dictionary*.

[2] Marine gastropod molluscs, or sea snails.

[3] Probably great shearwaters, *Puffinus major* (now known as *P. gravis*), although in these latitudes most often found in late summer and early autumn.

[4] Diatom that grows on a living plant; cells grow on a common stalk that is attached to rocks or algae. Kudela Lab. of biological oceanography, University of California Santa Cruz.

[5] Carpenter, *Microscope and Its Revelations*, p. 322.

[6] In south-western Greenland. T. R. Jones, ed., *Manual*, p. 350, lists the minerals to be found around the Arksut Fjord.

[7] Mineral aluminium and sodium fluorides, occurring in white or light-brown semi-transparent crystals; a valuable source of aluminium.

[8] James Berrie, ice quartermaster, HMS *Alert*.

which term the Davis Straits fishers apply to *Hyperoodon rostratus* Chem*nitz*.[1] It is stated by authors (v Alston Bells Quad. p. 423[2]) to be of shy and solitary habits, generally moving either singly or in pairs. Just before tea I heard that Bury had seen a corpse floating close to the ship about 3 o'c. p.m. On enquiry Bury insisted that it was so, and that the body was so close to the ship that he could have thrown a biscuit on it.

I read today M[r] Majors Voyage of the brothers Zeno Hakluyt soc. 1873.[3] At p.75, he points out very conclusively that the Gunnbiorn Skerries of Graah[4] in N.L. 65°.30′, cannot be those originally meant in the sailing directions of Ivar Bardsen,[5] as these islands according to the map of Johann Ruysch. 1507, states "Insula hæc A.D. 1456 fuit totaliter combusta".[6] But in 1574 Latra Clemens visits Gunnbiorn Skerries and finds plenty of Garefowl.[7] This means one of two things either, that three centuries ago the E. Greenland ice drift did not occupy its present position, (in which case the Danell I*sland* must have been inaccessible either to Clemens or the Garefowl) or else that Ivar Bardsen's skerries were not *totaliter combusta* in 1456, or that some portion had reappeared again where probably Clemens landed in 1574.

Saturday 26 June 1875 Dead Whale

E.N.E. W.N.W. S.W. Bar. 29.62. 29.416. Temp. 44. 52. 47 of sea 42. 41. 40. Lat obs. 58°.39 N. Long 46.4 W. D.M.G. 141 *miles*.

On deck during the middle watch with Aldrich. At 2 a.m. the sun began to glow the eastern horizon, and some small clouds, just tipped by the first rays, had somewhat the appearance of what I thought might be ice, but, with increased light they turned into vapour. At 2.20 a.m., we passed within sixty feet of a dead ♀ *Mysticetus* belly upwards. Quartermaster Deuchars, estimated it at a *five foot fish*, that is supposed length of the baleen, and the whale fishers always describe a fish by this standard. The only attendant on this whale which I reckoned to be about thirty five or forty feet long was a single Fulmar, apparently keeping guard over it, but no doubt as morning broke hundreds of these ravenous birds would assemble to the banquet. The solitary Fulmar is an instance of the repose of animals during the arctic night.

In the afternoon two Rorquals *? Balænoptera musculus*[8] (Linn.) were sighted, at least I specify them as such on the dictum of the quartermasters, who say that they can easily

---

[1] Flower, 'Instructions', in T. R. Jones, ed., *Manual*, p. 43. Chemnitz, 'Von der Balæna Rostrata'. Now known as *Hyperoodon ampullatus*

[2] Bell, *History of British Quadrupeds*, 2nd edn, p. 423.

[3] Zeno, *Voyages of the Venetian Brothers*.

[4] Gunnbjörn's skerries, lying between Greenland and Iceland, were discovered by Gunnbjörn Ulfsson in the 9th century; the islands were destroyed in a volcanic eruption in 1456. Graah, *Narrative of an Expedition*, 1837, summarized and excerpted in Zeno, *Voyages of the Venetian Brothers*, see esp. pp. lxxiii–lxxiv. The latter work also reproduces in an Appendix, Bardsen, 'Description', see esp. p. 41.

[5] DeCosta, ed., *Sailing Directions of Henry Hudson*.

[6] Ruysch's map of the world, the second oldest map showing the New World, published and widely distributed in 1507, in Tosinus, ed., *Geographia Cl. Ptholemæi*. Translation: "This island was totally destroyed by fire in AD 1456."

[7] Jones, ed., *Manual*, p. 110. 'The Gare-Fowl', p. 480; gare-fowl: the great auk, already extinct in the mid-19th century; Gaskell, *Who Killed the Great Auk?*

[8] Rorquals are the largest baleen whales. The blue whale was named *Balaenoptera musculus* in Linnaeus, *Systema Naturæ*, 10th edn, I, p. 75. 'Finners' are whales of the genus *Balaenoptera*, which includes the fin whale, *Balaenoptera physalus*, sometimes referred to as the common rorqual. The 'blast' of a whale is its blow or spout.

tell the "Finner" from the *Mysticetus* by its lower and rounder "blast". Observations on these animals from a ship and at a distance must necessarily be untrustworthy.

(The following passage from "Purchase's Pilgrimes" refers to the head of the *Mysticetus* "His head is the third part of him, his mouth (O! Hellish wide!) sixteene foot in the opening; and yet out of that *Belly of Hell*, yeelding much to the ornaments of our womene's backs.") For careful measurements of this v. Arc. voyage. R. A. Goodsir p. 97.[1]

Sunday 27 June 1875 First Ice

S.W. C.[2] N. 2.0.5. Bar. 29.29. 29.224. 29.55. Temp. 47. 54. 42. of sea. 40. 39. 36½. Lat. D.R. 59.36 N. Long. 48.46 W. D.M.G. 99 *miles*.

4.30 p.m. Came amongst loose ice. 6.30 cleared ice. 11.45 heard pack. 6.30 cleared ice. 11.45 heard pack.[3] About 1 o'c. saw several looms *Alca arra*.[4] flying in the direction of the Greenland coast. During dinner the officer of the watch came below and reported *first ice*, by 4 o'c. we were in the middle of drift ice, small pieces of old floe; the sea was dotted around with these fragments, and for singular beauty and strange effect, they quite came up to the standard of my imagination. The pieces of ice lapped by the warm sea-water, had taken to themselves the most extraordinary shapes, it required little effort to conjure up a likeness in one to a bird, in another to a massive coral, or a bear, or a house, indeed almost any shape ones fancy dictated. But the colour of the ice is lovely, in many pieces bright cærulean blue shone from the centre of the portion above water, the submerged part looking bright green, shining forth from the dull setting of the bottle-green sea. Standing on the forecastle I saw three *mergulus alle*,[5] seated on a piece of ice, they remained there until nearly touched by our cut-water. They were in full summer plumage.

Monday 28 June 1875 Cape Desolation

Wind N[b]W. N.N.W. S. 5.3.1. Bar. 29.62. 29.78. 29.72. Temp. 40. 46. 41. of sea 38½. 36½. 55½. 37. Lat obs. 60°.20 N. Long. 49°.31. D.M.G. 50 *miles*.

3 o'c a.m. passed out of detached ice. 3. a.m. observed an iceberg on port beam. 3.30 a.m. detached ice ahead. 4.40 Tacked. 6.30. obs*erved* a sail on lee bow which proved to be H.M.S. *Valorous*. 10 a.m. obs*erved* land on lee bow. noon under all sail. 4 p.m. steaming between two packs. 7.15 Passed through a stream of loose ice. Skirted the ice all day, which consisted of streams and packs of heavy floe, undoubtedly the outer edge of the East Greenland drift coming round Cape Farewell. At noon the coast of Greenland not far from Cape Desolation bore E. by N. distant forty-five miles by observation.

Saw several *Alca arra*, one or two gulls which I presume were Icelanders,[6] and a few skuas, these latter too [*sic*] far off to be certain of the species. The sea of a very dark bottle green colour.

---

[1] Feilden read the quotation from Purchas in Goodsir, *Arctic Voyage*, p. 127.
[2] C. is calm.
[3] i.e. heard movement of the broken pack ice, grating against itself.
[4] Brünnich's guillemot, known as the thick-billed murre in North America. Scientific name is now *Uria lomvia*.
[5] Little auk, scientific name is now *Alle alle*.
[6] Iceland gull, *Larus glaucoides*.

Tuesday 29 June 1875 <u>Walrus</u>
Wind. L.ᵗ air. C. NᵇE. Bar. 29.636. 29.47. 29.15. Temp. 38. 42. 46 of sea 35. 32. 38. Lat obs. 61°.52. Long 51.38. D.M.G. 106 *miles*.

4.5 a.m. altered course as requisite to clear pack. 6 a.m. steaming along edge of pack and through detached ice. 10 a.m. stopping, going ahead, astern and altering course as requisite to clear ice. 4 p.m. F. topsail carried away.

I remained on deck till 2 o'c. a.m. with Parr,[1] passed western edge of the pack. awakened at 7 a.m., by the jarring of the ship as she was driven at the ice. A walrus and several seals seen on the ice. By noon we were clear of the ice, at 7 p.m wind freshened and at midnight blew a gale, lay too [*sic*] under double reefed main topsail and fore and main trysails. Saw Looms, Little auks, Kittiwakes, Fulmars and Iceland gulls this morning in the pack.

Wednesday 30 June 1875
Wind. NᵇE. Calm. 6.7.0. Bar. 29.20. 29.58. 29.67. Temp. 44. 41. 49. of sea 37. 36. 38. 35. Lat. 61°.48 N. Long. 52°.41 W. D.M.G. 12 *miles*.

On deck middle watch with Aldrich, wind increasing at 3.30 a.m., a sea broke over the starboard quarter, and part of it went down the wardroom skylight. I ran down from the bridge to close my cabin door, but was rather late as a good deal of water had passed over the combing[2] as the ship rolled. The wind decreased and it turned out a fine day at 7 p.m., up steam. During the day passed several icebergs [see Plate 1], about 10 p.m., came up with the pack on our starboard quarter, coasted along it our course N.N.E. About 8 p.m. several "Finnies" were blowing some miles distant in a N.N.W. direction, the 'blast' of these animals, against a background of salmon coloured sky, was very like the smoke of a distant steamer. Sea dark bottle green, sky dull gray, towards night illuminated with bands of salmon pink.
[*Here Feilden inserted a watercolour sketch of* Discovery *in Baffin Bay; see Plate 1.*]

Thursday 1 July 1875 <u>Fiskernæs</u>[3]
Wind. L.ᵗ air N.W. C. N. 1.0.1. Bar. 29.72. 29.76. 29.74. Temp. 40. 49. 47 of sea 34. 38. 37. Lat obs. 63.16 N. Long. 52·39 W. D.M.G. 90 *miles*.

2 a.m. Steering along edge of pack. 7.40 Rounded a spit of thick hummocky ice. 8.30 obs*erved* land on starboard bow. Noon, land all along starboard beam. 12.20 Sounded, no bottom 130 fathoms 8.45 H.M.S. *Discovery* made her number under the land.

9.45. (Entered in log) [*Margin: Initialled by Lieut A. C. Parr R.N.*] ("Observed an active volcanic peak bearing S. 77° E".) This I doubt, I observed the phenomenon alluded to, and what was taken for smoke I imagined to be light vapoury clouds settlling on, and drifting off at intervals from a lofty peak. H.W.F.

2 a.m., steering along edge of ice, 7.40 a.m., rounded a spit of ice, course changed to N.E by N. At 9 sighted the Greenland coast near Fiskernæs. A beautiful clear day, and though thirty miles from shore we had a good view of the snow capped mountains, at 10 p.m., we were abreast of the fiord that leads to Godhaab.[4] At mid day sounded on a bank marked

---

[1] Lieutenant Alfred Arthur Chase Parr, HMS *Alert*.

[2] Coamings: The raised borders about the edge of the hatches and scuttles of a ship, which prevent water on deck from running below. *OED*.

[3] Now called Qeqertarsuatsiaat, SW Greenland, on an island off the shores of the Labrador Sea.

[4] Godthåb, now Nuuk and the capital of Greenland.

30 to 40 fathoms we found 100. No ice of any consequence was visible today between the coast and ourselves, so that we have cleared the northern limit of the E Greenland drift. The temperature of the sea water last night close to the pack was +33° this morning +38½°. Birds somewhat numerous today Kittiwakes, Fulmars, Arctic terns, Iceland gulls, and a Herring Gull?[1] with the tips of its primaries black.

[*Here Feilden inserted a watercolour sketch of Greenland coastal mountains observed on 1 July; see Plate 2.*]

Friday 2 July 1875 <u>Dredging</u>

Wind Lᵗ air. N.N.W–N.E. 1. 2. Bar. 29.718. 29.70. 29.60. Temp. 42. 44. 47 of sea 30. 38.57? 39. Lat obs. 64.44′. Long. 52.53. D.M.G. 88 *miles*.

9 a.m. communicated with *Discovery*. 2.30 sounded ¹⁄₁₂₀ fathoms. 5.10 stopped sounded in 30 fathoms hard bottom.

After breakfast the *Discovery* was alongside of us, a boat was lowered, and we went onboard of her. She experienced much the same weather as we had since separating on the 13ᵗʰ· June. They lost one boat, and injured another. All were well and hearty onboard. Hart[2] showed me the contents of the stomach of a Fulmar they had captured, which consisted of the horny mandibles, and gladius of a small *Cephalopod*. Walker, (Journ. Roy. Dublin. Soc. July. 60.)[3] mentions *Rossia palpebrosa*,[4] as found in the Stomach of a Gull. 6 p.m., Captain Nares stopped the ships over a 30 fath*om* bank in N.L. 65°.5 and about 23 miles from the Greenland coast, a dozen or more lines were immediatly put overboard, but without any result. The dredge was let down with swales attached. When hauled up it was half full of gravel and peebles,[5] as these banks must often be covered with grounded bergs, the moraine and detritus embedded in them, must during the summer be deposited in great quantities on them, and year after year the soundings will decrease on these spots. A careful series of soundings recorded from these banks would be of considerable value in the future. The majority of the peebles brought up were gneiss, and granite, more sparingly quartz and a few pieces of basalt, all were rounded, but I noticed no ice-scratchings. The swales were replete with *Echinoderms*,[6] *Star-fish*, *Ophiura*[7] six very large *Holothuria*[8] [*see Plate 5*] inside the net, & a few shells, *Buccinum*,[9] *natica*,[10] *Astarte*,[11] and *Saxicava*.[12] We passed many stems of *Laminaria*[13] with leaf and root attached. Brown (Arc. papers. p. 47.)[14] mentions that grounding bergs root up algæ in fiords.

---

[1] *Larus argentatus.*

[2] Henry Chichester Hart (1847–1908), educated as a botanist, naturalist on HMS *Discovery*.

[3] Walker, 'Notes on the Zoology', p. 70.

[4] A species of bobtail squid native to the North Atlantic.

[5] 'Peeble' is an obsolete spelling for 'pebble', which Feilden used consistently.

[6] Radially symmetrical marine invertebrates, including starfish, in the Phylum Echinodermata.

[7] A species of brittle star in the order Ophiurida.

[8] Soft-bodied limbless invertebrates, resembling cucumbers. Some are known as sea cucumbers.

[9] A sea snail in the whelk family.

[10] Predatory sea snails in the family of moon snails.

[11] A bivalve mollusc in the family Astartidae.

[12] A genus of marine bivalve shells.

[13] A genus of brown algae known as kelp.

[14] Brown, 'Physical Structure of Greenland', p. 47.

[*Here Feilden inserted watercolour sketches of the scenery observed on 2 July 1875, see Plates 3 and 4; and another sketch of a Holothurian caught in the dredge; see Plate 5.*]

Saturday 3 July 1875 <u>Coast of Greenland</u>
Wind N.E^bN. 3. 4. Bar. 29.54. 29.50. 29.65. Temp. 39. 40. 38 of sea 37½· 38. 39. Lat. obs 6526. Long 54·12. D.M.G. 55 *miles*.

Wind dead foul, tacked on and off the Greenland coast, a fine clear day. During the tacks when we neared the shore, we had splendid views of Greenland scenery. Very fitly did brave John Davis name it "The Land of Desolation".[1] Black bleak and forbidding, where not robed in snow, my eye never rested on a more melancholy land, but for all that grand and striking. When the sun dipped below the horizon, which it did for a few minutes at midnight, it departed in a blaze of glory, spreading a warm purple hue over the mountain tops, and lighting up ice-stream and snow drifted valley with delicate shades of pink and salmon colour. It reminded me somewhat of sunsets that I have seen in the Red Sea. At 11 p.m., 2 whales with back-fins passed near the ship. Of what species I cannot definitely say. I believe our ice-quartermasters to be most unreliable in identifying the species of *Cetacea*, they know a *Mysticetus*, but every thing else is either "Finner" or Bottlenose, of course they differentiate the "Uni".[2]

I noticed tonight, in opposition to what I have before written, that Fulmars were feeding at midnight, but tonight the sea was smooth, and no doubt the fine weather attracted *Sepias*[3] &c to the surface. Probably the crepuscular habits of many of the *Procellaridæ*[4] are dependent on the nature of the animals they feed on, and not due to any peculiar formation of their eyes. I wonder whether the attention of anatomists has been drawn to the eyes of these birds, and if so whether the contracting muscles of pupil are weaken*ed* and the dilating increased.

Sunday 4 July 1875 <u>Sukkertoppen. Arctic Circle</u>
Wind N.E.^bN.W. 4. 1. 3. Bar. 29.82. 29.93. 29.95. Temp. 39. 46. 48· of sea. 39. 37. 35. Lat 66°.00 N. Long 53.59 W. D.M.G. 35 *miles*.

7.30 p.m., Passed the Arctic circle.

On deck middle watch with Aldrich, continued on the shore tack till 1 a.m., were then nearly abreast of "Old Sukkertoppen", a very prominent, isolated round mountain close to the shore.

The colouring of the arctic summer nights is certainly glorious. When the sun tonight got to its lowest declination, the Heavens were tinted gold and amber, and for a couple of hours both before and after midnight, a most gorgeous display of colours revealed itself. The mountains previously shrouded with mist and gloom, completely changed their

---

[1] John Davis or Davys (?1550–1605), born in Devonshire, was the most significant Arctic navigator in the late-16th century. 'It seemed to be the true patterne of desolation, and after the same our Captaine named it, The Land of Desolation', in Janes, 'The first voyage of Master John Davis' in *The Voyages and Works of John Davis*, ed. A. H. Markham, p. 4. I don't know for certain that this was where Feilden came across this quotation, but he and Markham were together on *Alert*, and Markham may well have supplied him with a transcript of the work that he was editing, and published in 1880.

[2] The 'Uni' is the narwhal, *Monodon monoceros*; males usually have one tusk.

[3] *Sepia* is a genus of cuttlefish.

[4] Shearwaters and petrels.

appearance, the snowy summits were suffused with a warm salmon glow, deep purple shades climbed up the slopes, clothing scarre,[1] ravine, and precipice, with rich shades, and hanging like a warm tinted curtain over the valleys leading into the interior. Beyond, backed by a transparent veil of neutral tint, the line of the "inland ice" cut the horizon. It required the brush of Elijah Walton[2] to do justice to the scene. About 3 a.m., a whale, *Hyperoodon rostratus* (Chem*nitz*.) was blowing near the ship. Each emission of breath was accompanied by a stertorious grunt, which somewhat resembled the distant trumpet of an Elephant. This small whale was accompanied by a flock of thirty or forty *Rissa tridactyla*, who settled in its wake, and when ever the animal disturbed the water, rising or descending, these birds flocked to the spot, the agitation of the sea, evidently brought their food to the surface, as they were busily employed in feeding.

Moving rapidly through the water, as we are, is most destructive to the delicate organisms caught in the towing net, everything becomes mashed up into an *olla podrida*.[3]

At 10 p.m., we crossed the Arctic circle N.L 66°.32′.15″. Sighted Knight's[4] islands, a low group not far from C. Burnit. Passed Holstenborg at 10 p.m., I could just distinguish with a glass a few red painted houses.

[*Coloured sketch of a whale was inserted here; see Plate 6.*]

Monday 5 July 1875 Rifkol
Wind W–E.S.E–S.bE. 2. 4. 5. Bar. 29.90. 29.73. 29.65. Temp. 45. 48. of sea 35. 37°. 54? 38.

4 p.m. Passed several pieces of small ice and bergs. 6 p.m. numerous small bergs in sight. N. L 67°43′. W. Long. 54°37′.

At 11.30 a.m., five eider-ducks passed the ship off the mouth of Neksotouk fiord. In the afternoon many icebergs around us, some of the larger ones grounded, I counted forty large bergs in sight. When the thermo. in the afternoon fell to 39°.00 it felt very cold, owing to the wind. About 6 p.m., sighted the high land of Disco. In old times this part of Davis Straits gave good whale fishing which for long, the Dutch monopolized.[5] Quartermaster Thors gave me an old whaling dictum, which evidently refers to these <good> old times.
"Tak Riffkol hill and Disco[6] dipping
There you'll see the Whales a skipping"
Now the *Mysticetus* has abandoned these parts.

Tuesday 6 July 1875 Disco
Wind SbE. 3.5. Bar. 29.64. 29.67. 29.65. Temp. 46.52. of sea 37. 38. 40.

11.30 a.m., Found H.M.S. *Valorous* in Lievely harbour. Lashed alongside of her on the port side 19¾ fathoms.

---

[1] Scarred ground is the result of erosion, and F. could well be back-forming a noun from the adjective.
[2] Elijah Walton (1832–80), English painter, especially of mountain scenes.
[3] Originally a Spanish stew of assorted meat and vegetables; a hotchpotch.
[4] The Knight Islands are small and uninhabited.
[5] Vestergaard, *Whaling Communities,* 1990, p.15.
[6] Feilden writes Disco, not Disko. The latter is the modern spelling for this large island in Baffin Bay, off the coast of Greenland.

Plate 1.   Watercolour by Feilden of *Discovery* in Baffin Bay, captioned, 'Baffins Bay June 30th. 75. H.W.F.'

Plate 2.   Sketch made by Feilden on 1 July 1875 of Greenland, coastal mountains. 'Seneraratinia [Sanerâta Tinia] July 1 1875 HWF'.

Plate 3.   Watercolour by Feidlen 'Gothaab Greenland Coast. July 2ⁿᵈ 1875 H.W.F.'

Plate 4.   Watercolour by Feilden, captioned, 'Extraordinary iceberg, looking like a basaltic column, passed 2 a.m. July 2ⁿᵈ 1875 off Baalfiord
N. Lat. 64° 15'. Sketched during Arctic night. H.W.F.'

Plate 5.   Watercolour sketch by Feilden. 'Holothuria[n] with 10 tentacles dredged, Lat. 65°00′ Lon. 53°00′ July 2nd 1875. 30 fathoms H.W.F.'

Plate 6.   Watercolour by Feilden. 'Common Beaked Whale – *Hyperoodon rostratus* (Chemnitz). Off Old Sukkertoppen July 4th 1875. H.W.F.'

Plate 7.   Watercolour panorama on two sheets with annotations by Feilden. ~~Laterally~~ horizontally bedded Trap ~~Rocks~~ W. side. Disco. Blue Mountain. About 1200 ft high by guess. 6th July 1875. These cliffs are Blaa Fell, and just about the join lies Ovifak, the place where Professor Nordenskiöld found the meteorites & which I visited on the 11th July 1875. H.W.F.'

Plate 8.   Watercolour sketch by Feilden. 'Proven, N. Greenland 20.7.75 H.W.F.'

Plate 9.   Pencil drawing entitled, 'Berg. Entrance to Smith's Sound. July 27th 1875.'

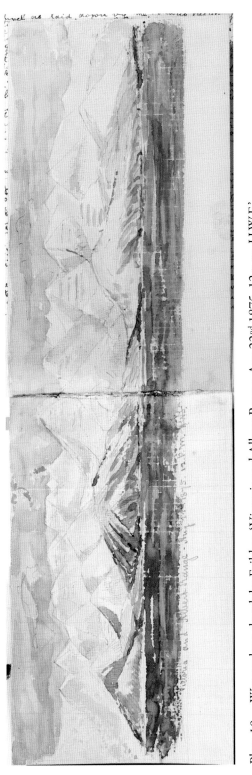

Plate 10.   Watercolour sketch by Feilden. 'Victoria and Albert Range. Aug 22nd 1875. 12 p.m. H.W.F.'

Plate 11. Annotated watercolour sketch by Feilden. 'View from Point Sheridan Flag Staff Oct. 25. 1875. The sketch is taken from nature, but the colour is put on by candle light, so that I have no idea of the shades. The sky was a dark smoke grey. The sun's reflexion clear bright amber. The Greenland mountains faint violet – obscured by band of soft white mist, showing open water & condensation – The pack had large expanses of white, relieved by shades of dark & light steel blue. The big shore hummocks, are enlivened by glimpses of cerulean blue,

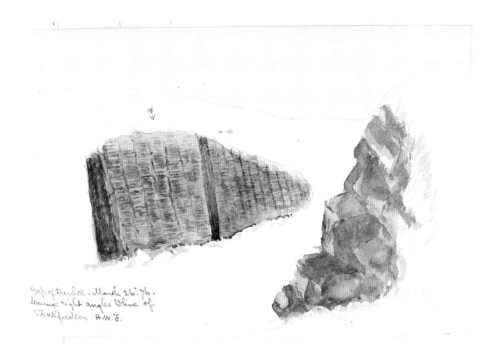

Plate 12.   Watercolour sketch by Feilden. 'Gap of Dunloe. March 26th. 76. Cleavage right angles to line of stratification H.W.F.'

Plate 13.   Annotated watercolour sketch. 'Alert Winter *Quarte*rs 82°28′. March 27th 76. Contorted strata in Big Ravine beds of argillaceous sandstone and clay slates. The cleavage of the beds on either slope being coincident with strike, cleavage must have taken place after pressure. Pressure N.W. by W. to S.E. by E.' There is additional data written on this sketch. Note the figure of the geologist working at the foot of the rocks. Feilden inserts himself into several of his sketches.

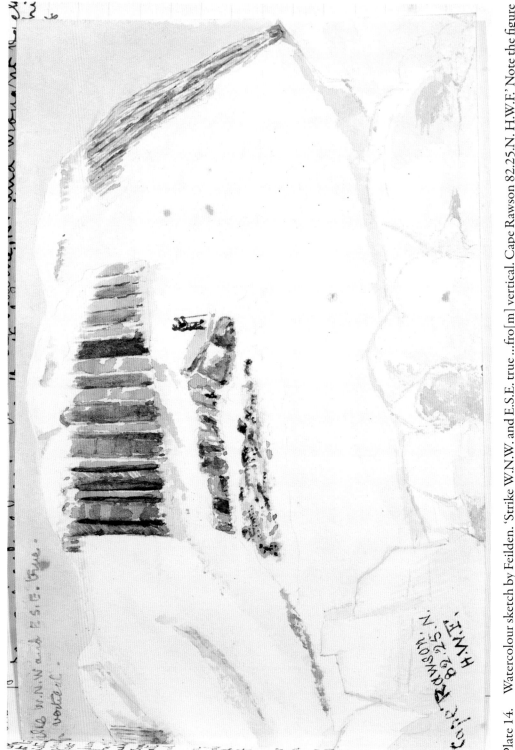

Plate 14. Watercolour sketch by Feilden. 'Strike W.N.W. and E.S.E. true ...fro[m] vertical. Cape Rawson 82.25.N. H.W.F.' Note the figure with a staff.

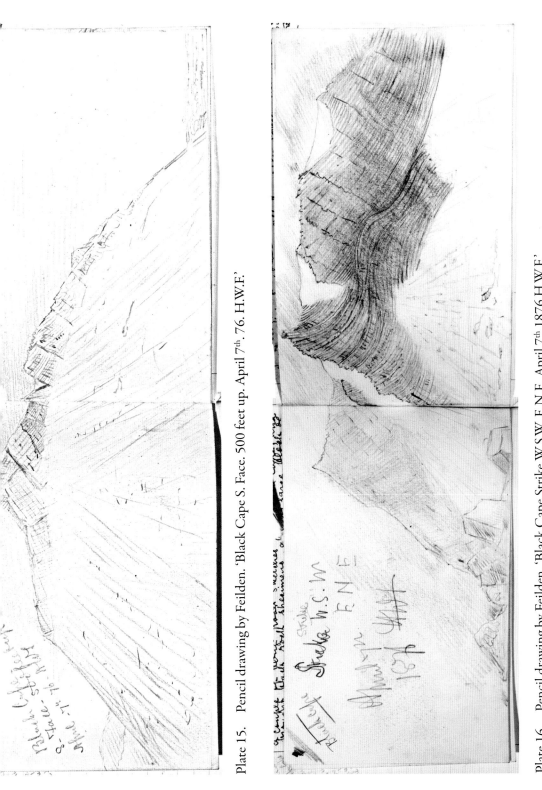

Plate 15.   Pencil drawing by Feilden. 'Black Cape S. Face. 500 feet up. April 7th. 76. H.W.F.'

Plate 16.   Pencil drawing by Feilden. 'Black Cape Strike W.S.W. E.N.E. April 7th 1876 H.W.F.'

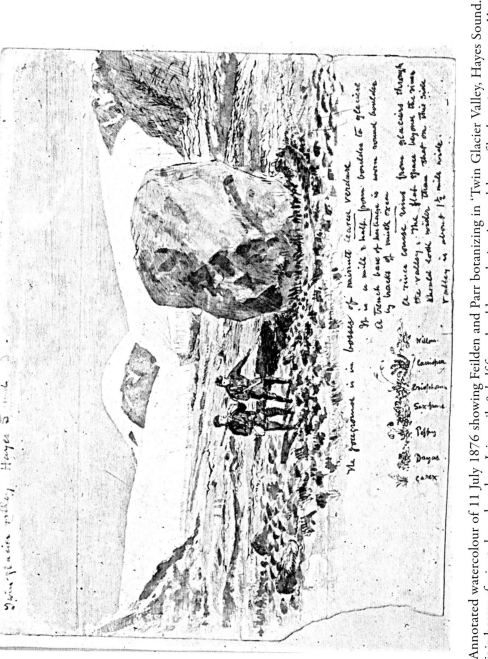

Plate 17.   Annotated watercolour of 11 July 1876 showing Feilden and Parr botanizing in 'Twin Glacier Valley, Hayes Sound. The foreground is in bosses of minute leaved verdure. It is a mile & half from boulder to glacier. A trench base of herbage is worn around boulder by tracks of musk oxen. A river course runs from glaciers through the valley. The flat space beyond the river should look wider than that on this side. Valley is about 1½ mile wide.' The flowers and shrubs sketched are *Carex* (sedge), *Dryas*, poppy, saxifrage, *Eriophorum* (cotton

Made the S.W. of Disco in the morning <under sail>, then steam was got up and we coasted to Godhavn, passing the steep mural cliffs of Ovifak. The basalt beds appear very horizontal, and the formation greatly resembles the Fäeroe Islands, then Laxe-bught, (the salmon bay,) opened, there the high lands descend on either side towards western termination of the bay, and from that point I understand a route leads across country to Disco fiord. Hundreds of ice-bergs dotted Disco Bay, the discharge of Jacobshavn glacier. by 10 o'c. we were moored alongside the *Valorous* in Lively harbour. The *Discovery* came in shortly after us. Lunched on the *Valorous* with Herbert Carpenter,[1] then went dredging with him and M[r] Gwyn Jeffreys, the proceeds of this operation belong to those gentlemen, I will merely say that there is no paucity of animal life in Lively harbour. Afterwards on shore, shot a ♀ *Plec. lapponica*,[2] breast bare, the ♂ bird flew close round. Saw several pairs of *Plec. nivalis*[3] and shot a ♂ for comparison of soft parts with the plates Dresser so kindly gave us.[4] The Greenlanders bring many *Som. mollissima*, and *Som. spectabilis*,[5] to the ship for sale, also a *Salmonoid*.[6] An officer of the Valorous showed me a *Ster. parasiticus*,[7] shot by him on land yesterday it was of the uniform dark type. I will not fill up my journal with the description of a place so well known as Godhavn, besides we shall get photographs of the place. The settlement is built on a low rounded gneiss island which forms the E shelter of the bay – the same rock crops up on the other sides of the harbour, standing out boldly on the W. face, and from that point forming the coast line to the W. of Fortune Bay. The line of junction between the gneiss and the overlying basalt is covered with a talus, which however plainly marks it. Called on Herr Inspector Karup [*sic*] Smith,[8] and gave him the parcel sent by Whymper.[9] I asked him to assist me with his advice about going to Ovifak and this he did most readily. At low tide the channel between Disco Island and the island on which Lievely is built, is passable on foot. On the rocks bared by the tide *Littorina*[10] are very abundant, and by dipping sprigs of algæ, which grows luxuriantly on the rocks, into a tumbler of fresh water I obtained a *Rissoa*[11] and some other small shells.
[*Here Feilden inserted two sketches side by side on facing pages, intended to form a single panorama; see Plate 7.*]

Wednesday 7 July 1875 <u>Disco</u>
Raining in the morning, after lunch landed on the mainland, and walked along the shore to the banks of a stream called the Red river which emptys [*sic*] itself to the N.E. of the

---

[1] Philip Herbert Carpenter FRS (1852–91), assistant naturalist on HMS *Valorous*, crinoid specialist.

[2] *Plectrophanes lapponica*, Lapland bunting.

[3] *Plectrophanes nivalis*, snow bunting.

[4] Henry Eeles Dresser (1838–1915), author of *The History of the Birds of Europe*, superbly illustrated by J. G. Keulemans and J. Wolf.

[5] *Somateria mollissima*, eider; *Som. spectabilis*, king eider.

[6] A member of the Salmonidae, a family of fishes including trout and salmon.

[7] *Stercorarius parasiticus*, parasitic jaeger, also known as Arctic skua.

[8] Sophus Theodor Krarup-Smith (1834–82) was the Royal Inspector of North Greenland (1867–82). See obituary, Steenstrup, 'Krarup Smith'1882.

[9] Edward Whymper (1840–1911), English mountaineer and author.

[10] *Littorina*: a genus of sea snails in the family Littorinidae, the winkles or periwinkles.

[11] *Rissoa*: a genus of very small sea snails.

settlement. The beach as far as the river is composed of fine sand <bitum*in*ous basalt>.[1] Many dead fishes, *Cottus*[2] were strewn along the shore, the grounding icebergs no doubt having been the cause of their destruction. Many great bergs were grounded all along this coast, and now and again they cracked with loud detonations, large fragments falling off, and sending the sea water up in columns of spray; the newly exposed portion of the berg is at once enveloped in mist, owing to its being so much colder than the air with which it suddenly comes into contact.

I saw several *somateria*, both *mollissima* and *spectabilis*, and a few snow buntings. A dead eider washed up on the beach was well picked by the ravens or gulls. The roots of the <washed up> algæ were full of *Saxicava*.

The Red river swollen by the melting snows came down a muddy torrent and its course seaward was visible for some distance, owing to the different colouring of the waters. The graveyard of the settlement lies a little inland from this beach. The graves are dug in the sand and then a heap of stones piled up. Near the graveyard met Captain Nares and Captain Jones of the *Valorous*, returned with them to the banks of the stream, skirted its right bank as far as we could get inland, and turning sharp to our left, crossed the hill, and came down to the harbour near the bay where the wreck of the *Wildfire* lies.[3] We came across many patches of red snow during the walk.[4] The flowers were rapidly bursting into bloom, the white blossomed *Cassiopeia tetragona*[5] gave quite a healthy look to the fells, the pink *Azalea*, the yellow poppy, the bright pink *Pedicularis*,[6] and the fern, *Woodsia*, were just undoubling their leaves. Down the valley of the Lyngemarken[7] by which we descended to the harbour, runs a stream said to be warm, but when I knelt down and drank, it was cold enough in all conscience. In this valley the willow grows somewhat luxuriantly, several acres of it over the knee, when walking through it. I picked up several specimens of *Zeolite* amongst the talus of the basalt cliffs. Near the spot where the boats came to take us off to the ship, the surface is covered with blocks of granitoid rocks, this has been the site of an ancient graveyard, the graves were simply wells or trenches sunk amongst the boulders, and covered over the top with flatter slabs, through the chinks the bones were visible but in most cases the graves had been broken in and rifled, last night I noticed one with two skulls in it, I left them, thinking that I might annoy the Greenlanders were I to turn resurrectionist, but I asked the govenor[8] about the graveyard, and he said it was quite disused, and he did not think any one knew, when it had been last

---

[1] Milner, *Gallery of Nature*, p. 653: 'Pitchstone, another basalt, containing a portion of bitumen, is of a glassy green, resembling obsidian or volcanic glass'.

[2] *Cottus*: a genus of the sculpin family of fish.

[3] *Wildfire* was an English whaler, which had been crushed in the ice and run on shore some years previously. See A. H. Markham, *Whaling Cruise*.

[4] John Ross brought some red snow back (as snow water) in 1818. See Levere, *Science and the Canadian Arctic*, pp. 66–7. Red snow is caused by *Chlamydomonas nivalis*, a cryophilic species of green algae containing a secondary red pigment. See H. G. Jones et al., eds, *Snow Ecology*, numerous references to red snow; see also Werner, *Roter Schnee*.

[5] A species of *Ericaceae* (heath).

[6] Lousewort or wood betony.

[7] 'The green "Lyngemarken", or heath-field, below is perhaps the most luxurious spot inside the Arctic circle, and is a well-known paradise for botanists. A small stream running through its centre is said to flow for the greater part of the year.' Moss, *Shores of the Polar Sea*, p. 11. Moss was surgeon in HMS *Alert*.

[8] Feilden consistently writes 'govenor' for 'governor'.

used. I went this evening to bring off the *crania*, but in the meantime some person with more "savez" or fewer qualms of conscience had forestalled me.

Thursday 8 July 1875 <u>Disco</u>
After breakfast went up the mountains facing Lively with M[r] Herbert Carpenter, our track can well be traced in the frontispiece to Rinks Greenland.[1] Landing at the head of the small bay where the wreck of the *Wildfire* lies, we followed the course of the small stream that runs down Lyngemarken, keeping the gneiss cliffs on our left, when we reached the overlying traps[2] and basalts, we turned sharp to our left, and ascended to where a mountain torrent cuts out a vast *cirque* through the soft traps. This spot is shown in Rink's picture, by a dark shade just over the brig. By aneroid[3] I made the highest point of the *cirque* 1000 ft., but from a lower point at about 900 feet which juts out into the *cirque* one obtains an excellent view of this remarkable result of snow and water action combined. The steep mountain side has been scooped out into an amphitheatre with perpendicular walls of at least 400 feet high. The bottom at the time of our visit was filled with snow, under which the cascade disappeared.

Passing above the *cirque* and keeping to the left bank of the stream, and gradually working up the ridge of the valley, we ascended without much difficulty to the summit of the centre peak, shown in Rinks picture; our aneroid gave here a height of 2400 feet. The view looking over Lievely was very fine. Whale fish and the Hunde Islands lay below us, though at least 14 miles off, and the opposite shores of Greenland were distinctly visible, the line of the great Jacobshavn glacier shone out under the brilliant sunshine, whilst a long stream of icebergs floated down Disco Bay to the southward. A little beyond this spot we crossed the snowline and made our way into it, losing sight of the sea, we plunged into the snow, which was very soft, and we sunk over our knees, plodding along we carried on for over two hours, the aneroid at this point marked 2800 feet, the snow sloped away gradually to the interior. Retracing our steps, we took nearly two hours to get out of the snow, then we walked rapidly down the hill, and finding some Eskimo children drawing water from Lyngemarken stream, they put us onboard our ships. The only birds we met with were *Plec. lapponica*, & *nivalis*, after reaching the snow line no animal life was observed, only the footprints of a hare. We suffered much from thirst. Moss fired on a Ptarmigan in Lyngemarken.

Friday 9 July 1875 'Ovifak' <u>Disco</u>
Every hour makes a difference in the quantity of snow visible on the slopes of the mountains, patches of considerable extent disappear with wonderful rapidity, and the melting of the snow continues throughout the twenty four hours.

This morning Herr Inspector Smith informed me, that two hours before, a young Greenlander, named Emil Propert, told him, that whilst passing Ovifak in his kayak, Spring of 1874, he saw at the same spot from whence Prof. Nordenskiold took the meteoric iron, two more round stones lying under water, but close inshore, of exactly the

---

[1] Rink, *Grønland*, I, frontispiece. Henrik Rink had been Inspector General (Royal Inspector) for South Greenland 1857–68.

[2] Step-like hills or cliffs.

[3] The aneroid barometer was used for measuring relative heights. See Plympton, *Aneroid Barometer*.

same description as those taken by the Swedish expedition.[1] After consulting Captain Nares, determined to visit Ovifak.

Left the ship at 5.30 p.m. in a whale boat in charge of M[r] Aldrich, with a crew of four men, and two Greenlanders, Emile and his uncle John Propert,[2] the latter the original discoverer of the meteoric iron at Ovifak. Wind moderate but foul, rowed to Fortune Bay, where we arrived at 7.15 p.m., landed in a little cove and made tea. The islets which form Fortune Bay, consist of rounded knobs of gneiss, the result of ice-action the tops of some are distinctly furrowed, the little valleys between the knobs are choked with rounded boulders now moss covered and hoary with lichens. Veins of syenite[3] in some places traverse the gneiss. Several traces of old Eskimo dwellings are to be found in sheltered nooks. A pair of *Glaucus*[4] *Gulls* hovered overhead croaking, their harsh note resembles the words Na-ya-kickee. Hundreds of Dovekies[5] were swimming round the shores, we shot several for supper, and took 11 eggs from chinks in the rocks, many we had to leave as we had nothing to fish them out with. A pair of Lapland Buntings were evidently breeding, but I did not find the nest, though I found a Snow Bunting's nest in a fissure of a perpendicular gneiss rock nine feet from the ground. I got on Simmond's[6] [*sic*] shoulders, and found half fledged young ones. The ♀ hovered close to our heads chirping. Left Fortune Bay at 8.45 p.m. shortly after I shot a young King Eider out of a flock, then a ♀ *Harelda glacialis*[7] out of a flock of five, then fired into a flock of King eiders killed one, and dropped two others, shot a Kittiwake in Laxebught out of a flock.

[Here Feilden inserted a MS sheet where he made a full list of the birds seen. The sheet is thin, and the text has bled through from both sides, making it hard to decipher:]

During my trip to Ovifak (July 9th & 10th. 1875) the following species of birds came under my observation.
Plectrophanes lapponica – one pair Fortune Bay
    „   *nivalis*   – seen wherever we landed
Rissa tridactyla – A flock, Laxe-bught, one shot
Larus Glaucus – [?] in cliffs. S.W. of Laxe-bught this [? spot] is called "Ka-ya-nek" after this bird
Stercorarius parasiticus. A few pairs

[1] Nordenskiöld, 'Account of a Voyage to Greenland', p. 439. 'The place where the iron masses were found was not, however, at Fortune Bay, but one of the shores most difficult of access in the whole coast of Danish Greenland, namely Ovifak, or the Blue Hill, which lies quite open to the South wind, and is inaccessible in even a very moderate sea, between Laxe-bugt and Disko-fjord'. See also Levere, *Science and the Canadian Arctic*, p. 266.

[2] Besides Emile Propert, the other Propert may have been Johannes Propert, nephew of the Danish interpreter Johan Carl Christian Petersen (1813–80), who took part in Kane's and M'Clintock's Franklin search expeditions.

[3] 'A crystalline rock allied to granite, mainly composed of hornblende and feldspar'. *OED*.

[4] Feilden uses Glaucus and Glaucous interchangeably; both spellings were acceptable then, but *Larus glaucus* is now the scientific name. Glaucous gull is the common name.

[5] In Feilden's day, this could refer either to black guillemots or to little auks, although the latter are probably intended here. Today 'Dovekie' refers only to the little auk.

[6] John Simmons, 2nd captain maintop, HMS *Alert*. The captain of the maintop was in charge of the crew handling sails and rigging on the upper portion of the mainmast, the maintop.

[7] Long-tailed duck, formerly oldsquaw.

Procellaria glacialis. Abundant. I did not notice any of the dark ['blaa'] variety called [?] by the Greenlanders [...]

Uria grille. Most abundant [...] laying its pair of eggs in the clefts of the gneiss rocks [...] [Among] the hundreds I saw there observed one going [?] black, entirely devoid of white on the scapulars. Holboll [Holbœl, *Ornithologiscehr Beitrag*, p. 81.] has remarked a similar instance before as occurring in Greenland. [...] The legs of the Dovekie in the breeding season are coloured brilliant carmine.

Alca arra. Abundant.

Alca torda. Not recognized by me. But an example shot on the 10th. on the way to Ovifak, by Captain Jones' party, and brought onboard the *Valorous*, where I saw it.

Harelda glacialis. Several parties of four or more seen, shot one ♀ juv.

Somateria mollisima. Perhaps.

Somateria spectabilis. Most abundant and all the Eiders we shot on this trip belonged to this species. They generally flew in flocks, in a course parallel to the coast. The six or seven examples we procured were adult or immature males; I counted one flock containing more than fifty individuals; the bright coloured males predominated and it might be hazarded that the rest were immature males. The Danish officials assure me that the King-[Eider] does not nest nearer Godhavn than some small islands in Disco fiord on the S.W. side of the islands

The prominent nasal protuberance in the adult males of this species is [a] bright gamboge colour when recently killed, after keeping a short time it turns into orange.

Note.

In addition I fancied I saw a pair of *Larus marinus* but will not be certain until I am satisfied that the immature Glaucus has not enough dark about it to make a mistake possible.

[*end of inserted sheet*]

Stuck to our oars and pulled, only with the stoppage of a quarter of an hour to Ovifak which [*continued next to marginal heading for date*]

10 July 1876]

we reached at 2 a.m. [*See Plate 7.*] The landing at Ovifak is a difficult operation, and quite impossible when the least swell is on, which is the case when any wind is blowing. The Swedish expeditions must have found it a hard task removing the meteorites from such an exposed situation. Aldrich dropped anchor, veered out line, and the men let the boat gently back in, keeping command of her with their oars; and as we neared the beach of a wave, leapt out and was followed by the two Properts. The horizontal basalt cliffs rise frowning over head to a height of at least 1000 feet, they are much serrated at the upper edge by the action of water and weather, and though at a distance they look mural, yet on closer acquaintance you perceive that they are fretted into most fantastic shapes, pillars, needles, land blocks of trap, standing out in relief against the cliffs. A talus with a very sharp angle extends from the beach to the cliffs about 300 feet up, this talus is removed between low and high tide marks, but this space is covered with heavy boulders, some of them large rounded masses of transparent gneiss. I and the two Greenlanders went to the spot from whence the Swedes took the meteorites, in 1872 (under command of Capt. Baron von Ober.)[1] There was no mistaking we were at the right place, for the two basalt ridges mentioned by Nordenskiöld (v. Arc. Man. p. 439.) were there, besides both my guides had accompanied the Swedish Professor to the spot. The two iron-stones said to have been seen by Emile Propert last spring, were not to be found. Emile pointed out the exact spot where he had seen them both under water. The sea was breaking somewhat, but we were clearly able to discern, that nothing like a meteorite was lying amongst the boulders, for several yards distance to seaward. My impression is, that the Properts were correct in the statement made, they jumped on shore with such alacrity, and ran to the spot with such rapidity, and showed such an amount of sincerity, in their regret at the absence of iron-stones, that, if they are rogues, they took me in. During this time Aldrich had taken the boat to a smoother spot a little eastward, had hauled up the boat, and pitched tent. The men went to sleep but A. and I sat smoking our pipes, old Propert constantly begging A. to start, as he was afraid of the wind freshening. Aldrich gave the men a short rest, then we put the things in the boat, launched her, let go anchor, and had tea; left at 5.15 a.m., and rowed back to Laxe-bught, ten minutes after leaving Ovifak, the wind came up gently from the E., so that again we had to stick to the oars. We reached a small bight on N.W. side of Laxe-bught, pitched tent, and turned in at 8 a.m., slept well, on the soft moss, covered by a single blanket, till 1 o'c. The Greenlanders who were in our tent, and had the same bed clothing suffered much, apparently, from cold. As I was putting on my shoes outside of the tent a ♀snow bunting, lit on the guy-rope within arms length. Whilst breakfast was preparing, I sauntered round the shores of the bay. Between the cliffs and the bay, stretches on this side, a considerable extent of flat land, about half a mile in width, and extending inland to the head of the bay, the present sea ~~level~~ <shore> is some feet below the level of this carse land,[2] so that here we have evident signs of upheaval. A considerable stream formed by the molten snow runs down into Laxe bught near its W. extremity. Rounded gneiss boulders are abundant in the river bed, and its sand and gravel is mainly composed of this rock. As boulders of gneiss are scattered over the flatland, and perhaps <may> have been transported <there>, when this land was below the sea, I walked up to near the spot where the river debouches from the hills, and convinced myself that any way, a good deal of the gneiss came from the interior. Therefore this stream must either cut down to the fundamental granite, during its course, or else the snow covered uplands of Disco, are strewn with <the> transported blocks, that during the melting of the snow melt down into the stream. Left at 5 p.m., in a fog – reached Fortune Bay at 7. got a fair slant of wind and reached the ship at 10 p.m. Heard, that Capt. Jones, and Lt. Wood[3] of the *Valorous*, Mr Gwyn Jeffreys, and Mr Herbert Carpenter, had visited Ovifak today, in the steam pinnace. Mr Carpenter was the only one of this party who landed. I brought away some specimens of the basalt ridges at Ovifak.

Sunday 11 July 1875 Godhavn <u>Disco</u>
Felt rather tired today and slept late. After lunch went onboard the *Discovery* and found that Hart and a party, had yesterday crossed the Red River to the N. of the settlement,

---

[1] See Nordenskiöld, 'Account of a Voyage to Greenland', p. 440n.
[2] Low alluvial land.
[3] Lieutenant Charles R. Wood

which stream they had to swim. They took a Halkett's boat[1] with them which they launched on a small lake, some way on the other side of the river. This piece of water is called Blaese Dalen, in Rink's map.[2] Here they shot six *Harelda glacialis* three ♂ and three ♀ evidently breeding. They also killed six Red-necked Phalaropes and found one of their nests with four eggs in it, shot as well a *Ster. parasiticus* and a Lapland Bunting, finding the nest of the latter with four young ones in it. Hart had also in his cabin an egg, found yesterday by Lieutenant Fulford,[3] in a cleft of the rock on Kjødø island at the mouth of the harbour. The bird was put off its nest, and two eggs found, one was eaten on the lower deck, and the other came into Hart's possession, it was supposed to be the egg of the King Eider, I think it is undoubtedly the egg of *Mergus serrator*.[4] Lieut. Wood of the *Valorous* showed me the skin of *Colymbus septentrionalis*,[5] which he got from a native on shore. Dined onboard the *Valorous* with Captain Jones, who asked me to look at a Puffin? killed by his party yesterday, it was a specimen of *Alca torda*.[6]

Captain Jones had many plants of holly fern[7] in his cabin which he had procured at Englishman's Bay, a day or two ago.

Monday 12 July 1875 Godhavn <u>Disco</u>
I feel a little disappointed at not finding meteorites or any specimen of meteoric iron, at Ovifak, but I do not begrudge the trip there. I forgot to mention that before joining Aldrich (at Ovifak) where the boat was pulled up, I ascended the talus to its junction with the strata above, in order to see whether the basalt ridges visible at the shore line appear again, at the higher altitude; they do not.

I am not able to follow out in their integrity the chemical analyses of Nordenskiöld, Nordstrom and others, of these Ovifak stones. Therefore I am unable to argue from the chemists point of vantage as to the probable meteoric or telluric origin of these iron masses.[8] But to my mind, they appear to be of telluric origin, and probably are embedded in the basalt dykes, below the water, and have been pushed up on the shore by the force of the sea. If Propert[9] really saw two more of them at the same spot last year, they must have been driven up there from below low tide mark since 1871.

---

[1] Sutcliffe, *The RIB*, p. 21: 'In 1843 a young lieutenant in the Royal Navy, Peter Halkett, constructed a boat-cloak or cloak-boat, so-called because it could be worn as a cloak until needed as a boat. Quickly inflated by bellows, its total weight including bellows and paddles was about 5 kg.' For further information, see Vine, *Pleasure Boating*, chap. 1.

[2] It is called Blæsedalen today. Rink, *Kaart over Disko-Fjorden*.

[3] Reginald Baldwin Fulford (1851–86), later Sir Reginald, lieutenant on *Discovery*. MS: SPRI collection GB 15, Fulford re the BAE 1875–6.

[4] Red-breasted merganser.

[5] Red-throated loon, red-throated diver.

[6] Razorbill

[7] *Cyrtomium* spp. (i.e. undetermined species).

[8] Flight, 'Meteoric Irons' in T. R. Jones, *Manual*, pp. 447–67 reports these analyses, as does Nordenskiöld, 'Account of Voyage to Greenland', in ibid., with Nordström's analyses reported on pp. 444–5. Rink, *Danish Greenland*, pp. 81–2, discusses the iron at Ovifak, and, referring to chemical analyses, argues that it is of native origin, not meteoric. After Nordenskiöld's observations in 1870, 'the Swedish government [in 1871] sent the gunboat, *Ingegerd*, Captain F. W. von Otter, and the brig *Gladau*, under the command of Lieutenant G. von Krusenstjerna, to bring these remarkable meteorites to Europe' (Leslie, *Arctic Voyages*, p. 179).

[9] Probably Johannes Propert, see p. 68, n. 2 above

When onshore this afternoon with Captain Nares, Inspector Krarup Smith showed us samples of the different nets used by the Eskimo. The Beluga or White whale net, is made of heavy sounding cord,[1] meshes 12 inches square with an average depth of 14 feet. The Beluga net is placed by the Greenlanders off points, and headlands, for this animal during migration hugs the shore very closely, especially when rounding points. Very likely this is to avoid the attacks of their enemy the *Orca gladiator*.[2]

The seal-nets are made of stout cord with 6 inch mesh, and 7½ feet depth. Captain Nares purchased both these description of nets.

The wooden houses of Danish officials are exactly like those of their countrymen in the Fäeroe Islands, with the exception of the turfed roofs which are so conspicuous in Thorshavn, or rather so indistinguishable from their similarity to the meadows in the back ground. The same love of flowers is to be noticed, but I have not remarked in Godhavn the pretty custom of training an ivy plant over the walls of a sitting room, as is common in Fäeroe.

I judge that the basalt beds of Greenland are probably contemporaneous with the Fäeroe Islands. An examination of the fossils and comparison of both, would settle the matter, but I only know one spot in Suderöe where any fossil remains (of vegetable matter) are to be found, and that is in a cliff to the E of Trangirvaag Fiord in Suderöe.

Tuesday 13 July 1875 Godhavn <u>Disco</u>

Writing letters home till midday. In the afternoon landed at Wildfire Bay, and walked over the gneiss rocks to Englishman's Bay, in company with Mr Clements Markham. We had a fine scramble down down[3] the steep cliff to the bay. Mr Markham had to go back to the ship for an appointment, but I remained behind collecting plants. This is the best spot for the botanist in the vicinity of Godhavn. The torrent that runs down into the bay makes a good section at the point of junction between the gneiss and the superincumbent basalt beds, at the point of contact, the gneiss does not appear to be altered which would be the case had the basalts been deposited as molten lava.

Returning to the ship, I saw several fragments of large spherical shell, lying on the hill side, probably segments of an 8 or 10 inch shell. As I am not aware of either the Danes or ourselves using smooth-bores[4] in ships, I fancy the iron must have been fired by the guns of the U.S.S. *Congress*, which escorted the *Polaris* to Disco.[5]

I made a drawing of the section alluded to above.

Wednesday 14 July 1875 <u>Disco</u>

In the afternoon I took Pullen[6] to Englishman's Bay,[7] it was most lovely weather, mosquitoes the only drawback, they were most virulent in their attacks. We got some

---

[1] i.e. cord suitable for sounding depths.

[2] A synonym for *Orcinus orca*, the orca or killer whale.

[3] 'down down' is what Feilden wrote.

[4] i.e. as opposed to rifled. See Hughes, 1969.

[5] Charles Francis Hall's third expedition (1871), the *Polaris* expedition, on which Hall died in questionable circumstances. There have been several accounts of the expedition, including Davis, *North Polar Expedition*; and Loomis, *Weird and Tragic Shores*.

[6] Rev. Henry William Pullen (1836–1903), see above, p. 19, n. 3.

[7] Just beyond Godhavn.

capital plants and were much struck with the beauty of a bed of *mertensia maritima*[1] in full bloom, its exquisite delicate blue blossom, dazzling the eye. *Angelica*, there grows abundantly, and two or perhaps three species of orchids. This spot is not visited so often as Lyng-marken by visitors to Disco. *Vitrina angelica, v. pellucida*,[2] was not uncommonly found adhering to the roots of ferns. A large berg in Englishman's Bay turning right over was a very fine spectacle.

Above the landing place at Watson's Bay, S.W. of Lynge-marken there is a small hollow about 100 feet above the sea, filled with sand, which has all the appearance of a sea deposit, though I found no traces of shells in it, but my examination was cursory, not having any digging implement with me. Taking this in conjunction with the evidence of coast elevation at Laxe-bught, I have no doubt that the Island of Disco, participated with the rest of Greenland, in the series of elevations which are so distinctly marked. Though it is stated <that> now a contrary depression is going on from a latitude N. of Upernivik to Cape Farewell.[3]

Thursday 15 July 1875 Disco
[*Margin*: "Godhavn"]
Wind S.W.–W.–S.E. 1. Bar. 29.93 Thermo*meter* 55°. of sea +49°.

5 p.m. Weighed and proceeded out of harbour, *Discovery* in tow. *Valorous* weighed in company. 7 p.m. Fog cleared, many icebergs in sight. Left Disco this afternoon under a salute from our kind Danish friends. The *Valorous* answered with 21 guns. Took the *Discovery* in tow. Inspector Smith took passage with us to *Ritenbenk*.[4] Our dogs 24 in number came on board at 2 p.m., 17 ♂ and 7 ♀. The Greenland mosquitoes are very troublesome, large striped gray fellows, they alight on one without any humming or note of warning, today I am sore with their bites. Steaming along the Disco coasts, we passed a fine glacier near Sinifik. The miocene[5] sandstones, yellowish-red coloured begin to show about this point, thickening towards the N.E.

The name of Ritenbenk is derived from the transposition of the letters in Count BERKE<N>TIN's[6] name. He was minister for Greenland about 1755, the time of the formation of the settlement. At midnight we passed close to a superb berg. It had a lofty arch piercing its very centre, through which the salmon tinted clouds were visible. The berg at least 200 feet high, was streaked with sapphirine [*sic*] blue, and close to the waters edge vivid green. Hundreds of *Procellaria* were perched on it, and many Arctic terns, and as we passed close alongside they flew into the air with loud cries, one solitary *Long tailed Skua*, remained on the ice. As the *Valorous* following us showed through the crystal arch, the effect was superb.

[1] Oysterleaf or sea bluebell, a plant in the borage family.
[2] Land shells belonging to the genus *Lymnophysa*. See Mörch, 'On the Land and Fresh-Water Mollusca', pp. 27, 28.
[3] See T. R. Jones, ed., *Manual*, 1875, pp. 482–97.
[4] Ritenbenk: a settlement on Appat Island.
[5] The geological period corresponding to the middle division of the Tertiary strata, divided by Charles Lyell (Lyell, *Principles of Geology*, I, pp. 136 ff., III, pp. 54–5) into four epochs distinguished by the percentage of fossil molluscs corresponding to those alive today. In Lyell, *Principles of Geology*, III, p. 370, there is an account of his use of the term.
[6] Christian August Berckentin (1694–1758) in 1755 was chairman of the General Trade Company, a Danish-Norwegian trading company which effectively governed Greenland 1749–74.

Friday 16 July 1875 <u>Ritenbenk</u>
Calm. Bar. 29.876 – 29.83. Temp. 50. 54.
1.50 a.m., stopped on account of fog. 2.30. Proceeded. 11 o'c. Let go port anchor near Ritenbenk in 17 fathoms.

Alert, *Discovery*, and *Valorous*, anchored in a fiord near the settlement of Ritenbenk at 11 a.m. Landed and called upon M[rs] Smith, at the stores got two white fox skins for which I gave £1.2.0. Two *Greenland Falcons*,[1] and various specimens of Eskimo skin work. In the afternoon walked with M[r] Clements Markham to the top of a hill on Arve Prince Island. These hills are ice worn and glaciated to an enormous extent, and dotted over with erratic boulders, some of them large basalts. Shot a young Wheatear, well able to fly, out of a family of 4; saw two other families of this species flying about; also shot a Lapland Bunting (juv.) able to fly, saw many Snow Buntings. We came across the scattered feathers of *Lagopus rupestris*,[2] no doubt shortly before fallen a prey to some hawk, and a little after we fell in with a brood of four young Ptarmigans just hatched. (Sent two of them to Newton[3] by Herbert Carpenter.) Returning to the shore we passed near an old deserted Eskimo burial ground, the tombs amounting to a dozen or so in number had originally been built up of blocks of gneiss, covered with slabs of the same material, all had fallen in and were very dilapidated; these tombs had originally been raised over the body, there being no trace of a grave, indeed the rocky nature of this locality would render it impossible for the Eskimos to have hewn ~~them~~ <one>. The few fragments of bones left, lay on the surface. I found a tolerably perfect cranium, which I secured. Probably these graves had been previously ransacked for now there is no trace of implements of any kind, in or about them. Two boats left the ship this morning to go Loom shooting at Swart vogel berg – the party returned at 10 p.m., bringing many *Alca arra* and *Alca torda*. A young Cormorant with extraordinary malformation of the wing was captured on its nest. One Glaucus Gull, two Kittiwakes, two King Eiders, and one Common Eider were also brought in. Many eggs of *Alca torda* were brought, but none of *Alca arra*, so that I surmise these two species at this place occupy different spots for incubating, or else <eggs of> both species would have been gathered indiscriminately; in addition there were four eggs of *Larus leucopterus*[4] many Kittiwakes and Cormorants in the bag.

M[r] Clements Markham left us this night at 12 p.m. to embark onboard the *Valorous* for passage to England.[5]

The crops of two of the young Ptarmigans, which I skinned this evening, were filled with the blossoms of *Vaccinium uliginosum*,[6] and the unfolded buds of *Cassiopiea tetragona*.[7] These young birds emitted from their flesh and down the same fragrant odour as our British Red grouse.

---

[1] Gyrfalcons, the largest species of falcon.

[2] Rock ptarmigan.

[3] Alfred Newton (1829–1907) was an English zoologist, Professor of Comparative Anatomy at Cambridge. *ODNB*. Newton was Feilden's friend.

[4] Iceland gull.

[5] The projecting paddles of HMS *Valorous* made the sloop unsuitable for forcing a way through Arctic ice, and determined the point at which she left the other ships. See Nares, *Narrative*, 1878, I, p. 25.

[6] Bog bilberry or western blueberry.

[7] Arctic bell-heather or white Arctic mountain heather.

Saturday 17 July 1875 <u>Waigat</u>[1]
Wind S.W. S.C. 2.3.4.0. Bar 29.880–30.066. Temp. 54. of sea 44½. Lat D.R. 69°51′. Long. 51·57 W.

Noon, ice extending right across the Waigat. *Discovery* in tow. 1 p.m. ice across channel from shore to shore. Observed an oomiak[2] come out of land off Sakkiak – 2 o'c. entered pack. 5.30 observed H.M.S. *Valorous*. 11 o'c. made fast to a berg. 12. Took *Discovery* in tow.

Working our way down the Waigat through streams of bergs, and floe ice, which were pouring out from the fiord of Itifdliarsuk, the bergs originating in the great glacier of Torsukatek. Many *Fulmars* flying around.

The *Valorous* left Ritenbenk before us and proceeded down the Waigat, with the intention of coaling at a station on the Disco side of the channel also called Ritenbenk; we had hoped to communicate once again with her, but at the time we sighted her the weather was so unpropitious, that all thoughts of so doing had to be given up.

The scenery of the Waigat is very fine, on our starboard side the Noursoak peninsula, rose in lofty terraced escarpments, topped with ragged, jutting peaks of basalt, peering through wreaths of clouds, in some places where the tops were flat, the lip of a glacier is to be seen curling over the edge. These cliffs are bright coloured, towards the base and half way up the sandstones are of a warm yellow colour, then come strata of deep ferrugineous red, and basalt. These strata appear very horizontal. The Disco side of the strait appears to be of similar formation, but by no means so striking as Noursoak, which having the advantage of a southern aspect, is brighter tinted.

[*Here Feilden tipped in a sketch of Waigat strait; see Figure 7, below.*]

Figure 7.   Rough pencil sketch of the Waigat strait, captioned, 'Waigat July 17th 1875'.

---

[1] The Waigat is a strait separating the island of Disco from the mainland of Greenland.
[2] A larger Inuit boat than a kayak, with skins over the frame.

Sunday 18 July 1875 <u>Hare Island</u>
Wind. S. – S.S.W.–W. 1.4.6.3. Bar. 30.02. 29.70. 29.83. Thermo 48. 56. 52. of sea 41. 42. 41. Lat. 70.42 N. Long. 55.7 W.
Passed Hare Island, in the morning, dull cloudy day. Divine service on the lower deck. One of our Eskimo dogs fell overboard, but a boat was lowered and it was picked up, it had swam sometime before it was noticed, and when brought onboard was greatly distressed, gasping for breath, and inflating the lungs with great difficulty. D[r] Colan and I carried it down to the galley-fire and restored it with heat and friction. I noticed one of the bitches licking it whilst it lay gasping on the deck. Foggy and gloomy all day.

Monday 19 July 1875 <u>Swarten Huk</u>
Wind W. S.S.W. 4.3.5. Bar. 29.83. 29.96. 29.99. Temp. 48. 51. 55 of sea 38. 41.
9.30 p.m. stopped to pick up boat, Govenor of Proven[1] came onboard. 10.50 came to anchor in 13 fathoms.
   In the morning abreast of Swarten Huk (The Black Headland). Fair wind and by 11 o'c. p.m., we were at anchor close to the little settlement of Proven. The navigation into Proven harbour is not easy for ships of our draught, but Captain Nares, went in with the *Discovery* in tow. The young Cormorant brought in on the 16th. from Swart vogel Berg, was dissected by me today, it was a curious instance of arrested development, the head of one humerus was rounded, and there was a complete absence of radius and ulna. This bird was large and well nourished, its stomach held a quantity of fish, also a large accumulation of peebles (weight   ).[2] A specimen of *A. torda* ♀, shot at the same place, and skinned today, had its hatching spot on one side, and not in the centre of the belly as usual. This bird during incubation must have laid on its side. The trap formation similar to that of Disco, extends close to Proven, which settlement is built on gneiss rock.

Tuesday 20 July 1875 <u>Proven</u>
Landed immediatly after breakfast, and called on the Govenor, Herr A. F. Möldrup. The number of inhabitants in the colony is 106 souls. Last years production of oil amounted to 350 tons Danish. The Danish brig not having as yet arrived from Copenhagen, the store is at a very low ebb. The colony is built on a small island of gneiss rock, and another island to the southward which forms the anchorage is of the same formation, but to the southward of this and also to the Eastern interior of Greenland the formation is most unmistakeably[3] trappean, its horizontal bedding and varied coloured stratas of tuff[4] being visible, and with the aid of a glass bands of columnar basalt can be detected. Roughly speaking a line drawn W & E a mile or two to the south of Proven would define the limit of the trap formation. The surface of the island of Proven to its summit is strewed with erratics, chiefly plutonic[5] rocks, and metamorphic,[6] some of these are of great size, and are poised, on apparently, very insecure foundations, many of them giving the idea that they would topple over with ~~very~~ little encouragement. On the very summit of Proven island

---

[1] A. F. Möldrup: see entry for 20 July 1875 below.
[2] Feilden leaves the weight blank.
[3] This is Feilden's spelling of 'unmistakably'.
[4] Rock formed from volcanic ash, as at Pompeii.
[5] Intrusive igneous rock formed from magma.
[6] Rocks produced from other rocks by the influence of heat and pressure.

are scattered several basalt erratics, with the sharp edges of the columns little worn by attrition, the hollows round about are filled with smaller fragments of the same material, many rounded but I did not detect any ice-scratchings, one small sandstone peeble which I picked up <when split> showed indistinct impressions of plant?

The means by which these erratics, (so plentiful on the land, and also the highest points uncovered by snow,) got there, requires a very great deal of consideration before I can give any decided opinion on the matter. If deposited by floating ice, we must assume that the Greenland coast, has been subjected to periods of intense elevation, since Miocene times, or else these <Miocene> basalts could not be found resting as erratics on the ice worn hills of gneiss and granite; but as the present elevation of these latter rocks is quite equal to that of the miocene deposits, we should also require to assume that the ~~elevations~~ <upheavals> have been local and spasmodic, or else the contiguous miocenes, would have been under water at the same time as the boulder covered hills. We may argue, however, that these basalt boulders may have been brought from a greater distance, this seems unnecessary, as we have ~~the~~ a matrix close at hand, and the sharp angles of the basalt boulders points to a small amount of attrition. It will be an interesting fact to discover whether the surface of the Miocene deposits are equally strewn with erratics as the metamorphic rocks of Greenland, or otherwise.

The flora of Proven is not as rich as that of Disco, but I noticed *Betula nana*[1] growing in considerable abundance. A solitary Raven came close to me when on shore. Snow Buntings abundant, a nest with well fledged young ones was found. Several broods of Wheatears were going about the rocks, their familiar "chuck chuck" resounding on all sides. A solitary Glaucus gull makes up my days list of birds observed.
[*Coloured sketch of Proven, Greenland, inserted here; see Plate 8.*]

Wednesday 21 July 1875 <u>Proven</u>
Wind N.N:E. C.1. Bar. 30.144–30.628. Temp +51 +48 – of sea +39½ +39¾.
5 p.m., weighed under steam took *Discovery* in tow and proceeded for Upernevik [*sic*].[2]

A small net let down to the bottom in 13½ fathoms brought up several small *Astartes*,[3] one star-fish, two crustaceans, and some mud for the microscope. By dipping over cans we captured hundreds of *Clio borealis*,[4] and *Limacina arctica*,[5] when the two species were placed in the same glass vessel, the Clio eagerly devoured the Limacina. The binding up of the Eskimo women's hair in a topknot wrinkles the scalp and seems to induce baldness in patches.

Went to the summit of the island that forms the south side of Proven harbour, the basalt boulders noticed by me yesterday are equally abundant there. On the top of the hill I picked up nodules of iron ore, or rather nodules composed of decomposed or altered gneiss largely impregnated with ferruginous matter. (v. Darwin Voy. Round. World p. 12–13.[6]). Yesterday I noticed on Proven a strange configuration in the gneiss, a

---

[1] A species of dwarf birch found on the tundra.

[2] Upernavik.

[3] Bivalve molluscs. See Jeffreys, 'Remarks on the Species of *Astarte*', pp. 233–4.

[4] *Clio* is a genus of small floating sea snails; *Clio borealis* 'swarms in the Arctic seas, and constitutes the principal food of the whale'. Roget, *Animal and Vegetable Physiology*, I, p. 258. See also p. 81 below.

[5] A predatory swimming sea snail, a sea butterfly. See Beneden, 'Mémoire sur la Limacina Arctica'.

[6] Darwin, *Journal of Researches*, 2nd edn, pp. 12–13.

perpendicular exposed surface was full of globular cavities arising in size from an apple to a round hole large enough to hold a man, if these ever contained any foreign substance, it must have been of a softer consistency than the matrix as the perforations into these holes do not by any means equal the largest diameter of the cavity, now however, not a vestige of any foreign substance is included. These cavities have all the appearance of having been formed when the rock was in a heated condition. The position of the settlement of Proven was fixed today at 72°22′N and Long 55.45′. W. Left at 5 p.m. By 12 o'clock p.m., we were abreast of Kasarsoak or Sanderson's Hope. The scenery between Proven and this point is superb the magnificent gneiss cliffs go sheer into the water, rising at least a 1000 or 1200 feet above the sea-level, whilst the rich colouring of rock and sunshine, backed by the snow, was almost inconceivably beautiful, to a person who has not visited these regions, in equally fine weather.

Thursday 22 July 1875 Sanderson's Hope and Upernivik.
Wind N.E. N.N.E. N. 1. 3. 2. Bar. 30.616. 30.55. 30.54. Temp. 46½. 49. 51. of sea. 37. 36. 35.
1.15 a.m. Stopped off Sanderson's Hope. 5.50 anchored off Upernivik in 9 fathoms 7 o'c. weighed, took *Discovery* in tow.

A little after 1.a.m the vessel stopped off <one of> the *Loomeries* (breeding place of Alca arra) of Sanderson's Hope. Boats were put out, and we hurried off to lay in a supply of fresh provisions, 122 guillemots rewarded our united exertions, had the sea been smoother we should have got many more, amongst the dead birds there was not a single Alca torda, nor did I recognise one of that species amongst the thousands of A. arra that flew close past me. There was a considerable swell on, but Captain Markham managed to land me on a ledge at the base of the cliff, minus boots and coats, I crawled up the face of the cliff a short way, and took three eggs, one of them from under the old bird.

The shelves on which the birds lay their eggs, are deep with excrement, and smell strongly. I brought away the eggs and some of the guano (the latter for diatoms) in my handkerchief, which I held between my teeth when regaining the boat. When we fired at the poor birds huddled together on the ledges, dozens of eggs were knocked into the sea, as the owners took wing, all these eggs contained young, nearly ready for hatching, and they all burst as they reached the water. Several pairs of Glaucus Gulls that were breeding high up in the cliff remained on their nests, and seemed to take no heed of the racket going on below. Nothing could excuse the wanton shooting and wounding of these beautiful birds, but the fact that they are excellent eating. Dropped anchor near Upernivik at 6.a.m. Landed and walked to the top of the island, rock formation hypogene,[1] patches on the extreme summit, show ice scratchings and peebles of basalt similarly marked were not uncommon. The surface of the island to its highest point is strewed with erratics. I noted a pair of *Char. hiaticula*,[2] and several snow-buntings.

The flora is more scanty than further south, but I observed *Ranunculus pygmæus*[3] growing abundantly in swampy spots near the settlement, and the diminutive *Betula nana*

---

[1] Lyell, *Principles of Geology*, III, p. 374: 'We propose the term "hypogene"... a word implying the theory that granite and gneiss are both *nether-formed* rocks, or rocks which have not assumed their present form and structure at the surface.'

[2] *Charadrius hiaticula*, ringed plover.

[3] Pygmy buttercup.

reaches the top of the island. At the settlement I found large numbers of the eggs of A. arra that had been collected by the natives at Sanderson's Hope, about ten days before. I bought a good few as specimens.

The natives stretch the seal skins in front of the igloo and fasten them down in a circular shape, by means of a great number of bone pegs, then the women set to work with their scrapers which are iron, of Danish manufacture. Sent our last letters on shore for the Danish brig, and left Upernivik at 7.p.m. These bone pegs are similar to those I have found common in the kitchen-middens of Benbecula,[1] where doubtless they served the same purpose.

Friday 23 July 1875 <u>Kangitok</u>
"Calm. S.S.W. N.N.E. 0. 1. Bar. 30.53. 30.56. 30.45. ~~Temp 45 + 48~~[2] Of sea 35–56. 1 a.m. Lying to by Kangitok Island, thick fog. 6 o'c. Two kyaks [*sic*] came off from shore. 7 o'c. took the ground. 8.59 sent hands on shore to wash clothes. 11.25 ship afloat, proceeded. 1 p.m, stopped and discharged Eskimo pilots. 8 p.m. Cape Shackleton bearing S 70 E. 11.30 lost sight of Cape Shackleton. S. Log[3]"

The island on which we landed is composed of red gneiss, thrown up at nearly a vertical angle: veins of quartz studded with large garnets, traverse the gneiss in a N & S direction true, brought away numerous specimens. The island was also covered with Eider-ducks nests, but they had evidently been gathered a few hours before, I came across any number of empty nests, but was not fortunate enough to find one with eggs and birds on them. Others of our party did, and killed both King & Common Eiders from the nest, but did not mark the eggs, so that they were useless for identification. Govenor [Fencker?][4] at Disco told me that the natives do not discriminate between the two species of Somateria, but call them by the same name. He considers well authenticated eggs of the King-Eider difficult to procure from this reason.

Saturday 24 July 1875 <u>Taking the Middle Pack.</u>
"At 12.45 a.m. steering north by compass, calm, Bar. 30.51. Temp of air +43°. observed ice ahead water fell to +33°. On entering the ice at 2 a.m., it proved to be a stream of open floe, varying in thickness from 8 to 24 inches, hummocky in some places, but to no great extent. This stream extended to about 3 miles to the southward and to the northward was joined to the main pack, between 3 and 4 passed through a stream of similar ice, but about 5 miles broad instead of two, this also extended about 3 or 4 miles south of us.

6.45 fired at a Walrus on the ice which escaped. From 8 to 10 the ice we passed through was in smooth thin pieces, offering no difficulty to our passage 10 to 11 ice became thicker rather hummocky from 1 to 2 feet thick, and more closely packed with some large floes.

---

[1] An island in the Outer Hebrides, west of Scotland in the Atlantic Ocean.

[2] These are air temperatures copied from the ship's log. Feilden sometimes copies such entries from the wrong column, hence the deletions. See Nares, MS Log book, HMS *Alert*, 1875–76. Feilden sometimes took his own observations of temperature, e.g. in his cabin. It is, however, striking that in the printed results of the expedition, the first part (Physical Observations) appear under Nares's and Feilden's names, although specific sets of observations therein, including magnetic readings and the temperature of sea water near *Discovery*'s winter quarters, are attributed to others.

[3] 'S. Log' is 'Ship's Log'.

[4] Edgar Christian Fencker (1844–1904) was Inspector for South Greenland 1892–9, well after the Nares expedition. However, Young, *Pandora*, p.104, states that Fencker was Governor in 1876.

11 to 12 ice heavier 1 to 3 feet thick & more closely packed with some heavy hummocky masses which had to be avoided, in one or two places where we tried, we could not force our way through the ice, but had to go round, only one iceberg in sight all the forenoon. We stopped twice, but on the whole found no difficulty in keeping our course. The ice was generally soft & rotten. At noon Lat. 73.33. Long. 63.19.W. 2 o'c. a Bear was seen, stopped the ship, went in pursuit Bruin escaped. During the first part of the afternoon watch, the thickest ice was not more than 2 feet, the thinnest from 2 to 8 inches, and apparently in a very rotten state, so much so that the water penetrated it, and melted the snow on top. There was generally a lead, but occasionally we had to break thro the thinner ice. There were also hummocky ridges across the ice which had to be avoided. The latter part of the watch the floes were large, and heavier, from 1 to 3 feet thick, but there was a good deal more water between them, and with only one exception when we had to break out and go round, found no difficulty in steering the ship on her course. 4–5, Ice rather more closely packed and about 8 in to 2 feet in thickness with more under the hummocks. We had no difficulty, however, in boring through into a fine lead, which we retained during the remainder of the watch, the ice becoming thinner and more open. 8 to 9 p.m., The ice was hummocky on the average from 1 to 3 feet thick with some large floes, heavy along their edges not very closely packed, with plenty of lanes through which enabled the ship to keep her course. At 9.30 came to an open piece of water about 1 mile square, after which same description of ice until 11 p.m., when it became much more open, no large floes but some heavy hummocky masses. Young ice forming along side. abstract Ships log"

At 6.40 a.m., a Walrus seen on the ice and fired at. 2 p.m. a Bear observed on the floe, landed on ice with others, in pursuit. Mr Bruin went much faster than we could. Animals observed today. Walrus, *Phoca hispida*, a large seal, Bear. Many Procellaria, 2 *Larus eburneus*,[1] – first observed. a Columbus?[2] species uncertain 1 Dovekie, several Little Auks and *Alca arra*. The water was filled with bunches of brown floculent [*sic*] matter, which under the microscope showed several forms of Diatoms. I shall long remember the beauty of this day.

Sunday 25 July 1875 <u>Cape York</u>
"Calm. E.N.E. N.E. Force 0 to 3. Bar. max. 30°.40. min. 30.20″. Temp of atmosphere +45 to +53. Temp of sea in the pack +32° – rising to +35½ when clear of the pack off Cape York. Lat at noon 75°20 N. Long. 66°19 W.

At 2 h. a.m. ice more open. From 12 h. p.m. till 2 o'c. a.m., the ice encountered was hummocky with large floes, but with considerable expanses of water between them which were more or less covered with bay-ice. From 2 h till 4 h. the floes were still more open and not more than one foot thick, passed several detached lumps which were several feet thick. Large quantities of young ice forming to the thickness of half an inch. Between 4 and 8 h, plenty of water between the small detached floes, which averaged about a foot thick. The speed with which we were going is the best criterion of the ease with which we avoided the few thicker pieces. 11 h, only occasional floes, several bergs to be seen 12 h meridian, no pack to be seen to the eastward from the masthead. at 12.15 h. cleared the pack!!

[1] Ivory gull.
[2] Loon or diver.

6 to 8 h steering along land between Cape York & Cape Dudley Digges many large icebergs around us.

8 h till 12 h midnight, steering about two miles from the land and inshore of a line of large icebergs, which were very numerous between C. York and Conical I. particularly near the latter. Only two or three were noticed with flat table tops and these were large ones but low. The Crimson Cliffs did not uphold their ancient renown. Glaciers stream down every ravine, ten large ones were passed between C. York and Conical I. abst*ract*. Ship's log."

A repetition of yesterday, bright sunshine, and glorious colourings on ice and water. Early this morning the lanes and leads of water began opening out wider, betokening our approach to the north water. At 9.30 a.m., sighted the high land about Cape York, and at 11 a.m, we were fairly in the N. water. Myriads of *Mergulus alle*[1] crowd this sea, bands of them diving just in time to avoid the ships stem. They use their wings vigorously under the water, I noticed that the diving flocks kept their individual bearings with as much ease as if they were on the wing, and all ~~came~~ <returned> to the surface within a few seconds of one another. At this season the pouch-like enlargement of the cheeks gives them a comical expression. A few Ivory Gulls sailing overhead several *Ster. longi*, and a few Looms and Dovekies[2] in the water. Went to crows nest at 5 p.m, as we neared Cape York. Melville Bay filled with immense Bergs, these extended along the coast from Cape York to Cape Dudley Digges, I counted from the deck over 200 immense ones in view at the same time; they were all grounded. At 7 p.m Discovery proceeded to Cape York to communicate with natives. Observed stems of *Laminaria*[3] floating. At 12 p.m., when I turned in C. Dudley Digges on our starboard bow Conical Rock ahead, and a line of bergs on our port quarter.

Monday 26 July 1875
"Wind throughout the day N.E to N, with a force of 1 to 2. Bar steady 30^{in}.20 Lat 76°19′N. noon. Long 70°33′W. Temp of atmosphere +40 to +52 of the sea from +34° to +40° at midnight stopped off the Cary Group. There was a thick fog all afternoon which lifted about 8.20 h. p.m. The icebergs extended up this coast, running parallel with it, but not more than seven or eight miles to seaward – abst*ract* ships log."

Sailing was tried during the middle watch, but when I went on deck at 6.30 a.m., we had made more westing than northing. A nasty fog came on, and steam was slackened; sounded in 200 fathoms, bottom mud. When the ship stopt [*sic*] for sounding I pulled in several examples of *Clio* and *Limacina*, when transferred to a glass vessel, the Clio[4] seized the Limacina, with their tentacles and devoured them slowly, under the microscope the powerful teeth of the Clio is plainly seen. At 10 p.m., the fog lifted and we were some six miles distant from the Cary Islands. <For information about Clio. Look up Macdonalds paper on *Clio australis*[5] which I have not got H.W.F.> Authors disagree about the mouth of *Clio borealis* being armed with teeth.

[1] Little auk.
[2] See above, p. 68, n. 5.
[3] A genus of brown algae, kelp.
[4] See above, p. 77, n. 4. Macdonald points out the confusion that has occurred between the species named *Clio australis* and *C. borealis*. Macdonald, 'On the Zoological Characters'.
[5] Ibid.

There is a fine paper by Steenstrup on the physiology of *Clio borealis*, that I have seen some where.[1]

Tuesday 27 July 1875 <u>Cary Islands</u>
"Calm throughout the day. Bar 30 to 29.90. Lat at noon 77°8′ Long 72°41′ Temp ~~+47 to~~ [~~+51~~°] of sea from +35° to +38°. Ships log."

At 12.15 a.m., close to the most eastern of the Cary Group. Stopped steaming, and lay to, in 22 fathoms, several fine Bergs in our neighbourhood. Day bright, warm, and clear. Noticed several large Annelids[2] wriggling near the surface, they looked like centipedes, and progressed with considerable speed. Secured one. Took Dingy[3] and landed with Moss. Formation of this island gneiss, thrown up at nearly a vertical angle dipping in places 80° from E to W. true. On the summit are many rounded drift sandstone peebles, judging from the colour, of the same formation as Northumberland and Hakluyt Islands. Many *som. moll* [Common Eider] were swimming inshore with their broods, killed 4 of them. Glaucus Gulls numerous and on a steep cliff, along some bright green covered ledges they were evidently nesting. Pulled to the spot and landed, off sea boots and coat. At the foot of the cliff the ground was covered with <the> ordure and castings of these birds, and it was a complete Golgotha from the skeletons of Mergulus alle strewn around: ledge after ledge that I ascended was thus covered, and it was dirty work getting up. The old birds numbering some 20 pairs attacked me vigorously, and swooped close to my head, their boldness and cries increased as I neared the summit, where I found about a dozen young ones able to run in a most provoking manner. (For colour of plumage and soft parts of these birds vide Bird book).[4] I noticed many shells of Dovekies eggs they must lay them in exposed situations at times or else the Gulls could not secure them. Little auks I found very shy, hundreds about only killed one. The gneiss rock was hoary with lichens. Flowering plants few, only gathered Potentilla,[5] Cochlearia,[6] Papaver,[7] Draba,[8] Salix[9] and two grasses. Back to the ship at 5 o'c. left at 6.30, having landed a dêpot[10] built cairn, and left letters.[11] At 12 m*idday* we were abreast of Cape Parry, Hakluyt and Northumberland Islands ahead, Inglefield Gulf stretching inland on our starboard beam. Sounded in 100 fathoms rock. These islands have a very striking appearance, at 4 p.m., we were passing between them, the geological formation is a highly coloured, massive, and evenly stratified sandstone, bright red at the base, but higher up the cliff alternating with lighter yellow coloured strata, the strata have a slight dip from N. to S. true. No appearance of intercalated basalts or traps. Many

[1] Johannes Japetus Smith Steenstrup. Feilden may have had in mind J. Steenstrup and Chr. Lütken, 1861.
[2] Segmented worms.
[3] 'Dingy' is an acceptable variant spelling of 'dinghy'. *OED*.
[4] I have not been able to locate this MS book.
[5] Cinquefoils, a genus in the rose family.
[6] Scurvy grass, a genus of herbs in the cabbage family.
[7] The type genus of the poppy family.
[8] Commonly known as whitlow grasses (which are not related to true grasses), a genus of flowering plants in the cabbage family.
[9] Willows: Arctic willows are low-growing or creeping shrubs.
[10] Feilden often, but not always, used this erroneous spelling for depot.
[11] This was standard practice on Arctic voyages in the 19th century.

glaciers pour down the ravines of Northumberland I. and at this season, rills and cascades were sparkling on its front, bathed by their spray and nurtured by the presence of thousands of sea fowl; the vegetation on the slopes and ledges, flourishes amazingly, shades of bright green alternated with the rich hues of the rock, the channel without a ripple on its surface was specked with myriads of little auks, the same birds flew ~~backwards~~ <up and down> in great companies, to their breeding haunts. On the east side of Hakluyt Island is a great loomery and there the rocks are coated white with their ordure. At 11 p.m. Sontag Bay was on our starboard beam.
[*Colour sketch inserted here, of an iceberg at the entrance to Smith's Sound. July 27th 1875; see Plate 9.*]

Wednesday 28 July 1875 <u>Port Foulke</u>
"Bar. 29.88 to 29.85. Wind E force of 3 to 5. Temp [*figure deleted*° *figure deleted*°] of sea +35° at 7.15 a.m, anchored off Jensen Point in 12½ fathoms. Ships log."
    At 2.30 a.m., we were abreast of Cape Alexander, Sutherland Island on our starboard beam, and about a mile and a half distant. This island marks the retreat of the glacier which now sinks beneath the waves, a considerable distance nearer the mainland. Sutherland I. estimated height 350 feet Cape Alexander 1400. Having feasted my eyes to the full on this fine headland and the noble Crystal Palace glacier, turned in. Not a speck of ice visible as far as the eye could reach up the sound, Cape Sabine in sight. Both ships anchored about a quarter of a mile from shore between Jensen and Reindeer Points. Landed immediatly after breakfast, and walked several miles into the interior, returning with numerous plants, insects, and geological specimens, my field pocket notes are too long to transfer to this journal. Returned to the ship at 5 p.m., got some food, and then started along the north shore of Foulke Fiord for the native settlement of Etah.[1] To the eastward of Reindeer Point are many remains of old Eskimo habitations, rings of stones mark summer residences, and green mounds old igloos. These spots are strewn round with multitudes of bones. The skulls, bones and horns of *Cervus tarandus*[2] were exceptionally abundant, every bone that had contained marrow, was split, the crania of the deer generally stove in through the forehead, others with the base of the skull smashed off, evidently for extraction of the brains. Foxes bones were common also Walrus, but from the skulls of these latter the tusks had in all instances been removed. Seals bones most abundant, a few hares, with myriads of the sterna of *Mergulus alle*. The settlement of Etah

---

[1] '[I]n July 1875, the village of Etah, on the north shore of Foulke Fiord, was found temporarily deserted. Etah is the most northern settlement of the Eskimo on the Greenland coast ...'. Feilden, 'Appendix I. Ethnology', in Nares, *Narrative of a Voyage*, II, p. 187. Etah, on an early (5th–3rd centuries BCE) migration route from the northern Canadian Arctic, was where the last migration of Inuit from Baffin Island reached the Greenland coast in 1865. Ehrlich, *This Cold Heaven*, pp. 26–7, 141, 239, 348. From around 900 CE to somewhat after 1100 CE, the Dorset culture, having moved in from Alaska, occupied the east coast of Ellesmere Island and the Greenland coast across what is now the Kennedy Channel; by 1300 CE, the Thule culture, ancestors of today's Inuit, had completely replaced the Dorset culture in those regions. By the mid 1300s, a colder climate forced the Inuit south from northern Ellesmere Island. Since Feilden did not find any Inuit remains in northern Ellesmere Island, his old and what he sometimes described as ancient remains are almost certainly post-14th century. Snow, 'The First Americans'; Damas, 'The Arctic from Norse contact'; Trigger and Washburn, *The Cambridge History of the Native Peoples of the Americas*; Damas, ed., *Arctic*; Maxwell, 'Pre-Dorset and Dorset'; McGhee, 'Thule Prehistory'.
[2] The genus Caribou (reindeer in Eurasia); the species that Feilden encountered here was barren-ground caribou, whereas the species on Ellesmere Island was (and is) Peary caribou.

The ARCTIC
Printing Office

Mesrs Giffard & Symons beg to inform the Public that they have obtained - at an imense cost & with infinite trouble - possession of the extensive premises lately occupied by Mr Clements Markham situated in Trap Lane within half a minutes walk of the foremost Quarter Deck ladder, and easily accessible to all parts of the City.

They have fitted up their new establishment - *regardless of expense*- with all the *latest inventions* and *newest machinery* to enable them to carry on the Noble Art of Printing in a Style & with a Rapidity hitherto quite unattainable.

They therefore expect from the Public that support & assistance which it always gives to the *truly deserving*.

Charges moderate. No credit given. All work required to be executed to be paid for in advance.

N B. Everything undertaken promptly and correctly executed.

H.M.S.Alert.
July. 28.th.
1875.

Figure 8. Printed broadsheet announcing the establishment of the Arctic Printing Office, H.M.S. *Alert*, 28 July 1875.

is placed in a sheltered little nook, overshadowed by gneiss rocks with a good lookout to S and W., it consisted of two or three stone igloos and one roofed over with canvas spread on spars, the place was deserted, but numerous traces of recent habitation were visible. We detected many relics of the *Polaris* scattered about. Aldrich and Parr brought in 50 *Som. moll.* Countless flocks of Little Auks were passing up and down the Fiord to and from their breeding places, unfortunately the line of country which I took did not lead me to their haunts, several aukeries were visited by members of the expedition, and Rawson[1] and others gave me most animated accounts of the scene. Hayes describes it well.[2] The young are little black puff balls. Some of our people visited My Brother Johns Glacier, a Reindeer was shot, and several hares. Egerton and Mitchell both came across ancient remains of Musk-ox. Captain Nares and Markham visited Littleton I and the scene of the wreck of the *Polaris* and brought back some books and gear that belonged to that expedition, also a flat bottomed scow.[3]

[*Here Feilden tipped in a broadsheet announcing the establishment of 'The ARCTIC Printing Office. H.M.S.* Alert. *July 28th. 1875'; see Figure 8, p. 84.*]

Thursday 29 July 1875 <u>Cape Isabella</u>
"Wind E.S.E force 4 to 1. Lat at noon 78°.29 Long 74°.45. Bar 29.80'. Temp. ~~+42° to +52°~~[4] of sea (after leaving Harstene B. which was +35°), +32°. +33½° off Cape Isabella, and +31° in the channel. 7.30 a.m., weighed and proceeded. 1.30 h. p.m. stopped off C. Isabella. Ships log."

We left our anchorage at 7.30 a.m. under sail, bound for Cape Isabella, where some provisions have to be left. Fog and snow, but no ice seen in crossing the sound, we passed many Little Auks, a few Fulmars and a few Dovekies. Abreast of the Cape between 1 and 2 p.m. Captain Markham landed to erect cairn, deposit record, and a small dêpot. I went on shore at 4.30. The geological formation is white and red granite in thick lateral beds. At a little distance one might easily take these rocks for alternating strata of red and yellow sandstones. The fog prevented me seeing up to the top of the cliff, but where I landed and took rock specimens the inclination of the beds was to the north true. Fragments of shore ice were here clinging to the coast and hummocks 30 feet high. Saw two *Procellaria glacialis*, at night.

Friday 30 July 1875 <u>Brevoort Island</u>
Payer Harbour
"Wind S.E. light. Bar 29.80 – 29.66. Temp. of sea. +33° to +31°. Position at noon by observation 78°48'N. Long 73°25'.W.

At 5.30 h. a.m., observed H.M.S. *Discovery* inside land ice in the vicinity of Cape Sabine. 10 h. entered pack steering in for land, ice passed through ranged from 3 to 5 feet thick with occasional heavier pieces. It was moderately open and rather rotten. 2.45 h. cleared pack 3.15 h made fast to land ice inside Brevoort I. 10 h. p.m. proceeded out under steam. ships log."

---

[1] Wyatt Rawson, lieutenant, HMS *Discovery*.
[2] Hayes, *Open Polar Sea*, has numerous references to Etah, esp. pp. 242–89 *passim*.
[3] Scow: a large flat-bottomed lighter or punt. *OED*.
[4] Air temperatures in log.

Snowing with fog, all around us pack ice, the *Discovery* ahead of us, near Brevoort I. Sounded at 9 a.m. 210 fathoms, bottom mud full of foraminifera.[1]

[*Margin*: *Foraminifera*] We forced our way through the pack and took shelter in an excellent harbour, between Brevoort and the mainland, in addition to the two islands marked on the chart there are two round-backed low skerries at the southern entrance which act as fenders to the ice, and afford much protection. These skerries are worn smooth with ice action [*Margin*: *Ice action*] and the red syenite of which they are composed is highly polished. In clefts the Eiders make their nests, these being composed entirely of down without any admixture of foreign material. Accustomed as we have hitherto been to bright patches of verdure this coast appears sadly bare and desolate, the granitoid rocks do not seem to disintegrate freely and consequently there is little soil formed. I gathered about 12 species of flowering plants [*Margin*: *Flowering* plants] none differing from those already procured on the Greenland side. A pretty little fern was rather abundant. Picked up a dead Snow bunting on shore. Glaucus gulls numerous in the harbour, and a few L. eburneus, a pair of Ravens [*Margin*: *Corvus corax*] were circling over Brevoort I, croaking.

Left the harbour at 10 p.m, and went into the channel and made our way into a large expanse of water which stretched in the direction of Cape Grinnell.

Saturday 31 July 1875 <u>Return to Brevoort I.</u>
Payer Harbour.
"Wind E to E.N.E. light. Bar. 29.64 to 29.67. Temp [~~+42° to +50°~~?][2] of sea +30° to +31°. 1.10 h. a.m., Cleared the pack, and stood along the edge, observed land. 2.40 h. a.m. stood back, as there was no open water right across the sound. Most of the ice passed thro was in small floes varying from 2 ft to 6 in, but some of the floes seen were very large, heavy and covered with hummocks. 11.30 h. a.m. made fast to land ice inside Brevoort I. ships log"

When I got on deck in the morning snow was falling and fog surrounded us, the vessels were steaming in the direction of Cape Sabine, Captain Nares finding the pack very close in the channel, had decided to return to our anchorage of yesterday. made fast between 11 and 12 m in the same place as before. Hart, Beaumont,[3] and Rawson, dined with us and afterwards I joined H. in a scramble up the hills behind our anchorage, on our way went onboard the *Discovery*, and saw the horn of the Narwhal [*Margin*: *Monodon monoceros* ♀] which they killed at Cape York, it was a ♀ and it is very seldom that the tusk is developed in that sex. H. has two nestling little auks [*Margin*: *Mergulus alle juv.*] in his cabin, which fed heartily on bread and milk. Bunyan[4] brought about 30 of these little creatures on board the *Disco[very]* when we lay at Port Foulke, but the dogs had eaten them all so that I could not procure a specimen.

[*Margin*: *Traces of Eskimo*] On landing we came across traces of the summer residences of Eskimo, seven circles of stones used for fastening down their skin tents, we picked up a few lichen covered bones of animals scattered around, including tooth of *Cervus*

---

[1] A class of amoeboid marine protozoa with shells.
[2] The double lines obscure the temperature readings; Feilden realized that he had copied from the wrong column in the ship's log.
[3] Lewis A. Beaumont, senior lieutenant, HMS *Discovery*.
[4] George Bunyan, ropemaker, HMS *Discovery*.

tarandus[1] bones of seal, and jaw of Fox. The ascent of the hill was severe, we estimated it at 1500 feet, its steep slopes were covered with blocks of Syenite, which had fallen down from the parent rock, all up its sides and on the summit are scattered boulders of foreign rocks chiefly yellow sandstone [*Margin*: *Erratic Boulders*]. I added considerably to my collection of flowering plants. Found [*Margin*: *Cistopteris fragilis*] *Cistopteris fragilis*[2] nestling between rocks at an altitude of 250 feet. From the top of the hill the prospect was anything but encouraging, to my inexperienced eye it seemed impossible that this mass of pack, which hemmed us in to our little harbour, and stretched unbroken as far as we could see, would ever ease off sufficiently to let us advance. We returned to the ship by 10 p.m., [*Margin*: *Larus Eburneus*] 6 *Larus Eburneus* were disporting themselves near our ship.[3]

Sunday 1 August 1875 <u>Brevoort I.</u>
Wind E. force 1 to 6. Bar 29.66 to 29.53 Temp [*deletion*][4] of sea +30°
"The ice passing the entrance of the harbour was very closely packed, heavy and hummocky with large bergs, fast in the floes, the whole moving rapidly to westward. No open water seen to seaward from top of island to foot of which we were secured. Ships log."

Outside, the pack was drifting southwest at a great rate, it appears of a very formidable description, great hummocks piled up on the floes. We are evidently in advance of the season.

Captain Nares lent me today a very interesting journal, picked up at the Polaris winter quarters, near Life Boat Cove, written by M[r] Henry Dodge, mate of Hayes schooner the *United States* who wintered at Port Foulke in 1860–61.[5] The ice at night drifting into our harbour, only light pieces, however, for Brevoort Island protects us from the pressure of the pack.

---

[1] Caribou.

[2] Brittle bladder-fern.

[3] In subsequent entries, Feilden enters the names of species in the margin, but where they are already in the text, I omit them.

[4] Air temperatures are given in the log.

[5] There is no mention in the journal of an insertion for 27 or 28 July, although Feilden placed his comment on and transcription of a passage from Dodge's journal there. The transcribed passage is a description of Cape Alexander, and refers to F's entry on 1 Aug. 1875. Feilden wrote: 'The following description of Cape Alexander is copied from the mss journal of M[r] Dodge, mate of the schooner *United States*, the ship belonging to D[r] Hayes, which wintered at Port Foulke 60 & 61.
"March 14th. 1861. p.155."
"Dodge journal."
"The Cape, which is wholly isolated from the mainland <by the glacier> pouring down on each side of its eastern extremity, is at its base, or at least from the water's edge, composed of a light yellow sand-stone, very coarse and soft. This formation extends half way up the declivity, being surmounted by a wall of very dark grey columnar basalt, which is again capped by a thin stratum of the yellow sand-stone, the debris of which in many places covers the sides of, and fills the crevices between the rocks. From half a mile north of the Cape to a point nearly opposite the western end of Sutherland Island, there was no floe ice at all, the open water washing directly against the ice-foot, undermining and crumbling it away in many places."
[*added subsequently by Feilden*:] <'Mr Dodge afterwards served as ice-pilot aboard the U.S.S.S. *Juanita* Commander Braine in the search for the *Polaris* 1873. V. Report Sect U.S. Navy'>.
See Dodge, Journals, 3 vols, 1860–73. The MS was kept by Feilden until it was given to General Greely in 1890. There is a typescript copy of vol. I in New York State Library, Albany. For the Hayes expedition, see Hayes, *The Open Polar Sea*; for the Hall expedition, see Davis, ed., *Narrative*.

The Captain, who ascended the hill we went up yesterday, and returned to the ship at 11 p.m, is of opinion that Hayes Sound is not a channel leading to the westward, but a deep bay. The ice now moving out of it is last seasons, and not the heavy description that would pass through a channel.

Monday 2 August 1875 Brevoort I
"Wind light. Bar 29.47 to 29.60. Temp. ~~+45 to +48~~ of sea +30° + 29½.
At 4 h. a.m Ice passing rapidly mouth of harbour to Eastward. 12 h. midnight, flow at entrance of harbour being driven in by the pressure outside. Ships log."

D[r] Coppinger[1] showed me today a specimen of *Tringa Canutus*,[2] [*Margin: Tringa Canutus*] procured at Port Foulke on the 28th July. He observed six of these birds flying along the edge of a stream, several miles inland, they were very shy, and he only succeeded in shooting one a ♂ in full breeding plumage.

After breakfast to Brevoort I. with Egerton, and visited a breeding place of *Larus Glaucus*. [*Margin: Breeding of Larus Glaucus*] The young birds were in much the same state of plumage as those we found at the Cary Islands, on the 27th July. Climbed up the rock and killed one young one, they were seated on a ledge not more than 20 feet from the water and a spot easy of access. During the disturbance occasioned by our intrusion, four Ivory Gulls [*Margin: Larus Eburneus*] made their appearance, one of these we secured. (For colouring of soft parts vide Orn*ithological* notes.) The contents of its stomach were a quantity of red flesh, probably seals. Many Eiders (*S. moll.*) [*Margin: Som. Moll*] nest on this island. Shot one off the nest with three eggs deep set. 3 or 4 seems to be the usual number of eggs laid by this species in these regions. [*Margin: Som. Spec. absence of*] I have seen no *Spectabilis* amongst the Eiders procured in the Sound, neither have I seen a ♂ bird. A raven [*Margin: Corvus Corax*] wheeled over head croaking, on the look out for plunder, Petersen saw him swoop down on an Eiders nest, and make off with an egg, as soon as the duck left her charge. A few *Uria grylle*[3] were fishing in the open spaces, and several Narwhals [*Margin: Monodon monoceros*] were seen playing near the edge of the ice, from the ship by the Quartermasters. On the top of Brevoort I are a few fresh water pools made by the melting of the snow, these were filled with the larvæ of a small diptera,[4] [*Margin: Diptera*] They were rapidly emerging from the larval stage, coming to the surface, sloughing off their integuments, and emerging as winged insects, to enjoy the short summer. Captured a small spider. [*Margin: Spider*] Near the summit the rocks were clad with a green confervoid,[5] [*Margin: Conferva*] in damp places.

Brevoort I is of the same granitoid formation as the adjacent mainland.

Tuesday 3 August 1875 Brevoort I.
"Winds calm & northerly 0 to 3. Bar 29.62. Temp. ~~30 56~~ sea +29½ +29° +30°.
1 h. a.m. Ice going to westward very slowly, part of floe at N. entrance of harbour broke up about midnight, and large pieces came in, between 2 & 4 ice cleared away from around ship and packed itself on floe at N. entrance which is closely shut up by ice. 9.30 h.

---

[1] Richard W. Coppinger, M.D., surgeon on *Discovery*, see also p. 10, n. 1.
[2] Red knot.
[3] Black guillemot.
[4] Flies and midges.
[5] Algae of the genus *Conferva*.

weighed and stood out under sail. 10.30 h. Found ice too thickly packed to proceed, hauled to the wind to beat back to the anchorage. 2.30 anchored in 20 fathoms. Abs*trac*^{t} of log."

An ineffectual attempt to round Cape Sabine under sail, returned to our anchorage by mid-day. Went on shore over the fragments of floe, which were jammed together. Where I scrambled up the ice-foot a circle of stones on the shingle behind, marked an old encampment. [*Margin*: *Eskimo Harpoon*] At the same spot Captain N. this morning picked up a harpoon head, it had grease adhering to it. In a niche of the rock close by was a small fire place, a thin slab of stone, had been used as the cooking apparatus, [*Margin*: *Cooking place*] this was blackened with smoke underneath, and stained with grease on the upper surface, with several long white hairs adhering to it. The droppings of the dogs around was composed of the same hair, which I took to be Bears. At Etah I noticed several of the same description of cooking places, there *Mergulus alle* had been the prevailing dish. The stems of Cass. tetragona had been used as fuel, and a large cache, closely packed with this plant, showed that the natives store it for future consumption. Crossing the ice of a bay to a peninsula which juts out from the mainland, found more traces of Eskimos, but these were very ancient. The circles which marked camps were hoary with lichens and moss surrounded. I discovered the greater portion of a large sledge scattered around. [*Margin*: *Ancient Sledge*] It had been a very composite structure, the bearers wood and bone, the runners bone, and the fore-runner was a carved piece of mica-schist with several holes bored through it. The cross pieces were portions of Narwhals tusks, but so ancient that the surfaces exposed were exfoliated, and so brittle as barely to stand transport.

Ascended to the highest point of the promontory, very clear. [*Margin*: *Extensive View*] Cape Alexander and the Crystal Palace Glacier showed distinctly. The coast above Rensellaar Bay with little snow on it. No trace of water outside.

Wednesday 4 August 1875 <u>Hayes Sound</u>

"Wind N.W. force 4 to 6. Bar. 29.60 to 29.65. Temp. 46̶ 50 [?] of Sea +30° +32° & +34° when at anchor at midnight in Hayes Sound. About 4.15 a.m. weighed and proceeded out of harbour 7.15 a.m., under steam. 5 h made sail. 7.15 h Furled sails proceeded under steam, stopping and sounding as required. The ice was blown off the south shore of Hayes Sound as far up as middle of Henry I, from which point it stretched right across the sound. The ice also appears to stretch across Smiths Sound from Henry I to East side. 2 h, came to anchor in 11 fathoms in a small harbour on south side of Hayes Sound. Abs*tract* of log."

At 4.30 a.m., left anchorage rounded Cape Sabine and anchored about 1 o'c. The coast on the south side of this sound is composed of lofty gneiss, syenite, mica schist with garnets and hornblendic schist hills rising to 1500 feet, but so denuded and covered with talus, and the strata so contorted that it would be rash to lay down the lie of these rocks without careful examination. [*Margin*: *Round Cape Sabine*]

Where we anchored a fine Glacier came down the head of the glen, it was immediatly christened the Twin Glacier, as a bare peak rising from its centre divided it into two before its final juncture. [*Margin*: *Twin Glacier*] This glacier descends into a strath,[1] reminding

---

[1] A wide valley; a tract of level or low-lying land traversed by a river and bounded by hills or high ground. *OED*.

me much of many Scotch valleys that I can call to mind. Its general shape is a broad triangle its widest part at the sea line about two miles and narrowing to about a mile where the glacier ends. A stream runs down the carse[1] land, at this date a clear rapid burn, which one could cross dry shod, but on the melting of the snows it must be a large torrent for the channel is not less than 100 yards wide, large patches of bright coloured epilobium[2] blossomed in this torrent course, and yellow flowered *Vesicaria*[3] on its banks [*Margin*: *Plants*] The sections of the banks showed that the stream cut through thin strata of sand, and glacier mud, filled with *Mya*[4] and *Saxicava* shells. These strata were in many places much crumpled up,   as if they had been deposited at a period when the snow   of the glacier protruded into the sea. We picked up the skull   of *Ursus maritimus* the antlers of *Cervus tarandus*, whilst traces of *ovibos*[5] were abundant and recent. [*Margin*: *Mammalia*] Killed a single example of *Char. hiaticula* near the shore, a ♀ with belly bare from sitting. Numerous traces of Eskimo. [*Margin*: *Eskimos*] The basement rock into which the glacier stream cuts is a hard conglomerate limestone [*Margin*: *Stratified Limestone*] which rests on the hypogene rocks above noted.

Thursday 5 August 1875 <u>Hayes Sound</u>
"Wind N.W. force 4 to 0. Bar. 29.60. Temp. ~~+46 +50~~ [?] of sea +30° +33°. Lat. 78°52 N. Long. 75°50′ W.
8.12 h. a.m. The ice as yesterday extended from East of Henry I. across Smiths Sound, between Henry I. and mainland it is loose, in some places rotten 2 to 3 feet thick. 9.40 weighed, made sail, and steered for west extreme Henry I. Entered loose floe ice between point and island. No wind 2.30 commenced steaming stopped at 3.30 the ice being too close to make any further progress. Abs*ract*. of log."

Left our anchorage at 9 a.m. with the intention of ascertaining whether there is a passage to the west of Bache and Henry Islands of the American charts, Albert and Victoria Land of Inglefield.[6] We were unable to decide this point to our satisfaction as we got jammed in the ice, which was moving out of Hayes Sound. This ice was nearly all last seasons, and much broken up. On several pieces of the floe, I noticed angular blocks of stone and rubble, which must have fallen this spring from the cliffs and settled on the ice-raft [*Margin*: *See rafts*] before it was detached from the shore. My own opinion is that Hayes Sound is merely a deep fiord, and not a channel as has been suggested, with the possibility of its connecting in some way with Jones Sound.[7] Vide p. 538. Report. Sec. U.S. Navy. 1873. Evidence of D[r] Bessels. "The natives of the west coast stated that United States Sound, as laid down by Hayes is in reality a sound connecting with Jones Sound, [*Margin*: *Connection between Hayes & Jones Sound*] and making Ellesmere Land an island … They informed us that

---

[1] Low alluvial land.
[2] A genus in the family Onagraceae, willowherb.
[3] *Carex vesicaria*, bladder sedge.
[4] A genus of soft-shelled clams.
[5] *Ovibos moschatus*, muskox.
[6] This is a reference to the English charts by the naval officer, Edward Augustus Inglefield (1820–94); English and American charts often used different names for some of the Arctic islands and also for places and features on those islands.
[7] Hayes Sound is indeed a fiord.

Grinnell Land is inhabited south of Cape Isabella, and that there are musk-oxen there, and a good deal of drift-wood, the drift-wood coming from the northward."[1]

Friday 6 August 1875 <u>Leave Hayes Sound</u>
"Wind light. Bar. 29.50". Temp. +50°+46° of sea +30° +31°. Lat. 79°00 N. Long. 76°.W. 9.30 h. a.m. Under steam. 10.30 stopped sounded in 57 fathoms mud and small stones. 1.30 p.m. Captain returned onboard, proceeded under steam towards Cape Sabine. A floe of ice extended from west of Henry I. to near Cape Sabine leaving room between it and land for ship to pass. 5 p.m. rounded south extremity of ice. 8.50 entered pack. 10.30 made fast to floe. 11. Iceberg drifted towards ship, cast off and tried to clear it. Beset and preparing for a nip. Pack consisted of floes about 3 or 4 foot thick. Abs*tract*. of log."

This morning a lead showing towards Cape Sabine got under steam, stopped at 11 o'c. for an hour, went ashore. (Ptarmigan Hill.) The base of the range, and half way up is of schistose rock thickly studded with garnets, but is capped by weathered yellow coloured limestone bedded nearly horizontally. The shores are dotted with old igloos, many caches and traces of summer encampments. [*Margin: Eskimo Settlement*] The bones of some large Cetacean, fragments over 5 feet long and one broad, had been used as rafters for the dwelling houses. I found bones of Seal, Walrus, Narwhal, Fox, Glaucus gull, and in one cache two small pieces of blubber. Picked up one or two morsels of human work, and I regretted much that I had only a few minutes to spare in investigating this interesting place. Hart found a skull of Ovibos, near one of the igloos. [*Margin: Muskox Skull*] Insects were abundant, a ptarmigan was shot. By 1 p.m., we were leaving Hayes Sound under steam and sail wind fresh from S.W. Saw numerous Dovekies and little Auks. We had in passing an excellent view of Victoria and Albert land, on its southern side its base is red syenite capped by massive horizontal limestone, but on the western face the Syenite entirely disappears. [*Margin: Geology*] The two noble headlands which flank this island or promontory, are almost perpendicular cliffs of thick bedded limestone dipping about 5° from S.S.E. to N.N.W. true.

Saturday 7 August 1875 <u>Beset off Victoria Head</u>
Wind 3 to 5. Bar. 29.76" to 30.12". Temp. of sea +30°. Lat.79°18′N. Long. 74°22′W. 0.30, Up propeller, unshipped rudder. 1 h Down propeller, made fast to Berg.

At midnight our position was somewhat critical as we were drifting down on a large berg, and pressed by a large floe piece. Hands on deck unshipping rudder, getting up propeller &c. [*Margin: Nipped in the pack*] We drifted past the berg all right, and made fast to it, lying in the slack water formed under its lee. On one edge of this berg about 20 feet from the water there was a considerable accumulation of rocks and stones, several tons weight. A flock of six *Strepsilas interpres*[2] flew round the ship. [*Margin: Strepsilas*] Landing on this berg I noticed many circular holes formed by the suns rays, on its surface.

Some of these holes showed curious ice crystallization. Long spicules of hard clear ice radiated from a common centre to the sides, and to the depth of 6 or 8 inches, below which was fresh water, some of these spicules were 6 inches long and thick as a lead pencil.

---

[1] *Annual Report of the Secretary of the Navy ... 1873*, p. 538.
[2] Turnstone.

They were easily detached from one another. The holes doubtless had been the result of the suns rays acting on a peeble or piece of stone, that had been exposed on the surface of the berg.

About midday loosened from the berg as it had begun to drift and endeavoured to force our way through the pack to Victoria Head. Though ramming and charging our progress was very slow, and at midnight we had not got more than two miles nearer the shore.

Sunday 8 August 1875 <u>Landed on Victoria Head</u>
Calm. Temp. ~~+47° +37°~~ of sea +32° and +31°.
0.45 floes opening slightly. 1 h went ahead 2–4 h going ahead and astern as requisite to force a passage. 4 h rudder head was sprung going astern against a floe. 7 h got into open water, proceeded for land. 1.30 Found we were drifting to the land, up steam and tried to get clear of the ice, nipping in from seaward. 6.45 Got into good open lanes, steered about N.E.

The ice opened somewhat this morning, and by dint of hard ramming aided on one occasion by blasting charges of powder, at 8 a.m. we were within half a mile of Victoria Head. Landed with Markham, it being low tide the ice foot was about 12 feet above the level of the water, but with a little trouble we managed to scramble up. The rock in this vicinity is a massive, hard, gray limestone, containing Silurian fossils, sparsely distributed. [*Margin*: *Fossils*] It is a noble headland some 1000 feet high. I picked up a *Cephalapod*, two or three *Brachyopod* [*sic*][1] shells and some *crinoidal*[2] remains. The strata appear to be nearly on a horizontal plane. The Flora on this hard limestone is much scantier, than on the granitoid rocks, which disintegrate much more easily, and form patches of soil, which supports vegetation. I only noticed *Salix*, and *Sax. oppositifolia*.[3] At the foot of the cliff the limestone passes into a conglomerate, similar to that which is exposed by the glacier stream, in the valley of the Twins. On the beach were traces of Eskimo encampments, and several fox-traps or caches. [*Margin*: *Traces of Eskimo*] Picked up a Foxes skull near cache. At midday a fall of snow, which froze and converted the pools into a tenacious sludge. The ship experienced a slight nip, as the floe set towards shore. At 4 p.m., on the commencement of flood tide the pack eased off, and we and our consort steamed over to Franklin Pierce Bay, where we made fast to the floes, under the lee of an island, [*Margin*: *Walrus Island*] which rises to an elevation of 350 or 400 feet, sloping gradually to the water from N. to S. and marked to its summit with lines of old sea levels. As we pushed through the ice, a small fish some six inches long was ~~pushed~~ <thrown> up on the floe.

Monday 9 August 1875 <u>Franklin Pierce Bay. Death of first walrus.</u>
Weather calm. Temp. ~~+38° +48°~~ of sea. +31° +32°. Lat. 79°25′W. Long. 75° [30].
4 h. Captain landed to erect cairn and leave record. 7.30 h proceeded under steam. 8.45 a.m., made fast to floe.

---

[1] Brachiopods are marine animals with hard shells or valves on the upper and lower surfaces, and hinged at the rear. On each side of the mouth they have a long spiral arm, used for feeding.
[2] Crinoids are a class of echinoderms (chiefly fossil), many of which resemble flowers with long stems.
[3] A saxifrage.

Figure 9.   Photograph. 'Stopped by the ice off Cape Prescott.' from Nares, *Narrative of a voyage to the Polar Sea during 1875–6 of H.M. Ships 'Alert' and 'Discovery'* ..., 1878, I, facing p. 84).

6.30 a.m. landed with Captain Nares, on the S.W. side of Franklin Pierce Bay. Captured two Lepidoptera. Flora, willow, dryas octopetala,[1] Saxifraga oppo. and the yellow draba. Rock formation Silurian limestone. From the spot where we landed to an elevation of three hundred feet, and at an angle of 45°, stretched upwards a series of terraces, casually looking, they might be taken for a series of ancient sea levels, but on closer examination it struck me that they must have been the submarine terminal moraines of extinct glaciers for as I followed the course of a small rivulet which cut through the terraces down to the basement rock, good sections were exposed, and a large proportion of the hard limestone peebles, and boulder stones showed ice scratchings, and where the basement rock was exposed by the stream its surface was splendidly marked with grooves, scratches and fine lines, all running parallel with the course of the stream, scattered throughout this moraine were abundance of mya, and saxicava shells. There are no glaciers discharging into this bay, but at its head a fine one debouches onto a plain but is at least three miles from the shore.

On one of the terraces one hundred feet above the present level I came across a well marked Eskimo tenting spot, a few crumbling bones in its vicinity, as a rule these people do not pitch their tents far from the shore, is it possible that the land has risen nearly a hundred feet since this tent was was pitched. Under steam by 8 a.m. trying to round Cape Prescott. [*See Figure 9, above.*] 3 Walrus on a floe, Markham manned whale boat secured one. Landed in the evening and geologized, the peebles of the conglomerate contain fossils.

---

[1] Mountain avens, in the family Rosaceae.

Tuesday 10 August 1875 <u>Dredging. Capture a ~~New~~ Crinoid</u> <*"Alecto glacialis?"*[1]>
Weather calm. Temp ~~42°~~ ~~47°~~ of sea +31° +32°.

Still fastened to a floe, dredge let down in 15 fathoms, when hauled up on floe, the contents rather surprised us. Echinoderms, Mollusca, Sponges, Crustacea, annelids &c. and a very beautiful crinoid.

James Barrie[2] quartermaster shot a ♂ walrus which was brought to the ship and cut up for dog meat. We eat [*sic*] its liver which was good, and the flesh though black and rather tough was decent eating. The length of this animal along curve of back from tip of nose to end of hind flipper was 12 feet 6 in., girth before fore-arm 11.6 immediatly behind ditto 11 ft. tusks 18½ and 17½ in. estimated weight over a ton. Bury gave me its head – the perquisite of the harpooner. I gave him 10/– for it.

Our dredgings today were over a peeble bottom composed of Silurian limestone. bottom temp. 29.50°. Specific gravity at surface 1007, bottom 1026.5.

Wednesday 11 August 1875 <u>Walrus Island</u>
Weather calm. Temp. ~~37°~~ ~~35°~~ [?]of sea +33° +31°.
11.15 p.m., cast off from floe and proceeded under steam towards Cape Prescott, *Discovery* in company.

After breakfast landed on the island provisionally called Walrus. It is composed of a close grained Silurian limestone. The dip is from S to N true and at a considerable angle as the island on its southern side rises from the sea as a cliff over 400 feet, shelving to the water on its northern face, which is well terraced with consecutive ridges of old coast line to a height of about 250 feet. On the summit of the island the limestone is marked with glacial scorings. The terraces are composed of angular fragments, not rounded, either the ice foot protected them from attrition during the periods of elevation, or else the component peebles have since weathered into their present shape. Walked for at least three miles along the northern beach, many traces of Eskimo residence, hundreds of weathered walrus skulls, all having had their teeth extracted lying about, mixed with them, seals skulls. Patches of green moss marked the sites of old igloos, round circles of stones summer habitations and numerous fox traps and cooking places pointed to a once prosperous settlement. After a careful but superficial search I found not a single flint, stone, or iron implement, only a portion of a bone lance and what might have been a bone knife holder. By the ruins of one habitation lay a large rib bone over five feet long, measured round outside curve. This with the remains used as rafters to the igloos in Hayes Sound shows that there was a time when cetaceans visited Smith Sound.

Thursday 12 August 1875 <u>Washington Irving I</u>
Wind light. Temp. ~~39°~~ ~~49°~~ of sea ~~32°~~ ~~33°~~[3] +31°.
2 a.m., Ice rapidly closing up leads ahead so made fast to floe to await opening. Floes covered with pools of water and very rotten. 2.15 made fast to floe. 4–6 no movement in the ice. 7.30 ice commenced drifting. 8.45 up rudder. 5.55 proceeded under steam. 6. Steaming as required thro ice for Cape Hawkes, ice very soft and rotten. 11 h. made fast

---

[1] A feather-star, now known as *Heliometra glacialis*.

[2] James Berrie, ice quartermaster on HMS *Alert*. Feilden often spells the name 'Bury'.

[3] I have no idea why Feilden crossed out these numbers for temperatures of the sea; they are accurately transcribed from the log.

to a berg in Dobbin Bay. We lay all day under the high conglomerate cliffs of Franklin Pierce Bay, but at 6 p.m. a lead showing to the N.E. up steam and fetched Dobbin Bay. Here the Discovery laid out a 1000 ration dêpot on the South side of the entrance to the bay about two miles beyond Cape Hawkes, and also a boat was left. The rock formation here changes its aspect. Hawkes is composed of massive limestone conglomerate bedded nearly horizontally, and belongs to the same formation as the cliffs we coasted along from Franklin Pierce Bay, but inside Dobbin Bay the conglomerate is capped by thinner beds of fossiliferous limestone, in some places contorted. At the entrance to Dobbin Bay, stands Washington Irving, approaching from the S, it bears a striking resemblance to a Sphynx, its geological formation is interesting, have notes about it in my pocket book. Captain Nares built a cairn on the summit of its outer headland, and we were much puzzled to find two old cairns built on it. If they had been placed there by Dr Hayes surely he would have mentioned the fact. They were covered with yellow lichen.

Friday 13 August 1875 <u>Dobbin Bay</u>
Wind light. Temp. ~~+46° +39°~~ of sea ~~+32° +33°~~ +31½°.
3.15 p.m., proceeded through ice to north shore of Dobbin Bay. 8 h. securing ship in ice. Young ice making.
    Turned in at 4 a.m. After breakfast we unmoored from berg and steamed across to N side of Dobbin Bay, cut a dock into a large floe. All hands at work till 10 p.m.
    The padre[1] remained onboard, and having let the stove in the wardroom out was chaffed accordingly.

Saturday 14 August 1875 <u>Cape Hilgard</u>
Weather calm. Temp. ~~+4~~[?]~~° +39°~~ of sea +32° +31½°.
    Left the ship at 10 a.m., with Captain Nares, and Aldrich for an excursion to C. Hilgard. Capt. Nares hauled the sledge, Aldrich and I and two hands took the Dingey across the floe, which was seasons ice, about a mile broad and full of hollows with knee deep water. There was a broad lead between this floe and the ice-foot which we ferried over.
    Before leaving the ship three *Strepsilas interpres* flew round, secured one, a ♀, its stomach was filled entirely with seeds. Landing on the ice-foot which was there from 50 to 100 feet broad, with pools of drinking water on its surface, we loaded the satellite sledge and proceeded northwards. The cliffs of limestone containing many fossils rose perpendicularly above us to a height of 1000 feet, a talus descended from about 400 feet to the present ice-foot, but wherever a point jutted out, or where the cliffs receded sufficiently far, to prevent the masses from the cliffs obliterating them, a series of well defined ancient sea beaches with shells saxicava scattered over them, rose above us in a series of horizontal lines to the number of six or seven tiers. The ice-foot at its edge is a perpendicular wall of ice reaching to the bottom, and varies of course with the abruptness of the coast, but inside it slopes off at an angle of 45° for each of the beaches above us sloped off about that angle; behind them extended a flat terre-plein of about the same extent as the present ice-foot. We got back to ship about 2 o'c. of the 15th loaded with fossils. At Cape Hilgard I found two stone built caches. Rawson and Aldrich walked to

[1] Rev. Henry William Pullen.

the glacier at the head of the bay beyond Cape Hilgard. Captain Nares and I were so heavily laden that we returned to the tent which had been pitched at the base of Cape Hilgard, and had supper.

Sunday 15 August 1875
Weather calm. Temp. [??~~+44°~~ ~~+48°~~] of sea +32° +30°.
8.30 proceeded under steam, *Discovery* in company.

I was very tired and ached all over from the unaccustomed exertion of hauling boat and sledge, and carrying a heavy weight of rock specimens. May[1] and Moss shot six *Tetrao rupestris*[2] yesterday, the old male and female with four young ones, they were all so soiled and dirty that I could not make specimens of any of them, contents of their stomachs Salix buds, and seeds. Towards evening a lead showing in the direction of Cape Louis Napoleon, we followed it, our consort touched the ground but got off without damage in a few minutes. Captain Nares taking advantage of every chance and after great exertions by midnight we were a couple of miles south of Cape Hayes.

Monday 16 August 1875
Weather calm. Temp. [+~~42°~~ ??][3] of sea +29½° +30°. Lat. 79°36′. Long. 72°24′.
1 a.m. stopped and made fast to floe. 1.15 cast off and lay to. 3.25 proceeded under steam. Made fast to very heavy floe, but cast off on account of a smaller floe closing in. The large floe drifted in shore, but the leads opened a little ahead so proceeded, some of the floes very heavy. 5 h steering as requisite between floes and through broken ice off the shore, ice setting in towards the shore. Floes very heavy 2 to 10 ft thick. 8. ice going south. Until 11 p.m. ice moving to the south, the floe to which the ship is attached drifting to the south.

The pack stretches away as far as can be seen from the crows nest to the N.E. without a lead or any water space showing. Captain Nares, Markham and I went on land and walked towards Cape Hayes. We came across the tracks of a Bear on the ice-foot. I procured a few Silurian fossils from the talus of the lofty limestone cliffs which skirt the shore. Fossils are not as numerous here as in the strata of Cape Hilgard. The yellow poppy, salix, one or two saxifrages, and the yellow draba were all the flowering plants I saw, but noticed a bee (*bombus*)[4] and captured a butterfly. It is difficult to imagine how lepidoptera ~~and~~ <can> exist in a climate which in July and August sinks below freezing point and where heavy falls of snow are of not unusual occurrence. About a mile to the south of Cape Hayes, a pair of Ivory Gulls, *Larus eburneus* were nesting in the precipitous limestone cliff. I was attracted to them by their shrill cries, and the movements of one of the pair, who, when I approached within a few hundred yards of the nest, came swooping down on me, passing within twenty or thirty feet of me.

Tuesday 17 August 1875
Weather calm. Temp. [??—] of sea +29° +30½°.
The ice seems to be of a totally different description, to that we have hitherto met with. It is much heavier and though in many places about the edges there are broken pieces, yet

---

[1] William Henry May (1849–1930), lieutenant, *Alert*; Admiral of the Fleet 1913. *ODNB*.
[2] Rock ptarmigan, renamed *Lagopus rupestris*.
[3] Log has air temperatures +40° – +44°.
[4] A member of the genus containing the humble-bees, now known as bumble-bees.

as a rule the floe is composed of smooth hillocks, which shows that the floe is due to accumulative ice, rather than to recent formation and nipping.

The small open space in which the *Discovery* and *Alert* are moored, is constantly changing its shape and size, and it requires great vigilance to prevent being nipped. Provisions, Seal-skins &c are now on deck ready to be thrown out, and I have not taken off my clothes on lying down since the 15th. This being Rawson's birthday, dined with him on the *Discovery*.

The dogs onboard the *Discovery* have been very bad, five have already died. Rawson's birthday, dined onboard the *Discovery*, on returning to the *Alert* at 5 p.m. the ice was in motion and the ship had to be warped out from between the berg and heavy floe that moved down on her from the northward.

Wednesday 18 August 1875
Wind light. Temp. +48° +40°. of sea +30° +29°. Lat. 79°37N. Long. 72°25′W.

This was a day of waiting, moored to the floe the two vessels remained in a pool of water. A party from the ship attempted to blast a passage through the ice, but its thickness fifteen feet rendered the effort nugatory. After one discharge two fishes '*merlangus*'?[1] were cast up on the floe and rescued. These fish must be abundant for the Dovekies *Uria grylle* that breed in the neighbouring cliffs, were constantly flying down to the pool in which we lay for food for their young ones, and seldom missed capturing one of these fishes at the first dive, this they held in their bills by the head as they flew back to the cliffs, but I did not observe them carrying more than one at a time. Ivory gulls *pag. eburneus*[2] also visited us and a Turnstone flew past the ship. I went out in the Dingey and secured three Dovekies. Depth of water 35 fathoms, I let down a circular net and hauled it up after being an hour at the bottom it contained many shrimps and several *Ophiuridæ*.[3]

Thursday 19 August 1875 <u>We round Cape Frazer</u>
Weather calm. Temp. +42° +37°. of sea +30½° +29°.
12.30 a.m. Shipped rudder, could not get the screw down on account of ice. 2.30 taken in tow by *Discovery*, 4 inch hawser carried away. 3.40 cast off, made fast to a floe. 0–4 Ice moving south. 5.45 got screw down. 3 p.m. cast off from floe and made sail. 3.45 under steam furled sails. 6.30 rounded Cape Frazer. 9.15 made fast to the floe in 22 fathoms. Commander[4] landed much open water reported to the northward.

Tried to go ashore by walking over the floes, but finding water between the floe and the shore, I and Moss returned to the ship. Egerton, Hart, and Coppinger got to land. Captain Nares went on shore and ascended Cape Hayes nearly 2000 feet. He saw the great Humboldt glacier on the eastern side of the strait distinctly, and leads of water apparently up to Cape Frazer. At 2.30 loosed from our moorings, and under steam and sail had the satisfaction of rounding Cape Frazer about 8 p.m. This is about the latitude where the Polar and Baffin Bay tides meet. At 9.30 we were close to Cape John Barrow. Markham and I landed, he ascended to look for a lead, I searched for fossils. The limestone cliffs as

---

[1] *Merlangius merlangus*, whiting.
[2] The ivory gull, named *Larus eburneus* by Constantine Phipps in 1774, was named *Pagophila eburnea* by Johann Jakob Kaup in 1829. Feilden uses both names in his journal.
[3] Ophiuroidea: a group of echinoderms that includes the brittle stars.
[4] Albert Hastings Markham.

hitherto, show a nearly horizontal stratification but the dip is from S.S.E. to N.N.W. true. One must bear in mind, however, that numerous landslips occur which vary the appearance of the beddings. I found the rocks of Cape J. B. highly fossiliferous. Before starting today I hauled up my circular net, and got several star fish also a delicate vitreous shelled, free swimming pecten.[1] A Phoca fetida[2] was killed. Two species of internal parasites, one in the stomach the other in the intestines.

Friday 20 August 1875 Cape Collinson
Light airs. Temp. +46° +34°. of sea 29½. Lat. 80°2′35". Long. 70°40′W.
1.15 a.m. Cast off from floe and proceeded under steam. Some very heavy floes about, but the ice in mid-channel going rapidly south and opening up leads. 4 h off Cape M'Clintock. 6.30 stopped and made fast to a floe off C. Collinson. 7.45 cast off and proceeded to northward. 8.45 stopped and made fast to floe. 6–8 p.m. ice moving to southward. Loosened from the ice at Cape John Barrow at 1 o'c. and after some tortuous, and at one point rather dangerous navigation we were brought up by heavy ice on the south side of Richardson Bay. Our observations this day put us in 80°.1′ N. and the *Discovery* 80°.3′. Walked across the floe to the *Discovery* and joining their people who were landing a depot of provisions went on shore. Found but few fossils saw bear-tracks, and droppings of foxes and hares. Vegetation salix, Sax. oppositifolia and *Draba aurea*. Hart dredged in 70 fathoms this morning and brought up several specimens of *Alecto glacialis*, and among the rejecta on the floe I found *Astartes* & a delicate *Terabratula* [*sic*].[3]

Saturday 21 August 1875 Morton's Open Sea?
Light airs. Temp. +47° +40°. of sea +29½° +28°.
5.15 a.m. proceeded under steam. 6 o'c. returned to former position, on finding leads closed ahead 7.15 made fast. 9.30 p.m. Cast off from floe and proceeded under steam. At 10.30 passed into open water extending for about 7 miles across the straits, ice visible all around.
    Still fastened to the floe off Richardson Bay unable to get on. Since passing Cape Fraser the tide flows to south and ebbs to the north, showing that Smiths Sound is not a *cul-de-sac*. When Egerton returned from shore on the 19th he told me that they had seen a pair of falcons and procured three linnets. On examination I found them to be the young of *Plec. nivalis*.[4]
    I have just returned from the crowsnest [*sic*] 5 p.m. and on the E side of Kennedy Channel there is a large amount of open water, so large that it is quite possible this or a similar polynia[5] might have been taken by Morton and Hayes for an open Polar

[1] A genus of scallops.
[2] Common seal.
[3] *Terebratula*, a genus of 'lamp-shells', brachiopods.
[4] Linnets are an Old World species. *Plectrophanes nivalis*, snow bunting.
[5] Open sea surrounded by sea ice; here used to refer to the suppositious open sea surrounding the North Pole. This hypothesis, dating from the 16th century, and revived in the 19th century, was accepted by the German cartographer August Petermann and the American naval officer, cartographer and oceanographer Matthew F. Maury, among others. For a brief statement of their views, see Potter, 'Open Polar Sea', and Hacquebord, 'Cartography', in Nuttall, ed., 2005, pp. 1578–80 and pp. 321–2. Hayes, *Open Polar Sea*, p. 419, states the case concisely: '5. That, with a reasonable degree of certainty, it is shown that, with a strong vessel, Smith Sound may be navigated and the open sea reached beyond it. 6. I have shown that the open sea exists.' The Admiralty, in giving Nares his orders, stated that reaching the North Pole was the main object of the expedition, but they clearly believed that sledging rather than sailing would be the way to get there. See Nares, *Narrative of a Voyage*, I, p. xiv.

Sea.[1] At 9.30 p.m. we cast off from the floe and bored our way for three or four miles through heavy broken up floe, by 11 p.m. we were in a large pool of water but the ice surrounded us with apparently no good lead to the N.

Sunday 22 August 1875 Pass Cape Constitution
Thermo. +50° +44°. of sea +27°. of sea +27° +29°. Lat. 80°21′ N. Long. 70°10′ W.
The ice in the centre (2 a.m.) of the channel is all small pieces with a small floe here and there. From 5.30 a.m. till 6.30 p.m. tacking to avoid ice, a great deal of open water up to Franklin I. where we had to haul to Western shore. 8 p.m., passed a few very extensive floes. No ice along east shore from Franklin I. but could only get into W. coast abreast of Hans I. which we were abreast of at 12 p.m.

Our situation greatly improved for the better, the ice opening up showed us clear water, or rather water with sailing ice far to the northward. We steered in a N.E. direction, Cape Jackson, Washington Land, on our starboard bow. Mt. Adams also. Cape Constitution, Franklin and Crozier Islands plainly visible from the deck. The wind was blowing stiff from the north, and with a strong southerly set of the current against us, our progress was slow. The East coast of Kennedy Channel as laid down by the *Polaris* people appears to be tolerably correct, but the West side as given by Hayes is all "no how". Between 2 and 3 o'*clock* a.m. we stood across the channel under steam and sail. By 9 a.m., we were in a great expanse of clear water, speckled with small ice-bergs and floes of no great extent. At mid-day we stood over again to the eastward, and at 6 p.m., we were between Franklin and Crozier Islands, looking into Lafayette Bay. Morton's description (v. Kane)[2] coincides with our view of the coasts only I think C. Independence of the chart must have been Morton's extreme, for at that spot the cliff descends sheer into the sea, forming a noble headland of 1500 feet.

The open water we have passed through during the last 24 hours is almost devoid of beast or bird life, we have carefully noted every bird seen, and the list sums up to about a dozen dovekies. Not a single gull, seal, whale, walrus or Narwhal.
[*Here Feilden inserted a coloured double-page panorama of the Victoria and Albert Range; see Plate 10.*]

Monday 23 August 1875 Bessel's Bay
Thermo. +52° +47° of sea +27½° +29°. Lat 81°8′N. Long. 64°13W.
2.45 a.m. Channel quite clear of ice, except a few loose pieces. No ice on east shore. On west side, Lady Franklin Bay full of ice. Ship could go close to East shore all along from Hans I. to C. Bryan, there being no ice. 5 h altered course, standing in for C. Lieber. 6.15 shortened sail, altered course, steering in a lead towards shore. 7 h altered for C. Bryan not being able to land on west shore for the ice. On the west side the ice is packed close without any lead through it. 10.30. Hove to off C. Morton. Captain started for the shore but as it came on thick to the north he returned; beat back to Bessel's Bay. 1.50 came to anchor there.

I remained on deck till 4.30 a.m., we were under sail, wind from S. Before us from Joe I. to Petermann Fiord the ice seemed heavily packed. Hall Land, winter quarters of *Polaris*

---

[1] William Morton in Kane, *Arctic Explorations*, appendix V, p. 378.
[2] Ibid.

99

visible some 30 miles ahead. On deck again before breakfast, found that we had lost ground. Finding the ice near Joe I. impenetrable the Captain stood over to west side of channel, no lead showing, made for Bessel's Bay, anchored about 1 p.m. in 7½ fathoms. *Discovery* joined us there. Bessel's Bay is a fiord cut by glacier action out of the limestone with perpendicular walls rising to over 1000 feet at the entrance. Further inland numerous glaciers pour down from Washington Land, and uniting in the fiord form one discharging glacier, owing to the small depth of water the bergs are very small. This bay and probably also Petermann fiord are the discharging points of the mer-de-glace which crowns the summit of Washington land extending nearly to Cape Bryan. In the open water around us bird-life was abundant, many Dovekies nesting in the cliffs flew up to their young with fish in their bills. A flock of fifteen Somateriæ and a Turnstone flew past the ship. At 1.30 p.m. landed with Parr on the west side of Bessel Bay the cliffs descend sheer an altitude of 1000 feet, but a talus in some places clings to the base reaching a height of 300 feet. We scrambled up the extreme point and looked out on Hall Basin, to the westward and towards Polaris Bay the ice appeared jammed, but open water down Kennedy Channel and a lead apparently to Lady Franklin Channel. The south wind blew strong and very cold though the thermo. marked +27°. At 11 p.m. a flock of eight eider ducks past [*sic*] the ship. Whilst returning from the shore shot a ♂ Dovekie flying with a fish in its bill.

Tuesday 24 August 1875 Lady Franklin Strait
Light air. Temp. +50° +40°. of sea +28° +29°. Lat. 81°7'. Long. 64°12'.
12.30 p.m. weighed and made sail. 7.55 passed entrance of Lady Franklin Bay.

Captain Nares went early this morning to the extreme point of land overlooking Petermann fiord, Cape Morton of the chart. He described the fiord on his return as an immense strait blocked with ice and apparently cutting deep into Greenland. As soon as the Captain returned we started for the western side of Hall Basin, passed the mouth of Lady Franklin Fiord but were brought up about 7 p.m. by closely packed ice and we were forced to retrace our course to Lady Franklin Sound.

A haul of the dredge this morning in Bessels Bay temp. 27½° in 7½ fathoms gave few results. The bottom was chiefly rounded limestone peebles, shed from the bergs and as they ground close to where we dredged and scrape the bottom, the paucity of animal life there may be explained. Large laminaria of two kinds were attached to the peebles, in the roots of the laminaria I found two examples of Tro. helicinus[1] a simple astarte, and 2 Aphroditæ[2] and a small starfish. Captain Nares noticed this morning an Eider duck, accompanied by her brood. During the night we neared the shore of Grant Land and entered a beautiful bay about midnight.

Wednesday 25 August 1875 Our First Musk-Sheep. Discovery Bay
Wind light. Bar. 29.78. 29.88. Temp. +40°. +42° +44° of sea +28½° +29½° +30°.
2.10 a.m. anchored in 16 fathoms in a bay on north shore of Lady Franklin Strait. Observed a herd of musk sheep.

I had just turned in, when at 1.30 a.m., I was aroused by the word being passed below that musk-ox were in sight onshore, on getting on deck found that we were within 150

---

[1] *Trochus helicinus*: member of a family of sea snails known as top snails.
[2] Sea mouse or sea aphrodita, a marine polychaete worm, i.e. a worm with bristles on the foot stumps.

yards of the land, and a quarter of a mile inland stood a group of nine musk oxen, at first they were taken for boulders standing out from the snow. A party of six landed and moved by twos to surround the herd. By this time the musk oxen were slightly alarmed and lead [sic] by an old bull were retreating quietly to the mountains, Markham and May killed two and Moss and Parr after a smart chase up a hill killed the remaining seven. The stomachs of these animals is very large that of the bull contained enough salix to have filled four stable buckets.

We have entered on a new geological formation at Discovery Bay, the surrounding hills are of slate, the dip of the strata much contorted in many places vertical.

Turnstones numerous, also Eiders, one Knot shot and I saw three or four more feeding on the beach at low water. Snow buntings flocking. Dabbling with a small dredge brought up Alecto glacialis and Pecten Groenlandicus.[1]

Thursday 26 August 1875
Our first Musk-Sheep. Discovery Bay. <Tern Island.>
Wind light S.E. Bar. 29.78 29.88 Temp. +40° +42° +44° of sea 29°½ +30° +28°½.
2.10 h. a.m. Anchored [in lee of a ?] bay on the north side of Lady Franklin Strait. Observed a herd of musk-oxen ~~12 a.m.~~ 11 a.m. ice outside commenced moving south. 9 p.m. ice outside moving south.[2]
"Wind light force 3 to 0. Bar. 29.90 to 30.07. Thermo. +48° to +43 – of sea +30° +29½. 8.30 a.m. proceeded under steam leaving *Discovery* at anchor. 9.20 found ice jammed at C. Beechey, rounded to inside a small spit off C. Murchison and touched the ground. Went astern and came off. 1.30 shifted berth a little further astern. 3.50 cast off and proceeded, ice jammed off Cape Beechey. 5 h made fast to bergs inside breakwater at the entrance of Discovery Bay. Abs*tract*. of log." Lat 81°41′N. Long. 65°21W.

Unmoored and left our consort at 8 a.m., both ships manned the rigging and cheered. The last I saw of Hart was his long figure clad in scarlet pyjamas and sleeping jacket, clutching the ratlins[3] and yelling enough to burst. Took on board from *Discovery* Rawson & eight men. By 10 o'c. a.m., we were brought up by the ice right across the entrance of Discovery Bay, stretching from Bellot I. to the mainland. Went with Markham and Rawson, about two miles up the coast in the whaler, ascended a hill, water to the south in Hall Basin ice jammed tight in Robeson Channel. Shot a Knot T. canutus ♂, feeding by the sea shore on crustacea. Saw snow buntings in flocks, also a flock of Eider ducks, and females or young. Back to the ship by 2 p.m., our vessel moved at 4 o'c. under the lee of Bellot I. On a little islet close to, some 8 pairs of *Sterna macrura*[4] were nesting found nestling in down.

Friday 27 August 1875 Tern Island, Discovery Bay
Wind calm. Bar. 30.10. Thermo. +47° to +43° of sea +29½ to +28½. +27½? H.W.F.
Ice tightly jammed off entrance to harbour.

---

[1] *Pecten groenlandicus*, now *Similipecten Winckworth*, is a small Arctic scallop.

[2] This short paragraph has been covered over by semi-transparent tape or paper, on which the heading 'Tern Island' has been written.

[3] Ratlines: small lines fastened horizontally on the shrouds of a vessel, and serving as steps by which to go up and down the rigging. *OED*.

[4] Arctic tern.

Had a haul of the dredge in 5 fathoms, temp. +28½, air +26, bottom composed of slate peebles. Several species of shells brought up, Astarte, leda,[1] mya, saxicava also several univalves amongst them examples of Trichotropis borealis,[2] several annelids and some Echinodermata. The stomach of T. canutus killed yesterday contained remains of *Anonyx nugax*.[3] I noticed this bird picking them up on the beach and running breast high into the water in pursuit of them.

The stomach of adult *S. macrura* ♂ shot yesterday was empty but that of the nestling [contained] remains of fish.

Landed on Bellot Island and did some skating. Found a piece of drift-wood on Bellot I. twenty feet above sea level. Caught a butterfly *Argonys*? [sic][4] and the feathers of a ptarmigan were also found. One of our Eskimo dogs ♀ died in parturition this morning, post mortem disclosed the pups in her 7 ♂ & 3 ♀.

Saturday 28 August 1875 Beset in the Pack
"Wind calm. Bar. 30.020 & 29.894. Thermo. +52° to +39°. sea +28° +29°.
2.30 h. p.m. Up steam, grounded on the mud. 5.15 proceeded under steam, passing thro loose ice. 6 h. p.m. steering as required through ice along west side of channel. The ice in the channel loosely packed with some leads along the west coast. 8 h. p.m. whilst going astern, rudder struck ice and got badly sprung. 10 h, there being no lead ahead turned back and steered for a small bay. Watch rigging derrick for getting spare rudder out, made fast to ice. Unshipped rudder. Log." Lat. 81°.41′ N. Long. 65°.22′ W.

In the afternoon we got under weigh and steamed through the ice out of Discovery Bay, keeping close in under the land, at 10 p.m. we rounded Cape Beechey, at 10 p.m., we passed a bay where on shore we saw six musk oxen feeding. We followed the lead for about three quarters of an hour but meeting with impenetrable pack, Captain Nares retraced his steps and returned to the Bay where we had seen the animals feeding. Pushing into the ice as near the shore as possible made fast, six of us were immediatly over the side with a ladder and a collapsible boat, with some difficulty got on shore.

[Aug. 29th 1852. Richards. P. P. p. 118. On a small island near Table island. N.L. 77°8′. Belcher channel. "The only animal life seen here were the grey tern, which, I believe, inhabit every part of the known earth; they were not very numerous, but extremely sociable and tame; two or three young ones unfledged were found, but, like most of the flowers we find here, they had blown too late, and would perish before they had feathers enough to protect them from the severity of the winter."][5]

---

[1] *Leda pernula*, now called *Nuculana pernula*, in the mollusc subphylum Conchifera.
[2] A cap snail.
[3] A small amphipod.
[4] *Argynnis*, a fritillary (butterfly).
[5] Square brackets in original. George Henry Richards (1844–1904) was second in command under Edward Belcher on HMS *Assistance*'s Arctic expedition of 1852–4, and carried out extensive sledge explorations to the north of Melville Sound and the Wellington Channel. See Belcher, *Last of the Arctic Voyages*, pp. 106–7. *Arctic Blue Books*, 1855, p. 118; Richards's papers from this expedition are in the Scott Polar Research Institute, MS GB 15 Sir George Richards. The 'grey tern' is the Arctic tern.

Sunday 29 August 1875 <u>Shift Rudder Bay</u>
"Weather calm. Bar. 29.81 & 29.71. Thermo. +39° +47°. Sea +29° +28½°.
4 h. p.m. A good deal of water along west coast, but to the eastward the floes seemed packed and closer. 4.20 proceeded under steam picked up the Captain & steered northward. Passing through open water on western shore with heavy pack outside. 8 h. steering close in along the west shore to the northward, with very heavy floes and large hummocks outside of us, ice going south. After passing Cape Frederick VII, the ice was in heavy loosely packed pieces up towards C. Union with no lead round the cape. 10.30 h. made fast to a large floe in a small bay north of C. Frederick VII. Ice still continued going south & opening out towards C. Union. Log." Lat. at noon 81°.52′. Long. 63°.45′ W.

Monday 30 August 1875 <u>Beset in the Pack</u>
"Wind calm. Bar. 29.73 to 29.93. Temp. +42° to +50°. Sea +29°.
1.30 h. p.m., cast off from floe. Party returned from landing depot. Proceeded steering as requisite between floes towards C. Union 2.45 h. stopped and made fast to some heavy pieces of floe ice 3.30 cast off from ice as it was closing round ship and made towards shore. 4.10 h. stopped, up rudder, beset with very heavy floes. 10.15 h. up steam and attempted to get out out of pack failed. 11.30 made another attempt failed. Drifting south in pack. Lat. at noon 82°.6′.44′. Long. 62°.45′."

Tuesday 31 August 1875 <u>Lincoln Bay</u>
"Weather calm. Bar. 29.86 to 29.60. Temp. +49° to +43° of sea +29°.
Lat. at noon same as yesterday.
12.30 h. a.m. Going ahead and astern as requisite, attempted to clear pack without success. 1.45 again unshipped rudder, 8.50 slipped rudder. 9.30 proceeded under steam cleared pack and entered Lincoln Bay."

[Geese migrating S.E, down Belcher Channel. v. Richards. P.P. 120. 1ˢᵗ. Sept 1852].[1]

Wednesday 1 September 1875 <u>The *Alert* rounds Cape Union. Most Northern Latitude Yet Attained by Any Ship</u>
"Strong breeze blowing up channel force 6–9. [*Bar. 29.53. Temp. +40° +47° +50°.*] of sea +29°.
12.30 h. Loose ice drifted up from south, 1 h pack began to move north quickly. 4 h, too thick to see the state of the ice. 5 h, squalls became more violent, ice moving NE as far as could be seen, for the thick weather. 9.0 read prayers. 9.15 Cast off from floe, and made sail to single reefed topsails and foresail. 10 set top gallant sails. 11.30 in T. Gᵗ. sails. Pack about 4 miles from shore (W. side) 12 h. meridian hoisted ensign being further north than any other ship. 12.20 Furled sails, proceeded under steam in one boiler until we came to the end of the lead, then returned and took shelter behind a line of big grounded hummocks."

---

[1] Square brackets in original. *Arctic Blue Books*, 1855, p. 120.

PART II: WINTER QUARTERS
2 SEPTEMBER 1875–1 APRIL 1876

[Sept 2nd 1852. Richards. P.P. p. 120.[1] Grove shot a walrus this evening, but could not decapitate him for want of tools. N. shore of Grinnell Land. Lat. 77.].[2]

Thursday 2 September 1875 <u>Winter Quarters</u>
"Wind very strong from S.W. [*Bar 29.40″ – 29.38″ Temp +48° +46°*] of sea +29°.
12.30 h. a.m., endeavoured to steam inside a line of grounded hummocks. Let go starboard anchor in 3 fathoms, a heavy squall struck the ship a few minutes afterwards, dragged our anchor, veered until we brought up with 6 shackles of cable. Unbent cable from port bower anchor and bent it to sheet anchor ready for letting go. 9.0 Wind suddenly shifting caused ship to swing on to grounded hummocks inshore. Up steam 9.30 weighed and shifted berth inside of grounded hummocks. made fast with 6 in 5 in & 3½ in hawsers aft. Pack closed the land rapidly, moving south at sametime."[3]

Early this morning I noticed a Dovekie pass the ship head to wind. About 9 a.m., wind shifted to the northward, pack closing in on us at the rate of knots, got up anchor and steamed inshore behind line of grounded hummocks at the same spot from whence we were blown out last night, shortly after we got into shelter the pack closed on our hummocks and sealed us in. A Turnstone flew past the ship. In the afternoon Aldrich called me on deck to see a large bird in a small pool about 150 yards off as far as I could make out it was an example of Colymbus septentrionalis. I lowered ice-boat and went in pursuit, we alarmed the bird which flew along shore to the southward and alighted in another pool about half a mile from the ship, getting on to the hummocks. I tried to work down to the bird but the fissures between the blocks were filled with soft snow, which let me through, and I very soon had to give up the chase.

This place looks like our winter quarters, Resumed playing whist in the Captains cabin. Lamps lighted below for first time. Turned in at 11o'c. and had a jolly sleep.

Friday 3 September 1875 <u>Floeberg Beach.</u>
Wind light or calm. Bar 29″.48. Temp. +47° +43° of sea +29°.
Ice moving to north all middle watch. Afternoon employed getting out 8 inch hawser and securing to hummock.

---

[1] See above, p. 102, n. 5.
[2] Square brackets in original, also for details in first line of 2 September entry.
[3] Feilden consistently writes 'sametime' for 'same time'. He used the information from the ship's log (Nares, Log Book, HMS *Alert*, 1875–1876) for his account of wind, temperature, and sea temperature, as well as latitude and longitude on the outward and homeward voyages. Sometimes, as in this entry, he transcribed further details from the log, and he often but not always used inverted commas to indicate that the log was his source.

An Eider duck cruising round, a flock of Harelda glacialis swimming in a pool 200 yards from the ship – these birds are still in their summer plumage. Thermo falling rapidly, ice forming round the ship. Our Eskimo dogs are turned out of the ship and put on shore.

Saturday 4 September 1875 Floeberg Beach.
Wind light. Bar 29.56 29.75. Temp +46° +38°. of sea +29°.
12.15 h. meridian, ice stationary, 1. h ice began moving to north and continued doing so all the watch, considerably quicker in shore than further out. Ice moving to the north until about 7 p.m. Very hummocky in passing pieces being piled up to a height of over 30 feet.

Sunday 5 September 1875 Floeberg Beach.
Temp +45° +40°. of sea +29°.
10.a.m. Commander and first lieut[1] left ship with dog sledges.

Monday 6 September 1875
A slight fall of snow beetwen 12 and 2.30 a.m. 6o'c. Wind freshening and snow falling – very thick. 8 o'c. Fog thick. 6 p.m., cleared a little. 8 p.m., ice moving very slowly north. Bar. 29°.734 to 29°.67. Max. temp. +14°, Min. +9°.
[Sept 6th 1852. Richards P.P. p. 122.[2] Saw two or three seals and some snow buntings today. N. shore Grinnell Land.]

Tuesday 7 September 1875 Floeberg Beach.
Bar. Max 30°.01. Min. 29°.642. Thermo Max. +18°½ Min. +13°.
Six a.m., heavy snow. Ten p.m., no motion apparent among the ice.

Wednesday 8 September 1875
Landing Martin's anchor,[3] ranging cables &c. No visible motion in ice. Weather almost calm. Bar. 30°.10 to 29°.998. Max. temp. +22°. Min. +15½. Snowing lightly, most lovely crystals falling. Temp. of sludge on surface of floe +26°.5.

Thursday 9 September 1875 Dog-Sledging
Left the ship with three dog sledges at 11.45 a.m, under the command of Lieut. Aldrich. Party, Dr Moss, Mr White and self. Sailors, Ayles and Simmonds, Petersen the Dane, and Frederick the Greenlander.[4] Thermo. at starting +17°. average weight of sledges 400 lbs. wind from N.N.W. true, blowing in our faces and lifting clouds of snow, made it rather difficult to see. The breath soon congealed, and the hair on our faces rapidly covered with icicles. In many places the snow was deep and soft, and our utmost exertions had to be used to haul the loads over and through the drifts. I was working with Petersen in the last sledge carrying the pemmican, and ran behind the sledge or pushed the whole 14 miles to camp.

[1] Pelham Aldrich.
[2] *Arctic Blue Books*, 1855, p. 122.
[3] François Martin's self-canting anchor (patented 1859), with swivelling flukes and shackles. Gay, *Six millenaires d'histoire des ancres*, p. 202.
[4] George White, engineer; Adam Ayles, 2nd captain foretop; John Simmonds, 2nd captain maintop; N. C. Petersen, Inuit interpreter; Frederick the Greenlander was in charge of the dogs.

Once our sledge went with runner under the ice which gave us a grand haul, Mr White's great strength coming in useful, as we three got the sledge out. Passing over rotten places in the floe hanging on to back of sledge got four times into the water up to the knees. Our course lay in a N.W. b[y] W. direction towards Cape Joseph Henry. Got into camp at 6 h.15 m. p.m, but had not our tents up till 9 h. 30 m. p.m, as we were rather green at the work. Temp. in tent rose during night to +30°. Slept well and warmly. Just before getting into camp Dr Moss shot a *Phoca fetida* at a small waterhole, which was secured, and added greatly to our supply of blubber. The greater part of the blubber was cached for future use, and the flesh gave our 24 dogs a good feed. These animals do not like the meat biscuit provided for them, they leave it on the snow, whilst anything made of leather left lying about such as harness whips, gaiters or mits disappears down their ravenous maws. My sub-lingual temp on getting into the tent was 98°.7.

Friday 10 September 1875 <u>Walden Lake</u>
It was 11o'c. before we got some cocoa and biscuit. At 12. m. Lieut. Aldrich started with two heavily laden dog sledges, Symmonds & Frederick the Greenlander, to put out a dêpot to the northward in the direction of Cape Joseph Henry. [*Here, Feilden tipped in a sketch map copied from Aldrich's chart of the route taken by the dog sledges to lay down a depot; see Figure 10, p. 107.*] Dr Moss, Mr White and I started for the head of the bay where our camp was. At its head is a deep ravine running up in a S. direction to the mountains. The channel course leading down to the sea, at an elevation of 40 feet, exposed beds of pulverized limestone, replete with shells – the majority retained the epidermis as fresh as if only just dredged up from the sea. Proof of recent elevation. In the ravine the dip of the rock was to S.W. true at an angle of 45°. The formation thinly laminated slate limestone with veins of carbonate of lime* [*Margin: ?Quartz. H.W.F.*] traversing it, and large quantities of cubes of iron pyrites. No trace of fossil remains. The rock here appears identical with the Silurian slates of North Wales. Crossing head of this bay to the north side, ascended 400 feet. About a mile and a half or two miles from the sea we (Moss and I, White having turned back) came on a lake of considerable size about 3 miles long and one and a half broad. There is one small islet in this lake, on which we built a little cairn. Found vertebra of a small fish in the droppings of a bird on this island, which leads to the supposition that there are fish in the lake. All over this district the exposed rocks are clad with the yellow lichen so abundant in Greenland, also several species of gray lichen. We then crossed the lake in a N.N.E. course, a very cold wind was blowing behind us driving the snow in clouds over us, its minute *spiculae*[1] stinging any exposed surface of our bodies, ascending to higher ground about 400 feet, we travelled along a ridge plentifully bestrewed with erratic boulders. *Gneiss, Granite, Quartzose* rocks with garnets, the formation *in situ*, being the Silurian slate which forms the whole of the neighbouring district. The absence of Glaciers in this country is worthy of remark and future investigation. The snow clad mountain peaks inland, rising to an altitude of at least 2000 feet high are as well fitted, apparently, for the birth place of the ice rivers, as the mountains of Greenland. Taking into consideration the very rapid elevation of the land, apparent to us at every step, it is just possible that the glaciers may now be forming in the mountain sides, but will take a long period to creep down to the present coast line. To my mind,

---

[1] Spikes.

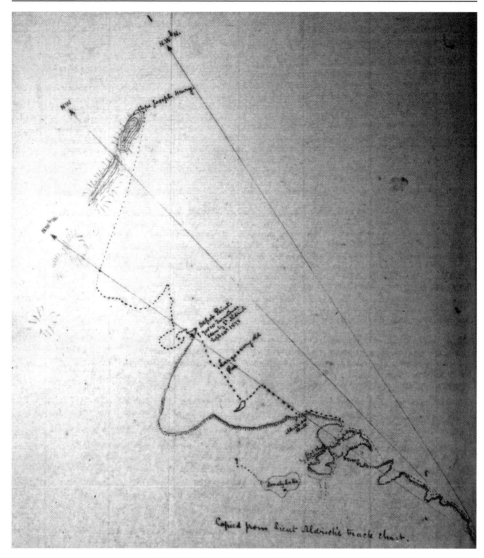

Figure 10.   Lieutenant Aldrich's sketch map of the route taken by dog sledges to lay down a depot.

however, there is unmistakeable [*sic*] geological evidence to show, that this portion of our globe has emerged from a much greater pre-glacial epoch than exists at present, and future observations may demonstrate that the retreat of the glacial epoch in Europe, was coincident with a similar change in the North Polar regions. We saw many tracks of Lemmings, and one Hare's near to the sea. Returned to camp by 3o'c. and eat some frozen seal liver which Petersen gave me. Rather oily but not bad. Crossing the bay to the tent, we passed the place where Aldrich had shot some Eider Ducks, <on 5th,> and which he was then unable to procure, as they were killed in a water hole, now the place was frozen over, but our dogs had been before us, and three holes in the young ice, and a few feathers all that remained, felt much disappointed, as it was carelessness on my part not having gone to look for these birds as soon as we got to camp last night, or early this morning. The ice on the above mentioned lake apparently never entirely melts, as a large surface was occupied by heavy floe which in one place was piled in small hummocks on shore. The structure of this floe [drawing] was crystals total thickness about 4 ft. On our return to the tent stockings firmly [drawing] frozen to the soles of boots though the temperature only marked +14°. inside [drawing] of the tent +22° which rapidly rose to +28°. Moss's sublingual temp was 99°.3.

Non melting of ice on fresh water lakes. see Parry 2nd. Voy. p. 313. Captain Lyon in his reports to the above mentioned officer records same fact. (id.)[1]

Saturday 11 September 1875 <u>Walk from Dumbell Bay</u>
Left camp with Dr Moss at 9 a.m. crossed the bay in front of our tent and walking towards the N. got to an elevation of 400 feet. Snow very heavy and soft, sinking up to our knees at every step. Found traces of Ptarmigans, on all the exposed ridges where the snow had some what drifted off, these birds had dusted down to the *Papaver*[2] heads, and eaten the seeds. Under the snow we found *Salix arctica*, in one spot withered *Potentilla*, and large quantities of *Sax. oppositifolia*. This flora with *Alopecurus alpinus*[3] & *Poa alpina*?[4] gave indications of sufficient verdure to support *Musk oxen* in the summer. *Lemming* tracks were numerous, and as usual the droppings of *Foxes* that we came across were entirely composed of the remains of these little animals. The *Foxes* pass the under jaws and feet of the Lemming, little altered by the action of the gastric juices. Getting to the crest of the hill, the great bay betweeen us and Cape Joseph Henry lay before us. The view was very striking far to the north and to seaward nothing but an ocean of frozen hummocks, towards the bight of the bay and extending for a mile to seaward, and for several miles along the coast was a border of tremendous floe, undoubtedly permanent, and the result of long periods of freezing. Its surface was peculiar, rising in round knobs, and humped back ridges, which were polished by the heat of the sun, and subsequent freezing, to an extent that prevented the snow resting on the exposed surfaces, and at a distance lead us to imagine that it was open water, walking down to the shore we took up Lieut. Aldrich's sledge-tracks, and followed them some distance on the floe, but finding the walking difficult, and slippery we made again for the coastline, making a mile or two more of northing. Here we had excellent examples of the pressure exerted by the sea and pack on fixed ice. The stupendous floe above noted, which extended as a natural breakwater nearly a mile to seaward, was driven on shore, its edge pressed up into enormous lumps, many of them 25, or 30 feet thick, before lifting themselves up they had ploughed into the shore, driving the shingle up into ridges 6 or 8 feet high. Near this point, which is in lat. 82°.35 N. (approximately) we picked up the skull of a ♂[5] *musk ox*, which gives good hope for our spring hunting parties. From this point we went on the back track rounding *Sickle Spit*, at this point we noticed some

[1] Parry, *Journal of a Second Voyage*, p. 313. George Francis Lyon, 1795–1832: see *ODNB*.
[2] The yellow Arctic poppy, *Papaver radicatum*. Feilden sometimes italicizes English as well as Latin names of flora and fauna.
[3] Alpine foxtail, a grass.
[4] Alpine meadow-grass.
[5] See above, p. 52, n. 1.

stones, that might have been artificially placed. [Very doubtful.] Three miles of tolerably smooth ice brought us back to camp by 3.p.m. We had walked 14 miles in this 6 hours. Changed stockings rested one hour, and as there was no further need of my remaining in camp, started at 4 p.m., for the ship, only carrying my gun. 7 miles from camp, met Lieut Parr, with sledge and men <proceeding N.,> time 6 o'c. That officer told me that on his journey he had picked up a Narwhal's tooth 4 ft 6 in., long. I reached the ship at 8.21 min. p.m., having done 14 miles in 4 hours and a half <21 minutes>. The Thermo. stood at plus 9°. Fahr. What little wind was blowing came from N.W, and favorable to me. I do not think that these kind of trips are wise on the part of a single traveller, had fog come on, or high wind with drifting, blinding snow, I should not have made the ship, and a day or two would probably have been lost in hunting up the missing one, entailing serious loss of time to the expedition. My sub lingual temp. before starting <from camp> was 98°. Though very warm when arriving onboard, found stockings frozen to soles of boots and handkerchief stiff as a board. Felt nearly overcome with thirst towards the end of my walk, having only had a cup of cocoa at 8 a.m, and a wine glass of rum and water at 3. p.m. Refrained, however from eating snow. Picked up Lieut. Egertons haversack some 4 miles from ship and brought it back, shortly after a small parcel belonging to one of Lieut. Parrs party, these articles were dropped from the sledge I met. Came across the place where this party had lunched found some small fragments of meat, and a piece of biscuit which I eat. I picked up some small droppings of an animal this morning containing Lemming bones which are probably those of *Musleta* [*sic*] *erminea*.[1] The majority of the lumps of piled up floe, which we looked at this morning were of cerulean blue colour. Not a single bird or any living wild animal did I see the whole day. The horns of the Musk-ox found today measured 25 inches from base to tip inside of curve, and 12 inches at broadest part of base. Richardson (F.B. Am. p. 277.)[2] remarks of this species "The horns are very broad at their origin covering the brow and whole crown of the head, and touching each other for their entire breadth from before backwards". This touching of the base of the horns I have not observed in any of the specimens, hitherto come under my notice. In the skull found today a considerable amount of the animals woolly hair was sticking between the base of the horns.

Sunday 12 September 1875 <u>Dog-Sledging Party Return</u>
Divine service in the morning. Walked with Captain Nares, Lieuts Giffard[3] & Rawson towards Cape Union, much open water extending in a belt along the shore from Cape Union to the N.W. At 10 p.m. began to blow strong from the S.W. gale continued throughout the night.

It seems to me almost certain that a diligent search will reveal gold in the quartz veins, which traverse the Silurian slates of this district, if we come across igneous rocks obtruding into, and altering the slates, we may rest assured that we shall. (Vide Murchison Siluria 5th. Edit. p. 449.)[4] If no opportunity occurs this autumn, which I am afraid will not as all

---

[1] *Mustela erminea*, stoat.
[2] Richardson et al., *Fauna Boreali-Americana*, I, p. 277.
[3] George Augustus Giffard (1849–1925), Lieutenant in HMS *Alert* (retired as Admiral).
[4] Murchison, *Siluria*, p. 449.

running water is now frozen up, I must next year do some diligent hand washing in the mountain streams. Lieut. Aldrich's party returned to the ship this afternoon, leaving old Michael the dog behind, who fell down in fit some miles from the ship.

Monday 13 September 1875

The S.W. gale continued to blow all day, causing us considerable anxiety as to the comfort of our sledging parties out under Markham. The snow came drifting from off shore covering the ship, and obscuring the land. The ice that keeps us in shows some signs of weakness today.

Tuesday 14 September 1875

At 2 a.m., Ice still setting out, and moving to south. Wind blowing a fierce gale strength B.[1] N. 10. Bar 29°.48″ Temp. +21°. 8 a.m., squalls very heavy blowing 10. This continued all day Bar. at 4 p.m., 29°.21″ lowest of the day. Temp +23°. whole gale blowing. this was a day of considerable anxiety, our sledging parties under Markham still absent, a fearful wind with heavy snow drift enveloping them, and the only hopeful feature the comparative high range of the Thermometer. The condition of the ship was also somewhat critical, every scrap of ice between us and the shore had drifted out, and we were lying broadside on to the grounded hummocks, striking incessantly against them with heavy thuds, the force of the wind canted us over in the direction from which it blew at an angle of 4° or 5°. The hummocks stood out bravely. We were fastened to the shore by a chain cable, anchor on shore and a hawser. About 4 p.m., the Captain during a temporary lull endeavoured to send a boat with another hawser on shore. 4 men left in a boat but the gale increasing, drifted them out to ~~wind~~<sea>ward, and as the only resource they made fast to a detached hummock. Captain Nares, Lieut Giffard and seven men landed on the berg against which the ship was thumping, hauling a boat and whale line after them, and by dint of two hours hard work got their boat again to leaward of the first one, which slipped from its fastening, and drifting down, was safely collared. All returned safe on board. About half past nine p.m., a man was seen on shore, shouting, evidently one of our sledging party. Lieut. Giffard and 8 men went ashore, (a desperately hard pull.) We then saw the boat returning with 8 men on board, whilst Lt Giffard and the other started along shore to the N.W. On the boat coming alongside we found that the late arrival was Commander Markham. The sledges under his command started from a point 4 miles N. of Sickle point or 18 miles from the ship at 9 o'c. a.m., His party had made first rate travelling and got within 3 miles of the ship, where Com. Markham intended camping, when one of his men, Shirley,[2] gave out, and had to be put on the sledge. Markham then pressed on with Shirley, and a single sledge to the ship, but about a mile and a half off, his men gave in, and he himself seeing the urgency of the case pressed on to the ship for assistance. When Giffard got to the sledge he found them all much exhausted, and trying to pitch a tent. Happily all were brought on board a little after 12 p.m. Com. Markham saw on the 11th four birds which he thinks a species of Loom, and picked up a piece of drift wood on a floe in N. Lat 82°31′. Lieut Parr picked up a Narwhal's horn on the 11th. This horn was found partly imbedded in shingle, to a depth of a foot or more and about two

---

[1] Feilden does not usually use this abbreviation. B. is for Beaufort, who devised a number system for strength of winds.

[2] John Shirley, stoker.

foot of snow over it, it measured 5 ft. 7 in, and apparently a foot at the tip had been broken off in removing it from the soil. its greatest thickness being 8 inches in circumference. From the discovery of this cetacean's remains we must not definitively state that the Narwhal is at present an inhabitant of these seas, for it is possible that it may be a fossil from one of the raised beaches so common in this part. The state of preservation in which we have found fossil shells, at considerable altitude, showing that no reliance can be drawn, as to the age of the fossil, from its state of preservation.

Wednesday 15 September 1875 <u>Drift Wood</u>
Lt. Parr and Egerton's parties arrived abreast of the ship at 10 a.m., and got onboard by 11o'c. The wind at this time had lulled. Orders were given to light fires in both boilers, screw and rudder to be shipped, before this was accomplished a snow storm came on, which prevented Captain Nares leaving our present anchorage, his intention being to have steamed to the N.W. and endeavour to find more secure winter quarters. The piece of drift wood found by Captain Markham's party on the 12th. inst., was brought on board this morning, it appears to be a portion of a branch torn off the trunk of a tree, and at the time of finding it, retained some bark, which was also brought away. This piece of drift measured about 3 foot in length, and 1 foot at its greatest circumference, it was in excellent preservation a section showing the ~~medullary~~ <annular> rings, over 70 in number and giving out an unmistakeable [*sic*] odour of turpentine. Shirley, the man who was overcome by his exertions yesterday, is much better today, under the kind treatment of Dr Colan, our fleet surgeon, who combines with his professional skill, the art of nursing his patient, with unceasing care. On making enquiries I found as a general rule that the men employed in the late sledgings did not open their bowels during their absence, four days, nor did they feel any uneasiness in consequence, the small allowance of fluid imbibed per day, and the great amount of perspiration induced by exertion, renders micturation seldom necessary. The urine passed is highly coloured, I suppose with bile. I have verified these observations in my own person. Lieut. Parr yesterday noticed a single Snow bunting, it is remarkable that this bird should remain behind its comrades to battle with such a tempest as has been blowing, how birds of this species obtain any water to drink is a puzzle to me. Every rivulet stream and lake is now frozen over, if shallow, frozen solid.

Thursday 16 September 1875
It blew a gale from the S.W. from midnight till morning when it gradually lulled. Spring tide at 1 o'c. a.m., and a whole gale blowing did not move the hummocks outside of the ship, so that we may look upon them as firm friends. All morning engaged in endeavouring to get shaft into screw. On hauling up the screw in the afternoon it was found that some ice had got inside the hole in the screw <boss>, and prevented the butt end of the shaft fetching home. When the shaft is withdrawn, (and screw elevated), it causes a vacuum, and the ice rushing through the aperture lodges in the orifice from which the shaft has been taken. During this time lost in getting the screw in order   the opportunity was missed of proceeding to the N.W., to a more secure   anchorage. One of the Marines who accompanied Commander   Markham's sledging party, is very ill today, and Dr Colan was   attending him all night, the poor man, I understand is suffering from   exhaustion, and collapse of the heart. It seems to me that cardiac complaints must   be engendered

111

by Arctic service, it is impossible that any men of ordinary physical strength can go through the labour and exertion requisite, without weakening their constitutions. I had a busy day in my cabin, there being no chance of landing. High temperature and consequently melting of condensation on roof of cabin. cleared all the ice I could off skylight, and stretched a cloth underneath to catch dripping, tacked a blanket over my bed, and cut off the supply of water that has been disturbing me at night, falling on my face. Tried to repack and arrange specimens, so as to give a little space for turning in. Hung up a few pictures and cleared up a good deal. I regret very much that I did not bring a couple of thousand cigars or cheroots with me. Pipes on sledge work are objectionable, they get frozen, baccy pouch gets full of snow [&c.?] A smoker wants a good cigar before turning over to sleep. one a day is sufficient as it is impossible to smoke whilst travelling.

Friday 17 September 1875
1 A.m., Ice setting north and off shore. Noon, floes outside setting to S.E. Blowing hard in squalls all day. Bar. max. 29.748. min 29°.60'. Max Temp. 36°½. Min. 29°. In the present state of the weather it was unadvisable to go on shore, though the Captain kindly offered to send me for an hour. The floe which has been driven off for the last few days by a continuance of S.W. gales, has reappeared outside of our sentinel hummocks. During the height of the late gales the snow was completely blown off the shore line, today we notice, that a bank of snow quite perpendicular and of some breadth fringes the shore, to the level of the beach, forming a snow-foot which will soon turn into an ice-foot. The hill tops in our neighbourhood are very bare of snow. The wind has regularly swept the exposed surfaces. Markham and Parr tell me that on the 14th. inst, when exposed to the full fury of the gale, pieces of stone as large as filbert nuts, were often flying about their heads, the bergs that form our protection to seaward, are now covered with dust and small peebles blown from the shore.

Saturday 18 September 1875
Calm throughout day with light airs from N.N.W. to E.N.E. Max. Temp. +36° Min. +19°. Bar. Max. 30.25", Min 29.646". 2 a.m., ice moving slowly north, 3.30 Wind fell and pack closed, one very heavy floe passed quickly to N. taking against the outside of our protecting hummocks, but without doing any harm. 1.45 p.m., ice began again moving to the northward. 7 p.m., ice moving south and off shore. 10 p.m. ice suddenly moved in, and considerable nipping took place against our protecting hummocks. This is copied from the prosaic leaf of the deck log. Words, however, can hardly explain to a person who has not been in these regions the power of ice in movement. Our ship lay in a bight formed by Cape Union to the S.E, and a spit running out to the N.W. on which the floes coach-wheeled and were deflected, whilst between us and the sea were several immense masses of grounded floe, which if seen in Baffin's Bay, would be called bergs. The height of these larger pieces was between twentyfive and thirty feet above the water level, and grounded so firmly as to have withstood to our knowledge, and safety, a full gale from the S.W. of four days duration, without drifting off the shelving bank on which they were grounded. The irresistible force of the ice was magnificently displayed on this occasion, slowly and solemnly the floe advanced, like well disciplined battalions to the attack, a sentinel berg of solid blue ice rising fifteen to twenty feet above the water, on feeling the presence of the floe, crumbled away and disappeared like a feather in a bowl of molten lead, or a house

opposed to a giant lava stream. Onwards the floe pushed and as it came in contact with our still bigger protecting hummocks, the mode of attack was changed, and the edges of the floe began to crawl up the sides of our friendly bergs, and at last deposited great lumps of ice on their summits, then as if by magic the signal of recall was passed along the line of battle, and the ice king withdrew his forces, just as slowly, just as solemnly, and leaving on our minds the same sense of his majesty as when he advanced to the attack. A specimen of *Arcturus* brought on board by one of the men it differs from plate in Wyville Thompson's ("Depths of the Sea" p. 128)[1] by having no spines on the back, and the third arm or thoracic plate, equal in length to the two preceding ones.
If a new species I propose calling it *Arcturus Mossii* after Surgeon
D[r] E. L. Moss Surgeon, R.N – and a member of the expedition.[2] The Quartermaster on watch at breakfast time informed me that he had seen a duck fly past the ship, during the morning. In the first watch, about 8 p.m, Lieut. Egerton saw thirteen birds, either ducks or looms[3] fly past the ship, outside our line of grounded hummocks and towards S.E.

Sunday 19 September 1875

On the 3rd of this month we noticed ten *Harelda glacialis* swimming in a lead two hundred yards from the ship. This morning about 7 a.m., two more of this species alighted in the vicinity of the ship. Lieut. Parr who was on watch, lowered the dingy and procured them both. I am much indebted to this Officer for the assistance he has invariably given me in the collection of objects of Natural History. The ice is again forming around the ship, but it will be several days before we shall be able to get on shore by walking. The moon in her third quarter was bright at 7.30 p.m in the N. The sun by that time had disappeared behind the high ground to the W. The difficulties that the collector in the various branches of natural history has to contend against in these regions are almost insurmountable. He can only hope for a month or six weeks in the year, when the ground is partially clear of snow, this is also the best period for navigation, so that he can only land for short and uncertain periods. From the time of entering Smith's Sound the use of the towing net has been almost prevented from the constant accompaniment of ice, and with the best intentions on the part of Captain Nares and his officers, it has been only feasible to lower the dredge three times in the same period, and then only in shallow waters. When the snow begins to melt in June, the ground becomes for three weeks or a month like a bog, and distances can no longer be traversed by sledges on account of the sludge. the ravines become impassable from the melting snow. To enable me to leave the ship for a few days in the summer, I must devise some means of transport, which will enable me to carry 100 lbs of *impedimenta*. The most likely plan that I can think of at present is to make pack saddles for some of the dogs, each dog will carry 20 lbs. and five of them would transport bedding and food for a weeks supply for two men. In reference to the use of the dogs, it seems to me that their services might be utilised in the chase of the Musk oxen, we are informed by authors that these animals when threatened by wolves,

[1] C. W. Thomson, *Depths of the Sea*, p. 128.
[2] *Arcturus*: a small isopod crustacean. Miers, 'Report on the Crustacea', p. 243, notes of *Arcturus baffini*: 'A single specimen was collected, with many of the variety I have designated *Feildeni*, by Dr Moss ...'. See Moss, *Shores of the Polar Sea*, p. 11.
[3] 'A name given in northern seas to species of the guillemot and the diver, esp. *Alca bruennichi* and *Colymbus septentrionalis* (Red-throated diver).' *OED*.

huddle together and show a firm phalanx of heads, to the agressors, if they can thus be brought to bay it will save an immensity of fatigue to the huntsmen. My impression is that all the fresh water lakes we meet with are old glacier beds, and we must therefore not omit to sound, and observe whether the greatest depth is to be found at the head or end of the lake. First star visible this evening about 9 p.m.

Monday 20 September 1875
Temp., still high so that the young ice does not form rapidly. skinned the two *Harelda glacialis*. killed yesterday, one was a ♀, the other I could not sex, so that it is probably a bird of the season. These birds were fat and in good condition, their stomachs contained remains of small crustaceans, and peebles of limestone and quartz. Put under a Queketts microscope[1] no trace of shells could be discovered. Michael one of the dogs returned to day, looking very poor and thin.ˣ [*Margin*: ˣPetersen's report to me after returning from shore feeding dogs] When Aldrich and his party returned last Sunday but one (the 12ᵗʰ) this dog had a fit, its trace was cut, and it was left on the *track*, the animal has now returned after an absence of eight days. One of the bitches died in labour this evening, this is the second case. I have hitherto refrained from making any remarks in my journal about the sickness of these dogs, as at present I have come to no definite conclusion in the matter.

Tuesday 21 September 1875
Captain G.F. Lyon, (Private Journal H.M.S. *Hecla* 1824.)[2] Gives the best account I have met with of the Eskimos, and their habits. At p. 375. id. Captain Lyon gives an account told by his friend Ooyarra of a bear killing a Walrus by dropping a block of ice, from a height on it. Hall in his "Life amongst the Esquimaux"[3] tells a somewhat similar anecdote in reference to Bears and Seals, and gives an engraving of the subject. We have also the following from the pen of the accurate and distinguished naturalist Fabricius (p. 23) "fragmenta enim glaciei prehendens in caput rosmari protrudens, vacillare facit, et sic facile occidit."[4] Taking all this independent testimony into consideration it would be hard to disbelieve this great sagacity on the part of *Ursus maritimus*. Went onshore with Captain Nares and Dʳ Moss for a couple of hours at mid-day. Dʳ Moss shot a fine *Hare*. Put a net overboard through a hole in the ice, baited with a *Hare's* head, only brought up a couple of small crustaceans. Old Michael came to me on shore, and wagged his tail, his feet were sound, and he does not seem out of condition.

Wednesday 22 September 1875
Lieut Aldrich with two dog sledges left the ship at 10.30 a.m., *en route* for Cape Joseph Henry. calm with light airs, a good deal of snow fell. The ice bears sufficiently to walk on shore. Helped to build a snow hut, and walked to the N.W. for a mile. Foggy.

---

[1] John Thomas Quekett (1815–61) was a histologist and microscopist, who invented a folding dissecting microscope *c*.1845.

[2] Lyon, *Private Journal*.

[3] Hall, *Arctic Researches*.

[4] Fabricius, *Fauna Groenlandica*. 'Indeed, seizing fragments of ice [and] thrusting [them] at the head of the walrus, it [i.e. the bear] makes it totter, and thus easily kills it.'

Thursday 23 September 1875

Left the ship with Capt. Nares and Lieut. Giffard at 10.30 a.m. returned at 2.30 p.m. We walked over Beacon hill towards Mount Pullen, getting within about 3½ miles of its base, then turning to our right we came back by the ravine that leads from Mt. Pullen and discharges into the sea about a mile and a half <N.W.> from our winter quarters. The snow was very heavy in this ravine, walking tedious. The day was fine, bright and clear. We had a good view of the mountains to the N.W. and the Congress Highlands, on the other side of Robeson Channel, looked quite close. In the bed of the ravine we came across a boulder of Syenite about 4 ft by 3. Nearly round, it was polished so smooth that passing the hand over it one could feel neither crack or flaw, indeed it looked as if it had come from a lapidarys lathe. Came across another small boulder which I recognised as being of Silurian conglomerate, a rock which I have not seen *in situ* since leaving Cape Hilgard. These boulders have probably been washed down from the slopes of Mt. Pullen, and so far point out that when its uplands were submerged the set of the glacial drift current must have been from S. to N. Dʳ Bessels records the same observation from Hall's Land. (vide "Bull. de la Soc. de Geo. Paris" – March 1875. p. 298.)[1]

We have been somewhat puzzled hitherto, to explain a curious noise which occurs in some places covered with snow, when walked over. I heard it for the first time today, and I think the reason can be satisfactorily accounted for. The noise resembled a heavy thud, then travelled along under the snow, sounding like a heavy gun fired at a distance, or far off thunder. Wherever the ground is covered with rocks, or as here, by great slabs of slate piled up promiscuously, the falling snow leaves caves or caverns underneath unfilled, the surface snow being sufficiently frozen to bear, prevents the walker from falling through, but the concussion of the feet is sufficient to detach the soft underlying snow from the harder upper crust, which dropping into the cavity produces the sound I heard today. This evening the Pole Star, and the pointers of Ursa Major were visible for the first time. The Pole Star appears directly over head and one has to throw the head back to observe it. I noticed that between the hours of 1 & 2 p.m. today that a beautiful pale violet colour suffused the Zenith, at the time it was bright and cloudless, this same tinge of colour I have frequently observed on the shaded side of snow clad hills, in these regions, on bright sunny days.
[23ʳᵈ. Sept. 1853. Shellabear P.P. p. 297. Shoots eleven ptarmigan E. shore Wellington Channel.][2]

Friday 24 September 1875

A single *Snow-bunting* flew past the ship today about 10.30, a.m, passing along the coast in a S.E direction. It blew a good deal last night from S.W which bared a great deal of the land in our neighbourhood, and gave the first chance of examining the surface, since our arrival here. The land in the bend where we are moored is covered with *angular* fragments of slate, some in large slabs the majority small pieces; about 100 yds from the ship is a fine polished boulder of granite, and the surface is scattered over with various kinds of erratic boulders, one of limestone contained a few fossils, I recognised coral and stems of a crinoid (Silurians). Walking to the point about a mile and a half to the N.W.

---

[1] Bessels, 'Notes on Polaris Bay'.
[2] W. B. Shellabear, Second Master, HMS *North Star*, *Arctic Blue Books*, 1855, p. 297.

which I refer to in my journal of the 18th inst., as giving us some protection, a series of sea-beaches ascend inland, as a rule these beaches are generally most prominently displayed on points extending into the sea. These beaches rise at this place to an altitude of 80 or 90 feet, in four or five well marked terraces, every constituent peeble is water washed and rounded, some spherical, a large proportion are erratics, none that I noticed showed any marks of glacial striae. By observing the presence or absence of ice markings I have learned to decide unhesitatingly, whether the terraces we meet with so frequently, are beaches or sub-aqueous terminal moraines. Beyond this point the ravine, (which in June must be a river) that descends from M[r]. Pullen, debouches from the hills about half a mile inland, and in its swollen state has cleared out a triangular <area or> dêlta, nearly a mile wide at the sea line, its surface composed of rounded water worn stones, many granites and erratics, which I presume have been washed down from the uplands, where doubtless they are plentifully bestrewed. This torrent course exposes a different formation of slates, which crop up in vertical ridges, exposure to the atmosphere gives this stone a glossy black, jet like hue, and differs also from the upper beds of grey slate in not laminating so thinly or easily. some of it is porous and contained [at one time] ^ cells ^ filled with mineral, most of them are weathered out, but I found specimens containing traces of what I took to be *asbestos* and some ~~nickel~~ ?. [*Margin*: Globular pieces of Iron Pyrites?] The vegetation of the land over which I walked is scanty, noticed *Sax. oppo. Pap. nud.*[1] *Potentilla nivea*[2] & one dried grass. Lieut. Giffard walked to the top of Mt Pullen, his observations I will record tomorrow.

Saturday 25 September *1875*
A fine bright day, Captain Markham, with Lieuts. Parr and May, left at 9.30 a.m. with three sledges for the N.W. A mile from the ship Lieut Parr's 12 men sledge broke through the young ice, got wet through, and had to be replaced by an 8 men sledge. The ice where the sledge broke through was 4½ to 6 inches thick. Memo. Don't attempt to haul a heavily laden sledge over young ice of less than six inches in thickness. Walked about three miles along the coast to the N.W. The ice in the first bay has not moved, in spite of the late heavy S.W. gales, and consists of a sheet of solid floe apparently frozen to the bottom, and never acted on by wind or outside pressure, being protected by the sides of the bay; at its mouth along the line of outside pressure huge hummocks are reared up. The ground being comparatively clear of snow, we walked inland finding all the surface composed of the slaty-limestone the same as near our winter quarters. Found a single stem of *Salix arctica*? and some withered plants of *Stellaria longifolia.*[x3] [*Margin*: [x] Plants additional to those noticed yesterday.] During a walk of five hours continuance we did not come across a trace of any animal save a *Lemming* or two. not a bone, piece of driftwood, or trace of Eskimo, all over the land erratic boulders are strewn. Near P[r]. Sheridan, the floe is pressed up on the shore and piled in hummocks of great thickness, the larger blocks being 30 to 40 feet high, the pushed in floe has driven the gravel inland, and above high water mark in wavy parallel lines of mounds, 3½–4½ to 5 feet high, which have been rounded off by atmospheric influences. At this point these ridges run parallel with the coast over half a

---

[1] *Papaver nudicaule*, Iceland poppy.
[2] Snow cinquefoil.
[3] Long-leafed starwort.

mile and extend inland over an area of 20 paces. I made a rough sketch of this interesting spot. (See Ramsay & Evans p. 77. Ad. Instructions.)[1] Re-*examined* the dark slate bed, which I came across in the bed of the ravine that discharges near P^t. Sheridan, all this slate is highly charged with mineral (iron pyrites) which emits a sulphurous smell on being struck with the hammer, the metal lies in rounded form, not in cubes. The temp. was zero or a little below, and the geological hammer chipped very easily, breaking off in flakes.

In the formations which are now making below the sea in these regions at the mouths of ravines, the future geologist will find a curious mixture. Beds of clay formed by the wasting of the limestones will be intercalated with beds of gravel, chiefly rounded limestone but also highly charged with erratics, washed down from the uplands. It will be a puzzle to the observer to understand how these erratics became embedded, not having had the adantage of knowing, that the country which is now [was] the parent of these formations, has in comparatively recent times been elevated, and is strewed with erratics, skulls of the Musk Ox will be lying side by side with seals. (Not far from the delta of the Ravine, in Discovery Bay, we found in one day four Musk ox skulls.) The strata will contain the shells of the testaceous[2] mollusks at present inhabiting these seas, and pieces of drift wood from Siberia or the rivers of America will not be wanting.

Sunday 26 September 1875
Divine service. Stayed on board most of the day.

Monday 27 September 1875
Walked to the S.E, passing through a small ravine which runs nearly N & S, and leads up to the plateaux above Cape Union.[3] Found traces of a Hare and a Ptarmigan.

Tuesday 28 September 1875
Went in the same direction with Wootton,[4] as I did yesterday. The ravine is full of Snow-drift in some places thirty feet thick, the summer torrent passing underneath – in fact it is a young glacier. Ascending to the plateaux we walked in the direction of Cape Union, and looked down on Robeson Channel, many cracks visible in the ice, and streaks of water, over these spots, heavy clouds hung. The uplands in this direction are most miserably bare of verdure, the soil produces no flowering plants, the rocks no lichens, underneath the feet the soil and fragments of slate, are raised by the frost into a series of low mounds, like half obliterated mole-hills, I dont exactly understand how the frost raises these mounds, but it is a common feature over all this country, wherever a certain amount of soil or clay covers the rocks. At midnight when I went on deck, overhead, to the south, and across the pack ice it was very dark, but low down along the northern horizon stretched a band of lurid light, [the sun] which gave an inexpressibly weird look to the scene, reminding me of a prairie fire.

[1] Ramsay and Evans, 'Geology and Mineralogy'.
[2] Having a hard shell.
[3] See Figure 22, p. 152, Aldrich's birthday menu on 8 Dec. 1875, on which a sketch has been drawn showing Aldrich and the Cooper Key Mountains, dated '27th. Sept. 1875'.
[4] James Wootton, engineer in *Alert*.

Wednesday 29 September 1875
A day of great rejoicing for me, as I have entered into the new work shop, made for my use forward, on the main-deck. My sleeping cabin has been cleared out today to the extent of one half, and a series of tin boxes which have caused a dripping on my face whilst in bed, for the last two months, have been removed.

Thursday 30 September 1875
Arranging my sanctum, and specimens all day.

Friday 1 October 1875
Worked at collection all day.

Saturday 2 October 1875
Just before dinner ran out for a little fresh air, noticed a large bird sitting on top of a hummock about <half> a mile from the ship – went back for gun. Snowing, and holes in floe very treacherous, as they were hidden, crept up to within 70 yards of the bird under the lee of another hummock, tide cracks very numerous, the snow and slush gave way, and I went in over the knees, fortunately scrambled on to floe again. as a last resource let fly, the big bird flopped its wing lazily, the snow falling prevented me making out the species, but probably it was a *Larus glaucus*, it might have been *F. candicans*.[1] The fact is only worth recording as showing that birds are to be found at this time of the year, on these inhospitable shores.

Now that I am well acquainted with flight of *Nyctea scandiaca* and general appearance of that bird on wing, I can unhesitatingly affirm that the bird I saw on ~~this date~~ 2nd Oct 75, belonged to this species. H.W.F. July 1st. 1876.[2]

Sunday 3 October 1875
Divine service. Worked at collection all day. Snow fell throughout the day, but the flakes were of a very light nature, so that the amount of atmospheric precipitation was much smaller than a person merely judging by the depth of the snow would imagine.

Monday 4 October 1875
All last night and throughout the day, the same description of snow fell as yesterday. By Dr Moss's experiments the amount of atmospheric precipitation during the past twenty-four hours has been ^{x}[0].*3 of an inch*. [*Margin*: ^{x}? – all bosh H.W.F.] The slushy nature of the young ice immediatly after, and continuous with the fall of snow, has been a matter of observation, and discussion amongst us today. Dr Moss enunciated the theory that the falling snow resting on the ice forms a non conducting covering, which permits the heat of the sea water to permeate the ice, whilst the mantle of snow prevents the radiation of heat into the atmosphere, and that this accumulation of heat disintegrates and melts the young ice. In this view I do not coincide for if it held good, how could solid floes of eighty

---

[1] Gyrfalcon.

[2] Feilden inserted this paragraph, dated 1 July 1876, between the entries for 2 October 1875 and 2 October 1876, referring to the former date. *Nyctea scandica* is the snowy owl.

feet in thickness be formed? for undoubtedly the floe increases in thickness by submarine congelation. The reason of the ice becoming slushy after a fall of snow is in my opinion as follows[:] the snow falling through an atmosphere of say +15°, alights on the ice at the same temperature, the young ice being little colder than the freezing point of water radiates its heat into the colder snow, forming slush before it has had time to freeze into ice of the temperature of the surface air.[1]

Tuesday 5 October 1875
Fine snow continues to fall, the young ice is very sloppy, over an inch of water under the snow. Captain Nares is of opinion that the pressure of the superincumbent snow causes the sea-water to percolate through the young ice. To my mind this does not satisfactorily account for the melting of the snow. Lieut Aldrich, who left the ship on the 22nd ult., with two dog sledges, returned this evening. He went beyond Cape Joseph Henry, and saw land on the other side, bearing W.N.W. from it. In a small lake about N. Lat. 82°.36'. he dug a hole through fourteen inches of <ice to the water> saw some fish, and with a crooked pin, a piece of white line which he had to untwist with a temperature of +10°, and a bit of bacon, he dextrously captured three, which he brought to the ship frozen in his telescope case. In N. Lat 82°.37' found a skull of ♂ Musk-sheep.

Wednesday 6 October 1875
Fine snow still falling. Young ice still more sloppy, in some places a layer of briny water several inches deep, separates the snow from the young ice. The largest of the Salmonoids brought by Aldrich yesterday measures 6¹/₁₀ in. No teeth on the vomer.[2] made a drawing of one in pencil. My birthday aged 37.

Thursday 7 October 1875
I am taking in hand to make a selection of small, almost microscopic collections of most of the specimens, ~~natur~~ illustrating the results of the expedition in the animal, vegetable and mineral kingdoms, so that in the event of our having to abandon our main collections, some fragments may be preserved. This will occupy my attention for sometime to come.

Friday 8 October 1875
Two of the Greenland dogs were ordered to be killed by Captain Nares, as Lieut Aldrich reported them as useless on his late sledge jouney, one of them being subject to fits, and the other not pulling his value in food. These two dogs were got at Proven, North Greenland, one was apparently a thorough bred Eskimo dog, of a light brown <&> wolfish grey colour which I designate A., the second B., was generally of the same colour, but showed a trace of cross of domestic dog, in an irregular white patch on one side of its face, though in shape and general appearance, it coincided with our other Eskimo dogs. *Ten grains* of solid stick cyanide of potassium enclosed in a bolus of meat were swallowed by each of these dogs, in eight to ten minutes they vomited the contents of

---

[1] Sea ice in the Arctic Ocean is the result of heat loss from the ocean into the atmosphere, and the surface of the ocean is covered in grease ice. Moss's explanation is accurate for the formation of ice; but Feilden's explanation accounts for the formation of slush and ice on land.

[2] A bone forming the front part of the roof of the mouth, and often bearing teeth. *OED*.

their stomachs, one A., staggered a little, B seemed none the worse. Both were then hanged. [*Margin*: If this had been pounded or mixed with a little acid, no rope would have been required H.W.F] I skinned A, for preparation as a skeleton. All the internal organs healthy. The intestines when opened showed no trace of any *entozoa*,[1] neither did the stomach. The head of B, I skinned and took to my cabin, as the cold on deck though +13° caused the forceps to cling to my fingers. I sawed this skull carefully through the nasal, frontal, and supra-occipital bones, dividing the maxilla, palatine & basic spheroids from below. Cerebrum and cerebrellum somewhat gorged with blood from strangulation. I made a very careful examination of the frontal sinuses of this dog, no trace in them of *Pentastomum*[2] or any other parasite. I continued the dissection carefully on both sides of the septum to the nostrils but no trace of any parasite. As far as my present observations go I am convinced that the fits from which our dogs suffer, have nothing in common with rabies, one form comes on with staggering, accompanied with foaming of the mouth, during these paroxsyms, the unfortunate animal, wanders about snapping, and with an extremely distressed expression, in aggravated cases the disease is accompanied with great constipation, which in some yielded to a drastic purge of croton oil, whilst the last stage of collapse was alleviated by warm soup and brandy. A milder form of fit is very common on the sledge journies, when driving rapidly, the dog gives one yelp, and rolls over in spasms, its harness is cut and the animal left lying on the snow, and in a few hours makes its reappearance at camp or the ship. One dog left behind in this condition some miles from the ship on the 12th of Sept, did not return till the 20th of same month. I have further observed some of these animals when walking on shore attacked by fits near to the waters edge, the beasts though falling down are aware of the proximity of the water which they dislike, and made efforts to get away from it, though in one case the animal fell in and would have been drowned, had not a bystander pulled it out. D[r] Moss made ~~an examination for me~~ drawing at my request of the contents of the stomach of one of the small *charr*, captured by Lieut. Aldrich. [x]Two species of insects were recognised under the microscope, which D[r] Moss painted with his usual skill and accuracy. [*Margin*:[x] One of them is a beautiful vermillion coloured *Hydrachnella*.[3] H.W.F.] It is fortunate that a person possessed of such skill in drawing microscopic details should accompany the expedition, as in case of losing the collections made, the official account of the expedition will be enriched by these drawings. D[r] Moss's sketch book contains amongst others made on the voyage, copious illustrations of *Clio*, a very beautiful new (apparently) sponge, taken in the dredge at Franklin Pierce Bay, a sketch of *Pentacrinus Naresii*,[4] captured at the same place, also the contents of its stomach, besides many sketches of *diatomacea* &c. &c.

Saturday 9 October 1875
Bright and clear, at 10o'c. a.m Temp. about zero, all hands on deck, the hatch ways, & skylights of the ward room were opened, the heated air and moisture from below, rose in the form of vapour, dense enough to be taken for smoke at a short distance. The skylight of the ward-room was kept open for about an hour, and every drop of moisture which

[1] Internal parasites.
[2] Internal parasites, formerly classed as trematode worms.
[3] Water mite.
[4] P. H. Carpenter, 'Preliminary Report', mentions this crinoid, named for Nares on the *Challenger* expedition.

clung to the beams was removed, the same result took effect in my cabin. The temperature sunk to −13 by 10 p.m. went on deck from the warm cabin without cap on, and waistcoat & trousers open, remained exposed for five minutes, or more, and felt no inconvenience from the cold. The round house at present in use is simply a tent stretched over the rudder-hole, open below to the wind and draught. The Eskimo dogs are great devourers of human ordure. When sledging with these animals, the person performing this function of nature has to provide himself with a stick or whip to drive the beasts away. It may be imagined how repulsive it is to make a dissection of the stomach and intestines of these dogs. Yesterday both Petersen and I were nearly overcome. One of the bitches a black and white one, I noticed today collecting and arranging straw, she was put in a sheltered place under the forecastle she was given plenty of material, and for a couple of hours was busily employed arranging a warm bed to pup in. I have been unable to determine accurately the period of gestation in these animals; all or nearly all the ♀ came in season end of July and beginning of August, and our upper deck during that time was a constant scene of *copula* between the sexes. The master dogs, reserved to themselves a couple of wives, (I did not notice this number exceeded.) over whom they watched with the most jealous care and vigilance, any attempt at intrusion on the rights of the harem being quickly resented with tooth and nail. Whilst employed fighting with an interloper the master dogs attention would sometimes be withdrawn from the other wife, an advantage quickly made use of by some of the bystanders. The bitches took the dog so often, and for such a prolonged period, and their consorts were so varied that my notes on gestation of this species are worthless.

From 8.45 until 9 a.m the sun showed half its diameter above the Greenland coast, but after passing Cape Rawson the highlands to the south shut him out from our view.

Sunday 10 October 1875
The bitch referred to yesterday gave birth to 6 pups, exposed to such a low temperature on the forecastle, and the mother having little or no milk they died shortly afterwards. When thrown to the dogs on the floe they were quickly devoured.

The upper limb of the sun showing at sametime and place as yesterday.

Monday 11 October 1875
Walked to Point Sheridan. The sun went today below our horizon.

Tuesday 12 October 1875
Walked to Point Sheridan. Splendid day. The sun refracted shining on the Greenland hills, and the Heckla[1] range; by calculation the sun is 5 minutes below the horizon today at noon.

Wednesday 13 October 1875
Egerton with dog sledge left at 10 a.m., to bring in the sledge left by Lieut. Aldrich some three miles and a half to the N.W. on the 5th inst. Captain Nares and I walked in the same direction as far as Pt. Sheridan, up to that point the floe inside of the line of grounded hummocks, was excellent walking and we moved along briskly reaching the

---

[1] Hecla. Feilden consistently uses the spelling 'Heckla'.

flag staff in twenty minutes, The morning was lovely, temperature below zero but no wind to speak of. Outside of the grounded hummocks was a broad lane of open water, which terminated at P^t. Sheridan. To my eye there appeared to be about the same amount of open water, and in identically the same place as when we arrived here on the 1st September. The small pieces of ice in this lane were setting to the N.W. but of course became jammed as they reached the head of the lead. To the northward about two miles out, was a large water hole, and beyond dark smoke coloured clouds, showed other spaces of open water. The sun though below our horizon illuminated the Greenland coast which stood out very distinctly the most northern point being highly miraged up, one conical point assuming a buttressed castellated appearance. the range of snowclad peaks to our west, which I believe forms the apex of Grants Land, were tinged with a most lovely roseate hue, fading away in the direction of Cape Joseph Henry, which stood out clear white and massive. In the river bed which extends a mile beyond P^t. Sheridan the snow lay from one to two foot deep, and we saw Egerton and his men pushing their sledge along with difficulty. He returned with the sledges just as we were finishing dinner, and reported that whilst driving in, two of his dogs fell down in fits, a third rolled over gave one yelp and expired, he very considerately brought me back this dog, which I at once took below to prevent its freezing, hoping to dissect it tomorrow. Rawson made a sketch of a peculiar stratification at Cape Union which he reached on the 5th. He describes a cliff rising to an altitude of 500 feet, through its centre rose perpendicularly a stratum of Reddish brown rock, on either side the slate strata branched off at a very acute angle. I presume that it is a later^x *eruptive* rock passing through the slates. [*Margin*: ^{x} Nothing of the kind Vertical strata. May. 1876. H.W.F.] In opening out my snow shoes, today, given me by Dr Rae,[1] I found inside a beautiful pair of moose hide mits lined with warm material and edged with fur. A note accompanying them informed me that they were the gift of Mrs Rae. [*2 lines inked out* ~~I am not ?? to say that ???~~ ══════════════]²

[*Here Feilden tipped in a sketch of Cape Union; see Figure 11, p. 123.*]

Thursday 14 October 1875
Max −8° Fahr. Min. −20°
After breakfast took the deceased dog C. on the forecastle and skinned him. When I took the body below yesterday, the animal had been exposed at the outside not more than ten minutes, and was perfectly limp. It remained in a cabin with a temperature from +33° to +38°. for seventeen hours, When I took it out this morning the stench of putrefaction was great, and required washing with Carbolic acid to make the cabin sweet again. Skinning at −7° to −10° is difficult work, blood, fat and fibre freeze on the knife. Finished by 12.30 m., took a brisk run out to P^t. Sheridan, ascended to the flag-staff, what was open water yesterday is now a grinding tumultuous pack, moving to the N.W. with the ebb tide. The floe between land and hummocks along which I travelled, groaned cracked, and fractured

---

[1] John Rae (1813–93), Arctic explorer. See *ODNB* and Richards, *Dr John Rae*. Feilden has pasted a note from Mrs Rae facing this entry: 'With Mrs Raes Kind regards and best wishes to Captain Feilden 22nd May 2 Addison Gardens South.' See also Appendix E, item 25.
² Indecipherable blacked-out passages are indicated in this edition by [══════════].

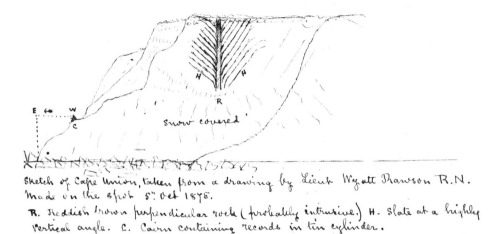

Sketch of Cape Union, taken from a drawing by Lieut Wyatt Rawson R.N.
Made on the spot 5ᵗ. Oct 1875.
R. Reddish brown perpendicular rock (probably intrusive.) H. Slate at a highly
vertical angle. C. Cairn containing records in tin cylinder.

Figure 11. 'Sketch of Cape Union, taken from a drawing by Lieut Wyatt Rawson R.N. Made on the spot 5ᵗʰ. Oct 1875. R. Reddish brown perpendicular rock (probably intrusive.) H. Slate at a highly vertical angle. C. Cairn containing records in tin cylinder.'

with the falling tide. At one p.m., the moon began to rise due north, full, looking very large, but somewhat obscured by fog. Made the following observations in [*sic*] the colour of snow. Drive your walking pole into a drift at any angle or in any direction, revolve it rapidly round making a cone shaped hole, whilst the stick is rotating the hole appears full of a dark smoke vapour, withdraw the staff and the hole becomes suffused with the beautiful cerulean blue colour seen so often in berg and floe ice. With your hand scoop out the snow below until the aperture becomes the shape of a bottle, the blue tint disappears, and snowy whiteness takes its place. The same happens when you press your foot into the snow, the gap in the snow looks quite white, but press your toe a little forward, making a nook, and a pale tinge of blue illuminates that spot. Moss walked on snow shoes to Sickle Point, and there met Captain Markham's party returning. He brings us back the good news, that all are well. They will be at the ship tomorrow perhaps tonight.

About 8 p.m., Lieut Parr arrived onboard and let us know that the rest of the party were about two miles off, several of us ran off and met them in the deep snow on the other side of Pᵗ. Sheridan, and gave a hand at the drag ropes. Great rejoicing tonight at all being gathered together once more. May is rather badly bitten in both big toes, and eleven of the men of the party, nearly fifty per cent have suffered more or less in the feet.

Friday 15 October 1875
Max +6° Fahr. Min −21°

A regular festival today, Musk ox meat, and other luxuries. We call these feeds "tighteners", as they act in that direction on the waistband. After breakfast walked to P^t. Sheridan and then about a mile along the edge of the ravine, came across fresh Ptarmigan tracks.

Saturday 16 October 1875
Max +21.2° – Min −12°
Walked to Point Sheridan, a few pools of open water visible. The twylight colours all round the horizon at meridian are most lovely.
The Greenland coast greatly miraged up.

Sunday 17 October 1875
Max −5° Min −17°
Walked to Point Sheridan with Captain Markham, between 12 and 1 p. m. The tints on the southern horizon of a beautiful roseate hue. To the north a delicate blue. Not a speck of open water to be seen. The Greenland coast much miraged.

Monday 18 October 1875
Max −9° Min −19°
Walked to P^t. Sheridan after morning quarters, this gives me from 10 till 12 m, out of doors.

Tuesday 19 October 1875
Max−8° Min −21°
Usual Walk to Pt. Sheridan.

Wednesday 20 October 1875
Max −9° Min −24°
Usual walk to Pt. Sheridan.

Thursday 21 October 1875
Max −3°. Min −25°
Walked to P^t. Sheridan. Roughly speaking the temperature in my cabin over my washing table is about 40° during day, sinking as low as +32° at night. On the side of my bed next to the ships side the condensation freezes solid, on the roof of the cabin the heated air condenses and drips in a continu*al* stream on my bed. The quilt is now soaking. I know perfectly well how this might be remedied but unfortunately it cannot be done. Either each cabin should be fitted with an air-tube leading to the uptake in the ward room or else communicating with the upper deck.

Transport by drift ice wont account for all the erratics strewn over this country & North Greenland, practically floe ice can but seldom be a raft for stones, and these in nine cases out of ten must be angular, not boulders. They must be the result of some great glacier, but where can the mountain tops be, from whence the ice rivers descended, and left the syenite boulders on the elevated limestones of this region.

Friday 22 October 1875
Max −8°. Min −31°

Thickness of young ice today 19 inches – 8 in. of this due to snow fall. We cannot expect to find in this country any fishes in fresh water lakes, that do not belong to species that migrate into salt water, such as Salmonoids for the land is of such recent elevation.

One of our Eskimo bitches coupled today for the first time this period with a big black dog called "Bruin".

Saturday 23 October 1875
Max −11° Min −17°
Walked to Pᵗ. Sheridan. The ♀ canis borealis[1] going the rounds of the ♂.

Sunday 24 October 1875
Max −11°.8 Min −20°
Light fall of snow during the night. Walked towards Cape Rawson. The young ice is now 19 inches thick, but ~~the~~ <its> surface is still slightly melted where it came in contact with the recent snow fall. Nearly a foot of the young ice is due to the old snow fall having consolidated into ice.

The bitch in heat coupled today with at least three different dogs, but I will date period of gestation from first copula the 22ⁿᵈ. inst.

Monday 25 October 1875
Max −8° Min −20.5°
Walked to Pᵗ. Sheridan. The moonlight is now very faint, the sun to the S.E. showed only a glow of pale amber, above smoke gray clouds. The ice and hummocks in shade dark violet, the flat floes white. A stratum of thick white mist hid the greater portion of the Greenland coast, the upper contour of the Congress Highlands, only showing backed by the sun's tints. Came across the fresh tracks of a Lemming, which I followed, they led across the ice-foot, every few yards it had burrowed down as if in search of water, the track led to the very verge of the loose pack, then burrowed again, and its return footmarks led straight again to the shore. A slight display of aurora in the E about 12 p.m. (v. Sherard Osborn. Sledge Journal. Par. Papers p. 212[2]).
[*Watercolour sketch of the view from Point Sheridan tipped in here; see Plate 11.*]

Tuesday 26 October 1875
Max −13°. Min. −21°.8.
Walked to Pᵗ. Sheridan. A marked difference in the amount of light. The moon though high is at the close of her last quarter. We shall lose her after tomorrow. Completed the ships awning, much darker below in consequence. Sunk a skinned Eskimo dog in a net through the tide hole. I have no doubt that when I return to temperate climates, I shall say that we never felt cold in the Arctic, and honestly believe that we made no difference in our clothing from England. My indoor dress is a thick wollen [*sic*] under-shirt and drawers, a chamois leather waistcoat – Baltic shirt, sealskin trousers, two pair

---

[1] *Canis borealis* is what Feilden calls the Eskimo dog, now called the Canadian Inuit dog; these dogs are working dogs, used in pulling sledges.
[2] *Arctic Blue Books*, 1855, p. 212.

stockings, a cardigan waistcoat and thick box cloth coat. If blowing at all outside, add, a sealskin jumper, sealskin cap with long flaps over the ears, a warm muffler, and thick gloves.

The position of Winter Quarters is given today by Capt. Nares as. 82°.27′.1".

Wednesday 27 October 1875
Max −11° Min −21°
Walked to P.^t Sheridan. Lemming track fresh, leading to the edge of the moveable pack, across ice-foot, traced it up with Nell the retriever, it came to a tide crack where the little animal had scratched and burrowed down to the water, and then returned to shore.

No moon visible this morning. A very heavy water pool cloud to the north, about 3 miles out, it looked like the smoke of a great conflagration. Robeson channel is evidently full of water holes today, judging from smoke. At 12 m., a meteor fell apparently close to the ship. Markham and Giffard and others who saw it, describe it as the most brilliant they have ever observed.

Thursday 28 October 1875
Max −18° Min −23°
Walked to P.^t Sheridan, found fresh Lemming tracks leading from the land across the ice-foot, to the junction of the moving pack, there the little animal had burrowed through the snow in the direction of the water, and afterwards returned to the shore.

Friday 29 October 1875
Max −15° Min −25°
To P.^t Sheridan with Aldrich. It is now getting very dark at meridian, having lost the moon, she will make her appearance again on the 8th prox. Quartermaster Bury reports that he heard the howling of a pack of Wolves on the shore last night. Moss to whom I lent my snow shoes, went a short distance inland, but found no tracks of *Lupus*, but plenty of *Lepus*.[1] He says that he does not think he could have shot a hare even if he had come across one, owing to the absence of light.

Saturday 30 October 1875
Max −9° Min −16°.2.
A regular turn out in my cabin, the drip from condensation has been so great of late, that my bed clothes are wringing wet, on the side of the bunk next the outside, very interesting miniature glaciers have formed which enable me to test the vicissitude of climate in corpore vili,[2] one part of my body enjoying a temp of 40° the other side −32°, a twinge of rheumatics in my right elbow set me to work this morning, and I have rigged up a blanket lining over head, and down the sides of the glaciers.

Sunday 31 October 1875
Max −14° Min −26°.8

---

[1] *Canis lupus arctos*, the Arctic or white wolf. *Lepus arcticus*, the Arctic hare.
[2] On a vile (or common) body.

After divine service, hauled up my net containing dead dog from the bottom of the fire-hole,[1] hundreds of shrimps had collected on it and though it has only been in the water for six days yet half of the carcase is already devoured. Some hundreds of these shrimps fell through the net on to the ice, temp about −15°. in five minutes they were all dead. Then walked to P^t. Sheridan, a faint glimmer of light in the S.E.

Monday 1 November 1875[2]
Max −11° Min −25° Temp of Earth 2 ft deep. +5°½
To P^t. Sheridan, at noon, Mount Pullen just distinguishable from the flag staffs a faint glimmer of light tinting the sky to the S.

We may date the commencement of real winter from today, ~~up till now~~ <still> we have ~~had~~ enough twilight, to read the Times leader at noon on the floe. Four long months before we see the sun again. I hope we may all be as well, and hearty at the end of that time as we are now. We are entering on our hybernation [*sic*] under excellent auspices. Nearly every body is in excellent spirits, and the health good. D^r. Colan, has just been in my cabin, to ask how I am, as this is his morning for monthly medical inspection. He showed me his report book which is very favorable. Number of souls onboard 70, which is 8 more than our complement, owing to Rawson and his sledge party. 15 men are under treatment for cough, cold and frostbite, but the D^r considers none of these serious. Our worst case is George Remmis, Wardroom Steward,[3] how he was passed for this service I cannot imagine, he is quite broken down in constitution, from the effects of climate &c. Has had several attacks of epilepsy, since we left England. was under treatment for a month in sick bay, with complication of Heart, Liver & Kidney. When one reads the very different circumstances under which Kane[4] commenced his conflict with Arctic winters, one cannot help feeling very sorry for the poor man and his companions. His whole book appears to me a pitiable record of inexperience, and ~~consequently~~ want of foresight in equipment, only relieved from disgrace, by the sad record of sufferings endured, and the individual exertions of some members of the expedition. I am convinced that a sailor only, can be put in command of an Arctic expedition, and that the absence of *naval discipline* must be fatal to obtaining the best results. In our little world the wheels go round with the smoothness of well adapted machinery, Every person knows his place, and his duties.

Tuesday 2 November 1875[5]
Max +12° Min −21°

---

[1] A hole cut through the ice so that water was always available in case of fire.
[2] Feilden has tipped in a scrap of paper: 'Monday Novr. 1 / <u>Breakfast. Preserved Beef & cold Pork sliced and grilled with currie powder / Cold [Corned] Beef / 3 lbs. cold mutton. Toast & Butter.</u> / Dinner / Chick Soup. Corned Beef. Mutton. 2 lbs flour. 5 oz. Suet pudding. Mutton Cutlets. [?] 1½ [? Cabbage]'
[3] George Kemish was the wardroom steward.
[4] Elisha Kent Kane (1820–57) was an American surgeon, naval explorer, and author. The second Grinnell Expedition, meant by Kane to go to the shores of a supposititious open polar sea via the route between Ellesmere Island and Greenland, was a disaster. Kane, *The U.S. Grinnell Expedition*, and *Arctic Explorations*.
[5] Tipped in: 'Tuesday 2nd / <u>Breakfast</u> / Fried Pork / Cold Beef /Bologna Sausages (2) / Toast & Butter / <u>Dinner</u> / Pea Soup / Boiled Pork / Bubble & Squeak / 3 lbs Mutton. 2 lbs [flour] / Suet & a little lard to be made into mutton pies. / 3 lbs cold mutton.'

Walked to P^t. Sheridan, less fog, and consequently much clearer than yesterday. Mt Pullen showing distinctly from the flag-staff. The newspaper column pasted on a board near the ships side, could be read at 10 a.m. There was a good deal of movement audible in the pack outside. It sounded today like the roaring of a great waterfall, at some distance. Noticed tracks of Hares on the ice-foot leading to the pack. Presumably Hares, and Lemmings go to the sea for water breaking through tide-cracks. For what other reason do they leave the shore, and towards the pack? The water from the tide-hole at a depth of 5 feet shows no organisms vegetable or animal, with the exception of a few minute *Entromostraca* [*sic*],[1] some of these Moss mounted as slides. A slight display of the Aurora this evening.

Since the darkness set in, I have adopted the following method of passing the twenty-fours which we call a day, as follows. Get up at 8, breakfast 8.30 – finished by nine. Pulling on warm clothes, perhaps a smoke, touching up a defect in one's cabin &c. passes the time till 10.15 – when we muster on the quarter-deck and prayers are read. Then outside till 12.30 or 1 o'c. Brush off accumulations of snow and ice, hang up garments in drying room, read a book and the bell sounds for getting ready for dinner which is served at 2.30 this meal generally lasts an hour, then comes a smoke and chat till 4.15. muster again on quarter-deck. Then I double down to my cabin lie down on my bunk with the pretence of reading and really sleep till 7 o'c. tea time.

After tea read and write in my cabin till twelve, then a pipe and chat till 1o'c. Go to bed and read till 2 or half past, then the "Land of Nod". Thus I get between 7 and 8 hours sleep in the twenty-four, and as it is always night between decks, it cant make any difference at what hours a person takes sleep. My reason for changing what we call night into day, is that during the last hours of the twenty-four and the first hours of the day, the ward-room is quietest, and one can work best.

Wednesday 3 November 1875
Max +12°. Min +7°.
It began to blow last night from S.S.E. but died away towards morning commencing again at 12 noon, during the previous twelve hours the temperature rose from −21 to +12 a difference of 33°. On the floe it felt warm and muggy. All last night and yesterday, I believe it blew a gale up Robeson Channel for heavy scud was passing to N.N.E. Outside of us say half a mile off, stretched a broad lane of open water increasing in breadth towards Robeson Channel, the extent of the water in that direction being lost in the gloom. Wind is certainly the main agent in moving Arctic ice. Smiths Channel is a great funnel down and up which the winds rush. We are fortunately placed just outside the neck of the channel, so I hope we shall not get the full force of the gales.

It is a subject of congratulation with me, that we are commanded by a man of previous practical experience in this region. Every day I see some practical result emanate from his store of knowledge. Eventually our officers will be equally capable, but without Nares they would have had to buy experience by a course of failures.

Depend upon it that in Arctic voyages, every amusement and luxury that can possibly be added to the expedition is a positive advantage. Luxuries should only be restricted by absolute want of stowage room. No fear in the Arctic of your ship

---

[1] *Entomostraca*: A class of crustaceans, whose name is no longer in general use.

becoming a Capua.[1] The enemy you fight flourishes on despondency, discomfort, ennui or short victuals. You must meet him with well lined bellies, warm clothing, good ventilation and cheerfulness.

Broke out the ice that has accumulated in my cabin, and which with increased temperature was dripping excessively. I half filled a large "pot-de-chambre", with chippings of ice.

Thursday 4 November 1875[2]
Max +18° Min +0.2
Temperature very high +12. at noon about that time a fresh breeze from S.S.E. came up, continued. It may savour of affectation but I can say that Egerton Rawson and I after a short walk, were glad to throw ourselves on the snow covered hummocks, and rest and cool ourselves. At eleven a.m. this morning the pack had completely closed the open water visible yesterday. The water in Robeson channel, and this long stretch from Cape Union to P^t. Sheridan, appears to be always influenced by the wind. I expect it will remain in the same condition throughout the winter. This open water in Robeson Channel will account for the higher temperature experienced by the *Polaris* to that of Kane's in Rensellaer Bay.[3] Whilst working at the fire-hole this morning I noticed "Bruin" the big Eskimo dog stagger, whilst digging with his companions, in the dirt heap, some 40 paces off, he gave a piercing yell and started off in my direction with a half paralyzed gait, pursued by three dogs, then he fell in violent convulsions. His companions fell upon him and worried and bit him, I drove them off with an ice-chisel, Bruin remained in convulsions five minutes, his four legs were contracted inwards and jerked outwards with great rapidity, foam ran from his mouth, and a <loud> gurgling proceeded from his throat, his eyes were open and fixed, gradually his legs stopped jerking the fit ended, the beast remained tranquil for about half a minute then rose to his feet, and ran round in circles head down, back somewhat arched, tail between legs still very unsteady, I had a lantern in my hand with which I had been exploring the contents of a net. Bruin now ran round this light in an idiotic manner, I changed my position five times, and the dog always followed and circled round the lantern, in a couple of minutes, he seemed to recover his faculties, gave a yell and made off to a hummock, where he coiled himself up. These fits have all the appearance of epilepsy in the human subject. I should like to know how Dr Brown-Séquard[4] artificially produced epilepsy in guinea-pigs, which disease was transmitted to their offspring [See Huxley Lay Sermon p. 270. ed. 72[5]].

---

[1] Originally an Etruscan, then a Roman city in Campania, where, according to Livy, Hannibal's troops were demoralized by luxurious living: 'Capua had been a Cannae to Hannibal ... there ... his hopes of future glory, were extinguished'. Livy, *History of Rome*, book 23, chap. 47.

[2] Tipped in: 'Thursday 4 / <u>Breakfast</u> / Devilled Beef. Cold Pork / 5 pots Sardines curried / <u>Dinner</u> / Pea Soup. Stewed Beef with carrots and onions / Minced collops Rissoles / Cold Pres^d. Beef. / Plum pudding. 1½ lbs flour. / Gooseberry Tart. 1 lb flour/ Coffee – 4 oz. suet.'

[3] T. R. Jones, ed., *Manual*, p. 608.

[4] Charles Édouard Brown-Séquard (1817–94) carried out researches on guinea pigs and epilepsy from 1869. Olmsted, *Charles-Edouard Brown-Séquard*; Huxley, *Lay Sermons*, p. 270.

[5] Huxley, *Lay Sermons*, p. 270.

Friday 5 November 1875[1]
Max [*blank*]   Min. −8°

Temperature high, wind which blew fresh between 12 and 2 a.m., died away by morning. It must have been still blowing up Robeson Channel, for at noon large dark water clouds were working north from in that direction, and from Flagstaff Point, I could faintly discern the Greenland coast, and open water, at least a streak of black, was taken by me for water. The wind has bared the uplands on shore, of snow, and this accounts I think satisfactorily, for the absence of vegetation in those quarters. Without the warm covering of snow, the plants cannot exist through the Arctic winter, and though the soil on the uplands is abundant enough to support vegetation, yet we only find it in the valleys and places where the snow remains during winter. This V[th] of Nov. was celebrated with the honours we used to pay to the memory of M[r] Guy Fawkes. A most rascally looking individual was made on the lower deck, after tea he was strapped to a sledge drawn round the upper deck, an impromptu band playing "the rogue's march", "Robinson Crusoe", and other appropriate melodies.[2] Guido was then hauled by the ships company, to the top of a hummock, and burnt with the aid of a pitch barrel &c. The lights and shades were very effective.

Saturday 6 November 1875
Max +19°.2 Min −9°

As I look upon this as a private journal, and have no intention of sending it to the Admiralty, I do not think it unfair to put down my private impressions, and make some remarks about my messmates.[3]

Old Colan our fleet-surgeon is a character. He is a dear kind old fellow, and if I was sick I should like him to look after me, [*2¼ lines blacked out* ═══════════════════════].
The old Doctor is very fond of speech making and never misses a chance of giving vent to after dinner oratory, which his position as President of the mess enables him to indulge in at times. He is firmly impressed with the idea that the chief responsibility of the expedition rests on his shoulders, and being most conscientious, this impression has clothed him with an air of austerity, quite foreign to his natural disposition. Any or all of our performances are styled by him "Unparalleled in the annals of Arctic travel". He tells us that he is keeping the medical comforts for the "Dead and the Dying", and cheers us by saying that he runs his eye over every one of us each day, to note our health, to observe whether there are any signs of incipient insanity in our midst, or precautions to be taken against suicidal mania. These remarks addressed to a party of very merry, contented Englishmen, are received with shouts of laughter. The old man comes in with a very absent air to breakfast, eats a little then balances his chair on two legs leans back and whistles a tune, combing his beard from left to right with his fork. When the servant comes for a helping of bacon, the same fork generally transfers the rasher from the dish in front of him to the waiters plate.

---

[1] Tipped in: 'Friday 5th / Devilled Beef. Fried Beef with currie powder / Cold preserved Beef / Toast. Butter. / Dinner / Hotch Potch Soup. 6 lbs of Steak. / 3½ lbs Onions stewed in two dishes. Cabbage 2 [Squares]'.

[2] 'The Rogue's March' was a tune used by the American army when drumming out undesirables from camp during the American Revolution. It may be heard at www.amaranthpublishing.com/rogues.html. I have not identified the tune of 'Robinson Crusoe', but it is likely that it came from an 18th-century pantomime of that name.

[3] Feilden, when disabused of his misapprehension about the private nature of his journal, subsequently went through it, inking out statements that he did not wish to become public.

Sunday 7 November 1875
Max +23° Min +7°
Parr tells me that he has found, that under similar circumstances, the ♀ of nocturnal Lepidoptera take much more killing than the ♂ of the same species, and that the gravid ♀ is very difficult to kill until she has deposited her eggs. He made this observation when at Harrow.

Monday 8 November 1875
Max +18° Min −12°

Tuesday 9 November 1875
Max −6°.4 Min −23°
Sutherland. Quart. Journ. Geol. Soc. vol. ix 1853 pp. 296–312, and Arctic Manual p. 352.[1]
Makes the following remarks on the geology of the west shores of ~~Baff~~ Greenland.
   "At Cape Cranstoune, situate on the north side of Omenak Fiord, and immediatly adjacent to the above two localities, the trap-rocks[2] again occur, and thence extend northward, apparently in one unbroken series, as far as Proven, in lat. 72°20′."
   This agrees with my own observation, and from the top of Proven Island, the line of demarcation between the traps and the granitoid rocks is quite appreciable to the eye. The trap-rocks with very horizontal beddings, run into the interior, many bold escarpments showing this unmistakeable [*sic*] formation. A line drawn through Proven Island from W. to E. would roughly separate the trap formation to the southward, from the denuded granitoid rocks to the northward. A casual observer would be struck by the marked difference in the landscape on either side of this imaginary boundary. To the north the hills are evidently much ice worn, the granite rises in peaks and serrations, but a second look will show that the angles have been rounded off all these projections. On parts where the snow had disappeared immense boulders are freely strewn. An immense one on the ridge of a hill just to the northward of Proven Island, looks as if it was so insecurely poised, that the slightest force applied to it would precipitate it downwards. I found rounded basalt blocks on the summit of Proven Island. To the southward the trap-hills rise in masses flat topped with an enormous talus stretching half way up their sides, above this talus the horizontal basalt beddings is easily recognizable.

Wednesday 10 November 1875
Max −20°.4 Min −34°.5
Moon up. The Doctor cut off a part of Self's[3] <big> toe today. [*2⅓ lines blacked out*] I happened at the time to be smoking in the next cabin, and had the benefit of the groans and cries.
   [*½ line blacked out* ~~Colan~~   ] the air between decks is too vitiated to risk the administration of anisthetics [*sic*], This is bosh, put your patient on the ward-room table, a four foot square skylight over head, and if required you can get in enough fresh air to drive a wind mill.

---

[1] Sutherland., 'On the Geological and Glacial Phænomena', reprinted in T. R. Jones, ed., *Manual*, pp. 352–67.
[2] Trap rocks are dark igneous rocks that are not granitoid, e.g. basalt.
[3] James Self, able seaman on *Alert*.

Menu.

Potages.
Mulligatawny.

Poissons.
Pegouse a la Couverture de laine.

Entrees.
Petits pates d'Homard a la Chasse.
Rognons a la pain roti.

Releves.
Mouton roti a l'Anglais.   **Tongues on gimbals.**

Entremets.
Pouding aux raisins.
Blanc-manger a la Hummock.
Petits pates d'Hahis a la place d'Eccleston.

Dessert.
Boudin glace a la Hyperborean.
Figues.   Noce.
Gateau a l'Irlandais.
Cafe et Liqueur a la Jesson.

11.11.75.   Feilden

Figure 12.   Printed dinner menu on the occasion of the first Thursday Popular Entertainment ('Thursday Pops'), 11 November 1875.

132

H.M.S. ALERT.

Thursday Popular Entertainment.

On Thursday the 11th of November 1875 will commence a series of Popular Entertainments, that will consist of Lectures Readings, Recitations, and Music, both Vocal and Instrumental &c. No trouble or expense has been spared in obtaining the services of a great number of the most talented men of the day. The Entertainment will be given in the airy and commodious hall situated in Funnel Row.

Programme.

Astronomical Lecture. (*with discussion*)	.	CAPT. NARES
Song	I knew that I was dreaming.	.	MR. GOOD
Song	Water Cresses.	. . .	MR. SHIRLEY
Reading	The Jumping Frog.	. .	DR. MOSS
Song	An Englishman am I.	. .	MR. CANE
Song	Broken down.	. . .	MR. BRYANT
Glee	The Wreath. MESSRS. ALDRICH PULLEN AND RAWSON
Song	The White Squall.		MR. MASKELL

GOD SAVE THE QUEEN.

No ENCORES.

Doors open at 7.30.   Sledges may be ordered at 9 oclock

MESSRS. GIFFARD AND SYMONS. Printing office Trap Lane.

Figure 13.   Printed handbill for the first Thursday Popular Entertainment, ('Thursday Pops') on 11 November 1975.

Thursday 11 November 1875
Max −11°.8 Min −33°.2
The moon is up, and giving us most pleasant, and cheering light. Still a faint light tinges the South. This is Commander Markham's birthday, and we had a good dinner in consequence. Among other good things an excellent cake which had been made for this occasion by one of his cousins. I only wish that the lady could have seen how much it was enjoyed.

Our "Popular Entertainments" commenced this evening and were a decided success.[1] The Captain's lecture was interesting and instructive, and explained the reason why we enjoy more moonlight here, than in southern climes. Moss's reading of the "Jumping Frog of Calaveras County",[2] brought down the house. [*See Figures 12 and 13 for the dinner menu and popular entertainment programme, pp. 132–3.*]

Cutting off big toes though a small, is yet a very painful operation. [*2 lines blacked out*] Oakley, a marine,[3] the poor devil gave tongue smartly. I left the ship, and on my return found he had served May the same way, keeping the poor fellow in agony for ten minutes whilst [*1 line and 2 words blacked out*]. A whiff of choloroform to these strong fellows would have saved all this pain. [*1 line and 2–3 words blacked out*][4]

Friday 12 November 1875
Max −8° Min −14°.8
Have had an Enfield Snider rifle, cut down and lightened from 9 lbs, to 6 lbs, it will be a useful weapon.

Our three pigeons are now placed in a coop on the upper deck, the door being left open, enabled them to fly about a little. Two of them are mating and seem fully occupied in billing and cooing. They are very hardy, for −30°, does not appear to affect them. If they survive the winter I shall train them as "homing" pigeons in the spring.

Saturday 13 November 1875
Max −13° Min −25°
Michael the Eskimo dog, of spoon eating notoriety, died today in a fit, he has had a continuance of them, and of the most violent description, hardly a day has elapsed for the last month, without his having had a seizure. This strange disease seems to me to be epilepsy. Bright and beautiful moon today, making up in a great measure for the absence of sun-light. Michael was frozen as hard as a board before I could get at him, no possibility of dissecting him.

Sunday 14 November 1875
Max −17° Min −28°
I never saw a more lovely moonlight than today shining overhead. The temperature more than fifty degrees below freezing. After service several of us scampered off to the point; the air was so exhilarating that we hurried over the crisp snow, singing, shouting and

---

[1] Markham, *The Great Frozen Sea*, pp. 415–23, Appendix A contains the 'Programmes of the Arctic Popular Entertainments' and those of 'The Royal Arctic Theatre', from 25 November 1875 to 17 February 1876. The 'Thursday Pops' generally began with a lecture by one of the officers.

[2] Mark Twain, *Celebrated Jumping Frog*.

[3] Thomas Oakley, gunner on *Alert*

[4] Given Dr Colan's name having been blacked out for the entry of 10 July, it is reasonable to surmise that Colan was the one who argued that the air between decks was too vitiated to use anaesthetics, thereby causing unnecessary pain to his patients.

laughing. When we reached the flagstaff we felt so warm that we had to stand about to cool ourselves. And what a moon! like a great mirror, or shield of burnished steel; not as you see her in the tropics or the Mediterranean, pale soft and warm, dimpling ~~the~~ land and sea with shadows, but cold bright and stern; not a cloud or fleck in the zenith, but towards the south, a pale delicate green shade with heavy lines of dark cloud brooding over it, told us where the sun many degrees below our horizon was giving light and heat to all we love. Our four pairs of eyes seemed to be involuntarily attracted in that direction, and for several minutes no one spoke. We all knew what each was thinking about, the subject was not broached. Then to break the silence I asked Aldrich about "Capella", "Arcturus" and other stars, glistening overhead. And then we looked at the great frozen waste in front of us, smooth ice, crooked ice, hummocks, floes, and packs all jumbled together in mystic confusions. If a man who looks out upon such a scene, cannot realize his insignificance, and the greatness of God, I pity him. A few animated specks looking forth on a world of frozen chaos, and the mind can scarce realize that more than a thousand miles of frozen barrier cuts us off from even the outskirts of half civilised man, a wall as high, <and> guarded by as potent a sword as kept our first parents from re-entering Paradise.

We trotted back to the ship, and as we gathered round our bright lighted social table, with many luxuries on it, we laughed and talked and were as jolly a party as could be found in Christendom.

Monday 15 November 1875
Max −16°.8 Min −32°
Like every other collection of fourteen individuals, our ward-room mess does not agree on the subject of ventilation. Of course all the rest of the ship is heated and aired according to the views of the Captain, but in the ward-room we have been allowed to have our own way. We all of us are aware that a moderate heat say +45° with ventilation, is the point to be gained, [*2 lines blacked out.*? ~~Moss~~], whose chief delight seems always to be in opposition to the opinions of others. [*2 lines and 2 words blacked out*] that poisoning by carbonic acid gas, was the certain result if we did not open the skylights of the wardroom at night. [*2 or 3 words blacked out.* ~~The~~ ??? ~~man~~] has for some time had his own way, and a wretched shivering crowd daily assemble round the breakfast table, with a temperature of +32° or +35, whilst in my cabin I have frequently had to dress with the thermo. below freezing. I held my peace knowing that like most diseases it would run its course and amend, however it gave me infinite pleasure to see that ~~Moss~~ seemed to suffer more from the cold than any one else. He must though be given the credit of possessing Spartan fortitude, for even with the skylights open at night, and a large copper cylinder leading from the upper deck, he rigged up an additional apparatus for his own benefit, consisting of an india-rubber hose passed through the skylights, which brought a whirlwind into his cabin, truth compels me to add that this freak only lasted for two nights.

Tuesday 16 November 1875
Max −24° Min −32°
Took up the net from the fire-hole this evening, the skeleton of the dog was picked perfectly clean. At the bottom of the net amongst hundreds of shrimps, I found about a dozen specimens of Arcturus, the largest of these had her antennae covered with young ones. One Annelid also in the net. Temperature <of air> −30° when we took up the net,

135

The Arcturus and Annelid died instantaneously when exposed to the air, a change of 59° being too much for them.

Wednesday 17 November 1875
Max −25°.2 Min −31°.8
Bright moon in the afternoon, but before mid-day noticed a very distinct paracelena[1] around the moon.

During the night there was very heavy pressure and nipping outside.

I placed in the mess book today a suggestion that the regulations for opening the sky-lights at night should be reconsidered ˣˣ " – Personally I would prefer a lingering death by breathing diluted carbonic acid gas, to freezing"ˣˣ
This little remark had due effect, for today the commander has had the skylights banked over with snow. [*7 lines crossed out.*]

Thursday 18 November 1875
Max −24°.2 Min −31°.8
The theatricals went off splendidly. Pullen's prologue written for the occasion was very good. The acting of both men and officers was above the average of private theatricals. The scenery by Moss was beautifully painted. Our caterers gave us a good supper afterwards. [*Feilden inserted the programme pages and the text of Pullen's prologue; see Figures 14–18, pp. 137–41.*]

Friday 19 November 1875
Max −24°.5 Min −30°
A faint streak of green pale light still visible in the south. A very beautiful Paracelina [*sic = paraselene*] visible today around the moon. A brilliant cross over the real moon, and three mock moons and a halo. This beautiful effect is due to the crystalization of the particles of moisture in the atmosphere, and the refraction of light from the prisms of the crystals.

Saturday 20 November 1875
Max −25°.8 Min −34°.8
Began a snow house with Petersens aid, for the storing of some of my effects. The star Aldebrahan[2] [*sic*] showed a peculiar optical delusion today, owing to refraction produced by fog, this star seemed to move up and down in the heavens, I have noticed the same phenomenon with other stars.

Sunday 21 November 1875
Max −29°.8 Min −37°.8
The moon showed up today for the last time this quarter. We shall not have her grateful light for another fortnight. Being foggy today no glimmer of light appeared in the Southern horizon, yesterday there was a faint light. This evening the thermo. registered 37° of cold or 69°. below freezing. Even with this degree of cold, the exposure of a large surface of the body, for several minutes to the air does not produce any feeling of intense cold, of course it would be very different were there a wind blowing.

On this date 1871, the *Polaris* was blown from her moorings and only saved from drifting helplessly into the pack, by being brought up by a berg. Not the least amusing

[1] A paraselene, a bright spot on a lunar halo.
[2] Aldebaran, the brightest star in the constellation of Taurus.

The

Royal Arctic Theatre

Will be re-opened on Thursday next the 18th inst.
by the Powerful Dramatic Company of

HYPERBOREANS !!!

Under the Distinguished Patronage of CAPTAIN NARES, the Members
of the Arctic Exploring Expedition and all the Nobility and Gentry
of the neighbourhood.

The world-wide reputation of this Company is quite unrivalled. The
Manager has spared neither trouble nor expense in forming this
Company, and he has selected none but the very best *artistes*, the
ladies being from England, and having numerous other engagements
can remain for a short time only.

The Scenic arrangements, under the control and manipulation of
that celebrated artist Professor Moss, *must* be acknowledged to be
unparalelled in the experience of ages and of the highest order.

The Orchestra, under the management of Signore Aldrichi (lately
from Milan),cannot fail to be appreciated by the audience.

Figure 14.   Printed handbill for the Royal Arctic Theatre, reopening, 18 November
1875.

137

PROLOGUE

Spoken at the re-opening of the Arctic Theatre,
on Thursday, 18th November, 1875.

KIND friends, with kindly greetings met to-day,
We bid you welcome to our opening Play :
You, whose indulgent smile forbids the fear
Of scornful wit or captious critic here.
To-day we welcome you, and not To-night,
For all is noon with us — all summer bright ;
And though the southern Sun has ceased to pour
His glittering rays upon our ice-bound shore —
H is ceased awhile to touch with drops of gold
T he crystal corners of our hummocks bold ;
We bear a warm soft light that never fades —
A lustrous light amid these Greenland shades ;
All trustful of each other's love, we learn
With steady flame our lamp of Hope to burn ;
And suns may set, and twilights disappear —
They shall not rob us of our Christmas cheer ;
Nor blinding drift, nor frozen wave, shall chill
Our laughter glad — for laugh, brave boys, we will ;
Kindling yet once again the genial glow
Of happy English homes on Arctic floe.

Yet once again ; for none would here forget
We are but sons of fathers living yet ;
In work and play alike, we but renew
The deeds of men who taught us what to do.
And though, more favoured than the rest, we soar

Figure 15.   Printed copy of Pullen's prologue for the reopening of the Arctic Theatre, 18 November 1875, side 1.

To loftier flights than their's who went before ;
Though ours the boast, by skilful guidance led,
In Virgin climes our shifting Scene to spread :
We love to read, on History's faithful page,
Of ancient triumphs on our Northern stage,
And boldly for our brave forerunners claim
An Arctic 'cast' already known to fame.

Now let the tell-tale Curtain rise, and say
What we have done to wile your hours away.
Such as we have, we bring you of our best,
And to your kind forbearance leave the rest.
One only grief is ours, and you shall share
With us the burden of that gentle care.
One cherished form we miss — one touch alone —
One glance of love — one tender thrilling tone.
Ah — in the sweet homes of our native isle,
The dear ones move, and minister, and smile.
We would not wish them here, but this we know —
Their thoughts are with us every step we go ;
Their life sets northward o'er the cold grey sea,
They live in wondering what our life may be ;
And heart draws near to heart, and soul to soul,
Till each has found its true Magnetic Pole.

God bless and keep them in His mighty hand —
Our wives and sweet-hearts, and the dear old Land!

H.M.S. ALERT.   H.W.P.
    Winter Quarters 1875.

MESSRS. GIFFARD AND SYMONS :
Printing Office, Trap Lane.

Figure 16.   Printed copy of Pullen's prologue for the reopening of the Arctic Theatre,
18 November 1875, side 2.

139

At 7.30 will Commence

The celebrated Nautical Farce,

THE CHOPS OF THE CHANNEL.

Characters.

LEANDER HELLESPONT	. . .	MR STUCKBERRY.
MR COUNTER BALANCE	. . .	MR WOOLLEY.
GRATINGS (STEWARD)	. . .	MR BURROWS.
MRS HELLESPONT	. . .	MDLLE FRANCOMBI.
MRS VENEER	. . . .	MDM MASKELLI.

Time . The Present Day.

Scene.   Saloon of a Boulogne Steamer

Interval of 10 minutes

During the Interval the renowned vocalist
MR STONE will sing THE IRISH BARBER.

Figure 17.   Printed 'Thursday Pops' programme of 18 November 1875. Part 1: 'The Chops of the Channel'.

140

After which will be performed the
Screaming Tragico-Comico Burlesque

~~~~~~

Entitled
VILIKINS and his DINAH.

Characters.

Master Grumbleton Gruffin.	COMDR MARKHAM.
a rich (Soap) merchant of London,	
the original Parient.	
Baron **Boski Bumble.**	MR EGERTON.
Ancestor of the celebrated Beadle,	
the original Lovier so galliant and gay.	
William **Wilkins.**	MR RAWSON.
Socially and convivially known as	
Vilikins, a youny apprentice in	
desperate love with	
Dinah Gruffin.	Mdlle BLANC.
The Sole feminine female offspring	
of the above mentioned Soap Merchant	
in love with the aforesaid Vilikins.	

Scene 1. Lawn of Gruffins House.
Scene 2. Interior of Gruffins House.
Scene 3. Lawn of Gruffins House.

GOD SAVE THE QUEEN.

MESSRS. GIFFARD AND SYMONS. Printing office Trap Lane.

Figure 18.   Printed 'Thursday Pops' programme of 18 November 1875. Part 2: 'Vilikins and his Dinah'.

141

result of our voyage would be a collection of the yarns spun by the members of the mess. Here is one of Egerton's. "On board the *Northumberland* was a Japanese middy rejoicing in the name of Matsuliro-Omura,[1] being ashore at Lisbon one Sunday in plain clothes – contrary to orders – he runs up against Admiral Hornby. Well young gentleman says the Admiral what are you doing in plain clothes, are you not aware it is against my orders for any officer of the fleet to be ashore in plain clothes unless he is going shooting. Me is going shooting, answered the young gentleman. And pray Sir, asks the Admiral rather amused, what are you going to shoot? Omura having a vague idea that he would appeal to the sporting instincts of a Briton, promptly replied, 'Me go Sir to shoot Fox.'"

Monday 22 November 1875[2]
Max −34° Min −44°
Petersen finished the snow-hut today. Temperature −37°. He and I set to work at 4.30 p.m., and by 6.30 p.m. we had taken over three sledge loads of gear from my sanctum, thus giving me some room on board. Though the temperature was so low both of us felt quite warm whilst working, and neither of us got frost bitten, though this morning whilst taking exercise several got slightly touched up.

About 2 p.m, whilst walking with Wotton [*sic*], we observed the Aurora, white coloured, and forming a perfect bow from N.N.E. to S.S.W.

Tuesday 23 November 1875
Max −34°.8 Min −42°.5
Temperature as low as -46°. Mercury frozen. Did not feel at all cold whilst walking.

Wednesday 24 November 1875
Max −28° Min −40°
Temp. −40°. Did not feel cold walking. There is still a very perceptible tinge of twylight in the southern horizon. So much so, that today one could discern the range of hills between us and the southern glow, quite distinctly. On Wednesdays, Captain Nares puts on the wardroom mess tables a couple of bottles of excellent wine after dinner, in addition to our regular allowance. Thus we have two glasses of white wine every day, Tuesdays, Thursdays and Sundays a glass of port additional. Began Danish with Petersen at nights.

Thursday 25 November 1875
Max −19° Min −33°
Temp. went down to −40°. We have had three pigeons, (brought from England) kept in a coop; they were on the lower deck, but were placed on the upper deck, and they flew about under the awning. Two of them disappeared yesterday, and the solitary one was killed today by order.

---

[1] *The Navy List*, 1873, p. 121 states that Ōmura Matsujirō was a midshipman on HMS *Northumberland* in May 1872; he was then on HMS *Bellerophon* in October 1873. Rear Admiral Geoffrey Thomas Phipps Hornby's squadron was cruising along the Atlantic shore of Portugal in late 1873 and early 1874, and did visit Lisbon; HMS *Northumberland* was part of the squadron: *Geographical Magazine* 1, 1874, pp. 33–4.
[2] Tipped in and partly obscured: 'Tuesday 22nd [Bre]akfast Cold Pork. Fried pork / [ ] Sardines to be devilled on toast w[ith] [ris]soles. [D]inner Pea Soup. Boiled Pork. [ ] rump steak with rem[oulade] of carrots. [ ] rolls ½ lbs. flour 1 oz suet. Rump steak in a pie 1 lb flour & [ ] suet. Potatoes. 2 [ ] Cabbage./ Dinner to be put on./ Feilden Soup & boiled pork. / Colan Rump steak & carrots. / Pullen Rump steak pie / Moss Pork rolls.'

THURSDAY POPS.

Programme.

Thursday November 25th 1875.

A few words on Magnetism.	Lt Giffard.
Song. *Serio Comic* "As thro the world you go"	Mr Rawlings.
Song. "Silver Moonlight"	Mr Radmore.
Recitations "Clanronald," and the "Twins."	Dr Colan.
Song. *Comic*, No smoking Allowed.	Mr Pearson.

The celebrated Brothers Chalkleburrosi, universally known as the Bounding Brothers of the Frigid Zone, will make their first appearance and exhibit a few of their astounding *feats* and *hands*.

Song. Far Away	Mr Hawkins.
Song. *Comic*, "Lieut Luff"	Mr Lawrence.
Glee. "Ye gentlemen of England"	Messrs Aldrich, Pullen and Rawson.

God Save the queen.

The Audience are respectfully invited to join in all Choruses when required.

Doors open at 7.PM. Performance to commence at 7.30.

Messrs. Giffard and Symons. Printing office Trap Lane.

Figure 19. Printed 'Thursday Pops' programme of 25 November 1875.

Friday 26 November 1875
Max +19°.2 Min −19°.2
The wind is from the S S.E blowing up Robeson channel. Absorbing the heat from the open water of that region, it came to us as a hot wind, the thermometer rising to +14°. highest during the twenty-four hours. Thus we see that a comparatively small space of open water exercises a very great effect on local temperature, consequently was there a Polynia or any space of open water to the north of us, the wind coming from that direction would be warm and damp, as it is, we find the contrary.

The absence of glaciers in Grant Land, is probably owing to its cold and dry climate, if the moist winds blow over Hall's Land and not over Grant Land it will account for one side having glaciers and the other not.

Saturday 27 November 1875
Max −11°.8 Min −20°.8
There is a very considerable twilight visible this morning in the southern horizon. Dark clouds are passing over the channel from the south. Stars bright and the ship distinguishable at a distance of half a mile.

D[r] Colan showed me a list, given to him at the Admiralty, of specimens collected by Surgeon Richard [*sic*] Anderson, of the *Enterprise* under Collinson. What became of the specimens is not known by Colan. He thinks they may still be at the Admiralty.[1]
Case marked C. addressed Sec. Admiralty London.
Contains eggs.
1.(4) Emberiza Lapponicus.[2] 2.(2) Emb. nivalis.[3] 3(2) Alauda alpestris.[4] 4.(2) Tringa pectoralis.[5] 5. (2) Tringa Schinzii.[6] 6. (2) Charad. Semipalmatus.[7] 7.(2) Tringa: ? No. 28. Cask A. 8.(2) Grus Canadensis.[8] 9.(2) Col. Septen.[9] 10.(2). Somateria Spec.[10] 11.(2) Harelda Glac.[11] } Winter Cove[12] No. 3.1852.

12.(2) Anser Hutchinsii.[13] 13.(2) Cygnus americanus.[14] 14.(2) L. Glaucus.[15] 15.(3) Char.Virginianus.[16] 16.(3) Strepsilas interpres. 17.(2) Tringa pusilla.[17] 18.(1) Phal.

---

[1] Richard Collinson (1811–83) commanded the Arctic expedition of 1850–55 that went via the Pacific Ocean and Bering Strait in a search for the Franklin expedition, see *ODNB*. Collinson, *Journal of H.M.S. Enterprise*; Barr, *Arctic Hell-Ship*. Robert Anderson was surgeon in HMS *Enterprise* under Collinson. Feilden transcribed the list of 106 items in his journal entry for 27 November 1875; it is a useful reference source for him. In transcribing this list Feilden initially wrote 'Richard', but correctly transcribed 'Robert' at the end of Anderson's list.

[2] *Emberiza lapponicus*: Lapland longspur.

[3] *Emberiza nivalis*: snow bunting.

[4] *Alauda alpestris*: horned lark, shore lark.

[5] *Tringa pectoralis*: pectoral sandpiper

[6] *Tringa Schinzii*: dunlin.

[7] *Charadrius semipalmatus*: semipalmated plover.

[8] Sandhill crane.

[9] *Columbus septentrionalis*, red-throated diver/loon

[10] *Somateria spectabilis*: king eider

[11] *Harelda glacialis*: long-tailed duck.

[12] Winter Cove is in Minto Inlet on Victoria Island, Nunavut.

[13] Hutchins' barnacle goose.

[14] Trumpeter swan.

[15] *Larus Glaucus*: glaucous gull.

[16] *Charadrius Virginianus*: American golden plover.

[17] *Tringa pusilla*: least sandpiper.

Lobatus.[1] 19.(1) Anser bernicla.[2] 10.(3) larus leucopterus. 21.(1) Larus argentatus. 22.(1) Larus sabini.[3]} Cambridge Bay[4] 1853

Case D. contains about 50 species of insects collected at Winter cove in 1852, and at Cambridge Bay in 1853.

Box Marked E with 4 Bottles.

No. 1. Vaginalis chionis[5] in spirits.No. 2. Fish lake, Winter Cove 1852. No. 3. Mollusca from Winter Cove 1852. No. 4. Sea fish and crustaceans. Winter Cove 1852.

Box F. 4 Bottles.

2. Som. Spect. And 2 som. Moll. (Var.) height of breeding season.

Box G.

No 5 & 6. Tringa? and 1 Phalarope — ? 6. Killed at Camb Bay in June 1854. Specimens of rocks. Marked 1, 2 & 3. Prevailing limestone around Winter Cove. 3 & 4. The Basalt with which many of the hills are capped.

6. Subjacent rock at point of contact.

7. ——— „ ———4 feet below.

8. ——— „ ———8 ———„———

9. ——— „ ——— 12 ———„———

10 & 11. From a very small coral deposit.

12, 13, & 14. – Rocks resting on the former, the basalt being about 12 feet above all.

15. Gypsum found about 40 miles from Winter Cove, and part of a very large deposit.

16 & 17. The prevailing rock from the north shore of Victoria land.

18 & 19. The rock of Sir R. Liston island.

20 to 63. Specimens of boulders collected at Cambridge Bay.

Signed Robert Anderson.

Aurora at night. ———————————

Sunday 28 November 1875
1st in Advent.
Max −10° Min −15°

There was a considerable haze today so that most of the stars were obscured, with the exception of the Pole Star, and the Pointers.[6] The mist or haze was, however, not opaque, and owing to the absence of clouds, objects at some distance were visible. At the end of our half-mile walk the ship loomed quite distinguishable, whilst the ridge of highland by Cape Rawson, cut the horizon, distinctly, bared cliffs, at least a mile distant, recognizable against the snow. No tinge of twilight visible in the S.E. at meridian. The moon being quite absent, and the stars obscured, I was prepared to find a pitch dark day, but so far in this dry region I have not noticed anything of the kind.

After dinner the conversation branched off on the subject of tombstones. Markham is responsible for the following, minus a little polishing by myself. Norfolk. I. churchyard.

[1] *Phalaropus lobatus*: Wilson's phalarope

[2] *Brenta bernicla*: brent goose, brant.

[3] Sabine's gull.

[4] Cambridge Bay is on Victoria Island.

[5] Sheathbill, a member of an Antarctic family. Clearly not all the birds listed by Anderson were collected in northern latitudes. The trumpeter swan, for example, goes nowhere near the Arctic.

[6] The two outermost stars in the bowl of the Big Dipper/Great Bear, which point to the Pole Star.

"Sacred to the memory of William Milbank, who convicted of murder, Departed this life in Jail, by hanging on the 13th. of May 17 – *Requiescat in Pace*. Go thou and do likewise."

Monday 29 November 1875
Max −7°.8 Min −15°
Hazy again today, but at half a mile distant, the ship was distinguishable. We have a nice flat piece of this seasons ice, lying beween the shore and the grounded hummocks, in the direction of Cape Rawson. Half a mile of this floe is marked off by little mounds, each surmounted with an empty meat can. By this means we manage to keep the track, and daily we get three or four miles brisk walking. It is quite impossible in the Arctic night as we have it now, to discern up or downs in the surface, lumps of ice or small hummocks, everything looks smooth, and white, and once off the level one goes tumbling and falling about, bringing up against hummocks and knobs of ice.

There are two journals to be found at the Admiralty which I feel confident will well repay perusal. That of D[r] Anderson,[1] surgeon of the *Enterprise*, under Collinson, and that of D[r] Rae, surgeon of the *North Star* under Saunders, when that ship wintered in Wolstenholme Sound.[2] I hope that Captain Nares will get me permission to consult these, on our return to England.

Tuesday 30 November 1875
Max −8°.2 Min −17°.8
More than 6 months from England, and the time has slipped past most pleasantly. This morning there was a marked tinge of sunlight at meridian. On the 8th of December we shall have the moon again visible, and that will carry us over the shortest day. Then the back of the winter is broken. People at home will hardly believe how difficult it is to find time to do things in the Arctic. I have no time to myself at all, suppose one gets up for breakfast at 8.30. quarters and prayers till 10 o'c. Out for exercise till 1 or a quarter past. Undressing washing, and a little reading, or perhaps a pipe carries one on to dinner at 2.30. Get away from the table at 4 or a quarter to. After a good dinner a cigar is more pleasant than study, and one feels little inclined to work until after tea at 7 o'c. At 7.30 school bell rings, and the classes last till 9 then generally two hours whist. Then a pipe. after that one has to keep up journal, read, prepare perhaps a Thursday lecture, work up theatricals and consequently I hardly ever get to bed before 2o'c. a.m.

This is the address of the man who sent us 6 doz of champagne. Fitzherbert Wright Esqr. 4. Oxford Terrace. Edgeware Road.

Temp. of sea-water today in tide-hole +28°.2. The water brought up today contained a beautiful little *Cydippe*[3] which Moss painted.

Wednesday 1 December 1875
Max +3°.2 Min −13°
A tinge of twilight visible today at noon. Ship distinguisable at half a mile distant. The Surgeon made his monthly inspection and report of health. General condition

---

[1] Anderson's MS 'Medical Journal', from Collinson's expedition survives; I have not located his natural history journal. See Feilden, 'Prince Albert Land', p. 1.

[2] *North Star*, Commander James L. Saunders, was a supply ship for Franklin search 1849–50. For Rae's journal, see Rae, *Narrative of an Expedition*.

[3] A typical genus of Ctenophora, transparent marine animals of gelatinous substance.

THURSDAYS POPS.

H.M.S. ALERT,

December 2nd 1875.

THE Manager has great pleasure in announcing to the Patrons, and others, of the deservedly Popular Thursday Entertainments, that, on the above date, there will be an entire change of programme, which he sincerely trusts will give general satisfaction and amusement. Having been successful in securing the services of the eminent talented Naturalist to the Expedition, CAPTAIN FEILDEN, the entertainment will commence with a Geological Lecture, delivered by that distinguished gentleman, and illustrated by Phantasmagorical assistance — to be followed by a series of Views, exhibited by means of the Magic Lantern, consisting of Tales and Comic scenes. Amongst the former will be the story of 'Aladdin and the Wonderful Lamp' 'the Settler and the Savages or Ingratitude punished' and the truly romantic history of 'Lord Bateman', set to music and sung by LIEUT RAWSON.

Our very able and renowned Pianist, LIEUT ALDRICH will, as usual preside at the Orchestra.

To commence at 7.30 precisely.

Children in Arms, not admitted.

God Save the Queen.

MESSRS. GIFFARD and SYMONS :
Printing Office, Trap Lane.

Figure 20.   Printed programme for 'Thursday Pops' of 2 December 1875, including Feilden's lecture on geology.

satisfactory. There is no doubt that we eat much less in the wardroom mess than we did, and I understand that yesterday several of the men reported to the Doctor loss of appetite. This is only what might be expected from the amount of confinement and lack of exercise that we have to submit to. Accompanying loss of appetite is the most disagreeable sleeplessness, I hardly ever get to sleep before 4 a.m., and at 8 o'c. when I am called I am scarcely able to get up. Immediatly after dinner any one of us could sleep, if we gave in to the feeling, but after tea we are all as lively as crickets. ♀ Canis familiaris[1] died this afternoon.

Thursday 2 December 1875[2]
[*The 'Thursday Pops' programme for 2 December 1875 was tipped in; see Figure 20, p. 147.*]
Max +29° Min −9°
Petersen tells me that the body of the bitch left out last night was much eaten by the other dogs, that they took it this morning and pushed it down the tide hole. No twilight and not a single star visible today, yet at half a mile distant the ship was distinguisable.

I gave a short lecture on how a piece of sandstone was formed, illustrating it with some slides in the Magic Lantern, and wound up with a disquisition on *Elephas primigenius.*[3]

I added to my comforts today, by unscrewing the dead-light in my cabin, and placing over it a box in which there is a tin lining with a hole in it, attached to this is an inch wide, india rubber tube which brings down a constant stream of fresh air into my cabin, and only reducing its temperature some 3° below that of the wardroom.

Friday 3 December 1875
Max +35° Min −9°.5
There has been an extraordinary variation in the temperature today. The maximum reached was +35°. At 5.30 p.m. (the wind blowing from S.S.E.) at an elevation of 18 feet on a hummock, the thermo. registered +28°.2. but during the lulls it fell at least one degree, a foot from the surface of the ice it registered +26°, on the ice +19°, at 2 inches in the ice +11 at 4 in. +8 at 8 inches +3°. The water in the fire hole at a depth of 8 feet showed +28.2° (the normal temperature). At 6 o'c. two thermos. taken simultaneously at the maintop and four feet from the floe, gave +24° for the higher elevation and +21° for the lower.

At meridian there was a tinge of twilight in the southern horizon, and at 5.30 p.m, there was sufficient difference to make the southern hills, stand out distinctly against the faint shade of light. The point of demarkation [*sic*] must be at least two miles from the ship. This shows that the strong warm wind from the S.E. must have been remarkably dry. No clouds were visible. The open water in Hall's basin cannot have influenced the

---

[1] Domestic dog, in this case sledge dog, i.e. husky.

[2] The 'Thursday Pops' programme for this date includes this announcement: 'THE Manager has great pleasure in announcing to the Patrons, and others, of the deservedly Popular Thursday Entertainments, that, on the above date, there will be an entire change of programme, which he sincerely trusts will give general satisfaction and amusement. Having been successful in securing the services of the eminent talented Naturalist to the Expedition, CAPTAIN FEILDEN, the entertainment will commence with a Geological Lecture, delivered by that distinguished gentleman, and illustrated by Phatasmagorical assistance.' Phantasmagorical assistance refers to projections and optical illusions produced by the magic lantern.

[3] Woolly mammoth.

temperature as its head is about +28°.2 and the wind +35°. Therefore this breeze must have arisen in the warm regions of the south, and during its course had deposited on Greenland its vapour, to form the glaciers, and hurried on to us as a dry but still warm wind. This is the only way I can account for the absence of glaciers in Grants Land. I noticed in the holes which I helped bore in the hummock today that if I placed the dark lantern with the metal back close to the augur hole, and stood in front of the glass, the light being reflected from my legs, shone down the perforations, which assumed a pale blue tint. By recovering the lantern and allowing the glare to fall on the hole, it looked quite black.

~~On the 11ᵗʰ Dec. 1875, I remarked that the bitch which returned on that date after a disappearance of nearly two months, carried~~[1]

Saturday 4 December 1875[2]
Max −8° Min −24°
There was a strong breeze all night from south. The thermo. continued to play most fantastic tricks. But after breakfast the wind lulled and the temperature soon went down to −9°. The ice around the ship made a cracking noise during the night. The fire-hole flooded nearly a foot of water over the ice forming the floor of the snow-hut.

Our difference of time here with Greenwich is 4 hours and 6 minutes, so that though we dine at 2.30 most of our friends are doing the same at home.

Yesterdays wonderful freaks in temperature, are ascribed by some of my messmates to heated air from the southward, and until I had revolved the matter over in my mind, was of the same opinion. But I find that Mʳ Murphy (Proc. Roy. Soc, XI, p.309)[3] enters fully into this question, and states that the phenomenon seems due to the breaking up of ice fields by a storm, and exposing the warmer water below, that, though the temperature at the surface of the water is +28° yet in the Polar Regions the temperature of the sea increases in descending until a stratum is reached of the invariable temperature of +39°, and we may suppose that in these storms the warmer water of the deeper strata is brought to the surface.

If this be so the breaking up of Hall's basin and Robeson Straits will account for the high temperature.

Sunday 5 December 1875
Max −2° Min −21°.5
Managed a little reading today, as it is too dark to keep one outside with any pleasure. I walked I daresay three miles before dinner.

"Temperature for November 1875. H.M.S. *Alert*. 82°. 27. N. L. 61°. 30. W. L.

Max.	Min	Mean	D°[4] Capt. Cab.	D° W*ard*.*Room*.	D°. Main deck
+23°	−46°.6	−17°	+51°.7	+44°.2	+44°.7

D° Mess Deck.	D° Drying room.
+56°.4	+60°.7"

---

[1] The entry is incomplete, and ends here.
[2] Scrap of paper with breakfast and dinner menus written by Feilden, tipped in.
[3] Murphy, 'On Great Fluctuations of Temperature', 1860–62.
[4] D° is Ditto.

Monday 6 December 1875
Max +4°.8 Min −12°.8
I very seldom recollect dates, but this is one that is especially engraved on my mind. viz. The defeat of the Gwalior contingent at Cawnpore in 1857, eighteen years ago. It was an impressive sight our night march back along the Calpee [*sic*][1] road towards Cawnpore. The moon shone out plainly at times, and illumined the dead bodies strewed along the road, but what affected me most was seeing several dead women with little infants in their arms, who had either been killed by retreating sepoys, to prevent them from falling alive into our hands, or else they had been speared by the Sikh cavalry in the heat of the pursuit.[2]

Walking with Parr on the floe, after breakfast, we observed a brilliant meteor, that came from a northerly direction, and burst seemingly over the ship. Rehearsal of "Aladdin the Wonderful Scamp." What with schools, lectures and rehearsals, I have not time for one tenth of the things I had planned to do this winter. The moon showed above the high land to the south at 6 p.m. more than half full.

Tuesday 7 December 1875
Max +1° Min −13°.2
The moon shone up this evening. [*4 lines blacked out*] some days ago [*name blacked out*] asked me to give him a piece of the drift-wood found by Markham's party in the autumn travelling. If any one else in the ship had asked me I would willingly have done so, as I had previously with the [*1 line blacked out*] knowing well that these officers had only the interests of the expedition at heart, and would make no outside use of information thus obtained.[3] [*Name blacked out*] on the contrary publicly enunciates, that he was accepted his appointment under the impression that he was to be [*2 words blacked out. Possibly the official*] naturalist to the expedition; that the appointment of an outsider to this post relieves him from all obligation to the public on that score, and that he is justified in amassing every item of scientific research or discovery – outside of his duties [*1 or 2 words blacked out*] for his own future advantage [*2 or 3 words blacked out*] My views [*22 lines cut out with knife or razor; see Figure 21, p. 151.*]
"Egerton do you know where the Captain keeps his paints and brushes for I want to return some" – and Egerton further tells me that he then cut off a piece of the drift-wood. I am quite sure that the Captain would have let him have the wood had he asked him for it. I object to this underhand dealing. He ought to have gone to the Captain and said "Feilden for some reason or other wont give me a piece of drift-wood, will you do so."

Wednesday 8 December 1875
Max −9°.5 Min −24°.8
[*The dinner menu for 8 December 1875 was tipped in; See Figure 22, p. 152.*]

---

[1] Kalpi.

[2] This was during the Indian Rebellion against the authority of the East India Company, 1857–8. In 1857 Feilden was an ensign in the 42nd (Royal Highland) Regiment of Foot, and accompanied his regiment to India, where he took part in the relief of Cawnpore (now Kanpur). In Cawnpore, the rebellion began on 5 June; Cawnpore was recaptured by the British on 16 July 1857. For the Gwalior Contingent, see Khan, 'Gwalior Contingent in 1857–58'.

[3] This entry, with all its deletions, refers to the disgruntled Edward Lawton Moss.

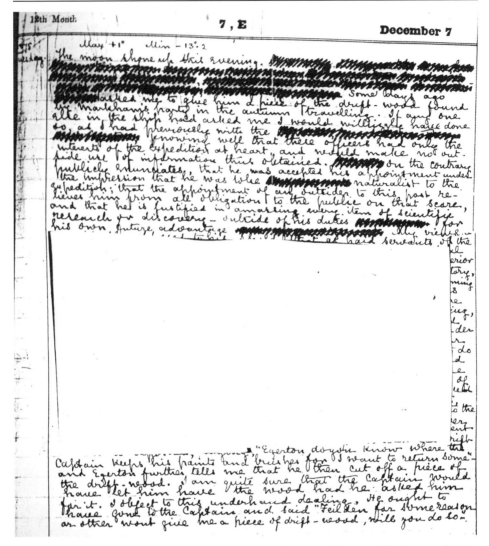

Figure 21. Photograph of the page for 7 December 1875 from Feilden's journal. This entry, concerning Feilden's relations with Moss, is the only one from which he physically excised a good part of the text with a knife or razor, as well as deleting other passages.

Aldrich's birthday.[1] The moon above the northern horizon shedding a most grateful light, around oure [sic] icebound home.

Captain Nares paid Aldrich a very pretty compliment today in naming the range of mountains beyond Cape Joseph Henry after Admiral Cooper Key,[2] to whom A. was

[1] Hence the handsome dinner menu, reprinted p. 152. On the menu for Aldrich's birthday dinner, Feilden added a sketch showing Aldrich and Adam Ayles, 2nd captain foretop, with Cape Aldrich and the Cooper Key Mountains in the distance; the date of 27 Sept. 1875 was added later. Nares, *Narrative*, I, p.155, and extracts from Aldrich's official journal, ibid., pp. 155–63, give an account of Aldrich's journey from 22 Sept. to 5 Oct. 1875.

[2] Admiral Sir Astley Cooper Key (1821–88). *ODNB*.

C. Cooper Key Mountains.
A. Cape Aldrich. N. Lat. 83° 45'.
B. Lt. Aldrich + Blue-jacket Ayles.
27ᵗ Sept. 1875.

MENU.
....
POTAGES

De Petits Pois a la Cuilliere de Michel.

Poissons

Saumon pris d'Epingles courbes.

ENTREES

Cotelettes a la Simmons avec Sauce Frederic.

Ragout de Bœuf a la Traineau de Chien.

RELEVES

Dindon de Marine a la Joseph Henri.

Huishe debris sur la Floe.

ENTREMETS

Pouding Anglais a la Pelham.

Confiteur de Marmelade a la Capato.

Blanc-manger d' Ayles.

Pouding de groseilles a la Challenger.

DESSERT

Biscuits.   Figues.   Peches.

Cafe.

H. M. S. 'Alert'   8th Dec. 1875.

Feilden

Figure 22.   Printed dinner menu for 8 December 1875, Aldrich's birthday, signed by Feilden, with sketch dated 27th. Sept. 1875, showing Aldrich and Adam Ayles, 2nd captain foretop, with Cooper Key Mountains and Cape Aldrich.

THURSDAY POPS.

December 9th 1875.

1

'A Few Words on Meteorology' :   Lieut. Aldrich.

2 Song.

'Norwood Gipsy at the Races' :   Mr. Harley.

3 Ballad.

'Shamrock of Ireland' :   Mr. Joiner.

4 Recitation.

'The Sailor and the Jew' :   Mr. Simmons.

5

Sailor's Hornpipe :   Mr. Cranstone.

6 Song.

'The Conductor of the Tramway' :   Mr. Symons.

7 Reading.

'A Night in a Railway Carriage' :   Rev. H.W. Pullen.

8 Song.

'My Maria was a Fairy Queen' :   Mr. Hindle.

9 Ballad.

'Beautiful Isle of the Sea' :   Mr. Winstone.

10 Song.

'Once I courted a Cook' :   Mr. Doidge.

11 Ballad.

'Union Jack of Old England' :   Mr. Francombe.

To commence at 7.30 precisely.

God Save the Queen.

Messrs. Giffard and Symons :
Printing Office, Trap Lane.

Figure 23. Printed 'Thursday Pops' programme, 9 December 1875.

153

flag-lieutenant in the Mediterranean, and the furthest point of land, approximate to be in 83°.15′ N. Lat. Cape Aldrich, after the discoverer.

Aldrich is one of the most loveable characters I ever met, perfectly unselfish, a thoroughly good sailor, industrious and hard working, with plenty of brains, and actuated by a desire to do to his neighbour as he would be done by, firm and honest, with plenty of courage, if I could praise him any more I would.

Thursday 9 December 1875[1]
[*The 'Thursday Pops' programme for 9 December 1875 was tipped in; see Figure 23, p. 153.*]
Max −18° Min −29°
Walking this day along the 'Lady's Mile'.[2] I heard a peculiar cry sounding from the hills, it must have been some of our dogs chasing hares or on the track of some animal, but it was certainly different to any note I have yet heard from our dogs, neither did it resemble the bark of a fox, but was a melancholy note.

Aldrich's lecture on meteorology was very good, describing the making and marking of the barometer and thermometer.
[*Margin*: 1876] This must have been a wolf in all probability H.W.F.

Friday 10 December 1875
Max −7° Min −17°
Moss has got under weigh rather an ingenious design, for collecting and procuring for microscopic investigation any foreign matter that may be carried in the upper currents of air. The apparatus is a weather gage with an open mouthed funnel, a pipe leads from this into a small box, fitted with a glass slide coated with glycerine which can be removed and subjected to the microscope.[3] If fastened to the mast head I do not think it will be a fair test for the vapour constantly rising from the ship must be charged with foreign matter, if placed on a hummock the snow drift will settle on the glass.

I placed today, in the thermometer stand, on the floe, a cigar box containing samples of about twenty different kinds of seeds. These I propose submitting to the cold for the whole winter and again the next, take them back to Kew, and see whether they will there germinate. A second lot of the same seeds must be treated for a single winter. Then I must place a variety of seeds in a bottle of water keeping it at a temperature of 50° or more for some weeks then expose them to the cold. Take them home also.

I try to get information from Petersen in regard to the habits customs and weapons of the Etah Eskimo, he had abundant opportunities of observation whilst wintering with Dr Hayes at Port Foulke, but, from my inability to speak Danish I cannot extract all I want. He says that those Eskimo were unable to kill the reindeer by their own means, this is at variance with my observations made at the ancient iglus of Etah, the bones and horns of *Cervus tarandus* were very abundant in the bone heaps, and these heaps must certainly be of great antiquity.

[1] The 'Thursday Pops' programme began with 'A Few Words on Meteorology' by Lieut. Aldrich.
[2] The 'Lady's Mile' was the exercise path across the snow from HMS *Alert* for the crew when they were not otherwise physically active. It was marked by tin cans.
[3] Exposing glycerine-coated plates to the atmosphere, and then examining them with a microscope, was a relatively new technique. See, e.g., *The Observatory*, 1 Dec. 1878, p. 257.

The arrow I found there was a sufficiently formidable weapon to tranfix a reindeer, and Petersen says that small bows and arrows were used by the children, to shoot birds &c. Now it seems improbable that a tribe should arrive at this knowledge of the use of the bow and arrow without applying it to ulterior purposes.

Petersen tells me, that these Eskimos are cognizant of the use of the drill. They take a disc of ivory the size of half a crown, with a round depression in its centre, this disc is held firmly between the teeth, a stick <or bone> of about a foot in length and about the thickness of a little finger is tipped with a square sided piece of stone ground to a point. – since intercourse with Europeans, iron has taken the place of stone – the other end is placed in the depression of the disc, and a rib of narwhal to which is attached a string of hide passes round the borer, is moved rapidly by the hand & makes a good drill. Petersen tells me further that this drill is stilled [*sic* still] used by the Greenlanders of Upernevik and the northern Danish settlements.

Saturday 11 December 1875
Max −7° Min −17°
The moon very bright, the heavens at noon, unobscured by a single cloud. I took "Darwin's Voyage of a Naturalist" Murray's edition 1873,[1] on to the floe and read a page of it with out difficulty. Cape Joseph Henry was discernible; the seasons ice measured today, through a hole cut in the floe one hundred yards from the ship 40 inches exactly. Aldrich when returning from <going on> his sledge journey to Cape Joseph Henry on the 25 Sept. cut loose a bitch that was constantly ill, and gave much trouble. When Commander Markham was returning on the same route during the second week of October, this animal hung about his party and though never approaching in the daytime, came to their tents at night and picked up scraps that were left out for her. She was noticed on the 13th of Oct, the night prior to the sledge parties arriving at the ship. Tonight she came back to the ship, but would not consort with the other dogs. Petersen caught her and she was a mere bag of bones. She did not appear very shy with us. On making enquiries, I am inclined to think that at least three days ago, that is the first day the moon rose above the northern horizon and consequently light at night, the same animal was seen prowling round the ship at night. The most probable supposition is that this animal must have for the last two months been stealthily visiting the ship at night, and picking up offal. It is possible that the product of the chase could have supported the animal. I look upon this as an instance of the Eskimo dog reverting to its wolfish descent. Perhaps the fits from which it suffered produced hallucinations, for all our dogs are treated most kindly, and would have thought their instinct would have at once brought them back to the ship. The weird howling heard on the 9th inst. probably came from this dog.

This bitch carries her tail in a drooping wolfish manner.

Sunday 12 December 1875
Max −7°.8 Min −21°.8
Misty today, with slight snow fall. The bitch referred to yesterday is today onboard, and being well fed seems quite contented on the upper deck.

---

[1] Darwin, *Journal of Researches*, new edn.

Monday 13 December 1875
Max −19°.8 Min −33°

The only pup that we have managed to rear so far, died today in a fit combined with cramps. A beautifully clear moonlight day.

The glycerine covered slide exposed to the current of air, showed under the microscope, numerous round sporules, with a centre ring; some are joined together. Moss says that he considers them animals. He has taken drawings of them however. He found that after melting a quantity of snow the other day that the residuum contained similar sporules.

The snow hut on the ice which has been used for holding salt pork, in order to see whether in the warmer atmosphere it would part with some of its saline properties, was opened today. temperature inside +11°. The roof of the hut was festooned with crystals.

Tuesday 14 December 1875
Max −21° Min −33°

It is curious, how, if one's mind runs on a certain train of thought evidences for or against ones argument, come to hand. On the 10th inst. I was much interested by Petersen's description of the drill used by the Eskimo of Port Foulke. Turning to Evans' "Ancient Stone Implements of Great Britain" p.p. 288–291"[1] no mechanical drills, appear to have hitherto been met with, these implements used as drills are simply flakes pointed, and turned by the hand. By mere accident, I today got a sight of a small collection of flints, found in an ancient grave at Upernuvik [*sic* Upernavik], and given by the Govenor's wife to Dr Colan. The first thing that met my eye in this collection was a stick of hard slaty stone about three inches long, of the size and shape of a slate pencil, that could be nothing else than the drill. This bespeaks for the Eskimo a considerable degree of mechanical ingenuity.

Wednesday 15 December 1875
Max −17°.8 Min −26°

Moss' birthday, as usual <on these occasions> we had a good dinner,[2] and we gave the hero of the hour a few little presents.

I was today able to clear up to my own satisfaction all doubts respecting the position of the lands to the northward of us, said to have been seen by them <the *Polaris* expedition> as far as latitude 84° N. See copy of despatch, addressed by the late Captain Hall, to the Sec. of the United States Navy, dated from Cape Perevoard [*sic*], 20th Oct. 1871. "From Cape Brevoart [*sic*] we can see land extending on the west side of the Strait to the north 22°. W., and distant about seventy miles, thus making land we discover as far as lat. 83°.5'. N.

---

[1] Evans, *Ancient Stone Implements*, pp. 288–91.

[2] Menu: 'This is the SOUP not − mulligatawny / KIDNEYS on toast − LOBSTER cutlets so prawny / A HARE shot by MOSS roasted to dish up / And a very nice CURRIE a la mode Bishop / The BEEF of Old England − salt boiled − not frest roast / None the less 'tis the best of which England could boast. / A Paraselenic PLUM-PUDDING comes next / 'Twixt shapes and cloths there's a question much vexed / BLANC-MANGE with Jam − and also MINCE-PIES / A la Eccleston Square − a regular prize / The Dessert's much as usual − you'll all know the reason − / 'Tis difficult here to get things out of season / But we seize on this festive occasion to say / Many happy returns to friend MOSS of this day.'

There is appearance of land farther north, and extending more easterly than what I have first noted, but a peculiar, dark nimbus cloud that constantly hangs over what seems may be land prevents my making a full determination."[1]

It is most satisfying to find, that the observations of this honest Arctic traveller, agree almost exactly with the results obtained by us. He hit off distance, bearing and latitude of Cape Joseph Henry, almost as we have since found it. On the dictum of some of the sailors of the *Polaris* expeditions, Hall's correct observations appear to have been shunted, and the American chart sticks Cape Joseph Henry nearly a degree to the northward of what it really is, while "the appearance of land" with "dark nimbus cloud" had procreated into President's Land. I must admit, however, that the appearance of this peculiar nimbus was most illusive, and it took days of patient watching, by many pairs of eyes, before we became certain, that no land, lay in that direction, within the scope of our vision, aided by glasses.

It is highly probable that the result of this voyage will be to show, that instead of an open Polar Sea, a disc of thick ribbed ice, caps this unknown part of our hemisphere. I therefore give the name of Paleocrystic to this area (*palaeios*, ancient – *Kruos*, ice), to distinguish it from what is generally called the Arctic regions.

Thursday 16 December 1875
[*The 'Thursday Pops' programme for 16 December 1875 was tipped in; see Figure 24, p. 158.*]
Max −19° Min −39°.5
The assumption of some reasoners, that an 'Open Polar Sea' exists cannot I think, with our present knowledge be upheld. We must first define the terms 'Open Polar Sea' and 'Open Water' in their true sense, and not as applied in a hap-hazard manner to Polynias, pools or spaces kept open in ice bound regions by the action of winds and tides. By open polar sea, I should define a large expanse of navigable water, in the vicinity of the Pole which admitted of regular navigation at certain seasons of the year, it is not necessary that it should for the whole year remain unencumbered with ice, but that the same area should be acted on yearly by the same influences and produce a similarity of results.

Such a result can only be attained by one force and that is an enormous warm current such as the Gulf Stream, which keeps open the Old Greenland Sea, and the West Coast of Spitzbergen. The term 'Open Water' is often misapplied by Arctic navigators, leads, lanes and pools in ice, which are only transitory, and due entirely to the shifting of the ice by wind, tide, local pressure, etc, are thus designated. To illustrate this, my idea is, that the north water of Baffin's Bay, Hall's Basin, and Lancaster Sound, may be correctly styled 'Open Waters' for the navigator may safely predict that in every season, a greater or less extent of open water will be found in these areas. Whilst the only real 'Open Polar Sea', with which we are acquainted is the 'Old Greenland', cleared, entirely by the action of the Gulf stream. Therefore we must consider 'Open Polar Sea', and 'Open water', as the maximum and minimum <result> of similar effects. Arctic travellers, particularly sledge

---

[1] Cape Brevoort. Hall, 'Copy of Draft of Captain Hall's Dispatch', 1871, in Hall, *Report of the Secretary of the Navy*, 1873, p. 294. Brevoort Island is off the SE coast of Baffin Island.

H.M.S. 'ALERT'

THURSDAY   POPS.

DECEMBER 16th 1876.

Great Attraction ! The Latest Novelty of the Season !!
The WIZARD OF THE NORTH !!! ☞ For One Night only!!!!

PROGRAMME.

The Entertainment will commence with
A FEW WORDS ON STEAM :   MR. WOOTTON.
After which the Only and Veritable
WIZARD OF THE NORTH,
en route to his Hyperborean Domicile,
will exhibit, and expound, some of his original and
inimitable illusions and feats of Prestidigitation, consisting
of the following Wonderful and Startling Tricks.

The Vanishing Egg.

The Magic Die.

The Mysterious Sixpence.

The Magic Shawl.

A startling Surgical Operation.

The Marvellous Watch Trick.

Tricks with Cards.

The Magic Bag Trick.

The Wonderful Generating Hat.

The Astounding Prestidigitorial Metamorphis,
performed with an Egg and Silk Handkerchief.

Our very able and renowned Pianist, LIEUT ALDRICH, will,
as usual, preside at the Orchestra.

To commence at 7.30 precisely.

God Save the Queen.

MESSRS. GIFFARD and SYMONS :
Printing Office, Trap Lane.

Figure 24.   Printed 'Thursday Pops' programme, 16 December 1875, including 'The Wizard of the North'.

voyageurs, should therefore be most careful in applying the term 'Open water'. The extent, the changes under the influence of the tides and winds should be carefully noted, and every Arctic traveller should make it an axiom never to use the term 'Arctic Water' in a slipshod manner.

There can be no doubt that the description of floe ice met with, by McClure and Collinson, on the eastward of Behring Straits, by the German expedition under Koldewey, by Parry north of Spitzbergen, by Payer and Weyprecht at Francis Joseph Land,[1] and by our expedition after clearing the north entrance of Smiths Sound is much thicker and heavier than that met with in Hudson Bay, Baffins Bay, and Lancaster Sound, and that it is similar to the drift of the East Coast of Greenland, which is the only true exit of the ice grown within the area of the unknown Polar region, and to which area I give the name Paleocrystic, or ancient ice. The limits of this Paleocrystic area may be defined with some degree of accuracy, and in those instances where our arctic explorations have not found this heavy ice impinging on the shores of the most northerly land attained by them, we may rest assured that beyond that point more land exists which acts as a 'breakwater' in warding off the Polar ice.

Friday 17 December 1875
Max −22°.8 Min −38°.8

The Palaeocrystic area, may be roughly defined as stretching across the north entrance of Robeson channel – <its ice> pressing on the north coast of Greenland, and pushing down the east coast of that continent, making the Greenland drift, which is met with south of Cape Farewell, the Gulf Stream pushes it back to the North shores of Nova Zembla[2] and Spitzbergen – its limits to the north of Siberia are not yet defined. At Behring Straits it attempts to push out, but is driven back by the Japanese warm current. This same thick-ribbed ice typhical [*sic*] of the area, is kept off the American shore, by the outflow of the great rivers, but still hugs it closely, it came on to the next shore of Prince Patrick I. Banks Land, a portion pushes through Banks Straits, making <further> navigation in that direction impossible and driving down McClintock Channel and Victoria Straits, finally jams between Victoria Land and King William Island, after rounding Cape Aldrich in Lat. 83.15, I believe that the general trend of the land will be S.W. in the direction of Prince Patrick's Island.

It will be seen from this that the drift wood brought down from the interior of both Asia and America is continually being pushed back by the polar ice – consequently it is a matter of extreme interest to find out from whence the drift wood found in the Palaeocrystic area comes from. I think we may rest satisfied that within this area no true

---

[1] Franz Josef Land. Robert John Le Mesurier McClure (1807–73), *Investigator*, Franklin search expedition 1850–54: see McClure, *Discovery of a North-West Passage*. Richard Collinson (1811–83), Franklin search expedition 1850–55: see Collinson, *Journal of H.M.S. Enterprise*. Karl Christian Koldewey (1837–1908) led two German Arctic expeditions, the first in 1868; Feilden is referring to the expedition of 1869–70, when Koldewey reached 75°30′N, off the east coast of Greenland: see Koldewey, *Die Zweite deutsche Nordpolarfahrt*. (William) Edward Parry (1790–1855): see Parry, *Attempt to Reach the North Pole*. Julius J. L. R. von Payer (1841–1915) and Karl Weyprecht (1838–81): see Payer and Weyprecht, 'Austro-Hungarian Polar Expedition', and Payer, *New Lands Within the Arctic Circle*.

[2] Nova Zembla Island is an uninhabited island off the north-eastern coast of Baffin Island. Feilden is here referring to Novaya Zemlya, in the Russian Arctic.

whales can exist, perhaps no cetacean. With the extinction of the *Mysticetus* in Lancaster Sound, Ponds Bay and Davis Straits, the British Whaling trade will come to an end.[1]

Saturday 18 December 1875
Max −14° Min −34°
Last appearance of the moon for more than a fortnight. Her light is most welcome. Whilst shining brightly, it has a good effect in increasing the appetites of our men – sitting always as vice at the ward-room table I can guage[2] very accurately my messmates appetites, and I am confident that even the reflected light of the moon, had a most wholesome action on the digestion.

The temperature of the fire-hole taken today was +28°.2 at the surface. +25.5 at the bottom, depth 36 feet.

In W. Henry Elliots account of the Fauna of the Pribilof Is. he comes to the conclusion that the Walrus of Behring Straits is distinct from the old world species.[3]

Sunday 19 December 1875
Max −32° Min −40°.8
I was mistaken in noting that yesterday was the date of the last appearance of the moon – She showed again this morning but this will be our last sight of her till next year. Rather seedy with a cold on my chest.

When we assemble for prayers on the upper deck in the morning, a lamp which is hung up close to the guy or ridge which supports the housing, is lowered for the use of the Chaplain, in certain positions, the atmosphere between the lamp and the eye of the observer, appears full of minute spiculae of ice, which appear to be constantly falling. I ascribe this to the greater cold of the lamp which condenses the breath of the bystanders. Parry remarks the same phenomenon, in his first voyage.[4]

Monday 20 December 1875
Max −31° Min −45°
Not allowed out on the floe today, by our good Doctor, owing to the cold in my chest.

The glycerine plates put up by Moss, have their surfaces scattered over with minute forms, but whether they are natural to the air, or come from the impurities in the vicinity of the ship, I cannot say. These forms consist of globes ×520 ⊙ inner part coloured red. some are entirely black. My microscope magnifies 🐛 about 520 to 530 diameters. Moss' about 450.

Tuesday 21 December 1875[5]
Max −21° Min −42°

[1] British Arctic whaling west of Greenland ended in 1914. For a general account, see Jackson, *British Whaling Trade*.

[2] Obsolete spelling of gauge.

[3] Elliott, *Affairs in the Territory of Alaska*, chaps 6 and 7, pp. 63–164, discusses the Pribilof Islands, their inhabitants, and the sea-mammals; his comments on the distinct species of walrus in those islands are on pp. 160–64.

[4] Parry, *Journal of a Voyage*, has numerous references to condensing breath and spiculae of ice, but I have not found one specifically referring to the action of a lamp.

[5] Scrap of paper with menu tipped in.

This is generally called the shortest day, but as the astronomical day counts from meridian to meridian, and not like the civil day, from midnight to midnight, it happens this year that the sun reaches its greatest southern declination, between midnight of the 21st and tomorrow morning.

What a pleasure it is to think that half of the darkness is gone. Still kept below by my cold.

Informed my class[1] this evening, that they would have no more instruction till Monday the 27th.

Wednesday 22 December 1875[2]
Max −31° Min −43°

The shortest day. Hurra! M[r] Sun on his way back to gladden our hearts. We had our final rehearsal of 'Aladdin or the wonderful Scamp' this morning on the lower deck.[3] Performance comes off tomorrow. Captain Nares tells me that he thinks he has observed the track of an ermine on the floe today.

[*There were three sheets inserted with the text for 23 December 1875, two parts of the printed 'Thursday Pops' programme for that day, and a sketch of Captain Feilden as Widow Twankay; see Figures 25–27, pp. 162–4.*]

Thursday 23 December 1875
Max −31° Min −43°.8   *This is not my own personal observation
At noon, type ¹¹⁄₅₀ of an inch in perpendicular height, could be deciphered:

Has it ever been remarked by Darwen [*sic*] or other writers on the same subject of variation of species by natural selection, that as the more perfect forms are reached, nature shows less tendency to depart from that type, or as the corollary, that when we meet with species long under domestication that do not seem to admit of great variation may we assume that nature in their cases ~~nature~~ has attained its highest phase of progressive development – Thinking of the differences between cats and dogs as I lay in bed this morning, caused me to reflect on this subject.

Friday 24 December 1875
Max −15° Min −43°.8
Last nights theatricals went off very well, the acting and dresses were excellent. The men's piece "Boots at the Swan" was most successful, Stone[4] as 'Boots' first rate.

---

[1] Feilden performed his share in instructing the men. A. H. Markham, *The Great Frozen Sea*, p. 101: 'Our school was opened on the 1st of November; from which date, until the reappearance of the sun, the attendance was regular and constant. It was composed of nearly the whole ship's company, and was divided into classes under the direct supervision of the officers. Reading, writing, history, arithmetic, and navigation were the principal subjects in which the pupils were instructed.'

[2] MS menu tipped in.

[3] The entertainment on 23 December was a double bill: first a farce entitled *Boots at the Swan*, followed by *Aladdin, or the Wonderful Scamp*, described as a burlesque-extravaganza in one act. Feilden has tipped in a printed cutting, beginning: '*The* WIDOW TWANKAY *comes on in a wild manner*. ... WIDOW. Aladdin! What's become of you, Aladdin? / Such conduct a young boy is very sad in; / ...' The scenery for *Aladdin* was designed and painted by Moss.

[4] For George Stone, see below, p. 184, n. 1.

ROYAL ARCTIC THEATRE

December 23rd 1875.

☞ Positively for the First Time in Lat. 82 27 N.

Her Majesty's Servants

Will have the Honour to Perform the

POPULAR AND LAUGHABLE FARCE

Entitled the

BOOTS AT THE SWAN.

CHARACTERS :

MR. HENRY HIGGINS, *a gentleman with an unfortunate name, and a fervent attachment to Emily Trevor* MR. STUCKBERRY.

FRANK FRISKLY, *a cavalry captain, with a genius for invention, a propensity for progression, and an attachment for everything but his regiment* MR. WOOLEY.

PETER PIPPIN, *a promising young gentleman in livery, with an inquiring mind, and an unfortunate attachment* MR. CHALKLEY.

JACOB EARWIG, *"the Boots at the Swan," a free-and-easy youth, with a talent for pantomime, a refined taste, and a strong attachment to refreshment* MR. STONE.

MISS CECILIA MOONSHINE, *a romantic lady, a victim to sentiment and light reading, with a fond attachment to extraordinary novelties* MDL. FRANCOMBI.

EMILY TREVOR, *a young lady, with a fortune in prospective, and a confessed attachment to Mr. Henry Higgins* MISS CRANSTONE.

SALLY SMITH, *a genteel housemaid, with a good character from her last place, and a slight attachment to a fancy baker* MISS MASKELLI.

Scene 1 A room in an Hotel
Scene 2 A Drawing-room.

Figure 25. Printed 'Thursday Pops' programme, 23 December 1875. Part 1, 'Boots at the Swan'. The original handbill is in poor condition.

After- Which,

Her Majesty's Servants

Will give an Operatic Representation of

ALADDIN, OR THE
WONDERFUL SCAMP:

A BURLESQUE - EXTRAVAGANZA

In One Act.

CHARACTERS :

THE EMPEROR OF CHINA, *A Monarch in difficulties, who
was under the necessity of marrying his
Daughter to the Richest Man about
Town.* MR. G. Le C. EGERTON.

ALADDIN, *A Lively Youth, but a Sad Boy, who was more
fortunate than he deserved to be.* MR. G. A. GIFFARD.

ABANAZAR, *A Magician, who had been round the world,
but could not get round Aladdin.* CAPT. MARKHAM.

THE WIDOW TWANKAY, *Aladdin's Ancient Mother, who in her
youth had never been beautiful, and who had
not grown more lovely in her old age.* CAPT. FEILDEN.

PRINCESS BADROULBADOUR, *The Pearl of the East, and the Light
of her Father's Eyes.* MR. WYATT RAWSON.

Scene 1	Pekin.
Scene 2	The Jewelled Cavern.
Scene 3	The Interior of Widow Twankay's Dwelling.
Scene 4	Hall in The Emperor's Palace.
Scene 5	Aladdin's Palace in the Suburbs of Pekin.
Scene 6	The Same transported by Magic to Africa.

The Beautiful Scenery wholly designed and painted by Professor Moss.

Music arranged and executed by SIGNORE ALDRICHI.

To commence at 7.30 precisely.

God Save The Queen.

MESSRS. GIFFARD and SYMONS :
Printing Office, Trap Lane.

Figure 26.   Printed 'Thursday Pops' programme, 23 December 1875. Part 2,
'ALADDIN, OR THE WONDERFUL SCAMP'.

163

Captain Feilden
as
Widow Twankay.

Figure 27. Sketch, tipped in to the journal, of 'Captain Feilden as Widow Twankay', initialled 'GleCE', i.e. George Le Clerc Egerton, Sub-Lieutenant, *Alert*.

To me it is a great effort to join in the troupe, but feel it my duty to aid in carrying out amusements up here, though it is rather hard lines at the age of seven and thirty, to make ones first appearance on the boards.

Finished reading a little book on Arctic voyages and discoveries, edited by M[r] Tomlinson F.R.S., and published by the Society for the Propagation of Christian Knowledge, it is a useful little work.[1]

Saturday 25 December 1875
Max −31°.5 Min −37°

Very dark outside, at noon I took 'Darwen's [*sic*] Cruise'[2] on the floe <at noon> but could not make out the letters on the title-page. I could distinguish black and white, the difference of colour between the print and the paper, but nothing more. I think it would be a useful thing if some capable person would institute a darkness scale, on the same principle as Admiral Beaufort's wind notation.[3] I find that there is no accord even amongst my messmates, as to the degrees of light or darkness, unless verified by comparison. Print of various types would easily be made into a scale, and hung up in a ship away from artificial light, could be logged by numerals, according to the intensity of the darkness. I asked two

[1] Tomlinson, *Winter in the Arctic Regions*.

[2] Presumably Darwin, *Journal of Researches*, new edn; there is no book by Darwin with 'Cruise' in the title.

[3] Devised in 1805 by Francis Beaufort, measuring wind speed (0 = calm, 12 = hurricane, 64 knots and over); first used by Fitzroy during the voyage of HMS *Beagle* (1831–6).

Figure 28.   Place card for Christmas dinner, with a drawing showing seals, polar bears and a goose. In the centre are the words, 'Captain Feilden. R.A. H.M.S. Alert.' Reverse side of card labelled: 'Admiralty House, Queenstown'.

or three today about the darkness, one replied that he thought it the darkest or one of the darkest of the season, another answered that he was struck with the amount of light.

Xmas day was kept up with great energy, and I think was much enjoyed by all. The lower deck was beautifully ornamented by the men. We all received letters and presents from kind friends, or thoughtful persons who had sent them onboard to be opened this day. Mrs Coutt [*sic*][1] daughter of Sir Edward Parry, is one of our greatest contributors. Her box of presents, having got damp was opened and distributed by Captain Nares, sometime ago, but I have kept mine stored away till now, and opened out the envelopes this morning. I got a paper-cutter and an ivory photograph frame, and many xmas cards from Mrs Coutt, a jumping frog from May's box, and little toys from other sources.

We sat down to a really sumptuous dinner at 6 [*See Figure 29, p. 166*], everything beautifully arranged by Aldrich & Giffard. The epergne[2] of flowers in the centre was lovely. A bottle of champagne between two, good port, sherry and madeira, ad lib. Such plum-pudding, and 'ye Gods', what a haunch of Musk-ox, tender and juicy, the gravy streamed from the brown mutton coloured flesh, with each draw of the knife, the beautiful fat, more than two inches thick on the flank. This is not a mode of speech, I took the trouble to measure this layer of outside fat and it averaged 2 inches. During the afternoon and after dinner Aldrich played on the lower deck, the ~~harmonium~~ <accordion> and flute joining, dancing was kept up with great vigour until 10.30 [*Place card with sketch tipped in; see Figure 28, above.*]

Sunday 26 December 1875
Max −29° Min −43°.2
This has been a very dark day, at noon the title page of my test-book quite indistinguisable. The ship was very quiet today, the reaction after yesterday. I hear that two or three of the

[1] Mrs Robert Coote.
[2] Tiered centrepiece.

H.M.S. 'Alert'.

A LA JULIENNE SOUP is the *Potage* we favour,
And SOLES fried *au naturel* serve us for FISH;
We have CUTLETS and GREEN PEAS of elegant flavour —
BEEF garnished with MUSHROOMS — a true English dish:

Then a MOUNTAIN OF BEEF from our cold Greenland valleys,
Overshadowing proudly BOILED MUTTON hard by;
Till our Appetite, waning, just playfully dallies
With a small slice of HAM — then gives in with a sigh.

For lo! a real British PLUM-PUDDING doth greet us,
And a crest of bright Holly adorns its bold brow;
While the choicest MINCE-PIES are yet waiting to meet us:
Alas! are we.Equal to meeting them now?

So we drink to our Queen; and we drink to the Maiden,
The Wife, or the Mother, that holds us most dear;
And may we and our Consort sail home richly laden
With the spoils of Success, 'ere December next year!

Figure 29.   Printed menu for Christmas dinner, 25 December 1875.[1]

men slightly exceeded yesterday evening, and these defaulters received a severe lecture from the Commander, he tells me that one poor fellow, cried like a child, he was so ashamed of himself, and another a most respectable man who somewhat exceeded is dreadfully down in his luck. My own testimony is that no body of men could under similar circumstances have spent a Xmas more decorously.

Monday 27 December 1875
A considerable tinge of twilight in the southern horizon, but at noon I could not make out the title page of my test-book.

Moss is making some calculations in reference to the amount of precipitation in the atmosphere. Last night a square foot of glass was exposed for twelve hours, atmosphere clear, and no drift. From the weight of snow precipitated Moss calculated that it was at the rate of nine tons per square mile, but do not think this experiment can by any means

---

[1] The menu was accompanied by a printed sheet with two stanzas of verse: 'On this glad Christmas day, / While happy bells are flinging / O'er bright lands far away / Their bursts of joyous singing; / We love to think that each sweet lay, / That sets those echoes ringing, / Hushed music from our icy bay / To loving hearts is bringing. // Hushed music that shall tell / How HE has left us never, / In whose dear sight we dwell, / Who aids our high Endeavour; / Who from the hearts that love us well, / Our short lives will not sever; / for whose good gifts our breast shall swell / With grateful praise for ever.'
On the verso, there is an invitation within a holly wreath: 'Fill this with your own imagination!!'

be considered conclusive, we are not certain indeed, whether the vapour arose from the ice and was condensed on the glass, which was exposed on a barrel on the floe, or was precipitated from the atmosphere.

I have been examining today, various species of mould, which have grown on damp objects in my cabin, set apart for objects of natural history which is the dampest place unfortunatly[1] in the ship. One of these moulds exhibited thousands of spores.

Tuesday 28 December 1875
Max −22° Min −30°.5

Captain Nares made a suggestion today which I think is worth taking a note of, namely that in the event of the ship being caught in the pack, and forced to winter there, any amount of valuable dredging could be done through the fire hole, by building a snow house over it as we have here, and the contents of the dredge being at once removed in a tub to the lower deck to prevent freezing.

Cutting out and keeping the fire-hole clear, has hitherto been considered, trying and arduous work. Our Captain's arrangement of having a lofty snow house built over it, and a covered way to it, has done away with an evil often complained of in previous expeditions.

Wednesday 29 December 1875
Max −23° Min −25°.2

Visibly lighter at noon today; at a distance of fifty paces, on the floe, at noon, one could detect people moving.

There is a large amount of sediment which collects in the melting apparatus, from the ice blocks used by us for making water for the ship, to the eye it looks like a fine grayish mud closely resembling in hue the strata around us. Under the microscope this sediment shows as small angular grains of rock, without any traces of Diatom skeletons in it. I am sure that the ice increases from above by the drifting of the snow, as well as from below by freezing.

Thursday 30 December 1875[2]
Max −15°.5 Min −28°.5

Captain Nares, let Buchanan's apparatus[3] down the fire hole depth 36 feet. Bottom temp. +28°.2 this is the greatest cold registered by any Arctic navigator as far as I am aware. This great cold has evidently an antibiotic tendency as the only minute living organisms found in this water were <a few> small Entromostracas. Let down a fifty pound lead to the bottom, little or nothing came up, a few grains of sand, however, mixed with three or four spindle shaped diatoms, but as this lead has been used before I place no reliance on these diatoms, belonging to this locality.

---

[1] Feilden consistently writes 'unfortunatly', 'fortunatly' for 'unfortunately', 'fortunately'.

[2] 'Thursday Pops' began with a lecture by Moss, on 'Mock Moons under the Microscope', followed by songs, ballads, readings, a recitation, and a part-song, see Figure 30, p. 169 below.

[3] A sophisticated apparatus for taking samples of seawater, devised by James Buchanan and used on the *Challenger* expedition, 1874–6. Nares had been the captain on HMS *Challenger* until ordered to prepare for the British Arctic Expedition. For details of Buchanan's and other water bottles, see McConnell, *No Sea Too Deep*, chaps 9 and 10, pp. 106–36.

For about a foot in depth from the surface of the fire-hole the water remains in a partly semi-congealed condition, if a person dip a vessel by hand into this, he will dish up nothing but ice, without any animal life in it. A simple arrangement which we adopt is as follows. Take a staff six or seven feet long, lash a bottle neck uppermost to one end, put a string through the plug, holding the line in one hand, push the staff and bottle perpendicularly into the water, withdraw plug, and fill the bottle; hurry between decks, and empty contents into glass beaker, but dont take the beaker on the floe, as they are liable to crack, on exposure. [*Margin: Sketch of Buchanan's water bottle.*]

[*Here Feilden tipped in a copy of the 'Thursday Pops' programme for 30 December 1875; see Figure 30, p. 169.*]

Friday 31 December 1875[1]
Max −16° Min −23°
Our year wound up most pleasantly, a few minutes before twelve we left the whist tables, and sat down to supper in the Ward Room. Ham, punch, &c. &c. Health of recent friends was drunk, and at five minutes to 8, we <also> drank a glass of punch to our friends at home, as that was equivalent to twelve oclock in England.

Persons at home judging of results obtained by Arctic expeditions, are wrong if they compare the work done, with the time spent in doing it. Practically the labours of the naturalist are confined to the short summer, this being also the season of navigation, advantage must be taken of every opportunity to push on. No man can say I will go on shore tomorrow, and do this or that, without adding "ice willing". Few persons have had the advantage of sailing with so thoughtful a person as Captain Nares, on no occasion has he ever omitted to send me on shore when feasible, or to give me every assistance. In spite of this I feel that the results in my department are somewhat meagre. From the 29th of July to the 1st of September, the date on which we attained our highest northern latitude, we were battling with the ice in Smiths Sound. The frequent delays were of great service to me as I was enabled to go frequently on shore, and I have traced the geology of the coast with tolerable accuracy. Cape Alexander and the environs of Point Foulke, consist of numerous strata of sandstones, intercalated with basalts, very horizontally bedded, and if I mistake not, of Miocene formation, these beds rest on plutonic and metamorphic rocks. The northern side of Point Foulke has been subjected to great glacial degradation, and the sedamentary [*sic*] strata have been denuded. Judging from Kane's work it would appear that these sandstones and basalts, appear again to the northward. Cape Isabella is formed of plutonic and metamorphic rocks, and this series continues till we reach Cape Sabine of Inglefield. Brevoort I, has <on its summit> a small deposit of tile with shells of existing mollusca, imbedded. From Cape Sabine the land bends abruptly to the W., forming the south side of what is called Hayes Sound on the chart. The predominant rocks are still plutonic and metamorphic, rising into mountains of considerable altitude, and they appear to extend without interruption into the westward. In the valley of the Twin Glacier[s] I came across the first sedimentary rocks <on that side> consisting of a hard, crystalline, unfossiliferous limestone. These beds are exposed by the action of the glacier streams which cutting down through the old moraine, and

---

[1] This entry runs without a break into 1 January 1876.

THURSDAY POPS.

H.M.S. ALERT.

DECEMBER 30th 1875.

PROGRAMME.

1. LECTURE   Mock Moons under the Microscope : DR. MOSS.

2. SONG   Irish Comic :   MR. PEARCE.

3. BALLAD   Maggie by My Side :   MR. SMITH.

4. READING   A Bashful Man :   MR. WOOLLEY.

5. SONG   My Friend the Major :   MR. CHALKLEY.

6. BALLAD   What I dreamed in my Old Arm Chair :

                                              MR. CRANSTONE.

7. READING   The Execution :   MR. EGERTON.

8. SONG   The Costermonger's Donkey :   MR. BURROUGH.

9. RECITATION   A Deed of Horror :   MR. MITCHELL.

10. SONG   Kill or Cure :   MR. SHIRLEY.

11. PART - SONG The Hardy Norseman : MESSRS ALDRICH,

                        RAWSON, WOOTTON, AND PULLEN.

To commence at 7.30 precisely.
God Save The Queen.

MESSRS. GIFFARD and SYMONS :
Printing Office, Trap Lane.

Figure 30.   Printed 'Thursday Pops' programme, 30 December 1875.

glacial beds, reaches the limestone. Looking north from this point, an entire change in the rocks is apparent. Bache & Henry I. (= Victoria Land) are Silurian limestones resting on red coloured plutonic rocks. From this point we carry on the Silurian limestones to about lat 81.N. At this point we moved over to West Greenland, and found almost similar limestones composing Bessels Bay, there can be no doubt that the same series runs continuously to C. Forbes the northern flank of the great Humboldt glacier. On regaining the opposite side at Discovery Bay, a great change ~~had~~ occurred<s> in the rock formation, the massive horizontal bedded fossiliferous limestones gives place to a highly crystalline, laminated and non fossiliferous limestone, the beds are tossed about at high angles, often distorted. I imagine that the line of demarcation exists, at what is called Lady Franklin's Sound. I trust that this very interesting question will be cleared up, by my fellow worker in the *Discovery*.

As far as possible I have taken notice of the effects of all the old glacial action that we have met with, and my journal is replete with references to this important subject. I believe I can claim as original <remarking> the difference between ancient sea-beaches and the terraces made by the snow-foot, a new fact for the geologist. A collection of several hundred specimens of rocks and fossils illustrating every point visited has been made and carefully labelled.

In plants my collection is considerable, at every point visited since entering Smith's Sound, I obtained as many specimens of the Flora, as lay in my power. I can see no variation in the flora of the American side from the Greenlandic.[1] The dredgings obtained, often full of diatomacea have been carefully preserved.

Invertebrates – our chances of dredging were limited, but we had the good fortune to obtain a new and beautiful species of crinoid, and amongst other good things two ~~or more~~ species of Terebratula hitherto unrecorded, from ~~arctic seas~~ <Smith's Sound>. All the results of our dredgings have been most carefully preserved. Insects required due share of attention and a tolerably rich collection has been made. Vertebrata. In fish we have not been fortunate as yet only four species, but one a Salmonoid discovered in a fresh water lake in lat. 82°.40′. ought to count for something, as it throws light on the question of migration.

Aves. – The collection is as yet somewhat limited, but I have added two new species to the avifauna of this area, viz *Tringa canutus*, and *Charadrius hiaticula*, also sighted a *Colymbus*, which eluded the gun.

In *Mammalia*, I think the most important observation made is one of a negative character, and that is, the non observance of any Cetaceans* since entering Smith's Sound with the exception of Narwhals at Cape Sabine. [*Margin*: A skeleton of a large whale observed near the deserted igloos of Hayes Sound. rafters of Igloos formed of the bones.] I have only seen two species of seals P. hispida, and P. barbata,[2] but the latter is included in my list only from seeing it on the ice; no specimen having been procured. We obtained specimens of Walrus as far north as Dobbin Bay, where they were tolerably numerous but the latitude of that spot, appears to be their northern limit. in these parts. We have found the traces of a species of Myodes <hudsonicus>[3] very common, but only obtained one living example.

---

[1] T. R. Jones, ed., *Manual*.

[2] Known in the 1870s as the great seal or the bearded seal; now the spotted seal.

[3] *Myodes hudsonicus*, now *Dicrostonyx groenlandicus*, the Arctic or collared lemming.

The range of the Reindeer [*Margin*: A shed antler found by *Discovery* in Lat 81°.44′] has been increased by us to N.L. 79° exceeding by three and half degrees the experiences of the German expedition on the east coast of Greenland.

The Reindeer has been obtained on the Seven Islands, [N., of Spitzbergen,] above 81°, but the mild climate of that Island is exceptional and due to influences absent here.

The Musk-ox, or better, Musk-sheep, has been found by us nearly as far as our explorations have extended <north>, but these animals have hitherto been collected <by us,> more for food than scientific purposes. Under the circumstances I can honestly say, that hitherto, it has been quite beyond the bounds of possibility to make any preparations of this species.

The only trace of Bears <in Smith Sound> that I have seen was the skull and most of the skeleton of an individual, lying some distance inland at Hayes Sound, and footprints near Cape Hayes.

Of the Eskimo we found numerous traces from Cape Sabine to Cape Hilgard, after passing that point our visits to the shore were less frequent, and consequently our opportunities for discovery more restricted. The finding of a very ancient sledge at Cape Sabine with the runners formed of schistose stone, is extremely interesting.

I have also come to the conclusion, founded on numerous observations, that we are now progressing in a period of increased glacial action, some of my principle [*sic*] proofs, are the abandonment of Eskimo settlements which must at one time have been numerously inhabited, the igloos in Hayes Sound, had been roofed with ribs and bones of large whales. These cetaceans are no longer found there. We found the so called horn of a Narwhal protruding from an ancient beach a few feet above present sea-level in lat 82°.30′. The narwhal I feel confident can no longer exist in this ice bound area. The numerous sea-beaches [*Margin*: This opinion subsequently modified H.W.F.] stretching in successive rows along the shores of this icy area, point to a time when their sea levels must have been washed with a comparatively open sea, for it is impossible to conceive that these miles of beaches formed of rounded pebbles could possibly have been formed under existing circumstances, for now a series of immense hummocks and permanent ice lines the shore. That these hummocks are permanent I have concluded from the fact of their being stratified and impregnated with dust formed of the same materials as the rocks on shore, with an absence of diatoms, and that their increase is attributable to growth by precipitation and snow drift. The Diatomaceous layers are confined to the lower & saline portions of the Floe.

Into my geographical and Physical deductions I shall not enter at present.
H.W.F. 1st. Jan. 1876. N. Lat. 82°. 27′.

    H.M.S. *Alert*.

List of the species of Birds collected between Lat. 78°. and 82°.27′ N during passage of Smiths Sound from 28 July 1875 to 19th Sept. 1875. By H.W.F.

July 28. Mergulus alle. juv. Port Foulke – Breed there in countless thousands.
  „   „   Som. mollisima ♀ Port Foulke – Very abundant.
Aug 2   Larus eburneus. Cape Sabine ♀ Several seen there, perhaps breeding.
  „   „   Larus glaucus juv. Cape Sabine – From nest.
  „   4   Char. hiaticula. ♀ Hayes Sound. Probably breeding. N.L. 79°
  „   11 Som. mollissima juv. Walrus I. One of three in the brood.

„ 12 Uria grylle. ♀.
„ 8 Uria grylle. ♂.
„ 23 Uria grylle. ♂. Bessels Bay.
„ 13 Strep. interpres ♀.
„ 13 Tetrao rupestris. – 5 shot Dobbins Bay only secured a foot.
„ 11 Sterna Hirundo ♀. Walrus I.
„ 26 „ „ ♀. Discovery B.
„ 26 „ „ nestling. „
„ 24 Tringa canutus ♀.
„ 31 „ „ „ . Found dead at Lincoln Bay.
Sept 19 Harelda glacialis ♀. Winter quarters.
„ „ „ „ juv. „ „

In addition to these species I have seen but not procured, a Diver, a Raven, a Fulmar, and a Snow-Bunting. Hart also thinks he has seen a pair of large white Falcons near Cape Hayes.

I might have procured a few more specimens of Glaucus gulls and Eider ducks, but otherwise these eighteen skins represent my best endeavours in this department.

The maximum and minimum temperatures recorded in my journal are copied from the ships meteorological record. The 24 hours included in each day, are astronomical not civil days, or in other words embrace the period from noon to noon, not midnight to midnight.

Corrected temperature for Dec. 1875. N. Lat. 82°. 27′.

Max	Min	Mean	Captains Cabin	Ward-room	Stoker Hold	After part mess deck	-Do- by foremast	Drying room	Means
+35°	−46.5°	−23°.4	+55°.48	+48°.67	+27°.1	+53°.7	+51°.99	+71°.95	
					[Captains Cabin]	[Ward-room]	[After part mess deck]		
H.M.S. *Assistance* 1850 Dec. 2nd					+52°	+45°	+55°		
H.M.S. *Intrepid*		„	„		+60°	+52°	+50°		
H.M.S. *Pioneer*		„	„		+50°	+50°	+50°		
H.M.S. *Resolute*		„	„		+30°	+30°	+39°		

Saturday 1 January 1876 Winter Quarters
Max −16° Min −23°. 82°.27′. N.L.

The New Year opens under most cheering circumstances. Dr Colan has made his monthly examinations and reports officers and men in excellent health. We have got over the worst of the darkness. We have so far enjoyed most delectable weather, since the ice around the ship commenced bearing there has not been a single day, up to this date, on which we could not have taken our regular exercise outside. We have been more than seven months cooped up, and I have not yet heard a cross, far less an angry word, fall between any of my messmates. Our expedition has attained a higher northern latitude both by sea and land, than any other recorded, at the time we left England. Moss was more fortunate in his haul of water, taken from the bottom of the fire-hole on the 30th ult. than I was, in the deposit formed at the bottom of the beaker he discovered a diatom of the genus *Tricerathium* [*sic*] <living> and a living example of a *Pleurosigma*.[1] The ♀ *canis familiaris* that came

[1] *Triceratium* and *Pleurosigma* are both genera of marine diatoms.

back to the ship after a lengthened absence, on the 11th Dec. 75 was today in copula with Bruin, the master dog, the ♀ referred to under date of the 22nd Oct. 75 is past her time, and is evidently <not> going to bring forth. For sometime past the two bitches <thought to be *with* pup> have been living on the upper deck, well fed, and a comfortable kennel built aft for their use.

Sunday 2 January 1876
Max −21°.2 Min −30°.2
It is worth recording, and examining into hereafter, the relation between the mean temperature of the sea water and the amount of animal life to be found in the lands bordering such seas in the Arctic regions. Captain Nares remarked to me this evening that off the Cape of Good Hope, where a cold and warm current <meet>, a regular jam of animal life occurs, that Porpoises, Birds, and Fish are innumerable – At the southern entrance of Smiths Sound, where the cold arctic current meets the comparatively warm water of Baffin's Bay, there also appears to be an immeasurable supply of life, little Auks in millions are cruising about. The land teems with Reindeer &c.
However, the moment one enters Smiths Sound proper all is changed.

Monday 3 January 1876
Max −19°.8 Min −37°
Between 12 noon and 1 o'c., the moon appeared above the eastern horizon there was also a marked tinge of twilight in the south at the sametime [*sic*].
Every day I draw water from the fire-hole and place it under the microscope, but so far have found little.

Tuesday 4 January 1876
Max −16° Min −31°.5
A little wind blowing, and a good deal of drift, so that it was considerably darker at noon than yesterday. Moon not visible. Walked between four and five miles. We have a track half a mile long marked out on the floe, from the ship to the southward, with empty barrels and meat tins. In dark weather it is an inward satisfaction to know that one walked a certain number of miles. At 6 p.m. when I went on deck it was much clearer, and the moon was visible.

Wednesday 5 January 1876
Max −10°.2 Min −24°.8
I have often noticed accounts of experiments made on sound by arctic observers, and the great distance at which we can hear persons conversing on the floe at great distances is remarkable, but the sense of smell appears to be excited in a corresponding ratio. With the wind in a favorable condition I have smelt cooking going on in the ship nearly a quarter of a mile off, while the evacuations of one of the Eskimo dogs dropped on our upper deck stinks the place until freezing has taken place. The same statement applies to the etiam ad cloaca hominum.[1]

---

[1] 'Also to the human sewer'.

Thursday 6 January 1876
[*The 'Thursday Pops' programme for 6 January 1876 was tipped in; see Figure 31, p. 175.*]
Max −10°.2 Min −32°.5
Beautiful moonlight, at 4 h. p.m. the planet Mars showed above the Southern horizon.
About 12 h. p.m., there was a puff of wind from S.W. which only lasted a few minutes, but
during that interval sent the temperature up over 20°.

We have a ♀ <white> cat in the wardroom, which is at present rather a disagreeable
shipmate, as she is in a peculiar state, and runs about the wardroom all night, entering
the cabins, rubbing against the chairs, and tearing at the curtains, uttering at the same
time plaintive calls to attract the attention of some ♂. Fortunately we have none of that
opposite sex onboard.

Some of our people remarked today a brilliant light on the floe to the N. which on
approaching turned out to be the moonlight refracted through a natural prism of ice on
a hummock. Moss Egerton and Giffard said they saw it.

Friday 7 January 1876
Max −14° Min −39°.5
Nice moonlight, walked four miles with Pullen. I can find little or nothing in the water
taken from the fire-hole, only a few minute Entromostraca, and a few species of living
diatoms from the bottom by Buchanan's water bottle. I draw a beaker full of water two or
three times a week from this fire-hole; the getting of it is a little troublesome. Armed with
a bottle apparatus attached to a staff, and lantern in the other hand, I sally forth minus
gloves temp. −30°. Have to put the lantern on the ground lift up a flap ~~leading~~ which
forms a door to the covered way, at its termination have to descend into a kneeling
position and push the lantern and apparatus through the small hole which leads into the
hut over the fire-hole, and then follow them; next chop a hole with an axe through the
newly formed surface ice, sink the staff and bottle, disengage the cork, wait until the air
has all been forced out of the bottle, – which seems to take a longtime – then haul up
recork, bolt to the ship as fast as one can, dive between decks, and then clap one's hands
together for five minutes to restore circulation. The reason I dont wear gloves on these
occasions is that with them on, I am so intolerably clumsy. Were it not for the snowhouse
built over the fire-hole it would be extremely disagreeable work ~~to~~ drawing a beaker of
water.

Saturday 8 January 1876
Max −12°.2 Min −39°
It blew fresh all night, and this morning our hands were not able to go out on the floe, as
usual, immediatly after prayers. Between 12 h and 1 p.m it fell quite calm. I walked with
Captain Nares some distance up the rising ground behind the observatory, and had a look
at the ice in the channel, but we did not discern any water. The moon shining on some
large even floes outside of the ship, gave them the appearance of water at first sight, but
on looking at them attentively, it was evident that no water was visible in that direction.
The direction of the Sastrugi[1] on the hill slope were from W. to E. showing the direction
of last nights gale. In the afternoon the wind freshened up from the same direction, and

[1] Ridges of snow formed by the wind on a snowfield.

THURSDAY POPS.

H.M.S. ALERT.
JANUARY 6th 1876.

PROGRAMME,

1. LECTURE On Light :   LIEUT. PARR.
2. SONG The hurdy gurdy man :   MR. STONE.
3. BALLAD Good old Jeff :   COL. SERGT. WOOD.
4. READING Curing a Cold :   MR. HUNT.
5. SONG Life under the Lights :   MR. RAWLINGS.
6. BALLAD My old friend John :   MR. RADMORE,
7. RECITATION Chestnut horse :   MR. SIMPSON.
8. SONG Yellow, White or Brown :   MR. PEARSON.
9. READING Story of the bad little Boy : LIEUT. RAWSON.
10. SONG Will a Monkey climb a tree ?   MR. BRIANT.
11. BALLAD Why chime the Bells so merrily ? MR. HAWKINS.

To commence at 7.30 precisely.

God Save The Queen.

MESSRS. GIFFARD and SYMONS :
Printing Office, Trap Lane.

Figure 31.   Printed 'Thursday Pops' programme, 6 January 1876.

as I write is whistling through the rigging. In spite of cold and wind old Bruin was *in copula* this morning on the floe with a small ♀ canis familiaris var. borealis called Topsy.

Our unfortunate wardroom steward,[1] I hear, had another fit last night, he has been drinking again, and I felt sure it would not be long before he had another seizure. I visited the poor fellow today, and I was much pained when he told me that there was not the slightest chance of his ever getting out of this place; and that it made no difference when he went. I tried to cheer him up, but his constitution is so undermined, that there is little doubt, but his prediction will be verified to the letter.

Moss considers that he has made a wonderful find in discovering (– on his authority I have not seen it –) the <sprouting> sporule of a fungus on his glycerine plate. He tells me that he considers it so extraordinary that he almost hesitates to record it. I cannot see anything so very wonderful, even granting that it is the sporule of a fungoid and was sprouting. After every gale or breeze of wind portions of the land are swept clear of snow, doubtless large tracts, beyond our ken. After the protecting mantle of snow is withdrawn the wind will carry with it seeds, sand, and the sporules of fungoids. This was observed and commented on by the late Admiral Sherard Osborn. v. p. 219. Parlia. Papers. (Journey 2nd June 1853).[2] The real point of interest to discover is, whether the willow <does not> put forth its buds, and seeds germinate under the snow, many weeks before the sun exposes the plant, and this will be elucidated by a careful examination of the crops of Ptarmigans and stomachs of Lemings [*sic*].

Sunday 9 January 1876
Max +4° Min. +16°.2[3]
The gale continued through last night, and has blown all day, so as to confine the people within the ship. On the upper deck the peircing wind forces the fine drift through the joins and crevices of the housing, so that a person exposed, even under the covering, becomes powdered over with minute particles of snow.

Outside of the ship is very dismal looking, the moonlight is strong enough to show the drift passing, so thick that objects which I know to be only twenty paces distant from the trap-hatch of the gangway are invisible. The wind howls as it passes through the rigging, and to my mind has a most disagreeable effect on the nerves, I have always disliked the noise of wind more than any other commotion made by the forces of nature; it invariably makes me feel sad. Earthquakes, I cant say I hanker after, but I dont mind them, and thunder and lightning is well enough in its way, but I am dead against old Boreas.

Below everything is jolly and snug, a good fire in the stove, two moderator lamps on the table, which is covered with red baize, tea is over, and the supper things are put out on the side board. Some of the fellows are reading, others writing in their cabins with the curtains open, the white cat is stretching and purring before the fire, and the steam issuing from a hook-hat attached to the stove bars, resolves itself into visions of a glass of hot after supper grog, and a pipe. My own cabin is as snug as possible, and I feel sure that I have been in many worse places during my travels, than the Arctic, in fact we are Sybarites.

[1] George Kemish, see above, p. 127 and n. 3.
[2] *Arctic Blue Books*, 1855, p. 219.
[3] Sea temperatures.

10.30 p.m. Have just come down from upper deck. "Auld Clutie is playing his cantrips",[1] outside.

Monday 10 January 1876
Max +8°.5 Min −23°.5[2]
The gale blew itself out before morning, and though the moon was some what clouded over, yet we were able to get good walks. Ascended the rising ground for some distance with Captain Nares to see whether any open water ocurred between us and Cape Rawson. None was to be seen. The temperature though about −9° was oppressive, and I felt as languid as if I were crawling along the Strada Reale, Valetta, during a Scirocco. There is no doubt of the debilitating effects of the Arctic winter, going up hill today I puffed like an old dowager, who has not been out of her trap walking for twenty years, and I perspired so that I had to change underclothes before sitting down to dinner.

The water last night forced itself up between the ship and the floe, by the stern post, and flooded the floe to the depth of several inches. The surface of the drifts is powdered with the dust from shore, which contains vegitable [sic] matter. I want to find the seeds of vegetables actually frozen in the floes, which if I do will prove the fact of the floes increasing from the top.

Tuesday 11 January 1876
Max −3° Min −24°.8
Weather calm, moon bright. The drifts of sand blown during the gale from the shore, and deposited on the surface of the snow, contain small particles of vegetable matter as was to be expected.

Wednesday 12 January 1876
Max 9°.8 Min −18°.8
Walked with Captain Nares to the flagstaff cairn, the moon very bright. Mounts Pullen & Rhoda* [*Margin*: *The Dean] showing plainly. The uplands are much bared of snow, the prevailing winds have been S.W.

There was a pleasant, unmistakeable [sic] tinge of honest twilight in the southern horizon at noon.

Thursday 13 January 1876
Max −8° Min −31°.5
Pullen tells me, that when he was at Malborough, between *1845 & 1848*, he was present at the slaying of two fallow deer, a buck with horns and a doe, in Savernake forest, by the schoolboys. The weapons they used were termed "Squalers".[3] i.e. a lump of lead run into a hens egg and moulded on to a piece of thick cane, and the destruction of the animals was

---

[1] 'Auld Clootie' is the devil, and his 'cantrips' are magic spells, in Scottish or Northumbrian dialect. See, e.g., Heslop, *Northumberland Words*, p. 191.

[2] Air temperatures, not from log. Feilden generally made his own measurements of sea and air temperatures, and it is not always clear which set of temperatures he entered in his journal. The ship's log enters degrees and half degrees; Feilden often used decimals to indicate smaller parts of a degree.

[3] Not in *OED*. But see Salisbury, *Glossary of Words and Phrases*, pp. 154–5, expanding on Feilden's correct definition.

compassed by 15 or 20 boys thus armed surrounding an outlying herd, and gradually closing on them, until they got within throwing range with the "Squalers", and sometimes breaking a deers legs. Of course this poaching would have been severely punished by the College authorities had it been detected, but the circumstance is interesting as illustrating how quickly boys revert to the savage type of chase, and with what a considerable degree of success.

The men <now> appear very pale and washed out looking when they come on the boards to sing.

[*Feilden tipped in a copy of the 'Thursday Pops' programme for 13 January 1876; see Figure 32, p. 179.*]

Friday 14 January 1876
Max −1°.8 Min −25°.2
A good streak of twilight visible today at noon, making us feel that the old sun has not forgotten us, but is trotting this way.
N.B. Examine spermatozoa of Eskimo dog in hopes of an opportunity ocurring of comparing it with those of wolf.
Ship had a slight list to port.

Saturday 15 January 1876
Max −23° Min −38°
Rather thick and cloudy. I find that the smaller and more delicate insects *Diptera* and *Arachnida*, that I collected last year, are not keeping well in alchohol. I have therefore mounted a few on glass slides. I was surprised on opening a box today, in which I had placed two cocoons, (that I found attached to stones at P.ᵗ Foulke on the 28ᵗʰ of July 1875,) that the cocoons were ruptured, and that two *Muscæ*[1] were in the box. I am not aware of any insect of this family weaving a cocoon around its pupa, I presume therefore that these flies make the larvae of some *Lepidoptera* the hatching bed of their eggs.

Sunday 16 January 1876
Max −29° Min −42°
The coats with hood, and trousers of Wapiti[2] hide, made for several of our expedition by Messrs Mills and Co. of Hanover Street, are worthy of great commendation. I find mine quite impervious to cold. It is too heavy for hard exercise, but for walking about in this winter on the floe it has proved excellent.

Monday 17 January 1876
Max −30 Min −43°.8
At noon, for the first time since the shortest day, I was able to distinguish by the twilight the inequalities on the floe, and put down my feet so as to avoid ruts and excrescences.
The feeble light which enlivened our hearts today is of the mildest character, the stars except exactly in the glow, where they were somewhat pale, were otherwise undimmed, the dark hill tops looked as if some giant hand had drawn a damp lucifer along their summits,

---

[1] Flies.
[2] North American deer, related to but larger than red deer.

THURSDAY POPS.

H.M.S. ALERT.
January 13th 1876.

Programme.

1. Historical Lecture :   Mr. White,
2. Song Fifty years ago :   Mr. Stuckberry.
3. Song   Keep a good heart :   Mr. Hollins,
4. Reading Paudeen o Rafferty's Say voyage :Mr. Lorimer.
5. Song Kiss me quick and go :   Mr. Mann.
6. Song   Up a Tree :   Mr. Self.
7. Recitation The Little Vulgar Boy :   Mr. Malley.
8. Song Semaphore, or danger on the Line : Mr. Hindle.
9. Reading Editorial Experience :   Lieut. Aldrich.
10. Song Wonderful Nose :   Mr. Gobe.
11. Ballad Ring the bell watchman :   Mr. Ayles.

To commence at 7.30 precisely.
God Save The Queen.

Messrs. Giffard and Symons :
Printing Office, Trap Lane.

Figure 32.   Printed 'Thursday Pops' programme, 13 January 1876.

179

which had left behind it a sheen of pale light. A little before noon there was an display of Aurora, very poor, but the best I have yet seen in these latitudes, it stretched in a bow from N.N.E. to S.S.W., colour pale white, and looking more like a twisted roll of fleecy clouds than the auroras I have seen in Scotland. The tide made considerable noise today rushing in under the floe. Working at microscope all day. Examined the intestines of two salmonoids captured by Aldridge [*sic*] near Depot Point, added another insect, Hydracnella [*sic*][1] to our collection.

Tuesday 18 January 1876
Max −9 Min −43°.8
Marked twilight at noon. From the top of a big hummock near the ship – 22 feet above the level of the floe – the Greenland coast was visible. A slight display of Aurora at 9 o'c. at night. The tide pole was removed today from its old position to another hole, the leads which kept it at the bottom, were full of soundings, grey mud. depth 36 feet.

Figure 33.   'Cony & Mammoth drawn from life. 1st. Lesson in animal sketches given me by Rawson. 18.1.76 H. W. F.'

Wednesday 19 January 1876
Max −29° Min −45°
Not so clear today, considerable amount of clouds passing up the Channel from the Southward.

   The formation of all or nearly all the bays along this Coast is singular, they are generally circular with narrow inlets to them, and often are composed of a series of circular basins connected with one another by narrows. When opening them up for the first time it is a question to the traveller whether they be lakes or salt water, and in some cases I have had to break through the ice and taste the water before coming to a conclusion. One thing is

[1] *Hydrachna*: water mite. Robert Maclachlan in Nares, *Narrative of a Voyage*, II, p. 238, lists '*Hydrachna*, probably two species' among the *Acaridae*. I have not found hydracnella.

certain, that the numerous lakes spread over the country, have been scooped out by the same forces as made the bays now connected with the sea, the mud deposits around them teeming with shells of recent testaceous mollusca,[1] shows that <it is> not so very long ago, since they were elevated above the sea-level, and in all probability before very long many of our bays will be converted into chains of circular fresh water lakes by the advancing elevations of the coast. I cannot conceive, however, of any natural force that could have gouged out these lakelets and bays but ice, and if I am right in this supposition we have evidence of alternations of depression and re-elevation of this district during the glacial period. We must suppose that glacial action scooped out the depressions, since that epoch <they> have sunk below sea level, and have again reappeared as lakes ringed with mud-banks containing recent molluscous shells. Why the majority of these lakes should be of circular form with narrow entrances is to me at present a geological puzzle. v. map. date 9th Sept.[2] also journal A.[3] p. 187.

But at the same time is it unlikely to suppose that the withdrawal of the glacial epoch from Britain and temperate Europe was contemporaneous with a similar change in the north polar regions?

Thursday 20 January 1876
Max −38.9 Min −46°
Reading the "Newcomes"[4] for the first time. I am glad that I have not read it before.
[*The programme for the 'Thursday Pops' of 20 January 1876 was inserted here; see Figure 34, p. 182.*]

Friday 21 January 1876
<observation hourly.> Max −45°.1 Max [*sic*] −48°
Very little twilight visible today owing to mist. I employed myself in marking up curves of temperatures for past months.

I have no patience with one of our number who is always announcing to his messmates some wonderful & original discovery.[5] Tonight it was the discovery of foreign matter in new fallen snow. No mention, however, was made to his auditors of Nordenskiölds experiments, (and their results), on the same subject.[6]

When we have more light I intend to collect a fixed amount of fresh fallen snow in well cleaned well stoppered glass vessels, and filter the sediment for examination at home.

Saturday 22 January 1876
<observation hourly> Max −45°.6 Min −49°.8
The thermo*meter* for the last twenty four hours registered a minimum of −49°.5.[7] During my walk the temperature was between −47° & −48°, but I cant say I felt any great degree

[1] Shellfish.
[2] This is Feilden's copy of Pelham Aldrich's map, Figure 10, p. 107.
[3] Not found.
[4] Thackeray, *Newcomes*, 1854–5 (there were numerous later editions).
[5] Almost certainly E. L. Moss, surgeon on HMS *Alert*. See Appleton and Barr, *Resurrecting Dr. Moss*.
[6] See Roscoe, 'Detection of Meteoric (Cosmical) Dust'.
[7] Although log had −49°.8.

THURSDAY POPS.

II.M.S. ALERT.

JANUARY 20th 1876.

GRAND PHANTASMAGORICAL EXHIBITION

AND

MUSICAL ENTERTAINMENT.

To Commence with

A Few Words on ASTRONOMY, by COMMR. MARKHAM,
Illustrated by the Aid of a Magic Lantern.
To be followed by a Series of
DISSOLVING VIEWS ;
Consisting of Coloured Representations of
Remarkable Places in England ;
Photographic Sketches of Foreign Countries &c.
After which, the Wonderful and Startling Adventures of
SINDBAD THE SAILOR
Will be related by the REVD. H.W. PULLEN.
In the next place, COMMR. MARKHAM will give a Lifelike and
Entertaining Display of Various Specimens in
NATURAL HISTORY ;
and
LIEUT. ALDRICH will recite the true and touching
TALE OF A TUB.
To Conclude with some highly amusing
COMIC SCENES.

To commence at 7.30 precisely.

God Save The Queen.

MESSRS. GIFFARD and SYMONS :
Printing Office, Trap Lane.

Figure 34. Printed programme for 'Thursday Pops', 20 January 1876, 'Grand Phantasmagorical Exhibition'.

of cold, except when facing the wind. After an hour and a halfs walk, I came in warm as a toast. There was a good deal of mist today, and not a streak of twilight visible.

Sunday 23 January 1876
<observation hourly> Max −52.3 Min −57°
The thermometer ranging very low, but well wrapped up I did my four miles across the floe.
    Rest of the day read the 'Newcomes.'

Monday 24 January 1876
Max −23 Min −54.5
Read in my cabin from after tea last night till five this morning and finished the 'Newcomes'. Very cold today but no inconvenience when walking. The ice made a good deal of noise outside today.

Tuesday 25 January 1876
<observation hourly.> Max −51.8 −Min -53.8
At noon today there was a considerable glow of twilight. Five of us, Parr, Egerton, Rawson, Wootton and self, tried to read "The Diary of the Besieged Resident in Paris," Second edition published by Hurst and Blackett 1871.[1] We all could make out lines of the Preface but could not read several consecutively. In the body of the book we could only make out words here and there but could not read a complete sentence. We may safely say that four of us have sight above the average, whilst Wootton, who is short sighted, is under present circumstances equal to any of us. I have heard some wonderful statements onboard, about reading type this winter. I am quite sure that on some occasions the reading has been due to the auroral glow suffusing the zenith, and nothing to do with the twilight.
    The ice made a good deal of noise outside today.

Wednesday 26 January 1876
Max −36 Min −50.5
Misty today, and not so clear as yesterday. I was thinking today over a letter which appeared in the Pall Mall Gazette[2] shortly before we left England, reflecting on the appointments of the naturalists and Chaplains appointed to this expedition and signed F.R.S. I understand from Mr Clements Markham that the author was Admiral Ummaney [sic].[3] I felt an inclination at the time to answer that letter, and would have done so, had I not been one of the parties referred to. That Admiral Ummaney should have written such a letter, shows great ill taste especially when signed F.R.S. showing that he was

[1] Labouchère, *Diary of the Besieged Resident*.
[2] *Pall Mall Gazette*, 24 April 1875, p. 5. 'two naturalists have been added to the complement– the one [*Feilden*] a collector of birds, with no higher qualifications than are possessed by several of the executive officers; and the other [Henry Chichester Hart on *Discovery*] a young gentleman from Dublin, who has studied botany, but who has never travelled, is not an artist, and has no special knowledge of Arctic problems. No geologist has been provided.' Feilden, although not formally trained as a geologist, was an outstanding field geologist. See Levere, 'Henry Wemyss Feilden'.
[3] Erasmus Ommanney (1814–1904), see *ODNB*. Ommanney continued to criticize the expedition after its return, and his criticism was countered in Richards, *Arctic Expedition*.

particularly proud of being able to attach such a signature to his letter. If the Admiral had reflected for a moment, I am bound to think that it would have occurred to him that he owed the proud distinction of F.R.S. to the courtesy of the leading society who had thus shown its approval of his services as an able Arctic navigator, and not on account of his additions to scientific knowledge. Consequently, however unworthy the selections of naturalists to this expedition may prove to be, yet Admiral Ummaney ought to have remembered that they were those of the council of the very society to which he owes so much, and under the shelter of whose fellowship he makes his anonymous attack. I have been informed however, that the Admiral was famous as a horticulturist at Gibraltar, and a great favourite at the Govenors table on account of his convivial proclivities.

Thursday 27 January 1876
Max −28.8 Min −46.2
Marked increase in the twilight today. Greenland coast visible, outline of the hills to our south quite distinct, outlines of large hummocks half a mile off distinguisable [*sic*]. I sat up writing and reading in my cabin till past 5 this morning and lay in bed till 11. I seldom if ever go to bed before 3 or 4 a.m. and give up my breakfast taking a cup of cocoa before going out for exercise. Between the hours of 12 p.m, and 4 a.m. one gets a quiet time.
　　In the farce of the Area Belle,[1] the acting of Chalkley and Stone was most commendable. [*A printed programme for* The Area Belle *was inserted into Feilden's journal; see Figure 35, p. 185.*]

Friday 28 January 1876
Max −37° Min −52.0
Increased twilight but we are not yet able to read ordinary type with any kind of ease. At noon today I could make out with great difficulty a few lines of Darwin's voyage.[2]
June 14th 1853. McClintock. Parl. Papers. 1855. p. 569. "We obtained some fresh water out of the holes in a mass of sea ice. These holes are formed by minute earthy particles blown off shore, and collected in hollows of the ice, which they rapidly thaw deeper by absorbing heat from the sun."[3]

Saturday 29 January 1876
Max −41° Min −48.8
Still unable to read on the floe at noon, though various shades of colour were visible in the twilight. All of us who have good eye sight are able to make out partly by guess, whole sentences in an article of the Times newspaper, but one cannot distinguish the individual letters in a long word. The duty of teaching on the lower deck is the most irksome thing that I have had to encounter in the Arctic. I voluntarily undertook it or rather my share of it like the others, but I am thankful that fate has not compelled me to be a schoolmaster.

---

[1] *The Area Belle* by Brough and Halliday (1864), a farce performed in the Royal Arctic Theatre on HMS *Alert*. George Stone is listed as 2nd captain foretop and Thomas Chalkley as able seaman, both on HMS *Discovery*: they joined *Alert* as part of a sledge crew with Lieut. Wyatt Rawson before the ships parted company on 26 Aug. 1875, to strengthen *Alert*'s crew, 'and as far as possible to share the honours of a struggle towards the Pole between the two ships': Nares, *Narrative of a Voyage*, I, p. 114.
[2] Darwin, *Journal of Researches*, new edn.
[3] F. L. M'Clintock in *Arctic Blue Books*, 1855, VI, p. 569.

ROYAL ARCTIC THEATRE.

H.M.S. ALERT.

On Thursday the 27th of January, 1876, will be Performed.

The Popular and Laughable Farce

entitled the

AREA BELLE.

CHARACTERS.

PITCHER *of the Police Force :*	MR. CHALKLEY
TOSSER *of the Grenadier Guards :*	MR. LAWRENCE
WALKER CHALKS *A Milkman :*	MR. STONE.
MRS. CROAKER *The Missus :*	MADAME. FRANCOMBE.
PENELOPE *The Area Belle.:*	MADLLE. MASKELLI.

Scenery by DR. MOSS. Music by LIEUT. ALDRICH.

To be Preceded by

READING :	Boots at the Holly Tree Inn. Dickens.
	REV. H.W. PULLEN.
COMIC SONG :	Never go without Mamma,
	MRS. HARLEY.

To commence at 7.30 precisely.

God Save The Queen.

MESSRS. GIFFARD and SYMONS :
Printing Office, Trap Lane.

Figure 35. 'Thursday Pops', 27 January 1876, printed programme for 'The Area Belle'.

185

The starting of the sledge parties and <consequent> abolition of evening school is looked forward to by me with much pleasure, but at the same time I intend to volunteer for the same duty next ~~spring~~ winter.

Sunday 30 January 1876
Max −39.9 Min −44.5
The moon showed this afternoon, the ice around us cracked a great deal with loud reports. Our ♀ cat is calling again for a ♂ at nights, and is very troublesome.

Monday 31 January 1876
Max −35. Min −45
The moon showing today. Ice cracking with tide. Afternoon and night engaged in examining mud brought up from the bottom of tide hole, depth 36 feet. Found two or three diatoms of the genus Tricerathium [*sic*] [*Margin: small sketch of Tricerathium*] and several of this form. I mounted specimens of each sort.

Temperatures for January 1876.

Corrected				Means not corrected							
Max A.421	Min. A.412	Mean A.222 & A.449	Captain's cabin	Passage outside cabin	Ward room	Abreast main hatch	Stoke Hold	After parts main deck	Mess deck by foremast ~~after part~~		Drying room
+8.5	−58.7	−29.83	+54.3	+47.2	+48.3	+45.1	+29.5	+56.1	71 in 55 in 17 in [lr deck] +54.2 +55.4 +44.5		+76.8

Mean temperature of lower deck without Drying Room.	+50.6
„ „ Mens mess deck	+52.6
Highest temperature registered in drying room.	+109.
Lowest „ Stoke hold	+22
Mean of Snow-hut for salt meat on floe	+4.5
„ „ „ on shore	−4.0
„ „ „ over Fire-hole	+0.3
„ Land	−5.2

Tuesday 1 February 1876
Max −7 Min −36
Overcast and hazy. Could only now and again, see the moon struggling through the mist. Twenty years today since I entered the service in the 42nd Highlanders. Eight years today since gazetted Paymaster 18th Hussars.

Wednesday 2 February 1876
Max −6 Min −19
Wind from N.N.E. with a good deal of drift, went out at noon but found it very disagreeable, so quickly returned to the ship. The wind felt quite warm being only −10°. this is certain proof to my mind that there is open water in that direction, I mean by

open water the ice has cleared away sufficiently to allow the wind now blowing over us to absorb some of the heat of the sea. I have been working away of late trying to condense some of the information I collected last year. Observations on Birds are completed as far as I am able, and I am now working at soundings. I find that where the coast-line is composed of hypogene rocks,[1] the soundings brought up, are very clean beautiful crystals of quartz, garnet etc, little or no life, but as soon as we get onto a calcareous rock bottom, the mud becomes much finer. *In soundings taken in Hayes Sound in <46 fathoms>* latitude 78°.52'., after some twenty trials, I gave up with out finding any trace of an organism, in latitude 79°.25' in about the same depth, but in the limestone area of Franklin Pierce Bay, the first grain showed *Foraminifera*, several diatoms, one of them a beatiful wheel-shaped *Coscinodiscus*.[2] Moss came into my cabin whilst I <was> examining the later. I hope he will not put down that they were found in soundings from our present winter-quarters.

Thursday 3 February 1876
Max −11 Min −33
A good deal of wind when I was out at first, but it died away after noon. Walked several times up and down the mile. Then to the hill where the thermometers are placed on shore. A good deal of haze in the channel, but the Greenland coast visible. No trace of water outside. The ships list to port is gradually increasing and the damp which collects on the sides of my cabin, runs down and collects under my bed and chest of drawers. This evening I had a crusade among the articles hidden there. Everything dripping, my gun-case full of water. The damp up here is very difficult to contend against. I often think that in after times I will be sorry that I kept so scanty a journal in the Arctic. Some of my messmates write every day a couple of solid hours in their log, but I am now of the opinion that it is a mistake. For every duty that is to be performed a qualified member of the expedition is told off to attend to it, for instance Rawson takes all the maximum and minimum temperatures outside, and the temperatures between decks. Aldrich takes the hourly temperatures, barometers, winds and meterological phenomena, and tabulates them. Egerton attends to the tides. Captain Markham in addition to his magnetic observations, pays the greatest attention to sledge equipment, Parr attends to the astronomy, electricity spectroscope &c. Giffard magnetism. May, navigation, plans, surveying, chronometers. Our old D[r3] is constantly at the meat [?] &c. Several officers join together for taking the declinometer.[4] Now the reason that I make no remarks in my journal on these subjects is that I have not the means or facilities that each of these highly qualified officers possess for making observations in their special departments. What therefore can be the possible good of my bringing together a lot of crude, unverified suppositions. Besides one cannot meddle in other persons work without becoming disagreeable. Moss has the analysis of air and water to look after, but he is in addition a regular free-lance meddling in every bodies business and thinks he can put the world right.
[*Here Feilden tipped in a copy of the 'Thursday Pops' programme for 3 February 1876; see Figure 36, p. 188.*]

[1] Formed beneath the surface; such rocks include granite and gneiss.
[2] A genus of diatoms in the family Coscinodiscaceae.
[3] Dr Colan, Fleet surgeon.
[4] Dip circle. Levere, 'Magnetic Instruments'.

THURSDAY POPS.

H.M.S. ALERT.

FEBRUARY 3rd 1876.

PROGRAMME.

1. LECTURE On our food in the Arctic Regions : DR. COLAN.
2. BALLAD   Men of Harlech :   MR. CANE.
3. SONG   Irish Wedding :   MR. LAWRENCE.
4. BALLAD Nora Mc. Shane :   MR. WINSTONE.
5. RECITATION Jack's cruise ashore :   MR. DOIDGE.
6. SONG Miss Lirriper's lodgings No. 2 :   MR. PEARCE.
7. BALLAD Janet's choice :   MR. MASKELL.
8. READING A pleasant day with an unpleasant
                   termination. Dickens :   LIEUT. MAY.
9. SONG Pull down the Blind :   MR. CHALKLEY.
10. BALLAD Castles in the Air :   MR. JOINER.

To commence at 7.30 precisely.

God Save The Queen.

MESSRS. GIFFARD and SYMONS :
Printing Office, Trap Lane.

Figure 36.   Printed 'Thursday Pops' programme 3 February 1876.

Friday 4 February 1876
Max −17 Max −24
Wind from N.N.W. all day. Hazy and altogether an unpleasant day. No twilight visible, and the moon much overcast. If our Eskimo dogs are the descendants of the wolf as they appear to be, why have they changed their colour in so many cases to black, and why do they not have a reasonable change of coat during the winter, like the hares, Lemmings, Ptarmigan &c.?
[*Margin*: Change of colour in Eskimo dog]

Saturday 5 February 1876
Max −14 Min −23.5
Wind greater part of the day strong from N.N.W. [*Margin*: *Winds.*] Before tea went outside for an hour with the Captain. After tea walked with Markham. Hazy, the moon

overcast, no stars visible. In looking through my journal I find that there is no record of our seeing [*Margin*: *Clio borealis*] *Clio borealis* or *Limacina arctica*, after leaving Port Foulke, apparently these disappeared with the colder waters of Smiths Sound. Snow falling between 11 and 12 tonight when I was on deck, it was of a fine description, the wind had subsided.

[*Margin*: *Appendicularia*] Plenty of Appendicularia[1] at Brevoort Island.

Sunday 6 February 1876

Max −12.5 Min −31

After morning service and divisions walked with Captain Nares in the direction of Cape Rawson. It was very cloudy, and passing over the moon from N to S. Not <much> twilight visible, no water visible in the sound, or anywhere else. We got within half a mile of the Cape, then ascended rising ground. The snow is nearly as bad to walk in as last September, most of the time I sink over the ankles, but perhaps this is owing to the fall of snow last night and the drift of the last few days. It is an extraordinary fact that Payer[2] should have observed thousands of Auks and Gulls in the cliffs of Kronprinz Land[3] in N. Lat. 80° on the 11th April, that the thermo should have been 10°R.[4] +54.5 Fahr. [*Margin*: Birds at Kronprinz Land in April. Payer.] The congregating of these myriads of birds at their northern nesting place establishes beyond a doubt that the water seen in their vicinity must remain permanently open for the rest of the season, sufficiently to provide these swarms of birds with food. I am sure that congregations of birds in the Arctic, means high comparative temperature of the sea, and greater abundance of marine life. In England in the beginning of May, *Uria* troile[5] resorts to the nesting places, but not before that date.

Monday 7 February 1876

Max −28 Min −45

Still clouded over, with wind from N. The list of the ship to port is 3½°. [*Margin*: List of Ship] The meat of the Musk-sheep served out today to messes and wardroom, was most preceptibly tainted with a strong musky taste and odour. It is the first carcase of those we have killed and eaten that has been so. I did not get the taste of musk out of my mouth for an hour after dinner, aided by a pipe of Cavendish,[6] whilst I eructated musk for several hours. It does not appear to be satisfactorily explained how this musky odour and taste originates. [*Margin*: Musk taste of. turned out to be the Old Bull.]

[*Feilden blacked out the remaining 32 lines he had written on this page; see Figure 37, p. 190.*]

---

[1] Small free-swimming planktonic tunicates, shaped somewhat like tadpoles.

[2] Payer, 'Notes on the Land', p. 30.

[3] The northernmost land in Franz-Joseph Land, which is an archipelago north of Novaya Zemlya in the Arctic Ocean.

[4] Réaumur scale, where freezing point of water = 0°R, boiling point = 80°R. At this date, the scale was used in several parts of continental Europe.

[5] Foolish guillemot, common guillemot, guillemot.

[6] Cavendish tobacco: '1886 Pall Mall G. 19 June 6/1 The cakes are … submitted to hydraulic pressure, and in the end a substance is obtained of great solidity, and which cuts like black marble. This is the cavendish which army men, artists, and others affect.' *OED*.

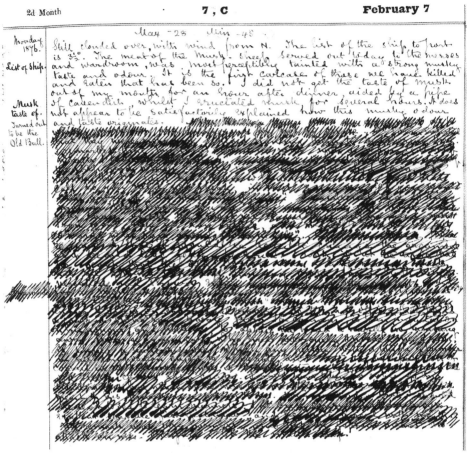

Figure 37.   Photograph showing journal entry for 7 February 1876, with 32 lines blacked out.

Tuesday 8 February 1876
Max −35 Min −50°

A beautiful calm day. Moon nearly at the full, temperature when I went out before dinner −43°. Walked to the top of cairn Hill. [*Margin*: *C. Joseph Henry*] Cape Joseph Henry distinctly visible – right in the lightest part of the twilight the planet Venus was twinkling brightly; all the stars in that direction were invisible. It felt warm and delightful. After dinner walked to Point Sheridan. I have not been there since the 14th of Nov last year. Along the line of raised beach at one extremity of which the signal staff is planted the wind has cleared off the snow, and one walks for a hundred yards or so over the round stones. When standing alone at a place like Point Sheridan, [*Margin*: *Stillness*] nothing can exceed the feeling of desolation ~~and solitariness~~ which comes over one, everything white, white, the moon shedding a weird light over the hummocks and floes to the north, not a sound audible except the crunch of the snow under foot, and now and again a sharp crack as some piece of ice splits with a noise like the snapping of a gigantic harp string.

In addition to the *Sastrugi*, the floe is covered with small markings exactly like the ripple marks we see on <the> shore~~, but at right angles~~ !

[*Margin*: Sastrugi] [*Here Feilden made some small sketches in the text.*]

 Sastrugi N and S

Ripple marks.

On the night of the 22nd of May 1853, eastern shore of Prince Patrick Island McClintock shot two musk bulls. extract from the Parl. Papers of 1855. page 559. The following glowing description of the scene from the pen of that distinguished officer. "At eleven o'clock we saw and shot two very large musk bulls, a well-timed supply, as the last of the venison was used this morning; we found them to be in better condition than any we have ever seen. I shall never forget the death struggle of one of these noble bulls; a spanish bullfight gives no idea of it, and even the slaughter of the bear is tame in comparison. This animal was shot through the lungs and blood gushed from his nostrils upon the snow. As it stood fiercely watching us, prepared yet unable to charge, its small but fixed glaring eyes were almost concealed by masses of shaggy hair, and its whole frame was fearfully convulsed with agony; the tremulous motion was communicated to its enormous covering of tangled wool and hair; even the coarse thick mane seemed to me indignant and slowly moved from side to side. It seemed as if the very fury of its passion was pent up within it for one final – a revengeful charge. There was no roaring the majestic beast was dumb, but the wild gleam of savage fire which shot from his eyes and his menacing attitude, was far more terrible than the most hideous bellow. We watched in silence, for time was doing our work, nor did we venture to lower our guns until, his strength becoming exhausted, he reeled and fell.

I have never witnessed such an intensity of rage, nor imagined for one moment that such an apparently stupid brute, under any circumstances of pain and passion, could have presented such a truly appalling spectacle. It is almost impossible to conceive a more terrific sight than that which was presented to us in the dying moments of this matchless monarch of these northern wilds. A mile or two farther we saw four milch cows and a very small calf."[1]

On 6th June 1853. McClintock is attacked by an old bull. v. id. p. 566.

Wednesday 9 February 1876
Max (mercury frozen) Min –51
Walked to Point Sheridan before dinner, temp –46 but no wind, then up the ravine as far as the first dêpot. Did not see or track of any wind. [*Margin*: Hare's track] Egerton and Rawson came across a hare track today. From Pt. Sheridan, Cape Joseph Henry and the Greenland coast was visible.

Thursday 10 February 1876
No max register mercury frozen.[2]
Min –~~49~~ 54.

---

[1] F. L. M'Clintock in *Arctic Blue Books*, 1855, VI, pp. 559–60.

[2] Alcohol thermometers are less accurate than mercury ones, but the mercury freezes at −38.83° C. Six's thermometer, the standard maximum-minimum thermometer throughout the 19th century, contains both alcohol and mercury. Six, 'Account of an Improved Thermometer'; McConnell in Sears and Merriman, *Oceanography: The Past*, pp. 252–65.

Left the ship at 12 m, with Egerton, walked to the gap of Dunloe, then ascended to the plateau by the eastern side as the snow appeared heavily and dangerously drifted in the ravine. Portions of the upland were bare or only lightly drifted over, but without altering our intended course much, we were able to steer over nice hard snow at a very brisk pace. We reached a point overlooking the channel <midway> between Cape Rawson and the next headland south, at a quarter to 2. We estimated this point at 4½ miles from the ship. We could see Repulse Harbour on the opposite coast, and a portion of the high lands south of it towards Cape Sumner, but Robeson Channel runs very nearly N.E. and S.W. true so that the next headland to our south cut off any further view of the channel. There was not water visible, a gray smoke hung over the channel but not at all opaque, so that we saw the floes and hummocks tolerably well. The ice appeared to be of the same description as that in the great area to the north of us. No flat place visible to us. Saw no trace of life on the uplands but between the ship and the gap of Dunloe, crossed a hares track. Venus was twinkling brightly in the twilight and the moon though full, was rather low to our northern horizon. Temperature −45° or 77° below freezing. We walked and ran on our return very briskly, reaching the ship a little after 3 p.m., our clothes were soaked with perspiration, but Egerton's nose and my left cheek were a little burnt, as a slight breeze was in our face as we returned.

We came across a small circular hole in the snow with a mouth about the size of penny piece, at the edges the inside snow had been thrown up in small particles evidently by some animal from the inside as no foot marks were to be seen. I presume a lemming had been peeping out to see how the sun was getting on.
[*The 'Thursday Pops' Programme for 10 February 1876 was tipped in; see Figure 38, p. 193.*]

Friday 11 February 1876
Min −55°
Walked up to flagstaff cairn. −50° no wind. The Captain and Parr walked up Sheridan ravine, and [*Margin: Hare.*] came across the track of a hare, this animal had been eating a plant of *Sax. oppositifolia* [*Margin: Saxifraga oppositifolia*] which was exposed. Here and there, I have lately come across this plant, in places where the snow has been drifted off, and where it is completely exposed to the lowest temperature. This shows that some of the Arctic plants retain vitality at extremely low temperatures. I placed some of the buds of this plant in glycerine.
"In fact, it is neither the mean annual, nor the summer (flowering), nor the autumn (fruiting), temperature that determines the abundance or scarcity of the vegetation in each district, but these combined with the ocean temperature and consequent prevalence of humidity, its geographical position, and its former conditions, both climatal and geographical." xxx "Phænogamic plants, however, are probably nowhere found far north of lat. 81°." v. Hooker. Arc. Man. pp. 202–3.[1]

Saturday 12 February 1876
Min −52.5
The sledging tents were pitched today, and inspected by the Captain. Aldrich, Rawson, and Egerton went out on the floe, and found the floes better fitted for travelling, than

[1] Hooker, 'Outlines of the Distribution of Arctic Plants', pp. 202–3.

THURSDAY POPS.

H.M.S. ALERT.

FEBRUARY 10th 1876.

PROGRAMME.

1. A Few Words on Arctic Plants : REVD. H.W. PULLEN.
2. RECITATION . An o'er true tale :   MR. WOOLLEY.
      After which the original, and only true

PALE-O CHRISTY MINSTRELS

will challenge all comers who may be in Latitude 82.27.N
to sing. !   ALERT's and DISCOVERY's only excepted. !
Musk Oxen, Hares, Ptarmigan &c. will meet with a warm
reception — and those who receive the most attention will
be expected to *come down* handsomely ! Failing competitors
the following programme will be *executed* !

1. Reminiscences of the old Land —   SHEEPSKIN !
2. Because others like it, why need we ?   BREAD DUST !
2. Commercial, Political, Amatory. &c.   PENDULUM !
4. Unknown's request.   BONES !
5. Several replies —   BEESWAX !
6. An old song a few extra words.   PEMMICAN FACE !
7. An Established favourite —   SHEEPSKIN !
8. A song which may have been sung before, but not in
   such a high latitude.   SCREAMER !

NB. THIS TROUPE NEVER SING'S IN LONDON.

To commence at 7.30 precisely.

God Save The Queen.

MESSRS. GIFFARD and SYMONS :
Printing Office, Trap Lane.

Figure 38.   Printed 'Thursday Pops' programme, 10 February 1876, including a talk by
Pullen on Arctic Plants, and a performance by the 'PALE-O CHRISTY MINSTRELS'.

might be expected from our shore observations. Others of our party wandering on shore found numerous traces of hares.

Sunday 13 February 1876
Min −55.5
A tuft of Sax. oppositifolia <gathered today when> exposed to the air without any protecting mantle of snow, showed signs of budding the little green buds visible, a small moss perhaps or *Phascum*[1] gathered under the same circumstances, also showed signs of vitality. Think of this with a temperature at −50°.

Portions of this plant when damped, and placed on a slide under a high power, showed hundreds of small bodies which moved rapidly in the liquid. Moss who had them under the microscope considered them to be Infusoria,[2] some of them were ciliated, but my impression is that they are the zoospores of some Confervoid Algae, perhaps Protococeus or Palmella.[3] vide journal of 15th inst, where I find the filter in the ward-room to be the source from whence these organisms came. May came off the list today, after four months confinement to his cabin and amputation of the first and second phalanx of big toe looking well and hearty. He kept up his spirits wonderfully and no one ever heard him complain during the long winter.

Monday 14 February 1876
Min −56
After breakfast I went out with my gun in the direction where Egerton told me, he had seen numerous hare-tracks two days since. Temperature −50° gun slung on my shoulder, as even through thick gloves, the heat of ones hands is abstracted by contact with metal at this temperature. I came across many tracks, and was debating with myself, whether or not to unsling and load my gun, when out started a fine hare almost from under my feet, of course it was out of range before I was prepared, it ran off for a hundred yards, then sat up and watched me. I followed its tracks for a long time but did not see it again. Returning to the place where it started from, I found that it was occupying a burrow about four feet deep dug horizontally into a snow-drift, I have no doubt that these burrows are occupied for some time, as this one was discoloured by the feet, and a good deal of hair was sticking to the sides. All about the neighbourhood this animal had been scratching and feeding, and always on the same plant *Sax. oppositifolia*. Even where exposed, without the slightest covering of snow, this hardy plant is now putting out delicate green buds all ~~over~~ <on> its brown surface, these knobs are grazed on by the hares who appear just to pare off the portions containing the buds. Lemmings tracks were also tolerably numerous. Egerton and Rawson were trying the sighting of their cut down Sniders, when I was on the hill, and they were firing out to the floe. The discharge of the rifle made little noise, but the bullets whistling through the air, sounded to me as loud as the noise of a shot from a field-piece.

Tuesday 15 February 1876
Min −53.8

---

[1] A genus of moss.
[2] A class of unicellular protozoa.
[3] Genera of green algae.

Went out again after Mr Hare, but he was not at home today. I have been much puzzled over the *Infusoria* stated to have been found by Moss in the stems of *Sax. op.* mentioned in my journal of the 11th inst. All yesterday and today I have been examining them in tufts of the same plant, certainly they were abundant, oblong creatures darting with great rapidity, and at the same time revolving on their own axis. magnified under the ¼ inch lens). I examined some fresh droppings of the hare, moistened with water from the filter, the same organisms abounded! then some soundings with the same result. [*Margin:* Infusoria −50°?] This sent me to the filter, and after twenty trials with different drawings off, I found each drop filled with these minute creatures. This shows how careful we should be, for the last two days Moss has been calling all hands in the wardroom, including the Captain, to look at the Infusoria, found in plants exposed to a temperature of −50°, and a little chaff has been expended at my expense, that the naturalist had been cut out. This fell harmlessly, as I have *ab initio*, protested that I laid no claim to pretensions of scientific knowledge, and was simply a smatterer and collector. I called Moss into my cabin this evening and he was instantly convinced that the filter was the origin of the infusoria.

Wednesday 16 February
Min −61
Thickness of winters ice this day 56 inches. Temperature of sea water taken through fire-hole.

Rawson and Egerton took the dogs out for a run, and sledged down to Cape Rawson. One bitch had a fit. Rawson brought me back some fresh animal droppings, I think they must have been of some species of *Mustela* as they struck me as too small for foxes. These droppings were made up of remains of lemming, the hair greyish white, and the big claws voided and digested. I can see no reason why the hare or lemming should be supposed to hybernate in these regions, we found the tracks of these animals numerous, last autumn as long as we had a glimmer of twilight, and this year as soon as returning light enables us to see a foot print on the snow we find them again. If they are moving about now when there is only feeble twilight for a portion of the day, equally well could they be so in December. For instance at 7 o'c. p.m. today our darkness is equivalent to that at noon on the shortest day. Finding as yet no tracks of Ptarmigan puzzles me, I noticed them last year a few days after the sun disappeared, I am inclined to think that they remain all winter, for whither can they migrate to.

8 of these abreast in a sledge firing volleys!

Figure 39. Drawing of sledge dogs from the rear captioned '8 of these abreast in a sledge, firing volleys!'

195

Thursday 17 February 1876
Min −62
Thickness of ice on 15th Feb. 55½ inches, of this thickness 6½ in. were above water.
Temperature of water this day.
Bottom in 6 fathoms mean of 7 observations − 28°.5′ −
    limits from 28°.4 to 28°.7′.
Water at about 2 feet from surface − 28°.5
Bottom of sludge covering surface of water 28°.0
Halfway through one inch of sludge − 27°.0.

   The corrected temperature when we were out this morning marked as low as −60°.35. Rawson and Egerton drove with dog-team in direction of Cape Union, went about 5½ miles from ship. They noticed that the fixed <land> ice was already splitting from the floe near Cape Rawson, in a fissure varying from 2 to 5 feet in width. On the floe I noticed a track which must be some species of *Mustela*, it is too large for lemming and far too small for hare or fox. Now that returning light enables us to see things things around us, objects of interest are cropping up, for investigation. The immense hummocks grounded along the coast, are often discoloured with foreign material, which runs in bands through them, but not always in parallel lines, the sediment from this ice consists of a greyish mud, which is often filled with Tricerathium [*sic*] and Gyrosigma. One of the hummocks I visited today was an immense block, at least 50 feet thick. The northern horizon to the zenith was a lovely violet tint.
[*Here Feilden inserted the 'Thursday Pops' programme for 17 February 1876; see Figure 40, p. 197*]

Friday 18 February 1876
Max −31.5 Min −59
The view from Cairn Hill was pleasing today, Towards the south a warm glow of Salmon, <violet to north> the planet Venus is decreasing in brilliancy by comparison with returning light. All the stars have disappeared at noon, and have done so for more than a week past. A belt of mist hung round the ship, and clung to the shore from Cape Rawson, at an elevation of 150 feet we were quite clear of this mist. The thermometer in the mist graduated lower than the one on the hill out of its influence. Petersen and Frederick took the dog-team to Rawson's snow hut 7 miles from the ship, they report many fox and hare tracks, a fox had burrowed into the hut and left some of his droppings behind which Petersen brought me, as usual it consisted of the remains of lemming. On Cairn Hill the tracks of *Mustela* are abundant. Where the hares had been scraping, the exposed plants of Sax. oppo. were budding, intermixed a moss was putting out tender green fronds, and a sprig of willow showed signs of buds. Fancy us walking about the hills and enjoying ourselves in a temperature of 90° below freezing. I exposed my bare hands for two or three minutes grubbing up plants, and in that short time they became stiff with cold, the Captain happened to have two pair of gloves on as well as ~~mits~~ [*sic*] <gauntlets>, and made me put a pair on as I only had gauntlets. Markham and Nellie put up my hare.

Saturday 19 February 1876
Max −31°. Min −58
Moss shot a fine ♂ hare 9½ lbs. he detected it by its black eyes in contrast to the snow. The stomach was full, I placed portions of it under the microscope, and I detected

THURSDAY POPS.

H.M.S. ALERT.

February 17th 1876.

Programme.

1. On Hydrostatics :   Lieut. May.
2. Song, Martha the Milkman's daughter : Mr. Francombe.
3. Ballad, Those single days of old :   Mr. Smith.
4. Reading, Gridiron :   Mr. Lorimer.
5. Ballad, Our Bugles sang truce :   Mr. Shibley.
6. Song, The Light Ship at the Nore :   Mr. G. Egerton.
7.   Clog dance :   Mr. Cranstone.
8. Song, Barrel of Pork :   Mr. Stone.
9. Recitation, The Soldier's pardon :   Mr. Mitchell.
10. Song, Kitty Wells :   Mr. Malley.
11. Duet, The Goddess Diana :   Messrs. Wood and
                                                                   Hawkins,

To commence at 7.30 precisely.

God Save The Queen.

Messrs. Giffard and Symons :
Printing Office, Trap Lane.

Figure 40.   Printed 'Thursday Pops' programme 17 February 1876.

parts of saxifrage, grass, moss &c, so that I imagine it eats whatever it comes across in a vegetable form. I opened the intestines from the pyloric duct to the rectum searching for parasites, 12 inches anterior to the junction of the cæcum[1] detected a worm (Filaria.)[2] and they were numerous in the fæces, to within three or four inches of the rectum. took out about 30 specimens. None were adhering to the coats of the intestine. Those that I examined under the microscope were apparently ♀ as they showed numerous ova, which under pressure from the slide circle, escaped through the vulva. Rawson and Egerton went south with the dog sledge and left a tent about 5 miles from the ship. Rather misty today. During the whole of this week the temperature has been about −50°, and all hands have been engaged at work outside of ship, bringing stores, coals, barrels, &c onboard, and there has not been any frost-bite. The weather has been remarkably calm.

Sunday 20 February 1876
[*Printed menu for dinner on 20 February inserted here; see Figure 41, p. 199.*[3]]
Min −59.2
A lovely day, temperature under −50°. Walked with Markham to No 2 Bay, about four miles out in a N.W. direction, found several tracks of hares and numerous tracks of lemmings. At noon it was very beautiful, and to us deprived of sunlight for so long, every sign of his return is most pleasing. To the south was a glow of amber light and above that, strata of thin fleecy clouds which were coloured delicate rose, and some rich lake colour, whilst much lower down and nearer to us was a string of disconnected watery looking clouds, with arched backs, which my fancy confused into a troop of whales arching their backs, as they descend from the surface, the northern horizon was delicate blue, merging into a darker shade and finally towards the zenith, becoming a splendid purple. Not a cloud or speck was visible in the north, the Heckla [*sic*] range, white & lofty stood out very clearly. We spun along over the hard snow at a good rate, and after 8 miles of it sat down to dinner with a good appetite. The perspiration had so condensed on me that when I took off my sealskin, my flannel shirt was frozen, and my under shirt dripping, the waist band of my trousers was also hard, and my drawers wet through. Cane[4] the armourer shot a fine hare today with a nondescript sort of pistol that he has, and Mʳ Goode the boatswain brought me in a pretty little lemming in its winter suit which he found dead on the snow.[5]

Monday 21 February 1876
Min −59.8
The shades of colour are certainly very lovely, The purple of the zenith uniting with the blue of the northern horizon is magnificent. The lemmings make burrows under the snow, and dig out spiracles by which they reach the surface. Our lemming here, must be I think

---

[1] The blind gut, first part of the large intestine. *OED.*

[2] Parasitic thread-like nematodes, roundworms.

[3] The menu is incorrectly dated at the foot. The dinner was on the occasion of Lieut George A. Giffard's 27th birthday, and the event was marked with a birthday toast. 'Poppie' was the name of Giffard's sledge.

[4] James Frederick Cane.

[5] Joseph Good is listed as chief boatswain's mate in Nares, *Narrative of a Voyage*, I, p. ix.

MENU
Le Vingt Février 1876.

That's French for what we're going to eat,
    On this bonniest of days.
Potage Julienne — that's Soup,
    With carrots, peas etc.
The daintiest *Gourmand* in the South
    Could hardly wish a betterer.
Poissons — Cod and Lobster Sauce ;
    (Oysters were more in season :
But the Guardian of their glossy beards
    Is deaf, alas ! to reason.)
Entrées — Kidneys in a stew,
    Or *Vol au Vent de Rognons* :
With Sausages and Mushrooms
    Of the sort they call Bolognian.
Tourts de Mouton (Mutton Pia)
    And *Langue de Boeuf* — that's Tongue ;
With the first Hare of the spring-time ;
    Neatly shot and nicely hung.
Strawberry Puffs ; *Compote de Pêches*:
    Blancmange *à la Vanille* :
With Puddings *à la Cabinet* —
    Thus ends our frugal meal.

Please to charge your glasses —
    Silence, pray ! now drink success
To the wittiest and the merriest
    Of our merry merry Mess.
May his 'Poppie' valiantly
    O'er distant ice-fields roam ,
And the 'Poppie' of his own true heart
    Be the bright flower of his home !

H.M.S. ALERT.   21st Feb. 1876.

Figure 41.   Printed birthday menu for Lieutenant Giffard.

from the description, *Mus Hudsonius*, the two middle claws on the fore-paws are so very singular, and Richardson mentions this feature as distinctive of the species.[1] At the mouth of a spiracle I found today some fresh droppings. Under the microscope I could not detect any particular plant, but the substance voided consisted entirely of vegetable matter. In both the lemmings and hare's dung are numerous claret coloured sporules, which <are> perhaps, the zoospores of Protococcus.[2] The way in which snow-drifts accumulate in ravines is somewhat singular. Where the prevailing wind beats against a perpendicular wall of rock, there the reflux eddy of the storm scoops out the snow in a semicircular gap with vertical sides, I came across one of these places today where the drift was at least 25 feet deep, and the gap scooped out as clean as if down by spade work. Giffard's birthday. Kept with a splendid dinner; Spiro[3] the Captain's servant volunteered his services as maitre de cuisine, on the occasion, and the result was excellent. Moss has been making experiments today on the amount of moisture in the air which I hope will be useful, as he has taken great trouble with them, bringing the air into his cabin from the mizzen-rigging. We have all noticed the peculiar mist or smoke which very often extends from the direction of Cape Rawson, clings to the shore and envelopes the ship, and which at an elevation of 150 feet we surmount, consequently I am somewhat afraid that observations made on the air in the vicinity of the ship will not be as valuable as if made beyond the influence of this mist, at present the impression is that the temperature marks lower in this fog than out of its influence.

[*Here Feilden tipped in his sketch of a snow drift in a ravine; see Figure 42, p. 201.*]

Tuesday 22 February 1876
Min −57.2
In the evening it blew strong from S.S.W. the temperature which up to this time had been as low as −40° to −50° rose with a jump in a quarter of an hour to −15°. When I went on deck it felt warm. The different bands that cross hummocks require strict investigation. I find that in many cases they cross one another at considerable angles.

Wednesday 23 February 1876
Max −2.2 Min −22.5
Blowing throughout the day in puffs from the S.S.W. a great deal of drift which prevented us going far from the ship. The sudden rises of temperature which invariably accompanies

---

[1] *Mus Hudsonius* is an earlier name for what Feilden elsewhere (see entry for 31 Dec. 1875, p. ??? and n. ???) refers to as *Myodes hudsonicus*, now *Dicrostonyx groenlandicus*, the Arctic or collared lemming. In Feilden, 'Appendix II. Mammalia', pp. 202–5, he uses yet another name for this species, *Myodes torquatus*, but he knows that this is the same species. Richardson et al., *Fauna Boreali-Americana*, I, p. 132, describe the Hudson's Bay lemming, *Arvicola hudsonius*. The British Museum, *List of the Specimens of Mammalia*, p. 120, lists the Hudson's Bay lemming as *Myodes hudsonius*; that lemming is most unlikely to be found as far north as northern Ellesmere Island. *Dicrostonyx groenlandicus*, the Labrador collared lemming, is the only lemming as far north as northern Ellesmere Island. Lemming taxonomy is complicated and disputed, and is reflected in the multiplicity of names.
[2] Nares, *Narrative of a Voyage*, I, p. 16. Aveling, *General Biology*, pp. 28–9. *Protococcus* is a genus of algae, a monocellular plant, which in the red form is responsible for the crimson colour of snow, observed by many explorers in the Arctic.
[3] Spero Capato, captain's steward.

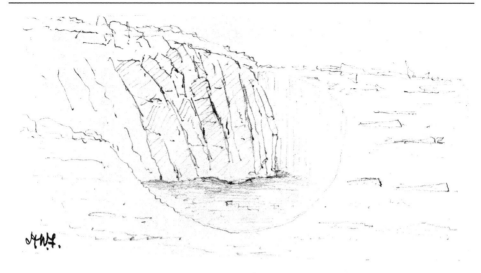

Figure 42.   'Sketch of a snow drift in a ravine, (made 21ˢᵗ. Feb. 1876) near winter quarters 82°.27. The drifted snow filling up this small ravine was about 25 feet deep, the prevailing wind having beaten against the perpendicular projecting rock, <about 30 ft high> made a reflux eddy, which ~~piled the~~ scooped out a semicircular trench with clean cut vertical walls of snow 25 feet in height and about the same in width.' 'H.W.F.'

the wind from this quarter is surely capable of some simple solution, I fancy when we compare our meteorological results with those obtained onboard the *Discovery* we shall find the clue, *viz*. open water in Hall's Basin.

Thursday 24 February 1876[1]
Max +2 Min −29
The last two days blow has exposed more ground in our neighbourhood than on any occasion since our arrival last autumn. I walked with Captain Nares inland to the second small lake; lake, however, is rather a misnomer, they are mere dips or hollows where the melting snows collect in summer, and now a few inches of ice frozen down to the mud represents the water. The gale had gouged out long strips of snow from W. To E. which also exposed portions of the muddy banks and shores. My attention was attracted to numerous valves of *Saxicava arctica*,? which strewed the surface, and on close examination I found several valves of *Astarte*?[2] alongside of these shells I came across a splinter of Pine?, about three inches long, and again another piece about six inches, a little further on, but still about the margin of extreme ~~depth~~ summer height of water I was surprised to find the ends of two logs of pine sticking up through the snow. [*Margin*: but lying flat and not embedded in the soil.] These logs measured respectively 3ᶠᵗ8ⁱⁿ × 1.8 and 3ᶠᵗ0ⁱⁿ × 1ᶠᵗ0ⁱⁿ. they

---

[1] The main event for this day's 'Thursday Pops' was a burlesque operetta written by Pullen and founded on Barham, 'Misadventures at Margate', which appeared as part of Barham's *Ingoldsby Legends*, pp. 321–4, and also in *Bentley's Miscellany*, 10, 1841, 620–22. Barham wrote under the pseudonym Thomas Ingoldsby, The operetta was announced as the last production of the Royal Arctic Theatre for the season, and thus for the duration of the expedition. However, the last entertainment was on 2 March 1876. See Figures 43 and 44, pp. 203 and 204.
[2] Bivalve shells.

were somewhat friable, and weighed 7 and 6 lbs. their exteriors showed the abrasion (silky fibre) peculiar to wood that has been long drifted in the Arctic. Of course there could not be the slightest hesitation in deciding how the wood got there to its present position, but these silent witnesses reveal to us a tale of most extraordinary interest. The distance the wood lay from the present sea-level is about one mile, and the height above it 200 feet or thereabouts, immediatly behind, the hill again rises to an altitude of 400 feet. [*Margin*:{200 by aneroid twice measured}]Surrounding the depression were numerous rounded erratic blocks, grains, granite, hornblendic gneiss, coarse sandstones, rounded and polished Silurian conglomerates, and many other description of rocks nesting upon the mud and the slaty limestone of the district which there is nearly vertical, and laminated into thin splinters by the frost. This wood therefore must have remained on the surface exposed yearly to the seasonal transitions of heat, <moisture> for the length of time that it took to elevate the land 200 feet above the present sea level, and the valves of the *Saxicava*,[x] though blanched, and minus the hinge ligament lay side by side on the surface unmistakeably [*sic*] showing that nothing had disturbed them from the moment they dropped to their present position. The two smaller fragments of pine floated buoyantly in fresh water.

Clumps of hypnum[1] – exposed, looked green and last years seed-vessels were attached.

[x] The thickness of the shells of these *Saxicava* is remarkable.

[*Here two printed sheets of 'Thursday Pops' were tipped in; see Figures 43 and 44, pp. 203–4.*]

Friday 25 February 1876
Max −25 Min −29
Wandering along the exposed patches. I found several places where valves of Saxicava and Astarte are exposed. The lines of old sea-beaches and upheaval, are very distinct in this neighbourhood. Rawson caught a lemming today which he brought to the ship alive it is a pretty little creature, in white dress. Parr brought me in valves of Astarte from the Shenandoah Ravine.

Saturday 26 February 1876
Max −11° Min −32
I found the captured lemming dead in its box, a tin biscuit one. It must have made great efforts to escape for its upper incisors were broken. I made a careful examination of it, but could detect no *entozoa* in any of its organs, or muscles. The cæcum is very large, and its *villi*[2] are of enormous comparative length, some of them three quarters of an inch in length. The stomach small. It was not a very inviting kind of day so I confined myself to walking on the floe, the measured mile, which perambulated for eight miles.

Sunday 27 February 1876
Max −29 Min −48°
After service, walked with my gun to the ravine leading up to the Gap of Dunloe. On portions swept bare by the wind, I found many traces of Musk-sheep, judging from the colour of the dung, I fancy some of it was not older than last season.

[1] Plait moss.
[2] Finger-like projections on part of the small intestine.

ROYAL ARCTIC THEATRE.

H.M.S. 'ALERT'.

Thursday 24 February 1876.

☞ *Last Performance of the Season.*

GRAND REPRESENTATION

of the

Original Pathetico-Comico-Burlesque Operetta

entitled the

LITTLE VULGAR BOY

or

WEEPING BILL.

Founded on the Celebrated Ingoldsby Legend —
'Misadventures at Margate.'
Written expressly for the occasion by
the REV. H.W. PULLEN.

Scenery by Professor MOSS M.D.
Music by LIEUT. ALDRICH.
Manager : LIEUT. MAY.

Preceded by

READING,	The Blessed Babies :	MR. HUNT.
SONG,	Fie for Shame :	MR. SYMONS.

Figure 43.   Printed 'Thursday Pops' programme, 24 February 1876, sheet 1, 'ROYAL ARCTIC THEATRE. H.M.S. 'ALERT'. 'WEEPING BILL'.

CHARACTERS.

MR. BROWN; an *Old Buffer, slightly green :*
COMMANDER MARKHAM.

MRS. JONES; *a Landlady, slightly cross, but with a keen eye to business :* G.LeC. EGERTON ESQ.

JACK ROBINSON; *a sea-faring man, slightly figurative in his language, and violently in love with Mrs. Jones :* LIEUT. GIFFARD.

WEEPING BILL; *a Little Vulgar Boy, slightly out at elbows, and fairly sharp for his age :*
LIEUT. RAWSON.

K. 55; *The irrepressible Bobby ; slightly self-important, and the natural enemy of Weeping Bill :* REV. H.W. PULLEN.

Scene 1 & 3 The Jetty at Margate
Scene 2 & 4 Mrs. Jones' Lodgings.

To commence at 7.30 precisely.

God Save The Queen.

MESSRS. GIFFARD and SYMONS :
Printing Office, Trap Lane.

I came across a lemming on a small bare spot, when he heard my footsteps, he raised himself up on his rump like a marmot and tucked his fore-paws into his breast, then apparently satisfied with the inspection, set to work again hunting for dinner. Whilst thus employed the lemming runs quickly, then suddenly halts puts its nose close to the ground and smells, in its movements it reminded me of a Guinea-pig. At this season the colour of its fur is grayish white, nearly white at the tips but darkening to mouse brown at the base, the general colour being very near that of the Chinchilla fur. I tried to capture the little animal with my hands, but he made off quickly to the snow, there tumbling into a depression I thought to catch him, but standing on his head, his strong fore-paws were set in rapid motion, and with great celerity the little creature burrowed a hole into the snow; being desirous of making sure of the species, I changed my cartridge for a small one of dust shot, and firing into the snow near to where the tail disappeared I secured the specimen. it was the same species as previously obtained, and a ♂. Some of the raised beaches in this ravine show the grounding pushing up marks of hummocks, as we see now going on at the present coast line. Many valves of Astarte are lying about on the surface in this ravine.

At 10 p.m the planet Venus was almost within the horns of the moon, which showed this evening for the first time this lunation. Do not astrologers say that this position of the planet, predicts the birth of some extraordinary being.

Monday 28 February 1876
Min −60.2
This was the day that we expected to see the sun, by refraction from the top of the hills, near the ship. It was misty which may account for not seeing him, though nearly all hands were out. Indeed Captain Nares gave a holiday to the crew on the occasion, and the blue jackets had a good run over the hills, several had guns, but only one hare was seen. I went with Egerton in the dog-sledge as far as Cape Rawson where I got off to geologise, and walk back to the ship, G. Giffard and Simmons going on to Rawsons Cairn, about ten miles from the ship. they returned between four and five, Simmons was frost-bitten in the arm, temperature being between −45° and −50°, with a little wind. The dogs now draw admirably, it is a pretty sight on a smooth floe to see them going, each dog is fastened by <with> a single cord from the collar, to a toggle which fastens into a loop in front of the sledge, instead of crowding into a pack each dog radiates out, like an open fan, each has his proper place, and if from a crack of the whip a dog dodges between his companions, his neighbours snap and snarl until he resumes his proper place.

Geologizing in −50° is not satisfactory, only here and there were the abrupt slopes, which I could reach uncovered with snow, and what with slipping, and the cold of holding a hammer I did not enjoy myself. It was too cold to make a sketch. The hard crystalline slaty limestone of the district seems destitute of fossils, cubes of iron pyrites are common, and bands of quartz and a yellow mineral are common. These veins of quartz appear to run parallel with the lines of stratification and are from a few inches to a foot in thickness. The strata are highly inclined, at Cape Rawson nearly vertical, but with the present mantle of snow, and intense cold, I cannot write definitely about the geology. At nearly every spot which I have visited in Grant Land and had a chance of observing the dip, the strata have been inclined at very steep angles. At 11 tonight Venus was looking a warm red colour. The rocks in this neighbourhood appear to be Azoic,[1] and lower Silurians, and are flexed or folded in a very complex manner at the headlands I have visited, the strata are always nearly vertical. I can therefore come to but one opinion, namely that owing to

immense lateral pressure these beds have been folded up and that enormous ice denudition has shaved off the upper folds, making the large flat plateaus so conspicuous a feature in

[1] Containing no organic remains. The term azoic period was used in the past to refer to the age of rocks formed before the appearance of life.

this neighbourhood, serial disintegration acting upon the exposed stratas [*sic*] has split up the slaty rocks in the lines of cleavage, so that the whole surface of the country is covered with thin fragments of slate. The melting snows have again cut out ravines at a lower level breaking up the country, and again to the westward beyond the plateaus rises a lofty range of mountains. Until I reach these mountains I can only speculate.

Tuesday 29 February 1876
Min −66°

Egerton and Rawson went with the dog-sledge some six miles to the south, and from rising ground had a sight of the upper part of the sun's disc for a few minutes. Several of us were up on Cairn Hill at twelve meridian, but a bright ray mounting towards the zenith was all we saw of old Sol. It was intensely cold, Captain Nares and I walked from Cairn Hill to Drift-Wood Lake and then on to the Shenandoah Ravine, to look at some furrows and gravel-heaps on a raised beach there, which the Captain thought might have been the result of hummocks pushing on shore. During the afternoon the corrected temperature was below −63° The second lowest temperature recorded by Arctic expeditions. Pullen's birthday a very good dinner,[1] and he invited us all to dine with him on his next birthday 29th. Feb. 1880. I hope the dinner will come off, and that I will be there to feed. The ♀ Canis familaris, mentioned under date of the 1st. January as being in copula, pupped today at 12.30 [p.] m, on the floe; Petersen carried this pup in and put it into a warm hutch, in the companion, prepared for her, at 5 p.m this pup was gone, Petersen says the bitch must have eaten this pup; it is just possible that Mr P. was careless enough to leave the door of the hutch open and that the cannibalism was perpetrated by some of the other dogs, for the bitch followed her pup onboard and was seen licking it by Captain Nares. The period of gestation according to my observation, which I believe is correct, amounts to 60 days. It is, <however,> a well authenticated fact that 63 days is the period of gestation with Dog and Wolf, therefore my single observation is not of much value.

The drift-wood I found on the 24th. being unfrozen and dry; I today sawed one of the logs through and put a small section under the microscope, it is evidently part of a conifer, as there is no assemblage of ducts near the inner part of each concentric layer. This wood is sound, and floats buoyantly. I am in hopes that the exact species of tree will be deduced in England from an examination of this wood by botanists, if so, it will throw great light upon the currents of the Paleocrystic[2] area in ancient times. If Siberian or Mackenzie River wood it cannot have floated up here by Smith's Sound, neither can the erratics that surrounded it.

---

[1] Printed menu tipped in: 'BILL OF FARE / At our board this day there's no gorgeous display / Of things that are rare for we can't get 'em there; / But all of our best you'll find nicely drest: / As we've told you before we cannot do more. // Our Soup's *Julienne*, or might have been – Then / A very nice dish of very good Fish – / Called *Soles* – *Lobster Patties* – and *Kidneys* hot, that is / They're curried – Beef boiled – and by odour not spoiled / The *Musk Ox* so sweet, which is always a treat. / A Willow fed *Hare*, we hope will be there: / He will if he's Shot, he won't if he's not. Our Second Course starts with some little *Fruit Tarts*, / And *Marmalade* nice in a *Pudding* with Spice: / *Blanc Mange* white and clear to the end brings us near, / *Roley Poley* so hot completing the lot. // Ain't Beauty unadorned, adorned the most? / So Poetry with our Poet must be lost: / For here our Bill of Fare must quite plain be, / 'Tis 'PULLENS' birthday – Sun rise – Februaree.'
[2] Old ice that took many years to form.

Wednesday 1 March 1876

Intensely cold and a light wind blowing, I thought of going up Cairn Hill in hopes of seeing the sun, but was deterred by the cold, so took a brisk walk along the floe. It is wonderful how human beings stand a temperature of over a hundred degrees below freezing as we are now doing. Going on deck from the warm cabins of +50°, one emerges into a temperature with a difference of 120°, and there is not the slightest feeling of oppression in the lungs, neither have I noticed any one holding his mouth shut, or in any way showing symptoms of discomfort from the low temperature. To perform the functions of nature in such cold without danger, seems nearly incredible, but no evils have arisen from an exposure of those parts for five minutes. On consulting with Petersen today I find that the bitch referred to in yesterdays journal was by his note-book first in copula on the afternoon of the 27th Dec. 1875, which gives 63 days as the period of gestation. Strong whisky exposed in a shallow dish froze; and rectified spirits of wine under the same influences became inspissated. Concentrated Rum 39° above proof froze in a shallow dish, glycerine in a bottle became perfectly solid, and transparent but there was no visible effect on choloroform.

On re-examination I find that the glycerine though solid, and showing no alteration of level when the bottle was turned upside down, yet was sticky where touched with the point of a hard pencil.

Thursday 2 March 1876

It is probable that we have to record today the most extreme minimum range of the temperature that has yet been noticed. Every care has been taken by our meteoroligsts [*sic*] and no less than ten thermometers are under observation, the means of all of these are noted by Aldridge [*sic*] and Rawson, at various temperatures and compared with the corrections given by Kew, on the whole they retain their relative differences, so that a most accurate mean may be safely deduced.

The upper disc of the sun was visible from the mizzen rigging at 9.45 a.m, just in the gap between the Greenland Coast and Cape Rawson, but he was soon hidden behind the southern hills, I went up Cairn Hill with Captain Nares, Pullen, and Aldrich at meridian, and our eyes were gladdened with another sight of the blessed sun*, [*Margin*: *Upper disc only. H.W.F. Rose tint thrown on floe to north, beyond the shadow of our hills.] I felt as if I had taken a new lease of life. I only now begin to realize how dark it must have been during the winter, one hundred and forty-two days is a long time to exist without the benificent [*sic*] rays of the sun, but Thank God, we all, on lower deck and wardroom, gathered round our dinner tables this day without a missing 'tally'.

The 'winter pops' came to a conclusion this evening with an admirable lecture from the Captain, on the ice of the Paleocrystic area,[1] and hints for the spring sledging. In concluding he said,' [*Margin*: to this effect] "There have not hitherto been many secrets between us, and I see no reason why there should be. My plan of operations is for the sledges of the *Alert* to investigate the N. shores of Grant Land, and at the furthest northern point to investigate the condition of the ice to the northward; the crew of the *Discovery* to do the same for the northernmost shores of Greenland, if entirely succesful,

---

[1] Besides the programme for the evening, the printing press provided the text of the chorus of 'The Palaeocrystic Sea', see Figures 45 and 46, pp. 209 and 210.

<and nothing more can be done up here> I intend retreating south this season, wintering with the *Discovery*, and carry on operations next year from that basis. I shall not winter with the *Alert* in the Polar basin again, unless the prospect of some great advantage to be gained, is tolerably certain (this of course, alludes to our attempt to traverse the ice to the Pole). And I promise come what may that you shall be back in England in the autumn of 1877." (This means that we should if we winter again up here, have to abandon the *Alert* on the return of the sledging parties in the spring of 77, retreat on the *Discovery*, and make our way to Port Foulke, and join the relief ships, in time for the navigable season.)

[*Two printed sheets containing the words of the chorus of 'The Paleocrystic Sea' were tipped in here; see Figures 45 and 46, pp. 209–10.*]

Friday 3 March 1876

The intense cold still continues, no wind, and we took our usual exercise. Employed myself the greater part of the day, in fixing up my cabin. Damp is the curse of the Arctic. My bedding is soaking, and my clothes, instruments, books specimens &c are covered with mould, drip drip all day long, when writing, down it comes on my head and on the paper. Just as one is adjusting a delicate microscopic specimen, a big drop spoils the work and one has to begin <over> again. ~~The pup *disappeared* today from the hutch and Petersen is of opinion that she *devoured* it.~~ At 9:30 p.m., beautifully clear, and the moon half full, a lovely light green glow, with flakes of tender rose light, in our N.Western horizon, marking the track of the sun.

Saturday 4 March 1876

Minimum temperature from noon yesterday to noon today (– Astronomical 3rd. inst)[1] was −73°.72 and the mean of the twenty-four hours −69°.68.

The lowest mean for any twenty-four consecutive hours as yet, is from 5 am. March 3rd to 4 a.m. March 4th. viz.

Uncorrected, −66°.71. *Corrected*. Kew 69.51. Cor. mean of Thermo. −70°.31. Walked up Cairn Hill, and had a good look at the sun, at twelve o clock his whole sphere showed above the hills. The action of this extreme cold on the human body has been exaggerated, I experienced no difficulty in breathing or any other annoyance, perhaps ascending the hill, my respiration was a trifle quicker than usual. Moss was out for 2½ hours after hares, found fresh tracks where the animals had been moving about, his sublingual temperature on his return as read by me was +37°.4 *Centigrade* = 99½° Fahr. (There must be some correction for this thermo) by his own Centigrade thermometer which he asked me to read.

There has been a great raking up in books of lowest temperature recorded, Herschel Phy. Geo. par. 261. gives Back −70° at Fort Reliance, and Gmelin at Kiringa in Siberia as recording −120°. on the authority of Thomson.[2]

---

[1] An astronomical day is the 24-hour period beginning at noon rather than midnight. Meteorological instructions for recording temperature are in T. R. Jones, ed., *Manual*, pp. 15–6.

[2] Herschel, *Physical Geography*, p. 238, referring to George Back (1796–1830) (see *ODNB*), expedition of 1833–5; D. P. Thomson, *Introduction to Meteorology*, p. 56, referring to Johann Georg Gmelin (1709–55), German naturalist and explorer, who joined Vitus Behring's 2nd Kamchatka expedition (1733–43). −120° is a flat impossibility. The lowest reliably recorded for Ellesmere Island was −50°C = −58°F.

H.M.S. ALERT.

MARCH 2 1876.

CHORUS.

Not very long ago,
On the six-foot floe
Of the palæocrystic sea,
  Two ships did ride
  Mid the crashing of the tide —
The 'ALERT' and the 'DISCOVERY.'

The sun never shone
Their gallant crews upon
For a hundred and forty-two days ;
  But no darkness and no hummocks
  Their merry hearts could flummox :
So they set to work and acted Plays.

There was Music and Song,
To help the hours along,
Brought forth from the good ship's store ;
  And each man did his best
  To amuse and cheer the rest :
And 'nobody can't do more.'

Figure 45.   Sheet 1 of the chorus of 'The Paleocrystic Sea', 2 March 1876.

Here's a health to *Marco Polo* —
May he reach his northern goal, oh !
And advance the flag of England into realms unknown !
May the *Challenger* be there,
All comers bold to dare,
And *Victoria* be victorious in the Frozen Zone !

May our *Poppie* be in sight,
With her colours streaming bright,
And the *Bulldog* tug on merrily from strand to strand !
And the *Alexandra* brave
See our banner proudly wave
O'er the highest cliffs and summits of the northernmost
land !

Here's a health to *Hercules*,
Whom the Autumn blast did freeze,
And all our gallant fellows whom the frost laid low !
Just wait a little longer,
Till they get a trifle stronger,
And they'll never pull the worse because they've lost a toe.

Here's a health, with three times three,
To the brave *Discovery*,
And our merry merry guests, so truly welcome here !
And a brimming bumper yet
To our valiant little pet —
The lively *Clements Markham* with its bold charioteer !

Here's a health to all true blue,
To the Officers and crew
Who man this Expedition neat and handy, oh !
And may they ever prove,
Both in sledging and in love,
That the tars of old Britannia are the dandy, oh !

Figure 46.   Sheet 2 of the chorus of 'The Paleocrystic Sea', 2 March 1876.

Sunday 5 March 1876

Very cold and some wind, started for Cairn Hill but when I had got up to the thermometer stand, 60 feet by aneroid, I found that my nose was turning white so ran back to the ship. I had already put my hand on one of the blue jackets faces, who had a white spot the size of a sixpence on his nose. No friction is required in these cases the application of a warm hand to the spot restores circulation at once. I find that cakes of glycerine soap, in paper boxes put away with clothes in the drawers, have either attracted moisture, or sweated, rendering things damp in their contact. Cakes of old brown Windsor[1] in the same drawer are hard and dry. The bitch that lost her pup lately was today frostbitten in her teats, which were gorged with blood milk, she was taken below to the Engine room, where there is a temperature very little below freezing. The late extreme cold seems to have had an effect upon the dogs, who shiver a good deal when standing still on the floe. These animals have been exposed during the late intense cold, without any shelter, on the floe, as they have been all winter.

I am surprised at Geikie (Great Ice Age p. 497) adducing as a proof of a mild climate having prevailed within comparatively recent times in the polar regions, the discovery of a tree <in 75°.02.N> supposed to have grown *in situ*, by *Sir Ed Belcher*.[2]

The late Sir R. Murchison in the Jour G. Soc. Vol. XI. 1855, to my idea explains this seemingly extra ordinary circumstance in a very simple manner. The reference to Mecham finding trunks of trees which had evidently grown in situ in Prince Patrick's Island is a misconception on the part of McDougall, Captain Nares informed me that he never heard Mecham express the opinion that the wood found had grown on the same spot. Bessels at 1800 feet found driftwood and *mya* shells lying on the surface of Hall's Land, and the wood, found here at an elevation of 150 feet with shells of *saxicava* and *astarte* shows that we require no amelioration of temperature to account for drift wood being found in these regions at elevations, or under circumstances incompatible with the transporting powers of water.[3]

Monday 6 March 1876

Walked up Cairn Hill and bathed in the sun's rays! I was given by one of the men a dried toe of a walrus, which I might have been lead [*sic*] to suppose had been picked up in this vicinity, but on ~~examination~~ <investigation> found that it had been discovered in one of the pantry drawers, so doubtless it belonged to one of the animals we killed at Walrus I, and had been stowed away, by one of the wardroom servants. A small hummock on the port bow, shows very distinctly the effects of grounding, it has evidently turned over, and now exposes the surface which was once in contact with the bottom, this surface is fluted and abraided [*sic*], and lumps of mud and pieces of slate are frozen into it, for several feet from the flutings, the ice is discoloured with mud, so much so that at a little distance it looks dark brown, on the top of this stratum the ice is clear. Evidently the mud must have got into the ice as the hummock froze downwards in shallow water. This mud was of the same colour as our bottom here, and contained *Tricerathium* [*sic*]. At 9.30 p.m the colours produced by the sun, were superb, the N.N.W, horizon

---

[1] Old Brown Windsor Soap; a popular soap, see Christiani, *Technical Treatise on Soap and Candles*, p. 406.

[2] J. Geikie, *Great Ice Age*, pp. 297, 497–8. Belcher, *Last of the Arctic Voyages*, I, pp. 380–81.

[3] Murchison, 'Occurrence of Numerous Fragments of Fir-wood', p. 540. George Frederick Mecham (1828–58), naval officer and explorer, see *Dictionary of Canadian Biography*. Bessels, 'Notes on Polaris Bay'.

being lighted up with a fine prismatic light the green colours extending many degrees to the zenith, the ice hummocks, stood out against this light in some cases like pyramids, ~~that~~

Thickness of Winters ice this day 64 inches, 4¼ inches of snow above it. Sea-water rose in hole to within 6 inches of surface of ice.

Tuesday 7 March 1876
Temperature went up today as high as −50, which ridiculous as it may appear to ourselves hereafter, is now considered a considerable change for the better, as this persistent low temperature, prevents Egerton starting with the dogs for the *Discovery*, and makes the prospect of an early commencement of spring travelling less probable. Having my nose pealed [*sic*], I found I could not face the wind today. Darwin (Nat Journal p. 318)[1] remarks that both in Tierra del Fuego and within the Andes, that where the rock was covered during the greater part of the year with snow, it was shivered in a very extraordinary manner into small angular fragments. Scoresby Arc Reg vol. 1. p. 122,[2] observes the same in Spitzbergen. The same is so striking a feature of the surface of the country around us, that every one remarks upon it. I have as yet come to no decided conclusion on the subject, it appears though, to have some connection with the strata being vertically protruded, and the action of frost on the laminations of the slate. How justly Darwin writes, id. p. 321

"Daily it is forced home on the mind of the geologist, that nothing, not even the wind that blows, is so unstable as the level of the crust of this earth."

Parr informed us today, that from this date our glass of port wine will be reduced from three <times> to twice a week.

Wednesday 8 March 1876
Darwin (p. 345 Nat. Voy.) with his invariable sagacity remarks "Considering the enormous power of denudation which the sea possesses, as shown by numberless facts, it is not probable that a sedimentary deposit, when being upraised, could pass through the ordeal of the beach, so as to be preserved in sufficient masses to last to a distant period, without it were originally of wide extent and of considerable thickness."[3] This reasoning accounts very satisfactorily I think, for our finding the beds of recent shells and sediment in this part of the world isolated, and not stretching in an unbroken line along the coast, we find them here in the heads of bays in the sides of valleys, and in depressions, but along the straight shores, where often lines of grounded stones at various elevations distinctly mark old lines of upheaval, the remains of shells are few, and generally fragmentary.

Thursday 9 March 1876
A very cold but beautiful day, the sun lighted up the hills splendidly, and from mirage and refraction the Greenland coast appeared quite near to us. A spirit thermometer placed against a block of patent fuel, with rays of the sun striking on the bulb, caused it to rise 22° above the temperature in the shade. The continuous cold weather prevents Egerton and Rawson starting for the *Discovery*.

I had a field-day in my cabin and again dug out several pounds of ice from the roof and corners<.> ~~of~~ At the table where I am now writing the temp is 53°, but up on the shelves

[1] Darwin, *Journal of Researches*, new edn, p. 318.
[2] Scoresby, *Account of the Arctic Regions*, I, pp. 122–3.
[3] Darwin, *Journal of Researches*, new edn, p. 345.

it marks 33°, whilst all moisture freezes into solid ice on reaching that part of the cabin formed by the ship's side, which of course has the lowest temperature. As long as the air saturated with the moisture of our bodies, damp clothes &c., can condense into ice in a temperature below 32°, it is all very well, and elegant glaciers form above my bed, but as soon as they protrude into a warmer temperature each icicle becomes a small stream and a persistent drip soaks the bed clothes. Over my head is a scupper from which I took out the glass, and <over the aperture> placed a metal box, covered with snow to act as a condenser, in intensely cold weather, the heated air saturated with moisture, when it came into contact with this condenser, let fall its particles of water in a shower of beautiful little snow crystals on to my writing paper. So even in my cabin I am able to study on a small scale, some of the beautiful laws that govern the formation of ice <& snow>, and to trace the first stage of the glacier in heated air.

Friday 10 March 1876

Now that we are enjoying again the light of the sun, it is perhaps as well to consider what I really felt during the period of darkness, and what effect it had on me. One hundred and forty-two days, or more than five lunar months without the sight of the sun appears, and is, very trying. I look back on it as wasted time, and look forward to next winter with the same feelings, but there is one thing that solaces me, and that is, one might have been in India. It is no affectation on my part when I say that two hot seasons in a bad Indian station is equivalent to *one* Arctic winter such as we have passed through.[1] Walked with Pullen beyond P^r. Sheridan. Markham found a small piece of wood on the floe, within a mile of the ship, it looks very like a fragment of a broom handle, (hazel?), but it is very light and its edges are rounder than if it had been broken lately, however it may possibly be a fragment from the ship. The lights tonight in the north were superb, one band of plum bloom along the horizon was exquisite. When the Commander went the rounds this evening, he found the man in charge of the drying room not right, he ordered the Sergeant of Marines, to have him relieved at once, when the Sergeant went back, the man [Cephas by name,][2] had fallen down, and some of the things were on fire. It was immediatly put out by the men forward, and extinguished entirely, before the Commander got back again. This shows how necessary the strict discipline of a man-of-war is. Suppose the Commander had not visited the drying-room, (which he invariably does) this man might have been suffocated and even greater misfortunes might have happened.

Saturday 11 March 1876

There can be no doubt that the great hummocks grounded on our shores are capable of marking peebles and pieces of slate with scratches and striations, and as some of these blocks of ice are as large as small bergs, it would be extraordinary if they did not. As I noticed in my journal of the 6th some of these hummocks that have been capsized show flutings and groovings on what has been their under surface at one time. Today Moss showed me a well marked, ice scratched piece of slate, which he got off one of these hummocks.

---

[1] Does not Feilden mean to say that *one* hot season in India is as bad as *two* Arctic winters?

[2] Square brackets in MS. The Captain's steward, Spiro Capato, was a native of Cephalonia or Kephalonia, the largest of the Ionian Islands, hence the name Cephas used here by Feilden.

We are now at the period of high tides, and as the tidal wave flows in at times with extra force, it raises the ice, splitting and rupturing it with loud reports. When standing on the ice during these pulsations or throbs, the movement is remarkably similar to what one observes during an earthquake [~~wave~~]. Some of the large detached hummocks are so firmly bedded that the rise of the tide does not affect them, but the seasons ice that surrounds them cannot resist the pressure, and splits in large circular rings large and gaping near to the hummock but decreasing, in width as the circles enlarge. I noticed one hummock today with four such rings around it. James Berrie ice-quartermaster, states that yesterday evening between 4 and 5 hrs. three birds past him close on the floe flying N.W., he describes them as the size of sparrows, white with black heads. I have my doubts about the correctness of this observation, as the only bird that could come any way near this description is a snow-bunting, which never has a black head at any season, & which I do not think is likely to appear here for another month or three weeks.[1] Berrie was also a great hand during the winter of hearing the wolves howling round the ship at night, he also <saw> *the corpse* floating in Davis Straits, "near enough to the ship to heave a biscuit on it," when he was quartermaster of the watch, and "did not think it a circumstance worth reporting at the time." Again, he did not mention seeing these birds for a day after the occurrence, and instead of telling me, told the old Doctor, who began at dinner by saying that it was the "outsiders" who found out facts in ornithology. I thought at the time it was some chaff on the part of the old gentleman, who is very fond of poking his jokes at me, but afterwards I understand Berrie adhered to his statement, but how they could be confounded with sparrows I am at a loss to understand.

Sunday 12 March 1876
Egerton, Rawson, and Petersen left a little after mid-day with dog-sledge *en route* for the *Discovery*.

Monday 13 March 1876
A disagreeable blowing kind of day. Removed ventilating box from dead-light in my cabin, and dug through the snow.

Tuesday 14 March 1876
A miserable day, blowing and unable to leave the ship for exercise. Dressed <for breakfast> by the streak of light that came through the dead-light of my cabin.
    Copy of letter from Mᵣ James Croll to Captain Nares, F.R.S., R.N. accompanying a presentation volume of "Climate and Time."[2]

"Geological Survey of Scotland. Edinburgh 23 April 1875.
    Dear Sir, I have much pleasure in forwarding you the volume which I trust may interest and please you for an hour now and again during your long winter night.
    In Chapter XVI I have given some details of a class of facts connected with the Arctic Regions which have, unfortunately, been too much overlooked, viz., evidence of a warmer

---

[1] Perhaps a Lapland longspur, a sparrow-sized bird with a black head and white underparts, which might *just* have arrived early.
[2] Croll, *Climate and Time*. See Feilden's journal entry for 5 March 1876 and notes. Osborn, *Discovery of the North-West Passage*, pp. 212–13.

condition of climate in Greenland during very recent Post tertiary times. According to theory we might expect that during the warm periods of the Glacial epoch Greenland was comparatively free of snow and ice, and the probability is that the ancient forests found by McClure, Mecham, and others, flourished during that period. Might I take the liberty of suggesting that when you are in those regions, to be on the outlook for any evidence bearing on this point, such for example as remains of trees, plants or shells which could not now live in such a climate. In chapter XVIII I have given all the facts which I could find relative to warm conditions of climate in Greenland during earlier geological epochs."

Wednesday 15 March 1876
Walked with Captain Nares up the ravine north of Cape Rawson, reached the plateau, but it being very misty we retraced our steps and finished up by a ramble amongst the hummocks. One immense block of ice at least 50 foot high, had split in two leaving a wide lane between the blocks, the lines of stratification were well marked, and showed plainly the growth of ice from above by the melting of snow &c on the top of the floe, and re-freezing. These strata of evidence of growth must not be confounded with rings, or belts of discoloured ice which often encircle blocks of ice that have been been floating free, at the waterline. The elastic qualities of ice are also shown by mushroom shaped fellows whose pent house roofs have bent over. Half a mile from shore, amongst the pack I found the droppings and urine of a lemming quite fresh.

Egerton and Rawson returned this evening, as Petersen had entirely broken down, cramp, frost bites, lungs, – Petersen very bad indeed, it is a wonder, how 'my boys' ever got him back to the ship alive, Egerton's fingers are all nipped from the frequency of taking off his gloves when endeavouring to restore Petersen.

Thursday 16 March 1876
Temperature high today, and I took a long walk, but the wind has not been strong enough to sweep patches bare <again>, all the ground in the hollows is covered with powdered snow, sufficiently deep to hide small objects. Out in the pack I noticed gusts of wind taking up drift snow in the air, and whirling it along in circling clouds like dust in an eddy. On visiting the hummocks that Moss is making his observations on, I find that the yellow band, from which I extracted diatoms, is a flotation growth not true ice. Consequently so far, I cannot yet positively state that I have extracted any diatoms from the lines of stratification. The word hummock in arctic parlance means, lumps of ice thrown up by some pressure or force on a field or floe, to confound the blocks of stranded ice that we meet here, with hummocks, will never do, so that it becomes necessary to coin a word to suit, until I can meet with a better term, I shall apply the name floe-berg to these masses of ice. [*Margin*: Floe-Berg]

12. p.m. I have just finished examining some yellow coloured ice which I got today from a floe-berg near Cape Rawson, it was embedded several inches into the solid blue ice and was without doubt part of the original floe, and it is replete with diatoms. H.W.F.

Friday 17 March 1876
Lemming ♂ captured today, colour white tip of fur, mouse brown at base. Length (entire) from snout to tip of tail 5.70 in. snout to apex of skull 1.20 in. Length of tail .50 in. Length

of longest claw on fore-foot .35 in. Stomach full of vegetable matter. [*Margin*: apparently digested buds of *Sax. oppo.*] Captain Nares and Parr found fresh tracks of two Ptarmigan in the ravine near Cape Rawson. Near drift-wood Lake, I came across a plant of Potentilla from off which the snow had been scraped, and on the plant was lying a single feather of a Ptarmigan, on our way back we put up a hare within half a mile of the ship. Measured the elevation of the spot, where I found drift-wood, both May's aneroid and my own made it 200 feet.

Saturday 18 March 1876
Bright sunny day, but wind from the north which made it very 'nippy', though the temperature was about −29°. I walked up a ravine near Cape Rawson, along the sunny side, in hopes of falling in with traces of Ptarmigan. In many places the flanks were swept bare, exposing the old line of beach rounded peebles, for at no very distant period this ravine was a shallow bay.

Small knobs of *Sax. oppositifolia*, are sparsely scattered amongst the shingle, at a little distance they appeared to be of a brown-russet colour, and one could scarcely hope that such withered looking tufts could be again the birth place of the lovely purple blossoms, which gladden the soul of the traveller, during the short Arctic summer. [*Margin*: Sax oppo] A closer examination revealed that the plant is rapidly sending forth its annual growth of leaves, and each stem is crowned by a bright green expanding bud, surrounded with a warm coating of last autumns dried foliage. The brown tuft of saxifrage no doubt absorbs all the heat of the sun, which today was sufficiently strong to melt a drop of water against the patent fuel, and the light precipitate of snow particles, constantly drifting over the plant, give it probably a means of absorbing moisture through its leaves, which the frozen earth denies to the rootlets.

I came across a beautifully striated stone on the top of a gravel ridge at our present sea-level, the grounded ice has pushed the shingle before it in ridges, and this stone resting on the top of the hillock, doubtless came from the bottom of the floe-berg.

Sunday 19 March 1876
A cold nippy day, walked down towards Cape Rawson and brought back the boulder referred to in yesterdays journal. It is rather an interesting piece of stone, as evidently it belongs to the hard slaty formation of the district being pitted outwardly with minute round holes which perhaps originally contained cubes of iron pyrites, now weathered out from its surface. Rounded by the attrition of the summer torrent, and in course of time reaching the sea, it must have been frozen into the ice, grated and pushed against the shore until the minute striations which now cover the boulder were engraved.

One of our Eskimo bitches dropped three pups today.

After tea, the wind having died away, Markham and I walked to Cape Rawson, leaving the ship at 8 p.m., and returning by 10 p.m.

Monday 20 March 1876
Egerton and Rawson, with blue jackets Simmonds and Regan,[1] left the ship with dog sledge, after breakfast, *en route* for *Discovery*. Captain Nares and I took a long walk,

[1] John Simmons, 2nd captain maintop. Michael Regan, able seaman, transferred from *Discovery*.

walking by drift-wood lake, where we noticed last seasons tracks of musk-sheep frozen into the mud, and covered by a thin layer of ice. Crossing the big ravine we walked northward about four miles, coming across the track of a fox, which we followed to a small hillock where Master Reynard had left fresh traces of his visit, and a little further off we saw where he had been scratching for Lemmings. Turning inland we skirted the base of the Mount Pullen range, at a distance of two miles, then recrossed the big ravine, and walked to the ship by Cairn Hill. At the ravine we noticed the fresh tracks of an *Ermine*?

The highest level we reached, by aneroid, was about 600 feet, and roughly speaking we may describe the geological features of the country as follows. At the period when the country was under its ice-sheet, the Heckla range and Pullen group must have been the centres from which it descended, and a long course of intense glacial denudation must then have ensued. How much further than at present, the ancient land area of that period extended, it is impossible now to say, but certainly beyond our present limits. This is shown by the configuration of the coast-line of today, for all along the shores from Cape Rawson to Cape Joseph Henry, at intervals of a few miles very peculiar bays run into the land,[x] [*Margin*: [x]and if we could explore under the sea no doubt an extension of the system would be observed] these have not been formed by the wearing out action of the sea, but by ice-action. These indents are circular in form, sometimes two or three connecting with one another by narrow entrances. Around their sides the slopes have been grooved down and in all cases a valley leads up from their heads towards the mountains, evidently pointing out the course of the old ice stream. This feature of the landscape is not peculiar to the coast line, at various over the country similar hollows are to be elevations and scattered noticed but now existing as lakes, or depressions in which the snow collects, and in summer form marshy spots. These evidences of old ice-scooping differ much in their character, from the fiords of Scotland Norway, and other regions, but undoubtedly the same agent, in both cases effected the work. After rising from the present sea-level by a series of slopes, often lined with old sea beaches, to a height of about 600 feet, the land assumes a plateau like form, sloping gently towards the base of the mountain ranges; this flatland is however cut up by numerous deep and in some cases precipitous ravines which diverge from the existing watershed, and have been cut out by the summer torrents of melting snow. These ravines are evidently of later date, than the period when the lakes were formed. The surface of our plateau land shows evidences of intense glacial action; the almost vertical strata of the hard limestones, slates, grits and schists of the district have been ground down to a level, or rather, plane off with, a gentle slope toward the sea, subjected to aerial degradation, the slaty cleavage of the rocks, assisted by the frost and snow, has been unable to resist the various agencies of destruction arrayed against it, and in consequence the surface everywhere consists of angular fragments of slaty rock, [most destructive to footgear,] varied by protrusions of some harder strata, which less impressionable than the contiguous rocks, have been able longer to resist the wear and tear of the elements brought against them. For ages the ice-cap must have rested on this Polar land, moulding the features of the rocks beneath into the shapes they now present to us, but a great change was at hand, the land commenced to sink, glaciers moraines and ice-cap sank beneath the waters, <and were obliterated> and nothing appeared above the floes, and pack, but the highest tops of the existing mountain ranges. How long this condition of affairs lasted is

217

not evident, but from reasons hereafter to be given, we must assume that the process of re-elevation dates its commencement from comparatively recent times.

Recrossing the ravine I came back to the ship by Drift-Wood Lake, examining every patch of exposed mud, bared by the wind in the hollow. I found a piece of drift-wood about six inches long, and in close proximity shells of five? different species, *Saxicava*, *Mya*, *Tellina*[1]? and two Astartes? Many of the latter retained their rich brown epidermis, and the two valves fastened by the frost to the surface of the mud, retained their proper positions, and looked so fresh, that one might have believed they had been left there by the receding tide last autumn, yet the spot where they now rest is more than a mile inland and elevated 200 feet. The drift-wood floated. It was there, whilst picking up the shells with my bare hands that my fingers became benumbed.

Tuesday 21 March 1876

A Ptarmigan seen near the ship by Aldrich and Pullen, it was flying over the thermometers on the shore. I took a walk to Point Sheridan, and passed some time in examining the old sea-beaches, the temperature at −35° with a light wind from the north was bitterly cold on the bare hands, and my fingers when picking up small objects were nearly bitten. The section of the old beach cut through by the stream, to which I gave special attention was about 30 feet high, the major portion of the stones and peebles being well rounded and polished, but no single specimen showed any ice scratchings. The lithological character of the constituent stones being most diverse. I did not find any shells of testaceous[2] mollusca in this section, I noticed *Potentilla*, *Saxifrage*, and *withered* tufts of grass growing some what abundantly on this section, and a fox had been hunting lemmings there, successfully too as shown by his traces.

Wednesday 22 March 1876

Left the ship shortly after nine with Parr. Temperature about −25°, a very pleasant day, no wind. Walking to near Cape Rawson, we then worked all the ravines in hopes of picking up a Ptarmigan. In No 2 ravine from Cape Rawson, came across a Saxifrage plant where one of these birds had been picking off the green shoots, and the foot marks quite fresh, hunted all round but saw nothing of him.

In number 1 Ravine from Cape Rawson, the old sea beaches <can be detected> flanking the sides as far inland as any part of the ravine is bared of snow.

They are there much abraided [*sic*] by aerial degradation, but upon the rounded bosses that jut into the valleys the gravel is thickly deposited, and though the terraces are not continuous yet sufficient of them remains to take in at a glance the various levels at which the process of upheaval has been stayed. Though I have not detected in these beaches a single glaciated stone, yet the presence of ice <to some extent,> during their formation is unmistakeable [*sic*], scattered along the ridges are large erratic blocks of gneiss, and granite resting on the surface of the shingle, which must have been transported there, and grounded by the agency of ice.

Up to this date I have not found a single shell of any mollusk in the beaches, the wave action to <have> rounded the component stones must have been great, and consequently

---

[1] A bivalve mollusc.

[2] 'Testaceous': having a hard shell.

fragile shells had but a poor chance of leaving their traces behind, but today in the highest beach visited at an elevation of not less than 500 feet, I discovered a few fragments of some thick shelled mollusca.

In No 2 Ravine from Cape Rawson, at an elevation of 50 feet or thereabouts, the grey Band deposit is charged with shells of two kinds of *Astarte* <without *Saxicava*>, whilst at Drift-Wood Lake, *Saxicava* is the predominant fossil shell. It is rather singular that in <recent> deposits of obviously the same age, and within a very restricted area, shells now living in the neighbouring sea, should be grouped as it were by species.

[*Margin*: 1853. Walrus] [23rd March 1853. Richards P. P. p.123. Queens Channel. Two walrus, an old and young one, were wounded today in a hole of water, but were not captured. 23rd March 1853. Ricard. P P. p.133. Walrus. They had been lying near a large hole in the ice, which, from the marks about it, had been most likely kept open by them all the winter.][1]

Thursday 23 March 1876

Left the ship at 10 a.m, with Captain Nares and May; entering the Big Ravine we followed its course for about 5 miles. The sides of this ravine are either covered with snow, or else scattered over with slabs of the slate rock or hard Sand-Stone of the district, which undermined by the summer torrents have slid down. The stratification of the neighbourhood is most complex, nowhere have I seen horizontal strata, it is nearly always vertical, and generally covered on the surface with *detritus*. At one point in the ravine, about three miles from the ship, an almost perpendicular wall [*Margin*: Dip. N.N.W to S.S.S. true] is exposed for some distance, fortunately its surface is in the same plane as its stratification and presents a beautiful example of *Ripple Mark*. The rock is a hard sandstone breaking into flags and with no sign of organic remains in it. The drifted snow in the bottom of the ravine is tolerably hard and made good walking. At two or three points in our journey we came across a peculiar ice formation, which at present I do not understand, the side of the ravine is flanked with an ice wall, showing plain marks of stratification, with an immense weight of superincumbent snow. Is it possible that pressure alone converts snow into ice? If so we have here the commencement of glaciers. About six miles up the ravine it debouches into a plain covered with soft snow which is very tiresome walking doubtless in summer this becomes a reservoir for the melting snow. The separation of *Mount Pullen* from *The Dean* is undoubtedly an old glacier groove, A line stretched along the rest of Mt Pullen, would align perfectly with that of *The Dean*, with the exception of the great hollow scooped out between the two hills, the flanks on either side being abrupt and quite different to the gentle slope of the other sides. The height of the plateau from which these hills rise is 750 feet. We ascended *The Dean*, its summit by my aneroid is 1390 feet. Its sides where not covered with snow are a mass of broken angular slates, looking like the debris shot from a slate quarry, completely hiding the bedding of the underlying rocks. Mixed with the fragments of slate were pieces of quartz

---

[1] *Arctic Blue Books*, 1855, pp. 123, 133. Edward Ricard, AB, HMS *Rattlesnake*.

and other minerals, which must have run in veins through the parent rock, some of the specimens contained beautiful little yellow crystals and specks of glistening metal. I filled my haversack with examples. I noticed that after 800 feet, *Umbilicaria*[1] was attached to all the stones, this lichen has not been met with by me at a lower level, several other lichens not hitherto observed were obtained on The Dean Mount by me. On gaining the summit a fine view was obtained into the valleys of the Heckla Range and the frozen waters of Dumb Bell Harbour, lay almost at our feet.

I was much interested in finding on the very summit of *The Dean* the characteristic erratic boulders of the lower land, a fine rounded block of gneiss, and a boulder of dark chocolate coloured Silurian conglomerate. Evidence of late submersion of this district any way to 1300 feet. The summit was hidden by the angular dark slate fragments the same as the side, and the only way that I could find out the bedding was by the ridges apparent on the top, looking some what like parallel waves, which marked the *strike*[2] of the various strata as E.N.E. and W.S.W. We came upon several tracks of Ptarmigans but did not see the birds. Returned to the ship by 5.20 p.m.

Friday 24 March 1876
Accompanied Captain Markham and Lieut. Parr with their sledge-crews, hauling boats out on the pack <for exercise>. Captain Nares and Pullen with the party.

Saturday 25 March 1876
To the ravine beyond Big Ravine of Cape Sheridan with Captain Nares, studying and sketching slate rocks. Petersen had half of his right foot amputated today.

[March 26th. 1853. Richards P.P. p. 123. Cape Lady Franklin. Bathurst Island. "The saxifrage and moss are very abundant on this shore, and we saw several recent traces of deer −1½°.] [from this summit we saw several deer, eight or ten feeding in pairs, in the valley westward of us; two passed within 50 yards of me, an old and a young one; none that I saw with a glass had horns; they were of a dirty whitish colour, with large brown or yellow spots, and were about the size of a large goat. id*em*"].[3]
[March 26th. 1853. S. Osborn. P.P. p. 127. C*ape* Lady Franklin. Capture a Lemming].[4]
[I got within 80 yards of a doe and fawn. Six more were counted, all does, apparently with fawns. The one I fired at was not much bigger than a large goat, hornless, with a short body and long legs; the colour a greyish white except from the shoulder to the crupper, along which a saddle of light brown extended. id].

Sunday 26 March 1876
To gap of Dunloe studying and sketching slate-rocks. Petersen had half of his other foot amputated today.
[*Here Feilden tipped in his coloured sketch of the Gap of Dunloe; see Plate 12.*]

[1] Rock tripe, a genus of lichens.
[2] The horizontal course of a stratum; direction with regard to the points of the compass. *OED*.
[3] Transcription of *Arctic Blue Books*, 1855, p. 123. Temperature is in margin of Richards' narrative.
[4] *Arctic Blue Books*, 1855, p. 127. Osborn refers to the capture of a small marmot, not a lemming.

Monday 27 March 1876
To the Big Ravine north of Cape Sheridan, where I examined, and sketched a very interesting section of slaty rocks showing contortion and convolution of the bedding. [*Feilden tipped in his sketch of contorted strata in Big Ravine; see Plate 13.*]

Tuesday 28 March 1876
To the big Ravine today where I again examined the singularly contorted rocks that I sketched yesterday. I am now thinking over these slate rocks and cleavage, and hope before long to come to some definite ideas on the subject. I was in company with <Capt.> Nares, and on our return to the ship we examined a very interesting hummock, on the top was a layer of snow, then a strata [*sic*] of ice four inches thick full of elongated air bubbles, then a 16 inch strata of half crystalline snow, then another ice strata 4 inches thick to ~~the~~ <a> dust band, then strata of solid ice.

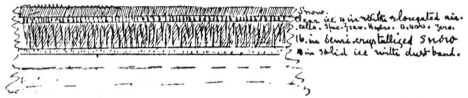

Reason of the imperfection of Geological records in reference to Evidence of Glaciation on Land-Surfaces. v. Croll. Climate and Time. p. 267.[1]

Wednesday 29 March 1876
Walked to Cape Rawson, and beyond. The pressure exerted by the ice at this point is astonishing, rounding the Cape one walks on the top of wall of hummocks abruptly reared up against the steep coast to a height of 100 feet above the water line, whilst for some distance on either side of the Point a <continuous> wall of hummocks and immense pushed up masses of floe-berg, rise to a height of 40 or 50 feet above the beach line. Looking to what ought to be seaward from the top of this wall, one gazes upon the very 'abomination of desolation'. Our poor fellows who have to attempt the pack next week, deserve all the credit that must redound on them. Fifty long nightless days on this waste of glacial conglomerate tugging, hauling, sweating, freezing. Each mile to be travelled and re-travelled three times.

The beds of rock exposed at Cape Rawson are vertical. Numerous veins of quartz, mixed with other minerals traverse them, sometimes running in beds six inches or a foot thick parallel with the stratification at other times traversing it in contrary directions.

Parr was out to the northward today, and saw a very large white bird flying lazily above, it alighted, but he was unable to get within anything like gun shot range. Parr says that it was larger than *Larus glaucus*, and rose from the ground unlike a gull, presumably it must have been "*Strix nyctea*".[2]
[*Feilden's colour sketch of Cape Rawson was tipped in; see Plate 14.*]

[*Enclosure: letter from Hart to Feilden, 29 March 1876; see Appendix A.*]

[1] Croll, *Climate and Time*, p. 267.
[2] Snowy owl.

Thursday 30 March 1876
Walked to the Ravine beyond Big Ravine, N. and brought back some rock specimens that I had collected there. This ravine is remarkably full of vegetation, and many tracks of Ptarmigan about.

Friday 31 March 1876
After dinner it being a beautiful afternoon I left the ship about 5 o'c. <4.30 p.m.> and walked round Black Cape in hopes of meeting our dog-sledge from the *Discovery*. Left a notice for them. Found rather a nice lake N. side of Black Cape, a little inland. Got back to the ship at 9.30 – distance travelled 12 miles in five hours.

At Cape Rawson the polishing and grinding action of the hummocks is visible on the face of the rocks at least 150 feet above present sea level, showing traces of elevation of the land as plainly as our mud-lakes and shell-beds. I have been at a loss to understand how it was possible for the raised beaches to have been formed on the borders of an ice-girt sea, such as we now have around, and surmised that there might have been periods of more open sea, but increased observation has shown me that I erred in this opinion. These beaches though traceable at many points along the coast, are more defined at the mouths of valleys and their flanks especially where torrents empty themselves, and the formation of the ridges is now going on around us. Closely sealing these shores is a line of the huge floe-bergs, which are pushed up to high water mark forming a complete barrier, when the summer torrents rush down charged with stones and boulders, it meets with this obstruction, and the pent-up water spreads out at the Embouchere of the valley in a fan like form, at the same time depositing all the debris. The numerous erratics of all sizes spread over the uplands are washed down the water shed of each stream and quite account for the lithological medley in the beaches. They are invariably rounded, so are the stones derived from the country and none show any ice markings, and the absence of shells in these formations is also very marked – by broken fragments.

The mud and shell lakes with driftwood, come under another category, no torrent rushes through them, they are of oval or rounded form, with usually the trace of a bar at their exit towards the sea, when they were at the sea-level they must have been bays occupied by young ice, and the ridge of grounded hummocks pushing up the mud and gravel, with the assistance of the small amount of debris washed seaward, raised the bar which now converts them into lakes. These bays must have been open enough at times to have admitted the drift-wood and also the erratic transporting ice, for these foreign rocks are equally as common on the borders of the lakes <& in the mud> as in the beaches, but I remark that in the lakes many angular fragments of erratics are to be found, which I have never observed in the beaches, also I have found in the lakes two well marked ice scratched boulders, showing me that these lakes were silted up quickly, and have not been disturbed since.

Saturday 1 April 1876
Wolves made their appearance around the ship today, one had the audacity to follow Captain Markham for more than two miles, at times coming within five paces of him, the Commander was accompanied by his retriever bitch, which must have attracted the animal, for though several of our sportsmen were out after them yet no one else got within 300 or 400 yards of a wolf. A small herd of either reindeer or musk-sheep passing in the vicinity of our winter quarters were recognized today by the tracks, these animals were not

seen, though their course was from N.N.W. as far as the Big Ravine, and from thence they struck inland to Mt. Pullen. I followed the track of a wolf round Cape Rawson, in company with Captain Nares, and Giffard, as far as the Black Cape, its droppings were chiefly composed of hair, (musk-sheep?) & splinters of bone, and fragments of *Tenia* [*sic*][1] were sticking to the excrement.

We descended Black Cape to enable Captain Nares to get some sights, and angles, its altitude by aneroid is 1050 feet, this cliff facing the east and S.E is precipitous almost a sheer 1000 feet down, the view from the summit on a fine day must be grand, but we encountered a cold nipping wind, which with a thermo. below −30° soon told, we all three were quickly frostbitten, on nose, cheeks and chin, one of the fingers of my right hand was frozen, but by nursing it in my parka, when we reached the bottom of the hill it came round. The Captain got his angles and a sketch, and I got a few rock specimens and a sketch. The strata composing Black Cape, though tremendously contorted, yet on the whole is vertical, the strike is from E to W. and on the summit which is not much covered with debris, the direction of the strike of each bed is easily noticed.

Captain Markham described the wolf he saw as of a whitish gray colour, about the size of one of our largest Eskimo dogs, with long fur, very dark eyes, long drooping tail, and extremely gaunt. He does not think that these animals could be confounded with the domesticated variety, from the tail alone, which in the dog curls upward in the wolf hangs down but does not touch the ground. In my journal of the 11th. Dec. 1875 I remarked that the bitch, who absented herself for nearly two months carried her tail in a drooping position.

Figure 47. 'April 1st. 1876. H.W.F. View from top of Black Cape 1050 feet high, looking S.S.E. towards Hall's Land', i.e. towards Greenland. In the foreground are Black Cape and Cape Union; across the straits are Repulse Harbour and Newman Bay.

[1] Tænia, a genus of tapeworm.

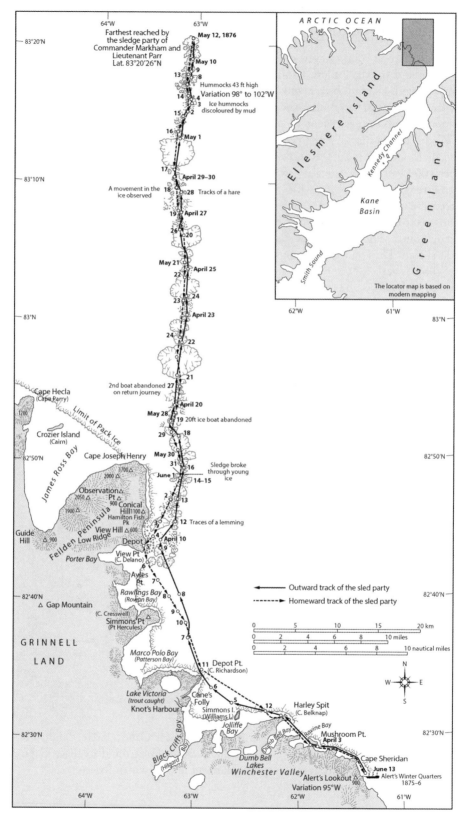

Map 6. Sketch map of the route of Commander Markham and Lieutenant Parr's northern sledge party, based on the map in Nares, *Narrative of a Voyage to the Polar Sea during 1875–6 of H.M. Ships 'Alert' and 'Discovery'*, 1878, vol. II, facing p. viii.

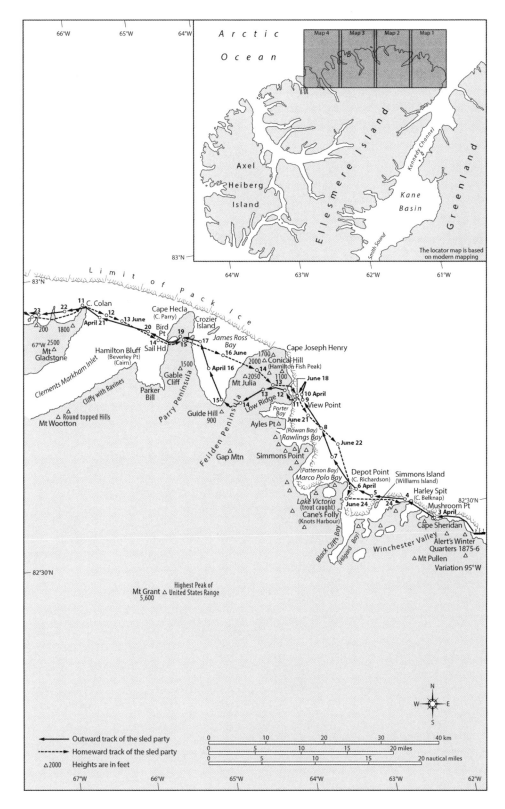

Map 7.   British Arctic Expedition 1875–6, chart 1 of the route of the western sledge party, led by Lieutenant Pelham Aldrich, along the northern shore of Grinnell Land from *Alert*'s winter quarters, 3 April to 26 June 1876, based on the National Map Collection, Library and Archives of Canada.

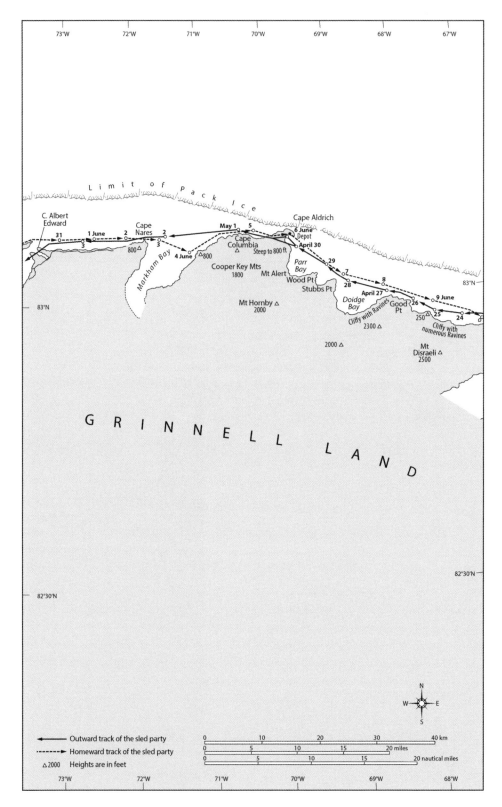

Map 8.   British Arctic Expedition 1875–6, chart 2 of the route of the western sledge party, led by Lieutenant Pelham Aldrich, along the northern shore of Grinnell Land, 3 April to 26 June 1876, based on the National Map Collection, Library and Archives of Canada.

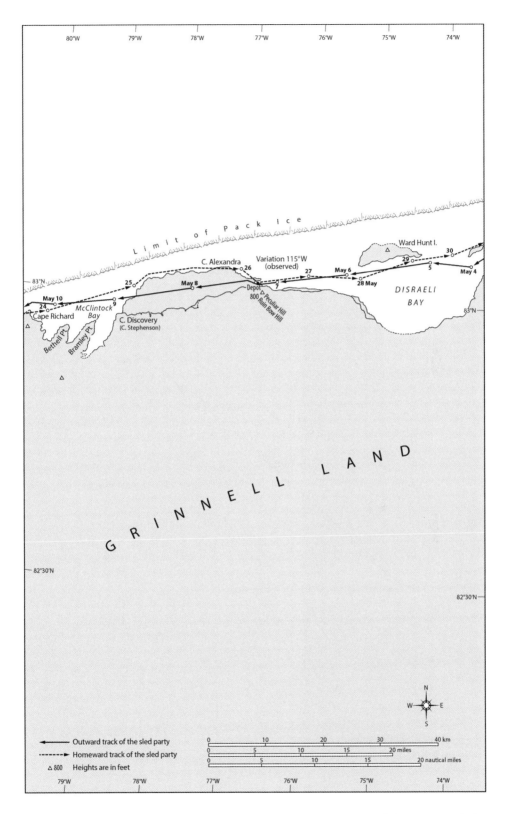

Map 9.   British Arctic Expedition 1875–6, chart 3 of the route of the western sledge party, led by Lieutenant Pelham Aldrich, along the northern shore of Grinnell Land, 3 April to 26 June 1876, based on the National Map Collection, Library and Archives of Canada.

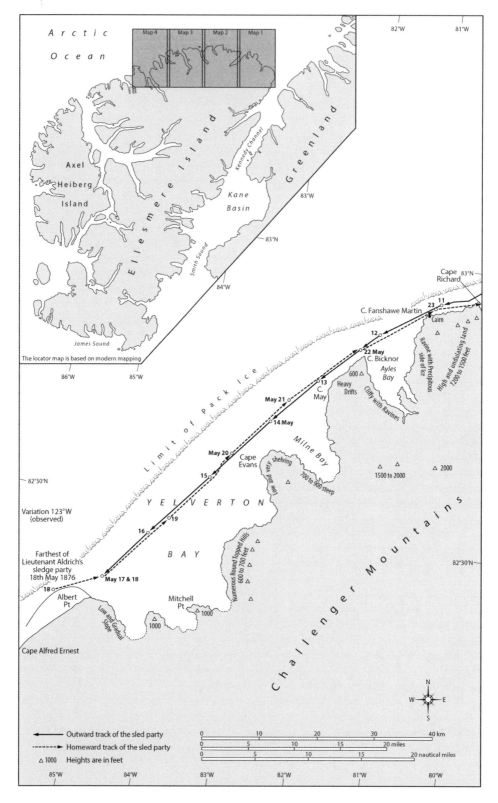

Map 10. British Arctic Expedition 1875–6, chart 4 of the route of the western sledge party, led by Lieutenant Pelham Aldrich, showing the farthest extent of the journey on 18 May 1876, based on the National Map Collection, Library and Archives of Canada.

PART III: SLEDGING IN EARNEST
2 APRIL–9 JUNE 1876

Sunday 2 April 1876

Wolves around the ship today. Our sledge parties are to leave tomorrow, final preparations are being made on all sides, we who remain behind cannot help feeling rather sad when we think of all the suffering, fatigue and dangers that these fine fellows are about to go through. All are in the best spirits, no officers could desire better crews than those which start tomorrow, and no body of men were ever commanded in an Arctic ~~expedition~~ <sledge exploration> by more worthy officers.

Markham and Parr command the parties attempting to force a passage over the ice toward the north, Aldrich and Giffard the exploring sledges to the N.W. Dr Moss and Mr White accompany them with auxiliary sledges, as far as Cape Joseph Henry and then return.

Unreflecting persons might imagine that the outfit for Arctic explorations as supplied in England to our vessels is so perfect, that intending sledgers have merely to summon their crews, fall in, and start at a days notice on a two months trip. In reality it is far different, days and weeks of anxious consideration and long calculations, have had to be passed by the responsible officers, to bring their crews and equipments to their present state of efficiency. Alterations, adjustment and improvements have been weighed, accepted or rejected during the winter months. The principal work of course falling on the Captain, Commander and Aldrich. The two latter the leaders of the main parties. I have been much interested and greatly pleased by the amount of actual supervision, I have seen expended by these officers of the sledges, in the equipment of their parties, to the least detail.

Two ♂ *Mus hudsonius*[1] brought in by the men; so far no ♀ captured.

Monday 3 April 1876

At 10.30 All hands mustered outside of the ship, sledges and boats packed, banners flying. Prayers having been read, and a verse of the "Old Hundred"[2] sung, Captain Nares wished the travellers God-speed, and off they started, half a mile from the ship the sledges stopped and gave three ringing cheers for the Captain. (The men call him Daddy!).

We are now 13 left in the ship 6 officers, and seven men including Petersen and the Greenlander – After tea the pumps were rigged, and buckets of water placed fore and aft of the ship between decks.

On an average our men were hauling today 235 lbs.

[1] Hudson's Bay lemming. See above, p. 200, n. 1, for lemming taxonomy.
[2] A hymn beginning 'All people that on earth do dwell', in a translation of the 100th Psalm.

Tuesday 4 April 1876

Walked with the Captain to Big Ravine before dinner, looking for what are supposed to have been traces of Reindeer (I think more likely Musk-sheep) seen on the 1ˢᵗ inst.

At 8 p.m., Egerton, Rawson with Regan, Simmonds and the dogs returned from the *Discovery*.[1] We were delighted to see them return in grand fettle, and they brought us most cheering news of how ~~are~~ our consort had passed the winter, and the good work they had accomplished.

Depth of seasons ice measured today 6 ft 3 in. Rawson and Egerton came across tracks of Bear near Shift-Rudder Bay, on their return journey.

Gave Petersen my Eider-down quilt, as he complained much to me of cold, he has three blankets, one under and two over. The stumps of his feet are melancholy looking articles, but they have been well amputated, and are already granulating. Plenty of carbolic ~~acid~~ has been used.

Edinburgh ought to be proud that two of the greatest aids to modern surgery, have been the result of the labours of two of her Doctors, I refer to Simpson and Lister.[2]

Wednesday 5 April 1876

Examining hummocks this morning, especially the one noted in my journal of the 28ᵗʰ March. In some parts what I call the 16 inch semi-crystalline band is converted into clear ice with long, and in some parts, oval, and oval-compressed air chambers in it. This  transition of snow into ice is apparently the result of compression, but why an upper band should solidify before a lower one is singular unless the thickness of the stratum has something to do with it. Sprig of saxifrage found in this band.

Bored holes in a blue topped-hummock on its upper surface, and placed in them glass tubes, of broken thermometers, the top of the tubing being exactly level with the surface of the ice, poured in fresh water round the glass rods, and they immediatly became imbedded in solid ice, this will I think give us a means of calculating the effect of the summer's sun on these hummocks.

Captain Nares walked out and examined the tracks referred to yesterday and came to the conclusion that they were those of Musk-sheep. This agrees with my diagnosis of the *Excreta* of the wolves. *vide. Journal.* 1ˢᵗ inst.

Thursday 6 April 1876

Walked with Captain Nares beyond Black Cape. Simmonds and the dogs accompanying us. We lunched down there by the snow-hut and got back to home by 6 p.m. We met with fresh tracks of a Wolf, Fox, Hare and Lemmings but saw no living object besides ourselves. I made a couple of very poor sketches of Black Cape, and brought back rock specimens, also a large block of quartz vein from Cape Rawson. [*Margin*: Next time on visiting Black

---

[1] Among the items they brought was a letter to Feilden from Henry Chichester Hart dated 29 March 1876, text reproduced in Appendix A.

[2] Joseph Lister (1827–1912), pioneer of antiseptic surgery. James Young Simpson (1811–70) introduced chloroform as an anaesthetic in surgery. See *ODNB*.

Cape Climb up and examine holes in cliff – Where [? *illegible pencil*] of submerged are [? *illegible pencil*]]

At 12 p.m., more than half of the sun's disc was above the northern horizon, a red glow suffused over our thermometer stand and yet the instruments were persistently showing –40°. This cold spell must break shortly.

Friday 7 April 1876
A disagreeable day, worked at home all day. Sun at 12 p.m. above the horizon, last night we saw it by refraction.

McClintock's age when he commanded the *Fox* was 39, that is about the limit of age for Arctic work.

Rawson informs me that he met with tracks of Lemmings *Myodes hudsonius*, on the floe, two miles from shore, off Lincoln Bay, this propensity of the lemming to wander on the ice seaward, easily accounts for Parr finding the skeleton of one of these little Rodents on a floe, near to the northward of Spitzbergen.[1]
[*Here Feilden tipped in two coloured sketches of Black Cape, see Plates 15 and 16.*]

Saturday 8 April 1876
Bryant returned with his sledge at mid-day having parted from Commander Markham yesterday morning, near Lake Victoria of Salmonoid fame. Considering the heavy loads the men were pulling and the great cold they experienced Bryant's report is favorable. Bury returned used up, and Malley changed places, going on to Joseph Henry. Goode has been frost bitten, Hill and another man having had attacks in the stomach. Domenic the cook returned with his heel frost bitten.[2] Last night the minimum temperature was –26°, Previously, since the departure of the sledges the temperature has marked between –40° & –50° at nights.

Rawson and May, with Simmonds Regan and dogs went south to Black Cliff, to work out a road through the hummocks for the Greenland party. R. and M. went to the top of Black Cliff surveying. R. brought me a drift sandstone boulder from its summit, over 1000 feet.

I walked over drift-wood lake, collected shells from the mud, bright and warm –20°. [*Margin*: Ice-scratched Erratics in Mud Beds] The first day this year that I have been able to lie on the ground, and look closely, the only position in which an observer usually gets anything out of the common. Then I walked on to the second lake, beyond the Big-Ravine, and collected in its neighbourhood many beautifully ice polished stones, some striated. These stones differ in their polish entirely from those in the raised beaches, they are all erratics, many glaciated, and evidently are lying in the same spot, as their ice raft occupied, when it deposited them there <& melted away> on the elevation of the land. I came across the tracks seen by Spiro [*sic*] Capato on the 1st inst, those I saw were of a middle sized and young musk-sheep.

---

[1] Rawson's identification is erroneous here, and I doubt that he could have distinguished between *Dicrostonyx* and *Myodes* by their tracks. See Blix, *Arctic Animals*, 151–2, and p. 200, n. 1, above.

[2] George Bryant, captain maintop on *Discovery*, transferred to *Alert*; Bury is James Berrie, ice quartermaster, HMS *Alert*; William Malley, able seaman; Joseph Good, chief boatswain's mate; Elias Hill, gunner; Vincent Dominics, ship's cook.

Sunday 9 April 1876

After service took the rifle out in hopes of getting some fresh meat for Petersen. Found tracks of Hare and Ptarmigan but saw no living creature. [*Margin*: Lemmings] The Lemmings appear to subsist on the *Sax. oppositifolia*, around these plants their tracks are numerous, and they nibble off the small green buds which are now showing in that plant. I have never ~~noted~~ <recorded before> how it is that in a country covered with snow, we are able to make some observations on the surface at all seasons; [*Margin*: Action of wind on Snow] which may appear strange to those who have not visited these regions and might perhaps imagine that a dead level canopy of snow covered the country on the tops of the hills and elevated ridges; the wind sweeps large spaces clear, whilst even in the hollows, the violent gales scoop out the drift to the bottom, sometimes several feet in depth, giving the appearance of a broken sea with breakers suddenly frozen, in these hollows we find plants exposed round which the lemmings congregate, as shown by their tracks, and in the mud of lakes and hollows we pick up fossil shells.

Monday 10 April 1876

Went out with the gun after breakfast, returned at 2 p.m., saw no living creature, temperature on my return marked −9°. [*Margin*: nine degrees below Zero oppressive] felt rather oppressive, though on the uplands where I had been walking a cold N.W. wind met me. Captain Nares was on the floe making observations, and there the wind was E. and also blowing up channel from the south. Cloudy this day, and great mirage to the northward where the ice on the horizon looked like lofty cliffs. The mirage did not extend to Cape Joseph Henry, and the Heckla range. The lichens are very numerous in quantity if not in variety, and one beautiful red species gives quite a warm glow to stones and rocks encrusted with it. I found that plates of glass coated with glycerine during the winter exposed to the breeze were crowded with sporules, and in looking over articles in my store room which had got damp, I found sheets of brown paper covered with lichen apparently of the same description as one very common species on shore. Whenever a wind blows the atmosphere becomes charged with vegetable spores, wafted on to the ice, successive breezes launch them forward, so that there is no difficulty in understanding how plant-life spreads. If there is land at the North Pole it is easy enough to believe that even there, we should not meet with any greater paucity of plant-life than in Grant Land. A difference of 400 miles, with a longer absence of the sun by 26 days (the calculation for latitude between our Winter hrs. and the Pole) can have but little effect on a flora, which survives, even when exposed to a temperature between −70° and −80°.

In Big Ravine I examined a very interesting exposure of rock. The strata were almost vertical, strike E.N.E. and W.S.W. The thicker strata though somewhat curved, and dipping at an angle of 88° to S.S.W. retained their relative thickness throughout, from bands 3 feet to as many inches, but a strata of rather finely laminated slates had suffered severely during the process of compression It was like a puckered ribbon. I was able to extract some of these bends and bring them home as specimens.

Rawson and Egerton with Bryant, Simmonds, Regan and Stone, left at 11 p.m. with dog and ladder-sledge to force a way across to Greenland taking their departure from Black Cape. Temp when they left −19°.

Figure 48.   Photograph of 'Floeberg and pressed up rubble ice', photograph from Nares, *Narrative of a Voyage to the Polar Sea during 1875–6 of H.M. Ships 'Alert' and 'Discovery'* ..., vol. I, facing p. 355.

Tuesday 11 April 1876
Light fall of snow. Dug out snowhouse. Packed up specimens. Opened the ward room skylight removed snow and let in the day-light making the cabin look rather dirty, but a pleasant change from the everlasting lamp-light.
(Clear snow from Wardroom Skylights)

Wednesday 12 April 1876
Worked at snow-hut bringing out boxes, painting directions and sending them down main-hold. A very beautiful bright day, just before dinner walked with the Captain down the mile to measure the big hummock. I tried to send a line over it with an impromptu bow and arrow made out of a tent-spreader and a piece of a rocket stick. Played whist in the Captain's cabin till 11 o'c. by sun-light. First time this year without lamp. Water melting on the ship's side. [*Margin*: Water melting on the ship's side].

[April 13th. 1853. Allard. P.P. p. 134. Penny Strait. at 10 h observed a bear approaching sledge: succeeded in capturing it, after its having killed a dog.][1]

Thursday 13 April 1876
Worked at snow-hut, cleared out most of the boxes. Everything put into this snow-hut last autumn is now in perfect order. No possibility of damp affecting it. Onboard a ship,

---

[1] *Arctic Blue Books*, 1855, p. 134; John Hillary Allard, master, *Pioneer*, 1852–4. This is Feilden's insertion, as are subsequent insertions in square brackets from the same source.

the greatest difficulty to contend with is damp, it is therefore advisable to put into a good snow-house as soon as one gets to winter quarters, all perishable articles, such as paper boxes, books &c. not required during the winter. The only alternative is to have everything in air-tight tin boxes. The Captain measured the big floe-berg at the end of the mile, Thickness of this block [*Margin*: Floeberg] protruding above surface

of pack being 65 feet, its whole thickness must be not less than 80 or 90 feet. A nice 'Open Polar Sea' to navigate which breeds this description of floe! [*See also Figure 49, below*]

Figure 49.   Photograph of 'HMS *Alert* at Floeberg Beach in Spring', frontispiece to Nares, *Narrative of a Voyage to the Polar Sea during 1875–6 of H.M. Ships 'Alert' and 'Discovery'*..., vol. I.

Good Friday 14 April 1876
After service went out with gun in the direction of Cape Rawson, but did not find a track of any animal, light powder snow has been falling for the last few days which has been sufficient to obliterate all the old tracks or to hide any exposed land surfaces. Captain Nares estimates the snow-fall of the last six weeks at 3 inches, which I think must be very near the mark.

[*Margin*: Moss & White return to ship.] Dr Moss and Mr White returned with their parties at 2.30 p.m., having parted with Commander Markham and Lieut. Aldrichs Expeditions at 2 p.m. on the 11th inst, at View Point N. Lat. 82°.46′. The ice northward from Cape Joseph Henry, looked very impracticable, and Moss seems to think that a progress over it of one mile per diem will be all that Markham can accomplish.

A wolfs track was noticed, and one Hare seen and shot by Moss, the same officer brought me a pellet of lemming's hair and bones which he found on a hummock in the floe. (probably owls?) he also brought me a specimen of what he describes to be the rock 'in situ' at View Point from an elevation of 3 or 400 feet. It is a small fragment of calcareous limestone, chiefly composed of corals and one small fragment of a shell, it appears to me to be the same rock. (Silurian). [*Margin*: Prospect of finding towards C. Joseph Henry Fossiliferous Rocks] as we met with at Dobbin Bay, and if it is from rock *in situ*, and not a mere fragment of drift boulder, we shall have the satisfaction, probably, of finding that the Heckla range has not been submitted to the same intense degradation as the district around us and south to Lady Franklin Sound, consequently we may have the satisfaction of finding various fossiliferous series of rocks developed in this fine range of mountains.

Saturday 15 April 1876
A very disagreeable day, cold wind blowing from N.N.W. After dinner walked to Cape Rawson to look out for Beaumont and the 'Discoveries', found it very cold facing the wind on my return to the ship. (At this time the Discoveries were weather-bound at Black Cape.)

[*Margin*: Very smooth stones on raised beach] I do not know where the rounding and glaciation of ice carried blocks is properly explained. It cannot be that attrition with one another effects it, for in such cases the stones though rounded are scratched and grooved, but we have another class, those that are nearly perfectly round, and polished as if they had just left a lapidary's shop. Is this done by their passing through ice only, without contact with other stones?

[*Margin*: "Starver" has pups, her sagacity] Starver one of our bitches has two nice pups, a white ♀ with black ears, and a gray ♂. They have been reared in the stoke hold in order to keep them from the kind attentions of the pack, who would feign [*sic*] take all stray puppies unto themselves, making them nice and warm inside of their bellies. Starver is a clever bitch, and can crawl up and down the iron ladder to the hold, at an angle of 60°, when going down she steadys [*sic*] herself against the hand rail with her curled up tail.

Sunday 16 April 1876
Just as we were going to service, Beaumont and Coppinger with two sledges came alongside,[1] so service was deferred till evening. [*Margin*: Beaumont's arrival] They left the *Discovery* on the 6th inst. Were weather bound the whole of yesterday half a mile south of Black Cape. The lowest temperature they recorded on their march was −45° and −48°. by B and C's thermometers respectively. They found the travelling bad, especially south side of Lincoln Bay.

Coppinger says that the Reindeers horns found at Discovery Bay, was considered doubtful <evidence of the presence there of those animals>, as it was first noticed by Beaumont, lying half way down the hill, and was subsequently carried by a man called

---

[1] Lewis A. Beaumont, senior lieutenant, *Discovery*. Richard W. Coppinger, MD, surgeon, *Discovery*.

Wyatt[1] to the cairn 1500 feet, [*Margin*: Reindeer's Horn.] Beaumont says that last autumn several reindeers horns, with other odds and ends were landed, and that probably either some man or dogs had dragged it from the dêpot [*sic*] to the spot where he noticed it first.

Archer and Coppinger left *Discovery* on the 28th March with Hans[2] two seamen and the dogs, arrived at Cape Lupton on the night of Thursday the 30th, and reached Thank God Harbour on March 31st. [*Margin*: Hall's Rest] Left on Sunday 2nd of April, arriving at *Discovery* at 9 o'c. on Monday evening the 3rd. [*Margin*: Thank God Harbour] Coppinger describes Thank God Harbour as a most cheerless looking spot, immediatly from the shore the land rises in a slope to the height of about 1000 feet almost bare of snow, and composed of stony debris, containing many coralline fossils, at Cape Lupton he noticed Graptolites[3] in the rock.

The stores left by the Americans were found generally in good order, but no arms or spirits were found. Halls grave was in good order with willows growing on it, the head board erect, and looking, Coppinger remarked, as if it might have been put up a month ago. Some remains of Musk oxen, *petrified* and which Hans mentioned he had brought in* [*Margin*: *From the south side of Thank God Harbour, at a spot called Salt Lake, where Hans states that are many bones of animals, about 10 miles from Hall's Rest] for Dr Bessels were noticed, also the skeleton of three small [dredges?]. Four miles from Discovery Bay on the floe, Dr Coppinger captured a ♂ Lemming – All the specimens of these animals procured at Discovery have been taken on the floe. Dr C. Further informs me that the fox after digging out the lemming from its hole, invariably pulls out the stomach and a part of the intestine and leaves them on the ground.

[April 17th. 1853. Herbert. P.P. p. 165, N. Bathurst I. – I observed five deer quietly browsing; they were fine animals, and appeared to be in good condition: their colour was of a brownish white; one of them, the largest, had horns.][4]

Monday 17 April 1876
After breakfast walked up Big Ravine then on to the plateau and down by False Fork Ravine. Came across the fresh track of a fox and a hare, the latter track I followed some distance but unsuccessfully. The snow which has fallen for the last three or four days, has rendered walking more tedious than at any time since the return of the sun. The scooped out hollows between the *sastrugi* are now filled with new drifted soft snow, and often I had to wade above the knee. In examining sections of the rock exposed in Big Ravine I noticed that there is very little tendency to split into slaty cleavage, some of the finer shales laminate very thin and split easily in the line of deposition. [*Margin*: Rocks Big Ravine] The thicker strata are a very solid hard rocks [*sic*], when freshly broken, sparkling with small grains of mica and specks of iron pyrites. Hour after hour I have spent in looking for fossils but have not yet been rewarded.

[1] Benjamin Wyatt, able seaman, *Discovery*.

[2] Robert H. Archer, lieutenant, and Hans Heindrich, Greenlander, both on *Discovery*. Hans Hendrik (*c*.1834–89) was an Inuk Greenlander, hunter, guide, and dog-driver, who had taken part in the Second Grinnell Expedition (1853–5) where he had played a major role in rescuing the survivors; he was a member of Isaac Israel Hayes's American expedition (1860–61); took part in the Polaris expedition (1871–3), and saved survivors from starvation; and, in his last Arctic sea voyage, served under Nares. (Hendrik, *Memoirs*; Holland, 'Hendrik'.)

[3] A fossil zoophyte, looking like pencil scratchings or markings on the rocks.

[4] *Arctic Blue Books*, 1855, p. 165. Francis B. Herbert, mate, *Assistance* 1852–4.

The veins of quartz and chert[1] that run through these rocks sometimes are coincident with the line of stratification but just as frequently running across it, in some cases the vein passing without any fault or dislocation through several distinct beds, and again running parallel with distorted strata, and adapting itself to the bends flexures and doublings of the compressed strata.

I noticed for the first time today, drops of water trickling down the face of the rocks exposed to the full glare of the sun. [*Margin*: snow & ice melting]

[April 18th. 53. Herbert P.P. p. 165. Bathurst I. sees three deer and a white hare −8½°.]

Tuesday 18 April 1876
A beautiful bright day, walked with my gun to the Gap of Dunloe. Saw no living creature, but returning to the ship came across the tip of a Musk-sheep's horn protruding from the earth, it was buried on the north slope of the ravine leading to the Gap. [*Margin: Musk-sheep Head*] After dinner returned to the spot with a pick axe and dug out the cranium, which appears very old. No other portions of the skeleton were to be found near it, though the snow of course prevented a close search. It is somewhat singular that though I have found several skulls of Musk-sheep, yet I have not found any other bones of the animal in proximity.

Whilst digging up this head, I uprooted several tufts of grass Poa cenisia?[2] buried under the snow, which retained their seeds, and a good deal of the juices in the Stalks.
At tea time Rawson and Egerton returned from Greenland, [*Margin*: *Rawson & Greenland party return*] Egerton brought me three rounded peebles which he took off the surface of floe in the centre of the Channel, and specimens of the rocks from the Greenland Side. [*Margin*: Stones on floe of Smith's Sound] They noticed a bird when crossing the channel on the [*blank space in original*] which they took for an owl.

Wednesday 19 April 1876
In the morning cataloguing the rocks brought back yesterday from Greenland by Egerton.

In the afternoon walked with Captain and examined floe-bergs. last autumn's snow is certainly now changing on the surface of the floes from snow to ice. We made marks at the junction of the snow and ice and took measurements for further observation. In some cases the snow appears to turn into long pendant crystals intermixed with snow, [*Margin*: Snow turning into ice] then under great pressure all the snow becomes ice, but long air cavities stretch downwards and appear to occupy the place of the snow, that lay between the crystals. Our shadows when cast upon the floe assumed a lovely violet colour, and the dog Nelly was reflected in the hues of the dog-violet. [*Margin*:Wonderful Purple glow] After tea walked up Cairn Hill.

This lovely shade of violet I can only compare to the liquid which exudes from a freshly caught *Ianthina fragilis*,[3] I think Ianthine here not an inapt term for this shade of colour.
Ianthine

---

[1] A variety of amorphous silica, possibly flint.
[2] A blue grass.
[3] Common oceanic snail.

Thursday 20 April 1876
Beaumont and Coppinger left with their sledges after tea, Pullen and I walked with them to Cape Rawson [*Margin*: Beaumont & Coppinger leave ship for Greenland] The men were pulling light loads, as they are to fill up from the dépôt below Cape Rawson. Beaumont returned to the ship a little after midnight, as there was some slight mistake in the numbering of the boxes, and some difficulty in the apportioning of the rations between the two sledges.

Friday 21 April 1876
Rawson left us after mid-day. The Captain and I walked to Cape Rawson, and saw the 'Discoveries' who had encamped near the depot. Beaumont very busy with the rations.
   Rather a cold wind though temperature −15 only, still there is a great difference between a wind blowing at −30° and −15°. Misty and overcast.

Saturday 22 April 1876
A disagreeable day, wind N.N.W., Moss was to have started with the dépôt for Cape Joseph Henry, but his journey was put off by the Captain. Rawson with Chalkley[1] returned from the floe beyond Black Cape <arrived just> after tea, his sledge having broken down, he was fitted out again with the dog-sledge and started in an hour back.
   Put the cranium of the musk-sheep that I found on the 18th inst. before the stove fire, and as it thawed, Moss noticed a small black spider crawl out from its hybernacula[2] underneath the horn, which he dextrously captured.

Sunday 23 April 1876
Captain Stephenson[3] and Mitchell, with Dugald,[4] Hans and Pettie[5] and 12 dogs arrived in the evening from *Discovery*. Left the ship on [*sentence left incomplete*].
   Came in today from the depot at Lincoln Bay, they must have done over 25 miles the last march. [*Margin*: Stephenson arrived at Floeberg Beach]
   Moss left with sledge and seven men to carry our dépôt of provisions to Cape J. Henry.

Monday 24 April 1876
One of Stephenson's dogs died this morning, I think it must have been overworked yesterday. Took its hide off in twenty minutes, temp −20°. put up some of its spermatozoa on a slide to compare with those of wolf and other dogs when opportunities arise. [*Margin*: Leave ship] Left the ship with party as per margin at 11.30 p.m., light breeze from S.E. force 2 to 3. Temperature −19°. White photographed the sledge before leaving. After rounding Cape Rawson the wind fell, and we had a fine night for travelling which was very good. The opposite Greenland coast was greatly miraged and looked very close, so distorted does mirage make land appear, that what we knew to be shelving land appeared in many places lofty cliffs with towers and buttresses jutting out, little hills appeared like

---

[1] Thomas Chalkley, able seaman, transferred from *Discovery*.
[2] Winter retreat.
[3] Henry Frederick Stephenson (1842–1919), captain of *Discovery*
[4] Presumably William Dougall, ice quartermaster, *Discovery*.
[5] Henry Petty, private marine, *Discovery*.

snowy Alps, and were ~~covered~~ <surmounted> with most eccentric looking caps, sometimes the image of the hill, turned upside down.[1] [*Margin*: Mirage of Greenland]

[*Margin*: Lieut. May. R.N.
Captain. Feilden, Naturalist
M[r] James Wooton. Engineer
Frederick. Greenlander.
King ♂ Boss ♂.
Soresides ♂. Ginger ♂.
Topaz ♂. Floe ♀. Sally ♀.
(7 dogs)
Canis familiaris, v. borealis]

[April 25th 53. Herbert P.P. p. 166. Bathurst I. many deer seen. one hare killed.][2]

Tuesday 25 April 1876
[*See Figure 50, p. 240.*]
At 12.10 a.m., reached Black Cape where we made tea temperature −17°. Very cold standing waiting about for an hour and a half for the water to boil, but warm tea certainly bucks one up. Reached the cairn where Rawson deposited his letters last autumn at 6 a.m., and the big ravine at Cape Union at 8.30 a.m., went into camp, Temp. whilst cooking in tent +40° at top of tent +70° outside −8°. Comfortably warm in the tent, but I had such severe cramps in my thighs, that I was forced to leave the tent and walk about outside, so I employed my time in scrambling up a hill, and chipping with a hammer. The talus I ascended on N side of ravine is very steep, many slates of thin sandstone, on it, fallen from above with peculiar markings. Still I could make out no definite fossil organisms. A curious looking mixed rock, gray with irregular black masses in it, was also abundant having slid down from above. These black lumps might be coral, but I don't think so.

From Cape Rawson to Cape Union the coast is a series of headlands divided by ravines from each other, the strata vertical or highly contorted, the dip irregular, but at Black Cape from N.E to S.W. The ravines are terraced with old beaches or sea-levels reared one over the other and cut out by the summer torrents during the process of upheaval. Not far

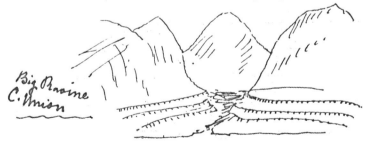

from Cape Union and about 20 feet above sea level, I noticed a limestone boulder say 3 × 3 feet. I do not think it could have rolled down from above, it contained many fossils I

[1] Such a mirage is often called *Fata Morgana*.
[2] *Arctic Blue Books*, 1855, p. 166.

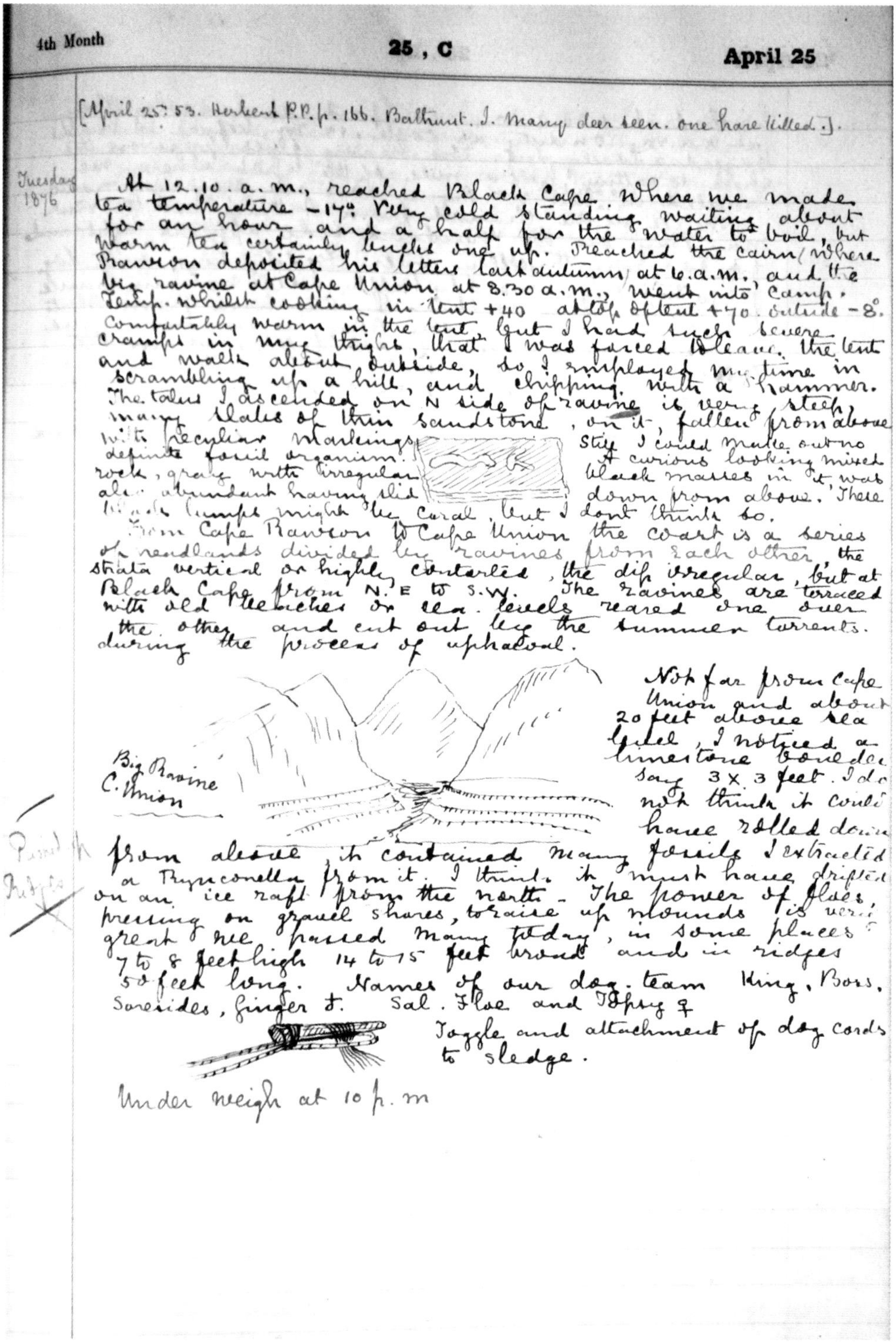

[April 25. 53. Herbert P.P. p. 166. Bathurst. I. many deer seen. one hare killed.]

Tuesday
1876

At 12.10. a. m., reached Black Cape where we made tea temperature −17°. Very cold standing, waiting about for an hour and a half for the water to boil, but warm tea certainly bucks one up. Reached the cairn where Rawson deposited his letters last autumn, at 6.a.m. and the big ravine at Cape Union, at 8.30 a.m., went into camp. Temp. whilst cooking in tent +40, at top of tent +70. outside −8. Comfortably warm in the tent, but I had such severe cramps in my thighs, that I was forced to leave the tent and walk about outside, so I employed my time in scrambling up a hill, and chipping with a hammer. The talus I ascended on N side of ravine is very steep, many slates of thin sandstone, on it, fallen from above with peculiar markings. Still I could make out no definite fossil organism. A curious looking mixed rock, gray with irregular black masses in it, was also abundant having slid down from above. These black lumps might be coral, but I don't think so.

From Cape Rawson to Cape Union the coast is a series of headlands divided by ravines from each other the strata vertical or highly contorted, the dip irregular, but at Black Cape from N. E to S. W. The ravines are terraced with old beaches or sea levels reared one over the other and cut out by the summer torrents. during the process of upheaval.

Not far from Cape Union and about 20 feet above sea level, I noticed a limestone boulder say 3 x 3 feet. I do not think it could have rolled down from above, it contained many fossils I extracted a Rhynconella from it. I think it must have drifted on an ice raft from the north. The power of floes pressing on gravel shores, to raise up mounds is very great, we passed many today, in some places 7 to 8 feet high, 14 to 15 feet broad and in ridges 50 feet long. Names of our dog team King, Boss, Sarcides, finger &. Sal. Floe and Ifprsy &

Toggle and attachment of dog cords to sledge.

Under weigh at 10 p. m

Figure 50. Copy of the page of Feilden's journal for 25 April 1876.

extracted a Rynconella[1] from it. [*Margin*: Pushed up Ridges] I think it must have drifted on an ice raft from the north – The power of floes, pressing on gravel shores, to raise up mounds is very great we passed many today, in some places 7 to 8 feet high 14 to 15 feet broad and in ridges 50 feet long. Names of our dog team King, Boss, Soresides, Ginger ♂ Sal, Floe and Topsy ♀. Under weigh at 10 p.m.

Toggle and attachment of dog cords to sledge.

Wednesday 26 April 1876
lunched at 1.30 a.m., camped at Lincoln Bay at 8 a.m. On duty as cook. 12 m., before I had bagged a lovely day. The heavy floes press on the shore to within half a mile of the spot where we hauled in <the *Alert*> last 30th August on our voyage north.

The ice in the channel from Arthur's seat to Newman Bay on the Greenland side appears light and fit for easy travelling over. Freddy says "with dog we go two day, one day half". [*Next to this date Feilden tipped in a sketch; see Figure 51, p. 242.*] I see no hindrance for active men walking by the shore from *Alert*'s winter-quarters to Lincoln Bay, in summer, save accidents from pieces of rock falling from the cliffs. [*Margin*: Rock that fall on floe of great size] Some of the fragments that have fallen this spring and have slid on to the floe, and are only awaiting the summer break up of the ice to raft southward, are blocks the size of a Billiard table.

Left camp with May at 11.30 p.m. Temp +3. Sent Fred to hunt the wily hare, many tracks about.

Thursday 27 April 1876
We struck across the brow inland, to the lake that lies behind conical Hill and runs W.S.W. This lake is about 2 miles long and on an average a quarter to half a mile broad. The ice on it is of two descriptions, heavy old floe rough topped and knobby, which doubtless represents the accumulation of several seasons, patches of smooth last seasons ice were interspersed but the old ice is in a proportion of twenty to one. About a quarter of a mile from the northern end of the lake the ice had cracked right across and shifted bodily south leaving a lane of about fifty yards wide of young ice right across the lake. Captain Nares mentioned to me subsequently, that when he looked down upon this lake in August 1876,[2] he noticed a band of water at this point, whilst the main body of ice still remained on the lake. I am particular in remarking on this because it accounts for a phenomenon visible at the south end of this lake, which would otherwise be inexplicable to me. This is a ridge of pushed up gravel along the whole south end of this lake, four five and six feet high with an abrupt face to the lake and sloping gently to the flat beyond, this ridge must be the result of the combined effects of strong prevailing N. winds, pressing the heavy floe ice of the lake against the shingle.

[1] *Rynchonella*: an extinct genus of brachiopods, molluscs with bivalve shells.
[2] This is the first indication in Feilden's journal that at least some entries were written subsequently from notes; the hand in this entry is uniform throughout.

Figure 51.   'Fred leaning on Dog Sledge. April 1876. H.W.Feilden.'

The bottom of the valley rises gently beyond this ridge and we walked for about half a mile over a sandy mud bottom from which most of the snow had been blown off, without a peeble on its surface, but thickly strewn with the shells of Astarte. Certainly it is not a very distant period since the sea covered this spot for the shells still retain their dark epidermis and many of the right and left valves were still in juxtaposition, resting on their umbones[1] and protruding half gaping through the frozen mud. We then got on to a second lake smaller and shallower than the one already crossed. After this we continued our walk through a series of small bottoms, which in summer are shallow lakes, but the erratics and sea shells were now left behind. Where there was any considerable difference in elevation the summer torrents had cut passages through the slate rocks, at one point I noticed a channel some 100 feet broad and 40 deep cut out as if by human agency. The strata were there vertical with the strike about E & W, the streaming flowing S to N, the strata being jointed parallel to the line of strike with the slate cleavage at right angles to the bedding. Consequently when the stream once began to pierce the rock the water flowed between the slates and removed them with great ease giving a straight up and down wall to the gully. We walked on until we reached an elevation of about 800 feet, where we killed a hare [*Margin*: Kill a Hare] and as it was 6 a.m. and we had been walking six hours without a halt we thought it time to return to camp. We noticed some tracks of Ptarmigan but saw no birds. Vegetation showed signs of tolerable abundance. Got back to camp quite worn out by 12 m., having been 12½ hours on the tramp without a drop of water, I carried the hare on my back from our extreme point, 10 miles distant. I had promised poor Petersen to bring him back some fresh meat if possible otherwise I should have left this hare. We were so exhausted on nearing camp, that when we threw ourselves down on the snow for two or three minutes rest, it was as much as we could do, to keep ourselves from falling asleep.
Cook called at 9.30 p.m.

Friday 28 April 1876
Started a few minutes after 12 p.m., of the 27th. Temp. +3°. A bright parhelion.[2] Went up hill close to our camp with May, who took round of angles whilst I sketched in Greenland Coast line. From looking at the lay of Halls Land I feel tolerably sure that the *Polaris* people made a mistake about their highest latitude. I believe their first Repulse Bay to be the gap between Cape Sumner and Lupton, and I do not believe they ever passed Cape Sumner in the steamer − 82°.16′ the highest northern latitude they claim, would have placed them in an area without any land to their north, whilst all of them when under examination agree that when in their highest latitude, they were in a channel with land ahead.[3] (v. Secretary Robeson's report to President U.S. 1873.[4])
Wootton and Fred went on with sledge to Stephenson's camp. May and I went up the large ravine near that camp it looked so favorable [*sic*] for giving a land route to Cape

---

[1] Umbo, plural umbones: The point at which a univalve shell, or each valve of a bivalve shell, is most protuberant. *OED.*

[2] A spot on a solar halo at which the light is intensified (usually at the intersection of two halos or bands of light), often prismatically coloured, and sometimes dazzlingly bright, formerly supposed to be a reflected image of the sun; a mock sun. *OED.*

[3] Feilden was right. Cape Sumner is at 81° 56′ N, 60° 00′ W.

[4] George M. Robeson, *Report of the Secretary of the Navy*, pp. 384–5.

Union that we decided to turn back, lunch and bring up sledge. Which we did, but as it came on very thick we had to camp three miles up. May and I walked on a couple of miles or so, and through the fog we thought we detected a dark headland which we recognized as the hill just north of Cape Union. If we were right in this surmise we had every prospect of finding the road we desired.

Left camp at 12 p.m.

Saturday 29 April 1876[1]

Very hazy, after two hours hard work we got to the dividing ridge, where the water flows on the one hand to Lincoln Bay and on the other to the valley north of Cape Union, following the latter we got to our encampment of the 25th inst., thus avoiding the bad travelling around Arthurs Seat, and finding a good land road between our ship and Lincoln Bay. [*Margin*: First good land road between Floeberg Beach and Lincoln Bay.] We reached camp at 6 a.m., May and I then started for the top of the hill on north side of Big Ravine with the theodolite. We estimated the height at 1300 feet took rounds of angles, sketches, gathered lichens. found it intensely cold. back to camp by 11 a.m. May had cramps after bagging.[2]

[*Here Feilden tipped in a sketch entitled 'Sledging in Grant Land', showing 'Ginger' and other sledge dogs; see Figure 52.*]

Figure 52. 'Sledging in Grant Land. H. W. Feilden. "Ginger" April 29th 76 H.W.F.'

[1] Letter tipped in: Coppinger to Feilden, Repulse Bay, 28 April 1876. See Appendix B.
[2] 'Bagging' is getting into a sleeping bag.

Sunday 30 April 1876
[30th April 1853. May P.P. p. 283. May. N. shore Bathurst I. shoots a Ptarmigan][1].
Reached the ship at 6 a.m. very tired and leg weary, drank four tumblers of lime-juice two cups of cocoa, <eat> half a tin of game pattie, preserved meat, a large basin of Mulligatawney [*sic*] Soup, and turned in, tried to sleep could not do so, legs aching. Got up, more cocoa, ready for dinner at 2.30. Unpacked sledge, dried gear, writing at log. Moss with his crew turned up at midnight from Cape Joseph Henry, in two days. He saw a Ptarmigan there <on 27th> and brought back some ~~Lower Silurian~~ <Carboniferous> fossils from View Point. [*Margin*: Carboniferous Fossils 82°.45′. *Productive encrinite*[2]]

I was extremely sorry to find poor Petersen had relapsed and had sunk much, since we left the ship. He seemed pleased poor fellow that we had brought him a hare.

Monday 1 May 1876
Examine stomachs of Isopoda from Arctic Sea. N.B. H.W.F.
Stuck to the ship, resting, writing, and marking up specimens. Emerson[3] returned in the afternoon from Greenland with his crew. Drip ceased in my cabin today.

Tuesday 2 May 1876
Resting, writing and preparing for Greenland trip. Emerson's crew under Egerton left this evening for Greenland, we are to pick up Egerton at Hall's rest.

Wednesday 3 May 1876
Packed sledge, got gear all ready, <Wootton> made bullets <for me>, mould a bath-brick.[4]
Went to bed till [*sic*] tea, ready for a start at 9. o'c. when Giffard and his men returned from the west head of C. J. Henry. Aldrich and he had passed over a Strait or Fiord and he came back for a boat. My trip put off.

He brought me specimens of the rock in situ forming C. Eugenie in N.L. 82°.56′ it is a fine <blue> gray calcareous limestone which is easily acted on by Hydrochloric acid.

[*Margin*: Ptarmigan 82.45] On the 30th April Giffard's party shot a Ptarmigan (one of a pair) near View Point Lat 82°.45′ N. It was so much torn by the Snider rifle bullet that I could not sex it but presume it was a male from the black orbital streak. It weighed 20 oz. Length bill to tail 15 in. Plumage white, with exception of tail feathers sixteen in number and two incumbent white ones. Colour of tail feathers pitch black, tipped with white, two centrals with broadest margin. 30 of an inch. Quills of tail feathers black ~~from~~ <on> two thirds of the way from tip, then to bare white. A patch of velvety black extending from nares to gape of mandibles and passing across the eye terminating .25 of an inch behind the eye, extreme length of this patch from nares 1.40 inch. Bill black, short, strong, culmen .40 in. Tip to gape .65 in. Toes black short feathered to base. Superciliary comb bright orange .70 in in length .30 in. in breadth. This bird differs from *T. rupestris* in possessing sixteen tail feathers instead of fourteen in addition of the white incumbent ones. [*Margin*: All wrong, it is T. rupestris] If I find on examination of more

[1] *Arctic Blue Books*, 1855, p. 283.
[2] Limestone made up of fossil crinoids.
[3] George W. Emmerson, chief boatswain's mate, *Discovery*.
[4] Bath-brick: a preparation of calcareous earth moulded in the form of a brick, used for cleaning polished metal. *OED*.

specimens this character is persistent enough to differentiate a new species I shall call it T. Newtonii, after the Professor of Zoology at Cambridge University. [*Margin*: Plants] The contents of the crop which filled a large wine glass consisted chiefly of stems, leaves & buds of Salix – Heads of Draba. Potentilla, Sax. oppositifolia &c.

Thursday 4 May 1876
Walked after breakfast in the direction of 'The Dean' got out about 4 miles, snow very ~~heavy~~ <general>. The sun came out about 11 a.m., and then to seaward a dense smoky coloured gray mist hung over the ice, which wreathed up into circular clouds as the sun's rays cleared it away. The snow is now as deep, if not deeper than we have had it before, but not bad to walk over. Last night there was hoary frost on the rigging, and skylights. Not a single track did I come across of any animal this morning. Back to the ship by 3.

May, Self & Freddy left for Greenland with dog sledge. I was to have gone with them, and the original intention was for us to visit C. Brevoort, Newman's Bay and Hall's Rest, but Giffard's return altered the programme. Went out after tea to Cairn Hill, and I strolled round a few short distances with the gun, not a track to be seen.

Thickness of season's ice today	79.25 in.
from surface of ice to water level	10 in.
Thickness of snow	4 in.

Friday 5 May 1876
Looking over and labelling a few geological specimens that Giffard produced from his sledge this morning, one specimen of limestone from 'Cavart I' mouth of Sail bay! N. Lat. 82°.56′ showed traces of fossil shells <*Spirifer*>.[1] This is most satisfactory as it shows that the fossiliferous strata have not been denuded from off the Heckla Range, as in our immediate vicinity. [*Margin*: Discovery of Carboniferous Fossils 82°.56′] Out with my gun north, from tea time till 12 p.m, Not a single track. Even the Lemmings had not been travelling over the snow, though I saw many of their spiracles. They must have a strong odour for Nellie the retriever bitch, who accompanied me at once spotted these holes and commenced shovelling the snow away violently. [*Margin*: *Spirifer*]

Moss tells me that, during his late sledge journey, on two occasions he noticed where a fox had scraped at a lemming's spiracle and had then burrowed up the passage until it came to the Lemming dead! The fox had left the dead Lemming. The first plant that has come to the front this spring is a lichen, in bare spots where a week ago a gray crust alone covered the service [*sic*] a new growth has appeared of delicate sulphur tinted leaves springing out of the old dry plant.

On almost the most western peak of the Heckla Range, their [*sic*] clung tonight, a cloud of gray colour, which might easily have been mistaken for the smoke of a volcanoe [*sic*].

Saturday 6 May 1876
Dug out snow hut and transferred dogs skins from rigging to it, as I am afraid of the heat of the sun putrefying them. Dug steps in the big hummock to reach sunken thermo. tubes when snow goes. Temp of dry bulb. +80°. Blowing from S. fresh, walked to the top of Cairn Hill, my aneroid makes it 500 feet. [*Margin*: Soil becoming soft.] Came back by

---

[1] A genus of marine brachiopods.

Drift-wood lake – several little patches of mud exposed there, are already feeling the effects of the sun and the mud is soft for 2 inches, I could extract the shells with my fingers, from the same place where it required blows of a sharp hammer to get them out a short time ago. Some of the Heckla range are showing black faces to day on their S.W. slopes. [*Here Feilden tipped in a sketch of Mount Pullen; see Figure 53, below.*]

Figure 53. 'Mt. Pullen from Cairn Hill. Elevation 500. H.W.F.'

[7th May 1853. Allard P.P. p. 154. N. of Grinnell Land. Whilst here we were joined by a wolf, the first and only one we have seen.[1]].

Sunday 7 May 1876
Windy and blowing strong up Robeson Channel. Greenland coast very clear, some of its hills are considerably denuded of snow. Towards evening the wind veered to the N.N.E. Giffard and his party left at 10 p.m for Cape Jos. Henry and the westward. The thermo at meridian showed +11°. The black bulb *in vacuo* +80 at same time at 12 p.m. +39°. Temp of earth at two feet −9½.

On examining carefully today a fragment of calcareous limestone brought by Giffard from Crozier & [Cavart Island][2] I find that it contains a fragment of a *Spirifer* a typical carboniferous fossil. I had already a fragment of a *Productus*[3] brought by Dr Moss from View Point N.L. 82°.45'. [*Margin*: Carboniferous Limestone Fossils] Finding these marine equivalents of the carboniferous formation after passing over the large section of

[1] *Arctic Blue Books*, 1855, p. 156. The original text differs slightly from Feilden's transcription: 'the first and only one we had yet seen'.

[2] Crozier Island is in Nares Strait, near Greenland; I have not found Cavart, and the reading is uncertain.

[3] An extinct genus of brachiopods, commonly found in carboniferous limestone.

Azoic rocks exposed in Grant Land is a most interesting discovery, but one for which the geologist must have been prepared, for the same formation (apparently) was pointed out by Salter to exist on the shores of Albert Land, lat. 77° to 77°.15′, (vide Belcher Voy. p. 378[1]) and Melville Island lat.76° by Haughton. *Proc. Royal Dublin Soc.*[2] [*Margin*: Carboniferous Limestone fossils] This discovery of Carboniferous fossils within 400 miles of the N. Pole, will open up a series of speculations, amongst geologists, of profound interest. N.B. D[r] Moss brought back several fossils from View Point, at which I had only a cursory glance, so could not determine them.

[May 8th 1853. S. Osborn. P.P. p. 205. N. Melville I. The first snow bunting was seen today flying about the sledges: this is nearly a month later than I observed them in 1851.][3]

Monday 8 May 1876
Left the ship at 10 a.m., walked up 'Big Ravine'. Markham's dog Nellie accompanied me, when half way up "The Dean" Nellie fell down in a very bad fit, precisely the same as attack the Eskimo dogs, this fit lasted about ten minutes, when she came too, she did not recognize me but ran snapping at me, then started off for about 100 yards and fell down in a second fit which lasted about five minutes, then she gave a howl, started off at the rate of knots making a bee-line for the ship, [*Margin*: Nellie has fits] I followed her tracks, thinking she might have further attacks, but she went very steady until I lost her footprints on the rocky ground on the left side of Big Ravine about two miles from the ship, I got back at 6.36 p.m., eight hours and a half which at two miles an hour means seventeen miles. About 7 p.m., Nellie was seen wandering about the ship in rather a distracted state, Moss went out and brought her in. I found fox droppings made of hare's fur, and its metatarsal bones, traces of Musk sheep near the 'Dean', and the fresh tracks of one Hare and one Fox. The Lemming must have a strong scent as Nellie spotted one through its spiracle, followed it up and caught it, a ♂. So far not a single ♂ has been brought to me. The weathered black slate of 'The Dean' and its adjacent hill 'The Minor Canon' produces quantities of quartz which contain beautiful little crystals of a yellow colour. The snow on the plateau was today hard, and easy travelling, this condition is dependent on the amount of wind that has passed over it, which by drifting, resorting, and packing the constituent particles, makes it firm; whilst in hollows it lies thick and soft.

Kane the armourer saw a small bird this evening near the ship which he described as a lark, probably a Snow Bunting. [*Margin*: Snow bunting]

Tuesday May 9th. 1876
Up the gap of Dunloe, and on to the plateau, found fresh footprints of a Ptarmigan. I have ~~frequently~~ found on the plateau at an elevation of 800 [*feet*] and upwards, fragments of a thicker and larger shell than in the Astarte beds, which hitherto I have not found higher than 200 [*feet*], today I picked up amongst other fragments the greater part of a valve of *Sax*[*icava*] *Norvegica*![4] and without doubt the fragments hitherto picked up

---

[1] Belcher, *Last of the Arctic Voyages*, p. 378.
[2] Haughton, 'Geology of the Parry Islands'; T. R. Jones, ed., *Manual*, pp. 550–52.
[3] *Arctic Blue Books*, 1855, p. 205.
[4] A bivalve mollusc in the family Hiatellidae.

belong to that species. The entire absence of this shell in the newer *Astarte* beds makes me think that a long period must have elapsed between the period when the 800 feet plateau emerged from the sea, and the subsequent rise to the present sea-level.

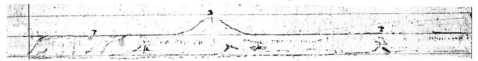

B. represents the 1700 feet level, with erratic boulders strewed over it, it appears as for instance, in the Pullen group to have escaped the tremendous degradation which ground the plateau. When B emerged P must have been a large expanse of sea, with a depth of over 200 fathoms, erratics are dispersed over its surface, and as above mentioned fragments of *Sax. Norvegica*, a shell of rather deep water habitat. that its remains are very rare is not wonderful when we reflect on the subsequent serial degradation that the Plateau has been subjected to, The large boulders of crystalline rock still remain, but no mud or earth, the vertical exposed slates have lost all their roundings and are now angular and split up. Below the plateau the land slopes very rapidly to the sea, and is cut out into ravines, and small hollows which at one time must have been indentations of the sea, in these places we find the *Astarte* beds and *Saxicava arctica*, embedded in the dark friable mud, and drift-wood on surface, at an elevation up to 200 feet. I came yesterday across a deposit just commencing to [*be*] bare of snow, it is exposed in a water channel leading into Big Ravine, it is about 20 feet thick and evidently lacustrine[1] as every few feet are marked with layers of semi-decomposed vegetation, "bands of *Hypnum*".[2] This deposit must be of later date than the *Astarte* beds, and apparently contains no shells, if it does I think they will prove to have been washed in, the peebles are small & rounded but not ice scratched.

May and Egerton returned at 9 o'c. this morning from Greenland, they left there 28 hours before and actually crossed and reached the ship in 12 working hours, May ascended a hill near Meyer's Repulse Gap 2000 feet, from its summit he had a magnificent panoramic view, down south to C. Lieber if not to C. Fraser. They met Coppinger returning from Beaumonts party, provisioned him and he started for Polaris Bay. The specimens of rock brought back by May, show that portion of Greenland to be of the same formation as around us in 82°.27′ here. Coppinger sent me specimen of the rock composing C. Staunton[3] [*sic*]. he mentions its strike is E by N. Dip 55° to S.S.E.

Wednesday 10 May 1876
At 1 a.m. this morning, Pullen was not onboard, and as he had left at 4 p.m. yesterday some little anxiety was felt about him, as it was blowing fresh from the S.W. Moss & White started South, Wootton and I to the north, Colan and Mitchell to Cairn Hill returned to the ship by 4 o'c., seen no traces of him. the Captain ordered breakfast at 6 o'c., and all hands to start after. At 4.30 our absentee returned he had been to the top of Mt. Pullen.

[1] A lake filled by sediment.
[2] A genus of moss, containing over 90 recognized species.
[3] Cape Stanton.

Found in a gap leading into Big Ravine an exposed section twenty feet deep of sand and mud, at an elevation of 180 feet. This formation must have been made in brackish water, for there are seams two or three feet thick of fine sand with layers of the very delicate Pecten (vitreus?)[1] which I found in 45 fathoms in Smiths Sound, and which we got abundantly in [10.4?] fathoms in Discovery Harbour, [*Margin*: Curious mud deposition] these fossil bivalves are resting with both valves attached, on their under sides, and a few other bivalves (Leda?)[2] with them. Two feet beneath them was a layer of semi decomposed moss (Hypnum?) 2 inches thick, and similar bands intercalated the deposit above the shells. Does this point to oscillations of upheaval and depression at the period of formation? On the exposed sand but I think fallen out of the Hypnum band I got a mandible of the lower jaw of a Lemming.

[May 11th. 1853. N. shore Grinnell Land. Allard. P.P. p. 156. "Observed a bear and cub coming towards us; did not succeed in capturing either, owing to the wolf which was still in our company, making an attack on them; an Esquimaux dog that was with us joined the wolf in the attack, and got a severe blow in the side by the bear, and would, no doubt, have been killed had it not been for the wolf, which came into the rescue by laying hold of bruin by the hind quarters: the wolf was then the object of the bear's attack, but the dog relieved, again acted in concert with the wolf; we were ready with our guns, but could get no chance of nearing either bear or wolf."][3] [First ptarmigan seen <May 12.> Grove. P.P. p. 266.[4]]

Thursday 11 May 1876
Visited the Pecten bed again today. Packed for trip to United States Range.
     Left the ship at 11 p.m. Party, Lieut. Egerton – in command Captain Feilden, Mr Mitchell, James Self A.B., Frederick, Greenlander. Sledge and 6 dogs 14 days provisions. Weight on sledge 900 lbs. Temp., at starting +18° Reached Murchison Point at [*entry incomplete*].

Friday 12 May 1876
One thirty a.m. Whilst tea was making walked to end of the spit. The hummock ridges are pushed up on the highest part of ridge Fifty feet at least above present sea-level. This is owing to elevation of land, and cannot be the effect of the ice driven on shore at present date. [*Margin*: Hummock ridges above [*illegible word*] Level] I picked up here a piece of fossiliferous limestone (coral) probably drifted from Cape Jos. Henry as it was a little rounded. I do not agree with Dr Bessels[5] in regard to the drift of Smiths Sound having once been from the south. The glaciation on the cliffs of Robeson Channel is certainly exhibited on the northern faces as if the pressure at height now two and three hundred feet above present level had come from that direction. [*Margin*: Bessels wrong in regard to S. drift] Brent geese feathers and dung of a prior season was lying round a small fresh water pond not covered with ice, as the south side of the Point. Met with snow and mist whilst crossing

---

[1] A fossil bivalve now known as *Delectopecten vitreus*, an animal of the scallop genus.
[2] Another fossil bivalve mollusc.
[3] John Hillary Allard (master, *Pioneer* 1852–4) in *Arctic Blue Books*, 1855, pp. 156–7.
[4] James Blair Grove (mate, *Assistance* 1852–4) in *Arctic Blue Books*, 1855, p. 266.
[5] See Bessels, 'Notes on Polaris Bay', p. 553: 'the current in Davis' Strait was to the North formerly, and not to the South as now'.

outer Dumbell[1] [*sic*] Harbour, travelling good. After Sickle Pt. snow heavy, camped near the boats at 6.45. Temp on going into tent +15 inside of tent +60°, James Self the cook complained of heat and took off his duffle coat. Distance made good 14 statute miles.

Left camp at [*blank*]. Temp +15, hazy but Cape Joseph Henry and Conical Hill visible at times.

[May 13th. 1853. Cheyne. P.P. p. 149. In Penny Strait sees two Snow Buntings first he has observed.] [Female bear and two cubs shot. id.][2]

[May 13th. 1853. S. Osborn shoots musk-sheep and lamb. Near Sherard Bay. Melville I. v. P.P. p. 207.][3]

Saturday 13 May 1876
Camp near Depot Point.
The so called ice-foot is greatly due to snow fall, in no other way can one account for its much greater height above the floe ice. The tidal crack in the neighbourhood of Boat Camp is very conspicuous. Cracking big lumps of ice where they have been pushed up on the snow-foot. [*Margin*: ice-foot]
This if I remember right is the day fixed by Captain Nares for the turning date of Markham's northern party. Not far from our last camp I found the dried <last years> dung of a bird in considerable quantities, it

was composed of *Sax. oppositifolia*. [*Margin*: Bernicla brenta] I take it to belong to *Bernicla brenta*[4] though we have not yet met with that bird. The dogs feel the heat greatly whenever we halted they threw themselves on their backs and rolled in the snow to cool themselves. Left the land a little west of the boats and steered across the floe in the direction of Depot Point. The floe deep with soft snow and heavy travelling, near Simmonds I there is a large Floeberg pushed up through a tide-hole about 25 feet showing above the ice and marked with some twenty or more distinct bands of stratification. Yellow diatom patches near under surface. Stopped for lunch at 12 p.m. (12th inst) started at 2 a.m. (13th) The sun came out for a few minutes temp −5°, soon became overcast, light wind but intensely cold from N. pitched camp south of Depot Point at 3.30 a.m., I started to examine cliffs. Too much snow to make out stratification, only points of rocks here and there projecting. It is a very hard gray rock, largely charged with iron pyrites, fine grained in some places; then passing into a coarse quartzose grit. I am getting very tired of these Azoic rocks, the snow about Depot Pt. lies more generally, is deeper and softer than about Floe-berg Beach. Went to the

[1] Standard spelling is 'Dumb-bell', Nares uses 'Dumbell', and Feilden is not consistent in spelling.

[2] John Powles Cheyne (lieut., *Assistance* 1852–4) in *Arctic Blue Books*, 1855, p. 149.

[3] Sherard Osborn (lieut. commanding *Pioneer* 1852–4) in *Arctic Blue Books*, 1855, p. 207. Osborn shot the animals on 12 May 1853. He here writes of cow and calf musk-oxen. Feilden, in his note summarizing Osborn's account, calls them 'musk-sheep and lamb', although the common name was, variously, musk ox, muskox, or musk-ox. But 'musk-sheep' was occasionally used. See e.g. E. Blyth, 'Suggested New Division', p. 428.

[4] Brant or brent goose, *Bernicla brenta*.

top of the cliff with Egerton and Mitchell height 300 ft. We looked down on Victoria Lake, it is separated from the sea by the usual bank of gravel, the result of ice-grounding and pushing up debris, and subsequent elevation of the land. We could not satisfy our selves which route to adopt for the westward. Saw tracks of a wolf near camp. [*Margin*: Wolf tracks] Lemmings wander far from land on the floe. The Greenland coast beyond the furthest point seems to run out in a long low peninsula.

Thought we heard the note of a Snow Bunting whilst in our tent. [*Margin*: Snow Bunting] The hummocks are dripping, they are now decorated with pendant icicles six feet in length. Temp +6° wind blowing from north soon got chilled whilst taking compass bearings.

Sunday 14 May 1876
Back to our tent by 9 a.m. 13th. Bagged and slept.

Egerton, Frederick and I started with empty dog sledge for the south, intending to ascend a hill which we had fixed on yesterday, for obtaining from its summit a good look out to the westward.

The ice in shore and under the base of the Black Cliffs smooth and of last seasons growth, we made good travelling passed under Black Cliffs and stopped to collect rock specimens. The formation is grey slates, charged with iron pyrites often in circular lumps, with intercalated black shales which when weathered crumbles into powder. We travelled on to a ravine south of Black Cliffs where we entered a bay, the snow had drifted off the land at its head, and showed us a surface of frozen mud studded with valves of *Astarte* and *Saxicava*, many erratics strewed about with them, two of these contained enchrinite[1] stems and corals. The torrent bed leading down to the bay exposed sections of the mud beds 30 feet in depth. Finding this ravine did not lead up to the hill we wished to ascend, we doubled back some two miles, and took up the first bay to the north of Black Cliffs. Saw two Ptarmigan *Lagopus rupestris* shot them ♂ & ♀. They were very tame. I killed the male first and his mate did not mind it, not leaving the spot. [*Margin*: Lagopus rupestris]

We next ascended the Ravine which we called Hare Ravine from the numbers of those animals we saw there. I saw six, and fired twice at them with bullets out of my gun but missed them. Frederick and Egerton with an Enfield rifle were equally unlucky, the former we found had been shooting with the 300 yards sight up at a distance of 80 yards, so his missing the animals was not extraordinary. We must have seen no less then 12 hares. There was a great deal of vegetation showing in exposed patches, and plenty of Musk ox dung. We ascended the hill 1450 feet by aneroid and called it Mount Constitution, the Ravine below us to the S. did not look promising for working to the W. The strata seem to diverge along this ravine, all to the south dipping S.S.W. all to the north dipping N.N.W. Back to camp at 9 a.m (14th inst.) During our absence Mitchell and James Self went to Victoria Lake and cut down through the ice 6½ feet but not having a proper weapon, only a pick, they were obliged to give the job up. The temperature at the lowest depth marking +22° on surface +10° and the ice becoming softer. Skinned the two Ptarmigans in the tent before going to sleep.

Cook called at 10 p.m.

[*Here Feilden tipped in a drawing of the profiles of the surrounding landscape from Depot Point; see Figure 54, p. 253.*]

---

[1] Also encrinite: a fossil crinoid.

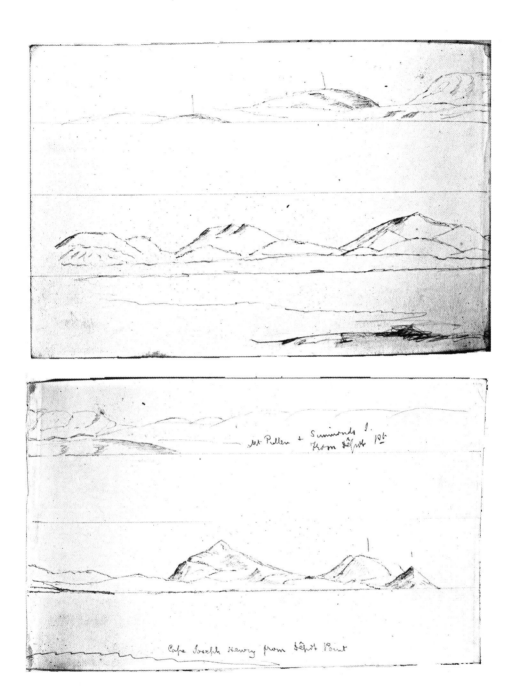

Figure 54. *Above*: 'Mt Pullen & Simmonds I. From Dêpot Pᵗ.' *Below*: 'Cape Joseph Henry from Dêpot Point.'

Monday 15 May 1876

Temp in tent +18° outside +10°. Bill of fare for breakfast, chocolate and devilled biscuits. Fried bacon and Ptarmigan. Left camp at 3.30 a.m. We were writing notes to be left in the Post office at Depot Point and depositing three days provisions in cache there. From Depot Point instead of following the land we struck across the large indentations, making for the mouth of the ravine which we hoped to ascend. The ice we travelled over was chiefly old blue topped floe, but much broken up by pressure, the vacancies between the hummocks filled up with soft treacherous snow. We stopped for lunch at 6.30, then continuing our march about two miles further by the coast, we came to the entrance of the fine ravine in lat. 82°.40′ which we had selected yesterday from the top of Mount Constitution, as the most likely looking one to give us a passage to the westward. We went three miles up it and camped at an elevation of 225 feet, in what appeared to be an old sea bottom about 2½ miles long and 1½ miles broad. The Ravelins[1] were on our left and showed the N.N.W. dip plainly at an angle of 25°.

About half a mile up the valley we sprung a Snowy owl it flew across our path, and alighted on the hill side. I went after it and got within 80 yards, the wary bird then rose flew about half a mile and again alighted, I went back to the sledge for Frederick and his rifle we vainly attempted to stalk the wily "oopik" [*sic*][2] there was no cover, there is a good deal of vegetation in this valley, of course all of last years but in spots where the snow had been blown off I came across several plants. Fox and Ptarmigan tracks were seen, and I noticed footprints of the Snow Bunting in the snow. Got to camp at 12. m*id-day*.

Called cook at 9.15 p.m.

Tuesday 16 May 1876

Temperature in tent during sleeping hours +20° of air outside +12°. Hoar frost clinging to the blades of grass sticking up above the snow. Left our camp at 1 a.m. very misty could see nothing a hundred yards in advance. Snow in some places letting us in to our knees, stopped for lunch at 3.30 a.m., it being too foggy to travel. Picked up the Vertebra of a musk-ox, a great deal of their dung lying about on exposed places. The stones which are uncovered by the snow are enamelled with lichens.

Remained in the tent till 11 a.m. left at 1 p.m., when the sun came out bright and clear. Travelling very bad owing to the soft snow. Wind came up from west very cold and right in our teeth sweeping the broad 'Westward Ho Valley' as we have christened it. We made about three miles by 4 o'c., when we came to the conclusion that it was a waste of time and strength attempting to drag our laden sledge any further to the west. We therefore halted and hitched permanent camp under the lea of a hillock that rose like an island from the centre of the flat valley.

This valley has been at one time a sea channel, and from the top of a hill about 800 feet on its northern border, I had a good view to the west, the valley seems to end in a slope of snow from which on either hand pyramidal peaks of hills, not less than 2000 feet high push their tops clear of this great white pall. [*Margin*: Plants] Among the withered tufts

[1] Ravelin: 'In fortification, an outwork consisting of two faces which form a salient angle, constructed beyond the main ditch and in front of the curtain.' *OED*. The term is readily adopted as a geological term, of which the meaning is apparent from Feilden's sketch and text.

[2] Oopick is Inuktituk for snowy owl.

of vegetation I came across today, I noticed *Sax. oppositifolia, Papaver, Draba, Sorrel*[1] and two species of grasses.

The droppings of Foxes are made up entirely of Lemming remains, whilst our own consist largely of wool fluff &c, derived from our gloves and duffel clothes. It would astonish a family physician. My barometer gives 300 feet higher than yesterday or about 500 feet above sea level,

Bagged at 6 p.m. the wind did not lull till midnight, could not leave the tent. The note of the Snowy Owl is not unlike a low one struck on a Jews harp.[2]

[*Here Feilden tipped in a sketch of 'Lepus glacialis when alarmed', although it shows behaviour observed on 18 May; see Figure 55, p. 256.*]

Wednesday 17 May 1876
Westward Ho Valley.
Temp. outside +16° lovely morning after 6 a.m. Temp of tent +18° to +20° during night. Left camp at 9 o'c. with Egerton, Freddy and empty dog sledge, carrying 100 feet of line for glacier work. We were in hopes of reaching the summit of Cheops, the great Pyramid, a noble peak, which rose from the northern border of our valley, apparently some seven miles distant. We proceeded to the westward but took advantage of the rising slopes on its northern face, so as gradually to work up to a valley, on the far side of which the immense snow slope which enveloped the 'Great Pyramid' seemed to abut, as seen from our camp, and by which slope we hoped to ascend. After 4½ hours travelling we got to this point at an elevation of 900 feet seeing on the way many tracks of Musk-oxen a good deal of withered grass two Ptarmigan and a Snow-Bunting, also the tracks of Fox Hare and Lemming. The rocks we passed over were formed of coarse quartzose grit. Here Fred and dogs halted, Egerton and I climbed the shoulder of the hill and ascended to its summit 1825 feet. From this point we had a good view as we looked to the northward across James Ross Bay, over the frozen Polar ocean, whilst directly below us was a tremendous ravine, which cutting through the ridge on which we were standing in a direction nearly N & S cut us off from the slopes of the next Pyramid, and evidently formed the outlet for the summer torrents of Westward Ho Valley, which empty into James Ross Bay. It was therefore evident that the attempt to ascend 'Cheops' was beyond our strength. Cheops is the finest mountain of the range, we were standing on an elevation of 1800 ft, and appeared so insignificant that I cannot estimate him at less than 5000 feet. A view from the top of this mountain on a clear day would tell us more than all our sledging parties will find out in a season! The extraordinary snow deposit which fills up the western end of Westward Ho Valley, looked so close that we determined to alter our route and try to reach it. The travelling was dreadful, snow soft and in very fine particles, not a sign of sastrugi or wind drift, down down went our feet sometimes we sank to the fork, the dogs were buried half way up their ribs, their tails wagging gamely as they dragged the sledge by a series of bounds. Hanging on to the back of the sledge was our only hope of progression. The dogs dragged the sledge faster than one could lift the legs out of the snow, and a heavy strain came on the arms and contracted the chest, so that every few yards it was a case of 'bellows to mend' We worked up to within 4 miles of the snow slope,

---

[1] *Oxyria digyna*, mountain sorrel.

[2] 'A musical instrument of simple construction, consisting of an elastic steel tongue fixed at one end to a small lyre-shaped frame of brass or iron, and bent at the other end at right angles'. *OED.*

but the depths of snow brought us absolutely to a stand still, we had deviated from a direct course some two miles by following the fresh track of a Musk-ox, [*Margin*: musk-ox] who in forcing his way through the soft snow must have sank belly deep, according to the track, on slopes were this animal had halted to procure food, the snow was rubbed up into heaps, and patches bared, as if the broad horns had been used as the weapons to push off the snow. We got within 4 miles of the huge snow slope (evidently a glacier covered) which terminated in a perpendicular wall. We got back to camp at 10 o'c. after 13 hours hard work. Did not a glass of lime juice and water go down. Three pannikins of pemmican went down my throat.

Lepus glacialis when alarmed

Figure 55.   Drawing by Feilden of 'Lepus glacialis when alarmed'.

[May 18th. 1853. Cheyne. P.P. p. 150. Sees a flock of ducks in Queens channel, flying to open water near Dundas.[1]]
[May 18th. 1853. Allard P.P. p. 158. North coast Grinnell land, notices 3 duck flying to the E. also the track of oxen passing from Exmouth I. to the land.[2]]

Thursday 18 May 1876
We got out of our bags at 9 of a.m., and went gunning. I saw two Hares which I shot, with my little gun and No. 4 shot. One was female and had 8 young ones in the placenta. They are curious looking brutes when disturbed, they stand erect on their hind legs, walk

---

[1] Cheyne in *Arctic Blue Books*, 1855, p. 150.
[2] Allard in *Arctic Blue Books*, 1855, p. 158.

two or three paces on their hind legs, fore feet tucked close to their bodies, then look around, and if not thoroughly frightened commence feeding again, If startled they make off in a series of bounds generally with one fore-leg tucked up. Two Arctic hares makes a great difference in travelling through snow, when slung on the back. I have three classes of snow in my category. Ankle deep 'bad snow', knee deep 'devilishly bad snow', over the knee 'damned bad snow'. Two Hares on ones back convert 'bad snow' into 'devilish bad snow'. The large intestine of these hares is filled with entozoa '*Filarians*'[1]? I saw a Snow-bunting as I left the tent this morning. Mitchell saw two Ptarmigan in the evening. James Self found enough water in a hollow of a rock to afford him a drink. This speaks well for returning summer.

[*Here Feilden tipped in a sketch of Westward Ho! Valley; see Figure 56, below.*]

Figure 56.　Feilden's drawing of 'Westward Ho! Valley, looking west from our camp 18th. May 1876 to edge of snow – 15 miles – Distant peaks – 40 miles – H.W.F.'

[May 19th. 1853. Cheyne. P.P. p. 150. Cape Becher sees flock of ducks, and a raven came hovering over the tent.[2]]

Friday 19 May 1876
Awoke cook at 10 a.m. Left camp at 12 o'c. with gun, hunted the ravines westward on south side of valley. I think we must have cleared out the stock of hares, as I saw no others, and no fresh tracks. Vegetation was so sparse and so confined to little valleys where a scanty soil is deposited and so dependent for exposure to the influence of the wind that

---

[1] Entozoa are parasitic animals that live within another. Filarians are slender nematode worms that are parasitic in vertebrates.

[2] *Arctic Blue Books*, 1855, pp. 150–51.

only a few hares can find subsistence in a large area. The dip of the strata in this valley is certainly N.N.W. but the strata are very confused. [*Margin*: Plants] Of withered plants I recognize willow, poppy, three kinds of grasses, Sax. oppositifolia has a long and strong root which runs deep into the ground. I find no erratic boulders in Westward Ho! Valley. Whilst crossing to north side of valley, on a bare rocky hillock I came across the fresh mutings[1] of a Snowy owl on the highest stone. The disgorged pellets lying around were entirely composed of Lemmings fur and bones. On north side of valley went up a ravine, there I picked up the scapular bone of a Musk-ox. The snow had drifted in places to a depth of 100 feet, where it had been beaten back by the eddies against a cliff. Egerton and James Self went up a hill on south side of valley carrying the theodolite for bearings, they gained an altitude of 2000 feet. It was so cloudy they could not do much. Mitchell, Fred and the dogs went up the valley with photographic camera, they saw a Snowy owl. It is wonderful what a difference the absence of the sun light makes in these regions, yesterday the valley glistened under the rays of a tropical sun, and the snow glowed with prismatic hues reflected from each crystal, the mountain slopes were bathed in violet and the zenith ran with colour, everything looked bright and cheerful. Today snow of largish flakes was falling, the sun was obscured the mountain tops were shrouded in gloomy gray mist, the wind came howling down the ravines, and made ones face smart, the change from yesterday was as sudden as from the tropics to the arctic.

Egerton returned at 8 p.m. tea and struck camp. Left at 9.30 got to near the shore by [*sentence left incomplete*].

(20th May 1853. Sherard Osborn P.P. p. 213. - Signs of the short and fleeting summer of these regions are now multiplying hourly, the S.E. breeze aiding the arrival of the birds now seen flitting past us. Snow buntings and ptarmigan have been seen winging their way north-west whilst the vegetation is fast throwing out green buds and showing symptoms of vitality. Temp +27°.)[2]

Saturday 20 May 1876
1 a.m. Camped. I shot a *Snow Bunting*, and on a bare patch found some Agarics,[3] last years of course, and a cup shaped lichen which I had not gathered before. The snow had melted from this piece of bottom land and had exposed several acres, it was sparsely covered with withered, last years tufts of grasses. Saxifrages, Papavers, Cerastium, Draba, Hypnum &c. I noticed many droppings of <musk-ox &> Ptarmigans, the footprint of Snow Buntings in the snow were very common.

The present water-course narrows near to where we camped, about a mile from the sea, and cuts its way through a wall of vertical black slates. Capping these slates is a continuation of the round pebbled fluviatile[4] deposit which makes the terraces, but at this point intercalated between the pebble series, is a bed of the very finest soft greasy feeling mud about 12 feet thick with badly preserved "Pecten islandicus".[5] [*Margin*:

---

[1] Droppings.
[2] *Arctic Blue Books*, 1855, p. 213.
[3] A genus of fungi.
[4] Produced by the action of rivers.
[5] A species of scallop.

Curious mud Bed] This bed is finely laminated but much contorted, and in a section of 100 yards that I examined I only found one pebble, a glaciated erratic.

Awoke cook at 11 a.m., under weigh at 1 p.m., before starting west up the valley, I have frequently noticed the intestines of the lemming *Myodus* [*sic*] *torquatus*[1] lying about, [*Margin*: Snowy owl & Lemming] I thought perhaps it was the work of foxes, today I find it is snowy owl, for round the blood and intestines of the lemming lying in the snow, were the distinct footprints of the Snowy owl. The Salix is today bursting into life, its Catkins are opening. [*Margin*: Salix in Bud] Freddy is seedy, and eats less than any of our party. He is a good fellow but delicate. Hans onboard the *Discovery* I hear eats more than any two men.

Whilst travelling the wind was W.N.W. very warm temp. between +25° & +30°. Saw a Snow Bunting which alighted close to us. Halted for lunch at 5.20 p.m., got to Hare Ravine at 10.15 p.m. I shot a ♂ Snow Bunting, they are quite numerous. Picked up our food at Dêpot Point found note from Wootton saying he passed on 18th (Shot 2 Ptarmigan saw 1 Hare). Double allowance of lime juice today, how we enjoyed it, after greasy pemmican. Receipt for the Gods ½ gill lime juice. Table spoon sugar ½ pint tepid water - stir till sugar dissolves, then fill pannican[2] with snow to suit taste. How much the Eskimo dog is to be admired, he is most admirably adapted for his work, patient cheerful and obedient he seems to delight in hauling. Our Duffle coats are not well suited for travelling in, and I never wear it then, but on camping it is most excellent, if cold or sweating, and to sleep in it is most comfortable. I believe this garment is an extra luxury to what the old arctic heroes had.

[*Here Feilden tipped in a sketch of members of the sledging party sleeping in a crowded tent; see Figure 57, p. 260.*]

Sunday 21 May 1876

Left camp at 1 p.m., and went up Hare Ravine with Egerton and Mitchell, we hunted for several hours but did not see a hare, on the same ground on which we saw several this day last week. Snow was falling throughout today, and no bright sun visible, this doubtless has an effect on the Hares and keeps them to their holes in the snow. Saw 3 *Snow-Buntings* killed one ♂, they are now mated. Contents of its stomach seeds of *Draba*. [*Margin*: *Draba*] The walking is very bad now on the slopes, the sun has glazed the surface of the snow, making it barely possible to stand on an incline, then every few paces it breaks in over ones knees, which sends one down with a drop that shakes every tooth in the head. The bottom of this ravine is covered with traces of Musk-ox, dung and wool. Where the snow has uncovered the mud the footprints of last season are quite plain frozen into the soil. Temp. outside +31°. inside +49°. The corkscrew in the knife that Alf Newton[3] gave me, came in very handy for opening lime juice bottles.

Monday 22 May 1876

It was snowing when we left camp this morning at 11.30 a.m. Just before starting a cock ptarmigan alighted close to our camp, we gave Freddy the privilege of shooting it. Intense

---

[1] Ringed lemming.

[2] Pannican: variant spelling of pannikin: 'A small metal (usually tinned iron) drinking vessel; a cannikin; also, the contents of such a vessel.' *OED*.

[3] Professor Alfred Newton (1829–1907), zoologist, *ODNB*.

Figure 57.   Members of the sledging party sleeping in a crowded tent, captioned, '21st . May 76. Egerton Mitchell Freddy J. Self H.W.F.'

excitement!, the poor bird ran about picking at the tops of the Saxifrage within twenty yards of us. Freddy aimed with his rifle for about two minutes, fired and missed, the Ptarmigan flew about fifty yards and again settled. I ran forward and stood watch over the bird with my gun until Fred reloaded. At the second attempt the Greenlander was quite successful. For a mile or more along the base of the Black Cliffs, and half a mile to seaward the ice was last seasons, and smooth, then we came upon heavy old blue topped ice which seemed not to have cleared out of the bay for many years, and this extended right to its head some four miles inland. In the centre of this bay is a small island Oopik. Hard slate, dipping N. on South end [*Margin*: Scratched Stones on Oopik I.] Many hummocks pushed up, the bottoms of these hummocks were studded with pieces of the slate frozen in, many of these were beautifully ice-scratched from the rise and fall of the tide.

The falling snow melted today on bare surfaces and the snow on the floe felt soapy and slippery, a great change from the crisp material we have been accustomed to. Egerton and I left camp with dogs and empty sledge and proceeded up the fiord which extends to the S.W. much further than we expected. We travelled up this valley some seven miles when it came to an end in the mountains. On both flanks of this valley we noticed the remains of great mud-beds, overtopped with thick gravel beds – As the land rose, the fiord with its deep marine mud bed turned into a valley, the summer torrents denuded out the mud beds, and what we saw left was only sufficient to point out what great accumulations of this fine mud had been deposited in modern geological times, for in some places these bands showed a thickness of 400 and 500 feet. [*Margin*: Mud beds 400 to 500 f^t thick] Back to camp at 11. p.m.

[*Here Feilden tipped in a drawing of a ptarmigan; see Figure 58, p. 261.*]

Figure 58. 'Hare Ravine – ♂. Tetrao rupestris [ptarmigan], as he appeared at our tent door. May 22nd. 76 Fred, distinguished himself on this occasion by his rifle shooting.'

Tuesday 23 May 1876
Temp. outside +24°. Left camp at a quarter to 3 p.m., lunched on Simmonds[1] [*sic*] Island, saw a *Snowy owl*, reached Dumbell at 12 p.m., where we camped.

Wednesday 24 May 1876
Before leaving Dumbell Harbour, we set up the tent which had been left in a snow hut by us there, last autumn. A fox had been inside and had torn open a bag containing dog biscuit, several dead lemmings also shook out from between the folds of canvas. It is hard work digging out and setting up frozen tent gear. Our work was concluded by 2 p.m., when we started for the ship. Three miles off we stopped, <melted snow> and drank every drop of the lime-juice on our sledge, we had an extra ration on hand as we were victualed for a day more. Got to the ship by 6 p.m. Distance travelled since 11th instant 140 miles. This means from Camp to Camp and does not include explorations.

Thursday 25 May 1876
Left the ship at 10.30 p.m. Saw a large grey *Wolf* crossing Ravine Bay. It walked up the hill side then lay down on a bare patch and watched us. Went a little way after it with my guns, but it was far too wary for that game. We halted at the tent at 2.30 a.m. (26th) for lunch. Temperature inside +35° outside +29°. I swapped my dirty sleeping bag, for a clean new one which I had left in the snow hut last autumn.

---

[1] Simmons Island.

Party.
Captain Nares.
Lieut May.
Capt. Feilden.
James Self.
John Hollins.[1]
Spiro Capato.[2]
Dogs
King ♂.
Sal ♀
Boss ♂
Ginger ♂
Topsy ♀
Floe ♀
Starver ♀

~~Wednesday~~ *Friday 26 May 1876*
We reached the boats at 5[h].40[m] a.m., where we camped. Called the cook at 4 o'c. p.m., temperature outside +26° inside the tent at breakfast +67°. There is something very soothing in a clean sleeping bag. I feel very proud of my exchange of a dirty stinking old one for a new one.

We left our camp at 7 p.m., weather misty, blowing the fag ends of a gale from the northward. Found considerable difficulty in following up tracks, it blew hard in our faces with mist and sleet. Captain Nares and I walked on in advance and had great difficulty in finding the road. We struck the young ice about a mile south of Depot Point.

A wolf followed us all morning. May and I dropped behind and hid ourselves under a hummock in hopes of waylaying the rascal, but he found us out and did not offer us a fair shot. The gait of this wolf was more shrinking than that of our dogs, and it carried its tail drooping, we reckoned him to be about half as big again as the best dog in our team 'King' Camped at 11.15. May got a finger frostbitten whilst waiting for the wolf. ~~Roused at 7 p.m., started at 8.45. The snow drift north of Dêpot Point very heavy result of last gale Stopped at 11 [grub] by 12. Saw a lemming running on the floe, too fast for me. Hollins sick had to camp.~~

~~Thursday~~ *Saturday 27 May 1876*
~~Barometer 29.80 Temperature +25 Cook called at 6.30 a.m., started 7.15, travelled over the floes in places the snow heavy, lunched just outside the shore hummocks south of Point Hercules~~[3]
Roused at 7 a.m., started at 8[h.]15[m.] The snow drift north of Dêpot Point very heavy, result of the recent gale. We stopped at 11 a.m., and lunched, as Hollins gave in, we hoped he would be better after getting something warm. Hollins being unable to travel nothing was left for us but to go into camp.

[1] John Hollins, private.
[2] Spero Capato, captain's steward, *Alert*.
[3] The barometric pressure and temperature match the entry in the ship's log. It is puzzling that Feilden deleted them.

~~Friday~~ *Sunday 28 May 1876*
3rd journey from ship.
Barometer 29″.80. Temperature +25°. Cook roused 6.30 a.m., Started 9h.15m. Travelling over the floes very heavy, The accompanying sketch made when halted for lunch is no exaggeration of the height of the hummocks. [*See Figure 59, below.*] On places the fresh snow-drift lay deep and gave us very severe labour hauling at the sledge. We lunched just outside the shore hummocks S. of Hercules Point, between the heavy floe and the shore was about 200 yards of squeezed up, frozen together rubble which gave us trouble. On the land the snow lay deep and soft the runners sunk in, and the sledge rested on the crossbars, entailing a constant succession of 'one two three' hauls. We found it no go, the dogs gibed and we were warm and so after rounding Hercules Point, we left half our gear, and by thus lightening our load were able to push on about a mile and a half, there we pitched our camp, and May and I went back for the half loads. We got to camp by 5.45 p.m.

Figure 59. '28th. May – 1876. Hummocks Point Hercules. Capt. Nares ascending to look for road for Traction Engine! or Bicycle!!'

Monday 29 May 1876
We got into our bags by 7.30 a.m., having previously spliced the main-brace[1] in commemoration of its being the anniversary of our leaving England. Captain Nares, Spiro and I left camp at 5 p.m., for the purpose of ascending Mount Julia. After a stiff walk of five hours, 10.20 p.m., we reached the summit with the theodolite. A most glorious panorama. A very fine day, what mist there was lay in the valleys below us and clung to the shore at our feet, but there was not sufficient mist to obstruct our view in any direction.

[1] Nautical slang for taking alcoholic drink.

Black Cape to the south of our winter quarters was discernible, also Mount Pullen & and the Dean. Greenland was quite clear, Cape Aldrich and the Cooper Key mountains to the westward easily ~~was~~ recognized from Aldrich's sketch of last autumn. To the south west a mass of snow covered peaks arose, Captain Nares called them the 'Five hundred Peaks'. Evidently the land continues to the S. and W. a long way. The summit of Mount Julia is composed of hard blue carboniferous limestone containing many fossils, its dip is very irregular, as far as I could judge from the small sections I examined bared of snow. From Cape Joseph Henry a flat valley snow covered runs to meet the head of James Ross Bay. From the top of Mt Julia we must have been able to see 50 miles to the north, we did not make out a crack or bowl, or water-sky, or any indication of water in any direction. Saw one Snow-Bunting on our way down the hill got back[1]

[*Here Feilden tipped in a sketch of Dana Valley; see Figure 60, below.*]

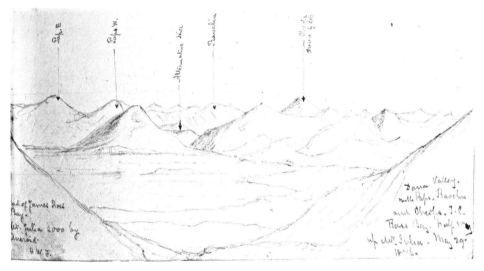

Figure 60. 'Head of James Ross Bay. Mt. Julia 2000 by aneroid. H.W.F.' and 'Dana Valley. with Paps, Ravelin and Cheops. J. C. Ross Bay. half way up Mt. Julia. May 29th. 1876.' From left to right, arrows indicate 'Pap. E', 'Pap. W.', 'Alternative Hill', 'Ravelin', and 'Cheops 5000 feet.'

Tuesday 30 May 1876

To the tent at 2 o'c. a.m. Took something to eat and then started in the direction of View Point with my gun. The country exposed over [?it] is carboniferous limestone dipping E resting on conglomerates. Shot a ♀ *Tetra rupestris* in summer plumage. Hollins killed two *Hares* one ♀ gravid contained 7 young ones with fur on them. He saw two Ptarmigan. I found a Musk-ox skull in lat. 82°45 N. much decayed. Got back to the tent at 7 a.m. May and James Self left at 5 p.m. (29th) for Depot Point, and returned at 11 a.m., 30th with provisions from depot, they found the travelling beyond Point Hercules very heavy.

This evening it began to blow, wind N.W. force 6. Temp. +18° a great deal of drift, it felt very cold. (Captain Nares went up a hill near to camp to take angles.) I went out and

---

[1] Entry incomplete.

found traces of recent submergence round our camp to an altitude of 300 feet. Mya, Saxicava, &c.

At 11 p.m., Captain, Spiro, Hollins and I went out to collect fossils, in the ravine just south of our camp the strata dip at an angle of 40° to E. and W., by following its course we got a good series of beds exposed. We collected a large number of Carboniferous fossils. Saw two Snow-Buntings we also saw the *Wolf* prowling about the camp. May and James Self went out with their guns but returned unsuccessful.

[*Feilden tipped in a sketch of 'geologising' alongside the entry for 30 May 1876; see Figure 61, below.*]

Figure 61. 'Geologising on an Arctic summer day. 30th. May 1876. Temp +18. Wind N.W. Force 6. Snow drift. Plenty of fossils. Dana Valley. N. Lat. 82°.44″.'

Wednesday 31 May 1876

We got into our bags at 8 a.m., Captain and I got up at 12 m. after four hours rest, as the weather appeared more decent, so we visited the fossiliferous strata again and collected a large number of fine carboniferous fossils. Returned to camp by 3 o'c. Breakfast. Captain Nares then started for Station Hill to bring back theodolite. I and James Self went with our guns towards View Point returned at 9.30 p.m. Saw no living creature. Wind, much drift and very cold. Brought back the horn off a musk-ox skull, old and rotten. Fed and bagged by 11 o'c. p.m. May and Hollins confined to tent with snow blindness, administered "Vini opii",[1] *conjunctiva*[2] much inflamed, eyelid swollen and painful.

There appears to be a fair sprinkling of vegetation (judging from wind cleared spots) in these parts. [*Margin*: Plants] Chiefly *Sax. oppositifolia*, *Draba*, and *Papaver*, the *Salix*

---

[1] Wine of opium, a solution of opium dissolved in sherry or diluted ethyl alcohol, used to treat inflamed eyes, conjunctivitis, etc.

[2] 'The mucous membrane which lines the inner surface of the eyelids and is reflected over the front of the eye-ball, thus conjoining this with the lids.' *OED*.

grows in recumbent plants many stalks are as thick as my thumb. Two species of grass gathered.

[June 1st. 1853. S. Osborn P.P. p. 219. +27°. A flock of wild fowl (geese), the first we have seen this season, were seen flying northward.[1]]
[S.O. Buddington. Report. See. U.S. Navy 1873. p.476. 'At Polaris Bay the summer began about the 1st. of June. There were some mild and very pleasant days in May. It began to get very well settled about the 1st of June.'[2]]

Thursday 1 June 1876
Strong wind and drift. Temp. of tent +28°. Roused cook at 3.30 a.m., intending to go on to Cape Joseph Henry. Wind increased to a gale could not leave the shelter of the tent, at 3 p.m., the gale broke, the snow wet and soft. Hollins is well of snow-blindness and May much better. My own eyes feel bad when first I awoke, cannot see for a few minutes, and a good deal of discharge. I wash them with snow warmed in my hand. Struck tent at 7 p.m. reached View Point Dêpot at 10 p.m. Very misty. Floe[3] had a fit I remained behind with her and tried to drag her into camp. (The wolf being about) but she was too much for me and I had to abandon her.

Close by the Dêpot a ravine runs down to the E from View Hill on N side of this ravine, the strata are exposed and they dip E at an angle of 80°. Many *corals, crinoidal stems* and large *Productus*.[4] A more dreadful day in June one can hardly imagine, snow, heavy drift and a gale from N.W. nothing discernible half a mile off, and as cold as charity. Not a living animal to be seen.
[*Feilden tipped in his sketch of '"Floe" having fallen down', alongside the entry for 1 June 1876; see Figure 62, p. 267.*]

[June 2nd 1853. S. Osborn P.P. p. 219. 'Picked up a marmot or two during the walk today; they soon became at ease, and ran about the tents eating biscuit dust.' Also a most interesting account on the migration of seeds in the Arctic, a subject not enlarged on by any other traveller with which I am acquainted.[5]]

Friday 2 June 1876
We left camp at 9.30 a.m. with empty sledge and dogs and crossed over View Hill, descended into the valley, crossed it and worked to the shore line again, in hopes of reaching Cape Joseph Henry. It was a most abominable day, sleet and mist temperature from +32° to +34° We got as far as Conical Hill, but it was useless to go on as the mist was so dense, we returned to camp by 1.30 travelling this time along shore line, and passing

---

[1] *Arctic Blue Books*, 1855, p. 219.

[2] *Annual Report of the Secretary of the Navy*, p. 219: Sidney O. Budington [Buddington], sailing master, *Polaris* (1871–3).

[3] One of the sledge dogs.

[4] An extinct genus of brachiopod.

[5] Osborn in *Arctic Blue Books*, 1855, p. 219. The passage in inverted commas, which are not used in the original, is Osborn's; the remaining sentence in this paragraph is Feilden's comment on a passage by Osborn, loc. cit. Charles Darwin spent a good deal of time studying the migration of seeds in general, and Hooker, e.g. 'Distribution of Arctic Plants', pp. 197–238, had considered the migration of plants and their seeds in the Arctic.

Figure 62. '"Floe" having fallen down in a fit, the General [probably Frederick, the Greenlander] remains behind to bring her to camp. She will neither be led or persuaded – kicking is the only means of making her progress, and then it is side ways like a crab, and of course off the track. 82°.45'. June 2nd. 1876. H.W.F.'

over what Moss described as a fearful chasm in the snow with edges of ice and a pitfall ready to swallow up men and sledges. The origin of this we easily ascertained, the pressure is very great at this point and what we were sledging over were pushed up hummocks with a heavy drift of snow covering them, a gap between the hummocks must certainly have been Moss' "great gulf fixed".

Slept and finished feeding by 10 p.m., snow falling thick, Barometer rising wind veered to N. no sun showing. Conical Hill is composed of dark gray hard limestone, its sea face is very steep. I had great difficulty in crawling up over the slippery snow, to obtain a specimen of the rock '*in situ*'. Picked up a few withered plants from under the snow.

Saturday 3 June 1876
We were ready to start south at 11.30 p.m. (2nd.). Captain and May rigging sail on sledge. I went with two hands, to deposit letters and dig a trench about the Cairn. Saw two Ptarmigan ♀ and ♂. Killed them same shot, ♂ in winter dress but moulting tail feathers, ♀ putting on summer garb. Weather beastly. Temp. just about or a little above freezing so that the snow that fell thickly wet everything. [*Margin*: Plant] Whilst digging at the dépot unburied a plant of *Cerastium alpinum*[1] from underneath the snow with its last years blossoms on it. Started under sail at 12 p.m. A mile S. of depot came across the skeleton of a musk-sheep partly protruding from snow, with a fine cranium and horns, which I put

---

[1] Commonly known as Alpine mouse-ear or Alpine chickweed.

on the sledge. We made a good run as far as N. end of Rawlings Bay, then the wind died away, and from there to Pt. Hercules it was 1, 2, 3, move her. Half way we had to divide our loads got to camp at 9 o'c. May and J. Self went back for left gear, returning at 11.30. The sun tried to struggle out at midnight but gave it up as a bad job. My skin trousers and May's came to grief today, the soft snow wet the thighs and one might as well have been clad in cold stewed tripe. Leather breeches are excellent in dry weather. Snow buntings common.

[Beside the entry for 3 June 1876, Feilden tipped in a sketch of the dog sledge in a summer shower, and a map of the area around Cape Heckla and Crozier Island; see Figures 63 and 64, below and p. 269.]

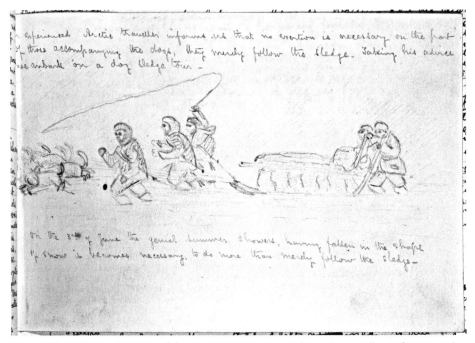

Figure 63.   *Caption at top of drawing*: 'An experienced Arctic traveller informs us that no exertion is necessary on the part of those accompanying the dogs, they merely follow the sledge. Taking his advice we embark on a dog sledge tour.' *Bottom caption*: 'On the 3rd. of June the genial summer showers, having fallen in the shape of snow it becomes necessary to do more than merely follow the sledge.'

[June 4th. 1853. S. Osborn P.P. p. 222. I am afraid to say how old the ice within Cape Fortune and Cape Ward appeared to be; the word very must suffice, for it might have been three or four years or half a century, there being, in my opinion, no certain clue to the age after it has seen a season or two of thaws.[1]]. I think that there is a possibility of arriving at some general conclusion as the age of permanent ice by an examination of the different layers of foreign material which we find imbedded in the ancient ice around us. These strata will represent seasons as rings mark annual growth in trees. H.W.F.

[1] See *Arctic Blue Books*, 1855, p. 222, for Osborn's comment.

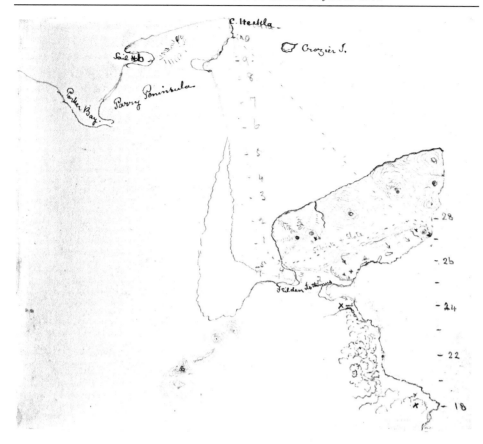

Figure 64.   Sketch map of part of Feilden's sledge route, showing the area around Cape Heckla and Crozier Island; note Feilden Isthmus.

[June 4th. 1853. Allard. P.P. p. 159. Princess Royal I. 1 deer, 1 hare, and 3 ptarmigan seen[1]].

Sunday 4 June 1876
Started at 11.30 hrs. 3rd. inst., with half load crossed shore hummocks to floe near Point Hercules, went back for second load, then placed both on sledge. The Musk sheep's skull that I took from the skeleton I found near View Point, looked so large that I felt ashamed to put it on the sledge, especially as there were several pounds of fossils on it already, cast away lower jaw, still it looked horribly large, then the Captain and I set to work with ice chisel and geological hammer, and we broke up the skull retaining merely frontal bone and horns, which are the finest I have yet seen. Halted for lunch (tea and bacon as usual) at 3.30, started at 5. Halted about a mile N of Dêpot Pt. on the floe at 6°.45′. The travelling today very heavy, extensive floes with deep snow, with barriers or hedges of hummocks, getting through these was severe work, the sledge sinking to the batten, and the slush and water well above our knees. On one large floe, a range of rounded blue topped hillocks rose above the surface of the floe, Captain Nares and I estimated them at 20 feet above

---

[1] See *Arctic Blue Books*, 1855, p. 159, for Allard's comment.

level of ice. It must have taken a long time to erode these hillocks out of the mass. All our gear wet above the knees, had to take off trousers before bagging, (N.B. take spare drawers in knapsack.) Starver one of our Eskimo bitches is a great adept at this and stole some pemmican, this made the other dogs vexed so out of jealousy they called out thief, which awakened us, J. Self went out to refasten the culprit, on his return he said to me "Lord bless me sir, that ere Starver, she is a regular Devonport twin." ? Davenport Brother.[1]

The rock about Pt. Hercules is a coarse quartzose gritstone almost a conglomerate, dipping <N.>E.

Monday 5 June 1876

Left camp at 10 p.m., 4th. inst., and reached Hare Ravine Bay at 1 a.m., 5th. inst. It was a lovely morning and the travelling along the young ice south of Dêpot Pt. though deep in snow was comparatively easy after "one, two, three, haul!" amongst the hummocks. The Captain decided to rest and shoot during the day in the heat of the sun, as no doubt the hares are easiest got during sunshine. I had just bagged, when the cook sighted a Ptarmigan on the hill slope, went out in my dry sleeping gear and secured him, a ♂. As I was returning to the tent I heard the cry of some wader the first this year, and looking in the direction it came from saw a flock of 14 *Tringa canutus*[2] circling over a small bare patch near the summit of the hill, they alighted and commenced picking. [*Margin: Tringa canutus.*] Went after them but fell down many times sometimes sliding back 20 or 30 feet again sinking up to the thighs in the sloppy snow, as often happens in like cases, just as I was getting in range the Knots gave a merry whistle and made off. [*Margin: Strepsilas interpres*] By this time I was dripping to the shirt with sweat and snow, so seeing three hares further on I thought it best to carry on, these animals when I got within a couple of hundred yards made off up the hill. [*Margin: Calidris arenaria*[3]] Returning to camp came across a pair of Knots, which I killed with No. 9 shot, both were in rich red plumage and turned out ♀ and ♂. their stomachs contained grit and buds of *Sax oppo.* the plant around which I had seen them feeding. Had to crawl in my wet shirt and drawers into bag, my travelling togs being also dripping from mornings work, soon got cold and cramps, Captain Nares gave me a gill of hot brandy and water, soon put me right. Some more Knots alighted near tent; May went out and secured one a ♂. At 7 o'c. shifted tent from snow to shingle, a great improvement as it obviates the necessity of brushing one's feet each time of entering the tent. Captain and May went off at 8 o'c. I remained and skinned birds, got off by 11. Walked along base of the Black Cliffs, snow disappearing in patches, saw a flock of Knots feeding in company with 4 *Strep. interpres*, and 2 *Calidris arenaria*, secured specimens of two last species. Found *Epilobium*[4] <withered leaves> and plant budding in a sheltered spot. [*Margin: Epilobium*] Hollins reported seeing flock of 12 or 14 duck pass over tent, "long necks black head and white underparts." Evidently *B. brenta*. Captain saw two flies, May brought in a hairy caterpillar, Snow-buntings paired, ♂ whistles sweetly, note some what resembles first bar of the throstle in early spring. I saw a Snow-bunting chase a Knot that passed too near his own peculiar mound.

[1] Ira Erastus Davenport (1839–1911) and William Henry Davenport (1841–77), the Davenport brothers, American magicians. Guiley, *Encyclopedia of Ghosts and Spirits*, pp. 81–3.

[2] Red knot.

[3] Sanderling, renamed *Calidris alba*, breeds on Ellesmere Island and North Greenland.

[4] A genus in the evening primrose family; most likely *E. latifolium*, broad-leaved willow-herb.

Tuesday 6 June 1876[1]

Left camp on spit, Hare Ravine Bay, at 1 a.m., crossed the floe which we found good travelling to south of Simmonds Island, where we entered a bay, struck the land, and hauled over the hills to Dumb-bell Lake, which we reached at 5 a.m. The first *Stercorarius* I have seen this season, passed us this morning. I fired at it and missed. I take it for *S. longicaudatus*.[2] [*Margin*: *Ster. longicaudatus*] After food and rest, May, James Self and dogs started back to our morning's camp for half load left behind, they left at 1 afternoon and returned at 6.30.

Captain Nares, Hollins, Spiro and I commenced making a hole through the ice of the lake about 50 yards from shore. Temp of snow on surface +20°, and a foot deeper +24°, at the depth of four feet came to the bottom. mud.

We then started a second hole further out in the lake, it was intensely hot the sun beating on us like in the tropics and right glad were we for the good water we made out of the melted lake ice. The thermometer is no criterion of the heat of the sun's rays which our coloured clothes absorb. The white surface of the snow reflects back again into space the sun's radiant heat, but our bodies and discoloured surfaces retain it. Before leaving camp this morning I shot a ♂ *Tetrao rupestris*, and found a sprig of *Sax oppo.* in bloom, the first blossom I have seen this year. [*Margin*: Saxifrage in bloom] How much it gladdened the heart and eye it is almost needless to say. Knots and Turnstones were calling and fresh life and animation seemed once more to have returned to this realm of the ice-King. My ears were today swollen and blistered with the heat of the sun. I should recommend the Arctic traveller to carry a small looking glass in his knapsack, it is useful for examining ones face for frostbites and gums for first symptoms of scurvy.

Wednesday 7 June 1876

Left camp at 7.15 a.m. (Dumb-Bell Lake) and crossing over the high land came down on the season's ice of Dumb-Bell Harbour, the snow was soft and sloppy and quite as bad walking as when I crossed over the same ground in Sept. last, as we were coming down the slope of the hill to the harbour we observed a seal lying on the ice, sunning and scratching itself, through the glass we made sure that it was *Phoca fetida*. [*Margin*: *Phoca fetida*] I tried to stalk it but it was too wary, I watched by the hole for some time, but it did not return. It is a question in my mind whether this animal has not wintered in this latitude.

Reached the ship at 2.15 p.m. We left May, J. Self, and Hollins with Spiro to dig out ice hole, they reached the water, and had a nibble from fish but caught none.

Ice Dumb-bell Lake
{
Snow 1 foot
Ice 7. 7½
Temp bottom   31°.2
Top   31°.5
Depth   18 feet
Mud, with fresh water diatoms.
}

Mays party Returning to ship in the evening. Day bright and glaring.

---

[1] Inserted here: second letter from Henry Chichester Hart to Feilden, dated 22 May 1876: see Appendix A.
[2] *Stercorarius longicaudatus*: long-tailed jaeger (in N. America), long-tailed skua (in Britain).

Thursday 8 June 1876

Busy all day working at the collections I have brought back from last journey. The insects that I procured on the island in Dumb-Bell Lake turned out badly, most of them being very minute, some were shaken to pieces, and spiders devoured others, I added, however, five new species, I am quite sure that a large field is open to the observer, who gives attention to the Arctic *insect*, the under surfaces of the stones, on warm exposed spots, seem to be the home of many species. This branch of Natural History in the Arctic regions, has hitherto received little or no attention. The amount of fat upon the skins of *Tetrao rupestris*, *Tringa canutus*, *Strepsilas interpres*, and *Calidris arenaria* is remarkable, they are so loaded with fat that it is difficult to keep their feathers free from grease. Three geese reported to me as cruising round the ship, and a couple of Boatswain birds (?Ster. longicaudatus.) they had gone when I reached the deck with my gun. At 6.30 p.m. Lieut. Parr arrived at the ship having walked in from View Point in 22 hours, the distance he travelled could not be less than 35 miles, [*Margin*: Parr returns from Northern Party] and what that means up here, only Arctic travellers can realize. Yesterday Captain Nares and I travelled in 10 miles of the same journey in 7 hours, and we had both felt quite tired. He brought dismal news of the northern party, all more or less affected with scurvy, 6 out of the 15 men on the sledges, 5 only able to crawl, and <only> 5 men besides Markham and Parr at the drag ropes. Had to leave their boats on the floe, and wait for assistance, not able to make a mile a day.

By 11 o'c. May, Dr Moss and James Self, with dogs were off, carrying medical comforts &c. By 12 p.m. Captain Nares with ~~two~~ 12 and 8 men sledges started for the N. 7 men in each sledge, Sub-Lieuts Egerton and Conybeare,[1] Mr Wootton and Mr White Engineers in the drag ropes, there being no more hands left in the ship fit for sledging. It was a most pleasing sight to me to see the quiet expeditious manner in which British naval officers meet an emergency. Every body sat down to tea as quickly as usual, by the time we had finished Cap$^{t.}$ Nares came in with a slip of paper detailing the sledges, parties, and supplies to go, and without the slightest noise or bustle, in four hours tents sledges and tackle were ready, and all hands sitting down to a cup of tea and a snack [*Margin*: 83°.20′.30″] before starting on this beastly night, as if it was the usual evening's programme. Markham's sledges found the travelling over the ice dreadful, constant pick and shovel, their highest point was on 12th. [*Margin*: 83°.20′.30″] May when sights were taken, the sledges having halted at 83°.19′.0″. There soundings were taken. 71 Fathoms, [*Margin*: Soundings 83.19′ in 71. Fath.] hard bottom, some *Shrimps and Entromostraca were brought up in a bread bag. On 27th. May Parr noticed *snow-bunting* in 82°.57′. [*Margin*: Snow Bunting 82°.57′.] A Hare's tracks on ice 20 miles from shore. Parr also tells me how in April, thermo at −40° he watched a little lemming struggling along the floe, it came towards him getting weaker and weaker, it then fell, and when he picked it up it was dead.
*Adult and young of "Anonyx nugax."[2]

Friday 9 June 1876

Sleet and drizzle temperature varying between +29° & +33°, slush and water round the ship, the land in the neighbourhood of the ship still deep in snow, no black patches visible,

---

[1] Crawford John Markland Conybeare (1854–1937), sub-lieutenant, HMS *Discovery*.
[2] A marine amphipod.

except above Cape Rawson. Parr seems to have recovered entirely from his tremendous march. Finished the birds skins, I brought back from last trip. Wrapped up fossils. The mud from the bottom of Dumb-Bell Lake contains fresh-water Diatoms.
Note subsequent
   Egerton killed 5 Brent Geese 2 at Ptarmigan Point and 2 at Canes Folly

Saturday 10 June 1876
Sleet and drizzle and mist, temperature varying from 29° to 33° slush making alongside of ship. Worked hard at my collections, up at 8 o'c. and did not go to bed till 4.30 a.m., (Friday morning.)
Ovibos Moschatus.
Mr Mitchell informs me that a ♀ was killed near Discovery Harbour on the 6th. of Sept., 1875 had two calves with her, they straggled away, but a party from ship returning the next day for the meat, found the two young animals standing by the dead ♀, and had been sucking her teats. One of these young ones was shot, and portions of its flesh put at once into the frying pan, which <meat> tasted so strong of musk that some hungry men of the party would not partake of it.
   Would it not be a good plan to differentiate between species that only straggle into the Arctic by getting beyond the 66° and those that come north of 80°. by calling them sub-polar species. By doing so especially amongst birds we should eradicate a lot of mere stragglers and in point of fact embrace only those species who really reproduce their ~~species~~ race, under the Pole. I imagine that a limit of 10°. around the Pole would produce about the same species of birds, on all sides.

273

PART IV: SLEDGING, NATURAL HISTORY, AND SCURVY
11 JUNE–25 JULY 1876

Sunday 11 June 1876
Mist, sleet and drizzle. Temp. 32°. Staid [*sic*] in the ship all day working. I have also got
to write some kind of report, to send down to the *Discovery* in case of our not getting
down their [*sic*] ourselves. This occupies my time much. It is quite impossible for me to
do justice to the subjects that have come under my notice in our present positions. It
entails all the labour I am capable of to arrange, pack up and stow away, the specimens I
bring onboard. [*Margin*: Scurvy.] [Most of *?*] hands left in the ship are scurvy stricken,[1]
and one has to do everything for oneself, from digging out snow houses, making box lids
and emptying ones slops.

[June 12th. 1853. S. Osborn P.P. p. 228. To-day was the first day we had had water fit to
drink off the floe, and dispensed with thawing water in consequence.[2]]

Monday 12 June 1876
Rather finer today, Temp 33°, the sun trying to struggle out through the mist, water
making on the floe round the ship. After breakfast took down my gear from the rigging
where it had been hanging since the 7th. and dried it below. Two geese passed over my
head, flying N. along the coast line. I took them for *Bernicla brenta*. Found a quantity of
cotton wool on deck wet and partly charred which the Doctor had condemned, set to
work and picked and dried it, got about 1½ lbs of clean wool out of it which is a good haul
for my taxidermy. Worked at specimens till dinner time. [*Margin*: *Ster. longicaudatus*]
Parr, who had been out for a walk on the floe brought in a pair of "Ster. Longicaudatus"
♂ & ♀, skinned them, contents of stomachs, Lemming fur and bones. Eggs in female size
of No 3 shot. [*Margin*: *Flies*] Mitchell brought in two flies which he caught on a bare
patch: put them in spirits. Parr also saw and fired at two geese but did not bring them
down. [*Margin*: *Dovekie*] 6.30 p.m. [*Ice*] Quartermaster Deuchars came below and told
me that a Dovekie was perched on the after bulwarks, it had flown away before I got on
deck.
    Went out after tea with gun towards Cape Rawson, 6 Brent Geese in pairs passed over
head out of shot returning south! [*Margin*: *Brent Geese*] These birds appear to have

---

[1] K. J. Carpenter, *History of Scurvy*, gives a general history of the illness. See also Smith, 'Historical Enquiry'.
Nares was to face serious criticism on his return for the way he had handled scurvy. See *Arctic Blue Books: Report
to the Lords Commissioners of the Admiralty, 1877*; Black, *Scurvy in High Latitudes*; and a counterblast to the
criticisms: C. R. Markham, *Refutation*, 1877.
[2] Osborn in *Arctic Blue Books*, 1855, p. 228.

reached their extreme limit, perhaps open water in Hall's Basin is the attraction, all birds so far seen have been coasting, no flocks have been steering across the ice due N. as one would have looked for were there land nearer the pole.

Tuesday 13 June 1876

About 7.30 a.m. May returned with dog sledge from relief party bringing in Pearson and Shirley,[1] they were carried at once to the sick-bay. Out after breakfast with Mitchell to Cape Rawson in hopes of getting geese, saw thirteen fly past us, none came within shot. seven were flying N., six south. Whilst sitting down waiting for these birds on a bare patch I collected several minute insects from under the surface of the stones, it is wonderful the amount of insect life in this country. I find the following method for collecting these private creatures, satisfactory, namely carrying a small tube half full of turpentine, and dipping up the insects with the head of a pin moistened in the liquid, the turpentine by removing the air, makes a far better medium, when transferring the objects afterwards to Canada Balsam, than spirits.

Where I lay on my stomach collecting insects, the strike of the slate rocks was well shown running E. and W., the slaty cleavage crossing diagonally.

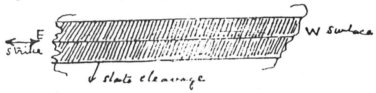

Ground down and placed under the microscope a section of the calcareous spine that I found in the mud deposits 300 feet thick, associated with *Pecten vitreus, Nucula*[2] &c, in valley head of Black Cliff Bay. It appears to me to be the sclerobasic axis of an Alcyonaria.[3]

Wednesday 14 June 1876

At 12 a.m. May returned [*illegible word*] 2[h].25[m]. a.m. Captain Nares with the relief sledges, and Markham with the northern party were alongside of the ship. Three hearty cheers were given, and the captain called on all hands to return thanks to God for the return of the party. We fellows onboard sighted the sledges, and ran out to meet them, joining the sledges at the flag-staff and giving a hand at the drag-ropes of the heavy sledges to the ship. Markham was in advance with the Marco Polo,[4] dragged by himself Radmore, Joliffe, and Maskell, Parr also hooked on and the northern party thus arrived alongside <5 out of 17>. Truly deplorable was the condition of the others, May at 12 o'c. had brought in Harley, Lawrence and Whinstone on the sledge, and yesterday morning Pearson and Shirley, who had to be carried onboard and below. On the twelve man sledge of the relief party were four men, Hawkins nearly dead, Rawlings, Simpson, and Pearce very bad, on the eight man sledge Francombe and Ferbrache, Porter succumbed at noon on the 8th inst

---

[1] John Pearson, able seaman, and John Shirley, stoker.

[2] *Nucula*, a genus of very small marine clams. *Delectopecten vitreus*, an animal of the Scallop genus.

[3] Sclerobasic: pertaining to calcareous or hornlike corals forming the central axis of compound alcyonaria, which are marine colonial polyps with 8-fold symmetry.

[4] One of the sledges.

and was buried by Markham on the floe, [1] I cannot pretend to write an account of the hardships and sufferings that these poor fellows went through. In latitude 83°.19′ they dug through the ice and sounded in 71 fathoms mud, the little they were enabled to obtain is full of foraminifera.[2] I guard this with a watchful eye as one of the most precious relics of the expedition. The highest latitude they reached was 83°.20′30″. I gave Moss sufficient of this sounding to mount on 8 slides. (H.W.F)

Egerton shot 2 geese (Brenta?) on Harley Spit, and White killed 4 more at Cane's Folly, unfortunately they did not even bring back a head. White shot <on 7th. inst> 2 *Calidris arenaria* ♀ and ♀. Eggs size of No 4 shot in ovary, contents of stomachs, grass seeds, and *Sax. oppositifolia*. Several Knots and *Ster. longicaudatus* were observed by the party whilst away. They also saw three *Phoca fetida* between the ship and Mushroom Point.

Thursday 15 June 1876
Working all day at collections, took a short walk towards Cape Rawson with Markham. Snow very sloppy, no geese or any other living animal seen. Noticed on a bare hummock-heap close to the floe a plant of *Sax. oppositi*folia in bloom. Temp part of the day +40°.

Friday 16 June 1876
After divisions this morning Captain Nares read out a memo, which was afterwards put up on the lower deck. I noticed what a wonderful effect it had on the crew, New life sprung into them, and one or two who cannot at present leave their hammocks, consulted me, in great tribulation whether or not I thought they would be sent home or allowed to stay out the next winter. The terrible malady which has come amongst us, certainly in some cases produced despondency, but it is only temporary, and as soon as most of the fine fellows realize that there is a prospect of their going home and leaving comrades to battle with another Arctic winter, they are as eager for the fray, as they were this time last year.

"Memo. H.M.S. *Alert*. Floe-berg Beach 16th. June 1876.
As we are not by any means the first who have suffered, we need not be alarmed at the deplorable sickness that has appeared amongst us, and which has evidently been brought to light by the heavy work entailed on our sledge parties. Hitherto it has always given way to a generous diet so, except in the severe cases which will naturally take longer, we may look for a speedy restoration to perfect health of those have been struck down.

However, it now becomes my duty to guard against a repetition of the attack, therefore, and I am sure greatly to the general regret, I have determined to give up all further exploration in a northerly direction.

Accordingly, both ships will go south this season to Port Foulke, where we know that fresh meat can be obtained in great abundance. One ship will then proceed home the other remaining there for the winter to examine Hayes Sound, during the following spring with a certainty of an early release from the ice in the summer.
(Signed) G. S. N., Captain, R.N."

[1] John N. Radmore, chief carpenter's mate; Thomas Joliffe, captain maintop; William Maskell, able seaman; Daniel W. Harley, captain foretop; Edwin Lawrence, gunner's mate; George Winstone, able seaman; John Hawkins, cooper; Thomas Rawlins, captain forecastle; Thomas H. Simpson, able seaman; Alfred R. Pearce, able seaman; Reuben Francombe, able seaman; William Ferbrache, able seaman; George Porter, gunner.
[2] An order of Rhizopoda (protozoan amoeba) with a shell, usually perforated by pores.

Started after breakfast at snow-hut with Conybeare's assistance, transferred all gear in it to ship, worked till 10 p.m. with two hours off for dinner. About 11 p.m. three *Sterna arctica* were flying about the ship, got a shot but failed in procuring one, White during my absence has enlarged my wife's carte that hangs up in my cabin, and has made a very nice photograph of it. The snow today, at a depth of four feet (that was to the ground) was quite sodden. The hut had sunk a good deal, and the roof slates of snow, three feet long by 6 inches deep and 8 broad were arched convex

Thickness of season ice	75½ inches.
Surface of ice to water	4¼ „
Thickness of snow	3 to 4 „

Saturday 17 June 1876

An example of *Ster. longicaudatus* flying round the ship this morning out of range. Towards Cape Rawson after breakfast, saw 2 *Ster. long*. Managed to secure one. ♀. These birds hunt the fells in pursuit of Lemmings and quarter the ground (snow?) like Harriers. The Lemmings are much given, to coming up through the snow and sitting on their haunches, I notice that their siphuncles[1] are now stained and dirty with their tracks as if they used the same holes for sometime. This may be accounted for by the greater density of the now sodden snow, which makes walking now very laborious. [*Margin*: Plants] Brought in a plant of *Sax. oppositifolia* in flower, which we put in a glass on the dinner table. The buds of the sorrel, chocolate coloured, are today showing through the withered leaves of last season. Captured a different species of the fly today, from those I obtained on the 12th. inst. I heard the cry of *Tringa canutus* on the high ground above Cape Rawson, and I saw a *Strep. interpres*. flying. Hunting for minute insects amongst the stones shows me that there are several species of mosses living here.

Sunday 18 June 1876

Markham and Parr brought back several specimens of the dark earth found in hummocks up to their highest latitude, it consists largely of quartz and other minerals, but abounds in Diatoms. (*Coscinodiscus*,[2] *Tricerathium*[3] &c.) [*Margin*: Dirt Bands N of 83°] Until I have seen the effects of the summers thaw on the Floe, I shall enter into no speculations about the origin of the dustbands, for at present our observations do not determine whether they are the result of melting and deposition of sediment, or snow turning into ice.

Several Arctic terns round the ship but none came within shot. Later on Giffard shot two, both ♀ stomachs empty. They must find great difficulty in procuring food here at present, the holes on the floe, not being ~~large~~ <deep> enough to allow Crustaceans to

[1] A small siphon; perhaps here a breathing tube through the snow.
[2] Radially symmetrical, disc-shaped diatoms.
[3] Also diatoms: see Brightwell, 'On the Genus *Triceratium*'.

come up to the surface in any number. Along with the moss in the mud-bed near big ravine I find shells of planorbis*[1] intercalated between beds of Pecten. This is a very remarkable discovery I am not aware of any Arctic travellers having discovered this fresh water mollusk alive, it points certainly to a period of milder temperature.
*I am all wrong about Planorbis v. J. 4th. July 1876. H.W.F.

Monday 19 June 1876 Leave Ship.
Parr and I left the ship, dragging satellite sledge at 9.30 p.m. Temp. at starting [*blank*]. Travelling good reached Mushroom Point 6 miles at 11.30 made a cup of tea at the tent. Saw three *Sterna hirundo* on our way cruising over the floes, and a dovekie *Uria grylle* in a pool, I fired a long shot but failed to secure it, also two *Ster. longicaudatus*. At Mushroom Point there were a pair of these birds seated on a bare ridge, we shot one which was feeding on a Lemming. In two pools we noticed seal-holes. [*Margin*: Plants] *Sax. oppositifolia* is now in bloom at Mushroom Point, and its purple blossoms are a great treat to the eye.

[June 20th. 1853. S. Osborn. P.P. p. 233. Temp. +31°. Cape Lady Franklin. Many birds flying about, especially wild fowl, such as ducks (eider and king eider), &c., Brent geese; they were evidently looking for a breeding place, and were very shy indeed. Ptarmigan were less wary, and we shot one or two walking up the hill, and I am led to think, from some of them we saw, which rather ran along the ground than flew, and whose legs were (unlike the majority) denuded of feathers and the feet very callous, and sinews of the leg much developed, whilst the birds themselves were lean and out of condition, whereas in some other ptarmigan nothing could have been finer than their flesh or plumage, that there are *two sorts* of ptarmigan in these regions, the one a migratory the other a stationary bird, which burrows in the snow during the winter, and braves an Arctic winter. One thing is undoubted, that ptarmigan have been occasionally seen throughout the winter by the "Investigators", "Resolutes", and "North Stars",[2] and it appears unlikely that the weak or sickly birds left behind by the broods on the approach of winter should be able to endure a climate which the strong full-fledged birds are known to avoid.[3]] 25th. March 1872. Two Ptarmigan seen on this date, at Polaris Bay, N. Lat. 81°36'.

Tuesday 20 June 1876 Travelling from Dumb-bell Harbour.
Left Mushroom Point at 12h.50m. a.m., from there to Dumb-Bell Harbour travelling not quite so good. After reaching tent, saw a pair of Brent Geese feeding on a bare slope, near by. We killed one a ♂, the other led Parr a dance, we also got a ♂ Ptarmigan, and a Sanderling, we hunted diligently for Ptarmigan's nest but failed in our search. Temp. at midnight +33°. Found that the large black and red hairy caterpillar which feeds on *Sax. oppositifolia* is the insect that weaves the delicate silky looking cocoons, which we find not unfrequently attached to stones. We bagged at 6 a.m.

Got up at 1.30 p.m. Had a wild goose chase before starting without any beneficial result to larder. Temp. inside of tent +53°. Outside +29°. Barometer fallen .15 of an inch since leaving ship. Started at 5 p.m. saw a *Phoca fetida*, lying on the ice in outer Dumb-bell Harbour, tried to get a shot but failed. Reached the boats at 8 o'c., and had some cold

---

[1] A genus of freshwater air-breathing snails with a flat spiral shell.
[2] Men from the three ships of these names during the expedition of 1852–4.
[3] Osborn in *Arctic Blue Books*, 1855, entry dated 21 (not 20) June 1853.

bacon and lime juice. The travelling was good, but we both felt hauling the little sledge, I was spitting blood from my gums most of the way, and somewhat stiff about the knees and ankles.[1] We took to the floe at the boats and crossed to Cane's Folly, by 11.20 p.m. leaving Simmonds[2] I. [*sic*] on our left. Travelling better than might have been expected at this season, but the cracks between the floes were extremely treacherous and "sold us a pup several times", by letting us down in the slush, and requiring a "one two three haul" to get out the sledge. Between Harley Spit and the boats saw several long-tailed Skuas, and observed that two species of minute *Diptera* harboured inside the expanded blossoms of [*Margin*: Plants] *Sax. oppositifolia*. We also secured a beautiful Ichneumon fly. No Pemmican in tent at Canes Folly so had to content ourselves with stewed Ptarmigan and potatoes. N.B. We found that it made a tolerable substitute for pemmican as we have not yet found our sledging appetites!

Note made 1st July 1876.[3] With all my care in transporting the minute diptera in tubes filled with both turpentine, and spirits of wine, they came to grief, and turned out very unsatisfactorily as microscopic mounts.

[June 21st. 1853. S. Osborn. P.P. p. 233. plants commencing to go into flower; the first saxifrage flower I have seen this season, forms, like the first of the sun, the first snow-bunting, and the first thaw, so many epochs in the monotonous round of the Arctic seasons.]
[Whilst scaling a glacier of small size, I was astonished on taking up a handful of snow to find the particles filled with living creatures, of a black colour, about half the size of a small flea, and very like them or shrimps in shape; they moved about rapidly. id. p. 234][4]

Wednesday 21 June 1876 Cane's Folly and Hare Ravine N. Lat., 82°.33′.
Up at 8.30 a.m., breakfast over, tent arranged, gear stowed, and off with our guns by 11 o'c. We saw 5 Brent Geese in bottom of Cane Valley, they were shy, having no doubt been previously initiated into the smell of gunpowder by our predecessors. We then shaped our course over the ridge to the S.W., that divides from Hare Ravine, on the brow suddenly came on two black heads and long necks peering over the slope, dropped on our bellies in the snow and wriggled up within shot, secured two Brent Geese, old Parr carried them. Saw several Knots their cry is wild something like *Numenius arcuatus* [*sic*][5] in the breeding season. "Tull a wee Tull a wee, wee wee." They are now mating as I saw several pursuing each other in the air, and soaring like *Gallinago media*[6] in the breeding season, the Knot has not the faculty of drumming like the snipe, but when descending it beats its wings over its back with very rapid motion, producing a loud whirring noise. Shortly after this we came on the track in the snow of two full grown musk-oxen accompanied by a young one, the footmarks of the latter were not larger than those of a small sheep.
　　These tracks at the outside could not have been more than a week old, the droppings of the beasts were soft and the footprints frequently held a handful of wool, which the

---

[1] Early symptoms of scurvy.
[2] Simmons Island
[3] Note made 1 July 1876, but written above entry for 21 June 1876.
[4] Osborn in *Arctic Blue Books*, 1855, pp. 233–4.
[5] *Numenius arquata*, Eurasian curlew, whose song is not altogether unlike that of the red knot.
[6] Great snipe, breeds in north-eastern Europe including Russia.

animals during progression had stamped off their winter coat. They must now be changing their coats. This incident gave us hope of meeting with musk-sheep soon; we followed the tracks well up Hare Ravine, until we overlooked the flat area that stretched to the base of Mount Constitution, this was deep in snow. The animals had stopped to feed at every bare patch on their route, and I noticed that several recumbent plants of *Salix*, which is now just coming into leaf, had been plucked up by them.

This accounts for the number of dead Salix plants that are scattered over the country. We caught a fly, a diptera, and a small spider. Found withered plants of *Sax. flagillaris*,[1] the old stems appear dead, but the tendrils bear at their ends a small bud, with accessory rootlets which are now spreading. Returning by southern slope of Hare Ravine spied a *Lepus glacialis* which gave us little trouble to secure. Two splendid snowy owls haunt the valley, they are most wary birds never alighting where it is possible to approach under cover. As one of these owls flew away from us, I saw it pass a spot where a **B. Brenta** was sitting. The goose rose and made straight at the owl, driving it some distance. We also observed two of these Geese depart greatly from their usual staid behaviour, they were courting and rose high in air with spiral flight and performed several strange antics. Next we came across a long neck and black head twisting about like an adder's walked up to it and secured a ♀ B. Brenta and 4 eggs in a warm nest of her down, the ground being slightly hollowed out below, and a good base of Sax. opp. stems, grass and moss for the down to rest on. The Gander was close by, and he ran about hissing, and fell a victim to his affection for his mate. We saw several Knots, several Turnstones and one pair of Sanderlings in our way back to the tent another Goose was taken in reverse and slung on to Parr's back making 5 he was carrying.

[*Entry continued in margin*] A stiff breeze from S.S.W. sprung up at 3.30 p.m., fortunately on our backs, which the barometer had given us ample warning of. Back to tent at 5 o'c. The Hare killed was a ♀ and had dropped her young for her teats had milk in them, and around the mammæ were suckling marks. A long-tailed Skua after hovering over tide cracks seated itself on the water. We got into our bags by 9.30 p.m.

Thursday 22 June 1876 Shooting in Hare Ravine
We bagged last night at 9.30 p.m, and remained in them till 12 m[*idday*], as it blew strong all night from S.S.W. rising to a gale about 4 a.m. The beacon flagstaff blown down. Whilst coiled up in our bags heard the notes of snow-bunting, Knots, sanderlings and Terns, and the "Honk Honk" of the Brent Goose passing near us.

By 2ʰ.45ᵐ. p.m. we left the tent having cleaned up and prepared another goose for dinner. First set up the flag-staff and built a substantial cairn round it. Walked to Hare Ravine crossed at the head of the bay, and went along its south side and the base of Black Cliffs – There is now plenty of drinking water running down the slopes. The number of Brent Geese is limited, today we saw five pairs, and we secured two pairs of them as well as a ♀ hare. Out of the six geese left one is badly peppered. The wind blew all day from the south sometimes with a force of 6, this made all birds very shy. We noticed a pair of Turnstones who seemed to be nesting, but though we watched them long and carefully, failed to see the ♀ go to her nest. I was greatly interested by seeing this bird actually turn over a piece of slate three inches in diameter and pick up the insects from underneath, it

[1] Whiplash saxifrage.

put its bill fairly under the centre of the stone and then chucked it over with a good toss of the head and neck. We saw two pairs of Sanderlings, and the same number of Knots, but no nests yet. [*Margin*: Plants] *Epilobium* under the Black Cliffs is in leaf. Found the cranium of a Fox. Two of the eggs of B. brenta which we eat this morning showed just a trace of sitting.

[June 23rd. 1853. S. Osborn P.P. p. 235. N.E. Bathurst I. Saw numerous herds of deer. Counted on one occasion not less than fifteen does with as many fawns. All these fawns had been but lately dropped.[1]]

Friday 23 June 1876 <u>We meet Aldrich's Sledge Party.</u>
Got to our bags at 3 a.m., aroused at 10.30 by J. Self and dog-sledge who had been sent on by Aldrich with Doidge and Stubbs both bad scurvy cases. Put them on our beds, fed them and made them comfortable, until arrival of their own sledge which reached Canes Folly at 11.30. Sergeant Wood on sledge Aldrich and Ayles in the drag-ropes, the only members of his party able to work. (May, Malley, & Thornback relief party assisting.) J. Self and Parr went back towards Depot Pt. with dog-sledge and gave Goode, Mitchell and Mann, a help in. Aldrich looking well, Ayles ditto,[2] the rest very bad, swollen faces and legs, weak and tottering scarcely able to put one foot before the other. I was employed getting breakfast ready for Aldrich and May stewed goose which they enjoyed in our tent. Parr and I had some preserved meat and biscuit under the lea of the tent. The two hares were cooked and eaten by the men. Parr and I went out at 3.15 p.m., in direction of Depot P^t half way across Cane Valley shot a goose, a very disagreeable wind blowing from S.S.W. On our return skirted Victoria Lake, and down by the valley, the water course has cut a channel through its centre, and good sections of the mud-beds are there exposed. up to 30 feet, as usual the river gravels rest on them. We found great numbers of *Mya* both valves attached and the hard epidermis of the syphons still preserved, *Saxicava* in multitudes, several examples of Trichotropis,[3] Pecten and several *Cylichnea* [*sic*].[4] thin beds of sea-weed. *Laminaria* stems and roots? were intercalated, and amongst this were round compressed objects which I took for shells of Planorbis, but which are really ~~Serpulae~~[5] Foraminifera also some bones.

Near the tent on a gravel flat found two *Ster. longicaudatus* who flew round us and darted at our heads, moved off a little distance and saw the ♀ alight on the gravel, walked to the spot and put her off two eggs laid in a depression without any attempt at nest making shot ♂ & ♀. Eggs rather pyriform[6] and of a delicate green <ground> colour not unlike those of *S. parasiticus*. Salix in leaf. [*Margin*: Salix] Fly and caterpillar bagged. Got back to tent at 9 o'c. skinned ♂ *B. Brenta* cooked and fed, then helped Aldrich's lot to pack up. We got some salt, lime-juice and pemmican gave them in return 7 geese and

[1] Osborn, *Arctic Blue Books*, 1855, p. 235.
[2] James Doidge, captain foretop; Thomas Stubbs, stoker; William Wood, colour sergeant; Adam Ayles, 2nd captain foretop; William Malley, able seaman; James Thornback, able seaman, seconded to *Alert* from *Discovery*; Joseph Good, chief boatswain's mate; David Mitchell, able seaman; Henry Mann, shipwright.
[3] A genus of small sea snails in the family of cap snails.
[4] *Cychlina*. A genus of marine bubble snails.
[5] A genus of marine annelid tube worms.
[6] Pear-shaped.

sundries. N.B. Virtue is always rewarded by playing the good Samaritan got a new pair of canvas boots from Doidge, who is not likely to want them again this season. Aldrich and his got off at 2.30 a.m.

Saturday 24 June 1876 <u>Sanderling and Snowy Owl breeding in 82°.33'.</u>
of the 24th. inst.[1] Two *Harelda glacialis* flew past ♂ & ♀. If it was not a deplorable, it would have been a ludicrous sight to see Aldrich's poor fellows start, they looked a compound of Christian in the Slough of Despond,[2] and Falstaff's army,[3] two were armed with paddles belonging to the Halkett boat, which they had been obliged to leave behind, and three with broken staffs with which they tried to support their tottering steps. Doidge had to cross a bad bit of broken snow-foot before getting on the ice, he took about a quarter of an hour to get fifty yards, tumbling down at each crack, his carriage the dog-sledge was waiting for him, however, on the floe.

Aldrich gave me a parcel of the rocks he had collected at his highest northern point 83°.6'. Mica schist, Serpentine, Quartz, Mica &c. Bagged at 4 a.m. Up at 11 a.m., it blew hard all morning from S.S.W. and continued during the day. The last 24 hours has marked a great change both on the floe and on shore. The former is now spotted over with patches of water, and rivulets are pouring down the slopes. Walking is now laborious on shore, the snow being sodden and at each step one sinks in over the knees or else plunge the feet into a bath just above +32°.

The condition of the floe warns us to be off ~~at once~~. Food 'scoffed' and tent cleared up by 1.30 p.m., Parr started for Hare Ravine, I went up Cane Valley, The strong breeze seemed to have driven the birds to seek shelter. A *Glaucus Gull* was hovering over the fresh-water pools a mile inland, but too wary to let me within range. Passed a *S. longicaudatus* feeding on a lemming, it allowed me to move walk within 20 paces of it, then backed away from me, making great efforts to gulph the lemming which it succeeded in doing, after that it flew about fifty yards and uttered its melancholy 'quirk, quirk'. Skirting the N. side of Hare Ravine, which is composed of old gravel terraces, and at a height of 800 feet, I spied a Sanderling running like a mouse, sat down and watched it return to its eggs. The nesting-place was a slight depression in the centre of a small plant of recumbent Salix and was lined with its dried leaves of last year, and a few catkins it contained two eggs, fresh. The sitting bird showed on dissection to be the ♂. On my way back was overtaken by Parr carrying 3 Brent Geese, he was also the bearer of the good intelligence that he had found the *Snowy Owls* nest in Hare Ravine with 7 eggs in it, but had left it for my inspection. [*Margin*: Plants] Yellow *Draba* in flower and *Sax. cernua*.[4] budding from last years stalk. Left tent at 9 p.m., went to Hare Ravine, a hundred yards from nest saw a snowy Owl leave it. The nesting-place was on a stony mound, simply a hole scratched out, like the dust holes of the domestic fowls, and about the area of a soup-plate. The eggs lying on the bare ground. Waited by the nest for the chance of a shot, the larger of the two birds alighted on the eggs, and I brought her down with a charge of No. 4. I left her lying partly in hopes of attracting the mate, and partly as I was afraid of injuring

[1] Entry continues from 23 June, to read 'got off at 2.30 a.m. of the 24th. Inst.', interrupted by date and heading.
[2] From John Bunyan, *Pilgrim's Progress*.
[3] In Shakespeare, *Henry IV*, Pt I, Act IV, Scene 2.
[4] Nodding saxifrage.

the beautiful plumage by shooting again, drew back and in about half an hour the other bird came, hovering round crying "whew" "whew". Imagine my disappointment when I saw the moribund bird as I thought, rise on its legs, get the wind under its wings and sail away to the other side of the valley. I went in pursuit, but a stern chase is a long one over deep snow, and I lost sight of my prize flopping some six feet above the ground over a low ridge. Got back to the tent at [*blank*]

Found mud-beds underlying gravel terraces at an altitude of 800 feet.

[June 25th. 1853. S. Osborn. P.P. p. 236. Passed a spot in which wolves had lately pulled down a deer and devoured it. Plenty of birds; we have eider ducks, brent geese, phalaropes, boatswain birds,[1] sanderlings, and glaucus gulls, which latter evidently feed, amongst other things, upon the lemmings or marmots so common in these regions. Saxifrage is now in full flower and leaf.[2]]

Sunday 25 June 1876
3.am. Whilst waiting for the owl found a snow-bunting nest with 3 eggs in it under a stone close to the owls. It was a well made structure of grass, lined with the feathers and down of *Nyctea scandiaca*. Blowing eggs and skinning till 8 a.m., beautiful morning, many blue-bottle flies about the tent attracted by refuse. They are now coupling. Got up at 12 *midday*, wind sprung up. Put gear back again into tent made everything ship shape, packed our sledge and fed. Started with sledge at 2[h].45 p.m., bringing Egerton's gun as we thought it possible this tent might not again be visited. The travelling over the young ice for about a mile from shore, though water above the ankles and very cold was tolerable, but when we reached the old floe and from there to Simmonds I. the travelling was truly execrable, the snow sodden, sunk often to the crutch, and had a foot of water round our feet and legs, fell on our faces now and again as we tugged at the sledge and she moved suddenly, then we found some little difficulty in regaining our footing. We reached Simmonds I at 6 p.m., took our guns, and walked over it. We found 4 or perhaps 5 pairs of Brent Geese breeding on it. Three geese were on their eggs and were slaughtered, one nest contained 5 eggs the other two 4, all were warm and comfortable structures of down. A fourth bird, a gander, was brought to bag, a fifth fell dead on the floe, but we were in no humour to go after it.

Back to sledge and got on drag-belts by 8 p.m., from Simmonds I. to the boats the travelling was equally as arduous as before over the blue-topped hummocks, there being many pools of water to wade through, and the sledge hanging back in the slush, requiring a succession of "one two three hauls". Very glad to get on shore where the travelling improved along the snow-foot. Reached the tent at Dumb-bell Harbour, by 12 o'c. I felt quite exhausted. Blowing half a gale from S.S.W. It is fortunate that Aldrich passed over this ice 24 hours ago, I hardly think his sick men could have travelled where we went along today. Saw a P[hoca] fetida at Simmonds I. and a *Glaucus Gull*. Got our supper a stewed Goose, it was no joke preparing this bird outside the tent for the pot. finished by 3 a.m. 26th. inst. (Aldrich and his party reached ship today 25th.)

---

[1] Arctic skua, parasitic jaeger.
[2] Osborn, *Arctic Blue Books*, 1855, pp. 236–7. Boatswain bird is another name for Arctic skua.

[June 26th. 1853. S. Osborn. P.P. p. 238. Eider Isles. Birds were numerous (eider ducks). but had only just commenced to form their nests, and consequently were very wild: we only shot one and got a nest of five eggs.[1]]

Monday 26 June 1876 <u>Dumb-Bell Harbour</u>
We had a fine sleep, the gale was blowing strong, and threatened our tent, but we were so snug under an upper robe, that we did not get out of our bags till 11.30 a.m. We had a good breakfast off goose eggs and preserved meat, and wound up with an egg-nog. Then the poles of the tent began to shift so we had to go outside and bank up. Packing up the gear, blowing eggs, and making our own sledge ship shape, and being besides in no particular hurry to start, we did not get under weigh till 6.45 p.m. The travelling to Mushroom Point was bad often to our waists a foot of water, then a foot of sludge, and the rest snow, our little sledge got buried in this muck, so we had to face about and get her out of these 'Sloughs of Despond' with standing hauls. Reached the tents at Mushroom Point at 8.45 p.m., made a cup of tea and left at 9.45. It was blowing strong from S.S.W., as we travelled between Mushroom Point and the ship we saw a *Larus glaucus*, several *Ster, longicaudatus*, several pairs of *Sterna hirundo*, and about 15 *Som. spectabilis*, a ♀ of which species we picked up wounded. A single *Procellaria glacialis* passed us at about 70 yards distance. Real rain fell.

[June 27th. 1853. S. Osborn P.P. p. 239. Queens channel N.L.76′.20. several female Walrus rose and snorted at us, and there were seen brent geese, duck, and tern in considerable numbers but very shy ... saw some deer grazing on the high land. ... 2 brent geese shot]. [Water Island. Great number of silvery gulls breeding here, and the island was covered with nests of one description of wild fowl and another. Picked up about 50 eggs, of different sorts; found most of them partially hatched and uneatable. id p. 241.][2]

Tuesday 27 June 1876 <u>Return to Ship</u>
Reached ship at 1.30 a.m.
Tired, and resting my limbs, just able to hobble about this morning. Whilst dragging at the sledge the last two days spit some blood. That kind of work comes heavy on an old fellow nearly forty.
   Working at the things I brought back on the sledge, skinning, labelling, and marking. There is very little to show, but the work seems never ending.

[June 28th. 1853. S. Osborn. P.P. p. 242. Had a regal supper of brent goose and preserved meats and boiled eggs. Temp +37°. Cooks volunteered to search the beach brought back a few small pieces of drift pine, 6 inches long, some good specimens of coal, and a small platter*, evidently scooped by manual labour out of pudding stone, no doubt lost here by some wandering Esquimaux in by-gone times.[3]]

---

[1] Osborn, in *Arctic Blue Books*, 1855, p. 238.
[2] Osborn, in *Arctic Blue Books*, 1855, pp. 239–40, 241.
[3] Osborn, in *Arctic Blue Books*, 1855, p. 242. The note about platters appears below, p. 285.

Wednesday 28 June 1876

Weight of King Eider ♂ 3¾ lbs. Weight of ♀ 3¾ lbs. Weight of Brent Goose 3 lbs. A small flock of these birds <King duck[1]> came near the ship, one of our sportsmen sallied out and obtained one example, a single *Harelda glacialis* was also seen. The stomachs of the *Somateria spectabilis* I opened today contained only gravel. The same with a ♂ Harelda.

The icicles that three weeks ago festooned our floe bergs and hummocks in long pendant array, have entirely disappeared, they were 10 and 12 feet long, two glass thermometer tubes which were buried in the floe-berg on the [*date missing*] by boring a hole with an augur and freezing solid around them with water, today were liberated, one 8 inches have [*sic*] fallen flat down, the other also 8 inches in length just holding to the ice by the base of its stem.

Egerton has shot and preserved a *Stercorarius* with very much shorter tail feathers than any I have seen <here> – I am inclined to consider it ——— but without a series to compare with, it is hard to pin a fellow up here to saying whether it is *S. parasiticus* or a young *S. longicauda*

I never realized until I had travelled over rotting floes, what a blackguard old Belcher was to move his ship down Wellington Channel, before Sherard Osborn's sledging party were safe onboard.[2]

[*Margin:* *]   Now a word about platters, the other day in Hare Valley at the height of 800 feet I took from a mud deposit, one and more platters that might easily have been palmed off as rude manual fashioned, in reality they were rounded platish nodules of clayslate, which had been embedded in the ~~clay~~ <mud>-beds, the core having disintegrated quicker than the platter with an even rim or edge half an inch high round it.

Giffard and Conybeare went on the plateau today beyond the Gap of Dunloe, to make observations in reference to land route to Lincoln Bay, they reported the snow as 3 ft. 4 in. in depth and very soft.

I worked hard all day and till 4.30 a.m. of the 29th. at my collections, skinning geese and ducks being severe labour ———

[June 29th. 1853. S. Osborn P.P. p. 243. Kills two reindeer. Remarks that the does have horns as well as bucks. The winter coat, now of a dull ash colour, was loose, and came away in handfuls, leaving underneath a handsome bay or dun colour.[3]]

Thursday 29 June 1876

After breakfast, went down south towards Cape Rawson to see whether a tide-crack would be suitable for dredging purposes. Malley[4] went on floe, whilst Captain Nares and I walked over the slopes with our guns. Saw 5 Brent Geese, 4 flying N along shore 1 flying S. No wader of any description was met with by us, and we did not hear the note of the Knot, only the merry chirp of the Snow bunting, the flora here is certainly poorer and at least ten days behind that of Hare Ravine in 82°.32′. Two or three pairs of Long-tailed

---

[1] King eider.

[2] Belcher, *Last of the Arctic Voyages*, I, pp. 283 ff., and Osborn, in *Arctic Blue Books*, 1855, p. 243, re difficulties of travelling over rotting floes.

[3] Osborn, *Arctic Blue Books*, 1855, p. 243.

[4] William Malley, able seaman.

Skuas are thinking of nesting in the neighbourhood but have not laid eggs yet. Parr shot a ♀ King Duck sitting in a pool with a cartridge, at a distance of at least 70 yards. A *Procellaria glacialis* seen by Captain Markham close to the ship in the evening. The ravines have now small streams running down them, and this water spreads out on the floe, over the surface of the ice; at the mouth of these streams a thin layer of mud and gravel is now deposited, but when the freshets break forth an enormous amount of alluvial gravel will be borne seaward, this to some extent will rest upon the shore ice and if piled up a foot or two in thickness will effectually prevent the sun acting on it, suppose that a secular elevation of the land being going on at the same time, there need not be any difficulty in comprehending the formation of intercalated beds of ice with alluviums, noticed in Siberia and N. America.

Malley reported the crack as five yards wide and of some length. Will take the small dredge there tomorrow.

We had an imposing dinner today, Soles, Lobsters, Ham, Champagne &c to commemorate the gathering together again of our Ward-room mess, after the trying sledging season. I think we all felt grateful, and thanked the kind Providence that permitted 15 of us to meet round the same table, (every member of our mess, and Conybeare and Mitchell[1] of the *Discovery*) apparently all in better health than when we left England, whilst so many of our men are prostrated with scurvy.

Captain Nares, spoke a few words to us after dinner, He remarked that he was sure the thought of returning to England this season would be a disappointment to us, but that we ought to remember that when we left England the current idea was that we should be home in eighteen months, that the two years had entirely originated with ourselves, when we were in the height of strength and vigour, that now this blight having fallen on us, the original programme would be maintained, and the season with healthy crews would certainly have increased our knowledge of N. Greenland. That the main object of the expedition had failed for reason of its impossibility, that the sledge-crews with the proverbial gallantry of British sailors, had tugged on and slaved, until they dropt, to be dragged by their comrades, little stronger than themselves. Our northern march and our western would be handed down in the pages of history, and that though we had commenced where other expeditions left off, yet our actual discoveries where [sic] of very considerable extent.

A lovely evening.

[June 30th. 1853. S. Osborn. P.P. p. 244. Wounds she bear and two cubs. Coal found in the ravines. deposits of coal and pipe clay!²]

Friday 30 June 1876
After breakfast took dog-sledge with Malley and Frederick and small dredge to tide-crack examined yesterday. Let dredge down in 10½ fathoms, bottom hard and stoney. Too short a haul to do any good. The swab brought up entangled, a Nymphon,³ some Protozoa, three Annelids⁴ and a small fragment of *Alva*.⁵

---

¹ Thomas Mitchell, assistant paymaster, *Discovery*.
² Osborn, in *Arctic Blue Books*, 1855, p. 244. Osborn wounded the adult female, not the cubs.
³ *Nymphon*, a genus of sea-spiders
⁴ Red-blooded worms.
⁵ *Alva*, an alga, sea-lettuce.

On shore with gun, snow rapidly baring the low lands, saw several Knots, they are still love making, two males were pursuing a ♀, their cry of "Tulla wee Tulla wee wee wee" is very shrill. The ♀ when she rose in the air was followed by the two males who cried incessantly, and as they hovered made a loud whirring noise with their wings, which they keep rapidly beating in an upright position. The ♀ when she alighted on a mound was joined by one of the ♂s, and the discarded suitor made off.

On a low flat, (rather boggy), secured an example of *Phalaropus fulicarius*, the only one I saw, it was picking about in the tame manner common to birds of this genus, and I had to step back to avoid over shooting it. The note is a low "peep peep". It proved on dissection a ♀ with ovaries not greatly enlarged, the largest ova size of a No. 3 shot. Contents of stomach digested insects. The colouring of this species in Dressers plate is too sombre, the bill is orange tipped with dark hair, brown, not yellow.[1] Two birds alighted in a pool near the ship during the afternoon, which I presume from the description given me where [sic] Phalaropes.

Walked on to Drift-wood Lake, and collected out of the exposed mud, at the same spot where I found it before a considerable quantity of drift-wood. Some larger stems are sticking up out of the mud, and will require a spade to remove them. This mud belongs to the same series as the other mud-beds so frequently alluded to by me, and from which I have procured various fossils. *Stercararious* [sic] *longicaudatus* is a very bold bird, when you approach its selected breeding haunts, if standing, it will remain motionless until you get within 2 paces, crying peevishly "Quirk, Quirk", when it rises on the wing it comes straight at one, as if desirous of investigating the make of one's head dress.

[*Margin*: Plants] Noticed withered plant of *Sax. flagillaris*, *Sax. oppositifolia* only now coming into bloom in this locality.

Shot a pair of *Sterna hirundo*, in close proximity to the ship.

[July 1st. 1853. S. Osborn. P.P. p. 245. Bear Point. Found every crack in the floe alive with terns.[2]]

Saturday 1 July 1876
Working hard all morning, did not go to bed till 5 a.m., and up at 8.30 for breakfast. My late collections, made whilst sledging, are slowly getting ship-shape. At 4 p.m. when I was ready to start with the faithful Malley armed with shovel, and bread-bag, for Drift-Wood Lake a breeze sprung up from S.S.W. Parr shot a *B. Brenta* and a ♂ and ♀ *Som. spectabilis*. Moss and Giffard went in the direction of Pt. Sheridan, they fired at 5 Brent Geese flying overhead, and brought one down, it had a large bare hatching spot on its belly and must evidently have been sitting on eggs. This shows that when leaving the nest in quest of food they join in flocks. M. and G. also obtained a ♀ *S. spectabilis*. Saw 2 Phalaropes and several Knots. The Lemmings are now driven by the melting snow to take refuge under large stones.

The habit of *B. Brenta* above alluded to accounts for what has been puzzling me the last three or four days namely seeing small flocks of these birds cruising N. and S. at the same time knowing that further north I had found them with incubated eggs a week ago, and it seemed strange to me if these birds were looking for breeding grounds.

[1] Grey phalarope in Europe, red phalarope in North America. Dresser, *History of the Birds of Europe*, VII, p. 538.
[2] Osborn, *Arctic Blue Books*, 1855, p. 245.

Aldrich gave me a lichen '*Umbilicaria*'?[1] from N. face of Cape Columbia. Lat 83°.6' and a withered stem of Papaver from same locality. A Ptarmigan's dropping, some Hypnum?, a calix of *Papaver* and some cases that look like *Serpula*[2] from a pushed up hummock-heap off Cape Discovery in Lat. 83°.

Out after tea in search of the wily Knots nest, I saw two pairs but they led me a Will of the Wisp dance. Why do not these birds settle down to nesting like reasonable creatures? They must rear their broods very smartly for here is the 1st. of July, and they are fooling about in the air still intent on their honeymoon, apparently quite thoughtless about the cares and responsibility of bringing up a family. The poor little lemmings have a bad time of it now, they are obliged to take refuge under stones, no safe, well chambered snow casemate to retreat into, they are very pretty now, gray on back, rufous on belly. When collared in the open they rise on their hind quarters and show fight, they are very easily killed, the slightest tap with muzzle of gun or haft of Knife, finishes them off. Caught 5, all ♂ as yet have not captured a ♀. A pair of Sanderlings that I watched for an hour were as wild and annoying as the Knots.

[July 2nd 1853. S. Osborn P.P. p. 245. A most interesting account of a she bear feeding her young on lemmings, and afterwards suckling them.[3] This account shows Admiral Osborn to have been an observer of no ordinary type.]

Sunday 2 July 1876
Got back to the ship at 5 a.m. Slept in till 2 o'c. Worked afterwards at collection. Went out after supper and tried to bring *T. canutus* to its bearings, saw a pair on the slopes half way up Beacon Hill, flying over a bare patch and hovering with quivering wings, when I got within a quarter of a mile they were off with a shrill "Tulla$\overline{wee}$ $\overline{wee}$", then I ascended Beacon Hill and walked along the edge of the plateau overlooking Drift-Wood Lake, saw another Knot which rose wild, then I descended into the flat valley, through which Big Ravine stream after cutting its way through the slate rocks flows to the sea. As this valley has preserved its original contour better than many of the larger ones, and elucidates several geological problems I may as well describe it.

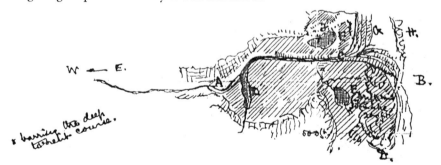

A to B is a flat valley about 150 feet elevation, at some not distant period it was an arm of the sea, the torrent course emerges from the mountains at A, about (800 foot high

[1] A genus of lichens; rock tripe.
[2] A genus of marine annelid tube-worms.
[3] Osborn, in *Arctic Blue Books*, 1855, p. 245. Osborn calls the animals marmots, but from his description, it is clear that lemmings are the prey.

mountain). As far as C. the valley is smooth, [*Margin*: barring the deep torrent course.] say 200 acres of nearly flat shingle, but at D a transverse stream has cut a gully, and exposed about 30 feet, underneath the two feet of shingle comes the stratified fine mud, with Pecten, Astarte, seaweed, and intercalated [*5 words heavily crossed out, possibly* ~~beds of hypnum and Planorbis~~] the lakes marked E are deeper than the surrounding shingles and have cut down into the mud, their margins are strewed with Astarte, Mya, Saxicava and drift wood. At F an elevation of 10 feet or so above the lake but still mud, great numbers of highly polished erratics the larger and harder ones being distinctly ice-scratched, I thought at one time these marked grounding ridges where ice rafts grounded on the rising of the coast but now I think they were deposited in the mud during its formation but have remained behind after its denudation. G series gravel terraces. H the polar sea.

[July 3rd. 1853. S. Osborn. P.P. p. 246. Much drift wood found on shores of Queens Channel[1]]

Monday 3 July 1876
Got back to the ship by 4 a.m. Up at 8.30. Out after breakfast, to Beacon Hill. This elevation 500 feet, on which we have a cairn built, flag staff and drum elevated is rocky. The hard gray blue limestone stratified, but not slaty cleaved, comes to earth at the summit, the strike being due E and W. and dipping south at an angle of 70°. Great slabs protrude from the ground, and many of these are splendidly marked with ripplings, also rain-drops, and I noticed some marks that might be annelid crawlings. However, I took as much of the ripple-markings as I could carry.

I remarked that on every slab, and in various planes of stratification where there were ripple marks the set of the wave mark was to the S. true.

Extended my walk to the small lakes, <(Drift-wood)> the snow though melting generally, is not running off in water with the rapidity I expected, as it trickles down the slopes in small gutters it is wonderful to notice what an amount of vitality the case hardened earth brings forth through its influence. Kneeling down I found that scum was acting as a raft to myriads of minute insects, the (little brown larvae looking fellows which I found previously under stones.) In the green confervoid, awakened into new life, hundreds of worm like creatures probably larvae of diptera, were wriggling and clinging. The buds or spores of the brown gelatinous confervoid, swollen to the size of boiled grain of tapioca floated with the miniature rivers, and the withered tufts of hypnum and mosses are assuming a brilliant green hue. Two King Ducks ♂ & ♀ were on each of these fresh water

---

[1] Osborn, in *Arctic Blue Books*, 1855, p. 246: 'The carpenter reports it all as drift pine larch (probably American); stacked it to dry for our return.'

lakes, and I walked over an old nest with the hatched eggshells of an eider, probably this species, close to the border of the lake. The Long-tailed skuas when hovering over a Lemming flutter with rapid beat of wings tail expanded and drooped after the manner of *F. tinnunculus*.[1] I tried to unravel the Knot, they are the most perverse birds I have ever met with. Saw 1 Turnstone. 2 Sanderlings and 3 *T. canutus*.

Tuesday 4 July 1876
The last two days have been beautiful for the Arctic, but today it was overcast, cold and snowing. The falling off the water supply in the ravines was very perceptible.

Two days ago Dr Moss came to the ship with the news that he had discovered a wonderful deposit of sea-weeds dead crustaceans &c in snow 14 feet above level of the sea – and that no hypothesis that he could imagine would account for the extraordinary phenomenon. I took the first opportunity and accompanied Captain Nares to the spot, which is where the stream from the N. fork of the Big Ravine (82°.29′) enters the sea, and on the gravel ridge and snow-foot which marks the line of spring tides, we found the deposit in question.

I felt no hesitation in solving the supposed problem; the sea-ware[2] and dead animals and some shells, were nothing more or less than the rejectamenta of last autumn's spring-tides, amongst the stuff, I picked up two pieces of stearine,[3] a few inches of White-line with dockyard brand in it, the Captain gathered some bristles of a tent-brush, and on enquiry I found that at this spot and close to the waters edge, Egerton camped last autumn. The sea-weed was chiefly semi-decomposed *Laminaria*, the animals Arcturus, Nymphon, and the various description of shrimps we got near the ship. In the roots of the Laminaria where some dead and much decayed shells of Trochus,[4] and Trichotropis,[5] and an annular compressed Serpula,[6] which I had frequently found in the Pleistocene mud-beds and had ignorantly considered a species of Planorbis, vide journal 18th. June. Saw 4 King Ducks on the lake, and on the borders of Drift-Wood Lake 11 *Tringa canutus*, feeding in company on the mud. When scared they rose in a flock but soon separated into pairs and took different directions, I augur from this that they are not yet sitting. Found two nests of lemming in the snow, comfortable round homes of grass about the size of a small cocoa-nut. Dug down into a burrow in the earth, about a foot horizontally and found a similar nest at the end.
N.B. Captain Nares picked up a small piece of drift-wood at the shore level it is a query whether or not this may not have been washed down by the stream from the mud-beds. Giffard & Conybeare left with dogs in direction of Lincoln Bay overland.

Wednesday 5 July 1876 Musk-Sheep Killed!!
Parr went out with his gun after breakfast, and 2 miles and a half from the ship sighted three musk-sheep a young bull and two cows; two of the seamen walking in that direction were sent back to the ship with the news, and about 12 m., several of our sportsmen left,

[1] *Falco tinnunculus*, European kestrel.
[2] Seaweed.
[3] A mixture of fatty acids used in making candles; presumably Feilden found candles or candle stubs.
[4] A genus of top-shaped sea snails.
[5] Boreal hairy snail.
[6] A genus of marine annelid tube worms.

they surrounded the beasts who moved in the direction of Parr, who shot two with bullets from his fowling piece, and the third with a ~~ball~~ <wire> cartridge.[1]

These animals were thin and in poor condition, and casting their fine winters wool which in summer drops off and gives place to long hair, this wove remains longer on the withers than else-where and at ~~the~~ a little distance gives the appearance of a white saddle.

An abundant supply of fresh meat is a real God-send for us, who are working, as hitherto every scrap of fresh meat has been given to the sick. Weight of meat [*blank*].

Engaged writing a report for Captain Nares on proceedings in my department since entering Smith's Sound last year.

Sunk net baited with pork through crack 8 fathoms.

Thursday 6 July 1876 Musk-Sheep
Just before breakfast a fine ♂ musk-sheep was alongside of the ship – several turned out and surrounded him, Dr Moss shot him, being close to the ship it was a good opportunity of preparing a specimen, hauled him alongside and took off hide, saved as much of the bones as possible and sunk them for shrimps to pick. Weight of flesh brought on board 211 lbs. light Heart liver Kidneys 12 lbs

The musk-sheep has a small gall bladder; large stomach filled with herbage, numerous large *taenia*[2] in big intestine, and *filaria*[3] in *duodenum*. Out most of the night saw a flock of 6 Knots and another of 24. Seemed to be paired but collect together for feeding, one pair of Sanderlings, 5 Brent geese in South Ravine, found a pair of Ster. longicaudatus breeding, merely a depression in the ground. ♀ so bold that she attacked me, coming within three feet of my head, threw stones at her until one hit her, not very hard but sufficient to make her alight some 30 yards off and recover her breath. Changed net to 10 fathoms. First day I have seen gnats flying in flocks only caught one though. Our blue-bottle flies quickly collected round the offal of the musk-sheep, one I captured, deposited her eggs in the bottle. Gathered a considerable number of lichens. My small gun came to grief today.

[July 7th. 1853. Drift wood abundant in Queens channel, some very aged pieces were found 40 to 50 feet above the sea level, on ancient beaches I expect. v. S. Osborn P.P. p. 249.[4]]

Friday 7 July 1876
Back to ship at 2 o'c. a.m. Weather turned over-cast and sleety. Poor old Bruin hauled in ice after breakfast, half an hour afterwards found dead in a pool on the floe, verdict "Found drowned", Egerton took off his hide, I opened him, all organs healthy. From stomach to rectum I slit up, not a sign of an Entozoa in him. These brutes dread water, I saw the old blackguard at 2 this morning seated on a floe-berg and giving vent to most dismal wolfish howls, this was because he was surrounded by water, in many places not requiring him to swim, and yet he was afraid to cross. I wonder if wolves show same antipathy to water. We know Eskimo dogs can swim well, for Boss proved it, on the way up. [*Margin*: Plant] Oxyria[5] in flower.

---

[1] The Eley patent wire cartridge was a paper-covered wire basket filled with lead shot and bone dust. Harding, *Eley Cartridges*.

[2] *Taenia*: tapeworm.

[3] Roundworms.

[4] Osborn in *Arctic Blue Books*, 1855, p. 249.

[5] *Oxyria digyna*, mountain sorrel.

Saturday 8 July 1876

Out after breakfast and back by 5 p.m. <in direction of "The Dean"> Giffard and Conybeare returned with dog-sledge from the direction of Lincoln Bay. They found the snow on the plateau almost impassable. It rained nearly all the time I was out, temperature about +40° it seems to have a great effect on the snow combined with the rain. Saw many Knots all flying high in flocks, coming from the Uplands to their feeding grounds near our lakes. Shot 3, also a pair of Ster. longicaudatus. 8 Brent geese killed and 5 Hareldas 1 ♂ & 4 ♀ by Parr and White.[1] White also saw two Ivory Gulls? Found a plant I do not know, an ichneumon fly, and some confervoids. Walking very disagreeable in the hollows up to waist in snow and water, acheing [*sic*] in every bone either from rheumatism or scurvy, damp weather brings it out.

At No 3 Lake across Big Ravine the snow has uncovered a section of mud-bed cut through <300 ft> by stream. Found several pieces of wood *in situ* in the mud, all this drift-wood I am sure that we find on the land has been washed out of the mud-beds, in confirmation with the drift wood found Astartes and Laminaria stems. The ichneumon fly was crawling listlessly on the snow. The little slate coloured insect is crawling in myriads on the snow, and floating in groups on the fresh water.

The night turned out beautiful, temperature +45°.

? White's description of an Ivory Gull, "About the size of tern slate coloured but without a black-head". Is it not lamentable that men should volunteer statements on subjects they know nothing about.

[June 9th. 1853. Grove P.P. p. 270. N. shore Grinnell Land, finds traces of an Esquimaux hut.[2]]

Sunday 9 July 1876

After service, skinned and cleaned head of musk-sheep the big ♂ and made it a<l>lready for going into pickle – skinning ♂ *Harelda glacialis* took up the dinner. ♀ *T. canutus*, after dinner, and mounting Anoplura[3] till suppertime, labelling and arranging. Can't make out the plant found yesterday. An ice worn pebble taken from mud-bed, *in situ* yesterday, shows under the lens minute Serpulæ attached! [*Margin*: Serpulae on ice worn Erratic]

From surface to	+32°.2.	Small crack outside of hummock.
6f[th] to 9f[th]	+31°.8	200 feet outside and clear of any
12f[th] to bottom	+29°.	floe-berg
about 12[?"] fathoms		
air	+37°.2	Temperatures taken by Captain Nares
Snow on ice	+32°.15	Casellas reversible Thermo.[4] acting.
Tide – half-flood.		well and agreeing with two others
		ordinary deep-sea, and mercurial.

Egerton found nest of *Som. spectabilis* 5 eggs – fresh, he kindly gave me two.

---

[1] George White, engineer.

[2] James Blair Grove, mate, *Assistance* 1852–4, *Arctic Blue Books*, 1855, p. 270.

[3] Sucking lice.

[4] The Miller–Casella reversible thermometer was a Six's thermometer with a double bulb, for measuring maximum and minimum temperatures. For Six's thermometer, see Austin and McConnell, 'James Six, FRS'. But see also Nares, 'Negretti's Reversible Thermometer', *Nature*, 7 Dec. 1876, p. 116. 'In obtaining some deep-sea

D[r] Moss has settled today to his own satisfaction that the northern part of Greenland is covered with a 'mer de glace' – No one else here is willing to hazard such an opinion, considering the distance we are off. It is contrary to May's opinion who ascended a hill 2000 feet high near Crossing Harbour,[1] and describes the back country of Greenland as round-topped hills covered with snow. I must add, however, that D[r] Moss's range of observation only extended to his range of vision from the 'crow's nest', and there was a very strong mirage. Giffard's aneroid gave an elevation of 2300 feet, as the high land he reached during his last trip.

Monday 10 July 1876
At 1 a.m., a strong breeze from S. set in, and continued. A shooting party left for Dumb-Bell Lake with satellite sledge. Markham, Pullen, May, Mitchell and Conybeare.

[July 9th. 1853. S. Osborn. P.P. p. 250. Picked up a piece of drift wood, a foot long and four inches in girth, half a mile from the sea, and fifty feet above highwater mark of spring tides. Saw many deer. seldom five miles of coast without a herd of deer upon it.[2]]
[July 10th. 1853. S. Osborn P.P. p. 251. Cheyne Islands. Any amount of Eiders breeding also terns which later laid their eggs on the bare and heated stones. Only trace of Esquimaux since leaving Northumberland Sound, found here.[3]]

Tuesday 11 July 1876
Got ♂ *Ovibos* into pickle, Captain Nares allowing me to draw the brine from two casks of Salt beef for this purpose. Headed up Musk-ox, and marked barrel No. 14. If it reaches England safely, it will be a noble specimen in a museum. labelling and putting away gear all day. D[r] Moss brought a ♀ *S. longicaudatus* which he had knocked down with a stone, he was so much pestered with the animals attacks that he was obliged to stone her off in self defence. Left the ship with Lieut. Parr at 8 p.m., carrying with our guns about 28 lbs each. The stream in north ravine running strong, we crossed at the shallowest spot we could find, where the stream spread out the water came to our knees, but was running so strong that we had just as much as we could do to keep our foot-hold. A few inches more would have been too much for me. The water nearly benumbed me. We took off our foot-gear after crossing, wrung it out and proceeded. A pair of geese (*B. Brenta*) and a flock of 28 Knots. (*T. canutus*) feeding in the bottom of the next ravine these last as wild as hawks. Took it easily and walked along the gravel ridges parallel to the shore, at No. 1 Bay turned a knee deep stream by crossing on the floe – low-tide, all the snow melted, the pools not above a foot deep, travelling good. Half a mile from Mushroom Point took Ster. long.

temperatures, which proved the existence of a sub-stratum of water warmer than that at the surface, the instruments used were the reversible thermometers of Negretti and Zambra's, not Casella's. The Casella thermometer was used on other occasions.' Nares was here correcting a mistake which he had made in his *Official Report* to the Admiralty. An abbreviated version of this report had been published in *Nature*: Nares, 'Captain Nares's Report'.It was also published separately by John Murray: Nares, *Official Report of the Recent Arctic Expedition*. The physical results of the expedition were published in *Arctic Blue Books*, LII, pp. 3–146.

[1] Egerton showed Parr and George Bryant (the captain of *Discovery*'s sledge crew) the 'Crossing Floe' from Cape Rawson on 17 March 1876; it stretched 'for a distance of six or seven miles across Robeson Channel': Nares, *Narrative* (1878) I, p. 272.

[2] Osborn in *Arctic Blue Books*, 1855, p. 250.

[3] Osborn in *Arctic Blue Books*, 1855, p. 251.

nest 2 eggs. Had to ward off the attack of one of the birds with my gun barrel, struck her once. Yellow and white *draba* in bloom, also *Sax. cernua*? *Oxyria, Salix*. Sax. oppo. is abundant and in glorious bloom, some of the brows are tinged purple with the flowers of this plant. The number of stamens in this plant is irregular varying from 9 to 11. At Mushroom Pᵗ. 3 *Hareldas* in a pool one ♂ and 2 ♀, they tried to elude us by diving, one of these birds got into the centre of the pond and stood a regular bombardment before it was killed. At high water mark many bleached shells of *Trochus helicina*?[1] shrimps and *Laminaria* cast up. Shot a ♂*Phal. Lobatus*,[2] one of a pair on the Harelda pond, doubtless they are nesting in the vicinity, the ♂ of this species is smaller and legs brightly coloured, than the ♀. The Captain saw a (the) wolf beyond north ravine just before we set out from ship, but we did not fall in with his tracks.

[*Continuation of text in margin*: White accompanied us to north ravine stream after leaving us he proceeded inland, and found the nesting place of Nyctea. 7 young ones, and one unhatched egg. he killed one of the old birds. I think <♀ from the plumage.]

[*Here Feilden inserted a coloured sketch of Feilden and Parr botanizing; see Plate 17.*]

[July 12th. 1853. S. Osborn. P.P. p. 252. Observed the skeleton of a large and old bear on the high ground.[3]]

Wednesday 12 July 1876

The brows along the coast are mostly clear of snow, and nice walking, but ankle deep rivulets fed from the melting snows higher up, occur frequently. Bagged at 5 a.m. Up at 1 p.m., a ♂ Harelda on pool bagged him. After breakfast started with our packs for Dumb-bell Harbour tent. Mid way got a *S. longi.* nest with 2 eggs passed skeleton of Musk sheep. Which must have been torn and scattered about by wolves. Four *Phoca fetida* were lying on the ice in Ravine Bay. During the walk added several plants to our herbarium, and a moth. Made a cup of tea at tent, then went along <south> side of inner harbour, we walked over mud-beds much over-layed [*sic*] with the washed down river gravels, found a considerable quantity of drift-wood in the mud 50 feet up. Multitudes of large Astartes scattered about. Another nest of Skua. two eggs. Saw a Snowy owl leave a hillock when we approached within a quarter of a mile, much such a position as we found them nesting at on 24ᵗʰ. June. Walked to the spot and there were 3 little blind owlets the colour of puff balls and 4 eggs with 3 dead lemmings resting in a hollow scooped out of the ground. The ♂ owl (the smaller bird) came towards us followed by a skua, which pestered it greatly, it passed within range, and fell dead to a charge of No. 6 from each of our guns. We waited by the nest long and patiently but the ♀ was too wary, she seated herself on a bank 4 or 500 yards off and though much disturbed by skuas would not leave the spot, as a skua made a swoop close past her head the owl jumped off the ground about a couple of feet, coming down on the same spot. Getting tired of waiting we ascended the hills, in the direction of Mt. Pullen. Mud-beds up to an elevation of 600 ft. These are much intersected with torrent courses. Found various bones in them and took one well ice-scratched erratic from the mud, near bye [*sic*] came [4]

[1] Now *Margarites helecinus*, spiral margarite, a species of sea snail.
[2] Wilson's phalarope.
[3] Osborne in *Arctic Blue Books*, 1855, p. 252.
[4] The entry for 12 July 1876 runs straight into that for 13 July, so text reads 'near bye came across', interrupted by date and heading 'Foxes'.

Thursday 13 July 1876 <u>Foxes.</u>

across considerable numbers of the four sided internal corals of some Alcyonarian[1] deposited in the mud with Astartes and Saxicava. Further inland heard yelping of Foxes, saw one standing on a rocky ridge. Parr went one side, and I the other, he knocked the ♂ over which crept in under some heavy rocks, and rushed the ♀ and he dropped her with the other barrel, she also crawled under the rocks, though she had a foreleg broken, and a hind-leg shattered, seeing her crawling into the recesses of the rocks polished her off with a charge of No. 9. We were unfortunate enough not to secure the ♂.

The foxes den was strewed around with dead lemmings, and evidently the foxes store them up. In one cache, I found 18, in another 14, several caches of 4 and twos and threes everywhere about buried lightly. All these lemmings were in summer pelt, and several were ♀. A ♀ lemming that I took from alongside the Snowy owls nest, had 6 foetal young in her uterus. Back to tent and bagged by 5 a.m.

Up at 1 p.m., went back to Snowy Owls nest, female as wary as yesterday, Parr lay in wait I moved up the hill, the owl returned to nest and was shot by him. One of the lemmings left alongside of the nest yesterday had been eaten, and half of the other devoured. The mud-bed out of which we took the corals yesterday is 200 f. by aneroid the foxes cairn 450 fᵗ. Looking round that spot today, we found a hole or holes that evidently had been tenanted by Ermines, and in one foxes cache of lemmings we found a dead Ermine (fly-blown) also the head of another, both had been bitten through the head. We came across portions of a hare hidden and indeed the whole place was a foxes larder. About half a mile further on heard the yelping of another pair of foxes, went to the spot, but the animals retreated under the rocks, and though they kept up a great snarling would not come out. After waiting sometime we walked on the plateau hoping to meet with Knots. No success but heard them. This plateau is extremely barren and cheerless as the snow has only just left. Returning by second Foxes den saw Mᴿˢ Reynard's bright eyes peeping out of a hole between the rocks, so I shot her, but her body slipped back into a position which we could not reach. The male came to investigate the cause of death of Mᴿˢ R. and I shot him, we managed to pull him out with our guns, minus head. One of their caches at this spot contained at least 50 lemmings in summer plumage, portions of Hare and Brent Geese were included in this larder.

Friday 14 July 1876

We found Ranunculus nivalis[2] very diminutive in flower at 250 elevation. Plenty of Oxyria – sorrel off which we grazed. White and yellow Draba grew luxuriously about the Foxes dens. The weather turned thick and cold so we made our way back to the tent which we reached at 10 o'c. <a.m.>. Picked up a large *Buccinum*[3] washed out of the mud beds on our way back. Saw a pair of Knots flying high, wild as hawks. In the foxes den one of the geese wings was that of a young bird, being speckled, and of course a bird of a former season, so that the foxes return to the same den yearly, the head of a Hare was pure white, winter garb and must have been killed early in the year as the Hare puts on a brown nose-patch in May, moreover we saw Foxes tracks with returning daylight, Musk ox bones had also been

[1] Soft corals.
[2] Snow buttercup.
[3] Whelk.

carried to the den. Began to snow shortly after our return, and the sun disappeared, mist enveloped us, and when I looked out of the tent at 5 o'c. our Snowy owls were covered in the water, and our gear on the tent guys was dripping. Not being able to see for mist, and having no change of clothes we were forced to spend the day in our bags. I skinned some birds and Parr did all the cooking, fetching water, cleaning up and putting the tent in order. When going to the shore to wash, we found a large *Hippolyte*[1] dead and a shell of *Trichotropis* attached to roots of laminaria, also *Astarte* and some Polyzoa.[2] The ♂ Phal. fulicarius is not so large or as highly coloured as the ♀. We also gathered close to high water mark a moss in fructification.

Saturday 15 July 1876

Our Lemming *Myodus torquatus* breeds early and often for in the Foxes caches we found them of all sizes down to that of a mouse and one female opened was gravid. I opened ♂ & ♀ Foxes could detect no *Entozoa* in them. Every Lemming killed by the Foxes, has had a tooth put through the skull, ditto the Ermines. During an interval of snowing we went out botanizing for a couple of hours, then skinned two Snowy Owls, and a Fox. Parr had a stalk after a Phoca fetida lying on the ice of Dumb-bell Harbour, but when struck it managed to slip down its hole, by 7 a.m. the sun came out, we made a cup of tea and started at 8 a.m., we returned to camp and bagged at 3.30 p.m.

Our tramp this day was a most weary and unsuccessful one, and devoted to the search for the nesting place of *T. Canutus*, we sprung several pairs from marshy spots, where they were evidently feeding, as they rose wild and flew away high, with a shrill cry. We saw a flock of a dozen or more feeding in company with a ♂ Snow Bunting near a small lake, but they did not allow us to approach within a hundred yards, when they rose wild as hawks.

Sunday 16 July 1876

We got out of our bags at 12 p.m. And left the tent at 1.45 determined to assault the highlands as the last hope of finding the Knot nesting. We ascended some 500 feet to the plateau behind our camp, misty, but steering by compass we walked some miles over a most dreary looking flat wilderness, the fog clearing we found ourselves near the base of Mount Pullen and the Dean. The plateaux over which we had walked was plotted off into beds by means of peebles taking pentagonal and hexagonal arrangement. This requires a great deal of consideration to work out. We ascended the Dean Mount, and saw two Knots, which were feeding on mossy swampy ground, they also rose wild without the slightest hope of their nesting place being anywhere in the neighbourhood. On our return route to the camp saw three Hares, we chased them but they were very wild, the Arctic hare when pursued always makes up hill.

At the Foxes nest, I stopped to look for insects under the stones and found many minute ones, and added a spider to the collection that I had not hitherto preserved.

Back to the tent by 10 o'c. found Egerton and 11 men camped alongside of us, on their way to bring in the boats. We got some pemmican from the crew, and made a hearty meal.

[1] A genus of shrimp.

[2] 'A class of compound or "colonial" aquatic (chiefly marine) invertebrate animals (sometimes reckoned as a group of Mollusca), of small size and various forms, often plant-like; popularly called moss-animalcules, sea-mosses, sea-mats'. *OED*.

Egerton had walked over to Captain Markham's shooting camp, leaving us a notice to quit as the tent we occupied was required for his party. E. returned at 6 p.m., with 4 Brent Geese on his back. Markham and his party had killed 13 of these birds yesterday on a Lake. These birds were all moulting and unable to fly. The sledge crew invited us to dinner we had a good feed, and then Parr and I left at 9. o'c. reaching Mushroom Point in one hour and a half, where we camped. [*Margin*: *Phalaropus fulicarius*] Put up a *Phalarope* from the pond near to the tent, and had a great chase after a pair of Harelda glacialis which we secured, after a large expenditure of shot. Then we saw two Brent Geese [*Entry runs on into 17 July*]

Monday 17 July 1876 <u>Mushroom Point</u>
with 3 young ones near the shore, we shot the old birds and took the downy young ones as specimens. Both of the old birds were in good feather and showed no signs of moult but the old birds were most assiduous in taking charge of the young, both goose and gander fluttered above the little ones, and urged them to the cracks in the floe, evidently thinking that once on the water they would be safe. It seemed very cruel to kill these poor birds but we wanted fresh meat. Then we left the shore and took a walk of a mile or two on the uplands but saw no living creature – we returned to the tent at 1 a.m. About 2 a.m., as we were getting one of the above mentioned geese ready for our meal. White hove in sight from the ship and he joined us at our meal, he had walked from the ship, and had found a nest of *Ster. longicaudatus* with 2 eggs and a nest of *Sterna macrura* with two eggs both of these lots he smashed. [*Margin*: Sterna macrura nesting] We sat talking till 4 o'c. on the night of the 11th. [*sic*] After parting with us at the stream, White went up the North Ravine, and found a Snowy owls nest containing 6 young ones, and one egg, he killed the old bird the ♂ and brought the young onboard.

We bagged till 8 o'c. a.m. and awoke bitterly cold, damp ground and no coverlid [*Margin*: *Bombus*] (Saw a *Bombus*) and started for the ship at 11 o'c. reached the ship at 2 o'c. we were able to walk over the ground most of the way only occasional patches of snow which we waded through. [*Margin*: *Trout*] Passing the lake in north fork of N. Ravine we saw many trout leaping and running from the shallows into deeper water.[1]

Tuesday 18 July 1876 <u>Floeberg Beach</u>
Busy during the day, skinning, mounting slides, and putting away gear. Aldrich took a party of men with the seine net on a sledge to a lake far side of Big Ravine they caught about 3 doz *Charr* 6 of which were given me for preservation. [*Margin*: *Salmo arcturus*] Norris[2] brought onboard some twenty *Lemmings* in summer the toes of these animals loose [*sic*] the under half of the double claw. Parr obtained a nest of *Som. spectabilis* containing three eggs shot female. Went out at night with my gun did not see a single living creature A large crack from Cape Rawson running E. To the ship by 2 a.m., 19th. instant.

---

[1] Arctic char, *Salvelinus alpinus*, then known as *Salmo arcturus*, is closely related to salmon and trout. It is the only species of lake fish on northernmost Ellesmere Island. Albert Günther in Nares, *Narrative of a Voyage*, 1878, II, pp. 221–2, also describes another suppositious char, *Salmo naresii*; this species has not been accepted.

[2] George Norris, carpenter's crew.

Wednesday 19 July 1876 <u>Floeberg Beach</u>
Skinned birds till 4 a.m. got up at 8 a.m., Worked at specimens all day. Giffard shot a *Sanderling* which he brought me. Moss walked to Black Cape and shot a Hare and 2 geese. The Hare was quite white, save tip of ears which were mouse-gray and a small streak of same colour from the apex of skull to snout.

Thursday 20 July 1876 <u>Floeberg Beach</u>
To bed this morning at 3 o'c., up at 8. Changed spirit in numerous specimens. It takes me an hour daily to arrange and change the papers of the small botanical collection.

Captain Nares, Parr and Giffard, started for Cape Union to have a look at the ice.

Went out after tea with my gun saw no living animal. [*Margin*: Plants] Gathered a few plants. Sax. opposi. is now wilting, S. flaggellaris [*sic*], S. Nivalis[1]? and *S. cernua*? coming into bloom. The two last are only sparsely found, all three last like damp spots. *Ranunculus* is in full bloom, *Oxyria* ditto. Stellaria just coming out. Taraxacum and *Papaver* not yet in flower.

A ♀ *Lepus glacialis* shot yesterday was pure white with the exception of ears which are mouse-gray, from apex of cranium to snout ditto, with a slight yellow tinge on forehead and bridge of nose.

Unless the Lemmings change their claws with the seasons there are two species here. The ones killed in winter had large bifurcating claws on their fore-paws, those procured during the summer, have fine pointed claws.[2] Norris carpenters-mate brought about fifty onboard the other evening, he put them in turned up empty barrels, they are confident ravenous little animals when *Sax.* or other flowering plant was presented to them they rose on their hind legs to receive it. Some got out on the deck, but our two cats though they hunted them refused to eat them. [*Margin*: Glaucus Gull] A *Glaucus gull* I observed sailing over the ship. A good deal of commotion amongst the floes outside. [*Margin*: Plants & insects] *Diptera* nestle at night in the blossoms of Sax. oppo., Ranunculus, and Draba. Mustard and cress on shore in leaf.

Friday 21 July 1876 <u>Floeberg Beach.</u>
Arranged plants after breakfast. Skinned *Calidris arenaria* killed on 19th. inst. ♂, with hatching marks on breast. Can find no *Anoplura* on skins of *Som. spectabilis*, nor have I discovered fleas or lice on Eskimo dogs, *Vulpes lagopus* or *Ovibos moschatus* <or Lemming> though I have searched diligently. Spring tide today Some commotion in the ice, a large piece of floe about stern moved upwards.

Moss was out at a crack yesterday 45 fathoms, getting water, on stuff brought up by lead I saw *Polycistina*, and he said that he had got *Globigerina*.[3]

Blew all day from S.S.W. and with spring tide caused considerable commotion in the ice outside of our protecting line of Floe-bergs. At 10 p.m. the floe (young ice) on our starboard quarter cracked about 30 feet from the ship with a considerable report, a rush

---

[1] *Saxifraga flagellaris*: whiplash saxifrage; *Saxifraga nivalis*: snow saxifrage, now known as *Micranthes nivalis*.

[2] The collared lemming, *Dicrostonyx groenlandicus*, occurs throughout the Canadian Arctic archipelago. Its foreclaws in winter experience significant seasonal growth. There is only one species, although there are local races. See Banfield, *Mammals of Canada*, p. 194; and Blix, *Arctic Animals*, pp. 151–2. See also p. 200 above.

[3] Polycistina: a class of radiolarians, protozoa with mineral skeletons. *Globigerina*: a genus of planktonic Foraminifera, which commonly have mineral shells.

of water came from below, the portion of the floe sticking round the ship, canted up, and became dry. The ship settled somewhat. At high tide about 11.30 p.m., there was a lane of water, running N & S outside of our Floe-bergs.

Put up insects on slides.

Saturday 22 July 1876 Floeberg Beach

At 1 a.m. four of Egerton's party, Simmonds, Cane, and two *Discovery*'s arrived dragging satellite sledge with over 200 lbs of Musk-sheep meat and 15 Brent Geese, killed by Markham's party during the week. 320 lbs in all.

When skinning birds shot off the nest up here, I find that though they are poor in flesh and flabby, the belly bare and skinned puckered, to compensate for the loss of feathers, a thick layer of fat remains on that portion of the body. It blew from S.W. the greater part of the day increasing about 3 p.m. and falling at 11 p.m. The crack outside of our floe-bergs is increasing in width. Captain Nares, Giffard and Parr returned from Cape Union at 11 p.m., having left the tent there at 3 p.m. 14 statute miles. The Captain seems satisfied with the condition of the ice, there was a lead along shore from a little south of Cape Rawson as far as Lincoln Bay. There was a lead on the other side of the channel from Newman Bay to Cape Lupton, south towards Cape Constitution, Captain N. thinks there was a water sky.

They brought skull of Musk-ox measuring 26 in. along curve of horns a single egg of Tetrao picked up on a ridge 2 Uria grylle, and some plants, also a slab of ripple marked stone from Cape Union.

They shot 1 Hare and 6 geese. Parr tells me that the coat of this animal was tinged with slate colour.

Sunday 23 July 1876 Open Water Outside of Ship. Floeberg Beach

Blowing fresh from S. all day. I have just been looking out from the main top. 6 p.m. and there is a lead of water stretching from beyond P^t. Sheridan to Cape Rawson, of half a mile in width and without any ice on it, when the wind lulls, the pack will close in again, but still it looks very cheerful and we may count on a release in good time.

[*Margin*: Plants] The flora north of Cape Rawson with the exception of Sax. oppos. is certainly more diminutive than that gathered on the shores of Robeson Channel, the plants I have collected between this point and 83° N. are certainly smaller than those brought by Parr from Cape Union.

Parr does not agree with me in this and says he only brought particularly good specimens.

I walked to Cape Rawson to-day and on the way put up two Knots from a piece of marshy ground, they rose very wild, with a shrill cry. [*Margin*: *Skuas eating insects*] 4 Long-tailed Skuas flew past me and alighted at no great distance, they then commenced a search for insects which they continued with great perseverance, hunting amongst the small stones. I shot one of these birds, and it disgorged a large number of spiders, diptera and caterpillars. [*Margin*: Skuas catching Lemmings] Shortly before I had been watching a bird of this species catching lemmings, it hovered like a Kestrel in search of mice and its rapid swoop and capture of the lemming was very graceful. [*Margin*: Lemmings] On turning over a large stone I found a gravid lemming I put her back into her retreat. She stood up on her rump and barked at me, they are bold little creatures. A number of these little rodents were brought on board a few days ago by the sailors, some 40 or 50, and were put in barrels, the old ones quickly killed the young ones by biting them in the neck. When bunches of herbage such as grass and saxifrage were thrown into the barrel, the lemmings ran to it and munched it up greedily uttering a satisfied little grunt.

Egerton and party came in with the boats at 10 p.m. He kindly brought my sack left at the tent, also several fine pieces of coniferous drift-timber, one large trunk, off which Egerton sawed some 3 feet. It was brought from Driftwood Bay, where Markham & Egerton say many tons are stranded. [*Margin*: *Fulmar*] E. picked up a dead *Procellaria glacialis*, at Harley Spit on 19th. inst, stomach empty and bird in very poor condition, he brought me head, wings, & feet. [*Margin*: *Shells*] Also a fine *Buccinum*[1] and several specimens of *Trochus* from North Dumbell Bay.

Monday July 24 1876. <u>Floeberg Beach</u>

Returned to the ship at 2 a.m., shortly before 4 o'c. Markham and his party returned having been 12 days out at the tent on Dumbell Lake. He brought me the cranium of a very large *Ursus maritimus* found at full 40 feet elevation at Drift-wood Bay. May shot a fine *Nyctea scandiaca* on the 15th. they found the nest with seven young ones in it, it was put into the cage on board ship along with the four young ones belonging to White.

A *Ster. longicaudatus* I shot yesterday though paired, was an immature bird – minus the long tail feathers – and mou*l*ted on forehead. During the day several 6 lbs charges of powder were exploded under the ice on our port quarter, with the object of freeing the ship from her cradle of ice. Mitchell brought me 3 Charr he found dead on the shore of Dumbell Lake, and a little one that he caught alive. Egerton also brought me a fish that he picked up on the floe or beach – a *Merlangus*?[2] By 9 o'c. tonight the pack had firmly closed on us. [*Margin*: *Ivory Gull*] At 9.30 p.m. a *Larus eburneus* passed the ship flying between us and the shore.

Tuesday 25 July 1876. <u>Floeberg Beach</u>

Dr Moss brought in a Knot which he thought he must have put off its nest. [*Margin*: *Knot nesting*] I skinned this bird for Markham, and found that it was a diseased bird, probably wounded, its inability to fly well, made him think it was nesting.

Out of a pair of *S. longi.* that I shot yesterday the ♀ was much longer than the ♂, and yet not an adult bird, its head and breast were barred. Contents of stomach a lemming several caterpillars spiders, flies & diptera. [*Margin*: *Dovekie*] Skinned a ♀ *Uria grylle* one of a pair shot by Parr in Robeson Channel Lat. 82°20′ N on the 21st. Stomach of *Uria Anonyx nugax*.[3]

Skinned a nestling Snowy owl for Markham. Went out after tea with my gun, searching for Knots nests remained out till 3 o'c. a.m. of 26th. Saw flocks <of 20 to 30> of Knots feeding near the borders of a lake, they rose wild & with a shrill cry, when I got within a quarter of a mile of them.

---

[1] A genus of medium-sized sea snails.

[2] Arctic whitefish, coalfish: not part of the expedition's report (Nares, *Narrative of a Voyage*), and probably misidentified, however tentatively, here.

[3] A small marine amphipod.

PART V: OUT OF THE ICE AND
HOMEWARD BOUND
26 JULY–28 OCTOBER 1876

Wednesday 26 July 1876. <u>Floeberg Beach.</u>
May has most kindly given me some excellent gold-leaf tobacco, enough to last me for three months. For some months past I have been smoking the shag tobacco supplied to the ship, which the blue-jacket call 'graveyard' from its peculiar smell.

The ships company engaged all day in trying to put in the propeller of the screw.

The following order was posted in the ward-room.

'No Officer is to absent himself from the ship for more than three hours without the Captain's permission' sg. A. H. Markham.

Again went out after tea, to follow up my long and weary search for the nest of the Knot. I must have walked some hundreds of miles on the errand. I spend nearly every night out with my gun, though the sun's altitude is not appreciably lowered, yet the mid-night hours seem more tranquil. All nature appears to be in a state of repose. It is the same feeling as comes over one when walking home from a London ball at 4 a.m. on a June morning. I saw several parties of Knots and one Turnstone, they rose a long way out of shot.

[*Margin*: Diptera] The small midge with feathery ostrich plumes to its head is now out in millions, they rest torpidly on stones when the sun is clouded over, but a little sun-light brings them to life again.

Thursday 27 July 1876. <u>Floeberg Beach</u>
Yesterday they were unable to get the propeller into the shaft, as the water froze in the hole of the boss. The propeller remained on deck all night and in a temp of +36° to 40° absorbed sufficient heat to prevent the water freezing close to it for several minutes. [*Margin*: Whale] Egerton gave piece of vertebra of true whale which he picked up at Harley Spit, at an elevation of 40 feet. Four species of diptera are very common. The largest erratic in the neighbourhood is a block of fossiliferous limestone, resting at some 20 feet elevation above high-water mark, and abreast of the ship. The portion above ground measures 3 ft. in height by 7 ft. 2 in. long and 7 ft. broad, it is rounded but shows no ice-scratchings.

Friday 28 July 1876. <u>Floeberg Beach</u>
A breeze of wind from S.S.W. commenced at 1 a.m. and a lane of water from Cape Rawson to outside of our position soon formed. This lane kept open all day. Blasting ice to make a channel. So busy all day labelling and stowing collections that I had no time to leave the ship – I am afraid we shall be off without having had a chance of using either dredge or trawl in the Polar Basin.

Saturday 29 July 1876. <u>Floeberg Beach</u>
Crew employed blasting passage through our barrier. A fine sunshiny day. Walked with Giffard and Egerton to the north fork of Big Ravine. On returning the torrent had swollen, so much, from the melting of the snow that the water reached above our knees and we got properly wet. [*Margin: Lychnis*] Found *Lychnis apetala*[1] growing abundantly, Ranunculus, we brought back some pieces of an erratic full of garnets. We caught two moths and chased a large Daddy-long-legs *Tipula arctica*,[2] which eluded capture, Egerton, with the net being some distance off. Many fragments of drift-wood with sea-shells and sea-weed, roots and stalks of *laminaria* are exposed in sections of the mud-beds, near the lakes north of the torrent at an elevation of 250 feet.

Cocoons of hairy caterpillars in my cabin brought forth numerous parasitical flies. Kemish[3] brought me two young blind lemmings which he took from their nest a day or two since, there were five in it and the nest was under a stone, a loosely made structure of grass.

12 p.m., the pack tightly jammed against our barrier of floebergs.

Sunday 30 July 1876. <u>Floeberg Beach</u>
Cloudy with snow. Harley, Gore and Lawrence[4] were out with others of the men walking, and near the lake they were attracted to a Knot which appeared very tame. Harley threw a stone at it, but the bird only flew a short distance, he threw another stone and this time knocked the bird over, which began calling its note brought three little 'cheepers' from amongst the grass by the water-edge, which they brought onboard to me. The pleasure of obtaining proof of the nidification of *Tringa canutus* in these latitudes, was enhanced by the good feeling displayed by the men. They were more pleased than I was with the capture. I gave the three a bottle of port wine for their after dinner *sederunt*. These young ones appear to be about 3 days old, they partake so much of the general character of plumage of nestling *Tringae* that I cannot describe them by comparison.[5]

"Iris black, tip of mandibles dark brown, bill dark olive, getting lighter toward base of lower mandible, Legs dark olive, toes black, soles of feet greenish yellow, back of legs ditto, under part of throat satin white, breast and belly white, back beautifully mottled tortoise-shell, a black line passing from angle of eye to nares, and another from the gape in direction of ramus of lower mandible. The old bird accompanying them was the male, showing no signs of sitting on the breast, very fat, stomach filled with insects, young ditto chiefly *Diptera*? Legs and bill of adult very dark olive brown."

Monday 31 July 1876. <u>Leave Floeberg Beach</u>
Breeze sprung up from S.W. at 4 a.m., pack outside began to move off, orders given to get up steam. From 7 a.m. till 9 o'c. blasting the ice-cradle around the ship, ship cleared herself by 9.30 and was afloat. Pushed out through the barrier of floebergs, a fresh breeze blowing up channel, but a good lead took us down abreast of false Cape Union Lat. 82°21′,

---

[1] Nodding lychnis, aka nodding campion.
[2] An Arctic crane fly.
[3] George Kemish, wardroom steward, *Alert*.
[4] Daniel W. Harley, captain foretop; William I. Gore, stoker; Edwin Lawrence, gunner's mate.
[5] Levere, 'Early Searches'.

brought up at mid-day by heavy pack. Moored to the shore ice. Markham went ashore – 8 p.m., the pack moving in. [*Margin*: Dovekies] 2 Dovekies close to us in a pool. Retraced our course to near Black Cape and moored to shore ice in a more sheltered position, tide setting north, the pack moving rapidly N. with wind and tide. Captain advised me to pack two or three small tin cases, with samples of my collection and put them on deck ready to throw out on the ice, in case of the ship going. Sounding alongside of ice-foot <Floeberg> 9 & 11 fathoms.

[*Margin*: Absence of Pinnacled Rocks] Passing along these coasts, one is struck by the entire absence of stacks or pinnacles which we so often see on Coast-lines of recent elevation. I account for this by the levelling grinding pressure of the ice, which at each stage of elevation rounded off the rocks. The floebergs along which we are moored are colossal 40 feet in height above water in some cases, it is easy to understand that McClure found it necessary to top in his boats[1] whilst the *Investigator* was passing along the west side of Bank's Land. [*Margin*: Thickness of Floeberg] These floebergs are grounded in about 3 fathoms making the thickness of the floe from which they were detached about 60 feet.

Tuesday 1 August 1876. <u>Robeson Channel</u>
A snow-bunting a this season's bird alighted in the rigging. We lay alongside of our friendly floeberg till about 3 a.m. The pack was sitting N, then the ice began to jam, and floe came poking its nose into our shelter, and gave us notice to quit, by some very smart handling on the part of the skipper, only Egerton and the watch on deck and myself, the ship was squeezed out through some loose rubble, between the advancing floe and the ice-foot, and we managed to scrape south as far as the point from whence we had to retreat yesterday.

The coast we are passing under rises above us to a height of 1,000 or 1,200 feet the strata composing it have been pressed up into a vast series of anticlinal ridges, the strata consequently dip in various directions and are in many places greatly contorted. The talus at the base of the cliffs and a good way up is very steep. The sombre colouring of the rocks, the contrast with the snow and ice, the sun hidden behind a leaden mist and a strong gale howling down the ravines and whistling through the rigging combined with the knowledge of our perilous position is anything but enlivening. I was pleased to see an Ivory gull soaring over the ship. 9.30 a.m. under steam again, cast off, attempted to press through the pack to a fairish lead off Cape Union, ice closed in too rapidly, so we had to return to our shelter, merely an eddy made by a torrent coming down a ravine and a slight indentation in the land. Several times the edge of the pack moving N or S. grated against the side of the ship. Screw & rudder up, cooking utensils and tents on deck. [*Margin*: dredging] During one ease off of the ice, Egerton & I took small dredge in the dingy, having run the line through a block, and carried it out to the edge of the moving jostling pack, let the dredge drop in 20 fathoms and hurried on board, then we hauled in before the pack closed again. To our disgust the dredge brought up nothing but sand, the delta forming in front of the ravine. We deserved better luck for I never heard of dredging being carried out under similar circumstances.

We dipped up a couple of beautiful hydroids, very delicate they fell to pieces almost immediatly.

---

[1] Top in, i.e. to hoist his boats upwards and inwards, to avoid damaging them on ice or cliffs. M'Clure, *Discovery*, 2nd edn, p. 197.

Wednesday 2 August 1876. <u>Robeson Channel</u>
Under weigh about 7.30 a.m., got down the coast abreast of Cape Union, a couple of miles south, there we were stopped by the pack, we hauled in alongside of the land hummocks in a most dangerous position, the pack outside drifting past at the rate of knots to the south, and if we are nipped the old ship must go like an egg-shell, between the floebergs and the pack. We are lying so directly under the cliffs of Cape Union that we can see the heaths of Union through the wardroom sky-light as we sit at table. At 4 p.m. Nares pushed the ship into the pack letting her drift south with the tide. It is a ticklish experiment but not more hazardous than remaining with one side of the ship jammed against the nether mill-stone, waiting for the upper to descend. One of the cocoons of the large hairy caterpillar so common about Floeberg Beach, hatched to-day and produced a fine gray moth, body an inch long. Drifted south with tide about 2 miles past Arthur's Seat, 11.15 p.m. up steam. May makes Union 82°.14′.30″. Ice loosened setting N with southerly wind. By fine handling on the part of Nares we got into a fair lead and at 2.30 we were abreast of Lincoln Bay depot. A heavy pack off Cape Fred*erick* VII, but beyond that point much open water. At times we passed so close between the pack and ice-foot, that the ship barely had an inch to spare, and it is no exaggeration that I could with a landing net have picked up objects from the ice-foot when passing.

Thursday 3 August 1876. <u>Shift-Rudder Bay</u>
With both boilers going and a full head of steam we pushed through the pack off Cape Fred. VII by 4 a.m., and ran through tolerably clear water till 7.30 a.m. then we encountered some tremendous bumps off Cape Beechey as the ship was driven full speed against the ice. By 5 p.m. we moored to the land-ice in Shift-Rudder Bay, in the open water-space between the pack and the shore. One or two *Phoca hispida* seen. The following birds I have seen since leaving Floeberg Beach.

> August   1 – 1 Ivory. 2 Dovekies & Snow-bunting
>   2   7 Dovekies.
>   3   several Dovekies and at S.R. Bay

about 40 Brent Geese including goslings, 2 *Sterna macrura* with nestlings (latter taken) 7 Turnstones two killed. 6 Long-tail-Skuas. 3 Snow-buntings. Parr brought me a fine antler of *Cervus tarandus* taken from the mud-deposits close to the lake, and a piece of wood evidently worked by man. The pack is jammed outside of us.

Friday 4 August 1876. <u>Shift Rudder Bay</u>
No alteration in the ice. Went ashore about 10 a.m., with Markham, Parr & May, Freddy with Kayak and two blue-jackets, [*Margin: Bernicla Brenta*] attacked the Brent geese on the second lake, drove them to a narrow lead between ice and land, where we lay in ambush, fired 10 barrels into them before they could scramble on to the ice out of range, killed 30, repeated the manoeuvre killed 27. total bag 57. Fresh meat for all hands! left 5 alive, returned to ship by 2 p.m. only one of these birds appeared able to fly, and it escaped. [*Margin: Salmonoid*] Found dead trout by lake side. Shot 2 Turnstones, saw 7. Cartridges being expended, came across a flock of 8 *Tringa canutus* quite tame, they have nearly lost their summer garb, and have put on the gray winter plumage. A miserable day, cold, snowing with alternations of sleet. The snow that falls lies at an elevation of 200 feet.

[*Margin*: *Pedicularis*] Found *pedicularis hirsuta* in flower: rather abundant, we had lost this plant at Floe-berg Beach. A single *Larus Glaucus* flying over the lake whilst we were slaughtering the geese.

Saturday 5 August 1876. <u>Shift Rudder Bay</u>
Egerton and Malley started at 10 a.m. to walk overland to Discovery Bay. Got up steam trying to get into a lead that showed near shore for about four miles south, the ice jammed us, however, into our little sniggling[1] hole, and we had to remain 'As you was'. Remained for the rest of the day with steam at a ¼ and one hour's notice, wind in the evening blowing down channel from the north, it felt very cold with a temperature at +31°½. The ice has packed very heavily and is pressing inshore. The floes are large and heavy say 20 foot thick, varying from 10 to 30, and I think some are 40 foot thick.

All hands feasted to-day on Brent geese, we secured the goslings for the wardroom table and found them rare 'belly-timber'.

~~SATURDAY~~ *Sunday 6 August 1876.* <u>Shift-Rudder Bay</u>
Between 1 and 2 a.m. wind N.E., the pack came pressing in heavily, jamming the rudder, blasted ice and unshipped the rudder. Our protecting floebergs behaved well. The whole body of ice in the channel is moving rapidly to the south, the pressure of the pack and rigging continued till 12 m*idday*. Sanderlings are flocking from the south, two lots passed the ship. Snowy owl for dinner on the wardroom table, not bad meat, have eaten better. The weather continued throughout the day beastly in the extreme, snow falling with a N.E. Wind. Rawson and 2 men arrived at 6.15 p.m. from the *Discovery*. Bad news from that ship. Scurvy attacked the Greenland party. Hand died on 3ʳᵈ. June, Paul on 29ᵗʰ. June both at Polaris Bay.[2] Rawson over from Polaris Bay between 29ᵗʰ. July & 4ᵗʰ. August, the passage must have been perilous. Beaumont and his men are still over there, or on the ice this evening. I feel most anxious for him. From 6 p.m. to 12 a.m. the movement of the pack was tremendous to witness, immense floes and large hummocks jammed together, seemed from the masthead to fill the channel, and travelled south with great rapidity under the combined influences of wind and tide. The enormous floebergs behind which we had crept for shelter~~ed~~ offered no resistance to the impact of the floes, they were hustled along and carried off like playthings, when the passing floes came in contact with them. One large floeberg 50 yards long and at least 40 feet thick which had grounded outside of us received the full force of the shock. Slowly it reared itself above the advancing floe then turned a complete somersault and alit on the floe a mass of rounded blue hummocks. Our position very precarious, spring-tide and top of high-water, the rubble from the pack pushing us onshore.

Monday 7 August 1878. [*sic*] <u>Shift-Rudder Bay</u>
At 2.30 a.m. on change of the tide the pack eased off somewhat, and relieved the strain on the ship. [*See Figure 65, p. 306.*] About 11 o'c. went ashore with Nares, he went up to the top of a hill to look out. The rocks capping the hills in this vicinity are strata of a reddish coloured limestone, more like sandstone, which rests conformably on blueish gray limestone and beneath it slates with quartz, its thickness appears to be 300 to 400 feet and in close proximity to the ship it dips to W. at 10° to 15°.

---

[1] 'Sniggling' is a mode of fishing by which the hook takes the fish, and not the fish the hook. *OED*.
[2] James J. Hand, able seaman; Charles Paul, able seaman.

Figure 65   Photograph of HMS *Alert* pinned near Cape Beechey, Robeson Channel, from Nares, *Narrative of a Voyage to the Polar Sea*.

Figure 66. 'View of Cape Beechey, Grin[n]ell Land, N. Lat. 81° 50′. With remains of Eskimo implements, found there by Captain H. W. Feilden, 7th. August 1876. [Drawn by and signed at bottom left] E. L. Moss.' Feilden added the caption with his signature.

I found about three hundred yards north of the ship and a little above high water mark some Eskimo relics, namely part of a sledge and a stone lamp and scraper. [*Feilden tipped in sketches of the Eskimo relics; see Figures 66 and 67, above and below.*]

Figure 67. 'Eskimo lamp found at Shift Rudder Bay. 7th. Aug 1876. by H.W.F.'

Our position this evening has altered much for the worse, a heavy piece of floeberg coach-wheeled in and grounding, hermetically sealed us up for the present. Wind changed about mid-day from N.E. to N.N.E., easing the pack off a great deal. [*Margin*: Ravens] Rawson tells me he saw two ravens nesting in a cliff at Polaris Bay, Knots seemed to breed there commonly, and he noticed one brownish bird there about the size of a snow-bunting, which elevated its crest, or as he described raised a top-knot, as it ran about searching for food. In all probability it was a shore lark,[1] as Rawson says it belonged to the bunting or finch tribe.

Tuesday 8 August 1876. Shift-Rudder Bay
We had some bad nips about 5.30 and 6.45 a.m. The ship was hove up about four feet the pressure then eased and she fell back about a foot. Although she groaned and squeaked a great deal, not a plank started in the decks, and I do not think the hull was at all injured. As for ourselves suppose the ship is crushed we have simply to step on shore, but I have my collections to look after, and unless I get the boxes out myself not a scrap will be saved. The nip eased off after breakfast with the ebb tide. Parr and I accompanied Rawson and his two men on their way to the *Discovery* for about 4 miles. Saw an Ivory gull, several Buffon's Skuas[2] accompanied now by 2 young birds, the old birds try to mislead by every device, crawling on belly &c., the young are in mottled plumage without tail feathers, these youngsters have an owlish flight. The white tarsus and piebald foot is as conspicuous in these young birds as in the adult. Saw two parties of juvenile *Calidris arenaria*. They were busy feeding with their parents running about and incessantly searching for insects. shot 3. Caught a young Turnstone. Many Arctic terns breeding at Brenta Bay. Found on N. side of Brenta Bay the remains of three or four Eskimo encampments. Very ancient, a few stones marked the sites, and some flat ones the floors of tents. Many fragments of bone musk-ox and seal scattered about, took a small fragment of wood from under one stone. Searched diligently for traces of handiwork. Only discovered rock-crystals which had evidently been worked, some were entire others in flakes. Two crania of musk-ox immensely old lying near. The sites of the tents were on a gravel bluff 15 feet above water. 69 Brent geese swimming out of range in a water-pool on Brenta Bay.

Wednesday 9 August 1876. Shift-Rudder Bay
Wind light from N.E. bright and clear, the *mer-de-glace* on the opposite or Greenlandic side of the channel beyond Cape Morton, looked most beautiful. Little movement in the pack outside. The stomach of a young Sanderling contained gnats and spiders, that of a young Buffons Skua, lemming. Position of our ship is Lat 81°.52'.56" Long. 63°.1'.15". Aldrich and Giffard went to Brenta Bay accompanied by Freddy and his Kayak. The wind freshened up towards 9 p.m. This persistent N.E. wind hemming us in with the pack is becoming monotonous. Procured a *Nymphon* from beach below high-water mark which differs from those I have got before. Caught a butterfly. Body black, ground colour reddish, black spots.[3] Aldrich and Giffard returned at 12h.45m. having slain all the geese

---

[1] *Eremophila alpestris*, known as the horned lark in N. America. This would be remarkably far north for that species. Lapland longspur, *Calcarius lapponicus*, breeds farther north.

[2] Parasitic skua, in N. America known as parasitic jaeger, *Stercorarius parasiticus*.

[3] Possibly one of the lesser fritillaries, or one of the copper butterflies. Robert MacLachlan in Nares, *Narrative of a Voyage*, II, p. 236, lists two species of fritillaries, *Argynnis polaris* and *A. chariclea*, and one copper, 'a pretty little *Chrysophanus* ... which appears to be a rather striking form (*Feildeni*) of our familiar *C. phlœas*'. The best match with Feilden's description is the Arctic fritillary, subspecies *arctica*, which occurs in northern Ellesmere Island.

in Brenta Bay, 70 in number, 29 adults and 41 young. Aldrich brought me back a lump of selenite. The ice slackened a good deal to-night. White & Moss out gunning shot a beautiful young Snowy owl, and several geese. Moss got 3 Hares.

Thursday 10 August 1876. <u>Leave Shift-Rudder Bay</u>
Weight of the three leverets killed yesterday after being cleaned was 6, 7 and 7½ lbs respectively. Weight of 6 goslings 16 lbs being about 2 lbs 8 ozs apiece, these birds, however, were wet in the feathers.

In the beginning of August the Knots began to change their summer garb, I noticed this on the 3rd. of August, on the 8th. only two or three red feathers were left on the breast, and today only a tinge of earth-red stain is left on the outer margin of breast feathers. Walked to the spot where I killed a musk-ox last year, which knocked me down. Found two or three species of flowering plants that I had not procured so far north before. Saw an adult Snowy owl, and a fox, shot a Hare 10½ lbs, could have secured another but would not have been able to carry it to the ship. One hill side I passed was white with disintegrated quartz, it appeared to be the strike of a vein coming to surface, and running N & S. Numerous rock-crystals in it. [*Margin*: Charr] The charr[1] were jumping like mad in the lake. Got back to the shore at 4.30 had leave till 5, from Nares. Ship had gone, saw her pushing her way through the pack a mile <or two> to the southward, ran abreast of her, the dingy was sent for me and I got on board with my hare and specimens. At the extreme limit of my walk to-day, I debouched on to a valley quite bare of snow, perhaps a mile wide and stretching 4 or 5 miles in a N.N.W. direction – We proceeded along pushing our way through the pack. Young ice formed last night ¼ inch thick. I noticed that family parties of Turnstones were numerous generally 2 old birds and three young in the flock. A young Snow-bunting had legs and feet dark slate, soles white-gray. 2 outer tail-feathers white outer margin toward tip dark brown, head & shoulders gray, bill gray, primaries brown, Snow-buntings flocking – Moss shot *phoca hispida* during the night, I shot two dovekies.

Friday 11 August 1876. <u>Cape Murchison</u>
Between 3 and 4 a.m. as we were pushing alongside of the shore and not far from Cape Murchison, several hares were seen, Moss and Parr landed and they bagged 4 of them, they saw several Snowy Owls. I saw one from the ship, perched on a projection of the Cape. We were brought up at 6 a.m. by the ice jammed against Distant Cape the entrance to Discovery Bay being in sight. Turned in and slept till 11. Under steam again boring through pack. We brought up under the lee of Breakwater Island, landed and shot 8 *Sterna macrura* found 5 downy young ones, and 5 eggs. The pack opened with the tide and we entered the harbour and steamed alongside of the *Discovery* at 7.30 p.m.

---

[1] Arctic char or charr, *Salvelinus alpinus*.

I was very glad to see our friends once again. Sat up talking with Hart all night. Bunyan[1] gave me a wolf's head he found to-day north of the Coal mine. Hans[2] had shot an Ermine.

Saturday 12 August 1876. <u>Discovery Bay</u>
I breakfasted with Hart onboard the *Discovery* and then started with him for the Coal-mine. This interesting deposit was discovered by Hart. It is beyond me after a cursory examination such as I undertook this day to define the limits of this formation. Hart of course will be able to do more. I was able, however, to place beyond doubt that this deposit is not belonging to the Carboniferous era. I was so fortunate as to obtain fossil leaves of hard-wood trees, analogous to those found in the Disco beds, I feel certain therefore that this is an extension of the Miocene lignites.

This deposit seems now to occupy a limited area, it is seen to greatest advantage in a valley running E and W. into Watercourse Bay, where the lignite bed is cut through by a stream. Where the main bed of lignite is exposed is at this level of the stream, and a stratum of 20 to 30 feet of black coal is visible, how much thicker, or how much deeper it extends below the bed of the stream, we have no means of judging. The bed dips E 10° to 15°. The black shales and bands of yellow sandstone resting on the lignite are 300 to 400 feet thick, these are capped with thick mud-beds containing glaciated stones and boulders and shells of *mya*, & *saxicava*. Fossil leaves and stems are not uncommon in the shales and sandstones as well as in the lignite itself.[3]

Sunday 13 August 1876. <u>Discovery Bay</u>
Stayed on board the *Discovery*, turned in until breakfast, ship underweigh at 7 o'c. Ice packed outside breakwater so we moored to the ice. Landed on Bellot I with Captain Nares, shot 2 long-tailed Skuas, 4 Turnstones, 1 young *Harelda glacialis*. Found ancient Eskimo tent-sites with broken bones, and fragment of wood, a Reindeer horn about 20 feet above sea-level. All these Eskimo traces are markers of summer encampments. [*Margin*: Birch bark] Egerton brought me birch-bark and driftwood from St Patrick's Bay.

Monday 14 August 1876. <u>Discovery Bay</u>
About mid-day Beaumont and his party were descried by old Thars[4] from the crow's nest, camped on the ice in Lady Franklin Sound, bearing S.E. from us and distant about 4 miles. Markham and May started with relief party from the ship and reached them about 7 p.m. Parr and I were up on the top of Bellot Island, at the time, and saw the meeting through our glasses. We shot 54 hares caught some moths, on our return to the ship got a bite then landed with Egerton and Nares crossed the breakwater met Beaumonts party on the ice and helped to drag, all got onboard the *Alert* by 1 a.m.

---

[1] George Bunyan, ropemaker.
[2] Hans Hendrik [Heindrick], (1834–89), Greenlander, took part in several other expeditions, including that of the *Polaris* (1871–3).
[3] Heer, *Flora Fossilis Arctica*, V, pp. 11–14; Heer, 'Notes on Fossil Plants', pp. 66–72; C. E. De Rance and H. W. Feilden, 'Appendix XV', in Nares, *Narrative of a Voyage*, II, pp. 327–45.
[4] John Thores, ice quartermaster, *Alert*.

Tuesday 15 August 1876. <u>Discovery Bay</u>
Nothing can exceed our joy at the safe return of Beaumont and his party, they drifted on the floes as far south as Cape Baird, where most providentially they made the shore, in this last spell to gain the land they worked 35 hours without a break.

In the afternoon I let down the trawl in 23 and 25 fathoms, good haul of crinoids, some few fish and crustaceans. A large boulder near sea-level on the breakwater seems to be Silurian limestone of the south. Now that we have seen the varying drift of the ice it is quite possible that these boulders may have been brought from either N or S. On the 14th. I found seal bones on Bellot Island at an elevation of 800 feet, they had probably been taken to the spot by gulls or foxes. Giffard shot 2 Ermines on Bellot I. Several Ivory Gulls are cruising about the harbour but they are very wild. Young Eider ducks and brent geese are now able to fly well.

Wednesday 16 August 1876. <u>Discovery Bay</u>
I remained onboard the ship the greater part of the day working up my captures of yesterday. Nares, Markham, Parr, May, and Egerton went to the Coal-seam. They brought back a good series of leaf impressions. They found them in the shales on the proper right bank of the ravine where I first found them. They measured the seam of lignite exposed and made it 25 feet. From Bellot Island the hare-hunters brought me several plants of Hesperis pallasii.[1] The visitors to the Coal-seam brought me back a *Colias*[2] and a Lepidoptera [*sic*] that I have not met with before. The Ermines killed by Giffard yesterday I skinned, one of them had *tænia*[3] in its stomach, contents of stomach lemming.

Thursday 17 August 1876. <u>Discovery Bay</u>
To the coal-mine with Nares and a party, *en route* I picked up ♀ musk-ox skull, and several butterflies. Nares and I landed on Dutch Island and found the ruined remains of an Eskimo hut on it. Got a tolerable collection of Miocene leaf impressions. Got a Bombus. An Eolis[4] came up on a piece of laminaria when the rudder grated against the ground at low-water Saw a Snowy-owl, Turnstones, and one hare. Moss picked up the fragment of a human femur.

Thinking it necessary to trace out the extent of the coal field, I walked round the valley it lies in, finding the basement rock cropping out on the hills all round, completely encircling the coal-fields.

The skipper during my absence detailed four blue jackets to hunt for fossils, during and on my return I got a considerable number from them – but I fancy friend Moss had relieved them pretty considerably before I put in my appearance.

Friday 18 August 1876. <u>Discovery Bay</u>
The *Discovery* moved over from her winter moorings and anchored behind the breakwater close to us. I went onboard of her to see Hart. Dined with him. Before dinner went out in dingy with grappling hook and brought up large quantities of laminaria. Coppinger showed me some of his Silurian fossils from Offley Island, they are very nice he promised

[1] A synonym for *Erysimum palassii*, Pallas's wallflower.
[2] Clouded yellow butterfly, one of the sulphurs; possibly the Northern or Hecla clouded yellow.
[3] A genus of tapeworms.
[4] A genus of nudibranch molluscs.

to send me a selection. The *Discovery* took the ground at low-water, when we sat down to dinner we had a heel to port of 16°. At 9 p.m. up steam and taking the southern passage between Bellot I. and mainland attempted to cross Lady Franklin Sound. Wind N.E. and still jamming the ice into the sound.

Saturday 19 August 1876. Discovery Bay
We moored to a large stationary floe on south side of Bellot Island, an enormous floe impinged on Bellot I. and filled up Lady Franklin Sound. Open water visible beyond Cape Baird to the southward. Landed on the south side of Bellot Island and botanised over the southern sunny slopes. The dark coloured cliffs of azoic slate, present a very bold escarpment to the south rising to an altitude of 800 or 1000 feet, a remarkably steep talus stretches up some 400 feet, on this slope *Hesperis* grew in great abundance, its stalks now covered with long seed-pods standing up 8 & 10 inches. I found Androsace septentrionalis[1] growing abundantly, also *Sax. oppo.*, „ *cernua*,[2] „ nivalis, „ cæspitora,[3] „ tricuspidata,[4] & „ flagellaris. A fern *Cystopteris*[5] common, a white daisy looking plant, and a fuzzy blossomed fellow with yellow centre likewise common. Finished skinning a young snowy owl and a young skua.

Sunday 20 August 1876. Bellot Island
Went ashore with Aldrich at 2.30 a.m., such a glorious morning, shot a hare which we saw feeding near to the beach. We ascended the hill about 400 feet to observe the state of the ice, much water visible south of Cape Baird, a lead opening from Cape Baird along the eastern face of the great floe which blocks up Lady Franklin Sound, this lead appears inclined to open to the mouth of Discovery Bay. We hurried onboard to acquaint the Captain. By 4 a.m. we reached the ship, up steam by 6 a.m., and both ships doubled back to the north entrance of Discovery Bay, and we got round the breakwater by 9 a.m. I noticed a flock of 20 Brent Geese winging their way south, down channel. The only birds I noticed between Cape B<aird>. and Cape Norton Shaw were 6 or 7 Dovekies.
Clear water off Cape Baird, and we ran down Kennedy Channel without interruption from ice. The day was magnificent and scenery superb. At Cape Lieber the rocks are highly contorted, south of that point, less so. There was very little snow on the shore-hills, and their colours were magnificent, a long line of strata appearing for miles in mountains and valleys, sometimes forming a jagged peak then doubling on itself becoming the bed of a valley.
    The colours of these strata were so intense that there was no difficulty in tracing their outcrop for miles. A black series, a carmine series, and an orange series.
    Sighted Cape Constitution at 11.30 a.m. and almost abreast of that position.

Monday 21 August 1876. Kennedy Channel
The ice was packed heavily off Cape M'Clintock and we turned back, running full speed some eight miles on the back track, and taking shelter in a magnificent fiord which was

---

[1] A member of the primrose family.
[2] Nodding saxifrage. Feilden used ditto marks for the repetiton of 'Sax.'.
[3] Tufted Alpine saxifrage.
[4] Three-toothed saxifrage.
[5] A member of the genus of bladderferns.

called Rawlings Bay. We moored to the land-ice, landed and found the rock in the vicinity a coarse gritty conglomerate, the large peebles being pink coloured, and showing traces of fossil corals but no organisms were detected in the strata itself. The tide rose and fell about 12 feet, a large floe piece coming across our bows pushed us on shore and at 9 p.m. we were high and dry, ship listing to starboard 25° [*see Figure 68*]. On shore with Parr found numerous traces of Eskimo, discovered sites of fifteen or twenty igloos, got some relics also a skull of musk-ox ♀, and a reindeer, both apparently having been killed by wolves. [*Margin*: Plants] Hart came onboard and I gave him all the plants I had collected on Bellot I. Rawlings Bay terminates in a discharging glacier, a smaller one runs down from the N. side near the head of the bay. I walked to within 6 miles of it. The ship got off by 12 p.m. The main dip of the strata in Rawlings Bay is W. Corresponding strata being conspicuously shown on either side of the fiord, the mountains forming the sides of the bay rise to 2,500 or 3,000 feet. *Phoca hispida* shot.

'ALERT' ON SHORE.

Figure 68. '"ALERT" ON SHORE', engraving from Nares, *Narrative of a Voyage to the Polar Sea during 1875–6 of H.M. Ships 'Alert' and 'Discovery'* ..., 1878, vol. II, p. 148.

Tuesday 22 August 1876
Left Rawlings Bay at 8 a.m., sleet, fog, and cold, the snow as it falls, rests upon the top of the mountains along shore, winter is rapidly approaching again. We worked down to about 25 miles from Cape Fraser in lat 80° by 2 p.m., when we made fast to berg pieces in a bay. Up steam at 8.30 p.m., but the tide having fallen 14 or 15 feet left us sticking. Engines broke down, tide began to rise, the ship was hauled off. Wind blowing very strong from S.W. and has driven a great deal of the ice off shore. Saw only a few dovekies (yesterday at Rawlings Bay I noticed two Snow-buntings, also the first undoubted icebergs.) At 6 p.m. Giffard went ashore and up a hill, a good deal of water ahead.

(Skinned *Phoca hispida*, stomach full of *Crustacea*. Engines repaired by 11 p.m., wind blowing strong, started, Scoresby Bay free of ice, quite a sea on. The snow that fell to-day is remaining on the tops of the coast-line mountains. Saw a single Glaucus gull. South cape of Scoresby Bay the rock alters becoming paler in colour the lines of stratification much deeper and more horizontal.

Wednesday 23 August 1876

The wind blew so strong directly in our teeth this morning that with 98 revolutions we could hardly hold our own. We took shelter in a small bay which I take to be Hayes' Gould Bay. If I am right then our next Cape South is Leidy and then Cape Louis Napoleon. A tremendous big floe is jammed against the shore and extends out into the channel, at 9 a.m. we moored to this floe waiting for something to turn up.

A fine falcon *Falco grœnlandicus* flew round the ship, but did not come within range. Parr shot a floe-rat *P. hispida* a female weight 65 lbs. Tip of hind flipper to snout 4′.3½″. Girth behind axillae 2′.4″. Front of fore-flipper to nose 1′.0″ girth round umbilicus 2′.4½″ occiput to nose 7 ins. Length between fore and hind flipper 2′2¼″ Length of fore-flipper 5½″ Length hind flipper 8 in. Dovekies are numerous in the pools around us, counted 27 in one party. The big floe to which we were moored drifted N. so we ran for shelter into the little bay we left this morning.

Landed with Nares & Hart, found many fossils – saw a Walrus. Parr saw a little auk.

Thursday 24 August 1876

1 o'c. p.m. up steam plenty of smoke as we are reduced to the culinary coal. Proceeded south. Brought up to the ice off Cape Frazer in less than an hour, moored to floe. Let down dredge in 80 fathoms, it came up after drifting along the bottom for sometime with the bag torn. The swabs were one mass of Echinoderms and *Comatulae*.[1]

Under weigh again at 8 p.m. and got round Cape Frazer, coming to shelter under the lee of two icebergs in Gould Bay by 11 p.m.

Friday 25 August 1876

At 3 a.m. the Captain called me and asked me to accompany him on shore and look at two old Eskimo camps that he had seen on the beach, from the crowsnest.

He and I and Malley landed. The Eskimo traces consisted of two rings of stones for summer tents, placed on a shingle beach raised 15 feet above high-water mark. The sea must have encroached at this particular point for half of one of the circles had been undermined and washed away.

Saw a magnificent *Falco candicans* sitting on the slope of Cape Leidy. Crawled up to him and let rip two barrels at him 70 yards off. No result. Walking towards the south, Malley picked up a broken Eskimo harpoon. Found a foxes skull, and a few fossils. (Trilobite.).

Back to the ship by 6 a.m. got under weigh and worked through the pack some five miles, moored to floe two miles north of Cape Napoleon. Several broods of Eiders were passed, the old birds became much excited. Landed in the evening with Nares, and walked along the beach round Cape Napoleon, until we saw well into Raised Beach Bay, this was

---

[1] Stalkless crinoids.

rimmed with heavy ice, and so was Dobbin Bay beyond. It appears to me as if a deal of heavy ice from the N. had drifted down here and stuck.

The ice-foot along this coast is beautifully wide and smooth. At this late period of the summer it is much cut up by water channels but in the spring it must be fine travelling.

Saw a circle of stones marking Eskimo encampment a mile and half N. of Cape Napoleon.

Saturday 26 August 1876
Went alongside of the *Discovery* and took from her ten tons of coal. Trawl put over in 25 fathoms. Temp. of bottom 29°.2. A very rich haul fish, Comatulae &c. a shell a *Trichotropis*, that I cannot make out. About 8 p.m. we left our moorings and sniggled about a mile nearer to Cape Napoleon.

The snow that fell to-day rests on the land.

Sunday 27 August 1876
In the evening the ice slackened and we got round Cape Napoleon, and crossed the mouth of Raised Beach Bay, rounded Cape Hilgard and moored in Dobbin Bay, not far from where we tied up last year.

Snow fell during the night, the rigging coated, and the decks sludgy.

The paucity of birds, noted by us coming down the sound is remarkable, only two or three Sanderlings and no Knots, How do these waders migrate?

Monday 28 August 1876. Dobbin Bay
A cheerless looking day. The snow has covered the hills with their winter garb. Several Ivory Gulls are cruising round the ship just out of shot, and picking up their livelyhood [*sic*] from the small pools still left open. The ice we are amongst is chiefly this years, but fragments of older floes are intermixed and some heavy pieces of berg. A large one is lying at the head of the bay inside of Prince Imperial Island. I suppose there must be a discharging glacier somewhere at the head of the bay. Depth 47 fathoms mud. Killed ♀ Ivory Gull.

Tuesday 29 August 1876 Dobbin Bay
In the middle watch a big iceberg near us took charge and during the morning watch we had to shift our berth higher up the bay. Dense fog which only now and again lifted. Moss and May landed in the morning the former shot two hares, two ptarmigan and a ♀ *Corvus corax*.[1] Moss got the Raven within range by laying down one of the hares and concealing himself until the bird came within shot of his rifle.

I landed with Parr in the afternoon we killed 4 hares, and I came across a brood of Ptarmigan 9 in number all of which I bagged, they were young birds changing into winter's plumage. They were quite unsuspecting and allowed me to shoot them as they ran amongst the stones. The Hares have now lost their gray faces and are pure white only the extreme tip of the ears being black. Weight of one hare 10 lbs 2 oz. weight of young ptarmigan 16 ozs. Shot two snow buntings saw many.

When on shore walked as far as the stratum of red sandstone which made so conspicuous an appearance in the cliffs, when we lay beneath them last year. I found the

---

[1] Common raven.

315

red stratum to consist of a coarse red-grit intermixed with a fine hard silicieous sandstone. The streams on shore are still running. [*Margin*: Plant] I found *Carex fuliginosa*[1] growing on shore.

Wednesday 30 August 1876. Dobbin Bay

The young ice is forming rapidly and consolidating the loose floe-pieces. Captain Nares after ascending a hill and looking round thought that we could reach some loose looking stuff outside of Cape Hawks. Under steam by 2 p.m. both boilers, *Discovery* and ourselves boring through the pack. We could make but little way. It is extraordinary the rapidity with which the young ice even when only an inch or two thick joins the floes together. We moored again between 4 and 5 p.m. after getting about three-quarters of the way across Dobbin Bay.

Thermo sunk to +18° it feels quite cold again. Markham landed on Prince Imperial Island, and brought from it a skull of the walrus, it had been broken by human agency.

Ginger the cat invaded my sanctum this evening tore off the head of a Ptarmigan I killed yesterday and which I took great pains to carry clean onboard and also destroyed two snow-buntings.

Thursday 31 August 1876. Dobbin Bay

Stuck in the ice, drifting slowly in and out with the tides. Sounded in 125, 113 and 110 fathoms, temperature of bottom +30°.8 +31° and +30°.75, mud bottom.

Discovery procured a large seal (Hans shot it) *Phoca barbata*, it weighed 510 lbs, on taking off its hide an Eskimo harpoon was found buried in the blubber of the back. The socket of the dart was made of ivory the blade being well wrought iron. Hans pronounced it to be a Greenland harpoon head, and suggested that it must have been struck in the Danish settlements. As this harpoon is exactly similar in construction to one I procured in Payer harbour in August last year, from a spot which I believe to have been a bivouac used of late years by the natives, I should not be at all surprised if this coast was not visited by some of the natives who wander up the west side. Dr Bessels informed Captain Markham that among the Eskimo of Etah was a man who originally came from the west side of the sound, and who stated that his former tribe hunted in the vicinity of Gale Point.[2] Went onboard the *Discovery* in the evening. A single Ivory Gull cruising around.

Friday 1 September 1876. Dobbin Bay

The weather continues dull, foggy, and no wind. With both boilers we pushed through the young ice and floe-pieces to a pool of water between Washington Irving Island and Cape Hawks, both ships made fast to a large grounded berg, which appears to be the same one as we tied up to in the same spot on the 12th. of August last year. Our boats got to shore and took off the greater part of the 2,400 rations placed in depot there last year.

---

[1] Short-leaved sedge.

[2] Markham, *Whaling Cruise*, p. 210, reports that Bessels 'considers that no expedition should go north without some Esquimaux for hunting and dog driving. He gave me the names of a man and his wife belonging to Etah, in whom he has the greatest confidence.' I have not found the record of Markham's report about the Eskimo from the west side of the Sound; this may well have been in conversation with Feilden.

The fresh snow lay about 8 inches deep, soft and powdery, temperature above freezing, it felt close and muggy and whilst the men were removing the depot I was glad to creep under the shelter of a rock and eat the ice hanging down. Numerous dovekies swimming in the pools. Some have nestlings still, as I saw them flying up and down from their nests. A single glaucus gull was wheeling about. Several broods of eider-ducks *som. moll.* swimming in the pools, young ones unable to fly, pinion feathers just protruding, down on parts of the body. We killed 18 including 2 old ones females. It is a somewhat curious fact that no one has seen a male eider since entering Smith Sound. The fact of these young Eiders being unable to fly, suggests that water-pools must remain open for sometime longer.

We had an anniversary dinner onboard the *Alert* to celebrate reaching highest northern latitude in a ship.[1] Rawson and Beaumont dined with us. The table was prettily decorated with flowers, a bottle of champagne between two, 3 most tender hares, and ten ptarmigan done to a turn. The snow lay too deep on the ground for me to obtain fossils.

Saturday 2 September 1876. Dobbin Bay

Beset off Washington Irving Island, tried to effect our escape with steam in both boilers, but we failed.

Sunday 3 September 1876. Allman Bay

At 4 a.m. again tried the ice. We got on as far as Cape Hawks there being no lead we were obliged to return and moored to iceberg. Started again at 1.15 and at 7 p.m. had worked round Cape Hawks about 7 miles, tying up in a bay north of Cape D'Urville. The newly formed ice hampered us so much that with both boilers going we did not push on more than a knot an hour.[2] The ice in the bay we are in is between 2 and 3 feet thick, perfectly smooth and no hummocks. Temp of water +32°. Water nearly fresh. Two glaciers at the head of the bay, neither of them discharge. The strata of the cliff from Cape Hawks to Cape D'Urville are massive and horizontal. A raven flying over Cape Hawks. Several dovekies, many seal-holes in the bay-ice. Moon very beautiful at night, also the planet Venus. Sick list clear. Consumed 2 tons of coals for 6 or 7 miles.

Monday 4 September 1876. Allman Bay

We are now left with 3 tons steaming coal, and the *Discovery* with two, and 46 tons for ships use, the *Discovery* with 45. Thus we have come nearly to the end of our tether, as far as steaming is concerned. The weather still remains warm damp and still, so that our chance of moving south under canvas is getting meagre. For my own part though I hate the winter, I look forward with delight to another summer to be spent in a latitude four degrees south of where I worked this year. A comparison between the two years collections would be of great interest. Some one or two of our people are very low about the prospect of a second winter.

We got up steam at 1 o'c. and moved to the south side of the bay, more out of the pressure of the ice and tied up to the floe. The bay we are in is called after the President of the Linnean Society[3] and the fine glacier at its head after John Evans[4] the President of

---

[1] 82°24'N

[2] Since a knot is a nautical mile per hour, 'an hour' is redundant.

[3] George James Allman, (1812–98), Irish ecologist, botanist and zoologist.

[4] (Sir) John Evans (1823–1908). See *ODNB*.

the Geological Society. The thinness of the ice in this bay and high temperature of the surface water is surely owing to the discharge from Evans glacier.

Tuesday 5 September 1876. <u>Allman Bay</u>

We remained fastened to the floe throughout the day. Snow sleet and hail falling, no wind to cause a disruption of the ice. Allman Bay is a fine indentation running inland about 3 miles, with a large valley at its end down which John Evans Glacier, pours. It is not a discharging glacier. The cliffs on either side are massive conglomerates rising 800 to 1000 feet. Talus runs up about half way. [*Margin*: *Falco candicans*] A very white *Falco candicans* was flying round the ship this afternoon.

Wednesday 6 September 1876

Landed with Captain Nares and Markham at 10.30 a.m. and walked along the coast as far as Cape D'Urville, between 3 and 4 miles. The walking was good along the ice-foot the snow about 4 inches deep but crisp. The sun shone out, and the clouds travelled from the westward, giving a decided warning of a change in the weather.

The cliffs formed of a conglomerate are constantly shedding peebles from their faces, which form the talus. These constituent peebles are some of them as large as a man's head, but they vary to the size of pears, all are well rounded, I have not detected a single gneiss or granite peeble in this formation, in some of the peebles I think I can detect fossil corals.

This same conglomerate forms the base of Washington Irving Island, but there the coralline limestone rests on it, it forms Cape Hawks and carries on to Cape Prescott. Walrus Island slopes with thinner strata 15° from S. to N. I think it is the same coralline limestone that caps Washington Irving I. However, I have a series of fossils from both points. I know also that at Victoria Head we have a massive fossiliferous limestone apparently the same as Cape Hilgard. Up steam at 5 p.m. and the ice slackening we moved into Franklin Pierce Bay. A walrus on a floe about 800 yards off, I could see through the glass that it was a fine tusker. It is singular that these brutes do not seem to go north of the meeting place of the Polar & Baffin's Bay tides.

This conglomerate formation produced but few plants. I found to-day some willow, *Sax. opp.*, *papaver* & yellow draba. Caught two lemmings, saw tracks of no other animals. Three eider with their broods in a tide-crack off Cape D'Urville, also 2 *Phoca hispida*. Water still running in rills on shore.

Thursday. 7 September 1876. <u>Franklin Pierce Bay</u>

Up steam at 9.30 a.m. and the ice slackening we moved into a large pool of water extending some distance to the eastern side of Walrus Island. Moored to a berg and landed on the island. Snow about 3 inches in depth, effectually concealed the Eskimo traces which we know to be so numerous on the Island.[1]

Here and there a cache or the walls of an unroofed igloo were to be seen. I took a pick with me but the soil was too hard frozen to make any impression. Numerous skulls of Walrus showed above the snow, these crania are interesting because they have all been broken in the same manner, the skull broken through across the eye-holes and the front part split in order to extract the tusks. I also found the skull of a large seal *P. barbata*.

[1] See entry 8 August 1875.

Several broods of eider ducks in a pool were still unable to fly. Giffard bagged 8, Malley was carrying them when the ice breaking, Malley let go the ducks, Giffard only managed to save one. I saw a pair of Ravens, and 2 Ptarmigan. A *phoca hispida* was shot in the afternoon.

Friday 8 September 1876
11.55 a.m. proceeded, 1 o'c. made fast. 3.30 p.m. proceeded, 4.40 made fast again. 8.10 p.m. proceeded. We have been dodging about all day, drifting with the tide, and endeavouring to escape being nipped.

During the middle watch a fox came alongside of the ship, which Parr shot. A female just changing into winter coat.

The cliffs on N. side of Bache Island show the greatest stretch of horizontal bedding that I have seen in the Arctic. They extend for miles with the strata as even as if laid with a level. The correspondence of the strata in the headlands of both sides of the channel is very remarkable.

Saturday. 9 September 1876. <u>Cape Isabella</u>
5.50 a.m. proceeded southward, a smart tuzzle[1] with the ice getting round Victoria Head. From there the ice slackened, with large spaces of smooth young ice two inches thick, through which the ships forced their way. Much diatom matter in the young ice. After passing Brevoort Island which we were abreast of at 6 p.m., we entered open water. The coast between Cape Sabine and Isabella is crowded with glaciers. The scenery of Baird Inlet is very fine. Not a single bird seen by me this day. Captain Nares saw a dovekie in winter plumage.

Three large glaciers discharge into Baird Inlet north of Mount Bolton. At 8 o'c. p.m. we were up to Cape Isabella, Markham and I landed a rough looking night, gloomy and sad appearance. I was desirous of taking a more careful survey of the rock formation, than I was able to do last visit. It is red gneiss, traversed irregularly with beds of white granite. Markham and Simmonds[2] ascended to the Post-Office and brought back a mail left there by the *Pandora*.[3] My letters were from William Leyland Feilden, Catherine Feilden, William Medlycott, Montague Joseph Feilden, and Edward Alston.[4] Newspapers to 29th May 1876. No sleep, happy to have such good news from home.

---

[1] Tuzzle is a variant of tussle. *OED.*

[2] John Simmons, 2nd captain maintop, *Alert.*

[3] The superseded Royal Navy gunvessel *Pandora*, on a private venture under Captain Allen William Young (1827–1915), sailed in June 1875 to look for the missing records of the Franklin expedition, intending to visit the N magnetic pole via Baffin Bay and Lancaster Sound, and then to navigate the North-west Passage; they were frustrated by ice, and returned to England in the autumn of the same year. See Cooke and Holland, *Exploration of Northern Canada*, p. 238. On their outward journey, they brought newspapers and letters for the Nares expedition. In 1876 Young returned with the *Pandora* with stores and supplies for the Nares expedition. C. R. Markham, *Threshold of the Unknown Region*, pp. 315–19; Cooke and Holland, *Exploration of Northern Canada*, pp. 240–41.

[4] Sir William Leyland Feilden (1835–1912), HWF's older brother and the 3rd Baronet Feniscowles; Catherine Feilden, possibly HWF's aunt, b. 1730 or 1728; see Assheton, *Pedigree of the Family of Feilden*, pp. 5, 10; possibly William Coles Medlycott, archaeologist (1806–82); Montague Joseph Feilden (1816–98), uncle of HWF; Edward Richard Alston (1845–81), zoologist (see *ODNB*). There were apparently no letters from his wife Julia, although theirs was a long and successful partnership. See Emerson and Stokes, *Confederate Englishman*.

It was a strange sensation standing alone on the point of Cape Isabella, to the north lay the channel to the unreached Pole, a route ever to be impressed on our minds by the recollection of our dangers and escapes. The ships were drifting with the tide along with heavy masses of ice to the northward, and to the south an open sea with dark lowering clouds hanging over it, the boom of the waves breaking against the granite shore, brought back a flood of recollections from the outer world that have not crossed my mind for 18 months. So interested have I been in my work that up till now, I have never let the thought of home enter my mind, but the southern wind and open sea brought back a strange longing for home, which our letters did not dispel.

Sunday 10 September 1876. <u>North-Water</u>
During the early morning we were passing through occasional streams of loose ice, from 3 feet to 12 inches above water. Very thick all day – a great deal of yellow diatomaceous matter in the rotten ice, every now and again bergs showing through the mist. Most miserable weather wind W.S.W. [*Margin*: Kittiwake] Saw a single Kittiwake & several fulmars.

Monday 11 September 1876
Sighted Hackluyt [*sic*] & Northumberland Is. wind blowing in squalls and gales from W. & S.W. dead foul., ran into Whale Sound for shelter, both ferrying all day between the Islands and Cape Parry, making leeway. Weather most beastily [*sic*], everything in cabins lost their sea-legs. Several Fulmars about. Water very phosphorescent, surface temp varied from +30° to +31° ½. Many glaciers on Northumberland I. Snow lying thick.

Tuesday 12 September 1876. <u>Barden Bay</u>
4 a.m. wore ship. 9.45 land observed on port-beam. 12 m. Northumberland island bearing S.E. by compass. 4 p.m. anchored in Barden Bay, *Discovery* made fast astern, anchored in 23 fathoms, during the afternoon the wind blowing in fresh squalls from S.W. We could see four or five Eskimo running along the shore with their dogs. Sea too rough to allow us to communicate with them. We anchored not far from the Tyndall Glacier of Dr Hayes.

I observed that the stripes of coloured matter in the face of the glacier are nearly vertical. A moraine at least 150 feet high flanks its western edge.

TRAP DYKES. KE-CAVE. MORAINE.
Tyndall Glacier.

15 or 20 glaucous gulls resting on the beach at the foot of the moraine which is of a rich red-colour and uncovered by snow. Between 11 and 12 p.m. the wind changed to N.N.E. we were obliged to up anchor and steam out as we were on a dead lee shore. Captain anxious to communicate with natives, but the bad weather rendered it impossible.

Wednesday 13 September 1876
4 a.m. rounded Cape Parry. Passed numerous icebergs 5 a.m. swell came up from the westward at 8 a.m. numerous icebergs at 2 p.m. icebergs very numerous off Wolstenholme Island. Wind dead foul. Fulmars Kittiwakes and Little auks in abundance.

Thursday 14 September 1876. Cary Islands
3 o'c. p.m. observed Cary Islands bearing E by N about 12 miles distant. 5.20 wore ship. Wind dead foul. Temp of surface +29°½ +31°½ +32° +31°½.

Friday 15 September 1876
Steering towards Lancaster Sound a few bergs in sight. Temp. of water varying from +31° to +34°. Colour of water dark brownish-green. 6 p.m. observed land on starboard beam – 9.30 p.m. wore ship. This is a most persistent foul wind.

Saturday 16 September 1876
Temperature of surface +32°. A few bergs in sight coming out of Lancaster Sound. At 11 o'c., off Cape Byam Martin. Tacked, stood off shore for an hour, tacked again in direction of Possession Bay, in order to take advantage of the southerly shore current. A considerable sprinkling of snow is now lying on the land. There appear to be some good valleys running down into the bays. Fulmars and Kittiwakes observed.
Noon Lat. 73°33′N.
Long. 76°59′W.

Sunday 17 September 1876
Noon Lat. 73° 40′N.
Long 73° 8′W.
3 a.m. passed 1 berg and also a few pieces of bay-ice. Surface temp. +30° to +34°.
5 p.m. Passed two icebergs and got amongst many Rotches.[1]

Monday 18 September 1876
Temperature of surface +34° in the morning +35° at mid-day. varied according to our proximity to bergs to +32½. Passed several bergs. Snow-buntings migrating south. Fulmars flying round.
Lat. at noon 73° 50′N.
Long. 67 44′W.

Tuesday 19 September 1876
At 3 a.m. passed five bergs, sighted twelve more during morning watch. 10 a.m. passed six bergs and a few pieces of loose ice. Temperature of surface +33½ +32 +34°.
Lat at noon   74°17′N.
Long   „   61°22′W.

Wednesday 20 September 1876
4.30 a.m. taken in tow by the *Discovery* at 9.30 Cast-off, 5.30 land observed on port beam. At noon passed through a line of very large grounded bergs. All afternoon

---

[1] Another name for the little auk, and a variant spelling of rotge.

surrounded by many bergs. Cape Shackleton and the Horse's Head in sight. Fulmars numerous.
Lat. at noon. 72°33′N.
Long. 58°48′W.

Thursday 21 September 1876
6.40 a.m. Sighted Sanderson's Hope. A very fine day. Temp of surface +34°.
Lat. at noon   73°7′W
Long.   „   58°26′. W.
Water very phosphorescent at night.

Friday 22 September 1876
A beautiful day. The water covered with looms and rotches, many Fulmars flying about and a few Kittiwakes. 2 *Graculus carbo*[1] flew past the ship. At 2 p.m. we came up to the pack, the *Discovery* took us in tow. At mid-day Lat. 71°58′ N. Long 60 19′W. *F. candicans* flew round the ship. at 4 p.m past a piece of floe stained with blood and having the backbone and several ribs of a seal lying on it, no doubt the debris of a bear's repast.

Saturday 23 September 1876. <u>Omenak Fiord</u>
A slight display of aurora during the middle watch. A very beautiful night. The Rotches crying much during the hours of gloom, their cry consists of two notes a shrill harsh one and a *w*himper. Went below at 3 a.m. After breakfast stood in towards the entrance of Omenak fiord, many bergs in sight, none of very great magnitude: some showed what I call 'crimped-cod markings' showing that they had not long left the parent glacier & had not yet turned over. Temperature of water +36°. Noon Lat 71°12′N Long 57.37.W. More than a hundred bergs in sight during the afternoon some of great size. Sea-water full of Entromostraca [*sic*]. The highland of Disco visible.

Sunday 24 September 1876. <u>Off Disco Island</u>
The *Discovery* in tow. A most lovely day, temperature of the air +40° of the surface water +36° and +38°. In the morning we were abreast of Hare Island, passed the entrance to the Waigat, and coasted along the western side of Disco Island. The strata are very horizontal. Many looms, rotches, Iceland Gulls, and some Eider duck flying about.

Monday 25 ~~August~~ September 1876. <u>Disco</u>
Passing Disco Fiord and Ovifak at noon. *F. candicans* alit on rigging mortally wounded him. Saw a very black fulmar ? puffinus.[2] Anchored in Lievely Harbour at 6 p.m. Krärup Smith and Fencker at once onboard, told us of the sailing of the *Pandora* four days ago. I do not know who were most pleased the good Danes at seeing us, or we to meet them again. Received late letters by last Danish brig from Copenhagen. Went on shore and called on Mrs Fencker,[3] I met her last year at Rittenbenk where she was staying with her sister Mrs Krärup Smith. Sat talking till 11 o'c.

[1] Cormorant.
[2] Shearwater.
[3] Nares, *Narrative of a Voyage*, II, p. 182, describes Mr and Mrs Fencker as his kind friends. Edgar Christian Fencker, a long-time resident in northern Greenland, became Royal Inspector of South Greenland in 1892.

Tuesday 26 September 1876. <u>Disco</u>
Last year I promised a reward to Johan and Peter Probert, if they brought me some of the Ovifak iron. It appears that they did find a block at or near the same spot, which the Inspector took and sent to Copenhagen. These fellows however, had found a smaller one which they kept for me. I of course took the specimen to Krärup Smith, and explained to him that I had no desire to obtain the iron surreptitiously, he replied that I was welcome to it, and he only wished it had been a better example. Fencker gave me a *F. peregrinus* in the flesh. I am afraid the natives of Lively have become demoralized by the numerous ships visiting the port, and the consequent distribution of money and clothes. I gave away any amount of clothing to these people, believing that I was doing them a kindness, but I found out that they at once take all clothing given them to the store and trade it to the Danish employés for a trifle.

I gave Peter Propert 10^s/[1] for the piece of iron from Ovifak in accordance with my promise of last year.

The ward-room mess gave Mr Krärup Smith and Mr Fencker and their ladies a dinner, the entertainment went off very successfully.

Wednesday 27 September 1876. <u>Disco</u>
Mr Krärup Smith asked me to his house by 8 a.m. and then most kindly allowed me to make a selection from his collection of Eskimo antiquities. I availed myself very freely of his generous offer.

In the afternoon received a box from the store sent to Disco by my wife via Copenhagen. Shot Dovekies, Little Auk, and *Tringa* maritima.[2]

Big dinner onboard the Discovery 25 of us sat down to table.

Mr Krärup Smith informed us that the settlement on the Whale Fish Islands had been withdrawn, owing to the mildness of the last few seasons, which preventing the formation of ice around the islands, deprived the inhabitants of their hunting areas.

Friday 28 September 1876. <u>Leave Disco</u>
We weighed and steamed out of the harbour before breakfast. Mr Krärup Smith accompanied us, with his boat in tow. Hans and Freddy also came to see the last of us.

Outside fog, steered for the cluster of islands in which Egedesminde is situated, after nightfall, islands and rocks about, and our native pilots knew not their whereabouts, so both ships anchored in what appeared to be a bay.

Friday 29 September 1876. <u>Arrive at Egedesminde</u>
The morning broke fine, and after getting up anchor, looking around, and wondering how we got into such a place without striking, we steamed through narrow tortuous channels between low gneiss islands, and shortly after breakfast came to anchor close to the settlement of Egedesminde.

I was soon on shore for a run, and picked up a good eider skin quilt and model oomiak. Nothing else to be got. The natives had never seen steamers before, and they were much excited, dozens of canoes came alongside bringing rock cod for sale, and the women came

---

[1] 10 shillings.
[2] Purple sandpiper.

in numbers to inspect us, oomiaks full of them came onboard at a time. There are many very loveable traits of character amongst the Greenlanders, they are scrupulously honest, the women are most chaste, and none of them beg. These girls will come into ones cabin and when asked to sit down, a couple will perch on the edge of the same chair, looking most demure, until I opened my drawers and let them see my clothes, woolen things they don't care for, but my red silk handkerchiefs and black silk neckties were quickly disposed of, and I only wished that I had had dozens more to distribute amongst these merry eyed, innocent little damsels of the far north.

The Govenor, Inspector, Secretary, and Mr Levenson [*sic*] [1] the naturalist dined with us.

Discovery taking in coal.

Saturday 30 September 1876. <u>Egedesminde</u>

I had a few things to arrange onboard today, so did not leave <the ship> until the afternoon when Egerton and I took the dingy and went to fish up a few shells. We found an old grave near to the sea, at some distance from the settlement. Returning to the ship, I afterwards went on shore with Markham and called on the Govenor, who kindly gave me a bow found in an ancient grave, Egedesminde district, and some eggs of *Anser albifrons*,[2] he described the goose as much like the common one with yellow feet. He also gave me some stone implements <from graves.>

Walked with Markham to the deserted cemetery where the coffins about fifty in number lying on the rocks, have fallen to pieces, leaving the bleached bones exposed. Moss took two skulls from this place today, but there is no surety that they ever belonged to full blooded natives.

Part of a haunch of *cervus tarandus*, presented by the Govenor was served up at our dinner, some of it near the outside was as musky as any *ovibos* I have tasted, but the rest was well flavoured.

Mr Levenson the Govenor's brother in law is a naturalist, at present he is studying the genus Turbellaria,[3] of which Fabricius discovered 9 species in Greenland, he has classified over 40 species.

For Turbellaria see p. 178. Arc. Manual.[4] Mr Krarup Smith told me that on one of the islands that we passed yesterday morning, are many ancient Eskimo graves, and extensive kitchen middens which would well repay search. From what I can learn it appears that Dr Rink the President of the Royal Greenland trade, is much averse to foreigners making scientific observations and the govenors have been instructed not to encourage them. For instance they could easily ship per Danish vessel from Copenhagen enough coal to supply all that Whymper[5] might require for his steam-launch, but Rink will not allow it.

Discovery got about 23 tons of coal in all.

---

[1] Dr G. M. R. Levinsen, subsequently a Danish inspector in Greenland

[2] White-fronted goose.

[3] A class of flatworms.

[4] T. R. Jones, ed., *Manual*, p. 178.

[5] Edward Whymper (1840–1911), *ODNB*. Whymper explored the interior of Greenland in 1867 and in 1872, when he examined the coasts around Disko Island: Whymper, 'Some Notes on Greenland', 1874. In 2011 there was a Whymper exhibition at the Scott Polar Research Institute, Cambridge: www.spri.cam.ac.uk/museum/exhibitions/whymper/

Sunday 1 October 1876. <u>Egedesminde</u>
At 10 o'c. The Govenor and his wife <Miss Jensen,> and two little girls, Mrs Fleisher,[1] Herr Insp & his secretary, and Levensen[2] came off to attend service. Many Greenlanders and some of the Danish employees were on the main deck. Pullen returned thanks for our safe return to civilisation and in his sermon touchingly alluded to the kindness of the Danes, which they appreciated much.

We gave the ladies a great lunch, but the Govenors wife and Mrs Fleisher returned onshore, I know the good souls went to prepare the dinner we are invited to this night.

The Govenor had got up a shooting match amongst the Greenlanders for our benefit, and after lunch we pulled over to an island on the opposite side of the harbour, where several tents were pitched, and all the hunters had collected. The shooting was at short range and not very good, we fired a few rounds at 250 yards just to show them the range of the Sniders. A good numbers of the young girls were present, but I missed several pretty faced ones, one little damsel came up to me and I recognized her as one of five who came into my cabin yesterday all at the same time, by one of my red silk handkerchiefs which I had given her, tied as a bandeau round her head.

After the shooting was over we went on board the *Discovery* and there Miss Jensen and the children were loaded with music, books toys, eau de cologne and sweetmeats. I dont believe any children ever enjoyed a day more & the little pretty governess never I am sure had so much attention paid to her before, as she has since the arrival of the Expedition at Egedesminde.

We mustered a party of six officers at the Govenors, and we had a right good dinner, instead of oysters, Pectens,[3] which are very good, these mollusks are abundant in the harbours.

Freddy came to me this evening with a seal skin as a memento, he was crying when he said good-bye to me. They are real good fellows these Greenlanders, for 15 months we have been shipmates, and many a night we have slept under the same blanket, and Fred has always been a good messmate.
Now that I am well acquainted with flight of *Nyctea scandiaca*[4] and general appearance of that bird on wing, I can unhesitatingly affirm that the bird I saw on ~~this date~~ <2ⁿᵈ. October 75, belonged to this species. H.W.F. July 1ˢᵗ. 1876.>[5]

Monday 2 October 1876. <u>Leave Egedesminde</u>
I was awakened at 6.30 this morning by Mr Krarup Smith, who had come onboard to say good bye, he sat down and smoked and drank cocoa, until the Captain and some of us had got on our clothes. I am sure the Danes feel very sorry at our departure. Krarup Smith has been so much with us, that we look upon him as an old friend. Govenor Boltroe[6]

---

[1] Perhaps the wife of Carl Fleisher, a Greenlander from Ilulissat, who carried out archaeological investigations into prehistoric cultures. Ilulissat Icefjord, which runs from the Greenland ice cap to Disko Bay, is now a UNESCO World Heritage Site.

[2] Brown, 'Florula Discoana', 1875, p. 259, writes that he was 'under obligations to Fröken Julie Levensen for most kindly presenting to us a small collection of Egedesminde plants'. This may refer to a relative of Dr Levinsen.

[3] Scallops.

[4] Snowy owl.

[5] Feilden had speculated on 2 October 1875 that the bird might have been a gyrfalcon or a glaucous gull. Although this sub-entry is physically placed on the journal page for 2 October, it is dated 1 July 1876.

[6] Carl August Ferdinand Bolbroe (1833–78) was Royal Inspector of North Greenland (1866–7).

brought me a baby bear skin as a parting gift, and the carpenter came off with several pieces of drift-wood, and pieces of squared timber, all more or less perforated by the teredo.[1] This drift-wood is generally put down as Siberian, I am a little doubtful about it being so, and think that the matter is worth a little investigation. Our young friend Knuhtsen, (alias ginger) Krärup's secretary was in great distress at our departure, "Oh! Captain Feilden I will never see you more farwell farwell [*sic*]."

We were under weigh by 7.30, and steamed off under a salute from the three guns of the settlement, many Kittiwakes, L. leucopterus, and Eider ducks, the last chiefly ♂ birds of the year, passed us.

We encountered a very heavy swell as we got into the straits, and a head wind, we rolled much, and the ship was very uncomfortable both during the afternoon and the night.

Tuesday 3 October 1876
A fine day, with light airs from S.E. some part of the day under steam.
Lat 67°.59′.30. Long. 55°. 37′ W.
Course & Dist*ance* 3.44.W. 57′. *Cape* Farewell 578′.[2]
Temp of sea. 35½° 36°. 38°. 39°.

Wednesday 4 October 1876. <u>Holstenborg and Arctic Circle</u>
<Today> Passed the Arctic Circle; this day 15 months ago we entered it. We are a good deal further out in the straits, than we were coming up, and the Greenland coast does not appear so striking. The weather beautifully mild and sun hot, little or no wind, under steam at midday. a few pieces of berg ice seen.
Lat 66°.40½ N. Long. 54°.30′.W. Made good S.16.E. 82′.
Temp of sea, 38½°. 37°. 36°

Thursday 5 October 1876
Blowing a gale of wind from S.E. moderated towards 5 p.m. barometer commencing to rise.
Lat. 65°.8′
Long. 56°.27′ Temp of sea. 36°. 38°. 39°.

Friday 6 October 1876
Wind light but sea tumultuous, ship rolling very much. Soundings no bottom 120 fathoms. Several pairs of *Hyperoodon rostratus*[3] playing round the ship, one pair came within 40 or 50 feet of our quarter and gave us excellent views of their heads both in full and profile. they were about 25 feet in length.

Many Kittiwakes round us, and a pair of Pomatorhine Skuas,[4] the first I have seen, were chasing them. Several Fulmars, a few Eider ducks, a loom or two, but no little auks noted today.

---

[1] Ship-worm, a genus of saltwater clams.
[2] 578′ is 578 miles. On 3 October, *Alert* was roughly 580 nautical miles from Cape Farewell, the most southerly point of Greenland.
[3] Bottlenose whale.
[4] *Stercorarius pomatorhinus*, in N. America known as the pomarine jaeger. But see also entry for 15 June 1875 and n. 3, p. 56 above, which suggest the difficulty of identifying these birds at any distance.

I was watching the *Hyperoodons* during the afternoon and I think there was only one pair of them about, as never more than two were visible at the same time.

Lat. 64°.46′

Long. 56°.29′ Temp of sea. 38°½. 36°. 34°. 33°. 38°.

Saturday 7 October 1876

Great numbers of Little Auks flying south in flocks of from ten to 100, stragglers between the flocks passing continually. Fulmars and Kittiwakes following the ship, a berg or two in sight this morning.

Beaumonts highest latitude in Greenland was 82°.26′ but he <thinks he> saw land in 83°.

Lat. 63°.42′

Long. 54°.32′ Temp of sea 38°. 37°. 39°. 40°. 41°.

Sunday 8 October 1876

Lat at noon, 61°.55′ Long. 54°.41′ *Compass & Distance*[1] S b W. 107 miles C. Farewell S. 68° E 389 [*miles*]. Observed no Little Auks today only Fulmars and Kittiwakes. 7.45 a.m. Sighted 1 small berg and two pieces of ice three miles by port beam. Probably this is the last ice we will meet with.

Temp of sea. 42°. 41½°.

Monday 9 October 1876

Barometer fell from 29°.02 steadily all day reaching its lowest point at 7 p.m. viz 28°.76 it blew strong all day from S.E. 5.15 a.m. up mainsail very squally. 10 reefed foresail, 11 up mainsail 11.30 furled mainsail, in Fore Topsails, reefed topsails. I only noticed Fulmars following the ship. We have left the Kittiwakes behind us.

Lat. 59°.35′

Long. 53°.25′ Temp of sea. 44°.

Tuesday 10 October 1876

A ~~fine~~ clear day, barometer began to move upwards during the night, wind fell light during morning doing about four Knots. With the fine weather a dozen or more of Kittiwakes following the ship.

Lat 58°.13′.N.

Long. 54°.7′.W. Temp of sea 44°.

C & D. to No 3. rendezvous. S.74 E. 480′. Dist to Portsmouth via rendezvous. 2041![2]

7 p.m. brilliant aurora in N.E. true.

Wednesday 11 October 1876

Weather turning fishy[3] again, Barometer going down, only noticed two or three Kittiwakes following the ship today and Fulmars.

5 p.m. shortened sail to double reefed topsails, Trysails, spanker, jib and topmast staysails.

Lat.57.49′

---

[1] Distance run over previous 24 hours.

[2] *Compass & Distance*. 480′ and 2041 indicate nautical miles.

[3] Unreliable.

Long.51.40'. Temp of sea. 44°–43°.

Thursday 12 October 1876
The barometer falling steadily since yesterday, blowing a full gale by morning, at 4 a.m. a heavy sea struck the starboard side, and a portion coming through the skylight flooded my cabin, gun cases, boots and clothes floating, had to remain in bed till afternoon, by which time I had borrowed a new stand of clothes.

Bar[*ometer*] as low as 28.60. No Kittiwakes and hardly a Fulmar, a tremendous heavy sea running.
Lat 58°.46'
Long. 51°.35'. Temp of sea. 43°.

Friday 13 October 1876
Lat. 57°.46' N. Long. 51°.33'. W. Dist to Portsmouth 1954.
Completed fixing up of rudder. Wind fair, but our consort lagged behind and lost us several hours. The barometer declines rising, we are in most probably for another gale, the sea has moderated since yesterday, but still it is almost impossible to write from the movement of the ship. A few Fulmars only in sight today. Cleaning up gun. Gun case spoilt. Very heavy sea.

Temp. of sea. 42°. 44°. 44½°

Saturday 14 October 1876
The bad weather still continues, low barometer and heavy sea, the ship rolling much, quite putting a stop to writing and making reading a bore. The wind changed today N. by W. true, the first symptom of a fair wind that we have met with since leaving Egedesminde.

Lat. 56°.44' N.
Long. 49°.42' W.
C & D. 3.44. E86. To Portsmouth 1888'.
During the afternoon force of wind 4 several land birds about the ship. Aldrich and Parr noticed several Redpolls during their watches. An owl, *Asio accipitrinus*[1] flew round us for a couple of hours it alighted on the rigging within twenty feet of me, once it lit with outspread wings on the water under the lee of the ship, it arose from the water with great ease. I noticed a similar case before in the straits of Singapore in 1860. An apparently tired out *Scolopax*[2] flew round the ship and alighted with outspread wings, under the lee bow, I got down into the mizen chains[3] with the hope of picking up the bird, but like the owl it flew off the water again, apparently greatly refreshed. Only a few Fulmars following the ship. Temp of sea 44°.

Sunday 15 October 1876
Barometer rising. Wind N. b. W. going on our course. Sun bright. Parr saw a Redwing *Turdus iliacus* flying around during the morning watch. Many Fulmars following. Clothes hung up in the rigging to dry.

---

[1] Short-eared owl.
[2] Woodcock.
[3] Chains attached to the mizzen mast, the aftermost mast of a three-masted ship.

Lat. 55°.14′
Long. 47°.51′. Temp of water +45°

Monday 16 October 1876
At daylight observed a barque right ahead. 10 a.m., Ship ahead bore up and hoisted the white ensign.[1] 11.45 *Pandora* made her number.
Lat.54°.41′
Long. 45.16′ Temp of sea.+45°.
Several gulls (Kittiwakes?) and many fulmars about the wake of the ship.

Tuesday 17 October 1876
Alert Discovery & *Pandora* sailing in company.

Wednesday 18 October 1876
Lat. 55° 14′ N.
Long. 39° 11′ W. Distance run 126′.
To Cape Clear 1088'.
Thick rainy day, a few Fulmars and seven or eight Kittiwakes following the ship. Captain Nares signaled [*sic*] to Stephenson "Will not risk *Alert* with damaged rudder up channel. If we separate rendezvous at Queenstown sighting Cape Clear."
The *Pandora* out of sight by 1 p.m. By 6 p.m. blowing stiff. 8 o'c. a gale. died away by midnight. Egerton saw a little auk.

Thursday 19 October 1876
Bright and clear morning a little wind from the S. Kittiwakes around the ship, most of them young birds. A single *Puffinus major* following the ship.
Lat. 55°. 44′ N.
Long. 35° 38′ W. Distance run 124′.
To Cape Clear 927′.

Friday 20 October 1876
During the morning watch a heavy squall came up from S.W. becoming almost a hurricane between 7 & 8 a.m. Then the barometer which had sunk to 29.40 began rising. Owing to our crippled rudder we cannot scud before the gale.
During the height of the gale I noticed *Puffinus major* and Kittiwakes as well as Fulmars. As the gale moderated these birds increased in numbers.
Since leaving Egedesminde we have only passed two or three days without seeing birds, and probably if I had kept a better look-out there would not have been one day.
Lat. 54° 59′ N. D*istance. Run*.[2]
Long 34° 35′ W. to Cape Clear 925′.

Saturday 21 October 1876

---

[1] Flown on Royal Navy ships and shore establishments.
[2] Distance run is not given here.
[3] On the nape of the neck.

Bright and fine day running with a fair strong S.W. breeze. Fulmars, Kittiwakes, and *Puffinus major*, following. The latter have white bellies, white under wings, tips black, white nuchal[3] mark, longer winged than Fulmars. Temp +50°. Wet bulb 47° Temperature of water 49°.

    Lat. at noon   54° 24′ N.
    Long   30° 3′ W.
Distance run 169′. To Cape Clear 765′.

This glorious weather continued throughout the afternoon, and up to mid-night we were doing 8 knots, under a starry sky. The old Polestar no longer obliges one to crane his neck to see him. 1800 miles of southing makes a vast difference.

    Anniversary of Trafalgar.

Sunday 22 October 1876
A lovely day, observed *Puffinus major*, Fulmars, and Kittiwakes.

    Lat. at noon.   54° 5′ N.
    Long   .,,   24° 55′ W.
To Cape Clear 582′.

Monday 23 October 1876
Early this morning the wind changed to S.E. blowing strong and dead foul, went on the other tack and stood S.W. Fulmars have entirely left us to-day. *Puffinus major* and Kittiwakes are following and an immature *Stercorarius pomatorhinus*.

    Lat. at noon   53° 59′ N.
    Long.   „   23° 5′ W.
Distance made 69′. To Cape Clear, S. 73E. 517′.

Storm petrels the first we have noticed following the ship. A small wader (*Calidris arenaria*?), two small land-birds, species uncertain about the ship. It will be a curious circumstance if it can be proved that in the Atlantic *Procellaria glacialis* does not cross south of the fifty-third parallel of north latitude. At 4 p.m. a starling *sturnus vulgaris*, tried to alight on the rigging but was blown to leeward. At 10 p.m wind shifted. Wore ship, went on our course wind S.W.

Tuesday 24 October 1876
    Lat. at noon   53° 12′ N.
    Long.   „   21° 6′ W.
Distance run 87′. To Cape Clear 438′.

During the morning watch an example of *Sturnus vulgaris* ♂ came onboard. Stomach empty. *Puffinus major* and *Thalass. pelagica*[1] following the vessel, also Kittiwakes. A bright and beautiful day towards evening breeze freshened and we were running 8 or 9 knots.

Wednesday 25 October 1876
After midnight we were becalmed. A snipe was seen close to the ship also a few small land birds. Steam up at 11 a.m.

    Lat. at noon   52° 14′ N.

---

[1] *Thalassidroma pelagica*, storm petrel.

Long.   „   17° 28′ W.
Distance run 143′. Skelligs distant 255′.
In the afternoon several small birds (finches) chirping and flying about in the upper rigging.
    Wind freshened towards night-fall. A heavy cross sea running during the night.

Thursday 26 October 1876
    Lat at noon   53° 15′ N.
    Long   „   13° 3′ W.
Distance to the Skelligs 129′. *Puffinus major* about. A common snipe and a skylark came onboard.

Friday 27 October 1876
Landed with Captain Nares, D[r] Moss and Rev[nd]. H.W. Pullen from H.M.S. *Alert*, at Valentia[1] 1 p.m.

Saturday 28 October 1876
Travelled with Captain Nares and D[r] Moss from Killarney to Dublin.

---

[1] Valentia, off the SW coast of County Kerry, is the most westerly point of Ireland, and since 1866 had been the eastern end of the first commercially viable transatlantic telegraph cable.

PART VI: HOME AGAIN: SCIENCE, POLITICS, AND THE MILITARY 29 OCTOBER 1876–7 JANUARY 1877

Sunday 29 October 1876. Arrival in London
Arrived in town 6 a.m., met by Clements Markham took breakfast at <21> Eccleston Square. To Woolwich by 12.30 m. train.

Monday 30 October 1876. Woolwich
Stayed at Woolwich, and made calls with the wife. Alston[1] came down from town.

Tuesday 31 October 1876
To town, ordered clothes from Joel Edwards,[2] met Alston at 3 o'c. To Jermyn Street, saw Prof. Ramsay[3] – To War Office saw Mr Milton[4] Accountant General. To Admiralty saw Captain Nares. British Museum saw Dr Gunther[5] and Bowdler Sharpe[6] – To College of Surgeons saw Prof. Flower.[7] Left my card on Prof. Huxley[8] at Jermyn Street.

Wednesday 1 November 1876
Remained at Woolwich writing. Colonel Douglas Smith[9] called.

Thursday 2 November 1876
Ned Alston and I went to Portsmouth.

Friday 3 November 1876
Alston and I went onboard the *Alert*, and packed up the things in my cabin.

Saturday 4 November 1876
In town, met Captain Nares, Captain Markham and Commander Parr at the Admiralty, Captain Nares was just starting for Sandringham.[10] Received a copy of Nares official

---

[1] Edward Richard Alston (1845–81), zoologist. *ODNB*.

[2] Joel Edwards, military tailor. The firm dated from the late 18th century, and continued until World War II. The *London Gazette*, 16 July 1880, p. 4006, gives 9 Hanover Square, Oxford Circus, as the firm's address.

[3] Sir Andrew Crombie Ramsay (1814–91), Professor of Geology, University College London, President of the Geological Society of London in 1863–4. *ODNB*.

[4] Sir John Milton (1820–80), Accountant General of the Army from 1871. See Fraser, 'A Publishing House and Its Readers', pp. 16, 37–8.

[5] Albert Charles Lewis Gotthilf Günther (1830–1914), ichthyologist and museum administrator. *ODNB*.

[6] Richard Bowdler Sharpe (1847–1909), ornithologist and museum curator. *ODNB*.

[7] Sir William Henry Flower (1831–99), zoologist and museum curator. *ODNB*.

[8] Thomas Henry Huxley (1825–95), biologist and science educator. *ODNB*.

[9] Probably Andrew William Douglas Smith (b. 1837), Honorary Lieutenant Colonel, Royal Marines.

[10] Sandringham was then the Norfolk residence of the Prince of Wales. See Mrs H. Jones, *Sandringham, Past and Present*, pp. 2–3.

report printed for Admiralty.[1] Gave my copy to the Prussian military attaché who I met in the club.[2] Called on Captain Evans Hydrographer to the Navy.[3] At the Royal, Geological and Geographical Socs. On to 6 Tenterden Street where Dresser has most kindly lent me one of Salvins rooms,[4] Alston helped me to unpack the arctic things we brought up from the *Alert* yesterday. There was an article in todays Athenæum about the Arctic,[5] the tone of which I did not admire, and an article in the Echo about Allen Young and *Pandora*,[6] which was simply vulgar and scurrilous.

Julie and I dined with the Frobishers and met Major and Mrs Barclay, we knew them at Aldershot when he was aide to General Maxwell.[7]

Sunday 5 November 1876
Wrote to Col. Lane Fox, Mr De Rance, The Marquis of Tweedale &c.[8]

Monday 6 November 1876
Dined with Col Brackenbury at the J.U.S. Club. Met at dinner Sir Garnet Wolseley, Major Butler and Col Baker and Mr Sandworth [*sic*] H.M.M. Consul for Crete.[9]

Tuesday 7 November 1876
To town with Julie, meeting of the Zoological Society. Slept at 6 Tenterden Street.

Wednesday 8 November 1876
Alston dined with me at the Club, and afterward we attended meeting of the Geological Soc. Returned to Woolwich.

[1] Nares, *Official Report*, 1876.

[2] Gustav Georg Hermann von Schrötter (1830–1919) was Military Attaché to the Prussian Embassy in London in 1873–6. His successor was not appointed until 1898. See Seligman et al., *Naval Route to the Abyss*, pp. 109–10.

[3] Frederick John Owen Evans (1815–85), Hydrographer to the Admiralty 1874–84. *ODNB*.

[4] Henry Eeles Dresser (1838–1915), leading ornithologist, zoologist, and all round naturalist. Osbert Salvin (1835–1908), naturalist. *ODNB*. 6 Tenterden Street, Hanover Square, was the house of the Zoological Society of London, and many naturalists gave this as their London address.

[5] 'Arctic Expedition', *The Athenæum*, 4 November 1876, pp. 596–7. The issue of 11 November 1876, p. 627, has a favourable article, 'Arctic Expedition', on the scientific results of the Arctic Expedition, based upon information supplied by Feilden.

[6] There is a critical account of the British Arctic Expedition in 'Passing Notes', *The Echo*, 3 November 1876, arguing that the outbreak of scurvy was preventable and needed investigation. 'Summary of Today's News', ibid., mentions the welcome of *Pandora* at Portsmouth. There is no article on Young and the *Pandora* in *The Echo*, 4 November 1876.

[7] I have been unable to identify the Frobishers. There are several Generals Maxwell at this date. The most likely are Edward Herbert Maxwell, CB, and W. R. Maxwell (d. 1892), Royal Marines. Major Barclay is probably Major Edward Barclay, in 1876 retired and unattached to a military unit. Feilden often calls his wife 'Julie'.

[8] Colonel A. Lane Fox, anthropologist. See Fox, *Catalogue of the Anthropological Collection*. Charles Eugene De Rance (1847–1906), geologist; see J. Geikie, 'Obituary'. Colonel Arthur Hay (1825–78), army officer and ornithologist, 9th Marquess of Tweedale, succeeded his father in the marquisate in 1876, see *ODNB*.

[9] Colonel Charles Booth Brackenbury (1831–90), see *ODNB*. The Junior United Service Club, 11 Charles St, Regent St, London. Garnet Joseph Wolseley (1833–1913), army officer, see *ODNB*. Major Thomas Adair Butler, VC, retired; see McCance, *History of the Royal Munster Fusiliers*, II, p. 244. Lieutenant Colonel James Baker (1830–1906), retired. Sandworth is Thomas Backhouse Sandwith (1831–1900), British Consul in Crete; see *The London Gazette*, 24 June 1879, p. 4086.

Thursday 9 November 1876
Remained at home in Woolwich Mr Freeman[1] called upon me in the evening.

Friday 10 November 1876
Remained at home in Woolwich.

Saturday 11 November 1876
To town and met Billy.[2] Bought from Ackerman's[3] a copy of the Illustrated Arctic News, and Browns sketches of James Clarke Ross' Ex. paid cash for them viz half a guinea for the one and a guinea and a half for the other.[4]

Sunday 12 November 1876
Billy came from town and spent the day with us.

Monday 13 November 1876
Dined with Uncle Montague at the Reform.[5] Leyland[6] and Billy there.

Tuesday 14 November 1876
Made calls with Julie on Woolwich people.

Wednesday 15 November 1876
Remained at Woolwich and walked with Julie in the afternoon.

Thursday 16 November 1876
To town and saw Captain Nares, dined with Maskyline [*sic*][7] at the Royal Soc. Club – Willis' Rooms.[8] Returned to Woolwich.

Friday 17 November 1876
From Euston to Mr John Evans, Hemel Hempstead, met D[r] and Mrs Hooker.[9]

Saturday 18 November 1876
To Cambridge, to Magdalene College. Dined with Cambridge Philosophical Society.[10]

Sunday 19 November 1876
Dined in Hall Magdalene College.

[1] Not identified.
[2] Billy is Sir William Leyland Feilden, 3rd baronet (1835–1912), HWF's older brother. *Debrett's Baronetage*, 1893, p. 205.
[3] Rudolf Ackermann (1764–1834) was a London publisher and lithographer, who transferred his business to his eldest son, Rudolf; the print business survived, becoming Arthur Ackermann & Son in 1855.
[4] Osborn and McDougall, *Facsimile of the Illustrated Arctic News*; Browne, *Ten Coloured Views*.
[5] Montague Joseph Feilden, 1816–98.
[6] There are several Leyland Feildens at this date; I do not know which one this is.
[7] (Mervyn Herbert) Nevil Story Maskelyne (1823–1911), mineralogist. *ODNB*.
[8] Formerly Almack's Assembly Rooms on King St, St James, and from 1871 Willis's Rooms; a social club.
[9] John Evans (1823–1908), archaeologist. *ODNB*. Joseph Dalton Hooker (1817–1911), botanist, and in 1876 President of the Royal Society of London. *ODNB*.
[10] A scientific society founded in 1819, and still extant.

Monday 20 November 1876
Left Cambridge and returned to Woolwich.

Tuesday 21 November 1876
Remained at Woolwich, and walked to the town and did shopping with Julie.

Wednesday 22 November 1876
Dined with the First Lord of the Admiralty.[1]

Thursday 23 November 1876
Went to Greenwich and dined at Royal Naval College. Slept in the College.

Friday 24 November 1876
Returned from Greenwich to Woolwich.

Saturday 25 November 1876
Went to Portsmouth. Met D[r] Rae[2] at Waterloo Station. Dined at the Royal Naval Club.[3]

Sunday 26 November 1876
Dined with Captain and Mrs Nares at their lodgings in Southsea. Met Captain Tizard late of *Challenger*.[4]

Monday 27 November 1876
Busy all day on H.M.S. *Alert* packing up gear. Dined with Colonel Digby and the officers of the R. M. Art*illery* at Eastney Barracks.[5]

Tuesday 28 November 1876
Busy all day on H.M.S. *Alert* packing. Dinner onboard H.M.S. *Excellent*[6] to the Arctic officers.
My name appeared in the London Gazette as transferred from 4th. Foot, to Royal Artillery.[7]

---

[1] George Ward Hunt (1825–77). *ODNB*.

[2] John Rae (1813–93), Arctic explorer. *ODNB*. Richards, *Dr John Rae*.

[3] The occasion was a banquet, at the Portsmouth Naval Club, for the officers of *Alert* and *Discovery*, along with Captain Allen Young of the *Pandora*. Feilden has tipped in a press cutting with a detailed account of the speeches at the banquet.

[4] Thomas Henry Tizard (1839–1924), naval officer and hydrographer. *ODNB*. Tizard joined Nares on HMS *Challenger* in late 1872, and remained with the ship until it was paid off in 1876; Nares meanwhile had been appointed to the British Arctic Expedition.

[5] Royal Marine Artillery, barracks at Eastney, near Portsmouth. G. S. Digby (d. 1877) in 1855 commanded the Royal Marine Artillery as Lieutenant Colonel in the siege of Sebastopol in the Crimean War; he became Colonel Commandant of the RMA in 1876. Feilden dined with him in the Royal Marine Artillery barracks at Eastney. *The Annual Register*, N.S., 1878, p. 140.

[6] HMS *Excellent* was a gunnery school in Portsmouth, formally established in 1869; in 1876 it was in the hulk formerly named HMS *Queen Charlotte*. It became a shore establishment on Whale Island in Portsmouth Harbour in 1891. www.royalnavy.mod.uk/our-organisation/where-we-are/training-establishments/hms-excellent/history

[7] Walker, *Bulletins and Other State Intelligence*, p. 946. The *London Gazette* of 28 November 1876. The *London Gazette* of 8 February 1876 p. 528, confusingly states that Feilden 'retires from the service', but this refers only to his transferring from the 4th Foot of the King's Own Royal Regiment to the Royal Artillery.

Wednesday 29 November 1876
Busy all day on H.M.S. *Alert*, getting out boxes from the hold and packing up. Reception at Admiral McClintocks in the evening.[1] Dined with Mr and Mrs Clements Markham.

Thursday 30 November 1876
Left Portsmouth by 2.50 train home by 8 o'c, going neither to the Mayor of Portsmouth's dinner or to that of the Scottish Society.[2]

Friday 1 December 1876
Remained at home, writing and working.

Saturday 2 December 1876
Rainy and stormy – 42 packages sent to me from the ship at Portsmouth. By Mr Boot.[3]

Sunday 3 December 1876
Very stormy and rainy remained at home.

Monday 4 December 1876
Very stormy and rainy, remained at Woolwich. Mr Freeman called in the evening.

Tuesday 5 December 1876
To town lunched with Alston. Went to Tenterden Street, ordered two cabinets through Mr Porter.[4]
    H.M. Ships *Alert* and *Discovery* paid off.

Wednesday 6 December 1876
Julie went to town with me. I left Carboniferous Arctic fossils with Mr Etheridge[5] at Jermyn Street. To British Museum, saw Maskelyne. Dined at Willis's Rooms with old Arctic officers sat between Roche and Toms.[6] Met Admiral R. Jenkins.[7] Went after dinner to Mr Clements Markham and slept there.

---

[1] At this date (Francis) Leopold McClintock (1819–1907) was Admiral Superintendent of Portsmouth Dockyard. *ODNB.*

[2] I have not been able to identify this society. Although Feilden did not attend the banquet given by the Mayor of Plymouth, he tipped in a press cutting, 'The Arctic Expedition', giving Nares's reply to the toast to himself and his officers.

[3] Not identified.

[4] Probably R. H. Porter, 6 Tenterden St, London, publisher of books on natural history, especially ornithology, who may have arranged for Feilden to purchase cases for natural history specimens.

[5] Robert Etheridge (1819–1903), palaeontologist to the Geological Survey and curator of the Museum of Practical Geology on Jermyn Street. *ODNB.*

[6] Richard Roche served as mate in the Arctic search expedition of 1852–4, and as lieutenant of the *Russell* in the Baltic fleet, 1855. Warren and Lean, *Royal Navy List*, p. 311. Possibly F. P. Toms, who had served as 2nd lieutenant on HMS *Queen* in 1852.

[7] Rear Admiral Robert Jenkins (1825–94).

Thursday 7 December 1876
Dined with Mr Gwyn Jeffreys[1] at the Roy. Soc. Club. Attended meeting of Linnean Society afterwards. Met Hart. Wrote to Sir George Nares in reference to collections of Arctic Expedition. Reported myself to War office for duty.

Friday 8 December 1876
Banquet at the Mansion House. I sat between Admiral Ommaney [*sic*] and Mr Alderman Finnis,[2] the latter is a fine old gentleman aged 76 and told me he had been 50 years connected with the Corporation of the City of London. His advice to me, which I acted on, was excellent, and proved valuable, "Eat whatever you see me take on my plate, and drink whatever I do, and partake also of all the things I order for you. I know the ways of the Mansion House, and what is good."

Saturday 9 December 1876
Went with Julie by train to Blackheath, called on Colonel Rich and Admiral Sir Crawfurd Caffin. the latter lives in a very pretty house with lovely cedar tree in the garden. (Vanbrugh Lodge)

Sunday 10 December 1876
To Christ Church, Shooters Hill with Julie. Arthur Pedder[3] came to dinner and stayed the night.

Monday 11 December 1876
Walked with Julie on the Eltham road.[4] Worked at sorting collections from Arctic.

Tuesday 12 December 1876
Meeting of Geographical Soc. at St James Hall. Sir George Nares, Captain Stephenson and Captain Markham read papers. The Prince of Wales in the chair.

Wednesday 13 December 1876
To London with Julie and lunched with the Martins, No 9 Montague Place.[5]

Thursday 14 December 1876
To town and took a photo of Musk ox to British Museum, and Disco plants.

Friday 15 December 1876
Working at fossils &c. all day. Mr Seccombe dined with us.[6]

---

[1] John Gwyn Jeffreys (1809–85), lawyer and conchologist, who in 1875 carried out dredging on HMS *Valorous* during the BAE. *ODNB*. See also Geikie, *Annals of the Royal Society Club*.

[2] Erasmus Ommanney (1814–1904). *ODNB*. Alderman Thomas Quested Finnis (1801–83), Lord Mayor of London 1856–7, and an enthusiast for voyages of discovery and exploration.

[3] Possibly Arthur Pedder, in 1883 residing in Barmston Rectory, Lowthorp, Hull.

[4] Now part of the A20, running down to Eltham, Greenwich.

[5] John Stapleton Martin, lawyer in the Chancery division (b. 1846). *Solicitors' Journal and Reporter*, 29, 1885, p. 717 (J. S. Martin, 'Obituary' of his father, Mr Marcus Martin).

[6] Possibly, in view of the Norfolk connection, Dr John Thomas Seccombe (1834–95). See *ODNB* article on Seccombe, Lawrence Henry.

Saturday 16 December
To town went to Horseguards to ask for leave. Called on Allen Young – and at the Admiralty.

Mr Freeman called in the evening and brought his spectroscope.

Sunday 17 December 1876
Walked with Julie in the afternoon on the Dartford Road. Arranging for a start to Scarborough.[1]

Fanny got out and was in copula with a vagrant dog that scaled the back wall.

Monday 18 December 1876
Paid White £7.7 for Belts. Peachery for dressing skins. Lewis & Allenby for Julie. Mr Edwards for rates – and Davis 6 for soldering a split ring.[2] Worked in my study and packed up and boxed 8 lots of fossils and Rock specimens for Mr Etheridge.

Tuesday 19 December 1876
Julie and I went to Scarbro. Much rain. Found my Father and Mother looking very well.

Wednesday 20 December 1876
Pouring with rain gale from S.S.W.

Thursday 21 December 1876
Rain and gale from S.S.W.

Friday 22 December 1876
Rain, but took a long walk with Billy.

Saturday 23 December 1876
Called on Mr Champley[3] – afterwards took a long walk with Billy.

Sunday 24 December 1876
Arthur Pedder, Mr Simpson and Banistre Parker[4] staying with Billy. Took a long walk with Simpson.

Monday 25 December 1876
(Went down before Church, and consulted Mr Dale[5] – not feeling at all well. He considers that I am suffering from scurvy. Read this for 24th.)

Xmas, as usual a very dull day in England.

---

[1] HWF's parents had two seats outside London: Feniscowles, near Blackburn, and Feniscowles House, Scarborough.

[2] George White, tailor, Regent St, London; Lewis & Allenby, ladies' outfitters, Regent St; Peachery, Edwards, and Davis not identified.

[3] Robert Champley of Scarborough had published on the great auk. See Champley, 'The Great Auk'.

[4] Hardwick, *History of the Borough of Preston*, p. 251, mentions a Banistre (some sources have Banastre) Parker of Extwistle Hall. In 1719 the family seat was transferred to Cuerdon Hall. I have not found the individual mentioned by HWF.

[5] Dr Frederic Dale.

Tuesday 26 December 1876
Wretched weather. Billy's friends left.

Wednesday 27 December 1876
Mr Harrison the contractor for the aquarium, took the Govenor, Billy and I over the place.

Thursday 28 December 1876
Called on Inglis[1] and took tea with him, in his workshop. Communication from War Office granting me leave till 31st. Jan prox. on condition that I found some one to do my work and held myself responsible for the same.

Friday 29 December 1876
Wrote to officer Commanding 1st. Brigade at Aldershot that I declined my leave till the 31st. Jan 1877 – and would prefer joining on Monday the 1st. prox.

Saturday 30 December 1876
Intended starting for London, packed up but felt very unwell so sent for Mr Dale, who forbid me to leave the house, as I have spitting of blood and congestion of right lung. A nice look out!

Sunday 31 December[2] 1876
Took a short walk on the parade.

Monday 1 January 1877
Returned from Scarbro to Woolwich with Julie. Left at 11.a.m., arrived at home, Shooter Hill, at 8 o'c. p.m. Much rain fell during our journey, and vast tracts of country in Yorkshire were under water on each side of the rails. Evening papers informed us that a terrific gale had been blowing this day on South Coast. Found a note awaiting me from Sir Wm. Gull[3] saying that he would see me at 11.45 tomorrow.

Tuesday 2 January 1877
To London by 10.10 train. Called on Sir William Gull at 74 Brook Street. Waited sometime but could not see him, as he was called off into the country. There being no certainty either that I should be able to have a meeting tomorrow, decided upon consulting some one else, so went to Mr Marshall in Savile Row.[4] He told me that there was slight congestion of right lung, but was more cheerful in his view than Dr Dale. Met Newton, Howard Saunders, and others at the Zoological Society.[5] Wrote to the War Office enclosing Mr Marshall's certificate, and applied for leave to appear before a medical board.

---

[1] Not identified.
[2] Feilden has written January [*sic*].
[3] Sir William Withey Gull, 1st baronet, of Brook Street (1816–90), physician. *ODNB*.
[4] John Marshall (1818–91), surgeon, 10 Savile Row. *ODNB* and Cassino, *Naturalists' Directory*, p. 241.
[5] Alfred Newton (1829–1907), zoologist. Howard Saunders (1835–1907), ornithologist. *ODNB*.

Wednesday 3 January 1877
Busy at home all day, finishing off delayed correspondence &c. Heard from Dr Hooker asking me to meet him at Burlington House[1] tomorrow at 4 p.m.

Thursday 4 January 1877
Went to London, to Tenterden Street and packed up my collection of Smiths Sound and Polar basin plants, and took them along with me to Burlington House, where I gave them to Dr Hooker. Talked for sometime with Dr Hooker and Professor Huxley, they were civil enough to me, but there was an undercurrent of ~~ill feeling~~ <coolness> running through them the whole time. They have taken an idea into their heads that the Arctic Expedition has treated them with want of courtesy and ingratitude, which is a most mistaken idea.

Friday 5 January 1877
Remained at home and made lids, and packed up boxes containing sea beasts &c. and sent them off to Burlington House. Dr and Mrs Roberts[2] dined with us.

Saturday 6 January 1877
To town very wet and windy; to Tenterden Street and packed up birds and miocene fossils in readiness to transport them to Burlington House.

Sunday 7 January 1877
Pouring all day wind S.W. remained in the house.

---

[1] Burlington House was the home of both the Linnean Society and the Royal Society of London. Hooker was at this date President of the Royal Society, and the meeting with Feilden would have taken place there.
[2] Identification uncertain. Possibly Sir William Roberts (1830–99), physician and physiologist. *ODNB*.

APPENDIX A

Letters From Henry Chichester Hart,[1] Naturalist in HMS *Discovery*, to Feilden, Received by Feilden in HMS *Alert*, and Inserted by Him in His Journal

Inserted facing entry for 4 April 1876

H.M.S. *Discovery*
Bellot Harbour
81.44 N Lat.
65.3 W Long.

29/3/76.

My dear Feilden

I was delighted to get *both* your letters and hear good news of you all; though the *Pole* seems a bad job However you have beaten the rest already, that is a comfort.

We have passed a comfortable and happy winter, only one hand has been really ill & he will scarcely recover from scurvy. We only did a little local survey sledging in the autumn, there was no ice foot & there was open water here & there till December, we had lots of skating. I was twice away sledging for a few days.

Musk Oxen occupied all our time in the little summer we had left, parties were away constantly either slaying skinning or fetching them down, so that I left botany for this year altogether. The flora is of course much richer than yours, and the land (except geologically) more interesting, it rises to about 3000 feet in one long Plateau from which we obtain a splendid view of your Hecla and Griper ranges. This plateau is about N E by S W true & is intersected by one deep valley about N W apparently to low land about the foot of the H & G ranges. This valley will prove a fruitful route for summer travelling & will probably afford a means for overland route to *Alert*, it is about 800 to 1000 feet above sea level, it is impassable from snow at present.

I have been up all the mountains in the neighbourhood, there are two or three fresh lakes of some size near us & with Aldrich's success in view, we fully expect to give you some good trout fishing when you pay us a visit. I hope however you will not wait for that season but put your noble face southern ere long.

---

[1] Henry Chichester Hart (1847–1908)), educated as a botanist, naturalist in HMS *Discovery*. He edited about 30 Arden editions of plays by Shakespeare. Parts of this letter are difficult to decipher because it was written on both sides of the paper and the ink has bled through.

Archer went under Coppinger's[1] medical supervision[;] dogs to Polaris Bay to take a survey of stores, they have had bad weather.

You must excuse me if I did not write you a long letter, but these fellows visit is too short & there is so much talking to be done that all sedentary or unsociable employments have been chawed up since their arrival.

We are about 250 yards from the shore & the first day we walked to it was Sept 5th. Hans has proved of great value as a hunter. He [?] freely & eloped to a snow hole at about −50° one night 4 miles away, he was ignominiously captured & brought back. Amongst the [stirring?] events may be mentioned the appearance of a seal three several times through the winter in the fire hole.

We are in a beautiful sheltered position, it is constantly [blowing] on the hills outside but we have only felt two gales of wind. The feel of this country is similar to yours argillaceous limestone and shales & clay flotz,[2] is all [shivery shaky?] & forms great beds of mud on the plain. There are pieces of quartz here & there but I have seen no [glacial?] markings anywhere However the atmospheric [?] is sufficient to have eroded them perhaps, there are several torrents about us which carry immense quantities of rock & mud in their active season downwards.

of *Birds* I have seen,

Turnstones
Knots } about 2 brace (fragment of egg on shore)

Snow buntings pretty common – (obtained one egg)

Eider ducks (old & young five)

Ptarmigan 10 brace

Snowy owl Hans has seen one three times

once this winter, I found a pellet composed of Lemmings –

I have seen no gulls nor Long-tailed Ducks –

Mammalia

Musk ox. plentiful.

Hares D*itto.*

Hudsons Bay Lemming Do. (8 or 10 obtained.)

Foxes one large blue one seen last autumn, one white caught in trap this year their tracks are numerous – I have seen three.

Seals

Phoca barbata[3] (2)
Pagomys fœtida[4] } Both shot here –

Botany

I have made no collection yet except of lichens, which I have not named. I have observed

3 *Drabas – Hesperis Cerastium alp*inum. *Papav.* nud*icaule* – [5]

---

[1] Richard W. Coppinger, MD, Surgeon, HMS *Discovery*.

[2] Argillaceous: clayey. Flötz: a term used by Abraham Gottlob Werner (1749–1817) to denote secondary (newer) fossiliferous rocks, lying horizontally.

[3] Bearded seal, *Erignathus barbatus*.

[4] Ringed seal, *Pagomys hispida*, *Phoca hispida*.

[5] *Drabas* whitlow grasses; a genus of flowering plants in the mustard family; Alpine chickweed; Arctic poppy.

Port Foulke Compositæ[1] (which I cannot identify)
*Taraxacum – Stellaria long*ipes. [?] subspic.[2]
*Alopecurus alp*inus. *Potentilla Multifida –*[3]
A couple of *Hypnums* & one *Conferva –*[4]
There has been no dredging done of course, but there are crinoids here, also a [b]ivalve
mollusc & abundance of red shrimps et al. These collections have been made & have been
examined thoroughly
  Fauna List since reaching w[inte]r Q[uarte]rs.
    to March 29.76
Musk oxen 32. (Muskiness appeared in animals of all sexes and ages)
Hares 20.
Seals 5 (~~2 of each kind~~) (2 Floe rats 3 [?Ground] seal)[5]
Ptarmigan 7.
Ducks 2.
So you see we have been pretty well supplied with fresh meat – most of us could go the
musk beef, but it was about half quite [fine firm] and first rate eating.
  I have not had time to examine all my collection yet so I cannot tell you as much as I
would like. There are shells (*Saxicava*)[6] to be found between 4 & 5 hundred feet above
sea level close to the ship.
  Wishing you every success in the coming season [?] hoping to see you soon.
      Believe me
      Ever yours sincerely
      Henry Christopher Hart
Please remember me to Moss & tell May if you like how deeply I sympathize with him but
who'd mind his loss of a toe! Best wishes to all the [?] of you. H.C.H.

Inserted facing entry for 6 June 1876

Discovery Bay
May 22 1875 [*sic*][7]

My dear Fielden [*sic*]
  Conybeare[8] is carrying letters to *Alert* & so here goes to wish you good luck and a
pleasant summer.
  I expected to have seen you last week (according to your prearranged plans) at Polaris
Bay, when the Capt. returned from your ship he offered to take me there – we left on
Wednesday 10th and returned on Thursday 18th, having had gales of wind all the time

---

[1] The daisy family.
[2] Dandelion; Longstalk starwort.
[3] Foxtail; cinquefoil.
[4] A cryptogam moss; a kind of algæ.
[5] There is no such species as a Ground seal, but that is what Hart has written. Perhaps he meant Grey seal.
[6] A bivalve mollusc.
[7] Should be 1876.
[8] Crawford James Markland Conybeare (1854–1937), sub-lieutenant on HMS *Discovery*.

(four days) we were there, It is a dreadfully exposed place & the men were confined to their tents from Friday to Tuesday; I got pretty well over the country around and behind the Bay, but it was under great disadvantages. I have written for Capt. Stephenson[1] a sort of remarks about the place which I suppose you will see & indeed there was precious little to find out.

The Limestone is very hard, close grained greyish blue rock, becoming shaly in many places above, it was only after a lengthened search I obtained (with help of a lens) any fossils which are minute – fragments of a Lamellibranch,[2] something of the *Modiola*[3] trib[e], and I think a Per[?] – several of these from Cape Lupton and 7 or 8 miles South East of it inland – also a single horizontal section of possibly a minute *Cyathophyllum*[4] – they are however all in situ and sound, capable I think of identification, but I have not had a chance of examining them yet, as I was cut down like a lily of the field with snow blindness the day after our return & my eyes are not O.K. yet.

If however you wanted a collection of fossils at hap-hazard P Bay[5] is the place – it is more densely covered with drift than an English meadow with buttercups. [here] are especialy boulders, & I brought home a lot of their fossils to amuse myself with, they are mostly Silurian.

The Limestone of the Country dips Easterly (Magnetic) 45° to 60° – I believe I will find it occur in this neighbourhood. Snow Buntings appeared there on 15th, here on 16th. travelling from N to S. have you any notice of them this year.

We have shot hares & ptarmigan (a few) the latter just on the change from W*inter*. dress then were shot with Sneiders![6] (10th)

No musk oxen have appeared here as yet here [*sic*] – 11 seen in Archer's Sound –

We catch Lemmings here, but they die, they are changing colour prettily, dark on head & back – Rufous flanks, bells, ear coverts shoulders –

Seen several owls, none procured – I have a great pet now, a caterpillar which I brought from P. Bay – quite tame

The P. vegetation is identical with that here, but much scantier and as far as the season will permit us to judge the Flora is considerably poorer –

I got a nice little floe-rat[7] the other day. Hans (our invaluable Eskimo) shot him in firehole.[8] A full grown female – [?] and spots according to Cocker – write me a line & love to all whom it may concern

Ever yours sincerely Henry C. Hart.

[*Note in Feilden's hand, written on Hart's letter above.*]

<I tell you no news from ship for obvious reasons. Please make for me a collection of *all* the plants your country contains, I will do as much as I have always hoped to do for you in return H.>

---

[1] Henry Frederick Stephenson (1842–1919), captain of HMS *Discovery*.

[2] A lamellibranchiate or bivalve mollusc, *OED*.

[3] A genus of mussels; a mussel of this genus, *OED*.

[4] A kind of fossil coral.

[5] Polaris Bay.

[6] Probably the .577 Snider-Enfield, which was a breech-loading rifle, adopted by the British Army in 1866.

[7] Floe rat is what sealers called the ringed seal, *Phoca hispida*.

[8] Hole kept open through the ice, so that sea-water could be instantly obtained in case of fire on board ship

APPENDIX B

Letter from Richard W. Coppinger, M.D., Surgeon in *Discovery*, to Feilden, Repulse Bay

28 April 1876
5 a.m.

My dear Feilden

Sorry to say that I have seen nothing as yet worth sending to you. I took a walk this morning about 3 miles inland & up a hill 1200 feet high, my main object being to reconnoitre a route towards Peterman*n* Bay, to meet future contingencies. Not as yet successful in this. Country very sterile. Undulating hills, showing [?] rock in situ, but undoubtedly same formation as in your vicinity. *Sh*ale, claystone, & a low [?] limestone, with in the lowlands numerous *small* rounder boulders of dark gneiss. Snow is in same amount as on your site, but much harder, affording a good footing for walking. Although I walked for about 4 hours I have seen a solitary fox ~~trap~~ track, as regards animal life. No droppings or such traces, we camped on the landfoot before midnight, & having arranged our cargo of provisions start for the eastward this afternoon. At present I am luxuriating in a smoke in my bag, preparatory to roasting. I take Emerson's [*sic*][1] 4 man, & he returns to you with my 8 man sledge empty. —There are some very fine sections of floe bergs with "dirt lines" stranded here: similar to those with you. Shall I bottle you up some of the dust from the lines, & send it by the next sledge? Let me know by Emerson [*sic*], I do not do so now, as I will have some opportunity of communicating a fortnight hence, & may then have something more interesting to put in the bottle.

Success to your Lincoln Bay trip

Yours very sincerely

R.W. Coppinger

---

[1] George W. Emmerson, chief boatswain's mate, *Discovery*.

APPENDIX C

Flora and Fauna in Feilden's Journal

Scientific Names of Mammals, with English Names

Arvicola hudsonius: obsolete term for Hudson Bay lemming
Balaena mysticetus: bowhead whale
Balænoptera musculus: blue whale
Balaenoptera physalus: fin whale, finback whale
Beluga: beluga, white whale
Canis borealis: husky
Canis familiaris: dog, domestic dog
Canis lupus: wolf
Cervus strongyloceros: wapiti, elk
Cervus tarandus: caribou, reindeer
Delphinapterus leucas: beluga
Dicrostonyx groenlandicus: northern or Arctic collared lemming
Elephas primigenius, Mammuthus primigenius: woolly mammoth
Hyperoodon ampullatus: northern bottle-nosed whale
Hyperoodon rostratus: beaked whale
Lemmus sibiricus: Siberian brown lemming
Lepus, Lepus arcticus, Lepus glacialis: hare, Arctic hare
Lupus: used by Feilden for Arctic wolf
Monodon monoceros: narwhal
Mus hudsonius: see *Myodes hudsonicus*
Mustela erminea: stoat or ermine
Myodes torquatus: ringed lemming
Myodes hudsonicus: Hudson Bay lemming
Odobenus rosmarus: walrus
Orca gladiator; Orcinus orca: orca, killer whale
Ovibos moschatus: muskox, musk-ox, musk-sheep
Phoca barbata: known in the 1870s as the great seal or bearded seal; now spotted seal
Phoca foetida, Pagomys hispida, Phoca hispida: fetid seal, ringed seal
Ursus maritimus: polar bear, Arctic bear
Vulpes lagopus: Arctic fox

Sources
Banfield, *Mammals of Canada*
Biodiversity Heritage Library, at: www.biodiversitylibrary.org/

EOL: Encyclopedia of Life, eol.org
Richardson, Swainson, and Kirby, *Fauna Boreali-Americana*, I, 1829
Smithsonian National Museum of Natural History, North American Mammals, at: naturalhistory.si.edu/mna/

Scientific Names of Birds, with English Names

Acanthis: redpoll
Alauda alpestris: horned lark, shore lark
Alauda arvensis renamed *Eremophila alpestris* skylark
Alca alle, Mergulus alle: little auk, dovekie, rotge, rotche (the last no longer used in English)
Alca arra: now *Lomvia arra*, thick-billed murre, Brünnich's guillemot
Alca torda: razorbill
Alca troile: guillemot, loom, murre
Alle alle, see *Alca alle*
Anser albifrons: white-fronted goose
Anser bernicla: see *Branta bernicla*
Anser Hutchinsii: Hutchins's Barnacle Goose, Cackling Goose
Asio accipitrinus: short-eared owl
Branta bernicla: brant, brent goose
Calcarius lapponicus: Lapland longspur, Lapland bunting
Calidris arenaria, renamed *Calidris alba*: sanderling
Charadrius hiaticula: common ringed plover
Charadrius semipalmatus: semipalmated plover
Charadrius virginianus: American golden plover
Colymbus glacialis, Gavia immer: great northern diver or common loon
Colymbus septentrionalis, Gavia stellata: red-throated diver/loon
Corvus corax: raven
Cygnus americanus: trumpeter swan
Emberiza lapponicus, see *Calcarius lapponicus*
Emberiza nivalis see *Plectrophanes nivalis*
Eremophila alpestris: shore lark, horned lark
Falco candicans, Falco grœnlandicus, Falco rusticolus: gyrfalcon, or Greenland falcon
Falco peregrinus: peregrine falcon
Falco tinnunculus: European kestrel
Fratercula arctica: puffin
Fulmarus glacialis, Procellaria glacialis: fulmar petrel, or mollemoke
Gallinago gallinago: snipe, common snipe
Gallinago media: great snipe
Gavia immer: great northern diver, or common loon
Gavia stellata: red-throated loon/diver
Grus Canadensis, Antigone canadensis: sandhill crane
Harelda glacialis: long-tailed duck, old squaw
Lagopus muta, Lagopus rupestris, Tetrao rupestris: rock ptarmigan

Larus argentatus: herring gull
Larus canus: common gull, mew gull
Larus eburneus, Pagophila eburnea: ivory gull
Larus fuscus: lesser black-backed gull
Larus glaucoides, Larus leucopterus: Iceland gull
Larus glaucus: glaucous gull, burgomaster
Larus marinus: great black-backed gull
Larus sabini: Sabine's gull, see *Larus eburneus*
Mergulus alle, see *Alca alle*[1]
Mergus serrator: red-breasted merganser
Numenius arquata: Euarasian curlew
Nyctea scandiaca: snowy owl
Pagophila eburnea: ivory gull
Phalacrocorax carbo: cormorant
Phalaropus fulicarius: in Europe, grey phalarope; in North America, red phalarope
Phalaropus lobatus: Wilson's phalarope, red-necked phalarope
Pinguinus impennis: great auk, garefowl
Plectrophanes lapponica, see *Calcarius lapponicus*
Plectrophanes nivalis: snow bunting
Procellaria glacialis, see *Fulmarus glacialis*
Procellaridae: petrels and shearwaters
Puffinus anglorum: Manx shearwater
Puffinus major, Puffinus gravis: great shearwater
Rissa tridactyla: black-legged kittiwake
Saxicola oenanthe: wheatear, northern wheatear
Scolopax: woodcock
Somateria mollissima: common eider
Somateria spectabilis: king eider
Stercorarius cataractes, Stercorarius skua: great skua, bonxie
Stercorarius longicaudatus: long-tailed skua or jaeger
Stercorarius parasiticus: Buffon's skua, parasitic skua or jaeger, boatswain
Stercorarius pomarinus: pomatorhine skua, pomarine skua or jaeger
Stercorarius skua: great skua, bonxie
Sterna hirundo: common tern
Sterna macrura, Sterna arctica, renamed *Sterna paradisaea*: Arctic tern
Strepsilas interpres: turnstone
Strix nyctea: snowy owl
Sturnus vulgaris: starling
Sula bassana: gannet
Tetrao rupestris: see *Lagopus muta*
Thalassidroma pelagica: storm petrel, Mother Carey's chicken
Tringa canutus: knot, red knot
Tringa maritima: purple sandpiper

---

[1] N.B. The same bird sometimes appears with different Latin and English names in Feilden's journal. See e.g. Dovekie, Rotge, for which his subsequently published accounts correctly use *Mergulus alle*.

Tringa pectoralis: pectoral sandpiper
Tringa pusilla: least sandpiper
Tringa schinzii: dunlin
Turdus iliacus: redwing
Uria grille: black guillemot
Uria lomvia: Brünnich's guillemot, loom
Uria troile: foolish guillemot, lesser guillemot, guillemot, common guillemot
Xema Sabini: Sabine's gull

Sources
Cramp, *Handbook of the Birds of Europe the Middle East and North Africa*.
Godfrey, *The Birds of Canada*.
Lockwood, *The Oxford Book of British Bird Names*.
Morris, *A History of British Birds*, 2nd edn.
Richardson et al., *Fauna Boreali-Americana*, II, 1831.

Scientific Names of Marine and Aquatic Organisms (Excluding Mammals), with English Names

Alcyonaria (also Octocorallia): sub-class of Anthozoa, colonial polyps, both extant and, for those that secrete skeletons, fossil
Alva: alga, sea lettuce
Alecto glacialis: feather-star
Annelida: phylum of segmented worms
Anonyx nugax: a small amphipod
Aphrodita: sea mouse or sea aphrodite, a marine polychaete worm
Appendicularia: small free-swimming planktonic tunicates
Arcturus: genus of small isopod crustaceans
Arcturus baffini, var. *feildeni*: small isopod crustacean
Astarte: small bivalve mollusc, extant and fossil
Asteroidea: starfish or sea stars, extant and fossil
Brachiopoda: brachiopods, class of marine bivalves not related to molluscs, extant and fossil
Buccinum: sea snail in the whelk family, extant and fossil
Cephalopoda: class of molluscs including octopus and squids, extant and fossil
Charr: char (*Salvelinus*)
Clio australis: southern sea snail
Clio borealis: northern sea snail
Comatula: feather star, a stalkless crinoid, extant and fossil
Coscinodiscus: genus of diatoms
Cottus: genus of fish in the sculpin family
Crinoids: class of echinoderms, extant and chiefly fossil
Cychlina: genus of small sea snails in the family of cap snails
Cydippe: genus in the order Cydippida
Delectopecten vitreus: a scallop
Diatomaceae: diatoms
Echinodermata, phylum that includes sea stars and sea cucumbers

Enchrinite (*Encrinite*): fossil crinoid

Entomostraca: obsolete grouping containing mostly tiny crustaceans including copepods and ostracods

Eolis: genus of sea slugs

Foraminifera: class of marine protozoa with external 'shells' called tests

Gastropoda: class of molluscs, mostly snails

Globigerina: genus of planktonic foraminifera

Graptolite: fossil worm (hemichordate)

Gyrosigma: genus of diatoms

Hippolyte: genus of shrimp

Holothuria: a genus of sea cucumbers

Hydrachna (Feilden has *Hydrachnella*): water mite

Hydroid, hydrozoa: small predators related to jellyfish

Hypalocrinus naresianus: a crinoid

Ianthina or *Janthina*: violet snail, pelagic; *J. fragilis* is now synonymized with *J. janthina*

Isopoda: order of crustaceans, characterized by seven pairs of equal and similarly placed thoracic legs

Lamellibranch: lamellibranchiate or bivalve mollusc

Laminaria: kelp

Leda, Leda pernula: in the mollusc subphylum Conchifera

Lepas anatifera: pelagic or smooth gooseneck barnacle

Licmophora: diatom that grows on living plants

Limacina arctica: sea snail, sea butterfly

Littorina: family of sea snails including winkles or periwinkles

Lucernariidae: family of sessile, stalked jellyfish

Margarites helecinus: spiral margarite, a species of top snail, a sea snail

Merlangius merlangus: whiting, Arctic whitefish, coalfish

Modiola: a genus of mussels

Mollusca: molluscs, soft-bodied unsegmented invertebrates; *testaceous mollusca*: molluscs with hard shells

Mya: a genus of clams; *Mya arctica* was renamed *Saxicava arctica* and was moved to the genus *Saxicava*. The genus *Saxicava* has been renamed *Hiatella*, so the species originally named *Mya arctica* became *Saxicava arctica* and is now *Hiatella arctica*.

Natica: moon snail

Nucula: genus of small marine clams

Nymphon: order of sea spiders

Octocorallia: subclass of Anthozoa, called soft corals

Ophiura: brittle star

Orthagoriscus: either *Orthagoriscus mola*: sunfish, sharptail mola, or *Orthagoriscus truncatus*: longer sunfish

Pecten: genus of scallops

Pecten groenlandicus, renamed *Similipecten greenlandicus*: small Arctic scallop

Pecten islandicus: Iceland scallop

Pecten vitrens: a scallop, no common name found

Pentacrinus naresii, Pentacrinus naresianus, renamed *Hypalocrinus naresianus*: sea lily (isocrinoid)

Planorbis: genus of freshwater air-breathing snails

Pleurosigma: genus of diatoms

Polycistina: group of radiolarians, planktonic protists; their skeletons are important as fossils

Productus: extinct genus of brachiopods

Rhizopoda: group of amoeboid protists, its members now reclassified into several phyla

Rissoa: genus of very small sea snails

Rossia palpebrosa: warty bobtail squid

Rynchonella: extinct genus of brachiopods

Salmo arcturus, renamed *Salvelinus alpinus*: Arctic char

Salmonidae: fish family including salmon and trout

Salpa: genus of free-swimming oceanic tunicates

Salvelinus alpinus: Arctic char or charr

Saxicava: genus of edible clams, also called *Mya*; fossil and extant

Saxicava arctica, Mya arctica: no common name recorded

Saxicava norvegica: no common name recorded

Sepia: genus of cuttlefish

Serpula: genus of marine annelid tubeworms

Spirifer: genus of marine brachiopods, fossil

Tellina: bivalve mollusc genus

Terebratula: genus of Brachiopoda, extant and fossil

Teredo: ship-worm, bivalve mollusc that bores into wood

Thalassicola: genus of sea snails

Triceratium: genus of diatoms

Trichotropis borealis: cap snail

Trilobite: one of a group of extinct arthropods with three-lobed bodies

Trochus helicinus, renamed *Margarites helecinus*

Turbellaria: non-parasitic flatworms (marine and terrestrial)

Sources

Richardson et al., *Fauna Boreali-Americana*, III, 1836.

WoRMS: World Register of Marine Species, at: www.marinespecies.org/index.php

Scientific Names of Insects and Other Terrestrial Invertebrates, with English Names

Anoplura: suborder of sucking lice

Arachnida: class of joint-legged invertebrates (arthropods), including spiders

Argynnis: fritillary butterfly

Argynnis chariclea: Arctic fritillary butterfly

Argynnis polaris: Polar fritillary butterfly

Bombus: bumble bee

Calliphora vomitoria: bluebottle fly

Chrysophanus: copper butterfly[1]

[1] 'There are three examples of a pretty little *Chrysophanus* ("copper"), which appears to be a rather striking form (*Feildenii*) of our familiar C. *phlœas*', i.e. the Red Admiral: McLachlan, 'Insecta and Arachnida', p. 236.

Colias: clouded-yellow butterfly

Culicidae: mosquitoes

Diptera: order of true flies

Entozoa: internal parasites

Filaria: parasitic thread-like nematode, roundworm

Hydrachnella: family of water mites

Hydrachna: water mite

Ichneumonidae: family of parasitic wasps

ichneumon fly: generally known as ichneumon wasp

Infusoria: class of unicellular protozoa

Lepidoptera: order of insects including moths and butterflies

Muscæ: flies

Pentastomum: genus of parasitic invertebrates, tongue worms

Polycistina: genus of beetles

Taenia: genus of tapeworm

Tipula arctica: Arctic crane fly

Vitrina angelica, and *Vitrina pellucida*: two species of land snails

Sources

Biodiversity Heritage Library, at: www.biodiversitylibrary.org/

Layberry et al., *The Butterflies of Canada*.

Richardson et al., *Fauna Boreali-Americana*, IV, 1837.

Scientific Names of Plants, Fungi, and Algae, with English Names

Agaricus: genus of fungi

Alopecurus alpinus: alpine foxtail grass

Androsace septentrionalis: member of the primrose family

Angelica: a genus of biennial and perennial herbs

Azalea: a genus of shrubby plants (family Ericaceæ)

Betula nana: dwarf birch

Carex fuliginosa: short-leaved sedge

Carex vesicaria: bladder sedge

Cassiopeia tetragona: Arctic bell-heather

Cerastium alpinum: alpine mouse-ear or alpine chickweed

Cerastium vulgatum: mouse-ear chickweed

Chlamydomonas nivalis: species of green alga containing a secondary red pigment, the cause of red snow

Cistopteris fragilis: brittle bladder-fern

Cochlearia: scurvy grass

Conferva: genus of plants containing species of filamentous cryptogams, now restricted to certain freshwater green algae

Cystopteris: member of the genus of bladder-ferns

Draba: whitlow grass

Draba alpina: Alpine whitlow grass

Draba aurea: golden whitlow grass
Dryas octopetala: mountain aven
Epilobium latifolium: broad-leaved willow-herb
Ericaceae: family of which *Erica* or heath is the typical genus
Erysimum palassii: Pallas's wallflower
Hesperis pallasii, renamed *Erysimum palassii*
Hypnum: plait moss
Laminaria: genus of brown algae, kelp
Lychnis apetala: nodding lychnis, nodding campion
Mertensia maritima: oysterleaf or sea bluebell
Micranthres nivalis: snow saxifrage, alpine saxifrage
Oxyria digyna: mountain sorrel
Palmella: a genus of green algae
Papaver: poppy
Papaver nudicaule: Iceland poppy
Pedicularis: lousewort or betony (old spelling bettony)
Pedicularis hirsuta: hairy lousewort
Phascum: genus of moss
Poa alpina: alpine meadow grass
Poa cenisia: soft or Mount Cenis meadow grass
Potentilla, Potentilla multifida: cinquefoil
Potentilla nivea: snow cinquefoil
Protococcus: genus of green algae; the red form of the alga (*Chlamydomonas nivalis*) is responsible for the red colouring of snow noted by numerous explorers
Ranunculus nivalis: snow buttercup
Ranunculus pygmæus: pygmy buttercup
Salix: willow
Salix arctica: Arctic willow
Saxifraga cernua: nodding saxifrage
Saxifraga caespitora: tufted alpine saxifrage
Saxifraga flagillaris: whiplash saxifrage
Saxifraga nivalis, renamed *Micranthes nivalis*
Saxifraga oppositifolia: purple saxifrage, purple mountain saxifrage
Saxifraga tricuspidata: three-toothed saxifrage
Stellaria longifolia: longleaf starwort
Taraxacum: genus of plants, dandelions
Umbilicaria: rock tripe, genus of lichens
Vaccinium uliginosum: bog bilberry or western blueberry
Woodsia: low, tufted ferns

Sources
Biodiversity Heritage Library, at: www.biodiversitylibrary.org/
The Plant List, theplantlist.org
Porsild, *Illustrated Flora of the Canadian Arctic Archipelago*
Werner, *Roter Schnee oder Die Suche nach dem färbenden Prinzip*

APPENDIX D

List of Enclosures in Feilden's Journal at the Royal Geographical Society

Feilden used his journal as a scrap book, pasting in cuttings, notes, sketches, both during and after the expedition, and keeping others apart from the journal; in addition, the RGS has a folder of MS sheets, apparently from field notebooks, and clearly rough and preliminary. These are in a separate list, following item 93, and, with two exceptions, insertion no. 1 (Plate 9) and insertion no. 2 (Figure 66), are not reproduced in this edition. The image in Plate 9 is on paper torn from Feilden's journal. The drawing in Figure 66 is a more finished and more informative sketch than the other images from his field notebooks, and more informative than item 80. Insertions made during the expedition and tipped into the journal are reproduced in this volume in the body of the text, with selected colour illustrations in a separate plate section.

1) Formerly inside front cover, now in separate folder. Printed sheet, 'HMS Alert Winter Routine'. See Appendix E.
2) First front flyleaf, recto, printed cutting headed 'Arctic Discovery and Research'. Added in violet ink, 'April 30ᵗʰ. 1875'
3) First front flyleaf, recto, printed sheet, 'Directions for Collecting and Preserving the Skeletons of Animals. Altered from those by W. H. Flower, FRS.'
4) 6 small pp. MS sketches and brief descriptions of plants. See Figures 1–6.
5) Pasted on p. iii listing Letts's publications and manufactures, '... cutting Hints for Collecting Cryptogamia by G. Dickie'.
6) P. iv, engraving of <Dog> Sledge ~~Travelling~~.
7) P. iv, offprint from *Bulletin de la Société de Géographie*, mai 1875: title: 'L'expédition polaire américaine, sous les ordres de Capitaine Hall: lettre du Docteur Émile Bessels, au Secrétaire Générale de la Société de Géographie de Paris , Washington, 19 juillet 1874', with various observations, flora, fauna, geography.
8) Coloured sketch 'Baffins Bay June 30ᵗʰ. 75. H.W.F.' Tipped in by page for 30 June 1875. See Plate 1.
9) Coloured sketch 'Seneratatinia [Sanerâta Tinia] July 1 1875 .HWF'. See Plate 2.
10) Water colour sketch, Godhaab, Greenland coast, July 2ⁿᵈ. 1875 H.W.F. See Plate 3.
11) Coloured sketch Holothuria[n] with 10 tentacles dredged, Lat. 65°.00′ July 2ⁿᵈ. 1875. 30 fathoms H.W.F. See Plate 5.
12) Coloured sketch, 'Extraordinary iceberg, looking like a basaltic column, passed 2 a.m. July 2ⁿᵈ. 1875 off Baalfiord N. Lat. 64°.15". Sketched during Arctic night. H.W.F.' See Plate 4.
13) Coloured sketch. Common Beaked Whale *Hyperoodon rostratus* (Chemnitz). Off Old Sukkertoppen July 4ᵗʰ. 1875. See Plate 6.

14) 2 Coloured sketches, forming panorama, [1] ~~laterally~~ <horizontally> bedded Trap ~~Rocks~~ W. side. 1 [2] Disco. Blue Mountain. 6th. July 75 H. W. F.
    [1] These cliffs are Blaa Fell, and just about the join lies Ovifak the place where Professor Nordenskiöld found the meteorites & which I visited on the 11th. July 1875. H.W.F.' See Plate 7.

15) 10 July 1875, two sides of sheet, ink, Feilden, 'During my trip to Ovifak (July 9th. & 10th. 1875), the following species of birds came under observation ...'

16) Pencil sketch, 'Waigat July 17th 1875'. See Figure 7.

17) Coloured sketch. 'Proven. N. Greenland 20.7.75 H.W.F.' See Plate 8.

18) Coloured sketch, 'Berg, Entrance to Smiths Sound July 27th 1875' See Plate 9.

19) Between entries for 27 and 28 July. Cutting, 1 column, printed. Clements R. Markham, 'Use of Arrows by the Arctic Highlanders.'

20) Transcription in Feilden's hand of passage from MS journal of Henry W. Dodge, 1860–61. Feilden placed this between entries for 27 and 28 July 1875, but referring to entry for 1 Aug. 1875. Dodge was mate of the schooner *United States*, the ship belonging to Dr Hayes. This MS was found by Nares 'amongst the debris left by the *Polaris* expedition at Cape Hatherton' and Port Foulke in 1872–3. See HWF insertion on 1 August 1875, which transcribes a passage from Dodge's journal for 14 March 1861, p. 155, describing Cape Alexander. The MS was kept by H. W. Feilden until it was given to Gen. Greely in 1890

21) 'The ARCTIC Printing Office'. Printed announcement by Giffard & Symons of opening a printing office on HMS Alert, 28 July 1875, tipped in for that date. See Figure 8.

22) Coloured sketch, 'Victoria and Albert Range. Aug. 22nd. 1875. 12 P.M. HWF.' See Plate 10.

23) [10 Sept. 1875]. Lieutenant Aldrich's sketch map of route taken by dog sledges to lay down a depot. See Figure 10.

24) Pen 'Sketch of Cape Union, taken from a drawing by Lieut Wyatt Rawson R.N. made on the spot 5th. Oct 1875.' Feilden has added geological information. See Figure 11.

25) In indelible pencil, short MS note by Mrs Rae, and insertion by an unknown hand about pair of snowshoes given by Rae to Feilden, between entries for 13 and 14 Oct. 1876.

26) Coloured sketch. View from Point Sheridan Flag Staff Oct. 25. 1875. See Plate 11.

27) 1 Nov. 1875. Breakfast and dinner menu tipped in, Feilden's writing.

28) 2 Nov. 1875, Breakfast and dinner menu tipped in, Feilden's writing.

20) 4 Nov. 1875, Breakfast and dinner menu tipped in, Feilden's writing.

30) 5 Nov. 1875, Breakfast and dinner menu tipped in, Feilden's writing.

31) Printed Menu dated 11.11.75. See Figure 12.

32) Printed programme for 11 Nov. 1875: HMS *Alert*. Thursday Popular Entertainment. (Begins with Astronomical Lecture (with discussion) by Nares. Then various songs and 1 reading.) See Figure 13.

33) Printed sheet:'The Royal Arctic Theatre will be re-opened on Thursday next the 18th inst.' See Figure 14.

34) Printed prologue by Pullen, 'Spoken at the re-opening of the Arctic Theatre on Thursday, 18th November, 1875.' See Figures 15 and 16.

35) Printed programme for 18 November 1875. See Figures 17 and 18.
36) 22 Nov. 1875, Breakfast and dinner menu tipped in, Feilden's writing.
37) Printed programme, 'Thursday Pops', 25 Nov. 1875. See Figure 19.
38) Printed programme, 'Thursday Pops', 2 Dec. 1875. See Figure 20.
39) Saturday 4 Dec. 1875. Breakfast and dinner menus tipped in, Feilden's writing.
40) 8 Dec. 1875. Printed dinner menu in French, e.g. Pouding Anglais a la Pelham. On it is a sketch by Feilden dated '27th. Sept.' showing Aldrich and bluejacket Ayles in front of Cape Aldrich and Cooper Key mountains. See Figure 22.
41) Printed programme, 'Thursday Pops', 9 Dec. 1875. See Figure 23].
42) 15 Dec. 1875. Printed menu in verse on Moss's birthday.
43) 16 Dec. 1876. Printed 'Thursday Pops' programme. Lecture by Wootton on Steam, then conjuring show by the Wizard of the North. See Figure 24.
44) 21 Dec. 1875. Breakfast and dinner menu tipped in, Feilden's writing.
45) 22 Dec. 1875. Breakfast and dinner menu tipped in, Feilden's writing.
46) 23 Dec. 1875. Printed Royal Arctic Theatre programme including a farce, 'Boots at the Swan', after which, 'Aladdin, or the Wonderful Scamp' with Feilden as the widow Twankay. See Figures 25 and 26.
47) 23 Dec. 1875. Pencil sketch, 'Captain Feilden as Widow Twankay'. See Figure 27.
48) 25 Dec. 1875. Feilden's place card, with sketch of seals, polar bears, goose. See Figure 28.
49) 25 Dec. 1875. Printed Christmas menu in verse. See Figure 29.
50) 30 Dec. 1875. 'Thursday Pops', printed programme, begins with 'Lecture: Mock Moons under the Microscope: Dr Moss'. See Figure 30.
51) 6 Jan. 1876, Thursday Pops' programme'. See Figure 31.
52) 13 Jan. 1876. 'Thursday Pops' programme. See Figure 32.
53) 18 Jan. 1876. Drawing by Feilden, 'Cony & Mammoth. See Figure 33..
54) 20 Jan. 1876. 'Thursday Pops' programme, including 'A few words on ASTRONOMY by COMMR. MARKHAM', who was also down to 'give a Lifelike and Entertaining Display of Various Specimens in NATURAL HISTORY'. See Figure 34.
55) 27 Jan. 1876. 'Thursday Pops' programme, farce, 'The Area Belle'. See Figure 35.
56) 3 Feb. 1876. 'Thursday Pops' programme. See Figure 36.
57) 10 Feb. 1876. 'Thursday Pops' programme, begins with 'A Few Words on Arctic Plants' by Revd Pullen. See Figure 38.
58) 16 Feb. 1876, sketch of rear of sledge dog, '8 of these abreast in a sledge, firing volleys' See Figure 39.
59) 17 Feb. 1876, printed 'Thursday Pops', programme, begins with 'On Hydrostatics' by Lieut May. See Figure 40.
60) 20 Feb. 1876, Menu in verse with birthday toast to Lieut Giffard. See Figure 41.
61) 21 Feb. 1876, Feilden's drawing of snow drift in ravine. See Figure 42.
62) 24 Feb. 1876, Royal Arctic Theatre, printed programme. See Figures 43 and 44.
63) 29 Feb. 1876, Pullen's birthday menu in verse. See above, p. 206, n. 1.
64) 2 March 1876. 'Thursday Pops' programme. *Positively the last Entertainment this winter.* Begins with Nares, 'The Palæocrystic Sea and Sledging Experiences'. Ends with 'the grand Palæocrystic Sledging Chorus, by the entire strength of the House'. See Figures 45 and 46.

65) Coloured sketch: 'Gap of Dunloe. March 26ᵗʰ. 76. Cleavage right angles to line of Stratification. H.W.F.' See Plate 12.

66) Coloured sketch 27 March 1876: 'Contorted strata in Big Ravine beds ...' Note Feilden geologizing in sketch. See Plate 13.

67) 29 March 1876. Coloured sketch: 'Cape Rawson. 82.25.N. HWF.' See Plate 14.

68) 1 April 1876. Pencil sketch: 'View from top of Black Cape'. See Figure 47.

69) Facing entry for 4 April, but dated 29 March 1876, letter from Henry Chichester Hart, HMS *Discovery*, to Feilden. See Appendix A.

70) 7 April 1876. Pencil sketch: 'Black Cape S. Face'. See Plate 15.

71) 7 April 1876. Pencil sketch, black and blue: 'Black Cape Strike'. Double page. See Plate 16.

72) April 1876, sketch, 'Fred leaning on a Dog Sledge. April 1876. H. W. Feilden.'See Figure 51.

73) 28 April 1876. Pencil letter, Repulse Bay, Coppinger to Feilden. See Appendix B.

74) 29 April 1876. Sketch, 'Sledging in Grant Land. H. W. Feilden'. See Figure 52.

75) Facing entry 7 May 1876. Pencil sketch: 'Mt. Pullen – from Cairn Hill. Elevation 500. HWF.' See Figure 53.

78) Between 14 and 15 May 1876. Field sketch, pencil, double page: 'Mt Pullen & Simmonds I. From Dêpot Pt.', and 'Cape Joseph Henry from Dêpot Point'. See Figure 54.

77) Facing entry 16 May 1876. Pencil sketch: 'Lepus glacialis when alarmed'. See Figure 55.

78) 18 May 1876. Pencil sketch: 'Westward Ho! Valley ...' See Figure 56.

79) 21 May 1876. Pencil sketch: Egerton and others sleeping in a tent. See Figure 57.

80) 22 May 1876. Pencil sketch: 'Hare Ravine' with ptarmigan. See Figure 58.

81) 28 May 1876. Pencil sketch: 'Hummocks Point Hercules. Capt Nares ascending to look for road for Traction Engine! or Bicycle!!' See Figure 59.

82) 29 May 1876. Pencil sketch: 'Head of James Ross Bay ...' and 'Dana Valley ...'. See Figure 60.

83) 30 May 1876. Pencil sketch: 'Geologising on an Arctic summer day'. See Figure 61.

84) 2 June 1876. Pencil sketch: '"Floe" having fallen down in a fit, ...' [kicking dog back to ship]. See Figure 62.

85) 3 June 1876. Pencil sketch: Sledge travel. 'An experienced Arctic traveller informs us that no exertion is necessary ...' See Figure 63.

86) Facing 3 June 1876. Pencil sketch map of Feilden's sledge route, from Parker Bay via Cape Heckla and Crozier Island, past Feilden Isthmus. See Figure 64.

87) Facing entry 7 June 1876, dated Discovery Bay May 22 1875 [*sic.*], letter from Henry C. Hart to Feilden. See Appendix A.

88) 7 Aug. 1876. Pencil sketch by Feilden: 'Eskimo lamp found at Shift Rudder Bay'. See Figure 67.

89) 6 Nov. 1876. Printed cutting pasted in: 'The Arctic Expedition./ Message from the Queen.'

90) Cutting 11 Nov. 1876, The *Athenaeum*. 'The Arctic Expedition. From the information kindly communicated to us by Captain H. W. Feilden, the naturalist of H.M.S. Alert, we are able to give the following brief account of the principal results obtained by him and by Mr C. H. Hart, of the Discovery, during the Arctic

Expedition of 1875–76.' (Two paragraphs each on geology and zoology, one on botany.)

91) 25 Nov. 1876. Cutting: 'Banquet to the Arctic officers' at the Portsmouth Naval Club.

92) Cutting: 'The Arctic Expedition', facing entry 30 Nov. 1876, describing the banquet hosted by Mayor of Portsmouth. Captn. Nares 'did not give up the hope of a British tar being one day triumphant at the Pole, if it was to be reached. They must not be in a hurry. The work was difficult, and the workers must not be hurried, and the country must not be disappointed if it was not obtained at one jump.'

93) Cutting facing 4 Dec. 1876, 'The Arctic Crews at the Mansion House'. 'The men appeared to enjoy themselves thoroughly; and altogether the evening was spent in a very pleasant and harmonious manner, at the Mansion House.' Musical selections, including a Sledging Chorus, and a duet and dance by Messrs. Birnyan and Emmerson.

Separate Folder Headed 'Enclosures' in 'Journal of a Voyage to Smith's Sound and the Polar Seas', LIB (387.B.)

The list of the dozen items in this folder was prepared by G. A. Langdon in July 1958. I have edited this slightly, where additional information is available.

1) 'Berg, Entrance to Smith's Sound. July 27th. 1875.' Blue crayon sketch, ink caption, unsigned. Mounted on fragment of F's journal. (*not* same paper as bound journal). See Plate 9.

2) Sketch: 'View of Cape Beechey, Grin[n]ell Land ... With remains of Eskimo implements ...7th. August 1876. HW Feilden'. See Figure 66.

3) One cover, with drawing on reverse, and 21 pp. from a small sketchbook, sketches and notes 1875–6, in pencil.

4) Sketch of a piece of limestone, dated Oct. 5th. 1875, signed 'Wyatt Rawson, HMS Discovery. For Captain Feilden.'

5) (a) Table in ink, in Feilden's hand, undated, showing 'comparative scale of number of days the sun is below south horizon at N. Pole and also at various latitudes where arctic expeditions have wintered ...' (b) Page, numbered 191, from a notebook, with figures relating to (a) compiled by Capt. Nares on Alert 17th. Jan. 1875. Ink in Feilden's hand. (c) Two more sheets similar to (b), the first page numbered 225. Ornithological notes, July 28th and October 2nd 1875, followed by list of officers and crew of H.M.S. *Alert* with particulars (of age, height, weight, chest measurement, and 'vital capacity') on leaving England 29th May 1875. (b) & (c) are probably fragments of MS of Feilden's 'Notes from an Arctic Journal'.

6) 7 engraved illustrations cut from Nares, *Narrative* (1878).

7) HMS *Alert* March 2 1876 Chorus (two sides, printed), duplicate copy.

8) Printed meteorological abstract for HMS *Alert* and *Discovery* 1875–76.

9) Press cutting, *The Chronicle*, Oct. 27th 1877. Report of lecture to Chester Society of Natural Science by C. E. de Rance.

10) Press cutting from (?) "Lantern Readings", 2nd edition, vol. 3, with list of 50 views illustrating lecture on the Arctic Expedition of 1875–6, published by [William] Pumphrey. Note in ink at foot "R.A. Canteen, Nov. 21st 1877, Aldershot R. W. F."

11) Proof copy of notice of a Linnaean Society meeting, from *Athenaeum*, 31 Nov. 1877.

12) Book post wrapper addressed to Capt. Feilden at Aldershot, from Dr Hooker Royal Botanical Gardens, Kew, March 30th 1878, with ½d stamp.

APPENDIX E[1]

<Lat. 82°.27′>   H.M.S. *Alert*
                         Winter Routine. <1875–76>[1]

A.M.
6.45   Call All hands. Lash up and stow hammocks. Call COMMANDER.
7.   Watch sweep upper deck, gangways, &c.
7.30   Breakfast.
8.10   Hands clean Lower Deck, and Steerage.
9.   Hands to Clean. Clear up Lower Deck.
9.15   Both Watches fall in, and "tell off" to duty.
9.45   Inspection of Lower Deck.
10   In off the ice – Issue lime juice.
10.15   Quarters for Inspection. Prayers – "All hands" fall in and told off, to work, outside
        the ship if possible.
P.M.
12.45   In off the Ice. Clear up decks.
1.   Dinner.
2.15   Both Watches fall in, and told off to work (when there is sufficient light.)
4.   Clear up decks.
4.15.   Quarters. (On days only, when the men have been employed during the
        afternoon.)
4.45   Supper.
8.15   Hang up hammocks. (Or when Evening School is over)
9.   Out Lights. (or according to the time Classes have been dismissed)
9.15   Rounds.
10.   Out Chief Petty Officers Lights.
11.   Out Ward Room Lights.

On the first Friday in every month, the hammocks will not be lashed up at the usual
time, but the bedding will be spread out, and aired, on the lower deck, remaining hung up
in convenient places until 12.30, when the hammocks will be lashed up and stowed.

The Quarter Master of the Watch will have charge of all Lights and Fires from 11 P.M.
until 7 A.M.

He is also responsible for the routine being carried out, reporting to the Commanding
Officer the necessary times.

---

[1] One printed page insert, inside front cover of Feilden's journal, with Feilden's insertions marked < >.

BIBLIOGRAPHY

MANUSCRIPTS

[Admiralty], Kew, London: The National Archives (TNA), PRO: MS ADM. 1/6313, 22 Oct. 1874.
—, PRO: MS ADM. 1/6328, 4 Dec. 1874.
—, PRO: MS ADM. 1/6361, 30 April 1875.
—, Memorandum, PRO: MS ADM. 1/6367, 6 Jan. 1875.
—, [Sailing orders for *Alert* and *Discovery*] are in TNA, PRO: MS ADM 1/6367, [Robert Hall to Nares], 25 May 1875, 9 pp. printed. Reprinted in Nares, *Narrative of a Voyage*, I, pp. xi–xviii.
—, Sailing orders for *Valorous*, TNA, PRO: MS ADM. 1/6337.
Anderson, Robert, Medical Journal of HMS Enterprize, from 14 December 1849 to 24 May 1855 by Robert Anderson, Surgeon, during which Time the Said Ship Was Employed in an Arctic Searching Expedition for Sir John Franklin, TNA, PRO: MS ADM 101/99/5.
—, 'A Contribution to the Natural History of Prince Albert Land. Derived from the Medical Returns of the Late Surgeon Robert Anderson, of H.M.S. "Enterprize", 1851–53': referred to in Feilden, 'Prince Albert Land', but not located.
Dodge, Henry W., Journals, 3 vols, 1860–73, USA, Brooklyn Historical Society Archives, MS ARC.020, vol. I, 1860–61.
—, typescript copy of vol. I of his manuscript journal, Hayes Arctic expedition, 1860–61. MS in New York State Library, Albany, NY, MS (NIC) NYKI590-940-0278.
—, Transcript of Dodge Journal 1860, edited. London, British Museum of Natural History (BMNH), Feilden collection, MS P(aleontology), 1 vol., pp. 37, [39], [44].
Feilden, Henry Wemyss, letter to P. L. Sclater, 25 Nov. 1874, London, Royal Society, RSL MS M C.10.172.
—, *Alert* Journal, 1875–7, London, Royal Geographical Society Library, MS 387B.
—, 'Arctic Expedition: Post-Pliocene & Recent Specimens from Arctic Localities', 1875–6, London, BMNH, Palaeontology MSS, Feilden Collection, MSS FEI.
—, Fishing and dredging specimens, 1875–76, London, BMNH, Feilden Collection, MSS FEI.
—, 'Rock Specimens and Collecting Sites Including Some Collected by H. C. Hart, and Some Deposited in the Museum of Practical Geology [1875–6]', included in Henry Wemyss Feilden, 'Diary of an Expedition to the Arctic', London, BMNH, Palaeontology MSS, Small Library, MSS FEI. pp. 44–77.
Fulford, Reginald Baldwin, Cambridge, UK: MS, Scott Polar Research Institute, Collection GB 15 Fulford, Correspondence etc. re BAE 1875–6.
Hooker, Joseph Dalton, London, Kew: MS, Royal Botanic Gardens, Kew, Herbarium Archives. J. D. Hooker Papers, Voyage of HMSS *Alert* and *Discovery*, Letters &c.
—, letter to T. R. Jones, 22 [Jan.] 1785, Cambridge, UK: SPRI MS 336.
—, letter to J. W. Dawson 4 Jan. 1879, Montreal, Canada: MS, McGill University Archives MG 1022, Accession No. 2211/65/38.
Linnean Society, Secretary of, to Secretary RGS, [1865], TNA, PRO: MS ADM. 1/5934, no date but in response to letter of 2 March 1865.

Markham, C. R. to J. D. Hooker 11 Jan. 1875, MS, RBG, Hooker papers, Voyage of HMSS *Alert* and *Discovery*, f. 174.

—, 'Arctic Expedition' 1875–76, MS vol., RGS MS CRM 65.

Nares, George Strong, Log Book, HMS *Alert*, 15 April 1875–2 October 1876, TNA, PRO: MS ADM 53/10624.

—, 'Letterbook', Nares to C.-in-C. 24 February 1875, Library and Archives of Canada (LAC), MG 29 B 12 vol. III.

—, letter to Henry Bolingbroke Woodward, 8 March 1899, Montreal: McGill University, Blacker-Wood Library, Woodward correspondence.

—, 'Remark Book', Ottawa: Library and Archives of Canada (LAC), MG 29 B 12, vol. III.

Rawlinson, H. C., to Benjamin Disraeli, October 1874, TNA, PRO: MS ADM. 1 6313.

Richards, George Henry, Expedition Diary and Correspondence, 2 vols, Cambridge: Scott Polar Research Institute, MS GB 15 Sir George Richards.

Royal Geographical Society MSS, Correspondence Block 1871–80.

Royal Geographical Society proposals, TNA, PRO: MS ADM. 1/5934.

Royal Society of London, Committee Minute Books, MS CMB/2/14/1 and MS CMB/2/14/2, Appointments of Arctic Naturalists and Compilation of Arctic Manual.

Royal Society of London, Secretary of, to President, Royal Geographical Society, 16 Feb. 1865, TNA, PRO: MS ADM. 1/5934.

Trevor-Battye, Aubyn Bernard Rochfort., 'A Noble Englishman: Being Chapters in the Life of Henry Wemyss Feilden, C.B. Colonel, 1838–1921', Athens, GA: typescript copy in Hargrett Library, University of Georgia Special Collections, Collection Number MS340(m).

PUBLISHED WORKS

Albury, W. R. and Oldroyd, D. R., 'From Renaissance Mineral Studies to Historical Geology, in the Light of Michel Foucault's *The Order of Things*', *British Journal for the History of Science*, 10, 1977, pp. 187–215.

Allen, David E., *The Naturalist in Britain: A Social History*, 2nd edn, Princeton, 1994.

Allman, G. J., 'Instructions on the Collection and Preservation of Hydroids and Polyzoa' in Thomas Rupert Jones, ed., *Manual of the Natural History, Geology, and Physics of Greenland and the Neighbouring Regions...*, London, 1875, pp. 51–2.

—, 'Instructions on the Construction and Method of Using the Towing Net, and Notes on the Animals which May Be Obtained by its Employment', in Thomas Rupert Jones, ed., *Manual of the Natural History, Geology, and Physics of Greenland and the Neighbouring Regions...*, London, 1875, pp. 52–60.

—, 'Appendix No. XI. Hydrozoa', in George Strong Nares, *Narrative of a Voyage to the Polar Sea during 1875–6 of H.M. Ships 'Alert' and 'Discovery'...*, 3rd edn, London, 1878, vol. II, pp. 290–92.

Amaranth Publishing, 'The Rogue's March', at: www.amaranthpublishing.com/rogues.html

The Annual Register: A Review of Public Events at Home and Abroad, New Series, London, 1878.

Annual Report of the Secretary of the Navy on the Operations of the Department for the Year 1873, Washington DC, 1873.

Anonymous, *The Aneroid Barometer, How to Buy and How to Use It, by a Fellow of the Meteorological Society*, London, 1869.

Anonymous, 'Appendix No. XVII. Game List', in George Strong Nares, *Narrative of a Voyage to the Polar Sea during 1875–6 of H.M. Ships 'Alert' and Discovery...*, 3rd edn, London, 1878, vol. II, pp. 352–3.

Anonymous, 'Appendix No. XVIII. Meteorological Abstract', in George Strong Nares, *Narrative of a Voyage to the Polar Sea during 1875–6 of H.M. Ships 'Alert' and 'Discovery'…*, 3rd edn, London, 1878, vol. II, pp. 354–5.

[Anthropological Institute], 'Report of the Anthropological Institute', in *A Selection of Papers on Arctic Geography and Ethnology, Reprinted, and Presented to the Arctic Expedition of 1875, by the President, Council, and Fellows of the Royal Geographical Society*, London, 1875, pp. 276–92.

Appleton, Paul C. and Barr, William, eds, *Resurrecting Dr. Moss: The Life and Letters of a Royal Navy Surgeon, Edward Lawton Moss MD, RN, 1843–1880*, Calgary, 2008.

Arctic Blue Books: British Parliamentary Papers, Accounts and Papers 1854–55. 28 vols. Vol. VI Arctic Expeditions. Session 12 December 1854–14 August 1855. Vol. XXXV. Further Papers Relative to the Recent Expeditions in Search of Sir John Franklin and the Crews of H.M.S. 'Erebus' and 'Terror', London, 1855.

Arctic Blue Books: Papers and Correspondence Relating to the Equipment and Fitting Out of the Arctic Expedition of 1875, Including Report of the Admiralty Committee. Presented to both Houses of Parliament by Command of Her Majesty, [C. (2nd series) –1153], vol. L, London, 1875.

Arctic Blue Books: Arctic Expedition. Further Papers and Correspondence. Continuation of Parliamentary Paper [C. –1153] of 1875, London, 1876.

Arctic Blue Books: Arctic Expedition, 1875–6. Journals and Proceedings of the Arctic Expedition, 1875–6, under the Command of Captain Sir George S. Nares, R.N., K.C.B. [In continuation of Parliamentary Papers C 1153 of 1875, and C 1560 of 1876.] Presented to both Houses of Parliament by Command of Her Majesty, 1877. [C. (2nd series) 1636.], London, 1877.

Arctic Blue Books: Report to the Lords Commissioners of the Admiralty on the Cause of the Outbreak of Scurvy in the Recent Arctic Expedition; on the Adequacy of the Provision Made in the Way of Food and Medicine; and on the Propriety of the Orders Given by the Commander of the Expedition for Provisioning the Sledge Parties. Presented to both Houses of Parliament by Command of Her Majesty, [C. (2nd series) 1722], vol. LI, London, 1877.

Arctic Blue Books: Results Derived from the Arctic Expedition 1875–76. I. – Physical Observations by Captain Sir George Nares, R.N., and Captain Feilden, &c. II. – Medical Report on the Eskimo Dog Disease, by Fleet Surgeon B. Ninnis, M.D. Presented to both Houses of Parliament by Command of Her Majesty, [C. (2nd series) 2176], vol. LII, London, 1878, pp. 3–146.

Arctic Blue Books online – consulted via www.umanitoba.ca/libraries/units/archives/digital/abb/

Armstrong, Alexander, *Observations on Naval Hygiene and Scurvy, More Particularly as the Latter Appeared During a Polar Voyage*, London, 1858.

Armstrong, Terence, Rogers, George, and Rowley, Graham, *The Circumpolar North: A Political and Economic Geography of the Arctic and Sub-Arctic*, London, 1978.

Ashwell, Lawrence T., *Companion to the British and American Homoeopathic Pharmacopoeias Arranged in the Form of a Dictionary*, 4th edn, London, 1890.

Assheton, Ralph, *Pedigree of the Family of Feilden, of the County of Lancaster*, London, 1879.

Athenæum, The, no. 2558, 4 November 1876, pp. 596–7.

—, no. 2559, 11 November 1876, p. 627.

Austin, Jillian F. and McConnell, Anita, 'James Six, FRS: Two Hundred Years of the Six Self-Registering Thermometer', *Notes and Records of the Royal Society of London*, 35, 1980, pp. 49–65.

Aveling, Edward B., *General Biology, Theoretical and Practical*, London, 1882.

Banfield, A. W. F., *Mammals of Canada*, Toronto and Buffalo, 1974.

Bardsen, Ivar, 'Description of Greenland in the Fourteenth Century', reprinted in the original Danish and in English translation in Nicolò Zeno, *The Voyages of the Venetian Brothers, Nicolò and Antonio Zeno …*, London, 1873, pp. 39–54.

Barham, Richard Harris, 'Misadventures at Margate', *Bentley's Miscellany*, 10, 1841, pp. 620–22

—, 'Misadventures at Margate', in *The Ingoldsby Legends; or, Mirth and Marvels, by Thomas Ingoldsby, Esquire*, London, 1841, pp. 321–4.

Barr, William, *Arctic Hell-Ship: the Voyage of HMS* Enterprise, *1850–1855*, Edmonton, 2007.

Barton, Ruth, 'An Influential Set of Chaps', *British Journal for the History of Science*, 23, 1990, pp. 53–81.

Belcher, E., *The Last of the Arctic Voyages; being a Narrative of the Expedition in H.M.S.* Assistance *... in Search of Sir John Franklin, during the Years 1852–53–54. With Notes on the Natural History, by Sir John Richardson, Professor Owen, Thomas Bell, J. W. Salter, and Lovell Reeve*, 2 vols, London, 1855.

Bell, Michael, 'Thomas Mitchell, Photographer and Artist in the High Arctic, 1875–76', *Image* 15, 1972, pp. 12–21.

Bell, Thomas, *A History of British Quadrupeds, Including the Cetacea*, 2nd edn, revised and partly rewritten by the author, assisted by Robert F. Tomes and Edward Richard Alston, London, 1874.

Beneden, P. J. van, 'Mémoire sur la Limacina Arctica', *Mémoires de l'académie royale des sciences, des lettres et des beaux-arts de Belgique*, 14, 1841, pp. 1–14.

Berly, J. A., *J. A. Berly's Universal Electrical Directory and Advertiser*, 3rd edn, London 1884.

Bessels, 'Notes on Polaris Bay', reprinted in Thomas Rupert Jones, ed., *Manual of the Natural History, Geology, and Physics of Greenland and the Neighbouring Regions...*, London, 1875, p. 553, from Bessels, 'L'expédition polaire américaine, sous les orders du Capitaine Hall, *Bulletin de la Société de Géographie, Paris*, 6th series, 9, 1875, p. 297.

—, 'Lettre au Secrétaire Générale de la *Société de Géographie*, Washington, 19 juillet 1874: L'expédition polaire américaine, sous les ordres du Capitaine Hall', *Bulletin de la Société de Géographie, Paris*, 6th series, 9, 1875, pp. 291–9.

Biodiversity Heritage Library, at: www.biodiversitylibrary.org/

Black, Patrick, *Scurvy in High Latitudes: An Attempt to Explain the Cause of the 'Medical Failure' of the Arctic Expedition*, London, 1876.

Blackadar, R. G., *Geological Reconnaissance, North Coast of Ellesmere Island, Arctic Archipelago, Northwest Territories*, Geological Survey of Canada Paper 53-10, Ottawa, 1954.

Blix, Arnoldus Schytte, *Arctic Animals and Their Adaptations to Life on the Edge*, Trondheim, 2005.

Blythe, E., 'A Suggested New Division of the Earth into Zoological Regions', *Nature*, 3, 30 March 1971, pp. 427–9.

Bockstoce, John, ed., *The Journal of Rochfort Maguire, 1852–1854. Two years at Point Barrow, Alaska, aboard H.M.S. Plover in search for Sir John Franklin*, 2 vols, London, 1988.

Brady, H. B., 'Appendix No. XIII. Rhizopoda reticularia', in George Strong Nares, *Narrative of a Voyage to the Polar Sea during 1875–6 of H.M. Ships 'Alert' and 'Discovery'...*, 3rd edn, London, 1878, vol. II, pp. 295–300.

—, 'On the Reticularian and Radiolarian Rhizopoda (Foraminifera and Polycistina) of the North Polar Expedition of 1875–76', *Annals and Magazine of Natural History*, series 5, 1, 1878, pp. 425–40.

Brightwell, T., 'On the Genus *Triceratium*, with Descriptions and Figures of the Species', *Journal of Cell Science*, s. 1, 1853, pp. 245–52.

British Museum, *List of the Specimens of Mammalia in the Collections of the British Museum*, London, 1843.

Brough, William and Halliday, Andrew, *The Area Belle: An Original Farce in One Act*, London, [1864].

Brown, Robert, 'Florula Discoana: Contributions to the Phyto-Geography of Greenland, within the Parallels of 68° and 70° North Latitude', *Transactions of the Botanical Society of Edinburgh*, 9, pt 2, 1865; slightly revised and reprinted in Thomas Rupert Jones, ed., *Manual of the Natural History, Geology, and Physics of Greenland and the Neighbouring Regions...*, London, 1875, pp. 256–68.

—, 'On the Mammalian Fauna of Greenland', *Proceedings of the Zoological Society of London*, 28 May 1868, pp. 330–62; slightly revised and reprinted in Thomas Rupert Jones, ed., *Manual of the Natural History, Geology, and Physics of Greenland and the Neighbouring Regions...*, London, 1875, pp. 1–34.

—, 'On the Physical Structure of Greenland' in *A Selection of Papers on Arctic Geography and Ethnology, Reprinted, and Presented to the Arctic Expedition of 1875, by the President, Council, and Fellows of the Royal Geographical Society*, London, 1875.

—, 'The Arctic Expedition. Its Scientific Aims', *Popular Science Review*, 1875, p. 159.

Browne, Janet, *The Secular Ark: Studies in the History of Biogeography*, New Haven, 1983.

Browne, W. H., *Ten Coloured Views Taken during the Arctic Expedition of Her Majesty's Ships 'Enterprise' and 'Investigator' under the Command of Captain Sir James C. Ross*, London, 1850.

Busk, G., 'Minute of the Linnean Society on North Polar Exploration', *Proceedings of the Royal Geographical Society of London*, 9, 1864–5, pp. 156–8.

—, 'Appendix No. X. Polyzoa', in George Strong Nares, *Narrative of a Voyage to the Polar Sea during 1875–6 of H.M. Ships 'Alert' and 'Discovery'...*, 3rd edn, London, 1878, vol. II, pp. 283–9.

—, 'List of Polyzoa Collected by Captain H. W. Feilden in the North Polar Expedition; with Descriptions of New Species', *Journal of the Linnean Society of London. Zoology*, 15, 1880, pp. 231–41.

Cambridge, O. P., 'On Some New and Little-Known Spiders from the Arctic Regions', *Annals and Magazine of Natural History*, series 4, 20, 1877, pp. 273–85.

Carpenter, Kenneth J., *The History of Scurvy and Vitamin C*, Cambridge, 1988.

Carpenter, P. Herbert, 'Preliminary Report upon the *Comatulæ* of the "Challenger" Expedition', *Proceedings of the Royal Society of London*, 28, 1878–9, pp. 383–95.

Carpenter, William Benjamin, *The Microscope and Its Revelations*, London, 1875.

—, 'Report on the Physical Investigations carried on by P. Herbert Carpenter, B.A., in H.M.S. "Valorous" during her Return Voyage from Disco Island in August 1875', *Proceedings of the Royal Society of London*, 173, 1876, pp. 230–37.

Carter, H. J., 'Arctic and Antarctic Sponges', *Annals and Magazine of Natural History*, series 4, 20, 1877, pp. 38–42.

—, 'Appendix No. XII. Spongida', in George Strong Nares, *Narrative of a Voyage to the Polar Sea during 1875–6 of H.M. Ships 'Alert' and 'Discovery'...*, 3rd edn, London, 1878, vol. II, pp. 293–4.

Cassino, Samuel E., *The Naturalists' Directory*, Boston, 1888 and 1890 [separate editions].

Caswell, J. E., 'The RGS and the British Arctic Expedition, 1875–76', *Geographical Journal*, 143, 1977, pp. 200–210.

Champley, Robert, 'The Great Auk', *Annals and Magazine of Natural History*, 14, 1864, p. 235.

Chang, Hasok, *Inventing Temperature: Measurement and Scientific Progress*, Oxford, 2004.

Chemnitz, J. H., 'Von der balæna rostrata oder dem Schnabelfisch', *Beschäftigungen der Berlinischen Gesellschaft Naturforschender Freunde*, 4, 1779, pp. 183–9.

Chester, Sharon, *The Arctic Guide: Wildlife of the Far North*, Princeton and Oxford, 2016.

Christiani, R. S., *A Technical Treatise on Soap and Candles; with a Glance at the Industry of Fats and Oils*, Philadelphia and London, 1881.

Collinson, Richard, *Journal of H.M.S. Enterprise, on the Expedition in Search of Sir John Franklin's Ships by Behring Strait. 1850–55*, ed. T. B. Collinson, London, 1880.

Cooke, Alan and Holland, Clive, *The Exploration of Northern Canada*, Toronto, 1978.

Coppinger, W., 'Appendix No. XVI. Report on Petermann Glacier', in George Strong Nares, *Narrative of a Voyage to the Polar Sea during 1875–6 of H.M. Ships 'Alert' and 'Discovery'...*, 3rd edn, London, 1878, vol. II, pp. 346–51.

Coues, Elliott, *American Ornithological Bibliography*, parts 1–3, *Bulletin of the United States Geological and Geographical Survey of the Territories*, vol. V, Washington, 1878–80, pp. 143–52, 521–1066.

Craik, Dina Maria Mulock, *Poems, by the Author of 'A Life for a Life', 'John Halifax Gentleman', &c.*, Boston, 1860.

Cramp, Stanley, *Handbook of the Birds of Europe the Middle East and North Africa: The Birds of the Western Palearctic*, 6 vols, Oxford, 1977–94.

Croll, James, *Climate and Time in Their Geological Relations: A Theory of Secular Changes of the Earth's Climate*, London, 1875.

Damas, David, ed., *Arctic*. Vol. 5 of *Handbook of North American Indians*, gen. ed. William C. Stuyvesant, Washington, 1984.

—, 'The Arctic from Norse Contact to Modern Times', in Bruce G. Trigger and Wilcomb E. Washburn, eds., *The Cambridge History of the Native Peoples of the Americas. Volume I. North America*, Cambridge, 1996, Part 2, pp. 329–99.

Darwin, Charles, *Journal of Researches into the Natural History and Geology of the Countries Visited during the Voyage around the World of H.M.S. 'Beagle' under the Command of Captain Fitz Roy, R.N.*, 2nd edn, London, 1845.

—, *Journal of Researches into the Natural History and Geology of the Countries Visited during the Voyage around the World of H.M.S. 'Beagle' under the Command of Captain Fitz Roy, R.N.*, new edn, London, 1873.

—, *On the Origin of Species by Means of Natural Selection, or the Preservation of Favoured Races in the Struggle for Life*, London, 1859.

—, *The Autobiography of Charles Darwin, 1809–1882*, ed. N. Barlow, London, 1958.

Davis, C. H., ed., *Narrative of the North Polar Expedition. U.S. Ship Polaris, Captain Charles Francis Hall Commanding*, Washington DC, 1876.

Davis, John, see Markham, A. H., ed., 1880.

Deacon, Margaret, *Scientists and the Sea, 1650–1900: A Study of Marine Science*, 2nd edn, Aldershot, 1971.

— and Savours, Ann, 'Sir George Strong Nares' (1831–1915), *Polar Record*, 18, 1976, pp. 1–15.

Debrett's Baronetage, Knightage and Companionage, London, 1893.

De Costa, B. F., ed., *Sailing Directions of Henry Hudson, Prepared for His Use in 1608, from the Old Danish of Ivar Bardsen*, Albany, 1869.

De Rance, C. E. and Feilden, Henry W., 'Geology of the Coasts of the Arctic Lands Visited by the Late British Expedition under Captain Sir George Nares, R.N.', *Quarterly Journal of the Geological Society of London*, 34, 1878, 556–67.

—, 'Appendix No. XV. On the Geological Structure of the Coasts of Grinnell Land and Hall Basin' in George Strong Nares, *Narrative of a Voyage to the Polar Sea during 1875–6 of H.M. Ships 'Alert' and 'Discovery'...*, 3rd edn, London, 1878, vol. II, pp. 327–45.

Dickie, G[eorge], 'Hints for Collecting Cryptogamia', *Transactions of the Botanical Society of Edinburgh*, 10, 1870, pp. 349–50.

Dictionary of Canadian Biography, Toronto, 1966– , available online at www.biographi.ca/en/

Dictionary of Geology and the Earth Sciences, 4th edn, ed. Michael Ashby, Oxford University Press, Oxford 2013.

Disraeli, Benjamin, letter to H. C. Rawlinson 17 November 1874, reprinted in *The Navy*, 22 May 1875, p. 482.

Dresser, Henry Eeles, *The History of the Birds of Europe: Including All the Species Inhabiting the Western Palaearctic Region*, 9 vols, London, 1871–96.

Duckers, Peter, *British Military Rifles 1800–2000*, Princes Risborough, 2005.

Dunbar, Moira and Dunbar, M. J., 'The History of the North Water', *Proceedings of the Royal Society of Edinburgh*, series B, 72, 1972, pp. 231–41.

Dunbar, Moira and Greenaway, Keith R., *Arctic Canada from the Air*, Ottawa, 1956.

Duncan, Martin, 'Report on the Echinodermata Collected during the Arctic Expedition, 1875–76', *Annals and Magazine of Natural History*, series 4, 20, 1877, pp. 447–70.

— and Sladen, W. P., 'Appendix No. IX. Echinodermata', in George Strong Nares, *Narrative of a Voyage to the Polar Sea during 1875–6 of H.M. Ships 'Alert' and 'Discovery'…*, 3rd edn, London, 1878, vol. II, pp. 260–82.

—, *A Memoir on the Echinodermata of the Arctic Sea to the West of Greenland*, London 1881.

Ehrlich, Gretel, *This Cold Heaven: Seven Seasons in Greenland*, New York, 2001.

Elliott, Henry W., *A Report upon the Condition of Affairs in the Territory of Alaska*, Washington, 1875.

Emerson, W. Eric and Stokes, Karen, eds, *A Confederate Englishman: The Civil War Letters of Henry Wemyss Feilden*, Columbia, SC, 2013.

EOL: Encyclopedia of Life, eol.org

Etheridge, R., 'Palæontology of the Coasts of the Arctic Lands Visited by the late British Expedition under Captain Sir George Nares …', *Quarterly Journal of the Geological Society of London*, 34, 1878, pp. 568–639.

Evans, John, *The Ancient Stone Implements, Weapons, and Ornaments, of Great Britain*, London, 1872.

Fabricius, Otto, *Fauna Groenlandica: systematice sistens animalia Groenlandiæ occidentalis hactenus indagata, quoad nomen specificum, triviale, vernaculumque: synonyma auctorum plurium, descriptionem, locum, victum, generationem, mores, usum, capturamque singuli, prout detegendi occasion fuit: maximaque parte secondum proprias observations*, Hafniæ et Lipsiæ [Copenhagen and Leipzig], 1780.

Feilden, Henry Wemyss, 'Arctic Molluscan Fauna', *Zoologist*, 3rd series, 1, 1877, pp. 435–40.

—, 'List of Birds Observed in Smith Sound and in the Polar Basin during the Arctic Expedition of 1875–76', *Ibis*, series 4, 1, 1877, pp. 401–12.

—, 'On the Birds of the North Polar Basin', *Proceedings of the Scientific Meetings of the Zoological Society of London*, 1877, pp. 28–32.

—, 'On the Mammalia of North Greenland and Grinnell Land', *Zoologist*, 3rd series, 1, 1877, pp. 313–21, 353–61.

—, 'Appendix No. I. Ethnology', in George Strong Nares, *Narrative of a Voyage to the Polar Sea during 1875–6 of H.M. Ships 'Alert' and 'Discovery'…*, 3rd edn, London, 1878, vol. II, pp. 187–92.

—, 'Appendix No. II. Mammalia', in George Strong Nares, *Narrative of a Voyage to the Polar Sea during 1875–6 of H.M. Ships 'Alert' and 'Discovery'…*, 3rd edn, London, 1878, vol. II, pp. 192–205.

—, 'Appendix No. III. Ornithology', in George Strong Nares, *Narrative of a Voyage to the Polar Sea during 1875–6 of H.M. Ships 'Alert' and 'Discovery'…*, 3rd edn, London, 1878, vol. II, pp. 206–17.

—, 'The Natural History of Prince Albert Land', *The Zoologist*, 3rd series, 3, 1879, pp. 1–9.

—, 'Geology of the Coasts of the Arctic Lands Visited by the Late British Expedition under Captain Sir George Nares, R.N.', *Quarterly Journal of the Geological Society of London*, 34, 1878, pp. 556–67.

—, 'On the Geological Results of the Polar Expedition under Admiral Sir George Nares, F.R.S.', *Abstracts of the Proceedings of the Geological Society of London*, 352, 1877–78, 17 April 1878, pp. 1–2.

—, 'Notes from an Arctic Journal', *The Zoologist*, 3rd series, 2, 1878, pp. 313–20, 372–84, 407–18, 445–51; 3rd series, 3, 1879, pp. 16–24, 50–58, 89–108, 162–70, 200–202

—, 'Note on the Birds Collected by Captain A. H. Markham, R. N.', Appendix B in Albert H. Markham, *A Polar Reconnaissance: Being the Voyage of the 'Isbjörn' to Novaya Zemlya in 1879*, London, 1881, pp. 333–9.

—, 'Appendix A. Contribution to the Flora of Russian Lapland', pp. 171–4; Appendix B. A Contribution to the Flora of Kolguev', pp. 175–86; 'Appendix C. The Flowering Plants of Novaya Zemlya, Etc.', pp. 187–225; 'Appendix D. Note on Lichens from Novaya Zemlya', pp. 226–7; 'Appendix E. Fungi from Novaya Zemlya, Waigats, Dolgoi Island, and Habarova', p. 228: 'Appendix F. Notes on the Glacial Geology of Arctic Europe and its Islands', pp. 229–310, all in H. J. Pearson,

'*Beyond Petsora Eastward*': *Two Summer Voyages to Novaya Zemlya and the Islands of the Barents Sea*, *with Appendices on the Botany and Geology by Colonel H. W. Feilden*, London, 1899.

— and Etheridge, Robert, 'On the Palæontological Results of the Recent Polar Expedition under Admiral Sir George Nares, K.C.B., F.R.S.', *Abstracts of the Proceedings of the Geological Society of London*, no. 352, 1877–78, 17 April 1878, pp. 3–4.

— and Jeffreys, J. G., 'The Post-Tertiary Beds of Grinnell Land and North Greenland', *Annals and Magazine of Natural History*, series 4, 20, 1877, pp. 483–94.

Flight, Walter, 'On Meteoric Irons Found in Greenland' in Thomas Rupert Jones, ed., *Manual of the Natural History, Geology, and Physics of Greenland and the Neighbouring Regions...*, London, 1875, pp. 447–67.

Flower, W. H., 'Instructions for making Observations on and Collecting Specimens of the Cetacea of the Arctic Seas', in Thomas Rupert Jones, ed., *Manual of the Natural History, Geology, and Physics of Greenland and the Neighbouring Regions...*, London, 1875, pp. 39–45.

Fox, A. Lane, *Catalogue of the Anthropological Collection Lent by Colonel Lane Fox for Exhibition in the Bethnal Green Branch of the South Kensington Museum. June 1874*, London, 1874.

Fraser, Angus, 'A Publishing House and Its Readers, 1841–1880: The Murrays and the Miltons', *Papers of the Bibliographical Society of America*, 90, 1996, pp. 4–47.

'The Gare-Fowl and Its Historians', *The Natural History Review: A Quarterly Journal of Biological Science*, 1865, pp. 467–88.

Gaskell, Jeremy, *Who Killed the Great Auk?* Oxford, 2000.

Gay, Jacques, *Six millenaires d'histoire des ancres*, Paris, 1997.

Geikie, Archibald, *Annals of the Royal Society Club*, London, 1917.

Geikie, James, *The Great Ice Age and Its Relation to the Antiquity of Man*, London, 1874.

—, 'Obituary: Charles Eugene de Rance' [in 'Anniversary Address'], *Proceedings of the Geological Society* in *Quarterly Journal of the Geological Society*, 63, 1907, pp. lxii–lxiii.

Godfrey, W. Earl, *The Birds of Canada*, rev. edn, Ottawa, 1986.

Goodsir, Robert Anstruther, *An Arctic Voyage to Baffin's Bay and Lancaster Sound, in Search of Friends with Sir John Franklin*, London, 1850.

Graah, Johannes Wilhelm August, *Narrative of an Expedition to the East Coast of Greenland ... In Search of the Lost Colonies*, trans. from the Danish by G. G. McDougall, London, 1837.

Greenland, at www.worldstatesmen.org/Greenland.html

Griffiths, Franklyn, ed., *Arctic Alternatives: Civility or Militarism in the Circumpolar North*, Toronto, 1988.

Grönlands Historiske Mindesmærker, udgivne af det Kongelige Nordiske Oldskrift-Selskab, 3 vols, Copenhagen, 1838–45.

Guiley, Rosemary Ellen, *The Encyclopedia of Ghosts and Spirits*, New York, 1992.

Günther, Albert, 'Instructions for Making Observations on, and Collecting Specimens of, the Mammalia of Greenland', in Thomas Rupert Jones, ed., *Manual of the Natural History, Geology, and Physics of Greenland and the Neighbouring Regions...*, London, 1875, pp. 36–9.

—, 'Appendix No. IV. Ichthyology', in George Strong Nares, *Narrative of a Voyage to the Polar Sea during 1875–6 of H.M. Ship 'Alert' and 'Discovery'...*, 3rd edn, London, 1878, vol. II, pp. 218–22.

Hacquebord, Louwrens, 'Cartography' in Mark Nuttall, ed., *Encyclopedia of the Arctic*, 3 vols, New York and London, 2005, vol. I, pp. 321–2.

Hall, Charles Francis, *Arctic Researches and Life among the Esquimaux: Being the Narrative of and Expedition in Search of Sir John Franklin, in the Years 1860, 1861, and 1862*, New York, 1865.15/472

—, 'Copy of Draft of Captain Hall's Dispatch', dated 20 October 1871, in *Report of the Secretary of the Navy, being Part of the Message and Documents Communicated to the Two Houses of Congress at the Beginning of the First Session of the Forty-Third Congress*, Washington, 1873, pp. 294–5.

Harding, C. W., *Eley Cartridges – A History of the Silversmiths and Ammunition*, Shrewsbury, 2006.

Hardwick, Charles, *History of the Borough of Preston and Its Environs, in the County of Lancaster*, Preston and London, 1857.

Hart, H. G., *The New Army List, Militia List, and Indian Civil Service List; Exhibiting the Rank, Standing, and Various Services of Every Regimental Officer in the Army Serving on Full Pay ...*, London, 1876.

Hattersley-Smith, G., 'The British Arctic Expedition, 1875–76', *Polar Record*, 18, 1976, pp. 17–26.

Haughton, Samuel, 'On the Geology of the Parry Islands and Neighbouring Lands', *Journal of the Royal Dublin Society*, 1, 1857, pp. 195, 210–14, 239–50; and 3, 1860, pp. 53–8.

—, 'Appendix No. XIX. Abstract of Results Obtained from the Tidal Observations Made on Board H.M. Ships 'Discovery' and 'Alert' in 1875–6', in George Strong Nares, *Narrative of a Voyage to the Polar Sea during 1875–6 of H.M. Ships 'Alert' and 'Discovery'...*, 3rd edn, London, 1878, vol. II, pp. 356–61.

Hayes, Isaac Israel, *The Open Polar Sea: A Narrative of a Voyage of Discovery Towards the North Pole, in the Schooner 'United States'*, London, 1867.

Hazard, John, *Army & Navy Calendar for the Financial Year 1893 –94; being a compendium of general information relating to the Army, Navy, Militia, and Volunteers, and containing maps, plans, tabulated statements, abstracts, etc., compiled from authentic sources*, 12th edn, London, 1893.

Heer, Oswald, trans. Robert H. Scott, 'On the Miocene Flora of North Greenland' in Thomas Rupert Jones, ed., *Manual of the Natural History, Geology, and Physics of Greenland and the Neighbouring Regions...*, London, 1875, pp, 368–73; reproduced from the *Report of the Thirty-Sixth Meeting of the British Association for the Advancement of Science held at Nottingham in August 1866*, London, 1867, pp. 53–5.

—, 'Notice of Heer's "Flora Fossilis Arctica" (Carboniferous Fossils of Bear Island and Spitzbergen, and Cretaceous and Miocene Plants of Spitzbergen and Greenland) communicated by Robert H. Scott', in Thomas Rupert Jones, ed., *Manual of the Natural History, Geology, and Physics of Greenland and the Neighbouring Regions...*, London, 1875, pp. 374–7; reprinted from the *Geological Magazine*, 9, 1872 pp. 69–72.

—, 'The Miocene Flora and Fauna of the Arctic Regions' in Thomas Rupert Jones, ed., *Manual of the Natural History, Geology, and Physics of Greenland and the Neighbouring Regions...*, London, 1875, pp. 378–89; reprinted from *Flora Fossilis Arctica: Die fossile Flora der Polärländer*, vol. III, Zürich, 1875.

—, *Flora Fossilis Arctica: Die fossile Flora der Polärländer*, vol. V, pt. I, *Die miocene Flora des Grinnell-Landes gegründet auf die von Capitän H. W. Feilden und Dr. E. Moss in der Nähe des Kap Murchison gesammelten fossilen Pflanzen*, Zürich, 1878.

—, 'Notes on Fossil Plants Discovered in Grinnell Land by Captain H. W. Feilden, Naturalist of the English North Polar Expedition', *Quarterly Journal of the Geological Society of London*, 34, 1878, pp. 66–72.

Hendrik, Hans, *Memoirs of Hans Hendrik*. London, 1878.

Herschel, John F. W., ed., *A Manual of Scientific Enquiry: Prepared for the Use of Officers in Her Majesty's Navy; and Travellers in General*, 2nd edn, London, 1851; 3rd edn, superintended by Robert Main, London, 1859.

—, *Physical Geography. From the Encyclopædia Britannica*, Edinburgh, 1862.

Heslop, Oliver, *Northumberland Words. A Glossary of Words used in the County of Northumberland and on the Tyneside*, vol. I, London, 1892.

Hoare, Michael E., ed., *The Resolution Journal of Johann Reinhold Forster, 1772–1775*, 4 vols, London, 1982.

Holbœll, Carl, *Ornithologischer Beitrag zur Fauna Groenlands, uebersetzt und mit einem Anhang Versehen von J. H. Paulsen*, 2nd edn, Leipzig, 1854.

Holland, Clive A., 'Hans Hendrik', *Dictionary of Canadian Biography*, vol. 11, University of Toronto/Université Laval, 2003–, at: www.biographi.ca/en/bio/hans_hendrik_11E.html (accessed 10 January 2019).

Hooker, J. D., 'Opinion of Dr. Hooker, C.B., on the Importance of Arctic Exploration: Speech delivered at a Meeting of the Royal Geographical Society on April 22nd, 1872', *The New Arctic Expedition: Correspondence between the Royal Geographical Society and the Government*, London, 1873, pp. 51–3.

—, 'The First Part of the "Outlines of the Distribution of Arctic Plants"', *Transactions of the Linnean Society*, 23, 1860, pp. 251–348; reprinted in Thomas Rupert Jones, ed., *Manual of the Natural History, Geology, and Physics of Greenland and the Neighbouring Regions...*, London, 1875, pp. 197–238.

—, 'Instructions to Botanists', in Thomas Rupert Jones, ed., *Manual of the Natural History, Geology, and Physics of Greenland and the Neighbouring Regions...*, London, 1875, pp. 62–7.

— et al., 'Appendix No. XIV. Botany. By Sir Joseph D. Hooker, C.B., K.C.S.I., President Royal Society. With lists of Flowering Plants, by Professor D. Oliver; Musci, by W. Mitten; Fungi, by Rev. W. J. Berkeley; Algæ and Diatomaceæ, by Professor George Dickie', in George Strong Nares, *Narrative of a Voyage to the Polar Sea during 1875–6 of H.M. Ships 'Alert' and 'Discovery'...*, 3rd edn, London, 1878, vol. II, pp. 301–26.

Hughes, Basil Perronet, *British Small-Bore Artillery: The Muzzle Loading Artillery of the 18th and 19th Centuries*, London, 1969.

Humphreys, Arthur Lee, *Piccadilly Bookmen: Memorials of the House of Hatchard*, London, 1893.

Huxley, Thomas Henry, *Lay Sermons, Addresses, and Reviews*, 2nd edn, 2nd printing, London and New York, 1872.

ITIS, Integrated Taxonomic Integration System, at: www.itis.gov/

Jackson, Gordon, *The British Whaling Trade*, Research in Maritime History No. 29, St Johns, NL, 2005.

Jeffreys, J. Gwyn, 'Instructions for Making Observations on, and Collecting the Mollusca of, the Arctic Regions', in Thomas Rupert Jones, ed., *Manual of the Natural History, Geology, and Physics of Greenland and the Neighbouring Regions...*, London, 1875, pp. 48–50.

—, 'A Few Remarks on the Species of *Astarte*', *Journal of Conchology*, 3, 1881, pp. 233–4.

Jones, H. G., Pomeroy, J. W., Walker, D.A. and Hoham, R. W., eds, *Snow Ecology: An Interdisciplinary Examination of Snow-Covered Ecosystems*, Cambridge, 2001.

Jones, Mrs Herbert, *Sandringham, Past and Present*, London, 1888.

Jones, Thomas Rupert, ed., *Manual of the Natural History, Geology, and Physics of Greenland and the Neighbouring Regions, Prepared for the Use of the Arctic Expedition of 1875, Under the Direction of the Arctic Committee of the Royal Society,... Together with Instructions Suggested by the Arctic Committee of the Royal Society for the Use of the Expedition. Published by Permission of the Lords Commissioners of the Admiralty*, London, 1875.

Kane, Elisha Kent, *The U.S. Grinnell Expedition in Search of Sir John Franklin: a personal narrative*, London, 1854.

—, *Arctic Explorations: The Second Grinnell Expedition in Search of Sir John Franklin '53, '54, '55*, 2 vols, Philadelphia, 1856.

Khan, Iqtidar Alam, 'The Gwalior Contingent in 1857–58: A Study of the Organisation and Ideology of the Sepoy Rebels', *Social Scientist*, 26, 1998, pp. 53–75.

Kofoid, Charles A., 'A Little Known Ornithogical Journal and its Editor Adolphe Bouchard', *Condor*, 25, 1923, pp. 85–9.

Koldewey, Carl, *Die Zweite deutsche Nordpolarfahrt in den Jahren 1869 und 1870 unter Führing des Kapitän Karl Koldewey*, 2 vols, Leipzig, 1873–74.

Labouchère, Henry du Pré, *Diary of the Besieged Resident in Paris*, 2nd edn, London, 1871.

Laudan, Rachel, *From Mineralogy to Geology. The Foundations of a Science, 1650–1830*, Chicago, 1987.

Layberry, Ross, Hall, Peter and Lafontaine, Dan, *The Butterflies of Canada*, Toronto, 1998.

Leach, Simon, Worshipful Company of Bowyers, at: www.bowyers.com/personalities_finnis.php, 2006.

Leslie, Alexander, *The Arctic Voyages of Alfred Erik Nordenskiöld, 1858–1879*, London, 1879.

Levere, Trevor H., 'Magnetic Instruments in the Canadian Arctic Expeditions of Franklin, Lefroy, and Nares', *Annals of Science*, 43, 1986, pp. 57–76.

—, 'Henry Wemyss Feilden, Naturalist on HMS *Alert* 1875–1876', *Polar Record*, 24 (151), 1988, 307–12.

—, 'Henry Wemyss Feilden (1838–1921) and the Geology of the Nares Strait Region: with a Note on Per Schei (1875–1905)', *Earth Sciences History*, 10, 1991, pp. 213–18.

—, *Science and the Canadian Arctic: A Century of Exploration, 1818–1918*, Cambridge, 1993.

—, 'Early Searches for the Nest and Eggs of the Red Knot', *Birders Journal*, 4, 1995, pp. 37–40.

Linnaeus, C., *Systema Naturæ per regna tria naturæ, secundum classes, ordines, genera, species, cum characteribus, differentiis, synonymis, locis. Editio decima, reformata*, 2 vols, Stockholm, 1758–59.

Livy [Titus Livius], *The History of Rome. Books Nine to Twenty-Six. Literally Translated ... by D. Spillan and Cyrus Edmonds*, London, 1887.

Lockwood, W, S., *The Oxford Book of British Bird Names*, Oxford, 1984.

The London Gazette, 24 June 1789 and 16 July 1880

Loomis, Chauncey, *Weird and Tragic Shores: The Story of Charles Francis Hall, Explorer*, Lincoln, NE, 1971.

Lyell, Charles, *Principles of Geology; Being an Attempt to Explain the Former Changes of the Earth's Surface, by Reference to Causes now in Operation*, 3 vols, London, 1830–33.

Lyon, George Francis, *The Private Journal of Captain G. F. Lyon, on H.M.S. Hecla, During the Recent Voyage of Discovery under Captain Parry*, London, 1824.

Mabberley, D. J., *Jupiter Botanicus: Robert Brown of the British Museum,* London, 1985.

Macdonald, John Denis, 'On the Zoological Characters of the Living *Clio caudata*, as Compared with those of *Clio borealis* Given in Systematic Works', *Proceedings of the Royal Society of Edinburgh*, 5, 1866, pp. 76–8.

McLachlan, Robert, 'Appendix No. VI. Insecta and Arachnida', in George Strong Nares, *Narrative of a Voyage to the Polar Sea during 1875–6 of H.M. Ships'Alert' and 'Discovery'...*, 3rd edn, London, 1878, vol. II, pp. 234–9.

Markham, Albert Hastings, *A Whaling Cruise to Baffin's Bay and the Gulf of Boothia, and an Account of the Rescue of the Crew of the 'Polaris'*, London, 1874.

—, *The Great Frozen Sea: A Personal Narrative of the Voyage of the 'Alert' During the Arctic Expedition of 1875–6*, London, 1878.

Markham, Clements R., *The Arctic Navy List; or, a Century of Arctic and Antarctic Officers, 1773–1873 together with a List of Officers of the 1875 Expedition, and their Services*, 1875.

—, *The Threshold of the Unknown Region*, 4th edn, London, 1876.

—, *A Refutation of the Report of the Scurvy Committee*, Portsmouth, 1877.

—, 'The Arctic Expedition of 1875–76', *Proceedings of the Royal Geographical Society*, 21, 1877, pp. 536–55.

—, *The Royal Geographical Society and the Arctic Expedition of 1875–76: A Report*, London, 1877; reprinted Cambridge, 2012.

—, 'Use of Arrows by the Arctic Highlanders', *The Geographical Magazine*, 4, 1 Nov. 1877, p. 303. [Markham was editor of this journal.]

—, ed., *The Voyages and Works of John Davis*, 'The first voyage of Master John Davis, undertaken in June 1585, for the Discoverie of the Northwest Passage, written by John Janes, Marchant, servant to the worshipfull M. William Sanderson', in *The Voyages and Works of John Davis the Navigator*, London, Hakluyt Society, 1st ser., pt II, 59a, 1880, pp. 1–14.

Martin, John Stapleton, 'Obituary of Mr Marcus Martin', *Solicitors' Journal and Reporter*, 29, 1885, p. 717.

Maskelyne, N. Story, 'Instructions for Making Observations on, and Collecting Mineralogical Specimens' in Thomas Rupert Jones, ed., *Manual of the Natural History, Geology, and Physics of Greenland and the Neighbouring Regions...*, London, 1875, pp. 77–82.

Matthew, H. C. G. and Harrison, Brian, eds, *New Oxford Dictionary of National Biography* [on-line], Oxford and New York, 2004.

Maxwell, Moreau S., 'Pre-Dorset and Dorset Prehistory of Canada' in David Damas, ed., *Arctic*, Vol. 5 of *Handbook of North American Indians*, gen. ed. William C. Stuyvesant, Washington, 1984, pp. 359–68.

McCance, S., *History of the Royal Munster Fusiliers*, 2 vols, Aldershot, 1927.

M'Clure, R. J. le M., *The Discovery of a North-West Passage by HMS Investigator*, ed. S. Osborne, 2nd edn 1857; 4th edn, 1865.

McConnell, *No Sea Too Deep: The History of Oceanographic Instruments*, Bristol, 1982.

—, 'Six's thermometer: a century of use in oceanography' in M. Sears and D. Merriman, eds, *Oceanography: The Past*, New York, 1980, pp. 252–65.

—, *Instrument Makers to the World: A History of Cooke, Troughton & Simms*, York, 1992.

McGhee, Robert, 'Thule Prehistory of Canada' in David Damas, ed., *Arctic*, Vol. 5 of *Handbook of North American Indians*, gen. ed. William C. Stuyvesant, Washington, 1984, pp. 369–76.

McIntosh, W. C., 'Appendix No. VIII. Annelida', in George Strong Nares, *Narrative of a Voyage to the Polar Sea during 1875–6 of H.M. Ships 'Alert' and 'Discovery'...*, 3rd edn, London, 1878, vol. II, pp. 257–9.

—, 'On the Annelids of the British North-Polar Expedition', *Journal of the Linnean Society of London. Zoology*, 14, 1879, 126–34.

McLachlan, R., 'Appendix No. VI. Insecta', in George Strong Nares, *Narrative of a Voyage to the Polar Sea during 1875–6 of H.M. Ships 'Alert' and 'Discovery'...*, 3rd edn, London, 1878, vol. II, pp. 234–9.

McNicoll, David H., *Dictionary of Natural History Terms with Their Derivations, Including the Various Orders, Genera, and Species*, London, 1863.

Miers, E. J., 'Report on the Crustacea Collected by the Naturalists of the Arctic Expedition in 1875–76', *Annals and Magazine of Natural History*, series 4, 20, 1877, pp. 273–85.

—, 'Appendix No. VII. Crustacea', in George Strong Nares, *Narrative of a Voyage to the Polar Sea during 1875–6 of H.M. Ship 'Alert' and 'Discovery'...*, 3rd edn, London, 1878, vol. II, pp. 240–56.

Milner, Thomas, *The Gallery of Nature: A Pictorial and Descriptive Tour Through Creation*, London, 1846.

Milton, John, *Paradise Lost*, ed. J. R. Boyd, New York, 1851.

Mörch, Otto A. L., 'On the Land and Fresh-Water Mollusca of Greenland', *American Journal of Conchology*, 4, 1868, pp. 25–40.

Morris, F. O., *A History of British Birds*, 2nd edn, 6 vols, 1870.

Morton, William, 'Mr. Morton's Report of Journey to North and East during the Months of June and July, 1854', in Elisha Kent Kane, *Arctic Explorations: The Second Grinnell Expedition in Search of Sir John Franklin '53, '54, '55*, 2 vols, Philadelphia, 1856. vol. II, pp. 373–80.

Moss, Edward Lawton, *Shores of the Polar Sea: A Narrative of the Arctic Expedition of 1875–6*, London, 1878.

Murchison, Roderick Impey, 'On the Occurrence of Numerous Fragments of Fir-wood in the Islands of the Arctic Archipelago; with Remarks on the Rock-Specimens Brought from that Region', *Quarterly Journal of the Geological Society*, 11, 1855, pp. 536–40.

—, *Siluria. A History of the Oldest Rocks in the British Isles and Other Countries; with Sketches of the Origin and Distribution of Native Gold, the General Succession of Geological Formations, and Changes of the Earth's Surface*, 5th edn, London, 1872.

Murphy, J. J., 'On Great Fluctuations of Temperature in the Arctic Winter', *Proceedings of the Royal Society of London*, 11, 1860–62, pp. 309–12.

Nares, George Strong, *The Official Report of the Recent Arctic Expedition*, London, 1876.

—, 'Arctic Expedition, 1875–6. Report of the Proceedings. Captain G. S. Nares. Between 22nd July 1875, and 27th October, 1876', in *Arctic Blue Books: Arctic Expedition, 1875–6. Journals and Proceedings of the Arctic Expedition, 1875–6, under the Command of Captain Sir George S. Nares, R.N., K.C.B. [In continuation of Parliamentary Papers C 1153 of 1875, and C 1560 of 1876.] Presented to both Houses of Parliament by Command of Her Majesty, 1877. [C. (2nd series) 1636.]*, London, 1877.

—, *The Official Report of the Recent Arctic Expedition*, London, 1876.

—, 'Captain Nares's Report', *Nature*, 15, 9 November 1876, pp. 24–48.

—, 'Negretti's Reversible Thermometer and the Arctic Expedition', *Nature*, 15, 7 December 1876, p. 116.

—, *Narrative of a Voyage to the Polar Sea during 1875–6 of H.M. Ships 'Alert' and 'Discovery'..., with Notes on the Natural History Edited by H. W. Feilden, F.G.S., C.M.Z.S., F.R.G.S., Naturalist to the Expedition*, 3rd edn, 2 vols, London, 1878.

— and Feilden, H. W., 'Physical Observations' in *Arctic Blue Books: Results Derived from the Arctic Expedition 1875–76*, London, 1878, pp. 3–146.

Navy List, Corrected to the 20th March, 1873, London, 1873.

Navy List, Corrected to the 20th September, 1874, London, 1874.

Navy List, Corrected to the 20th March, 1876, London, 1876.

Newton, Alfred, 'Notes on the Birds of Spitsbergen', *The Ibis, A Quarterly Journal of Ornithology*, New Series, 1, 1865, pp. 199–219.

—, 'Notes of the Birds which Have Been Found in Greenland' in Thomas Rupert Jones, ed., *Manual of the Natural History, Geology, and Physics of Greenland and the Neighbouring Regions...*, London, 1875, pp. 94–114.

Niles, Lawrence J., Sitters, Humphrey P., Dey, Amanda D., et al., *Status of the Red Knot in the Western Hemisphere*. Studies in Avian Biology No. 36, Ephrata, PA, 2008.

Ninnis, Belgrave, *Medical Report on the Eskimo Dog Disease*, in [Arctic Expedition], *Results Derived from the Arctic Expedition 1875–76. I. – Physical Observations by Captain Sir George Nares, R.N., and Captain Feilden, &c.*, in *Accounts and Papers: 1878*, vol. VII. Arctic Expedition [C. 2176], in *Accounts and Papers of the House of Commons*, vol. LII, London, 1878, pp. 147–54.

Nordenskiöld, Nils Adolf Erik, 'Account of a Voyage to Greenland in the Year 1870' in Thomas Rupert Jones, ed., *Manual of the Natural History, Geology, and Physics of Greenland and the Neighbouring Regions...*, London, 1875, pp. 389–446.

Nuttall, Mark, ed., *Encyclopedia of the Arctic*, 3 vols, New York and London, 2005.

'Obituary: Henry Wemyss Feilden', *Ibis*, 63, 1921, pp. 726–32.

The Observatory, A Monthly Review of Astronomy, no. 20, 1 December 1878.

Olmsted, J. M. D., *Charles-Edouard Brown-Séquard. A Nineteenth Century Neurologist and Endocrinologist*, Baltimore, 1946.

Osborn, Sherard, *Stray Leaves from an Arctic Journal; or, Eighteen Months in the Polar Regions, in Search of Sir John Franklin's Expedition, in the Years 1850–51*, London, 1852.

—, *The Discovery of the North-West Passage by H.M.S. 'Investigator', Capt. R. M'Clure 1850–1851–1852–1853–1854*, 3rd edn, London, 1859.

— and McDougall, George, *Facsimile of the Illustrated Arctic News Published on Board H.M.S. Resolute: Captn. Horatio T. Austin, C.B. in Search of the Expedition under Sir John Franklin*, London, 1852.

Oxford English Dictionary [online].

Page, William, ed., *The Victoria History of the Counties of England: A History of Cornwall*, 4 vols, London, [1906–].

Pall Mall Gazette, 22 April 1875 and 24 April 1875.

Parry, William Edward, *Journal of a Voyage for the Discovery of a North-West Passage from the Atlantic to the Pacific; Performed in the Years 1819–20, in His Majesty's Ships Hecla and Griper*, 2nd edn, London, 1821.

[—], *Supplement to the Appendix of Captain Parry's Voyage for the Discovery of a North-West Passage, in the Years 1819–20, Containing an Account of the Subjects of Natural History*, London, 1924. Appendix X, Zoology, by Edward Sabine, pp. clxxxiii–ccxlvi , including Shells (pp. ccxl–ccxlvii), by John Edward Grey; Rock Specimens (ccxlvii–cclvii), by Charles Konig; Appendix XI, Botany (pp. cclxi–ccxlv), by Robert Brown.

—, *Journal of a Second Voyage for the Discovery of a North-West Passage from the Atlantic to the Pacific Performed in the Years 1821–22–23*, London, 1824.

—, *Narrative of an Attempt to Reach the North Pole, in Boats Fitted for the Purpose, and Attached to His Majesty's Ship Hecla, in the year 1827, under the command of Captain William Edward Parry*, ..., London, 1828.

'Passing Notes', *The Echo*, no. 2457, 3 November 1876, p. 1.

Payer, Julius, 'Notes on the Land Discovered by the Austro-Hungarian Expedition under Lieut. Weyprecht and Lieut. Payer in 1872–74', *Proceedings of the Royal Geographical Society*, 19, 1874, pp. 17–37.

—, 'On the Newly Discovered Franz-Joseph Land', *Proceedings of the Imperial Academy of Sciences*, Vienna, 1874; partly reprinted in Thomas Rupert Jones, ed., *Manual of the Natural History, Geology, and Physics of Greenland and the Neighbouring Regions...*, London, 1875, pp. 596–9.

—, *New Lands Within the Arctic Circle; Narrative of the Discoveries of the Austrian Ship 'Tegetthoff' in the Years 1872–1874*, New York, 1877.

— and Weyprecht, K., 'The Austro-Hungarian Polar Expedition of 1872–74', *Journal of the Royal Geographical Society*, 45, 1875, pp. 1–33.

Pearson, H. J., *'Beyond Petsora Eastward': Two Summer Voyages to Novaya Zemlya and the Islands of the Barents Sea, with Appendices on the Botany and Geology by Colonel H. W. Feilden*, London, 1899.

Plant List, The, at: www.theplantlist.org

Plympton, George Washington, *The Aneroid Barometer, Its Construction and Use*, New York, 1878.

Porsild, A., *Illustrated Flora of the Canadian Arctic Archipelago*, National Museum of Canada, Bulletin 146, Ottawa, 1957.

Porter, Roy, *The Making of Geology. Earth Science in Britain 1660–1815*, Cambridge, 1977.

Potter, Russell, 'Open Polar Sea', in Mark Nuttall, ed., *Encyclopedia of the Arctic*, 3 vols, New York and London, 2005, pp. 1578–80.

Rae, John, *Narrative of an Expedition to the Shores of the Arctic Sea in 1846 and 1847*, London, 1850.

—, *John Rae's Correspondence with the Hudson's Bay Company on Arctic Exploration 1844–1855*, ed, E. E. Rich, London, 1953.

Ramsay, A. C. and Evans, John, 'Geology and Mineralogy: 1. General Instructions for Observations in Geology', in Thomas Rupert Jones, ed., *Manual of the Natural History, Geology, and Physics of Greenland and the Neighbouring Regions...*, London, 1875, pp. 68–77.

Rawlinson, H. C. 'Address', *Proceedings of the Royal Geographical Society*, 17, 1873, pp. clv–ccxviii.

Report to the Lords Commissioners of the Admiralty on the Cause of the Outbreak of Scurvy in the Recent Arctic Expedition; on the Adequacy of the Provision Made in the Way of Food and Medicine, and on the Propriety of the Orders for Provisioning the Sledge Parties, London, 1877. This paper was also in the *Arctic Blue Books*, LI, 1877.

Richards, George Henry, *The Arctic Expedition of 1875–76: A Reply to Its Critics*, London, 1877; reprinted Charleston, SC, 2011.

Richards, R. L., *Dr John Rae*, Whitby, 1985.

Richardson, John, Swainson, William and Kirby, William, *Fauna Boreali-Americana, or, The Zoology of the Northern Parts of British America: Containing Descriptions of the Objects of Natural History Collected on the Late Northern Land Expeditions, under Command of Captain Sir John Franklin, R.N.*, 4 vols, London, 1829–37.

Rink, Henrik [Hinrich Johannes], *Danish Greenland: Its People and Its Products*, London, 1877.

Rink, Hinrich [Johannes], *Kaart over Disko-Fjorden*, Gotthab, [Inspektoratets Bogtrykken], 1859, consulted in Royal Geographical Society, RGS CN18-OAR-GRL-S503.

—, *Grønland, geografisk og statistic beskrevet*, 2 vols, Copenhagen, 1857.

[Robeson, George M.], *Report of the Secretary of the Navy, Being Part of the Message and Documents Communicated to the Two Houses of Congress at the Beginning of the Forty-Third Congress*, Washington DC, 1873.

Roget, Peter Mark, *Animal and Vegetable Physiology Considered with Reference to Natural Theology*, 2 vols, London, 1834.

Roscoe, H. E., 'On the Detection of Meteoric (Cosmical) Dust in the Snow of the Arctic Regions' in Thomas Rupert Jones, ed., *Manual of the Natural History, Geology, and Physics of Greenland and the Neighbouring Regions...*, London, 1875, pp. 10–11.

[Royal Geographical Society], *The New Arctic Expedition: Correspondence between the Royal Geographical Society and the Government*, London: Printed by William Clowes and Sons, 1873.

[Royal Geographical Society], *A Selection of Papers on Arctic Geography and Ethnology, Reprinted, and Presented to the Arctic Expedition of 1875, by the President, Council, and Fellows of the Royal Geographical Society*, London, 1875.

Royal Navy, at: www.royalnavy.mod.uk/our-organisation/where-we-are/training-establishments/hms-excellent/history

Rupke, Nicolaas, *Richard Owen, Victorian Naturalist*, New Haven, 1994.

Sabine, Edward, Kirby, William, Gray, John Edward, Brown, Robert and Konig, Charles, *A Supplement to the Appendix of Captain Parry's Voyage for the Discovery of a North-West Passage, in the Years 1819–20. Containing an Account of the Subjects of Natural History*, London, 1824.

Salisbury, Jesse, *A Glossary of Words and Phrases Used in S.E. Worcestershire Together with Some of the Sayings, Customs, Superstitions, Charms, &c. Common in that District*, London, 1893.

Scoresby, William, Jun., *An Account of the Arctic Regions, with a History and Description of the Northern Whale-Fishery*, 2 vols, Edinburgh, 1820.

Scotsman, The, 13 February, 1 March and 17 March 1875.

Sears, M. and Merriman, D., eds, *Oceanography: The Past*, New York, 1980.

Seligman, Matthew S., Nägler, Frank and Epkenhans, Michael, eds, *The Naval Route to the Abyss: The Anglo-German Naval Race 1895–1914*, Farnham, 2015.

Six, J., 'An Account of an Improved Thermometer', *Philosophical Transactions of the Royal Society of London*, 72, 1782, pp. 72–81.

Smith, A. H., 'A Historical Enquiry into the Efficacy of Lime Juice for the Prevention and Care of Scurvy', *Journal of the Royal Army Medical Corps*, 32, 1919, pp. 93–116, 188–208.

Smith, E. A. 'On the Mollusca Collected during the Arctic Expedition of 1875–76', *Annals and Magazine of Natural History*, series 4, 20, 1877, pp. 131–46.

—, 'Appendix No. V. Mollusca', in George Strong Nares, *Narrative of a Voyage to the Polar Sea during 1875–6 of H.M. Ships 'Alert' and 'Discovery'...*, 3rd edn, London, 1878, vol. II, pp. 223–33.

Smithsonian National Museum of Natural History, North American Mammals, at: https:naturalhistory.si.edu/mna/

Snow, Dean R., 'The First Americans and the Differentiation of Hunter-Gatherer Cultures', in Bruce G. Trigger and Wilcomb E. Washburn, eds, *The Cambridge History of the Native Peoples of the Americas*, vol. I, parts 1 and 2, Cambridge, 1996, pp. 125–99.

Snyder, L. L., *Arctic Birds of Canada*, Toronto, 1957.

Solicitors' Journal and Reporter, 29, 1885, p. 717.

Steenstrup, J. Jap. Sm., and Lütken, Chr. Fred., *Bidrag til Kundskab om det aabne Havs Snyltekrebs og Lernæer samt om nogle andre nyer eller hidtil kun ufuldstændigt kjendte parasitiske Copepoder*, Kjöbenhavn, 1861. *Det Kongelige Danske videnskabernes selskabs skrifter. Femte Række. Naturvidenskabelig og Mathematisk*, V, 1861, pp. 341–432.

Steenstrup, K. J. V., 'Krarup Smith', *Geografisk Tidsskrift udgivet af Bestyrelsen for det kongelige danske geografiske Selskab*, 6, 1882, pp. 111–12.

Sturtevant, William C., gen. ed., *Handbook of North American Indians*, Washington DC, vol. V, 1984.

Sutcliffe, David, *The RIB: The Rigid-Hulled Inflatable Life-Boat and Its Place of Birth the Atlantic College*, Cambridge, 2010.

Sutherland, P. C., 'On the Geological and Glacial Phænomena of the Coasts of Davis' Strait and Baffin's Bay', *Quarterly Journal of the Geological Society of London*, 9, 1853, pp. 296–312.

Tammiksaar, E., Sukhova, N. G., and Stone, I. R., 'Hypothesis versus Fact: August Petermann and Polar Research', *Arctic*, 52, 1999, pp. 237–44.

Thackeray, William Makepeace, *The Newcomes. Memoirs of a Most Respectable Family. Edited by Arthur Pendennis, Esq.*, 2 vols, London, 1854–5.

Thistleton-Dyer, W. J., 'Lecture on Plant-Distribution as a Field for Geographical Research', *Proceedings of the Royal Geographical Society*, 22, 1878, 412–45.

Thompson, William, *The Natural History of Ireland*, 4 vols, London, 1849–56.

Thomson, C. Wyville, *The Depths of the Sea. An Account of the General Results of the Dredging Cruises of H.M.S.S. 'Porcupine' and 'Lightning' During the Summers of 1868, 1869, and 1870, under the Scientific Direction of Dr. Carpenter, F.R.S., J. Gwynn Jeffreys, F.R.S., and Dr. Wyville Thomson, F.R.S.*, London, 1873.

Thomson, David Purdie, *Introduction to Meteorology*, Edinburgh and London, 1849.

Tomlinson, Charles, *Winter in the Arctic Regions. I. Winter in the Open Sea. II. Winter in a Secure Harbour. III. Winter in a Snow-Hut*, London, 1846.

Thorsteinsson, R. and E. T. Tozer, *Geology of the Arctic Archipelago*, Geology and Economic Minerals of Canada, Geological Survey of Canada, Economic Geology Report No. 1, Ottawa, 1970, pp. 548–90.

Trigger, Bruce G. and Washburn, Wilcomb E., eds, *The Cambridge History of the Native Peoples of the Americas*, vol. I, parts 1 and 2, Cambridge, 1996.

Tosinus, Evangelista, trans. and ed., *Geographia Cl. Ptholemæi*, Rome, 1507.

Turner, Frank M., 'The Victorian Conflict between Science and Religion: A Professional Dimension', *Isis*, 69, 1978, pp. 356–76.

Turner, Gerard L'Estrange, *Nineteenth-Century Scientific Instruments*, London, 1983.

Twain, Mark, *The Celebrated Jumping Frog of Calaveras County and Other Sketches*, ed. John Paul, London, 1867.

University Education (Ireland). A Bill for the Extension of University Education in Ireland, *Parliamentary Papers 1873*, Bill 55, vi, pp. 329–62.

Vaughan, Richard, *In Search of Arctic Birds*, London, 1992.

Vestergaard, Elisabeth, ed., *Whaling Communities: North Atlantic Studies*, vol. II, Aarhus, 1990.

Vine, P. A. L., *Pleasure Boating in the Victorian Era*, Chichester, Sussex, 1983.

Walker, David, 'Notes on the Zoology of the Last Arctic Expedition under Captain F. L. M'Clintock, R.N.', *Journal of the Royal Dublin Society*, 3, 1860, pp. 61–77.

Walker, T., *Bulletins and Other State Intelligence for the Year 1876, in Two Parts: Compiled and Arranged from the Official Documents Published in the London Gazette*, Pt. II, July–December, London, 1876.

Warren, C. E. and Lean, F., *The Royal Navy List...*, London, 1881.

Werner, Petra, *Roter Schnee oder Die Suche nach dem farbenden Prinzip*, Berlin, 2007.

Whymper, Edward, 'Some Notes on Greenland and the Greenlanders', *Alpine Journal*, 6, 1874, pp. 161–8, 209–20.

—, *How to Use the Aneroid Barometer*, New York, 1891.

Winsor, Mary P. *Starfish, Jellyfish, and the Order of Life: Issues in Nineteenth-Century Science*, New Haven, 1976.

WoRMS: World Register of Marine Species, at: www.marinespecies.org/index.php

Year-Book of Pharmacy Comprising Abstracts of Papers Relating to Pharmacy, Materia Medica and Chemistry Contributed to British and Foreign Journals from July 1 1873 to June 30, 1874, London, 1874.

Young, Allen, *The Two Voyages of the Pandora in 1875 and 1876*, London, 1879, reprinted Cambridge, 2012.

Zeno, Nicolò, *The Voyages of the Venetian Brothers, Nicolò and Antonio Zeno, to the Northern Seas, in the XIVth Century, Comprising the Latest Known Accounts of the Lost Colony of Greenland; and of the Northmen in America Before Columbus*, trans. and ed. Richard Henry Major, London, 1873.

MAPS

Chart of Davis Strait and Baffin Bay Showing the Tracks of H.M. Ships 'Alert' and 'Discovery' 1875–6, National Map Collection, Public Archives of Canada, NMC-0009830 (C) 9929: H3/740/BAFFIN BAY/[1875–6].

Arctic Expedition, 1875–6. H.M. Ships Alert and Discovery. Captains G.S. Nares, F.R.S., and H.E. Stephenson, R.N. Northern Shores of Grinnell Land from H.M.S. Alert's Winter Quarters in Lat. 82.27 N. Long. 61.18 W to the 85th Meridian of West Longitude Explored by the Western Sledging Party, under the Command of Lieutenant Pelham Aldrich, R.N. between April 3rd and June 26th 1876, National Map Collection, Public Archives of Canada, NMC-0006155 (B) 9929: H3/740/ELLESMERE 1./ [1875 NMC-0006].

North America Polar Regions, Baffin Bay to Lincoln Sea, Hydrographic Office of the U.S. Department of the Navy, Bureau of Equipment, Washington, D.C., 1903. American Geographical Society Library Digital Map Collection, University of Wisconsin-Milwaukee Libraries, at: http://129.89.24.131:80/cdm/ref/collection/agdm/id/357 IIIF Manifest at: www.wdl.org/ en/item/15668/manifest.

INDEXES

GENERAL INDEX

Ackermann, Rudolf, 334

Adams, William Grylls, 6

Admiralty, xix, 1, 2, 4–7, 24, 47, 335; Admiralty Manual, 6; Arctic committee, 7, 9–10; Arctic journals held by, 146; HWF visits, 333, 335; instructions for expedition, 14, 18 n.3, 26, 52, 98 n. 5, 274 n. 1; reports given to, 292 n. 4, 333; specimens collected belong to, 15

African exploration, 3

Alaska, 83 n. 1

Albert and Victoria Land, 90–91, Plate 10

Albert Edward, Prince of Wales, visited by Nares, 332; visits *Alert* and *Discovery*, 49; chairs RGS meeting, 337

Aldrich, Pelham, senior lieutenant in *Alert* (retired as Vice-Admiral), 15, 104, 126, 135, 151, 207, 218, 312, 328; birthday menu, 151, 152; Cape Aldrich, see Cape; explores Cape Hilgard, 95; and Christmas festivities, 165–6; and HWF's collections, 120, 288, 297, 308–9; kept watch with HWF, 56, 59, 61, 63; HWF's admiration, 154; his map, 107, 181; takes meteorological readings, 187; lecture on meteorology, 154; Ovifak, 68–71; sledging, 17, 105–10, 114, 119, 155, 192, 22–8, 229, 235, 245, 281–3

Alert, HMS, 6, 14, 16; Cape Union, rounds ('Most Northern Latitude Yet Attained by Any Ship'), 103; coal stores, 14, 198; commissioned, 48; discipline on, 10, 127, 213; HWF boards, 48; Floeberg Beach, 234; Hayes Sound, 88–9; hull reinforced, 16; breaking through ice, 22–3; in ice at Hayes Sound, 168; ice floe, moored to, 95–7, 303–4, 314–18; nearly nipped in ice, 97; nipped in ice near Cape Beechey, 306; pack ice cleared at Cape York, 86; Most Northern Latitude, dinner to celebrate, 317; Portsmouth, departs from, 49; Proven, Governor came on board, 76; near Ritenbenk, 74; rudder and screw, 22–3, 91–2, 97, 102–3, 304–5, 328–9; steam engines, 6, 16, 313-4; towed by *Discovery*, 97; towing *Discovery*, 73, 75–8, 322; tracks of *Alert* and *Discovery*, xxvii–xxxi; at Upernavik, 102, 105; at Valentia, 331; ventilation, 18, 135;

winter quarters, 17, Plate 13, 313; winter routine, 360

Allard, John Hilary, HWF quotes from, 54, 233, 247, 250, 256, 269

Allen, David, 4n

Allman Bay, 317-8

Alston, Edward Richard, 59, 319, 332–3, 336

American expeditions, 1, 127, 236

anchor, François Martin's self-canting, 105

Anthropological Institute, anthropology, 13–14. See also ethnology

antiscorbutics, see scurvy

Archer, Robert H., lieutenant in *Discovery*, 236, 342

Archer's Sound, 344

Arctic archipelago, xix, 5

Arctic Circle, 15, 23, 28, 63–4, 66, 326

Arctic Ocean, xxx, 3, 21, 30, 119; HWF challenges theory of open Polar Sea, 18–19, 157, 234, 255. See also Paleocrystic Sea

Arksut Fjord, Greenland, 58

Armstrong, Alexander, 14, 18 n. 3

Armstrong, Terence, xx

astronomy, 182, 187

aukeries, near Foulke Fjord, 85

Austria, 5, 12

Ayles, Adam, 2nd Captain Foretop in *Alert*, 105, 151, 152; and dog sledging, 281

Back, Admiral Sir George, 208

Baffin Bay, xxix–xxxi, Plate 1, 26 n. 1, 30, 97, 157, 159, 173, 318, 319 n. 3

Baird, Spencer Fullerton, 46

Baker, Lieutenant Colonel James, 333

Banks, Sir Joseph, 7

Bantry Bay, 50–51

Barclay, Edward, Mr and Mrs, 333

Bardsen, Ivan, 59

Barentz Land, *see* Novaya Zemlya

Barham, Richard Harris (Thomas Ingoldsby), 201 n. 1

barometer: *see* instruments

Barrow, John (1808–98), 13

Barrow, Sir John, 2nd Secretary, Admiralty, 13

Beacon Hill, 115, 288–9

NATURAL HISTORY INDEX